Educational Dimensions of Acquired Brain Injury

Educational Dimensions of Acquired Brain Injury

Edited by

Ronald C. Savage
Gary F. Wolcott

pro·ed
8700 Shoal Creek Boulevard
Austin, Texas 78757

pro·ed

© 1994 by PRO-ED, Inc.
8700 Shoal Creek Boulevard
Austin, Texas 78757-6897

Library of Congress Cataloging-in-Publication Data

Educational dimensions of acquired brain injury / editors, Ronald C. Savage, Gary F. Wolcott.
p. cm.
Includes bibliographical references and indexes.
ISBN 0-89079-598-3
1. Brain-damaged children—Education (Elementary) 2. Brain-damaged children—Education (Secondary) 3. Learning disabled children—Education. 4. Brain-damaged children—Services for. 5. Acquired brain injuries. I. Savage, Ronald C. (Ronald Charles), 1948– . II. Wolcott, Gary F.
LC4580.E38 1994
371.91′6—dc20 93-27435
CIP

This book is designed in Sabon and Franklin Gothic.

Production Manager: Alan Grimes
Production Coordinator: Adrienne Booth
Art Director: Lori Kopp
Reprints Buyer: Alicia Woods
Editor: Debra Berman
Editorial Assistant: Claudette Landry

Printed in the United States of America

1 2 3 4 5 6 7 8 9 10 98 97 96 95 94

This book is dedicated to the parents and teachers who are joined together in the lifelong struggle to build a full and meaningful life for each child with an acquired brain injury.

More importantly, this book is dedicated to children with acquired brain injuries whose courage continues to challenge and change us.

Contents

Foreword

When I got my head injured I was riding my bike. I was leaving school. It was 3 o'clock. A man in a truck hit me on Walker Street next to the church. I was in the hospital and I was in a rehabilitation place for ½ year. I missed lots of school.

I am glad teachers have this book. They thought I wasn't right. I got messed up all the time in class. There was too much going on. I cried and the kids picked on me.

Now it is 2½ years later. I am in Grade 6 now. I feel alot better but my work isn't that good. My mom says I have to be "patient." I just want to be OK. Thank you to my teachers.

Maria, age 12, struck by drunk driver,
May 1989

The doctors told me in rehabilitation that I almost died. Now I'm not sure if it was that great for me to live. Since my traumatic brain injury, life has been hell. Everyone says I made a terrific comeback, but I ask "come back" to what? My old friends don't speak to me except to say "hi" and I'm in lower classes than I was before. They asked me to write about why this book is important to teachers. Easy. For me, and probably other kids my age, we made great progress. I walk, I talk, I eat, but that's it. My life has been trashed. When people say "Hey, get a life" they really should think about having a traumatic brain injury. Somebody stole my life.

Robert, age 16, head-on collision without seatbelt,
January 1991

I think this book is important for teachers to read for several reasons. When I almost drowned, I was only 5 years old, but the damage to my brain has followed me all my life. Elementary and high school were a struggle; college still is. But people never gave up on me. I had one of the first computers the school ever purchased. My classes were adjusted to "fit" what I needed. Today I'm studying to be a social worker or counselor.

My teachers cared. They reached out to me in every way possible even though we were in a tiny school system. I know that to succeed in this world you need to value yourself as a real person. All the special things they will tell you in this book are certainly important, but I feel the most important thing is to not be afraid of "me"—and to care about me. I can succeed. It just may take a little longer than usual. But I will succeed.

Maggie, age 20, near-drowning survivor,
July 1977

Preface

In the United States, acquired brain injury—not AIDS, not cancer, not disease—is the largest killer and disabler of our children. Each year thousands of children and adolescents are rushed to emergency rooms with some type of acquired brain injury. Fortunately, the medical care system is able to save the lives of most of these children. Unfortunately, many who sustain acquired brain injuries end up with problems that change the course of their entire lives. Acquired brain injuries through traumatic events (open or closed head injuries) or nontraumatic events (strokes and vascular accidents, anoxic injuries, infections, tumors, metabolic disorders, or exposure to toxic substances) affect all parts of a student's life: family, school, and community.

The impact of an acquired brain injury on a child does not occur merely at a point in time, but rather as a lifelong experience. It can affect the way the student thinks, feels, behaves, moves, learns, and participates in the world. Adults often think of children as wonderfully resilient beings who can adapt to severe injuries or overwhelming circumstances, but a child's brain is a brain that is still developing. In reality, children are just as vulnerable as adults, only it often takes longer for the effects of a brain injury to become clear. As the child grows and develops, previously damaged areas of the brain may not be able to carry out their normal functions. For example, a 4-year-old may leave the emergency room walking and talking, looking as if he or she has completely recovered from the fall off the swingset. Years later, long after everyone has forgotten about the brain injury, problems with outbursts, impulse control, and language development surface.

Ultimately, the schools are the primary provider of services for students with acquired brain injuries. The majority of children with brain injuries, whether or not they receive rehabilitation services, go home to their families and schools with little or no information to help teachers and parents. Only recently have the medical, rehabilitation, and educational systems begun to recognize the complex needs of children with acquired brain injuries and the need to develop more comprehensive educational programs.

This book is a compilation of the working experiences of professionals concerned about the educational dimensions of acquired brain injury. It is an attempt to provide teachers and parents with specific models and strategies to help respond to students' educational and lifelong needs.

Acknowledgments

The editing of a book is not without a great deal of effort by many people. The editors wish to thank the many contributors who gave up evenings and weekends to collect their thoughts and write about the issues affecting children with acquired brain injuries. We want to recognize Mark Ylvisaker, Jean Blosser, Roberta DePompei, and Ann Deaton for their special efforts in helping us to coordinate and organize this book. All are champions for the children about whom we write, and their ideas are woven throughout the book.

We also want to thank both the informal and formal networks of educators, rehabilitation professionals, and parents across the country with whom we have worked over the past dozen years. Informally, a wonderful array of people have helped us to better understand and shape our thinking about the tremendous needs of children and their families. Formally, the Special Education and Pediatric Task Forces of the National Head Injury Foundation helped to create the awareness within the federal government that led to the inclusion of "traumatic brain injury" as a specific category of children with special needs in the public education laws. Presently, schools across the country are developing programs to better identify and serve students with acquired brain injuries in response to these collaborative efforts.

We also wish to thank our families for allowing us the time to focus on a project that has become an important part of our efforts to improve services for children with acquired brain injuries and their families.

Contributors

Vivian Begali, EdS, NCSP
2676 Gatewood Circle
Charlottesville, VA 22901

Jean L. Blosser, EdD, CCC-SLP
Department of Communicative Disorders
College of Fine and Applied Arts
University of Akron
Akron, OH 44325-3001

Al Condeluci, PhD
United Cerebral Palsy Association of the Pittsburgh District
4638 Centre Avenue
Pittsburgh, PA 15213-1596

Ann V. Deaton, PhD
Children's Hospital
2924 Brook Road
Richmond, VA 23220-1215

James L. DePaepe, PhD
Office of the Dean, College of Education
University of New Mexico
Albuquerque, NM 87131-1251

Roberta DePompei, PhD, CCC-SLP/A
Department of Communicative Disorders
College of Fine and Applied Arts
University of Akron
Akron, OH 44325-3001

Timothy J. Feeney, MS
Southern Tier TBI Support Group
Broome-Tioga BOCES
Binghamton, NY 13760

John J. Feenick, MS
Physical Education Department
Castleton State College
Castleton, VT 05735

William F. Frey, PhD
Psychology Department
Middlebury College
Middlebury, VT 05753

Juliet Haarbauer-Krupa, MA
3172 Wicks Creek Trail
Marietta, GA 30062

Patrick Hartwick, EdD
Department of Special Education
SUNY at Geneseo
Geneseo, NY 14454

Patricia L. Janus, MEd
Montgomery County Public Schools
Services for Physically Handicapped Students
Lynnbrook Center
8001 Lynnbrook Drive
Bethesda, MD 20814

Dennis Judd, RPT
Health Care Rehabilitation Center
Brown Schools P.O. Box 43148
Austin, TX 78745

Ernest K. Lange, EdD
Division of Learning and Teaching
College of Education
The University of New Mexico
Albuquerque, NM 87131-1251

Lois Mishkin, MA, CCC-SLP
Lois Mishkin Associates, Inc.
1579 Rising Way
Mountainside, NJ 07092

Marcia R. Nordlund, MEd
200 North Linden
Westmont, IL 60559

Natalie Nussbaum, PhD
2980 Rosendale Road
Schenectady, NY 12309

Irwin W. Pollack, MD
Department of Neurology
Robert Ward Johnson Medical School
University of Medicine and Dentistry of New Jersey
New Brunswick, NJ 08901

Bradford Ross, PhD
New England Medical Center
Center for Children with Special Needs
750 Washington Street
Boston, MA 02111

Ronald C. Savage, EdD
Hilltop Manor of Niskayuna, Inc.
1805 Providence Avenue
Niskayuna, NY 12309

Shirley F. Szekeres, PhD
Nazareth College
4245 East Avenue
Rochester, NY 14618

Pattie Tworek, MS
36A Haswell Road
Watervliet, NY 12189

Beth Urbanczyk, MA, CCC-SLP
Hilltop Manor of Niskayuna, Inc.
1805 Providence Avenue
Niskayuna, NY 12309

Pamela Waaland, PhD
4807 Radford Avenue
Richmond, VA 23220

Gary F. Wolcott, MEd
Research and Training Center in Rehabilitation and Childhood Trauma
750 Washington Street 75-K-R
Boston, MA 02111-1901

Mark Ylvisaker, PhD
College of Saint Rose
432 Western Avenue
Albany, NY 12203

SECTION I

Introduction

CHAPTER 1

Overview of Acquired Brain Injury

RONALD C. SAVAGE
GARY F. WOLCOTT

Recent changes in U.S. public laws in education have attempted to clarify and identify a group of school-aged students who have sustained injuries to their brains at some point in their lives since birth. Educators and a number of other professionals have recognized that the largest killer and disabler of children in the United States is brain injury. Unfortunately, previous public laws and policies neither adequately described this population of survivors of acquired brain injuries nor helped in identifying, classifying, or developing educational programming for these students.

Questions had surfaced among an array of professionals from education, medicine, psychology, and other fields: Who are these children? What happens when the brain is injured? Does a child who sustains a closed head injury and a child who is stricken with encephalitis have similar problems and needs? Is a child who is a near-drowning survivor the same as a child who was strangulated in that both suffered a loss of oxygen to the brain? Are the effects of neurotoxins such as lead and crack cocaine really best described as brain injuries? What has happened to the brains of infants and toddlers who were violently shaken and impacted and are now entering the school system? Although many of these specific questions remain unanswered, significant progress toward answers has been made during the past decade by medical, rehabilitation, and educational professionals.

In an attempt to facilitate understanding and to clarify descriptions of acquired brain injury, we propose the following definition:

> An acquired brain injury is an injury to the brain that has occurred since birth. It can be caused by an external physical force or by an internal occurrence. The term acquired brain injury refers to both traumatic brain injuries, such as open or closed head injuries, and nontraumatic brain injuries, such as strokes and other vascular accidents, infectious diseases (e.g., encephalitis, meningitis), anoxic injuries (e.g., hanging, near-drowning, choking, anesthetic accidents, severe blood loss), metabolic disorders (e.g., insulin shock, liver and

> kidney disease), and toxic products taken into the body through inhalation or ingestion. The term does not refer to brain injuries that are congenital or brain injuries induced by birth trauma.
>
> Acquired brain injuries result in total or partial functional disability or impairment that adversely affects educational performance. The acquired brain injury may result in mild, moderate, or severe impairments in one or more areas, including cognition; speech-language communication; memory; attention and concentration; reasoning; abstract thinking; problem solving; sensory, perceptual, and motor abilities; psychosocial behavior; physical functions; and information processing.

This description of acquired brain injury is broader than the definition used by the National Head Injury Foundation (NHIF) (1986) and the regulations promulgated by the U.S. Department of Education (*Federal Register,* 1992). These definitions focus on the mechanism of injury—a physical force applied to the child's brain that results in a traumatic injury—but do not account for the other mechanisms that can cause injury to the brain and that result in similar impairments that lead to functional disability.

Acquired brain injuries can be divided into traumatic and nontraumatic as follows (Savage & Wolcott, 1988):

Traumatic Brain Injuries

1. *Open head injuries* caused by accidents, falls, abuse, assaults, and surgical procedures that result in a penetrating wound to the brain
2. *Closed head injuries* caused by accidents, falls, abuse, and assaults in which the skull and protective tissue surrounding the brain remain intact but damage to the brain comes from internal compression, stretching, or shearing actions

Nontraumatic Brain Injuries

1. *Anoxic injuries* caused by a reduction in the oxygen to the brain from anesthetic accidents, hanging, choking, near-drowning, severe blood loss
2. *Infections* of the brain, such as meningitis and encephalitis
3. *Strokes and other vascular accidents*
4. *Tumors* of the brain
5. *Metabolic disorders* that affect the brain, such as insulin shock, liver and kidney diseases
6. *Toxic products* taken into the body, including lead, mercury, crack cocaine, and other chemical agents, either ingested or inhaled

The functional consequences of the surgical removal of a brain tumor in one child often require the same rehabilitation and educational interventions as those of the child with a penetrating head injury due to a bullet wound. The widespread damage to multiple areas and brain systems caused by a closed head injury (when damage to areas of the brain is caused by bumping, twisting, or shearing movements of the brain itself within the skull) manifests itself in similar fashion to the very widespread brain damage due to loss of oxygen to the brain from a near-drowning incident. The efforts to develop a classification of brain injury that will be helpful to the educator and parent must focus on the resulting impairments and disabilities rather than the mechanisms of injury. Many states and school systems have adopted a functionally based definition of acquired brain injury similar to the one proposed above.

Because all learning is brain based, injury to a child's brain may have a significant impact on educational, vocational, and social performance throughout life. The brain is the student's "learning machine," and understanding how each student learns and what happens when learning does not take place has challenged educators for centuries.

HISTORICAL PERSPECTIVE

The human brain has long been misunderstood. As human knowledge has progressed through the ages, many attempts have been made to identify the physical and spiritual sources of consciousness and behavior. However, the brain was one of the last places examined. The great philosopher Aristotle thought that the skull was merely a reservoir for fluid; thus, our eyes cried, our noses dripped, and our mouths watered. At that point in human history, such ideas made sense. Most people felt that the blood was the seat of life; when a person's blood stopped flowing, he or she was dead. Even the ancient Egyptians opened the skulls of their deceased and discarded the brains when they mummified the dead; the skull was filled with jewels, precious metals, and mementos.

During the Middle Ages, when surgical interventions were becoming popular, holes were bored into peoples' heads to let out evil spirits (i.e., seizure disorders, mental illness). The barber–physicians were often confronted by people who did not want their "soul" cut by misguided hands. Later, in the middle 1800s, phrenologists were "feeling" peoples' heads for bumps to get a sense of who they were and what they were like. Phrenology became very popular, and elaborate maps of heads were displayed showing where love, honesty, trickery, and so on, were represented on individual people. Interestingly, at this time, one of the first medical terms—lame brain—was being used to describe a person with a brain injury. The term made sense, and "lame" remains in use today to describe a person with a lame leg or arm, or an individual who is experiencing intellectual slowness.

During the 20th century, understanding about the human brain has progressed significantly. The brain is clearly perceived as the seat of intellect, emotions, physical movements, and an array of other activities. The general understanding now is that who and what people are emanates from the brain and spreads through their entire lives and environment. It is the brain that learns new things, that feels emotions and reacts, that propels people through space, that makes human bodies run with precision, and that, when damaged by injury or illness, can bring complications to developing lives.

Finding a rational definition of injury or illness to the brain has been an ongoing challenge to physicians, psychologists, educators, and a host of other specialists (Savage, 1991). How should "brain injury" be defined? Are not all insults to the brain, whether by injury or disease or genetics, in a sense, brain injuries? Although medicine and psychology are equally uncertain about how best to define brain injury, in this chapter, we take a closer look at how educators have progressed in their definitions.

Corrine Roth Smith, in her book, *Learning Disabilities: The Interaction of Learner, Task, and Setting* (1983), presented a historical perspective in this evolving understanding. She noted the following:

> In the 1930's, Werner and colleagues worked with many mentally retarded children whose learning problems were traced either to biological events or to childhood accidents. They defined a brain-injured child as "a child who before, during, or after birth has received an injury to, or suffered an infection of the brain." Other educators and psychologists classified brain injury as organic drivenness (Kahn and Cohen, 1934), minor brain damage (Strauss and Lehtinen, 1947), organic brain disease (Bender, 1949), organic brain damage (Bradley, 1957), or minimal cerebral damage (Smith, 1959). (pp. 42–49)

In the 1960s, the term *brain injured* most often was reserved for children for whom the label could be validated. Thus, when brain injury could be proved, the label was more specific (e.g., cerebral palsy, hydrocephalus). Later, educators took greater note of the many children of average or above average intelligence who were not performing well in school, yet were not mentally retarded or brain injured. The term *minimal brain damage,* which was used for some of these children, was changed to *minimal brain dysfunction,* which later evolved into *learning disabilities.*

Thus, despite the efforts of many educators, the ability to clearly identify acquired brain injury has been elusive. Accepting the birth of a person as some type of beginning and end point helps in the process of categorizing brain injuries. Brain injuries that occur prior to or during the birthing process are defined as congenital; those that occur following birth are viewed as acquired (see Figure 1.1).

Brain function also can be disrupted by injury, disease, deformity, underdevelopment, and/or environmental factors. Not surprisingly, some brain injuries, whether

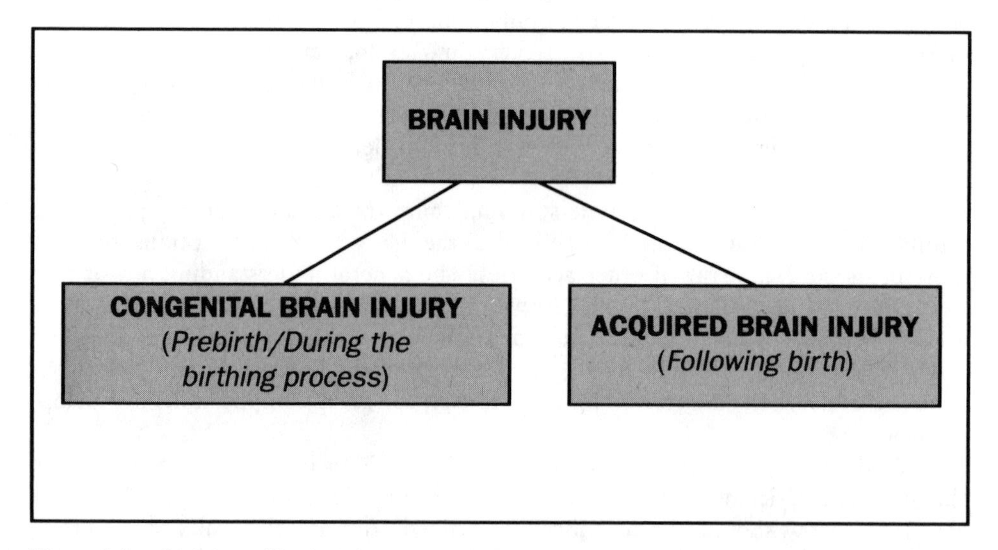

Figure 1.1. Division of brain injuries into congenital and acquired.

before or after birth, can be caused by nearly identical circumstances (i.e., neurotoxic poisoning by lead or crack cocaine can happen before or after birth; a pregnant woman could fall and injure her fetus's brain or a mother can drop her newborn infant). With 4 million preschoolers in our country subjected to lead poisoning and hundreds of thousands of babies born to drug addicted parents, educators are challenged to look at all children with acquired brain injuries, regardless of cause, and to seek to provide effective interventions.

EPIDEMIOLOGY

In scores of interviews, teacher training workshops, and seminars for special educators across the United States over the past dozen years, we have informally surveyed audiences. Consistently, when asked how many children with acquired brain injuries each educator has in his or her classroom, fewer than one in five reports having a single student. The vast majority indicate they have never been aware of any student in their classes with an acquired brain injury. However, upon further discussion and often follow-up with school records or parents, many more educators reported that students in their classrooms had cognitive, psychosocial, behavioral, or emotional difficulties that could be traced to an acquired brain injury.

How many students are actually affected by acquired brain injury? Is this a "low-incidence" disability as many educators suggest, or is it a "silent epidemic" as suggested by the National Head Injury Foundation and other advocacy organizations? Given the evolving definition of brain injury, one should not be surprised by the considerable debate over the actual number of students who experience acquired brain injuries each year, resulting in educational and functional disabilities. The incidence of acquired brain injuries in children is not well established. Many factors, including those discussed below, make it difficult to estimate the number of students affected by acquired brain injuries.

1. Within the medical care system, the diagnosis of acquired brain injury can be listed dozens of different ways (Cook et al., 1987). The standard means of establishing the number of people who experience a specific impairment is to review large numbers of medical records in hospitals. With dozens of different diagnostic codes that may or may not indicate an acquired brain injury, the results of these types of studies have ranged from 1 of every 40 (NHIF, 1989) to 1 of every 550 (Kraus, Fife, Cox, Kurland, & Laws, 1986) school-aged children each year.

2. Children do not access the medical system in the same ways as do adults. Large numbers of children with traumatic injuries are not admitted to hospitals but are seen in emergency rooms, physician offices, and local clinics, and are sent home. Records of these visits and follow-up care are not easily accessed; thus, brain injuries may be significantly underreported.

3. Rehabilitation and special education services following brain injury are new. Prior to the late 1970s, the vast majority of persons with brain injuries died. With the introduction and widespread application of new medical technologies, the vast majority of persons with severe brain injuries now survive (NHIF, 1986). Because physicians now can identify and monitor damage to the brain using computed tomography (CT)

scans, magnetic resonance imaging (MRI), and intracranial pressure monitors, and control the aftereffects of brain damage (brain swelling, bleeding, and chemical imbalances), the majority of persons with severe brain injuries survive.

Part of the difficulty in getting a clear picture of the disability group having acquired brain injuries is the wide variation found in occurrence from one geographic region of the country to another, from urban to suburban to rural areas, and within age ranges (see Tables 1.1 and 1.2). Gunshot wounds and blows to the head, which are common in some urban areas, are rare in suburban and rural settings. Similarly, acquired brain injuries caused by accidents with all-terrain vehicles are unlikely in cities. Some general patterns emerge, however, when age and cause of injury are examined (Annegers, Grabow, Kurland, & Laws, 1980; Di Scala, Osberg, Gans, Chin, & Grant, 1991; Fife, 1987; Goldstein & Levin, 1987; Kraus et al., 1984):

- Accidents are the leading cause of both death and disability for school-aged children.
- Traumatic brain injury is the most common result of such accidents.

TABLE 1.1. Common Causes of Acquired Brain Injury

Age	***Most Common Causes***
Infants	Abuse/neglect
Toddlers and preschoolers	Abuse and falls
Early elementary	Falls and pedestrian–motor vehicle accidents
Late elementary and middle school	Pedestrian–bicycle accidents, pedestrian–motor vehicle accidents, and sports
High school	Motor vehicle accidents

TABLE 1.2. Acquired Brain Injury Rates by Age Group

Age	***Rate***
0–4	1 of 667 children each year[1]
0–14	1 of 454 children each year[2]
15–24	1 of 181 adolescents and young adults each year[1]

[1] Data from "Incidence, Severity, and External Causes of Pediatric Brain Injury" by J. F. Kraus, D. Fife, P. Cox, K. Ramstein, and C. Conroy, 1986, *American Journal of Public Health, 140,* pp. 687–694.

[2] Data from "The Incidence, Causes, and Secular Trends of Head Trauma in Olmsted County, Minnesota, 1935–1974" by J. F. Annegers, J. D. Grabow, L. T. Kurland, and E. R. Laws, 1980, *Neurology, 30,* pp. 912–919.

- Twice as many boys as girls experience traumatic brain injuries.
- The greatest number of traumatic brain injuries occur in middle to late adolescence.
- A minimum of 1 of every 550 school-aged children *each year* will experience an acquired brain injury that may result in a long-term disability.

UNIQUE CHARACTERISTICS OF ACQUIRED BRAIN INJURIES

When students with acquired brain injuries are compared with students who experience disabilities due to congenital complications, clear differences are evident. The primary difference is the sudden onset of the injury, which often disrupts nearly all aspects of the student's and his or her family's life. Although much of the student's life experience, academic achievement, and personality often survive such an injury, this sudden intrusion into the individual's life leaves the student significantly altered, possibly for the long term. In many cases, the student is aware of these changes and some of their implications. The surviving skills and abilities are, in a sense, both a blessing and a curse. They serve as the basis for rebuilding the student's life. At the same time, that sense of "who I used to be" serves as a constant reminder of the loss that has occurred. In contrast, the student (and parents) who have "grown up" with impairments that occurred at or before birth have experienced the limitations of those impairments gradually at each developmental milestone.

Other characteristics of acquired brain injuries, which stand in significant contrast to the types of disabilities special education programs have served, are discussed in the following paragraphs.

1. *Severity of injury not necessarily equal to severity of disability:* In terms of broken bones, a compound fracture is worse than a simple fracture, as is more than one break in the same bone. This "broken bones" model of understanding injury, however, does not apply to the brain. As discussed in Chapter 2, the brain is a highly complex interconnected system. On the one hand, what may appear to be a minor injury involving a very small part of the brain can result in extremely severe disability. On the other hand, massive injuries to the head resulting in skull fracture and coma do not necessarily result in any level of disability following a period of recovery. Mild traumatic injuries, in fact, may be the most insidious. Parents, as well as medical and school professionals, may not recognize a brain injury in a child who had, for instance, a whiplash in an auto accident; however, it is clearly documented that brain injuries and resulting problems with memory, thinking, emotions, and behavior can occur without an actual blow to the head. Students often attribute their problems from this type of brain injury to fearing they are "going crazy" (see Chapter 11).

2. *Wide range of disabilities resulting from acquired brain injury:* Unlike many other types of children with special needs, students with acquired brain injuries defy easy categorization. Brain injury can affect all areas of a person's life and functioning.

Students with acquired brain injuries often experience disruption in cognitive, social, and physical functioning.

Cognitive Problems Involve

- Communication and language
- Memory, especially for learning new information
- Perception
- Attention and concentration
- Judgment, planning, and decision making
- Ability to adjust to change (flexibility)

Social and Behavioral Problems Involve

- Self-esteem
- Self-control
- Awareness of self and others
- Awareness of social rules
- Interest and social involvement
- Sexuality
- Appearance and grooming
- Family relationships
- Age-appropriate behavior

Neuromotor–Physical Problems Involve

- Vision and hearing
- Speed and coordination of movement
- Stamina and endurance
- Balance, strength, and equilibrium
- Motor function
- Speech
- Eye–hand coordination
- Spatial orientation

Such a wide range of configurations of functional problems requires a highly individualized program for each student.

3. *Dynamic nature of the resulting disabilities:* One of the most striking differences in comparing the general special education population with students having acquired brain injuries is the rate of change that can occur. Progress within the first 12 to 18 months following injury is often rapid compared with progress of other groups.

Students can "plateau" for a time and then suddenly make further significant progress. Given this dynamism, educators need to recognize such changes and to develop educational strategies that are responsive and flexible to the student's changing needs. Shorter time frames for evaluation and goal adjustment may be necessary within the student's Individualized Education Program. These spurts and stops can go on for years; thus, contrary to popular myth, substantial change can occur years after injury. The student can use prior life experience and preserved knowledge and skills (attained before injury) to continue to overcome his or her disabilities.

OVERVIEW OF BOOK

Although selective categories may help to better name the type of injury to the brain, they do not necessarily help determine what to do for the student. The remaining chapters of the book describe effective approaches and interventions that educators can use with students and their families. Chapter 2 looks at the brain from an educational perspective and discusses how the brain processes information, learns new material, and develops over time, as well as what happens to all these interrelated systems when the brain is injured.

This book, following the Introduction, is divided into four thematic sections. Sections II through IV are devoted to the brain-based processes of thinking, feeling, and acting. Section II, Cognitive Dimensions (Chapters 3–6), focuses on the cognitive issues that students with brain injuries experience and ways that educators can help these students both in assessment and intervention. Section III, Psychosocial–Behavioral Dimensions (Chapters 7–11), addresses the critical psychological effects of acquired brain injuries on socialization and behavior from a holistic perspective. Section IV, Neuromotor Dimensions (Chapters 12–13), presents information on physical assessment, intervention, and accommodations to help students better interact within their world. The last and largest section of this book (Chapters 14–20) is devoted to the overall school and community dimensions and their connections to students' experiences from the time they reenter school following a brain injury to the time they leave school and continue with their lives.

Thinking, acting, feeling, moving, and becoming an integral part of the real world are ever-critical issues and concerns that students, educators, and families face every day. Educators need to better understand how the brain works, what happens over time to children who have sustained acquired brain injuries, and how best to provide the array of educational services these students need and deserve. Such an understanding of the issues affecting students with acquired brain injuries will help educators collectively to develop the support services to help children and their families continue their lives after facing this most tragic experience.

CONCLUSION

Throughout the history of education, much confusion has been caused by terms that attempted to describe a person's brain that was not working the way it should. Many of these terms have been incomplete, unscientific, and often derogatory. When it comes to defining the brain, terms such as *congenital brain anomalies, head injury, traumatic brain injury, organic brain damage, minimal brain dysfunction,* and a host of others, have been used without consistency to define the injured brain. Recent changes in public education laws and practices identifying students with special needs who have traumatic and nontraumatic brain injuries have attempted to define more clearly what has happened to these children in hopes that better educational planning and programming will occur. In this chapter, we have provided a brief historical perspective of these definitional problems, the epidemiology and characteristics of acquired brain injury, and an overview of the major themes addressed in this book.

REFERENCES

Annegers, J. F., Grabow, J. D., Kurland, L. T., & Laws, E. R. (1980). The incidence, causes, and secular trends of head trauma in Olmsted County, Minnesota 1935–1974. *Neurology, 30,* 912–919.

Cook, J., Berrol, S., Harrington, D. E., Kanter, M., Knight, N., Miller, C., & Silverman, L. (1987). *The ABI handbook: Serving students with acquired brain injury in higher education.* Sacramento: California Community Colleges.

Di Scala, C., Osberg, J. S., Gans, B. M., Chin, L. J., & Grant, C. C. (1991). Children with traumatic head injury: Morbidity and postacute treatment. *Archives Phys Med Rehabll, 72,* 622–666.

Federal Register. (1992, September 9). Individuals with Disabilities Education Act (I.D.E.A.), U.S. Department of Education Regulations. Washington, DC: U.S. Government Printing Office.

Fife, D. (1987). Head injury with and without hospital admission: Comparisons of incidence and short-term disability. *American Journal of Public Health, 77,* 810–812.

Goldstein, F. C., & Levin, H. S. (1987). Epidemiology of pediatric closed head injury: Incidence, clinical characteristics and risk factors. *Journal of Learning Disabilities, 20*(9), 518–525.

Kraus, J. F., Black, M. A., Hessol, N., Ley, P., Rokaw, W., Sullivan, C., Bowers, S., Knowlton, S., & Marshall, L. (1984). The incidence of acute brain injury and serious impairment in a defined population. *American Journal of Epidemiology, 199,* 186–201.

Kraus, J. F., Fife, D., Cox, P., Ramstein, K., & Conroy, C. (1986). Incidence, severity, and external causes of pediatric brain injury. *American Journal of Public Health, 140,* 687–694.

National Head Injury Foundation. (1986). *Definition of traumatic head injury.* Washington, DC: Author.

National Head Injury Foundation. (1989, December). *Head injury update.* Presented at the National Head Injury Annual Symposium, Washington, DC.

Savage, R. C. (1991). Identification, classification, and placement issues for students with traumatic brain injuries. *Journal of Head Trauma Rehabilitation, 6,* 1–9.

Savage, R. C., & Wolcott, G. F. (Eds.). (1988). *An educator's manual: What educators need to know about students with traumatic brain injury.* Washington, DC: National Head Injury Foundation.

Smith, C. R. (1983). *Learning disabilities: The interaction of learner, task, and setting.* Boston: Little, Brown.

CHAPTER 2

An Educator's Guide to the Brain and Brain Injury

RONALD C. SAVAGE

The human brain is quite elegantly the supreme organ of learning. All that a person does, all that a person is, emanates from the brain. Nevertheless, few non–medically trained professionals receive detailed information on the brain or on how the brain learns and what is happening (or not happening) when the brain does not learn well. Ancient philosophers and scientists did not even recognize the importance of the brain as an entity. Even today in the "Decade of the Brain," researchers into this internal universe continue to try and gain an understanding of how people learn and who people are. An understanding of the brain is essential to gaining some knowledge of what happens to the brain after an acquired brain injury. This chapter highlights the present understanding of the brain from an educational perspective, rather than from a medical perspective. After all, the brain is the human "learning machine."

Webster's Ninth New Collegiate Dictionary (1988) describes the brain as follows:

> The portion of the vertebrate central nervous system that constitutes the organ of thought and neural coordination, includes all the higher nervous centers receiving stimuli from the sense organs and interpreting and correlating them to formulate the motor impulses, is made up of neurons and supporting and nutritive structures, is enclosed within the skull, and is continuous with the spinal cord through the foramen magnum. (p. 174)

This definition attempts to define the brain through its own neurology. Although the brain can simply be defined as a part of the central nervous system that can be found inside the skull, such a definition fails to describe the complexity and importance of this incredible organ that has evolved over time into a wonderful array of nerve cells that can adapt, create, and even change itself as necessary. This array of nerve cells and fibers has, in a sense, organized itself to become even more adaptable and creative in handling the most complex of tasks—thinking, moving, acting—and the most important task—maintaining life. Unfortunately, when the brain is injured, these systems break down, resulting in death or miscommunication among the numerous brain components.

The brain is not a hard muscle-like substance, but rather a soft gelatin-like organ that weighs approximately 3 pounds in an adult. Brain weight increases more than three times between birth and adulthood. The brain sits within a rough and bony skull and is bathed in a specialized cerebral spinal fluid. The brain is innervated by a sophisticated system of blood vessels that carry blood to and from the heart. Three membranes cover the brain: the outer *dura mater* (hard matter), which is like a heavy plastic sheet; the *arachnoid* (cobweb-like), which bridges the brain's many wrinkles and folds; and the *pia mater* (tender matter), which molds around every tiny crook and crevice on the brain's surface. Between the pia mater and the arachnoid, a teacup full of cerebrospinal fluid flows like millions of little streams, bringing nourishment and protection to the nerve tissue (see Figure 2.1). Internally, the brain also has four different reservoirs, called *ventricles,* for storing and circulating the cerebrospinal fluid. The ventricles are like tiny lakes within the brain that pools the fluid and helps cushion the brain and protect the brain tissue when swelling occurs (Lambert, Bramwell, & Lawther, 1987; Restak, 1979).

If, for example, a brain is injured by a sudden jolt or bang, it reverberates like Jell-O, often ripping, tearing, and stretching the blood vessels and delicate nerve tissues. To complicate matters, the brain rubs against the inside of the ragged and bony

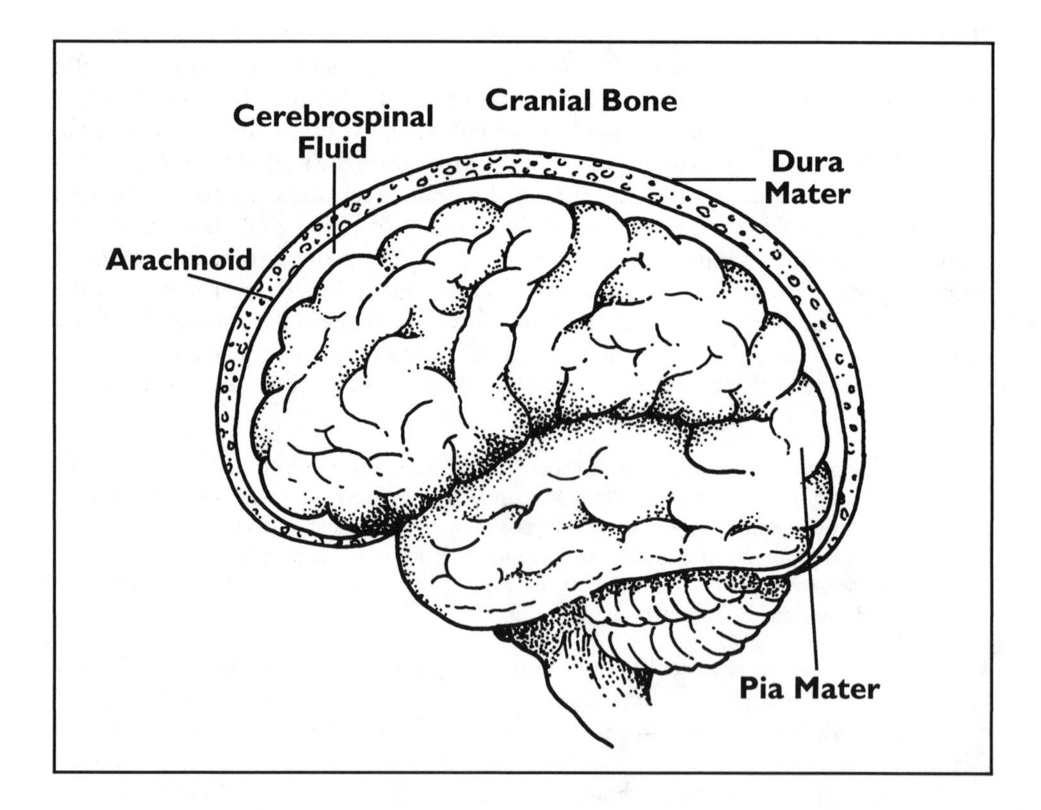

Figure 2.1. The three protective membranes that cover the brain and the fluids that flow between them.

skull, causing major bleeding. As with other body parts, the brain bleeds and swells with blood and fluid, causing tremendous pressure within the skull, which compresses the brain into itself and creates further injury. Thus, the brain sometimes receives two injuries: (a) the primary injury caused by an impact, stroke, disease, and so on, and (b) a secondary injury via brain swelling and bleeding. If someone were to trip and sprain an ankle badly, muscle, ligament, or blood vessels could be torn; the swelling created by all the bleeding and fluid accumulation causes additional problems, which is why ice or cold compresses are applied.

The brain reacts in a similar fashion, except the skull is not flexible like the skin on an ankle, which can stretch to handle the swelling. With a brain injury, physicians often need to relieve intracranial pressure by inserting specialized monitors into the skull and brain to control the swelling and to surgically operate and remove any accumulation of blood (*hematomas*). In some cases, the bleeds may be so small that the pressure on the brain builds up over time and may go unrecognized until the person starts to exhibit symptoms. The important issue is that the blow or insult to the brain is only part of the problem: The swelling, bleeding, and contusion (bruising) injure the internal neural network and are often pervasive and not simply localized at the site of initial impact. Like a 3-pound mold of Jell-O connected with billions of microscopic threads, a traumatic impact ripples through the entire brain, causing many complications. In addition, accidents that cause severe blood loss can cause a lack of oxygen to the brain, called *anoxia,* which quickly leads to brain injury. Many other nontraumatic brain injuries can cause anoxia. Victims of near-drowning, heart attacks, suffocation, smoke inhalation, asthma attacks, sudden infant death syndrome (SIDS), and strangulation suffer anoxia, which harms brain cells.

The billions of tiny cells making up the human nervous system are called *neurons*. Neurons are the "communicators." Other kinds of noncommunicating *glial* ("glue") cells support and nourish our neurons. Each neuron has three main parts: *cell body, axon* (a long, slim "wire" that transmits signals from one cell body to another via junctions known as synapses), and *dendrites* (networks of short "wires" that branch out from an axon and synapse with the ends of axons from other neurons) (see Figure 2.2). The neurons receive and transmit information in a relay through which electrical impulses alternate with chemical messengers. The electrical impulses flow through those nerve cell pathways to the axons and dendrites. Neurochemical transmitters leap the synaptic gaps between each neuron's axon and the other neurons with which an axon makes contact. Each neuron is its own miniature information center, which decides to fire or not to fire an electrical impulse depending on the thousand or so signals it is receiving every moment (Lambert et al., 1987; Restak, 1979, 1984). After a child sustains a brain injury, many of these pathways may be torn apart or stretched, thus preventing or slowing information processing. The study of nerve regeneration, repair, and creation will keep many researchers busy for years to come.

BRAIN GEOGRAPHY

A brief study in basic neuroanatomy—a geography lesson on our brain, so to speak—is necessary to better understand how the human brain helps people to think, move, and act. To better visualize how the brain looks geographically, take a golf ball in your hand and close your fist around it. Your arm resembles your *spinal cord,* which receives information from your skin and muscles and relays this information upward

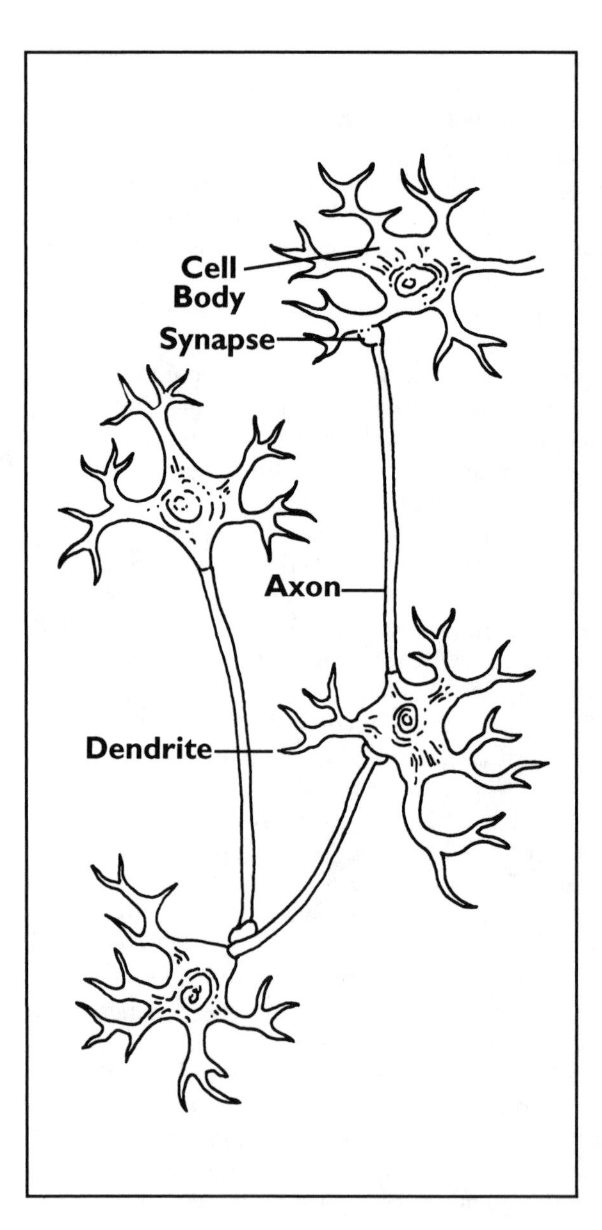

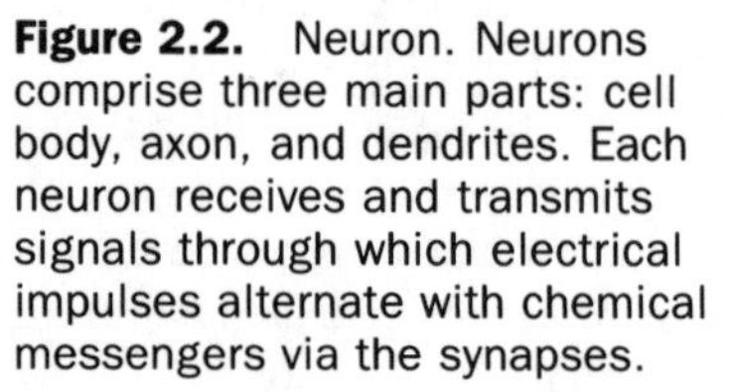
Figure 2.2. Neuron. Neurons comprise three main parts: cell body, axon, and dendrites. Each neuron receives and transmits signals through which electrical impulses alternate with chemical messengers via the synapses.

and, of course, relays information down and out from your brain. Your wrist is your *brain stem,* a small but important extension of your spinal cord. It is like the "point person" for all incoming and outgoing information and basic life functions. The golf ball you are holding represents your *limbic system,* a rim of cortical structures that encircles the top of the brain stem and is involved in emotions and basic elemental feelings, such as hunger, thirst, sex, and fear. Sitting atop and enveloping the limbic system, like your hand around the golf ball, is the *cerebral cortex,* which is divided into two hemispheres that are dedicated to the highest levels of thinking, moving, and acting. Lastly, situated in the lower back of the brain is the *cerebellum,* which coordinates, modulates, and stores all body movements (Brown, 1977; Harth, 1982; Restak, 1979). This interconnecting system of neural structures makes up your brain and who you are and are becoming. An understanding of this wondrous geography will improve understanding of what happens when the brain is injured.

The Brain Stem

A detailed look at the human central nervous system reveals a major trunk, the brain stem, which evolves from the spinal cord. The brain stem comprises four integral areas called the *medulla,* the *pons,* the *midbrain,* and the *diencephalon* (see Figures 2.3 and 2.4). In this array of structures in the brain stem, a collection of nerve fibers and nuclei called the *reticular activating system* (RAS) are housed. The RAS modulates a person's arousal, alertness, concentration, and basic biological rhythms (Hart, 1983; Restak, 1979, 1988). If you find yourself getting sleepy or have trouble attending to the information in this chapter, you need to "turn up" your RAS, which acts much like a dimmer switch that can be turned to make a light brighter or dimmer. After a brain injury, an individual may lose consciousness, which can result in coma. Because of the severity of the injury or the brain swelling, the person's dimmer switch may be turned down, leaving him or her unable to respond to even simple commands and unaware of surroundings. Unfortunately, the RAS can be depressed to a point at which life as the person has known it ceases to exist. The brain stem also contains the centers for the senses of hearing, touch, taste, and balance (but not for sight and smell).

The medulla and the pons, located in the lower part of the brain stem, are involved in many basic living functions. The medulla is about 1 inch of brain tissue that is vital to life and death, as is the rest of the brain stem. The medulla controls many basic metabolic responses: swallowing, vomiting, breathing, respiration and heart rates, and blood pressure (Lambert et al., 1987). Because this is the part of the brain struck by the polio virus, afflicted children of the 1950s had to be placed in "iron lung" machines that performed the functions that their medullas could no longer perform. When the medulla—or any area of the brain stem—is injured, life is immediately threatened.

Just above the medulla is the pons, a broad band of nerve fibers that connects the cerebral cortex and the cerebellum. This bridge of nerve fibers enables the "thinking" (cortex) and "movement" (cerebellum) parts of the brain to work together. Disruption to the pons can cause complete loss of a person's ability to coordinate and control body movements, possibly leaving him or her partially or totally paralyzed. Injury to the medulla and/or pons also can result in serious metabolic disturbances. Sometimes the upper regions of the brain can sustain catastrophic injury that results in "brain death," but the person continues to breathe and have a heartbeat even without life-supporting equipment. In this situation, the person is said to be in a prolonged coma or "persistent vegetative state." Unfortunately, the slang term "vegetable," which has been used to describe individuals in long-term coma, erroneously describes the circumstances.

The upper part of the brain stem contains the midbrain and the diencephalon and is responsible for alertness and arousal. The smallest part of the brain stem is the midbrain, which even makes possible elementary forms of seeing and hearing. Only centimeters above the midbrain is the diencephalon (comprising the thalamus, hypothalamus, and other structures), which is a master relay center for forwarding information, sensations, and movement. The hypothalamus, in particular, is the control center for eating, drinking, sexual rhythms, endocrine levels, and temperature regulation. It also is involved in many complex responses, such as anger, fatigue, memory,

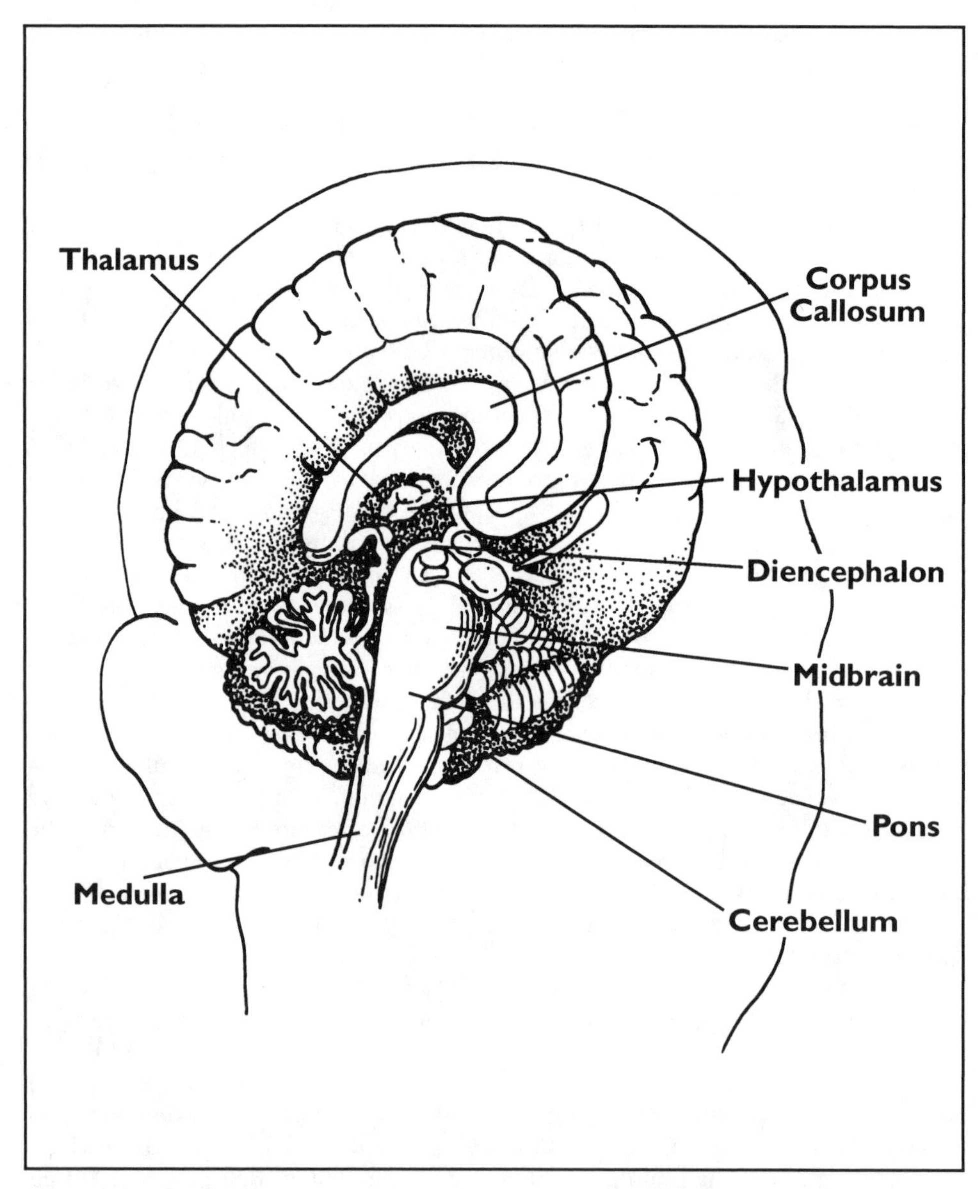

Figure 2.3. Brain stem. The brain stem serves as the master highway for motor and sensory nerve fibers. The four major parts (medulla, pons, midbrain, and diencephalon) make up the reticular activating system.

and calmness, and serves as the "conductor" of a person's emotional orchestra. The thalamus, which sits on the very top of the brain stem just beneath the cortex, acts as a major relay station for incoming and outgoing sensory information. Each of a person's senses (except smell) relays its impulses through the thalamus (Hart, 1975; Lambert et al., 1987; Restak, 1979, 1984).

Individuals who suffer injury to this upper part of the brain stem can experience severe attention and concentration problems, difficulty with memory storage and retrieval, weakened mental stamina, decreased sensory information, difficulty in reacting to stress, difficulty with hyper- or hypoemotional responses, and disorders in

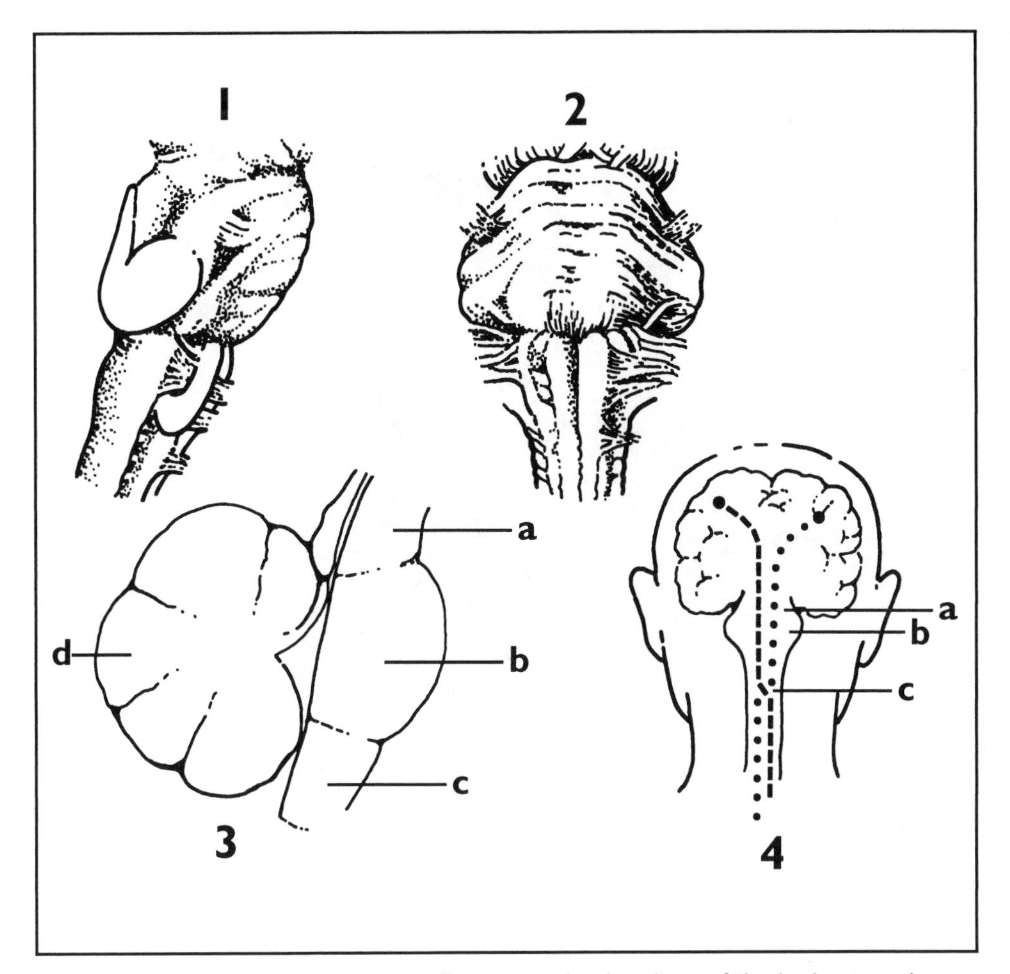

Figure 2.4. Views of the brain stem. Two representative views of the brain stem show also nerve fibers that end or start at this relay station and control center for vital life processes. (1) Representative side view. (2) Representative front view. (3) Diagram of side view to show the brain stem's three main parts: *a*, midbrain; *b*, pons; *c*, medulla. The cerebellum (*d*) (behind the pons) is not strictly a part of the brain stem. (4) Brain stem in action: The diagram simply reveals how the brain stem serves as a relay for signals that pass between cerebral hemispheres above and spinal cord below. Dotted lines show sensory signals flowing in to the brain. Dashed lines show motor impulses flowing out from brain to muscles. Note the crossing in the medulla, so that each side of the brain deals with the opposite side of the body. *a*, midbrain; *b*, pons; *c*, medulla.

eating and drinking, sleeping, and sexual functioning. Because the hypothalamus is the major brain region that manages the release of body hormones, survivors of brain injury may end up with many complex problems. The brain is also the largest "chemical" factory in the body. Disruption to hormonal, endocrine, and/or neurochemical systems can be just as devastating as injury to the neural network.

The Limbic System

Above, around, and interconnected with the diencephalon is the limbic system (see Figure 2.5), the area of the brain represented by the golf ball in the earlier analogy.

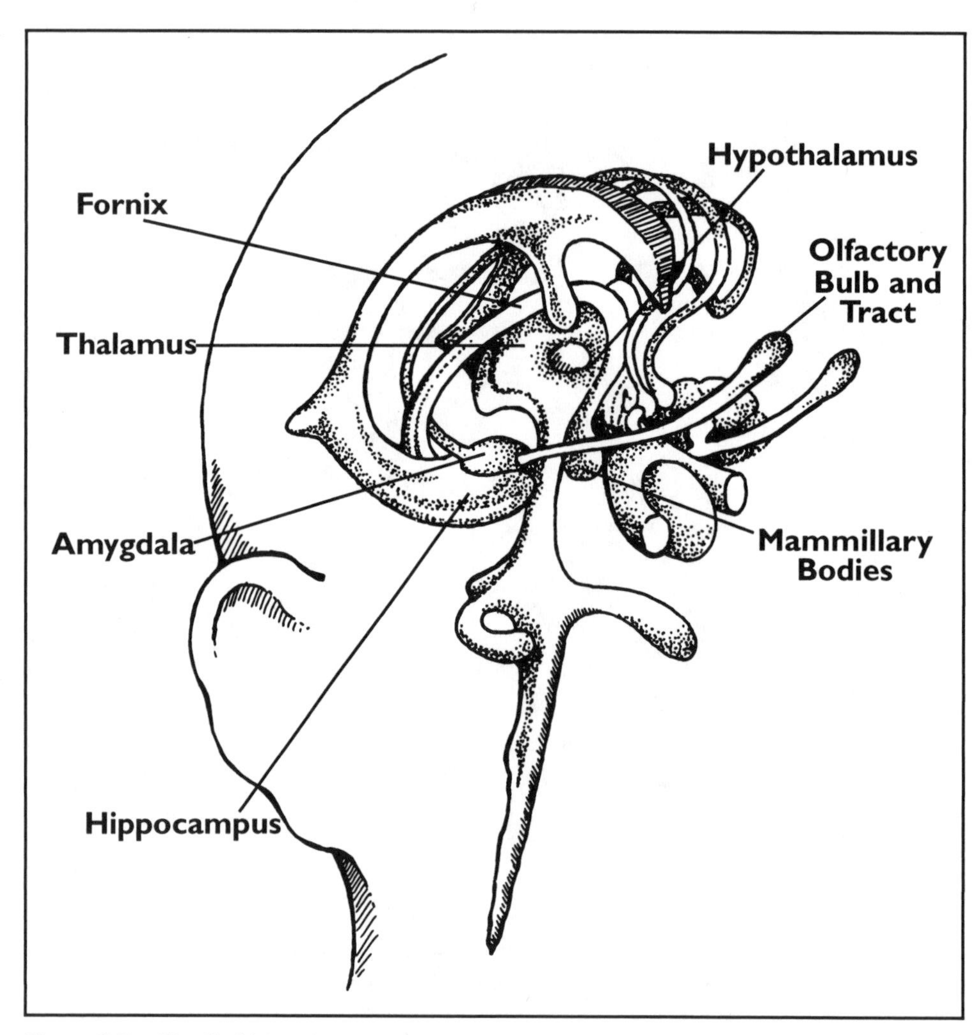

Figure 2.5. The limbic system.

Many "neuro" professionals (neurosurgeons, neurologists, neuropsychologists, neuroeducators, etc.) argue about which particular areas of the brain best fit into certain systems. Whether the diencephalon with its thalamus and hypothalamus is part of the limbic system or part of the upper brain stem is one of these debates. Arguments such as these are moot, however, if one believes that the brain is a highly interconnected and complex system that integrates many units into a beehive of internal and external responses and actions. Thus, the golf ball held in your hand is only a gross representation of the limbic system and its connectiveness to the other regions of the brain. Although dividing the brain geographically may facilitate understanding of the various components and systems, this division is only for convenience. No single part of the brain can be discussed accurately without connecting it to the whole. For example, a person's "attention" involves the brain stem, limbic system, and cortex.

The limbic system is complex and highly interconnected with other parts of the brain, especially the cerebral cortex. Some brain researchers have referred to this "middle" part of the brain as the mammalian brain, the evolutionary, animal-like part of the brain that houses basic elemental drives, emotions, and survival instincts (Restak, 1984). The two major structures usually associated with the limbic system are the *hippocampus* and the *amygdala.* Injury or damage to either of these structures can leave long-term and devastating problems for survivors.

The hippocampus is a paired organ, in that one is on each side of the brain within a temporal lobe. The hippocampus is most commonly associated with memory functioning and is particularly susceptible to loss of oxygen. Injury to the hippocampus causes students to have a great deal of difficulty with short-term memory, turning short-term memories into long-term memories, and organizing and retrieving previously stored memories (Lambert et al., 1987). The hippocampus is like the pole in your closet on which you hang your clothes. If the pole were pulled out, your clothes would fall into a heap, disrupting your entire system of hanging particular clothes in certain areas. When you wished to store new clothes, no pole (organizational structure) would be present to help you. Thus, your clothes would end up in a mess on the floor, which would make it difficult to find or store anything.

Close to the hippocampus is the amygdala, a structure that seems to be closely tied with emotional memories and reactions (i.e., fight vs. flight). There is speculation that, when a perception reaches the cerebral cortex, it is stored within the amygdala if it arouses emotions. A person's "fears" of snakes, spiders, and creatures of the night may cause him or her to run or stand his or her ground depending on the emotional response from the amygdala. Interestingly, both the hippocampus and amygdala are directly tied with olfactory fibers, which is why many survivors of brain injuries in the early stages of recovery benefit from smell stimulation (e.g., their mother's perfume, favorite food odors). Although all sensations—sight, sound, smell, taste, touch—evoke memories, smell and taste seem to be the most powerful stimulants for recollection.

Injury or disruption to the limbic system can produce a series of complex problems involving basic emotional responses to the world and oneself and how a person perceives and "feels." Actions, so often guided by emotions, can become uncontrollable. The person may become locked into over- or underreacting to even the simplest of situations. One minute, everything seems all right; the next, the world seems to be crashing down. Students may feel that they no longer have any control over their actions; they may become impulsive, haphazard, disconnected from their family and friends. The limbic system seems to run wild, and the injured cerebral cortex ("thinking" brain) cannot keep in balance the vast emotions that show themselves. As thinking, feeling, and moving beings, if humans are not in balance, their actions may bring only further complications.

Interconnected with the limbic system is a special group of brain structures called the *basal ganglia.* The four nerve cell clusters of the basal ganglia, or "nerve knots," help an individual handle physical movements by relaying information from the cerebral cortex to the brain stem and cerebellum (Restak, 1979). Most significantly, the basal ganglia centers serve as a "checking" system that comes to attention when something is not working the way it should be. An injured basal ganglia affects voluntary motor nerves and results in slowness and loss of movement (akinesia), muscular rigidity, and tremor, which can be localized or diffuse. When someone loses balance, the neurons in the basal ganglia tell the muscles to restore lost equilibrium.

The Cerebellum

The cerebellum is an excellent example of the interconnectedness of the brain. The cerebellum is wedged between the brain stem and the cerebral cortex, and is hitched to the back of the head (see Figure 2.6). (The golf ball analogy does not represent the cerebellum; you would have to glue the ball to the back of your wrist.) The cerebellum is about one-eighth of the brain's mass and has its own distinctive arrangement of brain cells. Medieval anatomists called the cerebellum *Arbor vitae,* the tree of life, because the layers of cells fan out in a striking foliate pattern. The cerebellum governs a person's every movement and monitors impulses from the motor and sensory centers (brain stem, basal ganglia, motor–sensory cortex) to help control direction, rate, force, and steadiness of movements (Lambert et al., 1987). It enables a person to develop and store the motor skills necessary to play sports, ride a bike, do aerobic exercises, perform martial arts routines, drive a car, brush teeth, and train the mind and body to accomplish amazing athletic feats. Many athletes who train rigorously over months and years coordinate their movements into "automatic" routines, ways to move without even thinking about what they are doing, enabling them to respond in milliseconds to an opportunity to score a winning point or set a new Olympic record.

Injury to or disease in the cerebellum does not produce muscle weakness, but rather disrupts a person's overall coordination of movements. A student with a damaged cerebellum may look "drunk" when he walks. He may not even be able to walk a marked straight line or sit without support. His eye–hand coordination, which is so necessary in life, may be disabled to the point that he cannot even reach out and pick up a glass of water. Or the child's movement may become so awkward that trying to

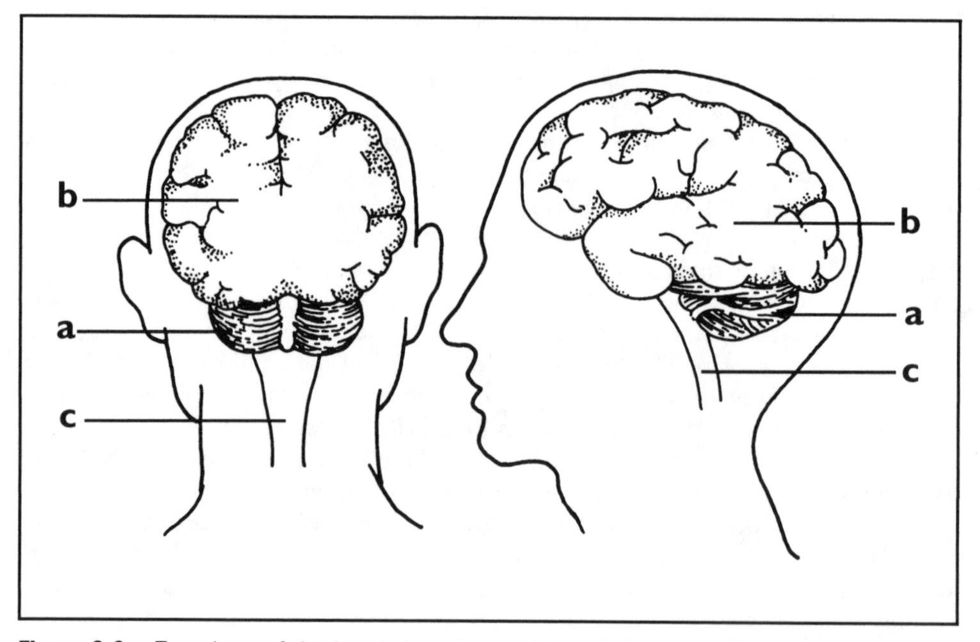

Figure 2.6. Two views of the head show the position of the cerebellum (*a*) between the cerebrum (*b*) and the brain stem (*c*).

write a simple sentence may result in a crushing blow to his own face. Because the cerebellum is responsible for coordinating muscle tone, posture, and eye–hand movements, damage to the cerebellum can seriously inhibit a student's movement within the school and community. Once-common routines, such as getting dressed, writing one's name, and getting from class to class within school, become frustrating and impossible to control.

The Cerebral Cortex

By far the most complicated structural component of the human brain is the cerebral cortex, which is made up of the *right and left hemispheres,* each with four lobes bounded by three fissures. As you make a fist out of your hand, the cerebral cortex is represented by your hand and fingers. The cortex is full of wrinkles and folds; in fact, if you could take your own cortex and flatten it out, it would be the size of a pillowcase. The wrinkling and folding of the cortex enables more brain to be packed into the skull. Of special interest is the fact that each person has, in a sense, two brains, that is, two hemispheres (see Figure 2.7). Having two cerebral hemispheres has led

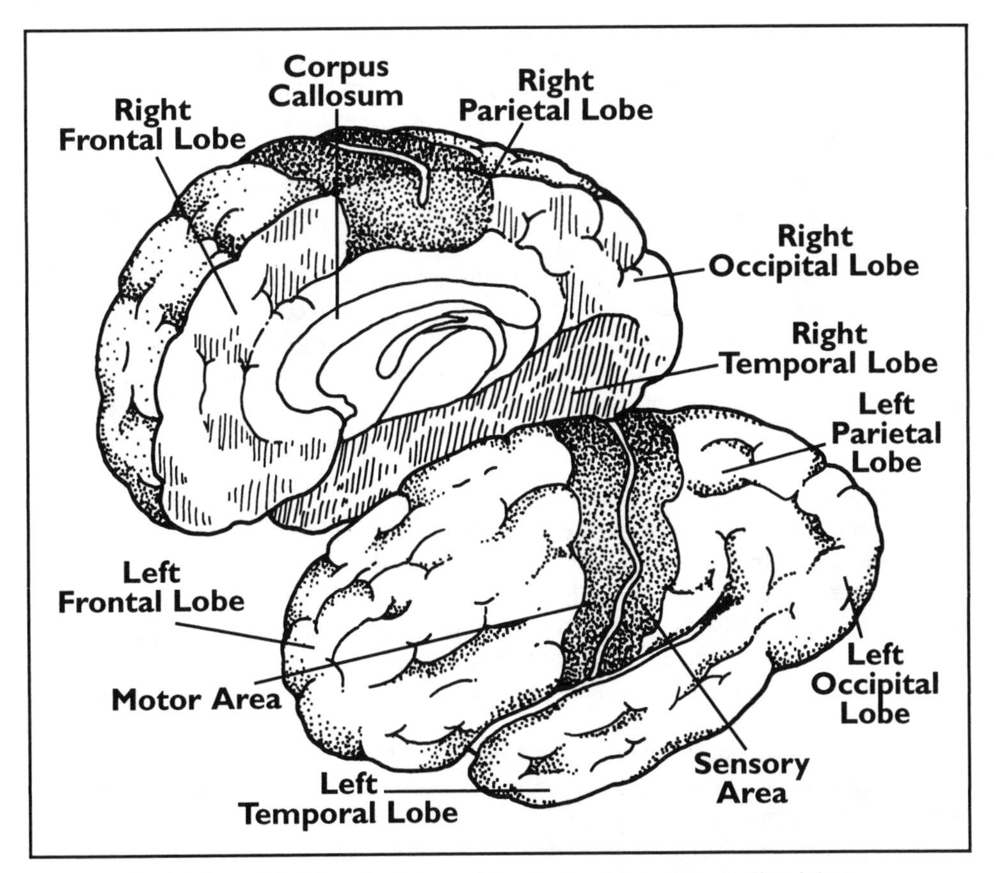

Figure 2.7. Right and left hemispheres of the brain with corresponding lobes.

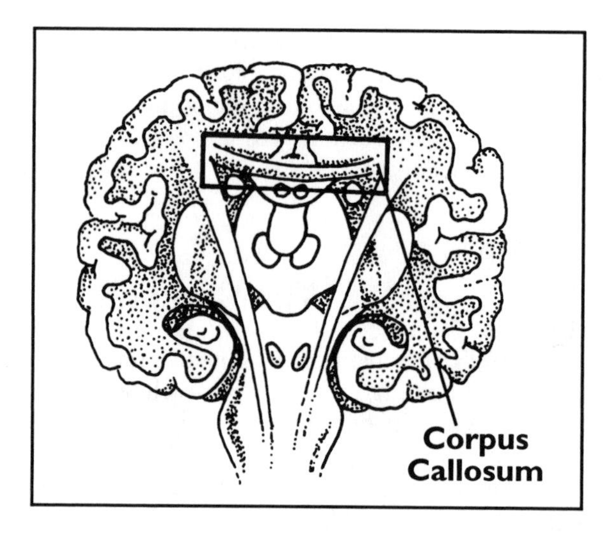

Figure 2.8. Corpus callosum. This thicket of fibers joins the right and left hemispheres, permitting the two sides of the brain to communicate with each other.

researchers to marvel at the cortex's information processing abilities and differences. History abounds with references to the "duality of the mind," but it was not until the 1960s that the duality became more clear. During that decade, Drs. Roger Sperry and Joseph Bogen gave detailed reports of significant changes in their patients whose seizures were alleviated by surgical cutting of the corpus callosum, a complex band of nerve fibers that exchanges information between the two hemispheres (Restak, 1979) (see Figure 2.8). Right brain–left brain differences soon became topics for common discussion. Additional studies showed that the two hemispheres of the brain, while seeming alike, had unique ways of processing information. The right hemisphere was more holistic, visual–spatial, and intuitive, whereas the left hemisphere was more linear, verbal–analytic, and logical. From a geographical perspective, comparing the two hemispheres is like comparing the states of Vermont and New Hampshire: They look alike except that they are "flipped around"; they have a major "connecting" river (the corpus callosum) running between them; and they specialize in certain things (Vermont is known for its marble quarries and New Hampshire for its granite), while sharing in other functions (both states make maple syrup). Interestingly, the right and left hemispheres control opposite sides of the body; thus, a person who receives an injury to the right hemisphere will have difficulty controlling the left arm or leg, and vice versa.

According to modern brain scanning, electroencephalograph research, and studies of people who have had their hemispheres separated by surgical sectioning of the corpus callosum, the left and right hemispheres do demonstrate both processing differences and similarities. The left hemisphere processes information in a logical and linear manner, which helps it better understand and use language (speaking, reading, writing, calculations), whereas the right hemisphere responds to information in a more holistic and spatial sense (shapes, faces, music, art). Although the right hemisphere can process simple words, such as *book* and *dog,* it cannot process words of higher conceptual demand, such as *honesty* and *perseverance.*

Despite the uniqueness of the cerebral hemispheres, they do communicate with each other a thousand times a second through the corpus callosum. This 4-inch long, pencil-thick band of complex nerve fibers allows the two hemispheres to work in tandem (Hart, 1983; Restak, 1988). When a person sustains a brain injury, the swelling or impact may seriously damage this precious relay system and result in impaired processing of information. Injuries can result in major damage to one or both hemispheres plus the corpus callosum pathway. Such injuries create very complex cognitive difficulties for people, and many compensatory strategies need to be developed to help students succeed in school.

To more fully understand the impact of an injury to the brain, one needs to remember that, when one part of the brain receives an impact, it reverberates throughout the brain like shock waves through a Jell-O mold. Students with traumatic brain injuries will not appear as "one-sided" people who have had a stroke in a particular hemisphere. Each brain injury manifests itself differently depending on the type and severity of the injury and the age of the student. Children before the age of 10, for example, may sustain an injury that affects the speech center in the left hemisphere, yet be able to develop speech in the opposite area in the right hemisphere. This does not mean, however, that language will progress normally because speech is only one small part of a child's overall language functioning. Nevertheless, during a person's early years, the brain can adapt and compensate for certain injuries.

Examining the roles of the four lobes–*frontal, parietal, temporal,* and *occipital*—will help in understanding the effects of an injury. Because the brain has two hemispheres, the lobes also have a left-side and a right-side involvement. Thus, the left and right frontal lobes work together, yet display many processing differences, as do the two hemispheres. These four lobes or areas of brain anatomy are named after the main skull bone that covers the brain. These landmarks help in mapping the surface of the brain. Like the interconnection of the hemispheres with corpus callosum, the lobes are interconnected by two types of complex neural fibers (see Figure 2.9). The *projection fibers* fan out from the brain stem and relay impulses and information to and from the cortex. The *association fibers* loop and link together different sections of the same hemisphere and modulate the cortex. These two neural fiber systems help the four lobes of the cortex work together and keep it connected intricately with both the limbic system and the brain stem (Lambert et al., 1987; Luria, 1973; Restak, 1979).

The frontal lobe, which includes everything in front of the central fissure, is particularly vulnerable to injury because it sits in the front of the skull. The frontal lobe also has extensive connections with the limbic system (emotions) and the other brain lobes. Injury or damage to this lobe severely compromises a student's ability to synthesize signals from the environment, assign priorities, make decisions, initiate actions, control emotions, behave and interact socially, make plans, and perform other executive-like functions (Restak, 1991). Although injury to any designated part of the brain creates problems, injury to the frontal lobe is especially debilitating because the frontal cortex is where ideas are initiated. Following a frontal lobe injury, a person's entire personality seems to change; the person does not seem to be like the person he or she once was. The prefrontal cortex in particular is responsible for various emotional responses a person has to circumstances. Rather than responding to situations intellectually, the person with frontal lobe damage may respond with delight, anxiety, hope, pessimism, or a range of other emotions.

Frontal lobe injuries in young children often go unnoticed because the caregivers are, in a sense, the child's frontal lobes—teachers and parents organize, plan, and direct the childrens' lives (Restak, 1986). As the child grows older and enters early adolescence, however, it may become obvious that the frontal lobe's ability to function more independently has been diminished by the earlier injury. The student may begin to experience a lack of control over a wide range of behaviors not because he or she is

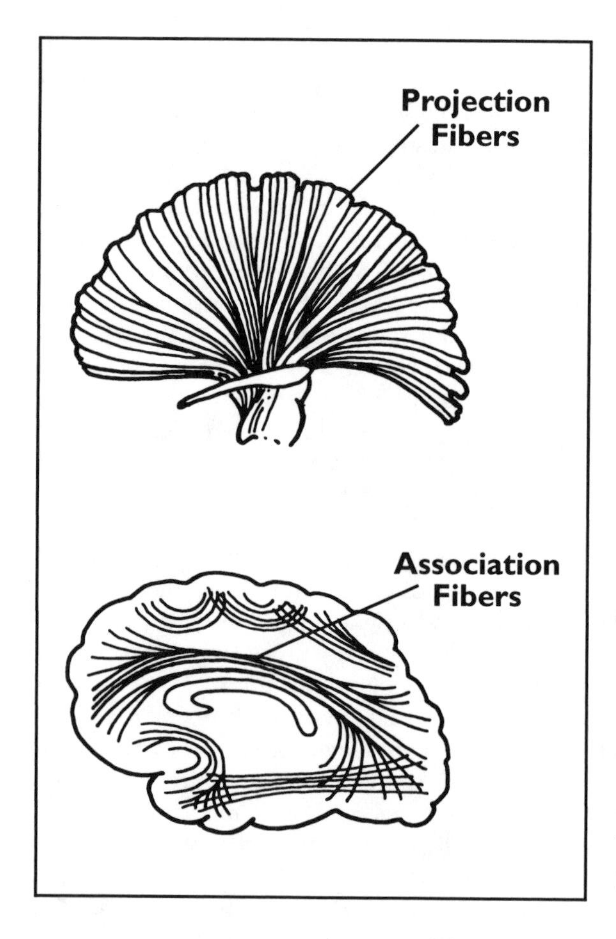

Figure 2.9. Fibers connecting the lobes of the cerebral cortex with each other and with the limbic system and the brain stem. *Top:* Projection fibers fan out from the brain stem and relay impulses to and from the cortex. *Bottom:* Association fibers link together different sections of the same hemisphere and modulate the cortex.

"misbehaving," but because the frontal cortex is not responding normally. Attempts to discipline or punish children with frontal lobe injuries do not help them to understand or compensate for the loss. Instead, ways to deal with complex behaviors need to be taught to students, just as new learning or memory strategies would be introduced to help them with cognitive problems.

Spanning the brain like earphones are two adjacent bands of cortex that trigger movement (*motor cortex*) and register sensations (*somatic sensory cortex*) (see Figure 2.10). This motor–sensory strip connecting the frontal and parietal lobes controls every voluntary movement from the simple pointing of a finger to the coordination of the lips and tongue to make sounds (Lambert et al., 1987). The parietal lobe caps the top of the brain behind the central fissure and merges into the occipital lobe. The parietal lobe is the "touchy, feely" part of our brain that responds to touch, heat, cold, pain, and body awareness. Injury to the parietal lobe can cause a loss of these sensing abilities. A student with damage to the right side of the parietal lobe may not recognize that anything is wrong with movement of the left side of the body because of basic neurology, not because of psychological denial. Even more complex functions such as attention can be affected by damage to the parietal lobe. The interconnectedness of the brain can impact a person's motivational states. For example, when a child smells food and turns her visual attention (eye movement) toward the source and responds by moving toward the food, a complex array of responses are generated through the

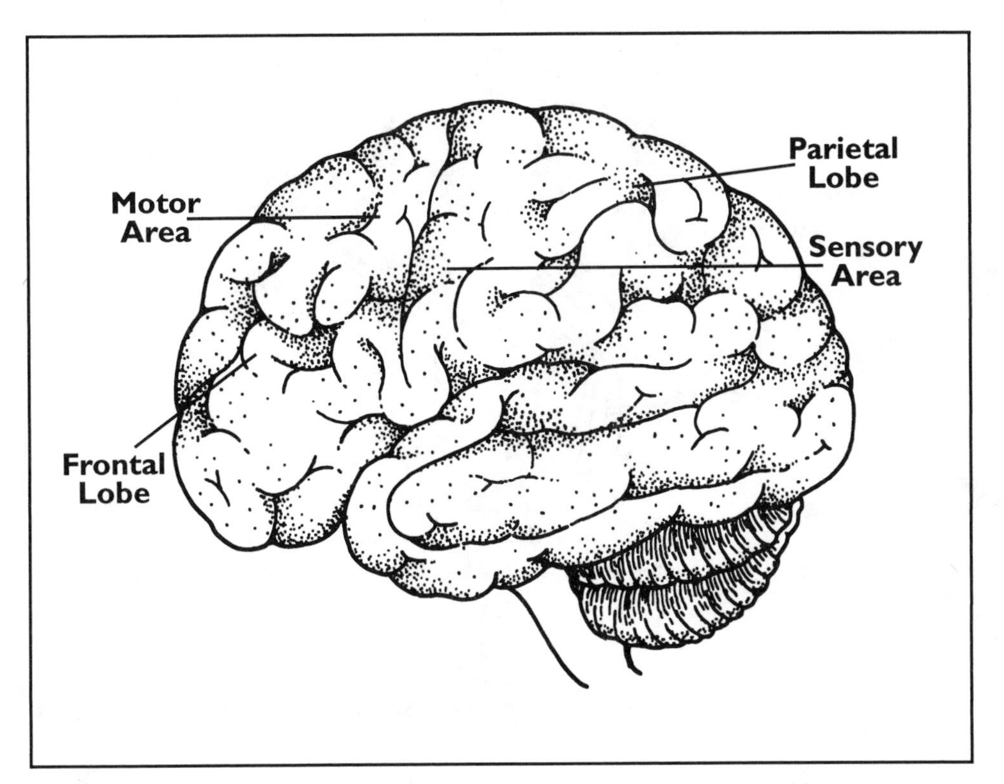

Figure 2.10. Motor–sensory strip that connects the frontal and parietal lobes.

limbic system to the frontal lobe, to the parietal lobe, and so on. Nerve cells that extend as far down as the brain stem provide the necessary arousal to the situation. Because much of school involves movement and motivational states, students with injured parietal lobes often experience a host of complex problems related to their motor–sensory systems.

The occipital lobe is the primary visual center, yet it is positioned as far away from the eyes as possible in the back of the skull (see Figure 2.11). This is why when you fall and hit the back of your head, you often see "stars"—in effect, you have stimulated your occipital lobe. The visual cortex is connected to the eyes by the optic nerves. Vision, neurologically speaking, is a very complex process; no other sense involves as many nerve cells. As incoming light rays pass through the eyes and are changed into electrochemical impulses, nerve fibers arrange and code these impulses. Near the back of the eyes, the optic nerves carrying these signals meet at a "crossing" called the optic chiasma. At this cross-point, optic fibers from the inner half of each retina cross to the opposite hemisphere of the brain (Brown, 1977; Lambert et al., 1987). Thus, the left optic track carries signals from the right-side field of vision, and vice versa, so that both sides of the brain in a sense "see" the same thing.

After these signals pass through a relay station in the thalamus and reach each occipital cortex, the whole image is reassembled and processed by different visual areas for size, shape, position, recognition, color, and so forth. Most of what you "see" derives its significance from what it means to you, based on your prior learnings and symbolic representations. As for other functions of the brain, if vision is separated from movement, or sound, or anything else, vision cannot be described in its broadest

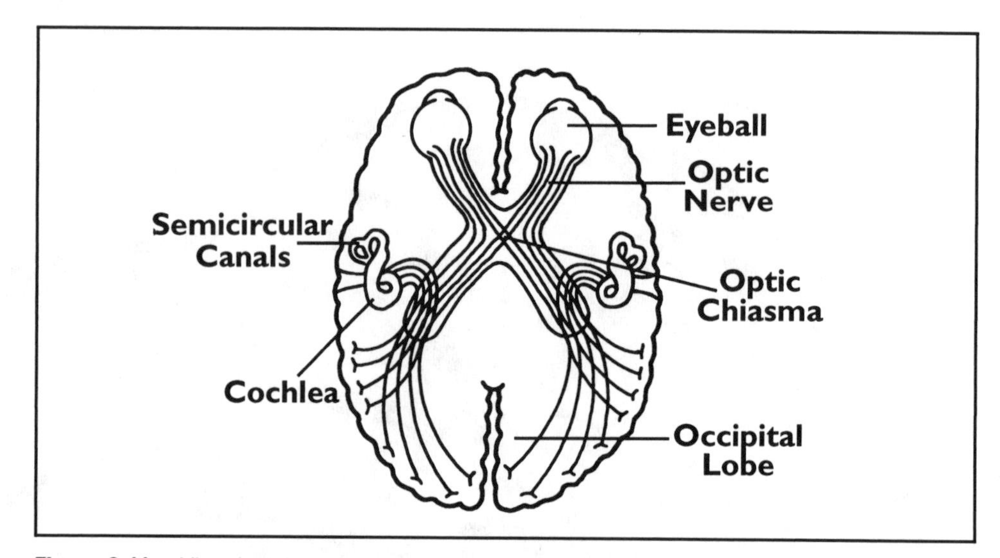

Figure 2.11. Visual and auditory pathways (viewed from top of brain). Two major visual pathways connect and cross, bringing information to the occipital lobes.

sense. Unfortunately, injury to the brain often disrupts what a person sees because of the complexity of this sense. Visual–perceptual–motoric damage can create many problems for students who have to learn in classrooms where much of the learning is presented visually.

The process of hearing also is very complicated, but it differs from that of seeing. As sound waves are picked up and passed through the outer and middle ears to the inner ears, a series of events takes place. The transmitted sound waves vibrate thousands of tiny sensitive hairs. Each hair is connected to thousands of nerve fibers that send signals through the eighth cranial (acoustic) nerve to the brain stem. There, many of the nerve fibers cross over before taking signals to the tops of the temporal lobes for analysis (Brown, 1977; Lambert et al., 1987) (see Figure 2.11). A brain injury can produce a breakdown of this process either neurologically or mechanically. Although many "mechanical" disruptions to the outer and middle ear can be restructured, damage to the inner ear and temporal lobe can produce serious consequences and have a direct impact on language and communication.

The temporal lobes rest on both sides of the brain and are the centers for language, hearing, and maybe the permanent storage of memories. More than a century ago, a French surgeon, Paul Brocca, and a German neurologist, Karl Wernicke, discovered that damage to particular areas of the left temporal and parietal lobes left people unable to speak or unable to understand language. The so-called Brocca's area of the brain is located in the lower portion of the motor cortex in the left frontotemporal lobe. This area controls muscles of the face and mouth and enables the production of speech. Wernicke's area in the left temporoparietal lobe governs a person's understanding of speech and the ability to make sense of thoughts when speaking. Together, these two areas direct the smooth transfer of thought, language, and expression into communication (Restak, 1979). Because language and communication are integral components in the learning process, many students with brain injuries need the long-term services of speech-language pathologists. A student's injured yet still developing language system can have a significant effect on his or her academic performance in school and interaction in the community.

The memory processing and storage capacities of the temporal lobes are not entirely understood. Whereas the brain can store short-term memories in the hippocampus, long-term memories seem to be holistically stored throughout the brain. The temporal lobes with their connections to the hippocampus may help in this long-term storage of permanent memories in terms of their meaning—that is, retaining concepts and relationships, instead of merely words themselves. Students with brain injuries often have difficulty with new learning but exhibit a good memory for information learned prior to the injury. Their memory system for understanding, storing, and/or retrieving new information has been disrupted by the injury to their brains. When attention, concentration, and memory are all disrupted by an injury, a student is unable to connect new learnings with prior knowledge and academic work seriously suffers. The student needs new strategies to help build the blocks to enable further learnings to take hold.

Human brain geography is amazing in its complexity and interconnectivity. Brains have evolved, and are still evolving, a neurological system that is continually adapting to make sense of "outside" and "inside" worlds. In working with students who have sustained brain injury, the more educators know about the brain and the effects of an injury on the brain, the better they will be able to help students live and adapt accordingly.

THE DEVELOPING BRAIN

Brain injury for a child is different from a brain injury for an adult even when precisely the same areas and systems of the brain have been damaged. A child's brain is still growing and developing; thus, an injury to a child's brain in the early years may not exhibit the same or as serious an array of problems as a similar injury might with an adult. Unfortunately, as the child develops and matures, earlier brain injuries can create more problems. A baby who falls and injures the frontal lobes may appear very normal in the ensuing years. However, when the child approaches puberty and the frontal lobes are being called on more and more to handle the complexities of life, the child's previously injured brain may not respond as it normally should. Brain injury in children must be viewed from a developmental perspective, and systems must be set up to monitor children over time.

Brain growth during development inside the womb and in the 5 years after birth is extremely accelerated when compared with other parts of the body (Epstein, 1979; Restak, 1986; Taylor, 1979). A newborn baby's brain has reached one-third of its adult weight although the baby is only one-twentieth as heavy as the adult it will become. Prebirth growth of the brain results from cells multiplying in the brain in a series of "spurts." After birth, the baby's brain grows not only in weight, but in complexity. Yet, even though the newborn baby's brain has almost all the neurons its brain will ever hold, they have not yet begun to form the connections and systems that develop the brain into an organized and integrated organ. This point is especially important in considering injury to infants and toddlers. It is difficult to assess the extent of damage to young children who have been abused, who fell, or who were injured in motor vehicle accidents because their brains are still immature. However, early damage to an immature brain does not mean that the child will simply "grow out of it." The often-held notion of brain plasticity and ability to rebound from serious injury does not necessarily hold true. Consequently, young children who have had brain injuries may end up with long-term neurologic problems that may never be overcome or compensated for because the basic neurological networks were damaged early in life.

Of equal concern are children who injure their brains at later ages. Many educators, pediatricians, psychologists, and child life specialists have presented the concept that children and youths are "developing" over time. Children are not merely miniature adults, but are beings in their own right with their own wants and needs. Unfortunately, many of the measurement instruments used to assess brain injury were developed for adults but are commonly used on children. Many of these devices provide false impressions of a child's injury and needs. In fact, many brain injuries that are determined to be "mild" may create a host of cognitive and behavior problems for children that go misdiagnosed and misunderstood.

Because normal brain growth occurs at significant times in children, an injury can have different consequences depending on the child's age when injured. Herman Epstein (1979), who researched brain growth in children by examining brain weight, theorized that children's brains grow in four 4-year cycles: 3–10 months, 2–4 years, 6–8 years, and 10–12 years and 14–16+ years. Each period of rapid brain growth is followed by a period of slower integration of that growth into the child's cognitive system. Interestingly, this period follows the growth stages of development identified by the biologist Jean Piaget. Epstein even presented information about sex differences in brain growth, which also may have implications for a child's injury recovery. The critical issues of brain growth and development and subsequent injury to a child's brain are areas in need of in-depth and long-term study. Although researchers have certainly begun to discover how brains work, they have scratched only the surface of our neurological abilities. The brain is certainly the most precious and complicated organ in the body. When the brain of a child is injured, the results can deeply affect the child and the family for a lifetime.

CONCLUSION

A better understanding of brain neurology and function can help educators better understand the complexity of the brain and what happens when the brain is injured. As medical professionals, educators, psychologists, and other specialists work together to understand how brains work, they will create new ways to help children and adolescents recover and compensate for acquired brain injuries. Unfortunately, researchers are only at the very beginnings of recognizing and appreciating the marvelous organ in the skull that defines who a person is and is to become, yet each day hundreds of people sustain brain injuries. An extraordinary effort is needed by all parties—the professionals, the survivors, and their families—to develop the services needed to help students recover, compensate, and adjust so they can more fully experience and enjoy the world around them.

REFERENCES

Brown, C. (1977). *Mechanics of the mind.* New York: Cambridge University Press.

Epstein, H. (1979). Growth spurts during brain development: Implications for educational policy. In J. Chall (Ed.), *Education and the brain: National Society for the Study of Education Yearbook.* Chicago: University of Chicago Press.

Hart, L. A. (1975). *How the brain works.* New York: Basic Books.

Hart, L. A. (1983). *Human brain and human learning.* New York: Longman.

Harth, E. (1982). *Windows on the mind: Reflections on the physical basis of consciousness.* New York: Morrow.

Lambert, D., Bramwell, M., & Lawther, G. (Eds.). (1987). *The brain: A user's manual* (2nd ed.). New York: G. P. Putnam's Sons.

Luria, A. R. (1973). *The working brain: An introduction to neuropsychology.* New York: Penguin Press.

Restak, R. M. (1979). *The brain: The last frontier.* New York: Doubleday.

Restak, R. (1984). *The brain.* New York: Bantam.

Restak, R. (1986). *The infant mind.* New York: Doubleday.

Restak, R. (1988). *The mind.* New York: Bantam.

Restak, R. (1991). *The brain has a mind of its own.* New York: Harmony Books.

Taylor, G. R. (1979). *The natural history of the mind.* New York: Dutton.

Webster's Ninth New Collegiate Dictionary. (1988). Springfield, MA: Merriam-Webster.

SECTION II

Cognitive Dimensions

CHAPTER 3

A Framework for Cognitive Intervention

MARK YLVISAKER
SHIRLEY F. SZEKERES
PATRICK HARTWICK

Cognitive impairment is a central theme in the treatment and education of children and adolescents with traumatic brain injury (TBI). In this chapter, we outline a conceptual framework that can guide cognitive assessment and educational planning for these students, illustrate classroom implications of cognitive deficits, outline approaches to cognitive intervention, and list principles of cognitive intervention and their classroom implications.

Understood broadly, *cognition* refers to the intellectual activity involved in the acquisition and use of knowledge, which includes processes such as attending, perceiving, organizing information, remembering–learning, reasoning, and problem solving. These processes operate within mental structures or systems, such as one's knowledge base and the "executive system" that directs and regulates cognitive activity. For as long as educators have been teaching, they have been searching for educational practices that are consistent with what is known about cognition. The resurgence of interest over the past two decades in cognitive approaches to education and, more recently, in cognitive rehabilitation for individuals with brain injury should not blind educators to the long history of philosophical, psychological, and educational theory and research in applied cognition (Mann, 1979). Those who forget the past are forced to relive it. Neglecting the lessons of the past may lead educators down garden paths known to be barren.

IMPORTANCE OF COGNITIVE FUNCTIONING FOLLOWING TBI

Attention to cognitive dysfunction is critical following TBI in children. This importance is underscored by the considerations discussed in the following five sections.

Vulnerability of Cognitive Functioning in TBI

Certain parts of the brain are more vulnerable than others in closed head injury (see Chapter 2). This is the physiological basis for the finding that children injured after infancy are more likely to have long-term cognitive and psychosocial needs than physical needs (Bigler, 1987; Ewing-Cobbs, Fletcher, & Levin, 1985; Perrott, Taylor, & Montes, 1991; Rutter, Chadwick, & Shaffer, 1983). Because children differ in their strengths and weaknesses before the injury and also in the severity and nature of the injury, no confident predictions can be made about which abilities will be spared and which impaired. However, some combination of problems described in Appendixes 3A and 3B are very common.

Importance of Cognitive Functioning for Children

With its emphasis on acquisition of new information and skills in a group setting, school places a heavy demand on a student's cognitive and self-regulatory abilities. An adult who returns to a familiar routine at home and on the job may not experience the impact of cognitive impairment to the extent experienced by a child returning to school. Particularly if the child has no easily observable physical effects of the injury, his or her return to school may be marked by a mismatch between the child's ability to perform cognitively and the teacher's performance expectations. This easily leads to failure, frustration, and increasing behavioral challenges.

Developmental Implications of Cognitive Deficits

Because children are a "work in progress" (Lehr, 1990), certain types of brain injury may have increasing functional effects over time or may first be manifest long after the injury. For example, an injured preschooler with impaired executive or self-regulatory control over behavior and cognitive processes may appear much like a normally developing preschooler. However, when the child reaches age 6 or 7, that injury may render the child incapable of meeting standard first-grade expectations, such as sitting quietly for extended periods of time and following directions. Similarly, a child injured at age 6 or 7 may appear to be well recovered within a few weeks or months of the injury, but show significant effects of the injury at age 11 or 12 given the cognitive demands of the increasingly abstract curriculum in middle school and the social demands of early adolescence. Furthermore, new learning problems, very common following head injury, have a relatively severe impact on young children because, unlike adults, they do not have a rich knowledge base on which to draw. Frontal lobe injury, very common in closed head injury (Katz, 1992; Pang, 1985), has long been known to have delayed consequences in children (Grattan & Eslinger, 1991; Mateer & Williams, 1991).

Assessment Challenges

Attention to characteristic cognitive profiles following TBI is particularly critical in an assessment context. Selective reacquisition of pretraumatically acquired knowledge and skills in the presence of significant new learning and organizational problems necessitates flexible interpretation of assessment results. Furthermore, the context and nature of formal testing circumvent many of the cognitive problems frequently experienced by children following TBI. Children often appear on testing to be better recovered than they are. Prefrontal injury may result in a profile that includes adequate performance on highly structured tasks but inability to perform effectively in the real world (Dennis, 1991; Grattan & Eslinger, 1991; Mateer & Williams, 1991; Stelling, McKay, Carr, Walsh, & Bauman, 1986; Welsh, Pennington, & Groisser, 1991). Good test performance predictably interferes with the acquisition of needed services and supports in school. These themes are further explored in Chapter 4.

Interrelationships Among Cognitive, Psychosocial, and Physical Domains

Cognitive weakness has clear implications for academic performance. In addition, cognitive functioning interacts dynamically with physical and psychosocial performance. These interrelationships are explored later in this chapter.

THEORIES OF COGNITION

Hresko and Reid (1988) outlined five overlapping but distinguishable cognitive approaches to research and intervention in the field of learning disabilities. These approaches have yielded distinct educational interventions for children with varied special education needs. Unfortunately, none of the approaches is yet associated with an instructional technology that has unequivocally demonstrated its effectiveness with any of the special education populations. Effectiveness of cognitive and educational intervention with children with TBI is largely unexplored territory.

Specific Abilities Approach

Associated with the well-known work of Samuel Kirk, Marianne Frostig, Newell Kephart, and others, the specific abilities approach emphasizes components of cognition (e.g., attention, perception, memory, association) as relatively independent building blocks that can be separately strengthened through remedial "mental muscle–building" exercises. The goal of remediating a weak building block, according to this approach, is to improve general cognitive and academic functioning.

Of all the approaches to cognitive intervention, the specific abilities approach has been subjected to the greatest amount of critical scrutiny. Empirical validation has, unfortunately, been disappointing (Kavale & Mattson, 1983; Mann, 1979). According to many recent critics, this approach (a) is overly simplistic in failing to account for the dynamic interaction among components of cognition; (b) neglects the active, strategic components of learning; and (c) fails to integrate cognitive remedial activities within the context of teaching academic content, thereby failing to produce generalizable improvements.

During the 1980s, there was considerable fascination with cognitive retraining for individuals with TBI. Although the methods have changed (e.g., computer programs vs. paper-and-pencil tasks), the underlying assumptions seem to be similar to the specific abilities approach in special education, that is, that separate components of cognition can be restored by exercising the impaired functions (Diller, 1976). Although some evidence indicates that test scores may improve modestly with process-specific retraining tasks (Ben-Yishay & Diller, 1983; Ruff et al., 1989; Scherzer, 1986; Sohlberg & Mateer, 1987), the effectiveness of this approach with adults with TBI has been no more encouraging than it was shown to be in special education (Ben-Yishay & Prigatano, 1990; Schacter & Glisky, 1986). Despite the impossibility of restoring to pretrauma levels all the cognitive processes that may be impaired by severe brain injury, evidence indicates that individuals can be taught to use their residual cognitive abilities with greater efficiency and to compensate effectively for cognitive loss (Ben-Yishay et al., 1985; Prigatano et al., 1986). Other models of cognitive intervention may be needed to provide a foundation for this endeavor.

Piagetian Structuralist Approach

According to Piaget, learning, cognitive growth, and, more generally, adaptation to the environment are products of two interacting processes: assimilation (interpreting experience in terms of preexisting knowledge and organizational schemas) and accommodation (adjusting the knowledge base and schemas to create a "better fit" with new experience). When assimilation and accommodation are balanced, the child has facility with a task and also takes account of new and unfamiliar information. This approach yielded a useful explanation for the importance of using tasks that are challenging, but within an appropriate instructional level of difficulty. It also provided educators with a helpful set of categories for describing cognitive activity at various developmental stages (sensorimotor, preoperational, concrete operational, and formal operational). Although Piaget's theory remains "a dominant force in developmental psychology" (Siegler, 1986) because of its useful descriptions of distinctive features of children's thinking, the rigid stage model of cognitive development in childhood has been largely rejected: "Children's thinking is continually changing and most changes seem to be gradual rather than sudden" (Siegler, 1986, p. 11).

Cognitive Behavior Modification Approach

The cognitive behavior modification (CBM) approach combines the useful technology of applied behavior analysis with covert methods of self-instruction and behavioral self-control (Meichenbaum, 1977). Most CBM programs include the following steps: (a) the instructor models task performance while uttering relevant task instructions; (b) the student performs the task while the instructor utters the instructions; (c) the student performs the task while talking through it; (d) the student performs the task while whispering the instructions; and (e) the student performs the task with covert self-instruction.

This approach has been shown to improve performance of students with learning problems in many areas of academic and behavioral functioning (Hallahan, Lloyd, Kosiewicz, Kauffman, & Graves, 1979; Hallahan, Lloyd, Kosiewicz, & Kneedler, 1979; Keogh & Glover, 1980; Kneedler & Hallahan, 1981; Kosiewicz, Hallahan,

Lloyd, & Graves, 1979; Meichenbaum, 1977). However, critics and proponents alike are not yet convinced of the generalizability and durability of these treatment effects (Meichenbaum & Asarnow, 1979). On the positive side, the approach does engage the student's active, self-regulatory function while maintaining an objective, data-based, behavioral orientation toward cognitive growth. Meichenbaum (1993) recently described the application of CBM procedures to rehabilitation after TBI.

Information Processing Approach

Investigators in cognitive psychology (e.g., Anderson, 1975), developmental cognitive psychology (e.g., Brown, 1979; Flavell, 1985; Kail, 1984; Siegler, 1986), and cognitive approaches to special education (e.g., Hagen, Barclay, & Schwethelm, 1982; Hall, 1980; Reid & Hresko, 1981) have emphasized the usefulness of information processing concepts for explaining cognitive performance. The information processing approach to classroom instruction and cognitive intervention is based on several critical beliefs: (a) that receiving information from the environment and storing it for later use are active processes in which students apply organizing schemas and old knowledge to the task of interpreting new experiences; (b) that component cognitive processes, such as attending, perceiving, organizing, learning–memory, reasoning, and problem-solving processes, interact dynamically in receiving and interpreting information and formulating a response; and (c) that cognitive activity is goal directed and component cognitive processes are controlled by an executive system (Anderson, 1975). Much of the recent work on learning strategies or compensatory strategies has evolved within this framework (Forrest-Pressley, MacKinnon, & Waller, 1985; Pressley, 1993; Pressley, Goodchild, Fleet, Zajchowski, & Evans, 1989; Pressley & Levin, 1983).

Metacognitive Approach

The metacognitive approach, closely related to the information processing approach, emphasizes students' awareness of their cognitive strengths and weaknesses, and their deliberate control over cognitive activity (Brown, 1975, 1978; Flavell, 1976; Wong, 1986). Students are taught and encouraged to assess their own strengths and needs, set goals for their performance, predict their success, monitor and evaluate their performance, and creatively solve problems when performance fails to meet their goals. The central themes include and extend beyond what traditionally fell under the "study skills" category. Later in this chapter, we highlight the importance of a metacognitive approach for many students with TBI.

Hresko and Reid (1988) completed their review of cognitive approaches to classroom instruction by arguing that, of the five, only the specific abilities approach is incapable of supporting creative and effective educational planning for students with learning disabilities. The remaining four, although different in focus and vocabulary, are generally compatible with one another and together offer educators a rich and comprehensive domain of educational possibilities. We have borrowed from all four in fashioning an approach to cognitive rehabilitation following TBI.

A FRAMEWORK FOR COGNITIVE INTERVENTION

Clinicians and educators need to approach cognitive assessment and intervention with a useful framework of descriptive categories. An organized conceptual framework helps to ensure a complete description of students' cognitive strengths and needs, guides exploration of interrelationships among cognitive deficits, helps diverse professionals understand the others' language, and serves as a source of intervention goals and principles of treatment. Clinical and educational activity, unstructured and without the direction of a conceptual framework, is blind; models and theories, uninformed by clinical experience and instructional skill, are empty (Szekeres, Ylvisaker, & Holland, 1985).

A descriptive framework is quite different from a theory or model of cognition. Commitment to a specific view regarding the actual mechanisms of cognitive functioning may easily stand in the way of a clear perception of a student's concrete needs. The goal of teachers and clinicians is to use productive theories and frameworks to select goals and generate sound treatment procedures, and thereby avoid a "hit-or-miss" workbook or "canned curriculum" approach to intervention. At the same time, each individual student's response and progress must be used as the ultimate guide in clinical and instructional planning.

The framework that we find most useful borrows concepts and principles from applied behavior analysis (Bandura, 1977; Miller & Dollard, 1941; Skinner, 1969) and cognitive behavior modification (Meichenbaum, 1977) approaches, the structural-organismic approach (Flavell, 1985; Piaget, 1983), the information processing approach (Dodd & White, 1980), and the metacognitive approach (Brown, 1978; Flavell, 1976; Wong, 1986). The categories of the cognitive framework are stated largely in information processing terms because of the comprehensiveness of this approach to cognition and the usefulness of the categories for clinical and instructional purposes. From this perspective, cognition is viewed broadly as a complex system with which an individual processes information, for particular purposes, within certain mental structures and environmental constraints (Dodd & White, 1980).

Aspects of Cognition

Appendix 3A includes a framework of descriptive cognitive categories (left-hand column) and descriptions of cognitive characteristics of children with severe closed head injury over three broad phases of recovery (early, middle, and late). The framework divides cognitive functioning under three headings: *Component cognitive processes* (attending, perceiving, learning–remembering, organizing, reasoning, problem solving) are involved in the individual's selecting, structuring, organizing, interpreting, storing, and applying information. *Component cognitive systems* include working memory (the short-term "holding space" within which active processing of experience occurs), the knowledge base (an elaborate system of information, relationships, rules, and principles that helps to guide cognitive processing), the executive system (that plans and directs cognitive, and other, activity), and the response system that controls output. Szekeres, Ylvisaker, and Cohen (1987) explained these framework categories in considerable depth.

We added descriptors (efficiency, level, scope, and manner) under the heading *functional–integrative performance* to capture the important fact that many individuals seem to have adequate cognitive recovery following brain injury, based on separate analysis of their component processes and systems. However, these individuals may still experience extreme difficulty in real-world tasks because (a) the demand for *efficient* processing (related to speed of processing or amount of information to be processed) exceeds their ability; (b) they are successful only with tasks limited in academic or developmental *level;* (c) they can maintain adequate performance only in structured or familiar environments (*scope* of performance); or (d) they are highly impulsive or perhaps dependent on others for direction, cuing, and initiation–inhibition (*manner* of performance). The description of outcome characteristics in Appendix 3A is based in part on our many years of clinical experience with this population and in part on the published outcome literature (e.g., Bawden, Knights, & Winogren, 1985; Campbell & Dollaghan, 1990; Chadwick, 1985; Chapman et al., 1992; Dennis & Barnes, 1990; Ewing-Cobbs, Miner, Fletcher, & Levin, 1989; Fletcher, Ewing-Cobbs, Miner, & Levin, 1990; Lehr, 1990; Perrott et al., 1991; Petterson, 1988).

In describing aspects of cognition, we need to highlight the many ways in which component processes and systems interact with one another. For example, memory may appear to be impaired, but only because the individual cannot attend adequately or organize information efficiently or perhaps because the individual does not direct himself to use his cognitive processes adequately (impaired executive functioning). Exploration of cognitive strengths and weaknesses must take account of interactions of this sort among components of cognition (see Chapter 4).

Stages of Cognitive Recovery

Recovery after severe TBI involves progression through a sequence of stages of cognitive functioning. The stages of cognitive recovery outlined in Appendix 3A must be interpreted cautiously. Beyond the earliest stage (i.e., no response or deep coma), different children may have very different sets of strengths and needs, based on their pretrauma characteristics and the nature and severity of their brain injury. Lists of common characteristics can never substitute for a careful description of individual children at any stage of recovery. Furthermore, each child experiences a large number of interestingly different stages of recovery, not merely three—or eight, as in the commonly used Rancho Los Amigos Stages of Cognitive Recovery (Hagen, 1981). Furthermore, lists of deficits, such as those in Appendix 3A, are not intended to suggest that children are adequately described by what they *cannot* do following the injury. Effective program planning requires thorough identification of a child's *strengths* and personality characteristics. Children with TBI are not mere collections of deficits.

The early stage of cognitive recovery generally occurs in a hospital or rehabilitation facility. Early in this stage, children have few responses to the environment and often do not recognize events, things, or people. Late in this stage, children respond differentially to external stimuli (e.g., turning to sound, tracking objects visually) and begin to show recognition of familiar events and people. They also may begin to respond to simple commands.

Although children rarely return to school at this early stage of recovery, educators and other school personnel may have responsibility for intervention through home-bound programming. From a cognitive perspective, intervention is designed to use sensory and sensorimotor stimulation to increase arousal and adaptive responses to the environment. The goal is to create an appropriately modulated sensory environment so that the child is neither over- nor understimulated. Furthermore, techniques for enabling the child to have effects on the environment (e.g., through the prompted use of remote switches to control toys, tape recorders, or other motivating events) are useful at this stage of cognitive recovery. Smith and Ylvisaker (1985) discussed issues in cognitive programming for children at this stage of recovery.

The middle stage of cognitive recovery is characterized by overall alertness and recognition of objects, people, and events in the environment, but also by some degree of confusion, disorientation, impulsiveness, severely impaired attention, and shallow processing of information. Superficial academic skills (e.g., ability to read and write words and short messages, do simple calculations, spell) may return quickly during the middle stage. However, comprehension, abstract thinking, organized expression, problem solving, and new learning lag substantially behind. Self-regulation of cognitive functioning (and of behavior generally) may be the most severely impaired aspect of cognition at this stage.

With children discharged earlier and earlier from hospitals and rehabilitation facilities, an unfortunate fact is that children often attempt to reenter their community school at this middle stage of recovery. In the absence of a solid set of individualized supports, the likely result is failure and possibly a downward emotional and behavioral spiral. The primary goals of cognitive programming at this stage are (a) to channel the child's spontaneous recovery through thoughtful environmental engineering, including simplification of the environment and routines, consistency in schedule, ample preparation for tasks and nonroutine events, and teacher expectations that are consistent with the child's ability to perform; (b) to systematically challenge components of cognition using tasks that gradually increase in difficulty, one aspect of cognition at a time; (c) to help the child recover familiar organizational schemes and thought processes that guided thinking before the injury; and (d) to prevent the evolution of maladaptive behavior by appropriately managing the child's confused, perseverative, inappropriate, and sometimes bizarre behavior. Haarbauer-Krupa, Moser, Smith, Sullivan, and Szekeres (1985) discussed issues in cognitive programming for children at this middle stage of recovery.

The late stage of recovery is characterized by generally appropriate and goal-directed behavior (relative to age expectations), but with specific constellations of cognitive deficits related to the child's injury and pretrauma status. At this stage, when they typically reenter their community school, children with TBI exhibit enormous variability. Following mild, moderate, and even many severe injuries, most children regain roughly normal global intellectual functioning (as measured by intelligence tests). However, severely injured children are generally left with cognitive deficits that may be permanent. Among the common long-term residual cognitive deficits are slowness in receiving information, thinking, and responding; distractibility; disorganized thinking and acting; inefficient learning; breakdowns in processing information and learning as the amount of information to be processed increases; unawareness of cognitive strengths and weaknesses; and generally weak self-regulation.

Following severe injuries, improvement can continue, at a decelerating rate, for several years (Klonoff, Low, & Clark, 1977). This may be confusing in a school setting because most children with special needs have a relatively fixed neurologic substrate. At a certain point after the injury, it becomes difficult to distinguish between the child's neurologic recovery, on the one hand, and, on the other, the child's learning to use his or her residual abilities more effectively. Many children with TBI had learning problems before the injury. This certainly places a constraint on the ultimate recovery;

however, it is generally impossible to identify clearly which challenges were a consequence of the injury and which were present pretraumatically. To complicate matters further, children injured early in life may experience delayed effects of the injury. Specific academic or social consequences may appear years after the injury at the developmental stage at which functions associated with the injured part of the brain are expected to mature.

Cognitive Deficits in a Classroom Setting

Appendix 3B includes illustrations of classroom manifestations of cognitive problems following TBI. This table is included for two reasons: (a) The cognitive framework that we are using will be easier for educators to appreciate with the concepts made concrete through these illustrations, and (b) it is useful to highlight ways in which the behavior of a student with traumatic brain injury can be misleading and easy to misinterpret.

Comparison with Other Disability Groups

Many of the illustrations in Appendix 3B could describe children with other disabilities, such as learning disability or mental retardation. To understand ways in which students with TBI may differ from students in other special education categories, it is instructive to compare central tendencies among these children with central tendencies among children with other disabilities, remembering that enormous individual differences exist within all disability groups.

Like students with learning disabilities, many students with TBI score within normal limits on tests of intelligence, despite uneven cognitive profiles and substantial difficulty learning new information. Children in both groups tend to have some problems from the following list: impaired attention; inefficient perceptual and organizational functioning; slow processing of information; disorganized thinking; poor awareness of disability; weak problem solving and strategic thinking; impulsive, disinhibited, and socially inappropriate behavior; and reduced tolerance for stress. Furthermore, children in both groups tend to profit from similar types of intervention, including task analysis, a multisensory approach to instruction, repetition and mastery learning, teaching to strengths, a focus on metacognition, teaching compensatory strategies, and teaching social skills.

Despite these similarities, many children with TBI differ from children with learning disabilities in some important ways (remembering that there is considerable individual variation within both groups):

1. Often children with TBI have an academic and cognitive profile that is not only varied, but also "gappy." For example, a student injured in ninth grade may remember much of the algebra learned that year, but be very weak with third-grade multiplication tables. This pattern—preserved islands of knowledge and skill at surprisingly high levels in combination with gaps at surprisingly low levels—may exist in many domains of knowledge and skill. The pattern has implications for assessment (requiring probes below basals and above ceilings on tests) and intervention (possibly

teaching in a "top–down" fashion that capitalizes on the student's motivation to be doing ninth-grade work and uses areas of strength in the remediation of weaknesses).

2. Early in recovery, children with TBI evidence a much greater degree of confusion, disorientation, and disinhibition than children with learning disabilities and may have persisting difficulty remembering personal experiences.

3. Children with TBI often reacquire basic academic skills and content (e.g., reading [word recognition and phonics], spelling, arithmetic) that children who have been learning disabled from birth have great difficulty acquiring. Therefore, much of the curriculum in a learning disabilities classroom may be irrelevant to the needs of the student with TBI. A similar pattern often exists in language reacquisition: Children with TBI may recover the surface features of the language code (phonology, morphology, syntax, and basic semantics) despite having substantial difficulty processing language efficiently, communicating in an organized manner, and communicating effectively in stressful social or academic contexts.

4. Children with TBI may have to "unlearn" academic habits that have been reinforced by years of successful use. For example, a child with TBI, who for years comprehended material well with only one reading, may have difficulty remembering to read assignments several times.

5. Children with TBI often struggle emotionally with profound losses, possibly including loss of ability, of friends, of goals and aspirations, of extracurricular activity, and many others. The emotional consequences of these losses, possibly including anger, depression, and withdrawal, must be addressed in the school setting.

6. Children with TBI may continue to experience neurologic recovery (at a decelerating rate) for months or years following the injury. This recovery demands much greater flexibility in planning and modifying programs for these children than for children whose neurologic potential is fixed. In the early months (and possibly years) following the student's return to school, reevaluation and Individualized Education Program updates must be more frequent than for children who are neurologically stable.

7. Because of recovery and because much of the child's learning is *re*-learning, the child may exhibit bursts of progress followed by periods of plateau. The progress may be incorrectly interpreted as efficient learning, leading to considerable frustration when progress slows.

Children with substantial brain damage and severe learning impairment may resemble, in global intellectual functioning, students with mental retardation. However, unlike most students with mental retardation, students with TBI typically evidence a sharply varied profile of skills and knowledge, and may continue to reacquire skills for years following the injury, occasionally in substantial leaps. Furthermore, placement in a setting for children with mental retardation is socially inappropriate and educationally counterproductive for most children with TBI. Such placement can also be very troubling for the family.

TYPES OF COGNITIVE INTERVENTION

The overall goal of cognitive rehabilitation and cognitive intervention in the classroom is to enable students to achieve goals—academic, social, recreational, and vocational—that are difficult to achieve because of cognitive deficits. Rehabilitation and special education efforts in pursuit of this goal may include (a) channeling spontaneous cognitive recovery, (b) retraining impaired cognitive processes (if there is reason to believe that the process can be improved with practice), (c) developing new skills to compensate for residual deficits, (d) creating classroom adaptations and other environmental compensations that permit effective performance despite residual deficits, (e) choosing instructional procedures that best fit the student's cognitive profile, and (f) promoting improved metacognitive awareness of strengths and needs so that the student can become an active participant in selecting goals and intervention strategies. Given the importance for children of education in a community school environment, a particular goal of teachers and other cognitive specialists is to identify and promote skills and supports that will enable the child to succeed in that setting.

Channeling Spontaneous Recovery

Spontaneous neurologic recovery may occur for several months and possibly even years (at a decelerating rate) following severe brain injury. Ensuring that the child is in an environment that is appropriately modulated with respect to stimulation and cognitive challenges helps to prevent frustration and consequent maladaptive behavior, and promotes the most effective return of cognitive function. In a classroom setting, this requires controlling the level of difficulty of academic and social tasks so that the child is challenged, but also experiences a great deal of success.

Retraining Impaired Cognitive Functions

Controversy persists regarding the potential to improve underlying cognitive functions through targeted drill and practice following cessation of spontaneous neurologic recovery. Studies of adults with brain injury tend to show that test scores in areas such as attention, memory, and problem-solving ability may be improved with extensive drill and practice, often using computerized "cognitive retraining" programs. However, the improvements are generally modest and it is rarely clear that they are transferred to functional academic or daily living tasks, or are specifically due to improved cognitive capacity as opposed to more efficient use of residual cognitive skill or acquisition of compensatory strategies. Schacter and Glisky (1986) argued persuasively that general cognitive functions, such as memory, cannot be directly restored through practice. However, many individuals with memory impairment can be helped to make more efficient use of their residual ability and compensate for lost ability.

Other cognitive processes may be more amenable to retraining. Organizational ability, for example, rests largely on organizational schemes that can be learned like any other content knowledge. Thus, it may be possible to improve organized thinking through the teaching of organizational schemes. However, this is quite different from the common practice of rehearsing components of organized thinking (e.g., sequencing, categorizing) independent of any specific meaningful content to be organized. The assumption in this case—that abstract "faculties" exist that can be separately strengthened and that, when strengthened, will enhance organized thinking in all domains—is not supported by current research in cognitive psychology (Singley & Anderson, 1989). However, improving organizational skill by teaching organizational schemes and highlighting the importance of using the organizational scheme when involved in learning or other organizational tasks can indirectly promote improved learning and memory, because well-organized information is easier to remember. Similarly, problem solving involves application of discrete procedures that can be learned. This suggests the likelihood of a practice effect with intensive practice, particularly if that practice is embedded in the practical contexts that will be the occasion for the individual's real-world problem solving. These treatment themes are explored in greater depth in Chapter 5.

Teaching Compensatory Strategies

A compensatory strategy is a procedure used to complete a task (achieve a goal) that is difficult because of cognitive (or other) impairment. In this sense, strategies are procedures used by students, not teachers. They may involve the use of external aids (e.g., tape recorder, calculator, memory book, schedule card), overt behavior (e.g., asking for instructions to be repeated), or covert behavior (e.g., elaborating or visualizing information mentally to make it more memorable). This approach to cognitive intervention is explored in Chapter 5.

Creating Environmental Compensations

An appropriately compensatory environment includes a variety of modifications designed to help the student succeed despite cognitive deficits. Modifications may include (a) consistent schedules and simple routines; (b) classroom arrangements designed to overcome cognitive barriers (e.g., ability grouping, preferential seating for distractibility, orientation cues, posted task reminders, rest periods, modified testing procedures, a "buddy" or peer mentor system for ensuring completing of assignments or getting from class to class); (c) verbal interaction consistent with the child's ability to comprehend (e.g., simplified instructions, increased processing and response time); (d) performance expectations (academic and behavioral) consistent with the student's ability to perform; and (e) the amount of coaching, cuing, prompting, and guiding needed to ensure generally successful classroom performance.

In the early months following the student's return to school, a generally useful rule of thumb is that staff should err, if at all, on the side of ensuring success. The primary goal of such a compensatory environment is to prevent the downward spiral that often sets in when students experience consistent failure on their return to school. However, real-world demands and performance expectations must ultimately become part of the school regimen, particularly if unawareness of deficits or denial come to be obstacles to academic and social progress, or if the student learns to manipulate the staff in ways that block progress.

Choosing Appropriate Instructional Procedures

An important contribution of cognitive specialists is the selection of instructional methods that are consistent with the cognitive profiles of individual students. For example, some students are poor candidates for a learning strategy approach. They may learn more effectively by being engaged in meaningful concrete activity that does not have *learning* as its explicit goal. Learning may be most critically influenced by number of repetitions, type of reinforcement, organization inherent in the material taught, and many other factors. Exploring these and other variables—and designing instructional programs based on this exploration—is part of cognitive intervention in a classroom setting. Ylvisaker, Szekeres, and Hartwick (1991) discussed this important aspect of cognitive intervention after TBI.

Promoting Metacognitive Skills

Students who are at a developmental level and stage of recovery at which it is possible to expect some awareness of their own academic and cognitive needs should be encouraged to develop a clear understanding of their own strengths and needs, and to participate in their educational planning. This entails an instructional focus on self-awareness of needs, realistic goal setting, planning, self-initiating, self-monitoring, self-evaluating, and problem solving. These are functions traditionally retained (often unconsciously) by the teacher or therapist, thereby depriving students of natural opportunities to grow in metacognitive maturity. Metacognitive and executive skills have increasingly become a focus in head injury rehabilitation for both children and adults (Ylvisaker & Szekeres, 1989). This important aspect of intervention is explored in Chapter 5.

Critical to intelligently planning a program of cognitive rehabilitation are distinctions within cognitive functions among *capacities* (i.e., structural capacities), *skills,* and *knowledge.* Impairments of structural cognitive capacities—for example, the amount of information that can be held in working memory at one time—may be comparable to sensory impairment in that they may not lend themselves to remedial exercises, but may be good candidates for compensation. A theme that has emerged from research in adult cognitive rehabilitation is that cognitive capacities of this sort are not like muscles that can be rebuilt with targeted exercises.

Organizational and problem-solving abilities, in contrast, have a procedural component that would seem to lend itself more readily to retraining exercises. Both abilities also have a knowledge component, knowledge of organizational schemas in the former case and knowledge of domain-specific relevant information in the latter. Therefore, functioning in these critical areas of cognition is likely to be improved by a combination of procedural practice in a relevant context and acquisition of domain-specific knowledge and organizational schemas.

Two themes that have emerged from research in adult cognitive rehabilitation and from explorations of cognitive intervention with children representing other disabilities merit special consideration: (a) Improvements in cognitive functioning are more likely a matter of *using* the system more efficiently than of increases in underlying capacity, and (b) improvements achieved in settings and tasks unlike those in which the skills will be put to functional use have little effect on functional performance.

Process, Strategy, and Academic Content

Teachers frequently ask whether they should focus on cognitive processes, learning strategies, or curricular content. When presented as mutually exclusive alternatives, the answer is generally academic content, because teachers and school districts are evaluated on the basis of student performance on tests of content. Fortunately, the opposition among these goals is misleading. Teachers sensitive to cognitive process and learning strategies routinely promote improvements in these areas within the context of teaching academic content. For example, comprehension strategies are best taught in the context of curricular reading assignments; strategies for organized expression of language are best taught in the context of writing themes for English class or, in the earlier grades, telling stories or reciting real-event narratives. Exercises to promote improved concentration or faster processing of information can be structured around math or reading content. Strategy instruction and exercises intended to improve the efficiency of information processing tend to fail the litmus tests of generalization and maintenance if they occur in settings and with materials that are unlike the setting and materials of functional application.

Given the importance of integrating these types of intervention, assigning "cognitive rehabilitation" to a specialist who is not a member of the classroom team makes little sense. Ideally, all of the staff who have a professional interest in the student's cognitive functioning should work with the classroom teacher(s) in identifying uniform goals and intervention procedures. Speech-language pathologists, for example, should use the student's academic materials and work with teachers in promoting strategies for improved comprehension and expression of language. Occupational therapists can use classroom-based fine motor tasks (e.g., writing, typing) and visual perceptual activities (e.g., reading and math worksheets) as a natural context for their intervention. Class outings and special events are a useful context for focusing on social skills and safety judgment.

INTERACTIONS AMONG COGNITIVE, PSYCHOSOCIAL, AND PHYSICAL DOMAINS

Teachers and other professionals who work with students with cognitive needs must have a keen appreciation for the variety of ways in which spheres of functioning interact. Physical impairment can have a variety of effects on cognitive functioning. For example, students with neuromuscular involvement may have to concentrate on movements (e.g., writing, walking) that for others are unconscious, thereby depriving themselves of cognitive energy and focus. In addition, physical impairment may eliminate compensatory options for cognitive deficits (e.g., note taking). For months or even years following injury, many students struggle with fatigue and its obvious effect on cognitive and academic performance. Students with spasticity may be distracted by pain. Antispasticity and anticonvulsant medications may interfere with cognitive functioning.

Cognitive impairment has comparable effects on physical functioning. For example, inability to perform complex movements may be the effect of impaired planning skill or inability to follow directions. Reduced attention to feedback may severely limit progress in physical and occupational therapy. Impaired attention or learning may make it difficult for a student to compensate for physical deficits by self-instructing (e.g., "Put the heel down before the toe") or by learning to use devices (e.g., power wheelchair, augmentative communication device).

Cognitive impairment can have a variety of effects on behavioral and social functioning. Students who cannot remain oriented to their tasks or remember assignments are often accused of noncompliance or laziness. Students who seek help from other students may be accused of cheating. Students who fail to meet their own expectations as well as those of their teachers predictably become frustrated, which may translate into behavioral maladjustment, or depression and isolation. Cognitive weakness, particularly in the area of social cognition, often results in awkward social interaction, which in turn leads to social isolation and behavioral maladjustment. Impaired social cognition includes difficulty interpreting complex social situations and "reading" others' social cues.

Behavioral and psychosocial problems can similarly affect cognitive and academic performance. When children return to school perplexed about their abilities and anxious about performance, the perplexity and anxiety, rather than primary cognitive deficits, may account for deficient performance. Depression, which is a common symptom following head injury in children, often emerges several months after the child has returned to school and compounds the effects of weak cognitive functioning on academic and social performance. Similarly, students with TBI who have adequate cognitive recovery but are disinhibited and impulsive predictably struggle academically and socially.

These examples of interactions among cognitive, physical, and psychosocial domains are certainly not exhaustive. However, they should alert teachers to the need to explore classroom problems from a variety of perspectives. If misinterpreted, the student's difficulties cannot be effectively addressed. Chapter 4 offers guidance for the systematic exploration of classroom problems that are often observed in children with traumatic brain injury.

TEAM INTERACTION AND COORDINATION

The complexity of cognitive functioning and its interaction with physical and social–behavioral functions mandate careful coordination of the student's total educational and therapeutic program. In a fragmented program, each classroom teacher decides independently which aspects of the child's needs should be stressed, and related services professionals (e.g., speech-language pathologists, occupational therapists, counselors, adaptive physical education teachers) address their own special areas of professional interest without integrating their intervention with other members of the team. The results of this approach are inefficiency (at best) and possibly an increase in the fragmentation and confusion that may already dominate the life of students with TBI. Programs that lack integration often overwhelm students with too many goals and objectives. Furthermore, intervention may be at cross-purposes, with one professional promoting compensation for a problem and another attempting to remediate the problem with remedial exercises. Finally, staff who work in isolation fail to exploit daily opportunities to promote generalization of other staff members' objectives.

The student's age, the size and nature of the school, and the number of professionals involved in the program all influence decisions about how best to integrate the cognitive components of the child's program. In elementary school settings, it may be possible to expect the classroom teacher to meet regularly with other professionals and thus to manage the student's program as a team. In high school settings, it may be more effective to appoint one person as a coordinator of the total program. This person would be expected to meet regularly with all members of the team to facilitate communication and to promote ongoing problem solving in an attempt to keep the educational program up to date and integrated.

The program coordinator must have a good understanding of the consequences of TBI, have a thorough understanding of education law and funding possibilities, be willing to be the student's advocate, be an effective communicator, be supported by the school's administration, be accessible to the team that works with the student and to the family, and have large stores of energy. Furthermore, the coordinator, who may come from inside or outside the school, must work well within an intervention framework that highlights interactions among cognitive, social–behavioral, and physical functioning. Schools that use a consultant teacher model may have little difficulty ensuring that this role is played effectively.

GENERAL PRINCIPLES OF COGNITIVE INTERVENTION

From a classroom perspective, cognitive intervention is designed largely to enable students to meet academic goals that are blocked by cognitive deficits. A broader and essential perspective includes the student's sense of self-worth and social success in progressively more "normalized" life situations. The eight principles listed below are guides to program planning for students with cognitive impairment.

Principle 1. *Success, resulting from appropriate expectations and planned compensation, facilitates progress while building a productive self-concept.*

This principle mandates systematic and carefully planned school reentry, as well as gradual introduction of academic demands, so that the student experiences a high level of success at every stage. Students who return to settings in which the demands on them far exceed their ability to perform become frustrated and predictably develop behavioral or emotional problems in reaction to repeated failure. Success may require a variety of supports in school, environmental modifications, compensatory cognitive strategies, and, above all, teachers and other professionals who have a correct perception of a student's needs and ability to perform.

Later, if unawareness and possibly also denial of deficits become obstacles to progress, carefully planned experiences of failure may be necessary to help the student recognize his or her needs. These failure experiences should, however, occur in a generally supportive environment and be accompanied by counseling so that what evolves is a balanced self-perception of strengths and needs.

The need for success extends beyond the classroom and into social life. Because social reintegration is often impeded by cognitive deficits, professionals responsible for the child's cognitive rehabilitation must actively promote successful social experiences. This process may require training in social skills, peer education and support, and psychosocial counseling for the student with TBI. Other children with a history of brain injury may become an important peer group and serve as the child's best source of understanding and support.

Principle 2. *The systematic gradation of activities can facilitate cognitive recovery and development.*

A cognitive approach to instruction requires frequent analysis of the cognitive demands placed on the student, as well as modulation of those demands so that the student can be successful. This principle does not mean that tasks must be at a developmentally or academically low level (which may be insulting to the student) or that teachers and therapists should proceed rigidly through a preestablished hierarchy of skills in a bottom-to-top manner. Rather, it means that supports are in place so that academic and therapy tasks can be completed successfully, whatever their level. These supports may include adjustments in time requirements, cues, environmental modifications, tutorial support, and the like. With appropriate supports, a ninth-grade student may work successfully within a ninth-grade curriculum despite gaps in academic content and substantial cognitive weakness. This approach capitalizes on the student's motivation and exploits preserved higher-level skills even as it addresses lower-level losses. As performance improves, supports are reduced and cognitive demands are increased until age-appropriate levels of cognitive stress are reached.

Principle 3. *Habituation and generalization training are necessary for learning.*

The true measure of successful teaching of a new skill is its transfer to relevant nontraining tasks, generalization to other settings and people, and maintenance over time. For example, a language comprehension strategy taught in a speech therapy session should be used in varied reading tasks in class and at home. Generalization must be specifically planned, either by designing a progression of activities to promote transfer of skills or by doing the original training with functional materials and in the contexts in which functional application of the skill is important. This principle supports the delivery of related services in the classroom whenever possible, with therapists collaborating with or consulting to classroom teachers. In addition, students with impaired learning require a large number of learning trials to improve a skill or internalize information or strategies.

Principle 4. *Student initiative, motivation, and problem solving are essential for effective learning and independent functioning.*

Frequently, students with TBI have, as part of their brain injury syndrome, reduced awareness of their disability. This may be compounded by emotional resistance to admitting disability or by depression in the face of reduced ability. These factors all contribute to apparently reduced motivation. The student may also have damage to that part of the brain associated with initiative and initiation of activity. Finally, school work may be harder and take more time than before the injury.

Professionals must, therefore, be creative in capturing the student's interest, motivation, and initiative. For younger children, this may entail more attention to concrete and meaningful reinforcement than is typically necessary. For older children, capturing motivation often requires making the student a partner in setting goals, determining strategies to meet the goals, evaluating performance, and solving problems. When these problem-identification and problem-solving functions are retained exclusively by the teacher, problems with motivation, initiation, and compliance are only exacerbated. In addition, older children may need a greater payoff for successful completion of work than is ordinarily needed by other students.

Principle 5. *Integration of intervention among all staff enhances learning and promotes generalization of learned skills.*

All staff—including ancillary professionals; art, music, and physical education teachers; and lunchroom aides—should be familiar with relevant cognitive needs of children with TBI so that their expectations are realistic and they contribute to consistent cognitive and behavioral programming.

Principle 6. *Chronological age must be considered along with developmental and academic levels in planning intervention.*

Children with TBI typically retain a self-concept based on pretrauma skills and achievement. Therefore, they understandably consider it disrespectful and infantalizing to be given materials and activities that may be at an appropriate academic level, but are designed for much younger children. It is generally most effective to group these children with socially appropriate peers and use materials that resemble those used by peers, but with modifications needed to ensure success. Similarly, reinforcement for older children and adolescents should be respectful of their social status (e.g., graphs of performance rather than stars or stickers) even though their performance may be at academically early levels. Because these children may have experienced incalculable loss, including loss of ability, loss of success, loss of friends, and loss of recreational activities, it is critical that educational practices do not highlight these losses and exaggerate the emotional responses.

Principle 7. *Individual and group interventions are both necessary to provide specificity of intervention as well as a natural social context for training in social cognition and social skills.*

Individual therapy and tutoring sessions have the obvious advantage of enabling the therapist or teacher to customize objectives, activities, and interaction to meet the specific needs of the individual. In addition, interacting individually with students may be necessary to explore cognitive functioning and compensations for cognitive deficits in the manner recommended in Chapter 5. Group intervention, in therapy or classroom settings, makes possible group peer support and practice in social skills. Group interaction is also a context for learning cooperation and inhibition skills, for learning to deal effectively with distractions, and for generalizing skills learned in other settings.

Principle 8. *Severity of cognitive deficits and improvement in response to intervention must be measured in functional contexts and activities.*

Chapter 4 includes a discussion of challenges to the ecological validity of cognitive testing with this population. With this as background, psychologists, teachers, and clinicians must pay particular attention to real-world performance in defining profiles of strengths and weaknesses, prescribing intervention, and evaluating progress.

CONCLUSION

In this chapter, we have outlined a perspective on cognitive intervention that is broad based in its theoretical foundation and wide ranging in its scope. The practical implications of this framework for assessment and intervention are explored in the three chapters that follow.

APPENDIX 3A
Aspects of Cognition and Stages of Recovery

Aspects of Cognition	*Early Stages*	*Middle Stages*	*Late Stages**
I. Component Processes			
ATTENTION: holding objects, events, words, or thoughts in consciousness. *Components:* span, selectivity, filtering, maintaining, shifting, dividing.	• Severely decreased arousal or alertness • Minimal selective attention, focusing, shifting • Attention may be primarily to internal stimuli	• Attention generally focuses on external events • Short attention span • Poor control of attention: highly distractible, inflexible	• Attention span may be reduced • Relatively weak concentration, selective attention, and fluid attentional shifts • Attending problems may reflect weak organizational processes, absence of goals, or both
PERCEPTION: recognition of features and relationships among features; affected by context (figure–ground) and intensity, duration, significance, and familiarity of stimuli.	• Begins to recognize (and perhaps use) familiar objects when they are highlighted • May perceive only one feature or aspect of stimulus • Adaptation to continuous stimulation	• Clear recognition of familiar objects and events • Inefficient perception in context • Sharp deterioration with increases in rate, amount, and complexity of stimuli • Difficulty in perceiving whole from part	• Possibly subtle versions of perceptual problems related to rate, amount, and complexity • Possibly specific deficits (e.g., field neglect) • Possibly inefficient shifting of perceptual set • Possibly weak perception of relevant features
MEMORY AND LEARNING: *Encoding:* Recognition, interpretation and formulation of information, including language, into an internal code; knowledge base, personal interests, and goals affect what is coded.	• Comprehension progresses from minimal responses to vocal intonation and stress to recognition of simple, context-bound instructions • No evidence of encoding or storage of new information	• Weak encoding due to poor access to knowledge base, poor integration of new with old information, or inefficient attention or perception • Inefficiently encoded information often lost after short delay	• Possibly subtle versions of earlier problems, particularly with increases in cognitive stress • Memory problems—any combination of comprehension, encoding, storage, or retrieval deficits

(*continues*)

APPENDIX 3A. *Continued*

Aspects of Cognition	***Early Stages***	***Middle Stages***	***Late Stages****
Storage: Retention over time. *Retrieval:* Transfer from long-term memory to consciousness.		• Recognition stronger than recall; receptive vocabulary superior to expressive • Disorganized search of storage system	• Memory problems—problems recalling information related to personal experience (episodic memory) or abstracted knowledge (semantic memory)
ORGANIZING: Analyzing, classifying, integrating, sequencing; identifying relevant features of objects and events; comparing for similarities or differences; integrating into organized descriptions, higher-level categories, and sequenced events. These processes are presupposed by higher-level reasoning and efficient learning.	• No evidence of these processes	• Weak or bizarre associations • Weak analysis of objects into features • Disorganized sequencing of events • Weak identification of similarities and differences in comparisons and classifications • Can integrate concepts into propositions; difficulty integrating propositions into main ideas • Major difficulty imposing organization on unstructured stimuli	• Possibly subtle versions of earlier problems • Difficulty maintaining goal-directed thinking • Ongoing difficulty discerning main ideas and integrating main ideas into broader themes • May easily get lost in details • Can impose organization on unstructured stimuli with prompting
REASONING: Considering evidence and drawing inferences or conclusions; involves flexible exploration of possibilities (divergent thinking) and use of past experience. *Deductive:* Strict logical formal inference. *Inductive:* Direct inference from experience. *Analogical:* Indirect inference from experience.	• No evidence of these processes	• Minimal inferential thinking; may deal with concrete cause–effect relationships, particularly if overlearned • General inefficiency with abstract ideas and relationships	• Fair to good concrete reasoning in controlled settings; disorganized thinking in stressful or uncontrolled settings • Abstract thinking remains deficient

(*continues*)

APPENDIX 3A. *Continued*

Aspects of Cognition	**Early Stages**	**Middle Stages**	**Late Stages***
PROBLEM SOLVING AND JUDGMENT: *Problem solving* occurs when a goal cannot be reached directly. Ideally involves goal identification, consideration of relevant information, exploration of possible solutions, and selection of the best. *Judgment:* Decision to act, based on consideration of relevant factors, including prediction of consequences.	• No evidence of these processes	• Inability to see relationships among problems, goals, and relevant information • Inflexibility in generating or evaluating possible solutions; impulsive; trial-and-error approach • Inability to assess a situation and predict consequences • Severely impaired safety and social judgment	• Possibly subtle versions of earlier problems • Impulsive; disorganized problem solving • Inflexible thinking and shallow reasoning • Poor safety and social judgment may be primary residual deficits; manifested in academic and social situations
2. Component Systems			
WORKING MEMORY (attentional focus): Storage or holding "space" where coding and organizing occur; limited information capacity; *functional* capacity is increased by making processes automatic or by "chunking" information.	• Severely limited capacity • Progression from single to multimodality processing of simple stimuli • Attention to internal stimuli may exhaust attentional "space"	• Gradual increase in attention span to near normal, as measured by digit span • *Functional* capacity remains severely restricted due to lack of automatic organizing processes • Therefore, processing deteriorates rapidly with increases in the information load	• Often normal digit span • Inefficient organizing processes may continue to reduce *functional* capacity as information load increases
LONG-TERM MEMORY: Contains knowledge of concepts or words; rules, strategies, or procedures; organizational principles and knowledge frames; goals, experience and self-concept.	• Emerging evidence of remote memory; recognition of familiar objects and persons • May assume that other contents are present but inaccessible	• Growing access to pretrauma contents • Recognition of strong associations (e.g., hammer–nail), basic semantic relations, and common two- or three-event sequences	• Recovery of access to pretraumatically acquired knowledge base stabilizes • Growth of long-term memory varies with type and severity of residual cognitive deficits

(continues)

APPENDIX 3A. *Continued*

Aspects of Cognition	*Early Stages*	*Middle Stages*	*Late Stages**
RESPONSE SYSTEM: Controls all output, including speech, facial expression, and fine and gross motor activity; includes motor planning.	• Severely limited; often perseverative responses • May use some gestures and speech toward end of this stage, but with motor planning problems or delayed responses	• Speaks or begins augmentative system • Possible motor-planning problems or general slowness • Impulsiveness and possible perseveration • Motor function varies with site and extent of injury	• Generally functional communication system—usually speech • Possible motor-planning problems or slowness • Possible rapid fatigue
EXECUTIVE SYSTEM ("central processor"): Sets goals; plans and monitors activity; directs processing and operations according to goals, current input, and perceptual–affective set.	• Minimal awareness of self and current condition • No apparent self-direction of behavior or cognitive processes	• Growing awareness of self; poor awareness of deficits • Weak metacognitive awareness of self as thinker • Minimal goal setting, self-initiation or self-inhibition, self-monitoring, or self-evaluation	• Shallow awareness of residual deficits • Mild to severe deficits in executive functions, related in part to anterior frontolimbic damage • Metacognitive level may permit strategy training
3. Functional–Integrative Performance			
FUNCTIONAL BEHAVIOR: Performance of "real-life" tasks and activities (e.g., reading a book or conversing). *Efficiency:* Rate of performance and amount accomplished. *Level:* Developmental or academic level of performance. *Scope:* Variety of situations in which patient can maintain performance.	• Cannot adapt to environment; activity level ranges from inactive to hyperactive; activity marginally purposeful (e.g., pulling at tubes, restraints, clothes; attempting to get out of bed); gives little or no assistance in daily care • May perform a limited range of routine tasks when prompted (e.g., brushing hair)	• Performs many overlearned routines (e.g., self-care, games) in structured settings with prompts; poor retention of information from day to day; severely impaired learning of new skills • Performs simple sequential tasks (e.g., dressing) in structured setting if stimuli are controlled for rate,	• Performance of pretraumatically acquired skills related to type and extent of residual deficits and ability to compensate; performance may continue to deteriorate sharply with increasing processing load; learning of new skills and strategies occurs at a reduced rate • Performance of complex tasks re-

(continues)

APPENDIX 3A. *Continued*

Aspects of Cognition	Early Stages	Middle Stages	Late Stages*
Manner: Dependence or independence (need for prompts and cues; impulsive or reflective style.	• Profound confusion or disorientation to person, place, time, and condition • Communication severely limited, inconsistent, and prefunctional; may begin to comprehend simple context-bound instructions • Minimal social interaction; little variation in facial expression; reflexive crying; may reflexively hold or shake hands • Agitated behavior at the end of this stage more pronounced in adolescents	amount, and complexity; organization of behavior deteriorates rapidly in uncontrolled setting • Continued confusion but growing orientation to person, place, and time in structured settings and with orientation cues; gross awareness of the structure of the day • Communication: *Expressive:* Usually verbal and functional (barring motor speech disorder), but often characterized by confabulation, word retrieval problems, excessive and often inappropriate output. *Receptive:* Rate amount and complexity of verbal input must be controlled to assure comprehension • Social interaction strained and often unsuccessful, due to disinhibition, inappropriateness, impaired social perception • Impulsiveness, agitation, and inability to set goals may result in minimal adaption to the environment	quiring organization, persistence, and self-monitoring continues to be deficient; efficiency continues to be low, with slow rate and low productivity • Solid orientation to person, place, and time, but disorientation may recur with sudden changes in routine • Communication is usually conventional in form, with possible word-finding problems, expressive disorganization, and comprehension limited in efficiency; social use of language may be strained or inappropriate • Social interaction and judgment may be dominant residual symptoms, related to weak awareness of social conventions and rules, persistent impulsiveness, and poorly defined self-concept (with shallow awareness of residual deficits) • Behavior generally goal directed, but goals may be unrealistic and social and safety judgment significantly impaired; needs prompts to set goals and subgoals

*Functioning also related to age and pretrauma developmental and educational level.

From "Cognitive Rehabilitation Therapy: A Framework for Intervention" by S. F. Szekeres, M. Ylvisaker, and A. L. Holland, in *Head Injury Rehabilitation: Children and Adolescents* (pp. 230–235) by M. Ylvisaker (Ed.), 1985, Austin, TX: PRO-ED.

APPENDIX 3B
Classroom Illustrations of Cognitive Problems Following Traumatic Brain Injury

	Illustrations of Cognitive Problems in a Classroom
1. Component Cognitive Processes	
Attention	• A student may fail to follow the teacher's instruction or to comprehend a lesson, not because of a willful failure to attend or an inability to understand, but because of an inability to filter out environmental distractions or internal feelings or thoughts. • A student may begin the task and then stop or change activity because of fatigue, underarousal, or disrupted attention. To maintain attention to task, the student may require regularly scheduled breaks. • Attentional problems may result in the student's talking out of turn, interrupting others, introducing irrelevant topics, responding inappropriately, engaging in random off-task behavior, or walking away. • A student may lose attention as tasks become more difficult, not because of resistance, but because the effort required places too great a demand on attentional resources. • A student may perform poorly at a new task because his attention is still focused on the previous task or on an upsetting event that took place earlier.
Perception	• A student may be unable to do otherwise easy math problems if they are presented on a worksheet filled with other problems. • A student may fail to read nonverbal signals from conversation partners because of perceptual problems. • A student may have difficulty finding items in her desk, books on a library shelf, and so on.

(continues)

APPENDIX 3B. *Continued*

	Illustrations of Cognitive Problems in a Classroom
	• A student may require preferential seating on one side c the room or the other because he cannot see or attend within one of his visual fields. Material may have to be placed on only one side of his desk. • Written assignments may appear to be extremely sloppy. • A student may need to use a finger or marker to maintai her place in reading or may require large-print materials despite adequate visual acuity.
Memory and Learning	• A student may fail to complete assignments, not becaus of negligence or lack of desire to comply, but because the assignment, if not written or repeated several times, is not remembered. • A student may miss classes, fail to bring materials to class, or do assignments incorrectly because of difficulty remaining oriented. • A student may require an unexpectedly large number of repetitions to learn simple motor sequences (e.g., tying shoes), classroom routines and rules, and textbook infor mation. The student may learn strategies to compensate for memory problems, but then forget to use the strategy • A student may need to be told to repeat information ove and over in order to place it in memory, and to "search memory" in order to find information that has been previ- ously learned. • A student may have difficulty learning routes in the school and finding rooms. • A student may have difficulty learning names of class- mates. • A student may do well on multiple-choice tests, but be unable to recall the information for an essay or short- answer test. • A student may repeat the same information over and ove (having forgotten that he said it earlier).
Organizing	• A young student, faced with the task of getting ready for gym class, may be unable to break the task into parts and decide what to do first. • A high school student may understand each part of a text, but be unable to analyze and integrate the infor- mation to determine the main ideas, prepare an outline, and write a summary. • A student may move unexpectedly from topic to topic in conversation because of an unusual set of associations. This may be interpreted as social strangeness or as re- sulting from a lack of knowledge about the subject.

(continues

APPENDIX 3B. *Continued*

	Illustrations of Cognitive Problems in a Classroom
	• A student may lose items or work inefficiently because of difficulty arranging items systematically and organizing the task. • A student's stories and descriptions may be hard to follow because she cannot maintain the logical or temporal sequence of the story or event. • A student may not profit from reviewing his notes because they lack organization. • A student may do poorly in math despite adequate comprehension of the rules because she does not adequately organize the numbers on the page. • A preschool student may refuse to play because it is too difficult for him to organize the materials.
Reasoning and Abstract Thinking	• A student who does well with basic mathematical operations may have great difficulty with their application in solving word problems or with the more abstract relationships involved in algebra. • A student may lose the train of conversation when a figure of speech is used (e.g., "She was *climbing the walls*"). • A student may fail to generalize strategies to new situations because of a failure to see relationships. • A student may fail to profit from experience because of difficulty seeing the relationship between the past experience and the current situation. • A student may do well on true–false and multiple-choice tests, but be unable to answer essay questions. • A student may comprehend the information in a reading passage, but be unable to answer open-ended questions requiring inferences. • A student may understand the facts in science class, but be unable to formulate rules or generalizations.
Problem Solving	• Having forgotten his locker combination and not having ready access to his homeroom teacher, a student may simply become upset rather than considering carefully who else may help. • A student who fails to comprehend a text with one or two readings may not use strategies to enhance comprehension (e.g., outlining the text, underlining key points, asking herself questions as she reads, discussing the text). • A student may use the same behavior (e.g., crying, withdrawing, hitting) in response to any and all problems. • A student may be unable to identify the critical information in a math word problem in order to solve the problem.

(*continues*)

APPENDIX 3B. *Continued*

	Illustrations of Cognitive Problems in a Classroom
2. Component Cognitive Systems	
Working Memory	• A student may not be able to follow a two- or three-step command, despite adequate comprehension of the language. • A student may comprehend only *parts* of instructions or statements and draw incorrect conclusions, making it ap pear as though he was not listening. He may require frequent prompts to complete the task. • A student may not be able to think about a compensatory strategy (e.g., "I must repeat this information in order to remember it") and listen to the presented information at the same time.
Knowledge Base	• Occasionally, a student gains access to pretraumatically acquired knowledge long after the injury. This may lead the teacher to infer that new learning is occurring at a more rapid pace than is actually the case. Alternatively, the inconsistency in learning rates may lead the teacher to infer that the student is often not trying. • Reading comprehension performance may vary more as a consequence of a spotty knowledge base than as a function of reading skill. • A student may have regained higher-level knowledge (e.g. ninth-grade algebra) despite having lost lower-level knowledge within the same content area (e.g., third-grade multiplication tables). • A high school student with academic skills at an early grade school level may have retained the self-concept and social sense of a high school student.
Executive System	• A student who lacks an awareness of her current cognitive limitations may complain that tasks are at too low a level and that restrictions on her activity are unnecessary. • A student may lack study skills (e.g., knowing how to divide tasks, how to prepare for exams, how to organize information for easy learning, how to check one's work and understanding). • A student with impaired initiation may appear lazy or resistive. • A student with impaired self-monitoring skill may not profit from feedback in social situations and, therefore, may behave in a socially awkward manner.

(*continues*)

APPENDIX 3B. *Continued*

	Illustrations of Cognitive Problems in a Classroom
	• A student with academic problems may attribute the problem to something outside of himself rather than attempt strategically to solve the problems. • Inability to inhibit inappropriate comments may cause social isolation.
3. Functional–Integrative Performance	
Efficiency	• A student scores at grade level on tests of reading comprehension that do not go beyond word, sentence, and short paragraph–length material, but cannot read and comprehend a several-page chapter in a history text. • A student performs well on quizzes, but poorly on essay exams that require recall and organization of large amounts of information. • A student demonstrates comprehension of academic material when given extra time to respond, to complete homework, and to finish tests; she demonstrates minimal comprehension when expected to respond within the normal time period. The student demonstrates frustration when expected to learn at a normal rate, but learns effectively with self-paced instruction. • A student appears hostile because he does not respond in conversation, when in fact he simply needs more time to process the information.
Scope	• A student may be well oriented and behave appropriately in a familiar environment, but become very disoriented and inappropriate in a new environment or with a sudden change in routine (e.g., transition from rehabilitation facility to school). • A student may perform well in a small group or small classroom situation, but withdraw or become aggressive in a noisy, disorganized environment (e.g., hallway, lunchroom). The student requires orientation cues, organizational strategies, and task reminders in busy or confusing environments. • A student may use learning strategies or social communication skills in the setting in which they were trained (e.g., therapy room), but not in other settings in which their use would be important (e.g., classroom).
Level	• A student may converse comfortably given simple and familiar topics, but evidence word-finding problems and significant disorganization when the topic is academically demanding.

(*continues*)

APPENDIX 3B. *Continued*

	Illustrations of Cognitive Problems in a Classroom
	• A student may perform well with academic materials a year below grade level, but be unable to perform with grade-level materials.
Manner	• A student may demonstrate good cognitive skills and perform well in school, but only with ongoing reminders from the teacher to begin work, stay on task, follow a routine, write down assignments, and so on. • An impulsive student may demonstrate mastery of academic material, but only when reminded to stop and think rather than saying whatever first comes to mind.

Adapted from "Cognitive Assessment and Intervention" by P. G. Burns, J. Cook, and M. Ylvisaker, in *An Educator's Manual* (2nd ed., Table 3.1) by R. C. Savage and G. F. Wolcott (Eds.), 1988, Southborough, MA: National Head Injury Foundation.

REFERENCES

Anderson, J. R. (1975). *Cognitive psychology and its implications.* San Francisco: Freeman.

Bandura, A. (1977). *Social learning theory.* Englewood Cliffs, NJ: Prentice-Hall.

Bawden, H. N., Knights, R. M., & Winogren, H. W. (1985). Speeded performance following head injury in children. *Journal of Clinical and Experimental Neuropsychology, 7,* 39–54.

Ben-Yishay, Y., & Diller, L. (1983). Cognitive deficits. In M. Rosenthal, M. Bond, E. Griffith, & J. D. Miller (Eds.), *Rehabilitation of the head injured adult.* Philadelphia: F. A. Davis.

Ben-Yishay, Y., & Prigatano, G. P. (1990). Cognitive remediation. In M. Rosenthal, E. Griffith, M. Bond, & J. D. Miller (Eds.), *Rehabilitation of the adult and child with traumatic brain injury* (2nd ed., pp. 393–409). Philadelphia: F. A. Davis.

Ben-Yishay, Y., Rattok, J., Lakin, P., Piasetsky, E. B., Ross, B., Silver, S., Zide, E., & Erzachi, O. (1985). Neuropsychologic rehabilitation: Quest for a holistic approach. *Seminars in Neurology, 5,* 252–258.

Bigler, E. D. (1987). Acquired cerebral trauma: Epidemiology, neuropsychological assessment, and academic/educational deficits. *Journal of Learning Disabilities, 20,* 516–517.

Brown, A. L. (1975). The development of memory: Knowing, knowing about knowing, and knowing how to know. In H. W. Reese (Ed.), *Advances in child development and behavior* (Vol. 10, pp. 103–152). New York: Academic Press.

Brown, A. L. (1978). Metacognitive development and reading. In R. J. Spiro, B. C. Bruce, & G. W. Brewer (Eds.), *Theoretical issues in reading comprehension* (pp. 77–165). Hillsdale, NJ: Erlbaum.

Brown, A. L. (1979). Theories of memory and problems of development, activity, growth, and knowledge. In F. I. M. Craik & L. Cermak (Eds.), *Levels of processing and memory* (pp. 225–258). Hillsdale, NJ: Erlbaum.

Burns, P. G., Cook, J., & Ylvisaker, M. (1988). Cognitive assessment and intervention. In R. C. Savage & G. F. Wolcott (Eds.), *An educator's manual* (2nd ed.). Southborough, MA: National Head Injury Foundation.

Campbell, T., & Dollaghan, C. A. (1990). Expressive language recovery in severely brain-injured children and adolescents. *Journal of Speech and Hearing Disorders, 55,* 567–581.

Chadwick, O. (1985). Psychological sequelae of head injury in children. *Developmental Medicine and Child Neurology, 27,* 72–75.

Chapman, S. B., Culhane, K. A., Levin, H. S., Harward, H., Mendelsohn, D., Ewing-Cobbs, L., Fletcher, J. M., & Bruce, D. (1992). Narrative discourse after closed head injury in children and adolescents. *Brain and Language, 43,* 42–65.

Dennis, M. (1991). Frontal lobe function in childhood and adolescence: A heuristic for assessing attention regulation, executive control, and the intentional states important for social discourse. *Developmental Neuropsychology, 7,* 327–358.

Dennis, M., & Barnes, M. A. (1990). Knowing the meaning, getting the point, bridging the gap, and carrying the message: Aspects of discourse following closed head injury in childhood and adolescence. *Brain and Language, 39,* 428–446.

Diller, L. (1976). A model for cognitive retraining in rehabilitation. *Clinical Psychology, 29,* 13–15.

Dodd, D., & White, R. M., Jr. (1980). *Cognition, mental structures and processes.* Boston: Allyn & Bacon.

Ewing-Cobbs, L., Fletcher, J. M., & Levin, H. S. (1985). Neuropsychological sequelae following pediatric head injury. In M. Ylvisaker (Ed.), *Head injury rehabilitation: Children and adolescents* (pp. 70–89). Austin, TX: PRO-ED.

Ewing-Cobbs, L., Miner, M., Fletcher, J. M., & Levin, H. S. (1989). Intellectual, motor, and language sequelae following closed head injury in infants and preschoolers. *Journal of Pediatric Psychology, 14,* 531–544.

Flavell, J. (1976). Metacognitive aspects of problem solving. In L. B. Resnick (Ed.), *The nature of intelligence* (pp. 231–235). Hillsdale, NJ: Erlbaum.

Flavell, J. (1985). *Cognitive development* (2nd ed.). Englewood Cliffs, NJ: Prentice-Hall.

Fletcher, J. M., Ewing-Cobbs, L., Miner, M., & Levin, H. S. (1990). Behavioral changes after closed head injury in children. *Journal of Consulting and Clinical Psychology, 58,* 93–98.

Forrest-Pressley, D. L., MacKinnon, G. E., & Waller, T. G. (Eds.). (1985). *Metacognition, cognition, and human performance: Vol. 2. Instructional practices.* Orlando, FL: Academic Press.

Grattan, L. M., & Eslinger, P. J. (1991). Frontal lobe damage in children and adults: A comparative review. *Developmental Neuropsychology, 7,* 283–326.

Haarbauer-Krupa, J., Moser, L., Smith, G., Sullivan, D. M., & Szekeres, S. F. (1985). Cognitive rehabilitation therapy: Middle stages of recovery. In M. Ylvisaker (Ed.), *Head injury rehabilitation: Children and adolescents* (pp. 288–310). Austin, TX: PRO-ED.

Hagen, C. (1981). Language disorders secondary to closed head injury: Diagnosis and treatment. *Topics in Language Disorders, 1,* 73–87.

Hagen, J., Barclay, C., & Schwethelm, B. (1982). Cognitive development of the learning disabled child. *International review of research in mental retardation* (Vol. II). New York: Academic Press.

Hall, R. J. (1980). Information processing and cognitive training in learning disabled children: An executive level meeting. *Exceptional Education, 1,* 9–16.

Hallahan, D. P., Lloyd, J., Kosiewicz, M. M., Kauffman, J. M., & Graves, A. W. (1979). *Self-monitoring of attention as a treatment for a learning disabled boy's off-task behavior* (Tech. Rep. No. 10). Charlottesville: University of Virginia Learning Disabilities Research Institute.

Hallahan, D. P., Lloyd, J., Kosiewicz, M. M., & Kneedler, R. D. (1979). *A comparison of the effects of self-recording and self-assessment on the on-task behavior and academic productivity of a learning disabled boy* (Tech. Rep. No. 13). Charlottesville: University of Virginia Learning Disabilities Research Institute.

Hresko, W. P., & Reid, D. K. (1988). Five faces of cognition: Theoretical influences on approaches to learning disabilities. *Learning Disability Quarterly, 4,* 211–216.

Kail, R. (1984). *The development of memory in children* (2nd ed.). New York: Freeman.

Katz, D. I. (1992). Neuropathology and neurobehavioral recovery from closed head injury. *Journal of Head Trauma Rehabilitation,* 7(2), 1–15.

Kavale, K., & Mattson, P. (1983). "One jumped off the balance beam": Meta-analysis of perceptual–motor training. *Journal of Learning Disabilities, 16,* 165–173.

Keogh, B. K., & Glover, A. T. (1980). The generality and durability of cognitive training effects. *Exceptional Education Quarterly, 1,* 75–82.

Klonoff, K., Low, M. D., & Clark, C. (1977). Head injuries in children: A prospective five year follow-up. *Journal of Neurology, Neurosurgery, and Psychiatry, 40,* 1211–1219.

Kneedler, R. D., & Hallahan, D. P. (1981). Self-monitoring of on-task behavior with learning disabled children: Current studies and directions. *Exceptional Education Quarterly, 2,* 73–82.

Kosiewicz, M. M., Hallahan, D. P., Lloyd, J., & Graves, A. W. (1979). *The effects of self-instruction and self-correction procedures on handwriting performance* (Tech. Rep. No. 5). Charlottesville: University of Virginia Learning Disabilities Research Institute.

Lehr, E. (1990). *Psychological management of traumatic brain injuries in children and adolescents.* Rockville, MD: Aspen.

Mann, L. (1979). *On the trail of process: A historical perspective on cognitive processes and their training.* New York: Grune and Stratton.

Mateer, C. A., & Williams, D. (1991). Effects of frontal lobe injury in childhood. *Developmental Neuropsychology, 7,* 359–376.

Meichenbaum, D. (1977). *Cognitive behavior modification: An integrative approach.* New York: Plenum Press.

Meichenbaum, D. (1993). The "potential" contributions of cognitive behavior modification to the rehabilitation of individuals with traumatic brain injury. *Seminars in Speech and Language, 14,* 18–30.

Meichenbaum, D., & Asarnow, J. (1979). Cognitive–behavioral modification and metacognitive development: Implications for the classroom. In P. C. Kendall & S. D. Hollon (Eds.), *Cognitive–behavioral interventions: Theory, research, and procedures* (pp. 11–35). New York: Academic Press.

Miller, N. E., & Dollard, J. (1941). *Social learning and imitation.* New Haven, CT: Yale University Press.

Pang, D. (1985). Pathophysiologic correlates of neurobehavioral syndromes following closed head injury. In M. Ylvisaker (Ed.), *Head injury rehabilitation: Children and adolescents* (pp. 1–70). Austin, TX: PRO-ED.

Perrott, S. B., Taylor, H. G., & Montes, J. L. (1991). Neuropsychological sequelae, familial stress, and environmental adaptation following pediatric head injury. *Developmental Neuropsychology, 7,* 69–86.

Petterson, L. (1988). *Sensitivity to emotional cues and social behavior in children and adolescents after head injury.* Unpublished doctoral dissertation, University of Minnesota, Minneapolis.

Piaget, J. (1983). Piaget's theory. In W. Kessen (Ed.), *Handbook of child psychology: Vol. 1. History, theory and methods* (pp. 103–128). New York: Wiley.

Pressley, M. (1993). Teaching cognitive strategies to brain-injured clients: The good information processing perspective. *Seminars in Speech and Language, 14,* 1–16.

Pressley, M., Goodchild, F., Fleet, J., Zajchowski, R., & Evans, E. D. (1989). The challenges of classroom strategy instruction. *Elementary School Journal, 89,* 301–342.

Pressley, M., & Levin, J. R. (Eds.). (1983). *Cognitive strategy training: Educational applications.* New York: Springer Verlag.

Prigatano, G. P., & Others (1986). *Neuropsychological rehabilitation after brain injury.* Baltimore: Johns Hopkins University Press.

Reid, D. K., & Hresko, W. P. (1981). *A cognitive approach to learning disabilities.* New York: McGraw-Hill.

Ruff, R. M., Baser, C. A., Johnston, J. W., Marshall, L. F., Klauber, S. K., Klauber, M. R., & Minteer, M. (1989). Neuropsychological rehabilitation: An experimental study with head injured patients. *Journal of Head Trauma Rehabilitation, 4*(3), 20–36.

Rutter, M., Chadwick, O., & Shaffer, D. (1983). Head injury. In M. Rutter (Ed.), *Developmental neuropsychiatry.* New York: Guilford Press.

Schacter, D. L., & Glisky, E. L. (1986). Memory remediation: Restoration, alleviation, and the acquisition of domain-specific knowledge. In B. P. Uzzell & Y. Gross (Eds.), *Clinical neuropsychology of intervention* (pp. 257–282). Boston: Martinus Nijhoff.

Scherzer, B. P. (1986). Rehabilitation following severe head trauma: Results of a three year program. *Archives of Physical Medicine and Rehabilitation, 67,* 366–374.

Siegler, R. S. (1986). *Children's thinking.* Englewood Cliffs, NJ: Prentice-Hall.

Singley, M. K., & Anderson, J. R. (1989). *Transfer of cognitive skill.* Cambridge, MA: Harvard University Press.

Skinner, B. F. (1969). *Contingencies of reinforcement.* New York: Appleton-Century-Crofts.

Smith, G. J., & Ylvisaker, M. (1985). Cognitive rehabilitation therapy: Early stages of recovery. In M. Ylvisaker (Ed.), *Head injury rehabilitation: Children and adolescents* (pp. 275–286). Austin, TX: PRO-ED.

Sohlberg, M., & Mateer, C. (1987). Effectiveness of an attention-training program. *Journal of Experimental and Clinical Neuropsychology, 9,* 117–130.

Stelling, M. W., McKay, S. E., Carr, W. A., Walsh, J. W., & Bauman, R. J. (1986). Frontal lobe lesions and cognitive function in craniopharyngioma survivors. *American Journal of Diseases of Childhood, 140,* 710–714.

Szekeres, S. F., Ylvisaker, M., & Cohen, S. (1987). A framework for cognitive rehabilitation therapy. In M. Ylvisaker & E. M. R. Gobble (Eds.), *Community reentry for head injured adults* (pp. 87–136). Austin, TX: PRO-ED.

Szekeres, S. F., Ylvisaker, M., & Holland, A. L. (1985). Cognitive rehabilitation therapy: A framework for intervention. In M. Ylvisaker (Ed.), *Head injury rehabilitation: Children and adolescents* (pp. 219–246). Austin, TX: PRO-ED.

Welsh, M. C., Pennington, B. F., & Groisser, D. B. (1991). A normative-developmental study of executive function: A window on prefrontal function in children. *Developmental Neuropsychology, 7,* 131–149.

Wong, B. (1986). Metacognition and special education: A review of a view. *Journal of Special Education, 20*(1), 9–29.

Ylvisaker, M. (1989). Cognitive and psychosocial outcome following head injury in children. In J. T. Hoff, T. E. Anderson, & T. M. Cole (Eds.), *Mild to moderate head injury* (pp. 203–216). Boston: Blackwell Scientific.

Ylvisaker, M., & Szekeres, S. F. (1989). Metacognitive and executive impairment in head-injured children and adults. *Topics in Language Disorders, 9,* 34–49.

Ylvisaker, M., Szekeres, S. F., & Hartwick, P. (1991). Cognitive rehabilitation following traumatic brain injury in children. In M. Tramontana & S. Hooper (Eds.), *Advances in child neuropsychology* (Vol. 1). New York: Springer Verlag.

CHAPTER 4

Cognitive Assessment

MARK YLVISAKER
PATRICK HARTWICK
BRADFORD ROSS
NATALIE NUSSBAUM

Cognitive assessment can serve several distinct purposes. In this chapter, we highlight assessment procedures that are useful in planning and refining classroom instruction and therapeutic intervention for children with cognitive needs following traumatic brain injury (TBI). Given this goal, cognitive assessment involves several professionals, requires the integration of formal and informal procedures, occurs in several settings (including classroom and social settings), and is ongoing. Assessment procedures that have been validated for other groups of children can be effectively used with children with TBI, but with qualifications based on the unique profiles and characteristics that these children often demonstrate. Prescription of educational services and prediction of academic, vocational, and social success should never be made solely on the basis of formal assessment.

Our goals in this chapter are (a) to present a broad and functional framework for cognitive assessment, one that integrates the assessments of several educational professionals, including psychologists, educational diagnosticians, and speech-language pathologists; (b) to discuss the strengths and weaknesses of both formal and informal assessment procedures for students with TBI; (c) to present informal assessment procedures that are useful in planning intervention; and (d) to discuss specialized assessment challenges, including the cognitive assessment of preschoolers and of children with mild TBI.

The role of cognitive assessment in determining a student's eligibility for special supports and services is well established. Equally important for children with TBI is the subsequent role of cognitive assessment in determining the nature of those services through planning interventions for the classroom and therapy sessions. To identify interventions that will be most helpful, cognitive assessment must be an interdisciplinary and pragmatic activity. It includes the administration of tests, but also requires creative detective work and hypothesis testing in instructional and other natural settings. Teachers and clinicians need more than a static description of isolated deficits. The most critical goal of cognitive assessment is a flexible intervention plan based on identification of (a) the student's strengths and weaknesses, (b) factors responsible for weak performance, and (c) interventions that are most effective in improving cognitive performance in academic and social contexts and capitalizing on the child's strengths.

Because TBI is now officially recognized as an educational disability category (PL 101-476, Individuals with Disability Education Act, 1990), school psychologists, special educators, and related services providers must be sensitive to modifications in the assessment process and interpretation of assessment results dictated by the characteristics of this population. Therefore, the focus of this chapter is cognitive assessment as it relates to securing appropriate services for children with TBI and also the pragmatic use of cognitive assessment to design effective interventions.

THE IMPORTANCE OF COGNITIVE ASSESSMENT

Cognitive and related behavioral and psychosocial problems are more common following head injury in school-aged children than are motor or other physical problems. Furthermore, children may be more vulnerable to the effects of cognitive impairment than comparably injured adults. For example, new learning problems may not be disabling for an adult who has good recovery of knowledge and skills acquired before the injury, and who returns to overlearned routines at home and work. Children, on the other hand, return to school, a setting that places significant demands on new learning ability and general cognitive and behavioral integrity. Children also face developmental challenges that may be extremely difficult to negotiate following the injury. The natural history following TBI is often characterized by return to school with undetected cognitive weakness. This creates a mismatch between teacher expectations and the student's ability to perform, which predictably leads to academic failure and maladaptive behavioral or emotional reactions.

Well-designed cognitive assessment may be needed to identify effects of the injury not captured by medical diagnostic procedures. Neuroimaging techniques (e.g., computerized tomography [CT scans] and magnetic resonance imaging [MRI scans]) are extremely useful in medical diagnosis, but may not detect every type of brain injury capable of producing cognitive deficits (e.g., diffuse axonal injury that is not severe). Furthermore, even careful psychological and neuropsychological testing may yield an overly optimistic prognosis for this group of children, particularly in the event of injury to the prefrontal areas of the brain. A child may return to school with good recovery of pretraumatically acquired knowledge and skills and with adequate ability to perform highly structured tasks in a controlled testing environment, yet have considerable difficulty regulating behavior and learning new information in the classroom. Therefore, cognitive assessment of these children must extend beyond the formal testing procedures routinely used in the schools. Also, because profiles of ability and need of children with TBI are often importantly different from profiles of children with other disabilities (discussed in Chapter 3), assessment guided by the characteristics of this group is critical for making appropriate decisions regarding services and supports.

THE SCOPE OF COGNITIVE ASSESSMENT

Cognitive assessment includes much of what traditionally falls within the assessment domains of school psychologists, neuropsychologists, special educators, speech-language pathologists, occupational therapists, vocational evaluators, and others. Chapter 3 presents a cognitive framework that can be used by diverse professionals to integrate assessments and speak to one another in a language that they all understand. This framework includes the categories *component processes* (attention, perception, memory and learning, organization, reasoning, and problem solving), *component systems* (working memory, knowledge base, executive system, response system), and *functional–integrative performance* (real-world performance in relation to the critical variables efficiency, level, scope, and manner of performance).

Although these may not resemble the descriptive categories traditionally used by school psychologists, educators, or related services providers, it is useful for all team members to consider their particular areas of focus from a cognitive perspective. Speech-language pathologists, for example, are accustomed to describing assessment results under the headings receptive and expressive language together with the various subheadings. However, following TBI, many children have adequate knowledge of the linguistic code, but have difficulty using language efficiently, communicating effectively in challenging academic and social contexts, and learning new language because of impaired cognitive processes or systems. Therefore, speech-language pathologists must be sensitive to the possible communicative effects of cognitive weakness and be able to probe communicative functioning from a cognitive perspective. Similarly, special educators must be capable of analyzing student performance on tests and in the classroom from the perspective of general cognitive disruption (e.g., impairments of attentional, organizational, problem-solving, or executive system functioning), as well as specific academic knowledge and skill.

Given the broad scope of cognitive assessment and the variety of professionals with a legitimate interest in assessing cognitive functioning, attention must be given to the *organization* and *integration* of these assessments. *Over*assessment is a likely consequence of several professionals testing in cognitive domains without integrating their assessment activity and results. Despite a great deal of testing, *under*assessment (i.e., resulting in an incomplete picture of the student's functioning) may result from professionals lacking a vocabulary and forum in which to communicate their findings with one another. Later in this chapter, we propose a model of interactive or dialectical cognitive assessment involving school psychologists and classroom teachers. We also present a sample of assessment probes using the categories of cognition introduced in Chapter 3. These probes may serve in part as operational definitions of cognitive terms, enabling professionals with different training to communicate with each other and to integrate their formal and informal assessments.

FLEXIBILITY IN INTERPRETING RESULTS OF ASSESSMENT

Because children with TBI often have unique profiles of ability and need, those professionals responsible for cognitive assessment must be creative and must flexibly interpret assessment results in light of what is known about this population. Although any combination of functions can be spared or impaired in TBI, these children can be confusing because of the strange juxtaposition of spared high-level abilities with major gaps in knowledge and skill at lower levels. Among other things, this necessitates probing knowledge and abilities below basal levels and above ceiling levels on tests. Furthermore, unlike other special education groups, students with severe TBI generally change neurologically over time. Neurologic recovery and reorganization can continue at a decelerating pace for months, and in many cases years, following the injury. Deterioration in some functional areas is also a possibility, due to a type of brain injury that remains "functionally occult" until the function subserved by the injured part of the brain is expected to mature or due to the delayed effects of a substantial new learning impairment. These three phenomena—unusual profiles, neurologic improvement over time, and shifting profiles resulting from improvements in some areas and deterioration in others—necessitate creative assessment, flexible interpretation of results, and well-planned follow-up, considering specific features of the child's injury and general features of TBI in children.

THE GOALS OF COGNITIVE ASSESSMENT

Form follows function. Answers to questions such as What type of assessment should I do? When should the assessment occur? Who should perform the assessment? Where should it occur? Should I use tests or other procedures? What tests should I use? presuppose an answer to the more basic questions, Why am I assessing this child? What purposes are served by this assessment? Cognitive assessment may serve a variety of purposes and, as a consequence, the procedural questions have many correct answers.

Diagnosis and Prognosis

Within medical and legal contexts, neuropsychologists and other professionals may be asked to evaluate a child with the goal of establishing the presence or absence of brain damage, localizing the damage, or determining the child's likely recovery and potential to respond positively to treatment. Diagnosing brain damage—particularly given the possibility of legal challenges—requires assessment tools and procedures that are specifically validated for this population in relation to this question. The informal probes and hypothesis-testing procedures highlighted in this chapter are in general inappropriate for this purpose. However, diagnosis of brain injury and prognosis for recovery are rarely the key questions that need to be answered in a school setting.

Classification and Eligibility for Services

A purpose commonly served by assessment in the schools is classification of children to determine eligibility for services. Many districts adhere rigidly to eligibility criteria, based on test performance, for granting special education and related services.

Therefore, psychologists, educators, and therapists must either use the prescribed tests or argue persuasively that these tests are not valid indicators of the need for the service in question. A problem in classifying children with TBI is that the test procedures most often specified to determine eligibility are somewhat insensitive to the full spectrum of cognitive problems frequently observed in this population and therefore yield an unacceptable rate of false negatives. Because the validity of available standardized tests in relation to the important question of need for services has not been formally determined for this population and eligibility criteria for TBI classification under PL 101-476 have not yet been established in many states, school psychologists and other decision makers must exercise sound clinical judgment based on performance on formal and informal measures and on thoughtful consideration of characteristics of this group.

There is, in fact, reason to believe that most tests commonly used for classification purposes would fail to identify those children with TBI whose recovery *on the surface* is quite good, but who have residual information processing and self-regulatory deficits of the sort described in Chapter 3 and who are consequently in need of some level of services and supports. Results of intelligence tests, such as the *Wechsler Intelligence Scale for Children–Third Edition* (WISC-III) (Wechsler, 1991), are substantially affected by the recovery of old learning. This is particularly true of the verbal portions. Therefore, a child may perform surprisingly well on such tests and fail to qualify for support services that he or she definitely needs. Furthermore, recovery of pretraumatically acquired academic knowledge and skill may result in a profile that lacks a significant discrepancy between actual academic achievement and achievement levels predicted by IQ (a criterion for learning disabilities services in many states). Indeed, it is not uncommon for severely injured children to return to school with a profile that is opposite that required for learning disabilities services; that is, they have reasonable academic achievement levels based on recovery of overlearned material combined with weak performance IQ resulting from pervasive slowness and impaired organization. After 3 or 4 years of academic failure due to significant *new learning* problems, the child's profile may reverse its pattern. However, requiring a child to experience prolonged failure before affirming the need for services or supports is unacceptable.

Ylvisaker (1989) reported data consistent with these cautions about the use of the *Wechsler Intelligence Scale for Children–Revised* (WISC-R) in determining need for services. Thirty-five children with severe closed head injury, all known to be within normal limits developmentally and academically before their injury, were followed 1 to 5 years postinjury (average 3 years). Of seven children who had posttrauma WISC-R IQs greater than 100 and who were given 1 year to recover pretrauma academic achievement levels, only one had academic achievement scores that indicated a year's improvement for every year in school after the first year following the injury. Although the number of children was small, this suggests that the WISC-R lacks predictive validity in relation to academic performance for severely injured children whose outcome is superficially good, and therefore cannot reliably identify those children in need of special education services.

Some test batteries are likely superior to others for the purpose of identifying children with special needs. For example, although not yet established empirically, clinical indications are that the *Woodcock–Johnson Psycho-Educational Test Battery–Revised* (Woodcock & Johnson, 1989) is more sensitive than the WISC-R to cognitive deficits frequently observed following severe TBI. The Visual–Auditory Learning Subtest, for example, is a useful measure of new learning capacity because it is unlikely that the items to be learned were familiar to the child before the injury and because the task embodies teaching with feedback, similar to classroom teaching. Similarly, the Concept Formation Subtest is sensitive to problems with conceptual flexibility and abstract thinking, which are often observed in children with frontal lobe injury, common in closed head injury. The *Woodcock–Johnson* is increasingly used with individuals with learning disabilities (Cuenin, 1990) and is a likely candidate for widespread use with students following TBI. The commonly used *Wide Range Achievement Test–Revised* (WRAT-R) (Jastak & Wilkinson, 1984) is notoriously ineffective in screening students with TBI. Because the reading portion contains no comprehension items and the math portion contains no application items, this test cannot be expected to identify students with TBI who are in need of further diagnostic exploration. The achievement portion (Part II) of the *Woodcock–Johnson* provides a more comprehensive assessment of academic achievement.

Knowledge of the common consequences of TBI and of the difficulty in detecting all of the child's cognitive sequelae by means of formal tests should help school professionals to secure appropriate support services for these children without relying on measures and criteria that have not been validated for this population. Such support is often necessary to prevent the child's failure in school.

A similar problem is faced by speech-language pathologists. Standardized tests of language, designed for children with congenital language delay or disorder, typically focus on knowledge of the linguistic code (i.e., the phonologic, morphologic, syntactic, and semantic features of language). This knowledge may return following TBI, despite significant difficulty using language efficiently under cognitive and social stress, interacting effectively in varied social contexts, comprehending abstract and indirect meaning, and learning new language. Therefore, speech-language therapy services or classroom support may be important for these children even if they fail to meet the criteria for these services based on test performance (see Chapter 6).

Because of the nature of standardized tests and the conditions of formal assessment, test results are often inaccurate or incomplete indicators of the student's habitual functioning in classroom and social settings. Reasons include the following:

1. The controlled and distraction-free testing environment may compensate for poorly regulated attentional functioning.
2. The use of short tasks and relatively brief testing sessions may compensate for reduced endurance, persistence, and attention span.
3. The use of very clear test instructions and examples may compensate for weak task orientation and impaired flexibility in shifting from one task to another.
4. The use of highly structured tasks and clear instructions, including instructions to start and stop, may compensate for weak initiation, inhibition, and problem solving.
5. Test items that do not include real-life *amounts* of information (input or output) or *rate* of delivery may compensate for weak integration and organization of information and generally reduced efficiency of information processing.
6. The use of tests that do not require the storage and retrieval of new information (not known pretraumatically) from day to day

(or longer periods) may compensate for significant new learning impairment.

7. The encouraging interactive style of the examiner may compensate for the child's inability to cope with interpersonal stress or perception of demands.
8. The basal and ceiling procedures of standardized tests may conceal gaps below basals and surprising strengths above ceilings, common features of head injury profiles.

Frontal lobe injury is notorious for resulting in a profile of adequate test performance, but serious difficulty learning and regulating behavior in the real world (Benton, 1991; Bigler, 1988a; Eslinger & Damasio, 1985; Grattan & Eslinger, 1991; Mateer & Williams, 1991; Stelling, McKay, Carr, Walsh, & Bauman, 1986; Stuss & Benson, 1986; Welsh, Pennington, & Groisser, 1991).

These considerations are illustrated by a seventh-grade student who scores within normal limits on tests of word recognition and sentence comprehension, but who is unable to read and comprehend a chapter in a seventh-grade social studies textbook because of significant organizational problems. Similarly, a third-grade student with good recovery of pretraumatically acquired academic skill may score within normal limits on all tests administered, but return to school with a substantial decrease in learning efficiency, difficulty controlling attentional functioning and remaining oriented to task, and great difficulty generalizing new skills from one setting to another. Or a preschooler may recover to the point at which it appears that he has all of the skills that he had before the injury, but over time may evidence developmental lags related to damage to parts of the brain associated with functions that mature later in development (e.g., behavioral self-regulation or abstract thinking). Optimal performance is predictably superior to habitual performance in the case of most children, with or without brain injury. However, severe TBI introduces a number of specific reasons to expect a more dramatic deterioration in performance in demanding contexts and also an inability to meet developmental expectations over time despite adequate performance several weeks or months after the injury.

In summary, poor performance on cognitive measures (psychological, neuropsychological, educational, linguistic) is generally predictive of poor school performance, although some children do surprisingly well in the classroom given the familiarity of the setting and materials relative to the unfamiliar setting and tasks of formal assessment. Adequate performance on tests of cognitive functioning, on the other hand, may not predict academic and social success. School psychologists, supervisors of special education, administrators, and others responsible for determining eligibility for special services and supports must interpret results of formal assessment in light of what is known about head injury and must be flexible in applying criteria for services. In the final analysis, there is no substitute for prescriptive teaching and diagnostic therapy, with careful monitoring of the child's response to instruction in natural settings.

Planning Intervention

Cognitive assessment within an intervention context has as its goals (a) determining the student's levels of performance in a variety of cognitive and academic areas for purposes of establishing instructional levels; (b) in the event of inadequate test performance, identifying which factors are responsible for poor performance and which of the weaknesses play the most critical role in depressing academic and social functioning; (c) setting baseline levels to measure progress in relation to the student's objectives; (d) determining which type of intervention is most effective in promoting improvement; and (e) determining what environmental, motivational, interpersonal, and task variables have the greatest effect on learning and other aspects of school performance.

Determining level of performance

Tests of academic and language performance are important in determining curricular levels and expectations for performance. They do not determine how to use the curriculum most creatively, but they do help teachers and therapists select tasks at the appropriate level of difficulty and identify which areas of performance are in need of support or remediation. Having established performance levels on tests, teachers and others must decide whether to translate those levels directly into a sequenced curriculum of teaching objectives or, alternatively, to place the student at a higher level, more consistent with the student's pretrauma expectations, and address weak areas in a "top–down" fashion. For example, a seventh-grade student who scores at third-grade reading levels within the first 6 months after the injury may respond best to a sixth- or seventh-grade reading curriculum with adaptations and supports (e.g., tutoring) designed to facilitate success. The latter approach is often effective with recently injured students because it mobilizes their motivation to be functioning at pretrauma levels, capitalizes on strengths in remediating weaknesses, and is consistent with the likelihood that recovery and relearning will enable the student to progress rapidly.

Explaining poor performance

Because most test items are multifactorial (i.e., a variety of possible deficits could explain why the child failed a particular item), considerable detective work may be required to explain poor performance on a test of academic or cognitive functioning. For example, the following are among the many possible explanations for a student's failure on a test of paragraph reading comprehension.

- *Attention:* The student may lack adequate physiologic arousal, may be unable to filter out external or internal distractions, may be unable to maintain attention to the task, or may be unable to shift attention from some event that occurred earlier.
- *Visual perception:* The student may have double vision, a visual field cut or neglect, impaired scanning, figure–ground difficulties, or some other specific perceptual impairment.
- *Organization:* The student may comprehend isolated details but fail to integrate them into a narrative that makes sense as a whole, or may comprehend the passage but be unable to organize a response.
- *Memory–learning:* The student may comprehend the passage but be unable to encode the information into memory, or store the information, or retrieve it when asked.

- *Reasoning and problem solving:* The passage may be at too high a level of abstractness or may require inferential skill beyond the child's level.
- *Working memory:* The student may understand the passage but be unable to hold in mind at one time the information from the passage and also the question to be answered.
- *Knowledge base:* The student may have no knowledge of the subject matter of the passage, and therefore may be confused and unable to comprehend the information. The child may lack the vocabulary and language concepts present in the passage.
- *Executive system:* The student may fail to grasp what is required of her, to initiate cognitive activity (e.g., searching memory) without prompts, to monitor comprehension, to evaluate performance to know that special effort is required, or to use available strategies to comprehend the passage.
- *Response system:* The student may be unable to retrieve words to express a response. He may be unable to speak or write effectively.
- *Efficiency factors:* The student may require shorter reading materials, extraordinary amounts of time to read and formulate a response, or extra processing time after every piece of information is presented.
- *Behavioral–emotional–motivational factors:* The student may be extremely anxious about her performance or may be bored with the task. She may refuse to respond because of oppositional behavior, or may simply require a promise of substantial reward before doing anything that requires effort.
- *Medical–physiologic factors:* The student may have subclinical seizures; levels of medication that are too high or too low, affecting arousal or other cognitive functions; pain related to bodily injury, headache, or spasticity; high or low blood sugar levels; or other factors. He may simply be exhausted.

Clearly, documenting impaired performance on complex tasks is only the first step in understanding how to help the child improve performance. Kaplan (1988) demonstrated that a correct answer on a test can result from successful application of a variety of cognitive processes and strategies; similarly, an incorrect answer can result from disruption of any number of processes. Whereas these considerations are valid for all children, there is a critical need for sensitivity to them in the case of TBI, due to the often unusual complexes of strengths and weaknesses observed in this population.

Appendix 4A lists assessment probes that may help to ferret out the specific disruption that is responsible for task failure. In the case of observed memory weakness, for example, it is important to determine the contributions to that weakness of various aspects of memory functioning (e.g., encoding, storage, retrieval), of related cognitive functions (e.g., attention, organization, executive functions), of characteristics of the information to be remembered (e.g., recent events in one's life vs. academic information), and of aspects of the presentation of the information (e.g., visual vs. auditory presentation, speeded vs. slow presentation). In many cases, this detective work requires examination of error patterns across many tasks, systematic variation of tasks by one factor at a time, and exploration of the effects of strategies to improve performance. The assessment probes in Appendix 4A are designed in part to assist in this process. Having clearly identified which of the many possible factors contribute most to success and failure, the efficiency of intervention will be enhanced.

Establishing baseline levels

Test scores can, in selected cases, also serve as baselines for measuring improvement. This must be done with caution, however, because it is possible that improvement can occur without being reflected in scores on formal tests. Alternatively, test scores may go up following training on a task closely resembling the test task, without the child's real-world performance being affected. This is the methodological problem that has plagued many investigations of the effects of cognitive rehabilitation in adults. Performance may improve on specific neuropsychological measures while performance of functional tasks in natural contexts may be unaffected by the training.

Often the best measure of improvement is pre- and postintervention performance on the functional task that is the focus of intervention (criterion-based assessment). For example, if the goal is to improve a child's comprehension of and memory for text by means of a summarizing strategy, using performance on standardized memory tests as the measure of successful intervention is invalid. It is possible, indeed likely, that a child could significantly improve memory for text using a text-processing strategy without demonstrating generalized improvement in memory as measured by any of the available standardized memory tests. Functional curricular measures are a reasonable alternative in this case.

Determining intervention approaches

Determining baseline levels of performance is only one component of planning rehabilitative and educational services. Subsequently, important decisions must be made. For example, should instruction be designed to improve academic skills and cognitive functioning through practice (remediation) or to equip the student with strategies to perform challenging tasks in a way that is somewhat different from pretrauma performance (compensation)? To determine if a student is a candidate for a deliberate cognitive strategy approach in the classroom often requires a period of diagnostic exploration, including exploratory teaching of strategies. This exploration is discussed in Chapter 5.

Similarly, decisions about classroom modifications and adaptations are best made as a result of experimenting in the classroom. Because there may be more time and flexibility for this activity in a rehabilitation facility than in school, rehabilitation professionals would be wise to simulate a classroom environment and explore the effects on academic performance, learning, and adaptive behavior of the following variables (Ylvisaker, Hartwick, & Stevens, 1991):

- *Environmental* (e.g., noise levels, activity levels, visual distractions, large group vs. small group vs. individual instruction, consistency in staff)
- *Schedule* (e.g., length of instructional periods, consistency in schedule, free vs. scheduled time, length of school day)

- *Cuing systems* (e.g., assignment book, task cues [e.g., advance organizers], repetition of instructions, written instructions, buddy system [for getting from class to class or for remembering assignments], maps for navigating within the school)
- *Modification in materials and tests* (e.g., large-print books, simplified worksheets, take-home tests, extra time)
- *Instructional variables* (e.g., task analysis, best sensory modality, compensatory strategies, self-paced instructional plans, competency-based instruction, precision teaching, computer-assisted instruction)
- *Classroom aids* (e.g., calculator, tape recorder, writing aids, positioning equipment, augmentative communication device, environmental control equipment)
- *Work expectations* (e.g., quality of work, length of assignments, independent work, rate of performance)
- *Motivational variables* (e.g., type and schedule of reinforcement, need for success and reaction to failure, need for immediate reward)

Traditionally, decisions about intervention approaches in special education and related services are based on inferences from performance on tests. This is certainly preferable to simply giving the child whatever type of instruction every other child in the classroom gets. However, careful hypothesis testing in actual or simulated classroom settings and with functional curricular tasks yields the most useful information for planning intervention. School personnel are well advised to request this type of information from rehabilitation centers prior to the child's return to school.

COGNITIVE ASSESSMENT IN THE SCHOOL

The type and amount of assessment needed initially in the school depends on the assessment results available from the rehabilitation facility. The last 2 to 4 weeks in rehabilitation can include the type of exploratory cognitive assessment described above. Anticipating the school's needs for test scores, formal assessment may also occur in the rehabilitation facility. If the necessary testing is not done before the child leaves the hospital, he or she may be forced to wait for weeks before the school psychologist can make room in a busy schedule for the testing. Therefore, rehabilitation professionals should offer to complete the required formal assessments to ensure appropriate and continuous services when the child returns to school.

Reassessment typically occurs relatively frequently during the early months of recovery and possibly for years following the injury. Because the goal of periodic reassessment is to ensure that the child's program continues to be appropriate, it need not include comprehensive testing.

Psychological–Neuropsychological Assessment

Traditionally, school psychologists provide initial and periodic psychological (intelligence and/or psychoeducational) assessment. The initial assessment may be critical in placement decisions and generally culminates in recommendations for instructional practices as well as placement. We have already highlighted the danger in using intelligence testing alone for placement decisions and in drawing firm inferences about instructional practices from test performance without confirming the hypotheses in the classroom. Later in this chapter, we describe a collaborative hypothesis-testing model that capitalizes on the assessment strengths and contexts of psychologists, as well as those of teachers and therapists, and integrates their results.

Neuropsychological assessment may include many of the same measures and address many of the same questions as traditional psychological assessment. However, it is more comprehensive in scope and involves the exploration of strengths and deficits using a model of brain–behavior relationships (Hynd, 1988). In this way, neurologic insights are added to behavioral observations to fill out the child's profile (Bigler, 1988b). Areas of assessment typically include motor and graphomotor functioning (including lateralization of motor functioning); attention, concentration, and orientation; sensory–perceptual abilities; memory (including old vs. new learning); language; problem solving and abstract reasoning; and executive functioning.

Approaches to neuropsychological assessment include (a) the use of fixed batteries, such as the children's versions of the *Halstead–Reitan Neuropsychological Test Battery* (Reitan, 1987) and the *Luria–Nebraska Neuropsychological Battery: Children's Revision* (Golden, 1987); (b) flexible batteries, adjusted to the needs of individual children (Lezak, 1983; Rourke, Bakker, Fisk, & Strang, 1983); and (c) a process approach to assessment (Kaplan, 1988). The latter emphasizes the means (e.g., strategies) that the child uses to arrive at an answer, rather than the correctness of the answer. Tests and other assessment tasks are selected and possibly modified to test hypotheses about the child's underlying neuropsychological strengths and deficits. This approach has advantages in pinpointing deficits, identifying the child's spontaneous strategies and processing strengths, and planning intervention. The disadvantage is that one sacrifices objectivity and the possibility of comparing performance with normative populations. The obvious advantage of both process and flexible battery approaches is that testing is customized to meet the specific needs of individual students.

In contrast to traditional psychological assessment in a school setting, an experienced pediatric neuropsychologist can use pathophysiologic information (i.e., information about the nature and location of the injury) to guide assessment and increase the accuracy of prognoses and recommendations, can dissect poor performance more completely, and can estimate the degree of organic versus functional contribution to the child's problems (Bigler, 1988b; Franzen & Berg, 1989; Hynd, 1988; Obrzut & Hynd, 1986; Rourke, Fisk, & Strang, 1986). For example, knowing that a child has a nondominant hemisphere lesion (i.e., damage to the hemisphere of the brain that is not responsible for language comprehension and expression) that affects organizational functioning across many domains, the neuropsychologist can alert the teacher and speech-language pathologist to likely organizational problems in language comprehension and expression that may not be evident in daily conversation or in language and reading tests commonly used in the school. Therefore, a neuropsychologist who has experience with traumatic brain injury in children can be a valuable member of the cognitive rehabilitation and special education teams, particularly if he or she is able to integrate neuropsychological assessment with the insights of the child's therapists and teachers.

Table 4.1 lists a number of tests that may be included in a comprehensive neuropsychological assessment of a child with brain injury. Some of these tests fall under the scope of practice of other professionals as well as psychologists; in these cases, members of the team should negotiate which tests should be administered by each professional. Begali (1992) presented a useful discussion of cognitive testing of children with TBI in a school setting.

Child neuropsychologists have recently begun to standardize and acquire normative information for assessment tasks specifically designed to assess the effects of frontal lobe injury in children (e.g., Dennis, 1991; Levin et al., 1991; Welsh & Pennington, 1988; Welsh et al., 1991). Some of these procedures involve the downward extension of tasks used to assess frontal lobe functioning in adults (e.g., *Wisconsin Card Sorting Task,* Heaton, 1981). Others are neuropsychological applications of procedures that have their home in developmental cognitive psychology (e.g., the Tower of Hanoi task; Matching Familiar Figures). Among the functions commonly tested by prefrontal batteries are attentional control, conceptual and perceptual flexibility, response inhibition, divergent processing and retrieval, problem solving, planning, and strategic thinking. Language tasks associated with frontal lobe assessment include controlled word fluency, processing of linguistic abstractions and indirect meaning (e.g., metaphor, irony), and conversational and monologic discourse tasks. Tests and other assessment procedures are listed in Tables 4.1 and 4.2.

Although systematic exploration of prefrontal (executive) functions is a welcome addition to neuropsychological assessment of young children, it is an enterprise fraught with peril. First, it has been known for some time that adults with prefrontal injury may score well on neuropsychological tests designed specifically to detect the effects of that type of injury (Bigler, 1988a; Eslinger & Damasio, 1985; Stuss & Benson, 1986). This appears to be true of children as well (Mateer & Williams, 1991; Stelling et al., 1986) and may be a reflection of what Lezak (1982) referred to as the paradox of executive system assessment—the paradox inherent in presenting prestructured tasks in an attempt to determine how effectively individuals can structure tasks for themselves in pursuit of their own goals. Second, because the frontal lobes undergo protracted neurologic development in childhood, a specific injury may not negatively affect test performance until years after the original injury. Third, certain types of prefrontal injury are associated with primary social disability and therefore may not be apparent outside of a social context. Fourth, many of the functions mediated by prefrontal areas are also subject to substantial developmental, cultural, and personality variability. Therefore, assessment results must be interpreted cautiously. Finally, the paucity of long-term outcome data following exclusive prefrontal injury in young children similarly demands caution in the interpretation of these tests.

Language Assessment

Although aphasia syndromes are uncommon following traumatic brain injury in children, they do occur (Ylvisaker, 1986). Tests developed to diagnose specific language delays and disorders in children are useful in the event of deficit knowledge of and facility with the linguistic code. However, knowledge of the phonologic, mor-

TABLE 4.1. Tests Often Used in Psychological or Neuropsychological Assessment of Children[1]

Cognitive Assessments

Kaufman Assessment Battery for Children (Kaufman & Kaufman, 1983)
Leiter International Performance Scale (Leiter, 1969)
McCarthy Scales of Children's Abilities (McCarthy, 1972)
Raven's Coloured Progressive Matrices (Raven, 1956)
Stanford–Binet Intelligence Scale–Fourth Edition (Thorndike, Hagen, & Sattler, 1986)
Wechsler Adult Intelligence Scale–Revised (Wechsler, 1981)
Wechsler Intelligence Scale for Children–Third Edition (Wechsler, 1991)
Wechsler Preschool and Primary Scale of Intelligence–Revised (Wechsler, 1989)
Woodcock–Johnson Psycho-Educational Test Battery–Revised (Part I) (Woodcock & Johnson, 1989)

Neuropsychological Test Batteries

Halstead–Reitan Neuropsychological Test Battery (Reitan & Wolfson, 1985)
Luria–Nebraska Neuropsychological Battery (Golden, Hammeke, & Purisch, 1985)
Luria–Nebraska Neuropsychological Battery: Children's Revision (Golden, 1987)
Neuropsychological Evaluation of Children (Reitan, 1987)
WAIS-R as a Neuropsychological Instrument (WAIS-R NI) (Kaplan, Fein, Morris, & Delis, 1991)

Measures of Prefrontal–Executive Functions

Concept Formation Subtest of the *Woodcock–Johnson Psycho-Educational Test Battery* (Woodcock & Johnson, 1989)
Contingency Naming Test (Taylor, Albo, Phebus, Sachs, & Bierl, 1987)
Design Fluency Task (Jones–Gotman & Milner, 1977)
Gordon Diagnostic System (1988): Vigilance, Delay, and Distractibility subtests
Matching Familiar Figures (Kagan, Rosman, Day, Albert, & Phillips, 1964)
Porteus Mazes (Porteus, 1959)
Tower of London (Shallice, 1982)
Trail Making B (child version in Reitan, 1955)
Wisconsin Card Sorting Test (Heaton, 1981; child norms in Chelune & Baer, 1986)
Word Fluency Subtest of the *Neurosensory Center Comprehensive Examination for Aphasia* (child norms in Gaddes & Crocket, 1975)

Achievement Tests

Kaufman Assessment Battery for Children (Kaufman & Kaufman, 1983)
Peabody Individual Achievement Test–Revised (Dunn & Markwardt, 1989)
Wide Range Achievement Test–Revised (Jastak & Wilkinson, 1984)
Woodcock–Johnson Psycho-Educational Test Battery–Revised (Part II) (Woodcock & Johnson, 1989)

Preschool Assessments

Bayley Scales of Infant Development–Second Edition (Bayley, 1993)

(*continues*)

TABLE 4.1. *Continued*

Hawaii Early Learning Profile (HELP) (Furons et al., 1985)
Kaufman Assessment Battery for Children (Kaufman & Kaufman, 1983)
McCarthy Scales of Individual Abilities (McCarthy, 1972)
Portage Guide to Early Education (Bluma, Shearer, Froham, & Hilliard, 1976)
Stanford–Binet Intelligence Scale–Fourth Edition (Thorndike, Hagen, & Sattler, 1986)
Uzgiris–Hunt Ordinal Scales for Assessment in Infancy (Uzgiris & Hunt, 1978)
Wechsler Preschool and Primary Scale of Intelligence–Revised (Wechsler, 1989)

Language Tests (see also Table 4.2)

The Boston Naming Test (Kaplan, Goodglass, & Weintraub, 1978)
Clinical Evaluation of Language Fundamentals–Revised (Semel, Wiig, & Secord, 1987)
Detroit Tests of Learning Aptitude–Third Edition (Hammill, 1991)
Peabody Picture Vocabulary Test–Revised (Dunn & Dunn, 1981)
The Token Test for Children (DiSimoni, 1978)
Revised Token Test (McNeil & Prescott, 1978)

Memory Tests

California Test of Verbal Learning (Delis, Kramer, Kaplan, & Ober, 1983)
Children's Verbal Learning Test (Drexler, Kramer, Pope, & Hough, 1986)
Continuous Visual Memory Test (Trahan & Larrabee, 1988)
Randt Memory Test (Randt & Brown, 1983)
Rey–Osterreith Complex Figure (Osterreith, 1944; Rey, 1941)
Selective Reminding Test (Buschke, 1974)
Wechsler Memory Scale–Revised (Wechsler, 1987)
Wide Range Assessment of Memory and Language (WRAML) (Adams & Sheslow, 1990)

Visual–Perceptual–Motor Tests

Benton Visual Retention Test (Benton, 1974)
Developmental Test of Visual–Motor Integration–Revised (Beery, 1989)
Motor Free Visual Perceptual Test (Calarusso & Hammill, 1972)
Purdue Pegboard (Purdue Research Foundation, 1948)

Behavior and Personality Scales

AAMD Adaptive Behavior Scale (Nihira, Foster, Shellhaas, & Leland, 1974)
Achenbach Child Behavior Checklist (Achenbach & Edelbrock, 1983)
Connors Teacher Rating Form (Goyette, Conners, & Ulrich, 1978)
Personality Inventory for Children–PIC (Wirt, Lacher, Kinedinst, & Seat, 1984)
Vineland Adaptive Behavior Scales (Sparrow, Balla, & Cicchetti, 1984)

[1]All of these tests are not equally sensitive to the effects of traumatic brain injury.

phologic, and syntactic features of language often returns to pretrauma levels despite difficulty with language related to more general cognitive and psychosocial dysfunction. For this reason, students with TBI often score within normal limits on language tests despite possibly needing specialized language–communication services or supports (e.g., classroom consultation).

Although some language tests are better than others in identifying needs of children with TBI (e.g., *Clinical Evaluation of Language Fundamentals–Revised,* Semel, Wiig, & Secord, 1987; *Test of Language Competence–Expanded Edition,* Wiig & Secord, 1988; *The Word Test,* Jorgenson, Barrett, Huisingh, & Zachman, 1981), no battery or collection of tests addresses all of the questions that must be asked about the language of these students. Table 4.2 highlights questions that speech-language pathologists should ask about the language and communicative abilities of children following severe TBI. It also suggests formal and informal techniques that might be used to answer the questions. It is particularly important to probe the effects of cognitive stress on language comprehension and expression (e.g., increasing demands for speeded performance or organizing activity), the child's ability to process linguistic abstractions and to maintain effective communication in varied social contexts, and the ease with which the child learns new language (Ylvisaker, in press). Procedures for evaluating these aspects of language functioning are described in Chapter 6. Because many of the language and communication problems following TBI are based on cognitive weakness, speech-language pathologists should also have facility with the conceptual framework and informal assessment procedures described in Appendix 4A.

Educational Assessment

Like other types of assessment, educational assessment includes at least two distinct goals: (a) to determine a student's levels of performance in academic and academic-related areas of functioning, and how these levels compare with those of students of similar age and grade level, and (b) to determine *how* the student learns, including his or her most effective information processing strategies and manner of handling materials, activities, and social demands in the educational setting. Formal educational assessment, including norm-referenced and criterion-referenced testing, is used to achieve the first goal. Informal procedures, including situational observation, curriculum-based probes, specific hypothesis-testing probes (see Appendix 4A), and diagnostic teaching are needed to make effective decisions about instructional practices and materials (see the earlier section called "Determining Intervention Approaches").

Standardized, norm-referenced tests reveal the student's major strengths and weaknesses by content area, thereby giving suggestions for further exploration. In selected cases, these test results can be a major indicator of progress. Norm-referenced tests not only allow one to compare the student's performance with that of the standardization group, but also permit comparison of postinjury with preinjury performance. For example, a child may score within normal limits on a test of academic functioning, but still perform well below pretrauma levels. In this case, despite grossly normal test performance, one can infer significant effects of the injury and the possible need for services.

Many educational diagnosticians use double scoring procedures on standardized tests to formulate hypotheses about what types of intervention might help the student. The first score is derived using standard procedures as described in the test manual.

TABLE 4.2. Cognitive–Language Assessment of Children

Area	***Assessment Focus***	***Possible Assessment Procedures***
Receptive language	Receptive vocabulary level; compare with comprehension as affected by:	*Peabody Picture Vocabulary Test–Revised* (Dunn & Dunn, 1981)
	a. increased length and complexity of utterance.	a. *Token Test for Children* (DiSimoni, 1978); *Clinical Evaluation of Language Fundamentals–Revised* (CELF-R) (Semel, Wiig, & Secord, 1987); *Detroit Tests of Learning Aptitude–Third Edition* (Hammill, 1991).
	b. increased rate of verbal input.	b. *Token Test* commands spoken rapidly (180 to 200 words per minute) compared with more deliberate rate.
	c. increased amount of information.	c. Paragraphs or longer reading passages from reading tests or graded readers used informally to assess auditory comprehension. *Free recall* tasks (e.g., story retelling) are more informative than *cued recall* tasks (e.g., wh– or yes–no questions). For well-recovered older students, reading and summarizing a chapter or more of age- and interest-appropriate material may reveal subtle language comprehension or integration problems.
	d. increased environmental interference.	d. Compare comprehension with and without distracting recorded conversation as interference; compare language performance in a quiet environment with performance in the classroom, lunchroom, or hallway.
	e. conversational demands.	e. Use the *Pragmatic Protocol* (Prutting & Kirchner, 1987) or similar tool to systematically document conversational behaviors; does the student detect and correctly interpret contextual cues and speaker's suprasegmental and nonverbal behavior?

(*continues*)

TABLE 4.2. *Continued*

Area	***Assessment Focus***	***Possible Assessment Procedures***
	KEY QUESTIONS: 1. What is the level of the student's basic language knowledge base (vocabulary)? 2. How is language comprehension affected by varied and increasing processing demands? *COMMENT:* With children, the demands of *new* concept formation and language learning may cause vocabulary levels to deteriorate, relative to age norms, over the years after brain injury.	
Expressive language	a. Expressive vocabulary level.	a. *Expressive One-Word Picture Vocabulary Test* (Gardner, 1979).
	b. Word retrieval under varying forms of stress (e.g., time pressure, teacher demands, social stress).	b. Word Fluency subtest from *Neurosensory Center Comprehensive Examination for Aphasia* (children's norms in Gaddes & Crocket, 1975)—includes time pressure with no visual cues; Word Association from CELF-R (Semel et al., 1987); *Rapid Automatized Naming Tests* (Denkla & Rudel, 1976)—time pressure with easy vocabulary and recurring picture cues. *Informal:* observe efficiency of word retrieval in conversation and in classroom recitation.
	c. Expressive organization of increasing amounts of information.	c. Complex picture description (e.g., "The Cookie Theft" from *Boston Diagnostic Aphasia Examination*, Goodglass & Kaplan, 1972); story generation or repetition; explanation of complex game; written summary of age- and

(*continues*)

TABLE 4.2. *Continued*

Area	Assessment Focus	Possible Assessment Procedures
		interest-appropriate chapter. Analyze for *main idea, presupposition, organization of ideas (discourse structure), expansion, accuracy, detail.* Discourse organization is quite different in stories, descriptions, and explanations. These should be compared. Story grammar analysis may be insensitive to organizational weakness because of the pretrauma overlearning of story structure. *Coherence* analysis (i.e., underlying conceptual structure) is more revealing than *cohesion* analysis (i.e., linguistic markers of organization) (Mentis & Prutting, 1991).
	d. Conversational competence.	d. Use the *Pragmatic Protocol* (Prutting & Kirchner, 1987) to document conversational and pragmatic skills with varied partners and in varied settings. Pay particular attention to *initiation, relevance, topic maintenance, logical topic shifting, "rambling," inhibition, social appropriateness.*
	KEY QUESTIONS: 1. What is the student's unstressed expressive vocabulary level? Compare with receptive vocabulary. 2. How do varying forms of stress affect naming and word retrieval? What cues and contexts best facilitate word retrieval? 3. Can the student organize adequately large amounts of language for clear and coherent expression (oral and written)?	

(*continues*)

TABLE 4.2. *Continued*

Area	**Assessment Focus**	**Possible Assessment Procedures**
	4. Is the student's conversation competent and appropriate in unstructured situations? *COMMENT:* Word-retrieval problems are common following head injury and different forms of stress can have different effects. Even mild word retrieval or language organizational problems may be handicapping in a busy classroom or stressful social situation.	
Integrative language and verbal reasoning	a. Cognitive–semantic system with increasing semantic complexity or abstractness.	a. *The Word Test* (Jorgenson, Barrett, Huisingh, & Zachman, 1981); *The Adolescent Word Test* (Zachman, Barrett, Huisingh, Orman, & Blagden, 1989); *Test of Language Competence* (Wiig & Secord, 1988). Analogy tests may yield inflated results because the analogies are often automatic; requesting an explanation of the analogic principle yields more useful results.
	b. Concept formation and cognitive–semantic flexibility.	b. Concept Formation subtest of the *Woodcock–Johnson Psycho-Educational Test Battery–Revised* (Woodcock & Johnson, 1989) is particularly useful for observing cognitive flexibility and ability to reorient in response to changing task instructions.
	c. Verbal reasoning and problem solving.	c. *Ross Test of Higher Cognitive Functions* (Ross & Ross, 1976). Informally, story and paragraph discussion can be used to assess the student's ability to detect main ideas, draw inferences, construct interpretations or explanations, and engage in organized problem solving and practical reasoning. "What would you do if . . . ?" tasks are not partic-

(*continues*)

TABLE 4.2. *Continued*

Area	Assessment Focus	Possible Assessment Procedures
		ularly revealing of problem-solving skill, because the questions may be answered appropriately on the basis of knowledge acquired pre–TBI.
	KEY QUESTIONS: 1. What is the student's level of abstract language processing? How well organized is the semantic system? Can the student detect subtleties of meaning? compare and contrast concepts? 2. Can the student efficiently form new verbal concepts and flexibly readjust the conceptual scheme? 3. Can the student use language to engage in higher-level abstraction and reasoning processes? *COMMENT:* Success with structured abstraction or problem-solving measures is no guarantee that the student will maintain an abstract and problem-solving attitude in the real world. In particular "What would you do if . . ." measures of problem solving are insensitive to real-world problem-solving difficulties.	
Verbal memory and new learning	a. Working memory: Immediate recall of unrelated items.	a. Digit span; unrelated word span.
	b. Immediate and delayed recall of semantically connected verbal material.	b. Immediate and delayed recall of short stories or paragraphs (e.g., Logical Memory subtest from *Wechsler Memory Scale–Revised*, Wechsler, 1987; for younger children, story retelling with immediate, 30-minute, and 24-hour delay retelling).
	c. Verbal learning with feedback.	c. *Selective Reminding Task* (Buschke & Fuld, 1974; unpub-

(*continues*)

TABLE 4.2. *Continued*

Area	Assessment Focus	Possible Assessment Procedures
		lished norms from H. Levin). The "Consistent Long-Term Retrieval" measure is a particularly good measure of the ability to learn rote verbal material. The Auditory–Visual Learning subtest of the *Woodcock–Johnson* is a useful indication of new learning ability in a simulated teaching context. *California Test of Verbal Learning* (Delis, Kramer, Kaplan, & Ober, 1983).
	d. Functional recall of daily events.	d. Informal probes.
	e. Prospective memory for scheduled events.	e. Informal probes.
	KEY QUESTIONS: 1. What is the student's level of attention, concentration, and "space" in working memory? 2. Can the student store and retrieve new information over extended periods of time? Are new concepts and words acquired at a normal rate? 3. Does the student make effective use of feedback in learning verbal information? 4. Does he or she spontaneously use strategies to aid learning and retention in deliberate learning tasks? 5. Does the student efficiently store and retrieve daily events (episodic memory)? 6. What variables appear to be particularly related to the student's memory efficiency: number of repetitions? intent to remember? interest level? familiarity? personal meaningfulness? attention? perceptual modality? inherent organization? con-	

(*continues*)

TABLE 4.2. *Continued*

Area	***Assessment Focus***	***Possible Assessment Procedures***
	text? mnemonic strategies? orienting task (i.e., instruction to remember vs. other instruction)? *COMMENT:* If memory performance is poor, many factors could be involved. See Appendix 4A for procedures for identifying the critical issues.	

Adapted from "Comprehensive Cognitive Assessment" by R. Baxter, S. Cohen, and M. Ylvisaker, in *Head Injury Rehabilitation: Children and Adolescents* (pp. 247–274), 1985, Austin, TX: PRO-ED. Adapted with permission.

This is the only score to which normative data can be validly applied. A second score is derived by varying administration in some way (e.g., clearer instructions, response modeling, alternate response mode, modified stimulus materials, additional time) to determine the possible effects of instructional options. For example, a sixth grader with visual perceptual difficulties may score at a third-grade level on a test of reading comprehension. However, presenting the paragraphs to the student one line at a time may increase the score to a sixth-grade level, suggesting that the primary obstacle to grade-appropriate performance on the test was perceptual impairment and that classroom reading materials need to be modified.

All of the cautions cited earlier about drawing confident inferences from formal test data alone apply equally to educational testing. In particular, educational diagnosticians must take care not to infer from normal performance on standardized achievement tests that the child does not require some level of service or support. In the early months after the injury, achievement test results may be misleadingly high relative to learning potential as a result of recovery of pretraumatically overlearned academic material. Baxter, Cohen, and Ylvisaker (1985) discussed additional considerations in educational testing and listed tests in common use in special education settings.

Criterion-referenced tests and probes are essential in determining which skills to assess further or to target for intervention. These assessment procedures also assist the teacher in placing the student in a curriculum and evaluating progress. Customized criterion-referenced probes are often the best means for evaluating progress because probes can be administered frequently and this measure of progress relates directly to the content of instruction. Frequent probes are important for students with TBI because these students may experience bursts of progress that must be reflected in the curriculum and because their performance may be inconsistent. Academic probes of this sort complement the cognitive probes listed in Appendix 4A and guide the teacher's planning in relation to critical decisions such as repeating a lesson, dropping a target skill, adding a new skill, or generalizing a mastered skill to another area.

Curriculum-based assessment is a type of criterion-referenced procedure that is used within the context of the school's curriculum and includes "any procedure that directly assesses student performance within the course content for the purpose of determining that student's instructional needs" (Tucker, 1985, p. 200). Its advantages include the following: (a) the assessment is related to the local school curriculum; (b) "normality" judgments are made in relation to locally developed norms; and (c) the assessment can be tailored in relation to the individual student's place in the curriculum. Curriculum-based assessment has been found to be useful with screening, identification, program planning, and progress monitoring of students with learning problems. Achievement in basic skills can be measured reliably and validly by using the school's curriculum to generate test items (Bigge, 1988; Deno, 1985; Fuchs, Butterworth, & Fuchs, 1989; Fuchs, Deno, & Mirkin, 1984; Fuchs & Fuchs, 1988).

Behavioral checklists are also useful in the ongoing evaluation of students, particularly those with inconsistent performance and unusual profiles of ability. Checklists may include behavioral statements in a variety of areas, including attention, orientation, on-task behavior, frustration tolerance, questioning behavior, comprehension of instructions, and social interaction. Teachers can use these customized checklists to track their exploration of instructional procedures designed to identify those procedures that match the student's strengths. Checklists could also be designed to reflect a sequence of skills in a curriculum, and thus become the measure of progress.

Checklists are particularly useful in the evaluation of social skills, which require situational assessment. Students with TBI often have difficulty with conversational competence, comprehension of social cues, and peer relations in general. Ideally, teachers, speech-language pathologists, and counselors should collaborate in the classroom assessment and treatment of social skills. Selected curricula for teaching social skills are described in Chapter 6.

Hypothesis Testing and Interdisciplinary Assessment

Regardless of the skill and expertise of the psychologist, neuropsychologist, educational evaluator, speech-language pathologist, and others, many interesting questions regarding cognitive functioning are not answered until treatment and classroom instruction have begun. These include questions about the student's learning rate and style; which deficits are primary and which secondary; factors that influence learning (including the environment, types of tasks, cuing systems, strategies, and behavior management systems); relative contributions of various cognitive impairments to functional problems; interaction of cognitive and psychosocial issues; and effectiveness of various types of intervention. Intervention, especially in the early stages, includes a series of experiments designed to define the child's problems as precisely as possible and to isolate the most effective approach to intervention.

The initial assessment report by the school psychologist should, therefore, conclude not with a set of confident prescriptions regarding intervention strategies, but rather with recommendations for how the teachers and therapists can test hypotheses generated by formal psychological assessment. Classroom instruction is the ideal environment in which to explore many of the cognitive issues outlined in Appendix 4A. In addition to answering questions and testing hypotheses that emerged during the psychological evaluation, classroom instruction frequently results in additional questions that might best be answered by the psychologist. Follow-up psychological assessment can then be used to refine intervention by answering the additional questions that have arisen in the classroom.

Table 4.3 illustrates how this dialectical or interdisciplinary hypothesis-testing assessment can occur. The type of dialogue illustrated in the table typically occurs

TABLE 4.3. Two Illustrations of Interdisciplinary Cognitive Hypothesis Testing

Illustration Number 1

A. *From the recommendation section of the initial psychological evaluation report:*

It is clear that JP has impaired memory. This impairment cuts across input modalities (e.g., auditory and visual) and types of information (e.g., linguistic and nonlinguistic). This deficit will make it very difficult for JP to demonstrate his comprehension of material. Poor performance on memory tests cannot be explained by weak attention or lack of comprehension of the material to be remembered. JP's performance was adequate on Digit Span, *Speech Sounds Perception Test*, and *Seashore Rhythm Test*, indicating adequate attention and concentration. Language testing (see Speech-Language Pathology report) suggests adequate comprehension of words and sentences.

It is not clear at this point what effect the following variables would have on JP's ability to remember information that he reads or that is presented to him verbally.

1. *Encoding of information into memory versus storage versus retrieval:* The teacher should routinely approach memory tasks by having JP first try to freely remember the information, then respond to cues present in wh– questions, then respond to multiple-choice or true–false questions. If JP consistently does much better on the latter two tasks, it is reasonable that intervention should focus on retrieval of information that JP is able to encode into memory.
2. *Characteristics of the information:* The teacher should explore the effects on memory of variation in *type* of information (e.g., factual information vs. biographical information vs. procedures vs. routes) and *personal significance* of the information. If personally significant information, for example, is consistently remembered much better than nonsignificant factual information, then the teacher should find ways to attach meaning to information that is presented.
3. *Aspects of presentation:* The teacher should explore the effects on memory of additional processing time during presentation of information, the nature of the instructions (e.g., instruction to *learn the material* vs. instruction to *engage in an interesting activity*, with learning the byproduct), reinforcers, repetition, and feedback.
4. *Suggested strategies:* The teacher should carefully observe to see if JP uses any memory strategies spontaneously (e.g., taking notes, repeating information, asking for repetition from the teacher, asking questions about the information for purposes of elaborating). In addition, the teacher should recommend that JP use a strategy and document its effect

(*continues*)

TABLE 4.3. *Continued*

on performance of a meaningful memory task. If the strategy does improve performance, does JP subsequently use it in related tasks?

We should have a follow-up meeting in 2 months, after the teacher has had an opportunity to explore these variables in the classroom.

B. *From the teacher's reply to the psychologist after JP's first 2 months in the classroom:*

1. JP clearly does much better on true–false questions than free recall. He remembers personally interesting information much better than other types. He seems to do better when he has extra time to process the information, when I repeat the information several times, and when I tell him to think about the information in a variety of ways.
2. I am not certain what type of memory strategies to recommend for JP. Sometimes he seems very disorganized and when I recommend that he organize information in his head in a certain way, he remembers it much better. However, he never does this on his own. Could you give me recommendations?
3. Is JP's memory going to get better on its own? JP seems to be doing better in class, but I don't know if this is because of our work or because of physical recovery in his brain.

C. *From the psychologist's reply to the teacher:*

1. I saw JP for brief reevaluation to try to answer your questions. His scores on the *Wide Range Assessment of Memory and Learning* have not changed. Therefore, the improvements that you have seen in class are probably a result of your intervention rather than spontaneous neurologic recovery.
2. JP scored relatively well on tests of organizational ability when I made clear what his job was. I suggest that you continue to tell him that he has to organize the information in his head in some way. Because JP is very concrete, you may need to practice organizing actual physical things so that he gets the idea of what organizing is all about; it should then be easier for him to know what he is supposed to do with information in his head. Always ask him *how* he is organizing the information in a text. It may be useful for him to make diagrams of how he is organizing the information. It is worth a try. In the case of any strategy of this sort, give him an active role in deciding what to do and also in determining its effectiveness. Remember, strategic behavior is problem-solving behavior. Be careful not to assume all of the problem-solving responsibilities yourself. Daily talk about organizational strategies—in very simple and concrete terms—should help JP understand what is expected of him. Also, including him in decision making about strategies should help overcome resistance. Make sure he knows that the effort that he puts into organiz-

(*continues*)

TABLE 4.3. *Continued*

ing the information in a text has a payoff in improved comprehension and better grades.

Illustration Number 2

A. *From recommendation section of initial psychological evaluation report:*

DJ is a 12-year-old male, currently in the sixth grade. Results of the *Wechsler Intelligence Scale for Children–Third Edition* and the *Wide Range Achievement Test–Revised* are within normal limits. DJ appears to have experienced nearly complete recovery from his head injury. Prior to his injury, he had difficulty in several academic areas, particularly writing. His fifth-grade teacher reported that written syntax, punctuation, and spelling were significantly substandard. This writing delay was observed in today's evaluation and should be a focus of instruction. DJ is not a candidate for special education services at this time.

B. *From the teacher's reply to the psychologist after DJ's first 2 months in the classroom:*

DJ's problem with writing is much more significant than it was in fifth grade, before the injury. He is extremely slow and his poor spelling, punctuation, and grammar negatively affect all written work, including worksheets and tests. However, I am more concerned with his written stories and essays. They are extremely disorganized, almost a jumble of isolated thoughts. There is no evidence of planning, organizing, or editing. His reading skills as measured by the *Woodcock Reading Mastery Test–Revised* are at grade level, although he sometimes has trouble understanding longer reading assignments. I do not understand what accounts for the extremely poor writing, and therefore I do not know how to help. I think DJ needs more than I can give him. Because he has failed all of his writing assignments, he is becoming very frustrated. Could you help?

C. *From the psychologist's reply to the teacher:*

The speech-language pathologist and I have seen DJ in an attempt to determine the source of his extreme writing difficulty. Most areas of language functioning test within normal limits. However, DJ does have word finding problems, which are particularly severe when he is under stress. The speech-language pathologist's informal assessment indicates that all aspects of language comprehension and expression deteriorate badly when DJ is under time pressure or social pressure. Under these circumstances, he does not do as well as we expected based on our initial test results.

The problem with written organization that you observed appears to be a much more general organizational problem. DJ has as much difficulty with organization when he gives a narrative orally as when he writes it. For example, having him tape record a theme rather than write it did not improve the organization. Furthermore, he has difficulty organizing nonlanguage tasks,

(*continues*)

TABLE 4.3. *Continued*

such as putting together a complex car model. When we gave him a very simple outline to follow, his writing improved.

Recommendations:

1. DJ should receive speech-language pathology services. The speech-language pathologist should work with the classroom teacher to give DJ very concrete organizing strategies that will help him to organize his written themes and to organize texts that he is assigned to read so that he does not get lost in the details. Initially, DJ should receive as much support as he needs to succeed. The speech-language pathologist should use classroom materials and assignments in an effort to promote generalization of skills that are achieved.
2. DJ should start with very simple strategies that allow him to organize a sentence to express his thoughts clearly. Models should always be present and initially there should be no time pressure. Self-monitoring of the sentences in relation to the goal of clear expression should be a constant expectation. When working on organization of thoughts, errors in other aspects of writing (e.g., grammar, spelling, and punctuation) should be overlooked or corrected by the teacher without comment. The focus must stay on clarity of writing, not the mechanics.
3. Because word retrieval problems contribute to DJ's poorly organized expressive language, writing exercises can be part of semantic feature analysis exercises (explained in Chapter 5).
4. In moving from sentences to multisentence essays, DJ's tasks should have the following components:
    a. A clear description of the task and its purpose
    b. A model to which DJ can refer for guidance
    c. Adequate time to complete the task
    d. Mastery at each level of difficulty before moving on
    e. Self-evaluation: DJ should always evaluate his writing in relation to his goal
    f. Generalization: If a procedure (e.g., an outlining procedure) is found to work in therapy with a type of writing project, then that same procedure should be added to DJ's classroom routine

I propose that the three of us get together in two months to review DJ's progress and the effectiveness of these suggestions.

---

more informally, in a staff conference or during impromptu conversations in the teachers' lounge or hallway after school. The goal is to *experimentally* identify the best instructional methods for the child, as opposed to drawing tenuous conclusions from test performance or proceeding in a "canned" curricular fashion that may be inappropriate for individual children. This type of communication from school psychologists has much greater meaning and practical significance for teachers than more typical reports that summarize test data and speculate about what will work best in the classroom.

INTRODUCTION OF FORMAL COGNITIVE ASSESSMENT

Early in recovery, behavioral checklists and guided observation forms are useful for rehabilitation team members to track changes in alertness and responsiveness. Standardized tests should not be used until attention has improved and confusion has decreased to the point at which one can have confidence that the test is measuring what it was intended to measure. Furthermore, formal tests should be used only if questions about the child can be answered by the test and if the answers will influence the course of treatment or instruction. Tests of receptive vocabulary (e.g., the *Peabody Picture Vocabulary Test, Revised,* Dunn & Dunn, 1981) and basic reading ability, for example, may be useful fairly early in recovery in that they yield relevant information about how to interact with the child and about appropriate treatment activities.

Comprehensive cognitive assessment should be deferred until the child demonstrates good orientation to task, is clearly able to follow test instructions, can attend to a task for 20 minutes or more, and is no longer in a phase of rapid recovery. Assessment results achieved during times of cognitive change are quickly outdated and, therefore, serve little purpose.

COGNITIVE ASSESSMENT OF PRESCHOOLERS

Children in the 2- to 5-year range present interesting challenges to those responsible for cognitive assessment following head injury. Less is known about long-term outcome in this group than in older children and adolescents (Ewing-Cobbs, Miner, Fletcher, & Levin, 1989). Furthermore, the absence of reliable pretrauma baselines make it difficult to determine which aspects of the child's current functioning, if any, are due to the injury. Because children with pretrauma learning and behavior problems are disproportionately represented in the population of children with TBI, it is possible that observed delays were present before the injury. Furthermore, given their natural desire to have the child return to pretrauma levels, parents may exaggerate the similarities between posttrauma and pretrauma functioning. Also, great variability in performance is evident among normally developing preschoolers and the relationships between brain and behavior are still developing, both of which contribute to difficulty identifying effects of the injury and predicting long-term outcome.

Standardized tests of cognitive functioning are available for this age group (see Table 4.1). For children at an early stage of development, the *Bayley Infant Scales of Development–Second Edition* (Bayley, 1993) provides a global assessment of development and contributes to the identification of specific problem areas (e.g., vision, language, basic concepts). Measures of cognitive development based on a Piagetian framework, such as the Uzgiris–Hunt Scale (Uzgiris & Hunt, 1978), provide additional information about the child's understanding of basic concepts such as object permanence and cause–effect relationships. These scales include naturalistic play tasks that tap early problem-solving abilities (e.g., going around a barrier, applying foresight vs. simple trial and error). In addition, these assessment tasks flow more naturally into intervention activities than do the items on many norm-referenced tests.

The *Kaufman Assessment Battery for Children* (Kaufman & Kaufman, 1983) and *The McCarthy Scales of Children's Abilities* (McCarthy, 1972) provide attractive materials designed to capture a preschooler's interest and attention and to assess a variety of areas relevant to cognitive development. The Fourth Edition of the *Stanford–Binet* (Thorndike, Hagen, & Sattler, 1986) is normed for ages 2 through adulthood, thus providing a broad scope for longitudinal assessment. For the younger age levels, test designers paid attention to interest and appeal of the tasks, and sequenced the tasks to optimize a young child's attention and interest. However, subtests at the early ages provide relatively few items before reaching an upper threshold, especially for preschoolers with areas of delay or deficit. Therefore, the utility and reliability of the *Stanford–Binet* is limited and must be supplemented by other materials.

Developmental scales commonly used in preschool settings (e.g., *Portage Guide to Early Education,* Bluma, Shearer, Froham, & Hilliard, 1976; *Vineland Adaptive Behavior Scales,* Sparrow, Balla, & Cicchetti, 1984) assess a variety of domains, including social–emotional development, language, self-help, and motor skills. These scales are relatively efficient to administer and, in conjunction with the parent interview and developmental history, can help provide a broad profile of the individual child.

As with older children, however, performance in readily testable areas, such as physical and perceptual–motor functioning and language comprehension and production, may return to pretrauma levels despite damage to those parts of the brain associated with new learning and self-regulatory behavior. Therefore, cognitive, academic, and behavioral problems commonly emerge years after the preschooler's injury, either because of the delayed effect of new learning problems or because the injured part of the brain is associated with functions that are not expected to mature until a later developmental stage. The latter phenomenon is well illustrated by the child injured at age 2 who predictably has all of the behavioral characteristics of a 2-year-old following the injury (impulsiveness; silliness; fluctuating attention; oppositional behavior; inflexibility; lability; egocentric thinking; concrete thinking; poor judgment, planning, and problem solving) but who continues to have those same characteristics at age 6 when a higher level of executive functions is necessary to succeed in first grade.

The most important component of cognitive assessment of very young children who appear to have recovered well involves teaching them information, rule-governed activities (e.g., games), and vocabulary items that are known to be new for the child, and systematically documenting the child's rate and manner of learning. In addition, diagnostic exploration should include observation of the child in representational play and social interaction with gradually increasing cognitive and social stress to detect possible deficits of organization, planning, problem solving, and communication, including word retrieval, that may not be evident in normal interaction or in testing. Because no norms exist that are associated with these functional probes, care must be taken not to overinterpret marginal deviations from expected performance.

In preschool assessment, data should be combined from norm- and criterion-referenced measures, naturalistic observation, diagnostic intervention, and family interview. In that prediction of recovery and development remains hazardous even with these varied sources of information, follow-up is critical. Preschoolers with significant TBI should be carefully monitored into the early grade school years, even if their functioning appears to be within normal limits within weeks of the injury. Particularly careful monitoring should occur when the child begins formal education, to rule out the need for special supportive services to ensure academic success.

MILD TRAUMATIC BRAIN INJURY

Many children with mild injuries (and some with injuries that appear initially to be more severe) recover quickly and return to school with no apparent special needs. However, because there is not a necessary connection between duration of altered consciousness (or other neurologic signs) and outcome following TBI, an apparently mild injury may be followed by a prolonged period of depressed cognitive or behavioral functioning. This period may range from a few days to a few weeks or longer. Standardized assessments may be insufficiently sensitive to detect consequences that could have implications for the child in school. Therefore, a monitoring system should be established for these children, using real-world academic and social performance as the measure of recovery. This system should include the school nurse or school psychologist, who periodically interviews the classroom teacher(s) about the student's performance. The interview is designed to detect red flags in the following areas:

1. *Attendance:* Unexpected absences from school or from specific classes
2. *Academic Performance:*
   - Inattentiveness beyond what is normally expected of the student
   - Difficulty getting started or staying on task; need for more supervision than expected
   - Weak orientation to task ("spacey"); difficulty shifting from task to task
   - Academic performance lower than before the injury
   - Relatively slow performance; delayed responses
   - Difficulty remembering new information or assignments
   - Assignments uncharacteristically late or incomplete
   - Difficulty organizing large tasks
   - Evidence of struggle in oral expression (e.g., word finding problems) or written expression (e.g., poorly organized essays); unexpectedly poor comprehension of large reading assignments
3. *Social–Behavioral Performance:*
   - Unexpected conflicts with peers or teachers
   - Resistance to schoolwork; strong negative reaction to correction
   - Unexpected inappropriateness in behavior; socially inappropriate language; social withdrawal

(*list continues*)

- Apparent depression; sadness; moodiness; little initiation
- Excessive tiredness

If any of these behaviors are reported, teachers should be counseled to provide appropriate adaptations and to make their expectations fit the child's ability to perform. Consultation with the school psychologist and, if symptoms persist for more than 3 or 4 weeks, a neuropsychological evaluation by an experienced pediatric neuropsychologist should be considered. It is extremely important that students receive the supports they need to be successful during this transitional period. Typically, special supports and adaptations are necessary for no more than a few weeks at the most. Care must be taken not to encourage long-term reliance on special accommodations. Chapter 11 presents a more extensive discussion of mild TBI.

CONCLUSION

In this chapter, we have described a perspective on cognitive assessment as it relates to educational planning for students with TBI. We emphasized the importance of an interdisciplinary assessment that supplements test results with contextual observations and a hypothesis-testing approach to diagnostic teaching. Suggestions were offered for dealing with special assessment problems, including assessment of preschoolers and students with mild TBI.

APPENDIX 4A
*A Conceptual Framework and Selected Probes for Exploring Cognitive Functioning in Children with Traumatic Brain Injury**

Codes: **E** = early childhood (roughly 2–5 years)
M = middle childhood (roughly 6–11 years)
A = adolescence (roughly 12–18 years)

Component Processes

Attention

1. Is the child adequately *alert/aroused?*
   a. Observe level of arousal in relation to time of day, people in the environment, varying sensory modalities, level of environmental–sensory stimulation, deliberate attempts to arouse (e.g., presenting novel toys or games; varying interactive style; using the child's name; playing favorite music) (E,M,A)
2. Can the child *maintain attention* for a sufficient length of time to accomplish age-appropriate tasks? If attention span is short relative to age expectations, what factors appear to improve attention span?
   a. Time continuous attention during formal assessment tasks. (E,M,A)
   b. Time continuous attention during group therapy or classroom tasks. (E,M,A)
   c. Ask parents or caregivers how long the child usually and/or maximally attends to most interesting activities (e.g., play, TV watching) in natural settings. (E,M,A)
   d. Does attention span increase when the same task is used in a less distracting environment? when the task is more interesting or enjoyable for the patient? when the task is an actual practi-

* From "Rehabilitative Assessment Following Head Injury in Children" by M. Ylvisaker et al., in *Rehabilitation of the Adult and Child with Traumatic Brain Injury* by M. Rosenthal, E. Griffith, M. Bond, and J. D. Miller (Eds.), 1990, Philadelphia: F. A. Davis. Reprinted with permission.

cal activity rather than play or some other representational task? when there is a reward for task completion? when the task instructions or expectations are made clearer, or when the child is instructed to pay attention? when the task is made easy to accomplish? during specific times of day? following medication? (E,M,A)

3. Can the child attend to *selected* stimuli and disregard stimuli that are not relevant to the task? If the ability to selectively attend is not age appropriate, what are the effects on selective attention of the variables listed in 1a?
   a. Observe responses to distractions in a variety of tasks and settings, such as reactions to abrupt topic shifts in conversation, deterioration in comprehension with background noise, and sharp deterioration in performance on computer tasks with distractions. (M,A)
4. Can the child *shift* attentional focus in a manner that is adequate for classroom or social functioning?
   a. Can the child flexibly change activity in a classroom or nursing unit? interrupt TV watching for a short conversation and return to the show? play videogames that require rapid shifting of attention from stimulus to stimulus? shift from topic to topic during conversation? follow the speaker in a multiperson conversation? (E,M,A)
   b. Is perseveration observed during formal assessment, such as during rapid naming tasks or set shifting tasks (e.g., *Wisconsin Card Sorting,* Heaton, 1981; Concept Formation of the *Woodcock–Johnson Psycho-Educational Test Battery,* Woodcock & Johnson, 1977)? (M,A)
5. Can the child *divide* attention in a manner that is adequate for age-appropriate academic and social functioning?
   a. Can the child maintain conversation and/or comprehend instructions while engaged in a motor activity (e.g., walking or eating)? (M,A)
   b. Can the child pick up objects with one hand while holding the container in the other? (E,M,A)

Perception

Care must be taken to distinguish visual perceptual problems from visual acuity problems, limited ocular range of motion, and cognitive problems such as impaired attention, organization, or executive functions.

1. Does the child *focus* on selected objects?
   a. Observe eye movements and duration of visual fixation with familiar people and highly meaningful objects or pictures in the child's visual field. (E,M,A)

2. Does the child visually *track* objects or people?
   a. Observe sustained fixation on moving objects or light source. Does the child track across midline? Does tracking systematically end or begin at certain points in the visual field? (E,M,A)
   b. Observe visual regard while attempting to have the child rapidly alternate visual fixation from one object to another (*saccades*). Gradually move the objects into different quadrants of the visual field. (E,M,A)
3. Can the child *identify and discriminate* among objects and features of objects?
   a. Have the child find familiar photographs in a photo album. (E,M,A)
   b. Have the child complete large-piece inset puzzles; place shapes into sorting boxes; stack stacking boxes by size; complete pegboard designs; color selected shapes on a page. (E,M,A)
   c. Have the child match increasingly complex pictures; identify which of four increasingly complex shapes is different; complete math problems on increasingly (visually) complex worksheets (does child notice changes in operation signs?); decode words and/or sentences on increasingly full pages; select correct coins from a group in a money exchange task. (E,M,A)
   d. Figure–ground mechanisms: Observe the child's search for a specified toy in a toy box, a specified item of clothing in a drawer, or a specified object in a complex picture. (E,M,A)

Memory and Learning

1. Is there a "memory problem" to be explored?
   a. Interview teachers, family members, and nursing staff about the child's functional ability to remain oriented (person, place, time), retain information from day to day about personally experienced events, and learn new information or skills at an age-appropriate rate.
   b. Observe the child's (1) recall of events from day to day; (2) recognition of the examiner, the examiner's name, and the route to office from day to day; and (3) prospective recall of interesting events that have been planned for the next day. Observe the effects of cues. (E,M,A)
   c. Assess performance on a sensitive measure of memory–learning, such as the *Selective Reminding Test* (Buschke & Fuld, 1974) or Visual–Auditory Learning from the *Woodcock–Johnson.*
2. Because *encoding, storage,* and *retrieval* are all evaluated by testing for retrieval of information, it is not possible to obtain a clear and quantified picture of the relative contributions of each of these aspects of memory to memory problems. However, significant disparities between free versus cued versus recognition memory do

give insight into this issue. If performance on recognition memory tasks is dramatically better than performance on free recall tasks, then the problem may be largely at the retrieval stage. If performance is poor even on recognition memory tasks, then encoding or storage may be weak. If immediate recognition memory is good, but delayed recognition memory is poor, then *perhaps* storage is weak. Only if differences are extreme can inferences be drawn. Qualitative analysis of *what* the child recalls (e.g., significant vs. insignificant details; main idea; sequences) is often more revealing than assessing the quantity of information remembered.

   a. *Immediate versus delayed recognition memory (visual):* Show the child a small number of objects or pictures (have the child name the pictures); then show a larger set and ask the child to identify the objects or pictures viewed earlier. Repeat after 30 minutes. (M,A; for preschoolers, use same task, but in context of real activity)
   b. *Immediate versus delayed recognition memory (auditory):* Read a story that is well within the child's ability to comprehend; ask yes–no or multiple-choice questions immediately after reading and again 30 minutes later. Compare results. (M,A)
   c. *Free versus cued recall:* Read a story that is well within the child's ability to comprehend. Ask the child to retell as much as he can remember. Then read another story (same level and length) and ask wh– questions about the information. Compare results. (Could add a yes–no condition to compare recognition memory.) (M,A; for preschoolers, act out the story with props, and then ask questions)
   d. *Show a picture of a room* with furniture and accessories; take the picture away and ask the child to recreate the room arrangement with flannel-board props; does performance improve substantially when you guide placement to the correct general area? (E,M,A)
   e. Use tests of *naming and word retrieval* (e.g., controlled word fluency) to measure the child's ability to access stored lexical items. (E,M,A)

3. *Attention versus memory:* Is the observed memory problem specific to memory processes or is it a result of weak attention?
   a. Using the same task (e.g., story recall or nonverbal task) with materials at the same level, compare results (1) when the task is administered in a nondistracting environment, one-on-one, with attempts to guarantee attention (e.g., manipulating the objects, having the child name the objects, orienting the child to the salient aspects) and (2) when the task is administered in a more distracting setting, in a group context, and with no special attempts to guarantee attention. (E,M,A)
4. *Comprehension versus memory processes:* Is the observed memory problem specific to memory or is it a result of weak comprehension?

a. Compare recall of stories that are marginally challenging in terms of academic and/or language level with recall of stories that are below the upper limits of the child's academic and/or language level. Alternatively, use two stories at the same academic and/or language level, but allow the child to act out or draw aspects of the story in one case but not the other. Compare results. (M,A)

5. *Executive system versus memory processes:* Is the observed memory problem specific to memory processes or is it (in part) a failure of the executive system (e.g., to deliberately pay special attention to material that has to be remembered or to initiate and maintain an organized search of memory)?
   a. Using a story recall task, compare results when the child is simply read a story and then asked to recall versus when the child is encouraged before hearing the story to pay attention and remember. (M,A)
   b. Using a story recall task, compare results when the child is simply asked to retell the story versus when the child is given repeated encouragement to search his memory and told to ask himself questions that might help the search. (M,A)
   c. Using a word retrieval task (e.g., listing words in categories or starting with a specific letter), compare results of uncoached performance versus performance with some encouragement, rewards, and suggestions to approach the task systematically. (E,M,A; for preschoolers, use words in concrete categories)
6. *Characteristics of the information to be remembered:* Is it substantially easier for the child to remember one type of information than another?
   a. Compare the child's ability to remember (1) *recent episodes in her own life,* (2) *factual information presented verbally* (nothing to do with her own life, (3) *procedures to accomplish a task* (e.g., learning the procedures to operate a videogame machine, assuming this is new learning), (4) *routes and locations in the building,* (5) *new faces,* and (6) *new names.* (E,M,A)
   b. Compare the child's ability to remember (1) information that is emotionally *significant* versus (2) information that is interesting, but not at an emotional level, versus (3) information that is neither (bearing in mind that personally meaningful information is normally easier to remember). (E,M,A)
7. *Aspects of presentation of the information:* Does the child's ability to remember vary with variation in the way the information is presented?
   a. *Input (and output) channels:* Compare, for example, recall of a story that is read to the child versus that of a story of the same level and length that the child reads. (All combinations of input and output channels can be systematically varied to detect relative strengths and weaknesses.) (M,A)

b. *Processing time:* Compare recall of a story that is read with normal pauses after clauses with recall of a story of the same level and length that is read with extended pauses after clauses. (Time the pauses to track progress.) (E,M,A)

c. *Task orientation:* Compare recall performance of word list learning when (1) the child is told that his job is to remember as many words as he can from the list versus when the child (2a) is told to listen to the words and indicate each time he hears a word of a certain sort; or (2b) is told that his job is to get a set of items to accomplish some activity; or (2c) is engaged in an activity with the items and in the context of the activity each item is named once; the child is later asked to recall what things were used in the activity. Each condition can be used with all age groups, recognizing that preschoolers would be expected to perform significantly better on 2c. (E,M,A)

d. *Incentive to remember:* Compare recall when the child is simply asked to remember something versus when the stakes are high—for example, make a bet that the child cannot remember more than five items and have something "valuable" riding on the bet. (E,M,A)

e. *Repetition and spacing:* Compare recall of a story that is read only once versus a story of the same level and length that is read twice (or more) and at planned intervals. How many repetitions are necessary to make a genuine difference? What amount of spacing seems to be optimal? (E,M,A)

f. *Feedback:* Does the child profit from informational feedback in a learning task? The Visual-Auditory Learning subtest from the *Woodcock–Johnson* is useful. (M,A)

8. Does the child *spontaneously use strategies* to learn–remember (recognizing that the child may use strategies that are not observable)?

a. During memory–learning tests (e.g., the Visual–Auditory Learning subtest from *Woodcock–Johnson;* paragraph recall) or functional activities, does the child show evidence of rehearsing or organizing information? Does she ask for repetition or clarification? Does she ask to take notes? (M,A) Does the child pay extra attention or handle objects in a special way when instructed to remember? (E) Present a set of pictures (from four categories and arranged in a circle) to the child; ask the child to study the pictures so that she can remember them; tell her that she can move the pictures. Observe what she does to organize or learn the pictures. (M,A) Ask the child to read a text and write a summary. Encourage the child to underline and take notes. Analyze the notes and underlining for evidence of strategic procedures, such as highlighting essential details or topic sentences. (M,A)

b. Ask the child what he did to help himself do well on the test. (M,A) Ask the child what he would do to remember what he got for Christmas last year. (E,M,A) Ask the child what he would do to remember to go to his friend's birthday party. (E,M,A)

c. Go through a list of common strategies and ask the child if she does any of them to help herself. (M,A)

9. *Effects of memory strategies:* Does performance improve when the child is instructed to use specific strategies? Which strategies seem to be most effective?

   a. Compare results of a paragraph recall task (using paragraphs matched for length and level; reading or listening) with and without the following strategy instructions (M,A):
      - repeat important information in your head as you listen
      - Reread or ask for repetitions
      - Draw a vivid picture of the story in your head as you listen, or draw little pictures on paper to represent important events
      - Find something in your own experience to which you can relate the information
      - Take notes
      - Ask yourself questions during pauses

   b. *Elaboration:* Use two paragraphs of the same level and length. Read one to the child twice, and then test recall 24 hours later. Read the other once and then discuss the information, including relevant elaboration of the key points; then test recall 24 hours later. Compare results. (M,A) With preschoolers, analogous probes can be constructed using play materials; elaboration is accomplished by relating the objects in play. (E)

   c. *Organization:* Use same procedure as in 9b, only this time, instead of elaborating the information with the second paragraph, propose a system for *organizing* the information (e.g., determining who, what happened, where, when, why). Compare results. (M,A)

   d. *Mnemonics:* Compare memory for names or word lists with and without instruction to use "tricks" such as unusual associations or the method of loci. (M,A)

   e. *Retrieval strategies:* Compare recall (e.g., for recent events or story detail) with and without suggestions on how to search memory. Base suggestions on the strategies that were suggested at the time of encoding. (M,A)

Organizing

As in the other areas of assessment, it is necessary in testing organizing processes to try to eliminate the confounding effects of other cognitive processes and/or systems; for example, in probing organizing processes, avoid straining attentional abilities, perceptual abilities, comprehension abilities, memory abilities, and executive direction–control.

1. Can the child *analyze* objects into their component parts? concepts into their component features? tasks into their component steps?
   a. Ask the child to describe a familiar object to a person who has no idea what it is. (M,A)
   b. Ask the child to explain a very familiar activity or game to a person who has no idea about the activity. (M,A)
   c. Present a novel task; can the child determine (tell or select) what materials/tools are needed to complete the task? (E,M,A)
   d. Have the child explain what he is doing throughout a block design task. (M,A)
2. Can the child *compare* features and *identify* similarities and differences?
   a. Use concept formation–analysis tasks (e.g., the Concept Formation subtest from the *Woodcock–Johnson;* the Similarities subtest from *Wechsler Intelligence Scale for Children–Third Edition,* Wechsler, 1991; the Likenesses/Differences subtest from the *Detroit Tests of Learning Aptitudes–Third Edition,* Hammill, 1991). (M,A)
   b. Use sorting tasks (by perceptual features or semantic relations). (E,M,A)
3. Can the child *classify–categorize–associate?*
   a. Use semantic association tests (e.g., the Associations subtest from the Word Test, Jorgenson et al., 1981). (M,A)
   b. Give the child a set of pictures that could be sorted *categorically* or *sequentially–thematically;* which way does she sort? (E,M,A)
   c. Have the child organize furniture in a room for a snack; for watching a movie; and so forth. (E,M,A)
   d. Ask the child how he would pack grocery bags at a supermarket. Give a list of items and a set of conditions (e.g., it is hot outside; the customer is small; the customer has to put things away in a hurry). (M,A)
4. Can the child *sequentially* organize events?
   a. Use the Picture Arrangement subtest from the WISC-III. (M,A)
   b. Determine how many sequence cards (and at what level) the child can appropriately order? (M,A)
   c. Propose a script for play (e.g., let's go to the store; let's make a sandwich). Observe how effectively the child directs the events. (E,M,A)
   d. Does the child progress through routine daily events in correct sequence without cues (e.g., get up, get dressed, eat breakfast, brush teeth)? (E,M,A)
   e. Have the child describe her daily schedule in a correct sequence. (M,A)

f. Can the child follow the sequence of steps in a structured activity (e.g., cooking)? with (or without) a guide? (M,A)

(*See also planning tasks under Executive System.*)

5. Can the child *integrate or synthesize* events into *main ideas, themes, or scripts?*

a. Preschoolers: Present an increasing number of toys that relate to one another thematically. How many can the child organize into a play theme? (E)

b. Put a set of construction toys on the table. Ask the child to make something. How many of the objects are used? Is the construct an identifiable, organized whole? (E,M,A)

c. Give the child three easily identifiable symbols standing for an object, action, or relationship (e.g., block, jump, and over). Ask the child to act out a sentence using these ideas. (M,A)

d. Use the Object Assembly subtest from the WISC-III. (M,A)

e. Can the child answer main idea questions from paragraphs read or listened to? (M,A)

f. Telegram task: Have the child select the best words to express a complex idea in a short telegram. (M,A)

g. Have the child explain a favorite game: Does he start with a general orienting statement about the overall nature of the game? (M,A)

Reasoning and Problem Solving

Again, in assessing reasoning and problem-solving processes, it is necessary to rule out the confounding effects of attentional problems, perceptual problems, comprehension problems, memory problems, and executive control problems.

1. *Inductive reasoning:* Can the child make appropriate generalizations, given a set of instances? see single principles in a set of instances? see the rule that guides a progression or a grouping of things?

a. Use concept formation–categories, types of tasks (e.g., the Categories Test from the *Halstead–Reitan,* Reitan 1987, or the Concept Formation subtest from the *Woodcock–Johnson*). (M,A)

b. Use *Raven's Progressive Matrices* (Raven, 1956). (M,A)

c. Preschoolers: With a set of objects that could be sorted in a variety of ways (e.g., toy animals), begin sorting into two bins according to a rule (e.g., two-legged in one, four-legged in the other). Can the child continue the sorting? (E)

2. *Causal reasoning:* Can the child infer causes from effects? predict consequences from causes?

a. Using picture cards or descriptions of hypothetical events, have the child (1) predict what would happen if a certain event occurred and (2) explain why a certain event occurred. (M,A) Preschoolers: Place a desired object in a precarious position, in which an undesired event is likely (e.g., a favorite doll on the edge of a table); cause the event to occur (the doll falls); repeat. Does the child do anything to prevent the event from occurring? (E)

3. *Deductive reasoning:* Can the child draw logical conclusions on the basis of formal logical relations signaled by terms such as *all, some, if–then, and, or,* and *not.*
   a. Use the *Ross Test of Higher Cognitive Functions* (deductive reasoning and missing premises subtests) (Ross & Ross, 1976). This test is best used informally; have the child explain why she selects the answers she selects. If she cannot do the task, teach the task with one or two items—then probe again. (A)
   b. Use graded reading comprehension materials, especially "drawing conclusions" components. (M,A)
4. *Analogical reasoning:* Can the child detect indirect relationships among words, ideas, and events?
   a. Use word analogy tests. Used informally, the largest amount of information is obtained through the following progression: (1) having the child complete some items in the standard way; (2) having the child describe the relationship as he sees it; (3) and then, if necessary, teaching the type of thinking involved and trying additional items. (M,A) Preschoolers: The *Illinois Test of Psycholinguistic Abilities* (Kirk, McCarthy, & Kirk, 1968) has analogies for preschoolers; these relationships may be best tested with objects. For example, the clinician (1) shows the child a foot and a sock and (2) gives the child a hand and asks what should go with it, given a choice of objects. (E)
   b. Have the child explain proverbs. Again, use the following progression: (1) child attempts to explain proverb; (2) examiner teaches the process involved in explaining proverbs; and (3) child tries again. (A)
5. *Divergent thinking:* Can the child suggest varied solutions to problems? varied interpretations of events or actions?
   a. Present a number of concrete problem situations (e.g., candy in a jar with a tight lid); how many possible solutions does the child explore to solve the problems? (E,M)
   b. Present hypothetical problems and ask for as many possible solutions as the child can imagine. (M,A)
   c. Give the child a selection of animal or person figures; ask the child to make the figure do as many things as she can think of. (E)
6. *Problem solving and decision making*
   a. Using Tasks 5a and 5b, have the child select and justify the best solution. (M,A)
   b. Using Task 5a, note whether the child recognizes the problem.

Look for patterns in the child's problem solving (e.g., does the child use a trial-and-error strategy? ask for help? give up? exhibit random ineffective or impulsive behavior?). (E,M)

c. Give math word problems. Look for recognition of the problem, selection of appropriate operations, and calculation. (M,A)
d. Use the Categories Test from the *Halstead–Reitan*. (M,A)
e. Ask family members if the child spontaneously engages in organized problem-solving behavior in natural settings. (M,A)

Component Systems

Working Memory

1. What is the child's immediate memory span for unrelated items (e.g., digits, unrelated words, visual symbols)? (E,M,A)
2. Compare memory span for unrelated items with memory span for related items (e.g., semantically related words, sentences). (E,M,A)
3. Does the child frequently need directions repeated? (E,M,A)

Knowledge Base

1. What is the child's level of language knowledge and organization?
   a. Use a picture vocabulary test (receptive vocabulary). Start testing well below anticipated basal and look for gaps in the child's vocabulary knowledge base. (E,M,A)
   b. Use tests of word definitions, multiple definitions, antonyms, and synonyms. (M,A)

   (*See also earlier tasks under Organizing.*)
2. What is the child's level of general knowledge?
   a. Specifically probe knowledge in the child's areas of pretraumatic interest, activity, and/or education. (E,M,A)
3. What is the child's level of academic achievement?
   a. Use tests of academic achievement. Compare with pretraumatic achievement levels. (M,A)
4. What is the child's level of knowledge of pretraumatically acquired social and nonsocial skills, rules, and procedures (e.g., how to ride a bike, use a calculator, play a game)?
   a. Specifically probe skills and knowledge of rules and procedures in areas of pretraumatic interest, activity, and education. (E,M,A)

Executive System

1. *Awareness of strengths and weaknesses:* Is the child's awareness of his own strengths and weaknesses age appropriate?

a. Use a self-report questionnaire. (A)
b. Ask the child open-ended questions about why she is in a rehabilitation center; what sorts of activities she has had trouble with since the accident; whether she is ready to go back to school. (M,A)
c. Ask more specific questions about the child's ability to remember; to understand what others say; to understand what he reads; to concentrate. (M,A) As part of the probing, assess the child's comprehension of cognitive terms. Can she meaningfully discuss cognitive strengths and weaknesses? (M,A)
d. Before administration of a test, ask the child to predict how well he will do. After administration of a test, ask the child how well he thinks he did. (M,A)

2. *Goals:* Does the child understand and engage in goal-directed activity?
   a. Does the child accept and work toward short-term goals (e.g., attempt to achieve a set goal within a therapy activity) and intermediate goals (e.g., attempt to achieve a set goal within a few days or weeks)? Compare goal-directedness with and without incentives. (E,M,A)
   b. Ask about long-term goals (e.g., What do you plan to do when you are done with school?) and mid-term goals (e.g., What courses do you plan to take next term at school?). Compare goals with abilities. (A) Ask family members the same questions about the child's goals. (A)
   c. Does the child set goals for herself and pursue them in play (E,M,A) and in therapy or school (M,A)?
3. *Planning:* Does the child give evidence that he actively creates plans to achieve his goals?
   a. Ask specific questions about what the child plans to do to achieve long-term and/or mid-term goals. (M,A)
   b. Give the child a complex task that requires some planning (e.g., baking a cake); observe for evidence of spontaneous planning. If the child begins without a plan, ask her to stop and create a plan. Evaluate the plan for organization and completeness. Compare performance with intrinsically structured tasks (e.g., baking a cake) versus unstructured tasks (e.g., making something out of Tinker Toys). (M,A)
4. *Self-initiation:* Does the child evidence age-appropriate initiation of activities and of cognitive processes?
   a. Ask family members about the child's initiation of activity at home or in other natural settings (e.g., "Does he seem to think up things to do as much as before the accident?"). If the child is an inpatient, ask a similar question of nursing staff. (E,M,A)
   b. Observe the child's initiation of social interaction, play, and activities of daily living. (E,M,A)

c. In testing sessions, does the child initiate conversation? spontaneously offer information? Does she need a direct command to begin the task? (E,M,A)

d. In therapy tasks, does the child require cuing to use the cognitive abilities that he has (e.g., to search his memory, to organize a task, to use his log book or other compensatory device/strategy, to ask questions when he needs information)? (E,M,A)

5. *Self-inhibition:* Does the child demonstrate age-appropriate ability to inhibit behavior, thoughts, and emotions that are inappropriate or nonfunctional?

   a. Is there evidence of perseveration? Observe performance during tests that can illicit perseveration (e.g., confrontation naming or rapid automatized naming tasks). (E,M,A)

   b. Does the child exhibit perseverative motor behaviors? (E,M,A)

   c. Does the child's conversation remain fixed on a given topic or set of topics? (E,M,A) Does she wander from topic to topic with no orientation for the listener? (E,M,A)

   d. Does the child do things that are considered socially inappropriate? Does he recognize that the behavior is inappropriate but continue to do it anyway? (E,M,A)

   e. Use specific probe tasks (e.g., "Hit the button, but only when the flashlight goes on"). (E,M,A)

6. *Self-monitoring:* Does the child demonstrate age-appropriate ability to monitor (attend to) her own behavior during tasks? monitor her orientation to the task? monitor the adequacy of her own knowledge to accomplish a task? monitor the adequacy of her own remembering?

   a. Is there evidence during testing or other structured activities that the child notices and tries to correct mistakes? (M,A)

   b. Does the child request information when needed? For example, when the examiner leaves out needed information in barrier communication tasks, does the child request clarification? (M,A)

   c. Talk too rapidly to the child; does he request repetition or slowing of rate? (M,A)

   d. Give incomplete instructions for task completion (written or oral); does the child recognize the need for more information? (E,M,A)

7. *Self-evaluating:* Does the child show age-appropriate ability to evaluate her own performance?

   a. Ask the child, "How do you think you did?" following a test or other structured activity. Are the answers accurate? (M,A)

8. *Ability to change set:* Does the child demonstrate age-appropriate ability to consider alternate hypotheses or courses of action?

a. Observe the child's flexibility in problem solving during tests such as the Concept Formation subtest of the *Woodcock–Johnson.*

9. *Strategic behavior:* Does the child demonstrate age-appropriate ability to use strategies?

   a. *Spontaneous use of strategies:* Look for use of pre–TBI rehearsed strategies in informal activities such as card or board games. Look for spontaneous use of strategies during testing (e.g., does child ask for help? rehearse or organize information in obvious ways during memory testing? use sentence completion to help with word finding?). (M,A,)

   b. *Ability to describe strategies:* After a test in which strategic behavior was observed or was at least relevant, ask the child what he did to help himself accomplish the task. (M,A)

   c. *Ability to recognize strategies:* After a test for which strategies are useful (e.g., memory or learning test), give the child a list of possible strategies and ask if she used any of them. (M,A)

   d. *Ability to profit from strategy suggestions:* See strategy probes under Memory and Learning processes.

Functional–Integrative Performance

Descriptions of a child's component processes and systems may not yield an accurate or complete description of the child's performance on demanding functional tasks (that require the efficient integration of many processes and systems) in unstructured settings. Observation of functional–integrative behavior in natural contexts is both the beginning and the end of cognitive assessment. Assessment begins with such observations because exploration of component processes and systems is largely for purposes of discovering why performance of functional–integrative behavior in real-life contexts is less effective than it should be. Assessment ends with such observations because the effectiveness of cognitive intervention must ultimately be measured against real-life criteria.

We have found it useful to track four broad dimensions of functional–integrative behavior.

1. *Efficiency* (including the *amount* of work accomplished and the *time* required, holding quality constant). Efficiency can be probed in a number of ways, such as (a) holding all else constant, systematically increase the *amount* of information to be processed (or work to be accomplished) and observe the rate of decline in performance, and (b) systematically increase the *rate* at which information must be processed (e.g., compare timed vs. untimed performance) and observe the rate of decline in performance. Input and output channels can be systematically varied.

2. *Scope.* Scope of performance includes the variety of settings in which effective functional performance can be maintained. Probes involve comparing the child's performance on functional–

integrative tasks in simple and structured settings versus complex and unstructured settings; in one-on-one versus group situations; in familiar versus unfamiliar settings; and with familiar people versus strangers. Generalization of newly learned skills should be tracked carefully from the context of learning to other functional settings.

3. *Level.* Determine at what levels (academic level, language level, general developmental level) the child can maintain functional performance.
4. *Manner.* Manner refers to the characteristic way in which the child performs a task. Probes involve observing the child and noting characteristics of behavior along the following dimensions: impulsive versus reflective, rigid versus flexible, dependent (needing cues) versus independent, passive versus active, and egocentric versus nonegocentric.

REFERENCES

Achenbach, T., & Edelbrock, C. (1983). *Manual for the Child Behavior Checklist and Revised Child Behavior Profile.* Burlington: University of Vermont.

Adams, W., & Sheslow, D. (1990). *Wide Range Assessment of Memory and Learning* (WRAML). Wilmington, DL: Jastik Associates.

Baxter, R., Cohen, S., & Ylvisaker, M. (1985). Comprehensive cognitive assessment. In M. Ylvisaker (Ed.), *Head injury rehabilitation: Children and adolescents* (pp. 247–274). Austin, TX: PRO-ED.

Bayley, N. (1993). *Bayley Scales of Infant Development–Second Edition.* San Antonio, TX: Psychological Corp.

Beery, K. (1989). *Developmental Test of Visual–Motor Integration–Revised.* Chicago: Follett Educational Corp.

Begali, V. (1992). *Head injury in children and adolescents: A resource and review for school and allied health professionals* (2nd ed.). Brandon, VT: Clinical Psychology.

Benton, A. (1974). *The Revised Visual Retention Test (fourth edition).* San Antonio, TX: Psychological Corp.

Benton, A. (1991). Prefrontal injury and behavior in children. *Developmental Neuropsychology, 7,* 275–281.

Bigge, E. (1988). *Curriculum-based instruction for special education students.* Mountain View, CA: Mayfield.

Bigler, E. D. (1988a). Frontal lobe damage and neuropsychological assessment. *Archives of Clinical Neuropsychology, 3,* 279–297.

Bigler, E. (1988b). The role of neuropsychological assessment in relation to other types of assessment with children. In M. Tramontana & S. Hooper (Eds.), *Assessment issues in child neuropsychology.* New York: Plenum Press.

Bluma, S., Shearer, M., Froham, A., & Hilliard, J. (1976). *Portage Guide to Early Education–Revised edition.* Portage, WI: Cooperative Education Service Agency.

Buschke, H. (1974). Components of verbal learning in children: Analysis by selective reminding. *Journal of Experimental Child Psychology, 18,* 488–498.

Buschke, H., & Fuld, P. A. (1974). Evaluating storage, retention, and retrieval in disordered memory and learning. *Neurology, 24,* 1019–1025.

Calarusso, R. P., & Hammill, D. D. (1972). *Motor-Free Visual Perception Test (MVPT)*. Novato, CA: Academic Therapy.
Chelune, G. J., & Baer, R. A. (1986). Developmental norms for the Wisconsin Card Sorting Test. *Journal of Clinical and Experimental Neuropsychology, 8,* 219–228.
Cuenin, L. H. (1990). Use of the Woodcock–Johnson Psycho-Educational Battery with learning disabled adults. *Learning Disabilities Focus, 5,* 119–123.
Delis, M., Kramer, J., Kaplan, E., & Ober, B. (1983). *California Verbal Learning Test.* New York: Psychological Corp.
Denckla, M. B., & Rudel, R. (1976). Rapid "automatized" naming (R.A.N.): Dyslexia differentiated from other learning disabilities. *Neuropsychologia, 14,* 471–479.
Dennis, M. (1991). Frontal lobe function in childhood and adolescence: A heuristic for assessing attention regulation, executive control, and the intentional states important for social discourse. *Developmental Neuropsychology, 7,* 327–358.
Deno, S. L. (1985). Curriculum-based measurement: The emerging alternative. *Exceptional Children, 52,* 219–232.
DiSimoni, F. (1978). *The Token Test for Children.* Allen, TX: DLM Teaching Resources.
Drexler, M. L., Kramer, J. H., Pope, D., & Hough, D. G. (1986, February). *Developmental norms on a children's verbal learning test.* Paper presented at the International Neuropsychological Society Meeting, Denver, CO.
Dunn, L., & Dunn, L. (1981). *Peabody Picture Vocabulary Test–Revised.* Minneapolis, MN: American Guidance Service.
Dunn, L., & Markwardt, F. (1989). *Peabody Individual Achievement Test–Revised.* Circle Pines, MN: American Guidance Service.
Eslinger, P. J., & Damasio, A. R. (1985). Severe disturbance of higher cognition following bilateral frontal lobe oblation: Patient EVR. *Neurology, 35,* 1731–1741.
Ewing-Cobbs, L., Miner, M. S., Fletcher, J. M., & Levin, H. S. (1989). Intellectual, motor and language sequelae following closed head injury in infants and preschoolers. *Journal of Pediatric Psychology, 14,* 531–547.
Franzen, M., & Berg, R. (1989). *Screening children for brain impairment.* New York: Springer.
Fuchs, L., Butterworth, J., & Fuchs, D. (1989). Effects of ongoing curriculum-based measurements on student awareness of goals and progress. *Education and Treatment of Children, 12,* 63–72.
Fuchs, L., Deno, S., & Mirkin, P. (1984). The effects of frequent curriculum measurement on pedagogy, student achievement and student awareness of learning. *American Educational Research Journal, 21,* 449–460.
Fuchs, L., & Fuchs, D. (1988). Curriculum-based measurement: A methodology for evaluating and improving students' programs. *Diagnostique, 14,* 3–13.
Furons, S., O'Reilly, K., Hooka, C. M., Instauka, T., Allman, T. L., & Zeislott, B. (1985). *Hawaii Early Learning Profile (HELP).* Palo Alto, CA: VORT Corp.
Gaddes, W. H., & Crocket, D. J. (1975). The Spreen–Benton Aphasia Tests: Normative data as a measure of normal language development. *Brain and Language, 2,* 257–280.
Gardner, M. F. (1979). *Expressive One-Word Picture Vocabulary Test.* Novato, CA: Academic Therapy.
Golden, C. G. (1987). *Luria–Nebraska Neuropsychological Battery: Children's revision.* Los Angeles: Western Psychological Services.
Golden, C. G., Hammeke, T., & Purisch, A. (1985). *The Luria–Nebraska Neuropsychological Battery.* Los Angeles: Western Psychological Services.
Goodglass, H., & Kaplan, E. (1972). *Boston Diagnostic Aphasia Examination.* Philadelphia: Lea & Febiger.

Gordon Diagnostic System. (1988). *Model III instruction manual.* DeWitt, NY: Author.
Goyette, C., Conners, C., & Ulrich, R. (1978). Normative data for Revised Conners Parent and Teacher Rating Scales. *Journal of Abnormal Child Psychology, 6,* 221–236.
Grattan, L. M., & Eslinger, P. J. (1991). Frontal lobe damage in children and adults: A comparative review. *Developmental Neuropsychology, 7,* 283–326.
Hammill, D. (1991). *Detroit Tests of Learning Aptitude–Third Edition (DTLA-3).* Austin, TX: PRO-ED.
Heaton, R. (1981). *Manual for the Wisconsin Card Sorting Test.* Odessa, FL: Personality Assessment Resources.
Hynd, G. (1988). *Neuropsychological assessment in clinical child psychology.* Newberry Park, CA: Sage.
Jastak, J. F., & Wilkinson, G. (1984). *The Wide Range Achievement Test–Revised.* Wilmington, DE: Jastak Associates.
Jones-Gotman, M., & Milner, B. (1977). Design fluency: The inventions of nonsense drawings after focal cortical lesions. *Neuropsychologia, 15,* 653–674.
Jorgenson, C., Barrett, M., Huisingh, R., & Zachman, L. (1981). *The Word Test.* Moline, IL: Lingui Systems.
Kagan, J., Rosman, B. L., Day, L., Albert, J., & Phillips, W. (1964). Information processing in the child: Significance of analytic and reflective attitudes. *Psychological Monographs, 78*(Whole No. 578).
Kaplan, E. (1988). A process approach to neuropsychological assessment. In T. Boll & B. K. Bryant (Eds.), *Clinical neuropsychology and brain function: Research, measurement, and practice* (pp. 129–167). Washington, DC: American Psychological Association.
Kaplan, E., Fein, D., Morris, R., & Delis, D. (1991). *WAIS-R as a Neuropsychological Instrument (WAIS-R NI).* San Antonio, TX: Psychological Corp.
Kaplan, E., Goodglass, H., & Weintraub, S. (1978). *The Boston Naming Test.* Boston: E. Kaplan & H. Goodglass.
Kaufman, A., & Kaufman, N. (1983). *Kaufman Assessment Battery for Children.* Circle Pines, MN: American Guidance Service.
Kirk, S. A., McCarthy, J. J., & Kirk, W. D. (1968). *Illinois Test of Psycholinguistic Abilities* (rev. ed.). Urbana: University of Illinois Press.
Leiter, R. (1969). *Examiner's manual for the Leiter International Performance Scale.* Chicago: Stoelting.
Levin, H. S., Culhane, K. A., Hartman, J., Evankovich, K., Mattson, A. J., Harward, H., Ringolz, G., Ewing-Cobbs, L., & Fletcher, J. M. (1991). Developmental changes in performance on tests of purported frontal lobe functioning. *Developmental Neuropsychology, 7,* 377–395.
Lezak, M. D. (1982). The problem of assessing executive functions. *International Journal of Psychology, 17,* 281–297.
Lezak, M. (1983). *Neuropsychological assessment.* New York: Oxford University Press.
Mateer, C. A., & Williams, D. (1991). Effects of frontal lobe injury in childhood. *Developmental Neuropsychology, 7,* 359–376.
McCarthy, D. (1972). *The McCarthy Scales of Children's Abilities.* New York: Psychological Corp.
McNeil, M., & Prescott, T. (1978). *Revised Token Test.* Austin, TX: PRO-ED.
Mentis, M., & Prutting, C. A. (1991). Analysis of topic as illustrated in a head-injured and a normal adult. *Journal of Speech and Hearing Research, 34,* 583–595.
Nihira, K., Foster, R., Shellhaas, M., & Leland, H. (1974). *AAMD Adaptive Behavior Scale (Revised).* Novato, CA: Academic Therapy.
Obrzut, J., & Hynd, G. (1986). Child neuropsychology: An introduction to theory

and research. In J. Obrzut & G. Hynd (Eds.), *Child neuropsychology* (Vol. 1). San Diego: Academic Press.

Osterreith, P. (1944). Le test de copie d'une figure complexe. *Archives de Psychologie, 30,* 206–356.

PL 101-476. Individuals with Disabilities Education Act. (1991). Washington, DC: U.S. Department of Education, Office of Special Education and Rehabilitative Services.

Porteus, S. D. (1959). *The maze test and clinical psychology.* Palo Alto, CA: Pacific Books.

Prutting, C. A., & Kirchner, D. M. (1987). A clinical appraisal of the pragmatic aspects of language. *Journal of Speech and Hearing Disorders, 52,* 105–109.

Purdue Research Foundation. (1948). *Examiner's manual for the Purdue Pegboard.* Chicago: Science Research Associates.

Randt, C., & Brown, E. (1983). *Randt Memory Test.* Bayport, NY: Life Science Associates.

Raven, J. (1956). *Guide to using the Coloured Progressive Matrices (revised edition).* London: H. K. Lewis.

Reitan, R. M. (1987). *Neuropsychological Evaluation of Children.* Tucson, AR: Neuropsychology Press.

Reitan, R. M., & Wolfson, D. (1985). *The Halstead–Reitan Neuropsychological Test Battery: Theory and Clinical Interpretation.* Tucson, AZ: Neuropsychology Press.

Rey, A. (1941). L'examen psychologique dans les cas d'encephalopathie traumatique. *Archives de Psychologie, 30,* 286–340.

Ross, J. D., & Ross, C. M. (1976). *Ross Test of Higher Cognitive Processes.* Novata, CA: Academic Therapy.

Rourke, B., Bakker, D., Fisk, J., & Strang, J. (1983). *Child neuropsychology: An introduction to theory, research, and clinical practice.* New York: Guilford Press.

Rourke, B., Fisk, J., & Strang, J. (1986). *Neuropsychological assessment of children: A treatment oriented approach.* New York: Guilford Press.

Semel, E., Wiig, E. H., & Secord, W. (1987). *Clinical Evaluation of Language Fundamentals–Revised.* San Antonio, TX: Psychological Corp.

Shallice, T. (1982). Specific impairments of planning. *Philosophical Transactions of the Royal Society of London, Series B; Biological Sciences (London), 298,* 199–209.

Sparrow, S., Balla, D., & Cicchetti, D. (1984). *Vineland Adaptive Behavior Scales.* Circle Pines, MN: American Guidance Service.

Stelling, M. W., McKay, S. E., Carr, W. A., Walsh, J. W., & Bauman, R. J. (1986). Frontal lobe lesions and cognitive function in craniopharyngioma survivors. *American Journal of Diseases of Childhood, 140,* 710–714.

Stuss, D. T., & Benson, D. F. (1986). *The frontal lobes.* New York: Raven Press.

Taylor, H. G., Albo, V., Phebus, C., Sachs, B., & Bierl, P. (1987). Postirradiation treatment outcomes for children with acute lymphocytic leukemia: Clarification of risks. *Journal of Pediatric Psychology, 12,* 395–411.

Thorndike, R., Hagan, E., & Sattler, J. (1986). *Stanford–Binet Intelligence Scale–Fourth edition.* Chicago: Riverside.

Trahan, D., & Larrabee, G. (1988). *The Continuous Visual Memory Test.* Odessa, FL: Psychological Assessment Resources.

Tucker, J. A. (1985). Curriculum-based assessment: An introduction. *Exceptional Children, 52,* 199–204.

Uzgiris, I., & Hunt, J. (1978). *Assessment in infancy: Ordinal scales of psychological development.* Urbana: University of Illinois Press.

Wechsler, D. (1981). *Wechsler Adult Intelligence Scale–Revised.* San Antonio, TX: Psychological Corp.

Wechsler, D. (1991). *Wechsler Intelligence Scale for Children–Third edition.* San Antonio, TX: Psychological Corp.
Wechsler, D. (1989). *Wechsler Preschool and Primary Scale of Intelligence–Revised.* San Antonio, TX: Psychological Corp.
Wechsler, D. (1987). *Wechsler Memory Scale–Revised.* San Antonio, TX: Psychological Corp.
Welsh, M. C., & Pennington, B. F. (1988). Assessing frontal lobe functioning in children: Views from developmental psychology. *Developmental Neuropsychology, 4,* 199–230.
Welsh, M. C., Pennington, B. F., & Groisser, D. B. (1991). A normative-developmental study of executive function: A window on prefrontal function in children. *Developmental Neuropsychology, 7,* 131–149.
Wiig, E. H., & Secord, W. (1988). *Test of Language Competence–Expanded edition.* San Antonio: TX: Psychological Corp.
Wirt, R., Lachr, D., Kinedinst, J., & Seat, P. (1984). *Multidimensional description of child personality: A manual for the Personality Inventory for Children (Revised by D. Lachr).* Los Angeles: Western Psychological Services.
Woodcock, R., & Johnson, M. (1989). *Woodcock–Johnson Psycho-Educational Test Battery–Revised.* Allen Park, TX: DLM Teaching Resources.
Ylvisaker, M. (1986). Language and communication disorders following pediatric head injury. *Journal of Head Trauma Rehabilitation, 1*(4), 48–56.
Ylvisaker, M. (1989). Cognitive and psychosocial outcome following head injury in children. In J. T. Hoff, T. E. Anderson, & T. M. Cole (Eds.), *Mild to moderate head injury.* London: Blackwell Scientific.
Ylvisaker, M. (1993). Communication outcome in children and adolescents with traumatic brain injury. *Neuropsychological Rehabilitation.*
Ylvisaker, M., Chorazy, A. J. L., Cohen, S. B., Mastrilli, J. P., Molitor, C. B., Nelson, J., Szekeres, S. F., Valko, A. S., & Jaffe, K. M. (1990). Rehabilitative assessment following head injury in children. In M. Rosenthal, E. Griffith, M. Bond, & J. D. Miller (Eds.), *Rehabilitation of the adult and child with traumatic brain injury* (pp. 558–592). Philadelphia: F. A. Davis.
Ylvisaker, M., Hartwick, P., & Stevens, M. B. (1991). School reentry following head injury: Managing the transition from hospital to school. *Journal of Head Trauma Rehabilitation, 6*(1), 10–22.
Zachman, L., Barrett, M., Huisingh, R., Orman, J., & Blagden, C. (1989). *The Adolescent Word Test.* East Moline, IL: LinguiSystems.

CHAPTER 5

Cognitive Intervention

MARK YLVISAKER
SHIRLEY F. SZEKERES
PATRICK HARTWICK
PATTIE TWOREK

In this chapter, we discuss a variety of approaches to intervention for students whose academic and social functioning is impeded by cognitive weakness following traumatic brain injury (TBI). Chapter 3, which includes a discussion of cognition, descriptions of common cognitive symptoms following TBI, a framework for cognitive intervention, and general principles of treatment, should be read as a background for this chapter. Because intervention for language disorders is often an important component of cognitive intervention with this population, Chapter 6 should also be read in conjunction with this chapter.

Our primary focus in this chapter is children and adolescents whose recovery is generally quite good (e.g., they may walk and talk and score within normal limits on tests of intelligence), but who have residual cognitive weakness that interferes with successful school and community reentry. In this chapter, we present a functional and integrative approach to cognitive rehabilitation that is thoroughly integrated within the student's educational program; present specific intervention suggestions in selected areas of cognition—attention, organization and memory, strategic abilities, and metacognitive–executive functions; and suggest procedures for cognitive intervention with preschoolers.

Many of the procedures that we discuss are equally applicable to children with learning disabilities. Indeed, many of the intervention strategies and instructional methods developed for other special education populations are useful for children with TBI. These procedures may require modification and flexible application, however, given the unusual profiles of strengths and needs that many children with TBI evidence (see Chapter 3).

COGNITIVE CHALLENGES FOLLOWING TBI

Children return to school at varying stages of recovery and with varying constellations of strengths and needs. Some children reenter community schools while still in the middle stages of recovery, dominated by confusion resulting from general disruption of cognitive functioning (see Table 3.1 in Chapter 3). These children tend to be poorly oriented (relative to age expectations), to have sharply reduced attentional ability, to process information inefficiently, and to have difficulty retrieving old information and learning new information. Unexpectedly sharp breakdowns in performance often occur with increases in the amount and complexity of information and in the rate at which it is presented. Children at this stage may be extremely impulsive and disinhibited, resulting in behavior that is inappropriate—sometimes bizarre or aggressive—and difficult to manage in a classroom. They tend to profit from a highly structured environment and may require considerable cuing and behavioral support to benefit from their school experience. Some children never progress beyond this stage of cognitive recovery.

The general goals of cognitive rehabilitation for children in these confused stages of recovery are (a) to reduce confusion; (b) to increase orientation, adaptive behavior, and organized interaction with the environment (including communication); (c) to increase gradually the ability to attend, to process information, and to organize responses; (d) to reestablish basic organized thinking; and (e) to begin to use external aids (e.g., simple memory book, schedule card) to compensate for major cognitive deficits.

More commonly, children return to school following TBI having progressed beyond the stages of obvious confusion and disorientation. Many of these students *appear* to have returned to pretraumatic levels of functioning. However, when examined more closely, or when subjected to academic or cognitive demands or social stress, they are likely to evidence some combination of deficits from the following list (Haarbauer-Krupa, Henry, Szekeres, & Ylvisaker, 1985):

- Impaired attention, concentration, and ability to shift attentional focus
- Greater than expected disorientation caused by unanticipated changes in routine
- General inefficiency in processing information (e.g., slowed processing) and in learning new information or skills
- Relatively marked deterioration in performance caused by increases in the amount, complexity, and abstractness of information and in the rate of presentation or response
- Inefficient retrieval of information and of words
- Gaps in knowledge or academic skill at surprisingly low levels despite good performance at higher levels in some areas
- Poorly organized behavior and language expression
- Difficulty with abstract reasoning
- Impulsive and socially awkward behavior
- Difficulty interpreting social cues and "reading" social behavior
- Disorganized problem solving
- Impaired "executive" functions, including self-awareness of deficits, goal setting, planning, self-initiating and self-inhibiting, self-monitoring, self-evaluating, and problem solving

Even if relatively subtle, deficits of this sort can interfere with academic and social functioning. In some cases, specific residual problems are related to focal brain damage (e.g., perceptual neglect of the left visual field associated with right hemisphere damage; problems with comprehension and/or expression of language associated with left hemisphere damage). More commonly, general symptoms (some combination from the list above, particularly under stress) are present, related to multifocal and diffuse brain damage, often including some damage to the frontal lobes, which are highly vulnerable in TBI.

GOALS AND SCOPE OF COGNITIVE INTERVENTION

The general goal of any rehabilitation program is to enable people who have disabilities caused by injury or disease to successfully achieve their goals. In pursuit of this general goal, rehabilitation professionals may help individuals recover lost capacities, knowledge, and skills (if this is possible); compensate for lost capacity and skills that cannot be recovered; and adjust to their new life as it has been affected by the injury. It may also include changing the environment so that they can succeed despite impaired functioning, changing their tasks to fit their abilities, and adjusting the expectations that teachers, parents, and others have for these individuals' performance. People with *physical* disabilities, for example, may be taught to walk again, possibly using a modified gait, or to use a wheelchair. Modifications may have to be made in their home, school, or work environments. Teachers, family members, and employers may need education regarding realistic expectations and techniques for helping the individual with difficult tasks. And the individual may need intensive counseling regarding adjustment to his or her disability.

The goals and scope of cognitive rehabilitation are parallel to those of physical rehabilitation. The barriers in this case are cognitive rather than physical. Rehabilitation efforts may focus on

1. Channeling spontaneous recovery by means of general stimulation (in the early weeks after the injury)
2. Retraining impaired cognitive processes (if there is reason to believe that the process lends itself to a training effect)
3. Developing new skills or procedures to compensate for residual deficits
4. Creating environmental compensations that permit effective performance despite residual deficits
5. Identifying instructional procedures that best fit the student's profile of cognitive strengths and needs
6. Promoting improved metacognitive awareness so that the individual can become an active participant in selecting goals and intervention strategies (see Chapter 3)

In addition, individuals may need intensive education and counseling to help them understand and adjust to the many ways in which their lives may be changed by residual cognitive deficits. Family members, teachers, and employers may also need education and counseling so that their expectations are consistent with the individual's ability to perform.

Professional disputes in the area of cognitive rehabilitation often center around the extent to which impaired cognitive processes can be remediated by means of targeted remedial exercises. To use the physical rehabilitation analogy again, can general cognitive functions such as attending effectively or learning–remembering efficiently be restored by "mental muscle–building" practice in attending or remembering? Evidence from adult cognitive rehabilitation is not particularly encouraging (e.g., Ben-Yishay & Prigatano, 1990; Moffat, 1984; Schacter & Glisky, 1986). Similarly, special education studies do not support functional memory improvement through rote memory drills (e.g., Belmont & Butterfield, 1977). In general, narrowly targeted exercises designed to improve basic-level processes (e.g., attentional, perceptual, and rote memory processes) have not been shown to have a generalized positive impact on functional cognitive or academic performance for children with learning disabilities or developmental delays (Kavale & Mattson, 1983). With this research as a background, teachers and therapists must (a) be thoughtful in their decision to approach a cognitive problem through remediation or compensation or some combination; (b) monitor their intervention carefully to ensure that there is a payoff in important functional tasks, not merely improvement in isolated therapy tasks and formal tests; and (c) place primary emphasis during intervention on transfer of skills from therapy tasks to functional tasks, generalization to functional settings, and maintenance over time.

Because everything a child does has a cognitive dimension and because cognitive rehabilitation is ideally delivered in the context of concrete academic, communicative, daily living, or social activities, several professionals are generally involved in delivering this service. In a school setting, these may include teachers, speech-language pathologists, occupational therapists, counselors, psychologists, and others. An effectively integrated program requires that all of the team members integrate cognitive goals into their intervention and that they integrate their interventions with one another. For example, if a child's organizational functioning is impaired, the speech-language pathologist should address the organizational impairment as it affects comprehension of language (e.g., comprehension of extended text) and expression of language (e.g., organized narratives, coherent conversations). The speech-language pathologist should also ensure that the organizational strategies that are used are consistent with strategies used in the classroom. Indeed, school therapists increasingly report that the effectiveness of their intervention increases if they work collaboratively with classroom teachers, preferably in the classroom.

INTERVENTION PROCEDURES

Attention

Difficulty with attention is common following TBI. In the early stages of recovery, individuals lack arousal and alertness, probably due to damage to the reticular activating system (see Chapter 2). This underarousal or lack of focused attention may persist, despite good recovery of cognitive function. More commonly, however, children return to school adequately alert, but with attention problems that more closely resemble those of children with attention deficit disorder. They may have a short attention span (sustained attention), difficulty filtering out competing signals (selective attention), difficulty shifting the focus of their attention (alternating attention), and difficulty attending to two activities or thoughts at the same time (divided attention).

The focus of attention is often externally controlled by environmental stimuli. On the other hand, a person may *deliberately* direct attention to stimuli if this serves a particular purpose (e.g., studying a text in preparation for an exam). Deliberate control over attention is necessary for efficient processing of information and classroom learning. Because adequate attentional control forms the basis for higher-level cognitive processes and academic skills, it is the focus of considerable discussion in the literature on cognitive rehabilitation and special education. Classroom consequences of attentional deficits are described in Chapter 3.

Poorly controlled attention can readily lead to a variety of difficulties with memory and learning, language comprehension and expression, and social interaction. It is equally important to recognize that *apparent* attention problems may be the consequence of other deficits, including impaired language (e.g., the child lacks the inner language to direct attentional focus or simply finds the content too difficult to concentrate on), weak organizational skills (e.g., the child lacks the ability to "chunk" incoming experiences and is therefore overwhelmed by too much stimulation), or impaired executive self-regulation of cognitive processes (e.g., the child simply does not "turn on" his or her concentration when needed or cannot "turn off" attention to concerns that interfere with the task at hand). Identification of the critical factors in cases of apparent attention deficit disorder is necessary for selecting appropriate training or management strategies.

Approaches to intervention following brain injury include (a) specific retraining exercises, (b) environmental management, (c) deliberately applied compensatory strategies, and (d) pharmacologic management. Sohlberg and Mateer (1989) described retraining exercises designed to remediate specific processing weakness in adolescents and adults with TBI. For example, cancellation exercises (cancelling one or more specified items, such as numbers, letters, words, or pictures, in an array of similar items) are used to facilitate sustained attention. Vigilance and reaction time exercises (e.g., "Prepare yourself, wait, and respond quickly when a specified signal appears on the screen") are a common component of cognitive retraining software focused on attentional skills. Selective, alternating, and divided attention exercises can easily be constructed by adding foils, distractions, shifting stimulus or response requirements, and stimuli that must be simultaneously processed.

Sohlberg and Mateer (1989) presented data supporting the usefulness of retraining exercises of this sort in improving attention and, derivatively, memory functioning in adults with TBI. In evaluating the merits of this approach, one must consider the litmus test of all intervention, namely transfer to functional tasks. In the case of school-aged individuals with brain injury, if there is a rationale for approaching attentional problems in a process-specific retraining manner, it makes sense to use functional educational software to present the stimulus items for the cognitive exercises. The same processes exercised by cognitive retraining software can be targeted using readily available educational programs, thereby addressing the transfer of training issue in the selection of the training tasks; that is, speeded processing, shifting and dividing attention, organized scanning, and other basic cognitive processes can be engaged in the context of meaningful academic exercises. The need for functional training tasks is particularly acute in working with young and concrete, stimulus-bound children. As discussed in Chapter 3, controversies persist in connection with decontextualized cognitive retraining programs designed to restore processes impaired by brain injury. Later in this chapter, we discuss the uses and limitations of computers in cognitive rehabilitation, an application often associated with this process-specific approach.

Because attention deficits have been a focus of applied educational research for many years, teachers and therapists should consider intervention approaches that have been validated for other groups of children. For example, several studies have documented the value of a cognitive strategy approach to attention deficits for students with learning disabilities (Brown & Alford, 1984; Douglas, Parry, Marton, & Garson, 1976; Hallahan & Reeve, 1980; Kendall & Finch, 1979). Children with attention disorders but otherwise good cognitive recovery following TBI may likewise benefit from procedures for self-management of the attentional weakness.

Environmental management can be useful with children whose attentional problem is largely a result of external distractions. Reducing distracting features of the environment until adequate attention to task is achieved and subsequently reintroducing distractions in a program of gradual desensitization may be effective for these children. As with other interventions, however, this approach must be used experimentally and cautiously. We have worked with highly distractible young children with TBI who have become *less* attentive in a distraction-free environment. It may be that the familiarity and organized routines of a normal classroom promote improved attentional functioning rather than serving only as a source of distractions. Well-understood routines, possibly supported by pictured or verbally rehearsed scripts, and clear time frames, possibly supported by timers, are an important component of environmental management for many children. Novel and highly engaging materials also help to capture the attention of these children.

Some children with attention deficits benefit from stimulant medications. Because a research literature does not yet exist on the effectiveness of stimulants (e.g., Ritalin) with children following TBI, trials of the medication must be closely monitored to determine effectiveness in individual cases. Some practitioners report, based exclusively on uncontrolled clinical observation, that stimulants are particularly useful with those children with TBI who had some degree of attention deficit disorder before the brain injury. This observation awaits experimental verification.

In some cases, Tegrotol is used with children with extreme impulsiveness and attention deficit after TBI. One child who fit this description was admitted to a rehabilitation facility 10 years after a severe TBI at age 2. The stimulant medication that he had taken for several years appeared to have no impact on his behavior and was discontinued with no noticeable effect on attention or activity level. The use of Tegrotol, combined with an intensive program of behavior modification and saturation teaching of self-control scripts and routines, resulted in a sufficient increase in attention and decrease in impulsiveness that he was again able to benefit from classroom instruction.

In Case Study 5.1, we describe a child who had attention deficit following TBI. Various techniques were used to enable the child to return to and succeed in school.

CASE STUDY 5.1

Attention Deficit Following TBI

JB was 5 years old when she fell in her home and struck her head against a table. Initially, she simply complained of a headache, but her neurologic condition worsened. A computerized tomographic scan revealed a bruise and bleeding within the brain. She underwent two separate surgical procedures to stop the bleeding and remove the collected blood. For a period of 4 weeks following injury, she was minimally responsive and unable to walk, talk, or eat.

When she was transferred from an acute care hospital to a rehabilitation facility at 5 weeks postinjury, she was still in a wheelchair because of right-sided weakness, she spoke with a soft and breathy voice, she was alert and followed simple commands, and she was reasonably well oriented to her situation. She had a severely reduced attention span; was fiercely distractible; had impaired visual perception; was emotionally labile, with frequent unprovoked crying; and was extremely dependent on her mother. Evaluation over the first 2 weeks of admission indicated excellent recovery of language and preacademic skills. She had good organizational skills, kindergarten-level concepts, and adequate problem-solving ability. The primary cognitive and psychosocial goals were to improve attentional functioning and reduce dependence on her mother, both with a focus on school reentry.

Initially, attention problems were approached environmentally. JB's desk in the rehabilitation facility's classroom was removed from the center of activity, often blocked with a visual screen. To capture attention, learning–relearning tasks were couched in motivating play activities, manipulative objects were part of all activities, and activities shifted focus at least every 5 minutes, prior to her losing attention and becoming demanding. Subsequently, JB's desk was moved to the mainstream activity area, activities were gradually extended to 15 minutes, and some paper-and-pencil tasks were introduced to decrease reliance on toys. However, the teacher continued to sit next to JB to ensure on-task behavior. The mother gradually phased out of the classroom and several different staff members were used in JB's classroom to generalize attentional control. The final stage included varied kindergarten tasks in a setting that resembled a regular classroom. JB worked on her own worksheets and other materials obtained from her school.

As stated, phasing her mother out of the classroom was gradual. Initially, she sat next to JB. As soon as possible, she shifted to a chair behind her daughter. She next left the area for segments of the therapy or instructional time, and finally reduced her role to taking JB to class and picking her up. Meanwhile, the staff gradually evolved their responses from extremely supportive and nurturing to more standard kindergarten teacher responses to manipulative or tantrum behavior.

Systematic school reentry began with a school representative visiting the rehabilitation facility to meet with the staff and family. Subsequently, a facility special educator visited JB's school and met with the instructional staff. Prior to her injury, JB had attended a private parochial school that was inaccessible to wheelchairs. Therefore, her options were restricted to (a) changing schools or (b) receiving her initial instruction through a homebound program. The second option was selected by the family despite strong arguments made by staff for changing schools. To ensure academic continuity, JB's kindergarten teacher was hired to provide 1 hour per day of tutoring and to monitor JB's emotional dependence on her mother.

The initial Individualized Education Program (IEP) was written for a 3-month period. At that point, JB was able to return to her regular class. She was subsequently promoted to first grade in a regular education classroom. Classroom management recommendations that accompanied her to first grade included the following:

1. JB should be positioned close to the teacher, not too close to peers or to the doorway (because of distractibility), and on the right side of the room since she was visually more attentive to her left than to her right.
2. She should be given immediate feedback to help keep her oriented to task and should be allowed to use manipulative objects as needed during instruction to help focus her attention.
3. She should receive cues as needed to ensure success with academic material.
4. Because of visual perceptual deficits, visually "busy" workbook exercises were to be avoided.
5. Artificial barriers in the classroom were *not* recommended as part of the attention management system. In addition to the stigma factor of such an approach, staff believed that JB could profit from good peer modeling and maintain her attention. This turned out to be true, and she succeeded in her first-grade placement.

Organization and Memory

Treating organizational deficits is important for its own sake, because disorganization can interfere seriously with academic success and with daily living activities. Improving organizational skills also has a positive impact on memory and learning. One of the most solid conclusions that has emerged from recent research in memory functioning is that a close relationship exists between organization and memory. The better organized the information is, the easier it is to learn and the longer it is remembered (Bower, 1972). There is some value, therefore, in considering these two cognitive processes together.

Organizational and memory impairments are very common following TBI (particularly closed head injury) and merit considerable attention in intervention programs. General difficulty with organization may be manifested by disorganized activities of daily living (e.g., inefficient dressing), poorly organized expressive language (e.g., disjointed conversations and narratives), weak language comprehension because of difficulty integrating the information in a text and seeing the main point, and weak retention of new information because it was not adequately organized and coordinated with existing knowledge at the time of encoding.

The term *organization* may refer to a *process* (i.e., organizing people, objects, events, or ideas), a *product* (i.e., the relationship that obtains among people, objects, events, or ideas when they are organized), or a *conceptual structure* (i.e., the mental representation of organizational schemes which is hypothesized to explain an individual's organizing of objects, people, events, or ideas into patterns) (Pellegrino & Ingram, 1978). Young children can learn more effectively when information is organized for them in a way that fits with their internal organizational schemes and, later in development, when they are required to organize the information themselves in ways that make it meaningful and memorable for them.

Objects, people, events, and ideas can be organized in countless ways. The following examples of common organizational schema tend to dominate the organizational activity of children (Ylvisaker, Szekeres, & Hartwick, 1992):

- *Perceptual similarity:* Organizing items according to color, shape, size, texture, taste, and the like.
- *Semantic similarity:* Organizing items according to features such as supraordinate categories (e.g., cookies, cakes, and pies are desserts), part–whole relations, action–object relations (e.g., kick–ball), opposites, and the like.
- *Function* (use): Grouping items that share a function (e.g., glove, bat, and ball go with baseball).
- *Main idea and detail:* Grouping related facts under the main idea that holds them together.
- *Story schema:* Grouping people and events in a story under headings such as setting, characters, episodes, barriers, and solutions.
- *General life scripts:* Grouping biographical events under broad categories, such as time and place of birth, time and place of education, and time and place of marriage and jobs.
- *Specific event scripts:* Grouping people, things, and events according to sequences of events that are common in one's life. For children, specific event scripts typically include getting up and getting ready for school, going to school, routine events at school, organized play after school, eating meals, preparing for bed, going to a birthday party, visiting the doctor or dentist, going to camp, going to church, playing games, and many more.

Improving a child's organizational functioning after brain injury involves three phases (Ylvisaker, Szekeres, Henry, Sullivan, & Wheeler, 1987):

1. Reestablishing or developing an organized knowledge base, including specific-event scripts relevant for that child, and establishing an organized and consistent pattern to daily living activities. For preschoolers, this may exhaust the possibilities for intervention.
2. Teaching children to recognize the distinction between organized and disorganized behavior, objects, or events and to appreciate the usefulness of organization. This "metacognitive" focus presupposes that the child is at least at the developmental level of an early grade schooler.
3. Developing organizing strategies (e.g., a note-taking procedure for studying a text or an outline form for writing an essay) that the

student can differentially impose on material to facilitate efficient encoding, storage, and retrieval of information. Considerations relevant to teaching compensatory strategies are discussed separately below.

Table 5.1 describes treatment activities that may be useful in reestablishing the seven organizational schemes listed above. The specific activities were developed for adolescents with significant cognitive weakness. Using developmentally appropriate objects and activities, the same approach can be used with younger children. For example, preschoolers can be given a doll house and a large container filled with an assortment of furniture. The child's goal is to sort and arrange the furniture (functional scheme) within the context of a play script such as helping Mom clean house (thematic scheme). Scripts can be varied initially using the same settings, and later using different settings and props (e.g., arrange items to sell in a store and then play store). All of these tasks give the child opportunity to impose organization on the environment in meaningful activity. Grade school–aged children can use similar activities; however, at this developmental level, the concept of organization and the usefulness of organization should be explicitly introduced in discussion with the child (e.g., "How are the toys organized?" "Why did you organize them that way?" "Why does a shopkeeper organize products the way he does?").

The reflection questions in Table 5.1 are designed to promote an understanding of the reasons for organizing things or ideas in certain ways and an understanding of the situations that require one type of organizing rather than another. This metacognitive knowledge is necessary if students are expected to use organizing procedures as deliberate compensatory strategies.

Whether the goal is to establish unconscious application of organizational schemes or deliberate use of organizational strategies, treatment for organizational deficits includes the following steps (Ylvisaker et al., 1987):

1. Selecting a functional task that is meaningful to the child (e.g., reading a short story; writing a paragraph on an interesting topic; making a cake).
2. Presenting an organizational scheme as a means to get the job done (e.g., a form for note taking when reading a story; an outlining form for writing a descriptive paragraph; a guide for making a cake).
3. Completing the task using the organizational scheme, with whatever cuing may be necessary.
4. Discussing the task, how it was done, and how well it was done. This discussion focuses on the organizational scheme, how it made doing the task easier, and what other tasks may require this or related types of organizational schemes.

Reestablishing specific event scripts

Preschoolers organize things and information in a variety of ways (e.g., using perceptual, categorical, and thematic forms of organization), and their memory performance can be enhanced by using these schemes in organizing the information to be remembered. It appears, however, that these young children prefer *thematic* organiza-

TABLE 5.1. Reestablishing Organized Semantic Memory

Organizational Schema (means for attaining the goal)	***Task and Goal***	***Activity***	***Reflection***[a]
Perceptual similarity (e.g., color, shape, size, texture, rhyme)	"The shop asked us to organize these left-over pieces of sandpaper so they can easily be found. Let's find a good way to do this."	1. Label small boxes for different grains (extra fine, fine, medium, etc.). 2. Sort the pieces according to their "texture" and put them into the labeled boxes. 3. Call out the textures and time how quickly they can be found.	How did you sort? Why this way? Was it "good"? In what other situations might one sort by texture? What would have happened if you had sorted by size? How could this help you remember where your tools or other possessions are kept or at least help you always locate them?
Semantic similarity (e.g., supraordinate category, opposites)	"We got a job to set up the layout of a new department store. We have to make it easy for customers to find what they want."	Make a floor plan specifying the location of departments. Place labeled items into the departments, grouping them by similarity (e.g., TVs, stereos, radios) in one area, but subgrouped within the area. Make display arrangement to entice people to buy (e.g., comfortable chair, flowers, glass of wine, and stereo).	How did you arrange the store? Why did you use that arrangement? In what other situations would you group things this way? When would this arrangement be inconvenient? How could knowing this arrangement help your memory of a visit to a store? How did the display arrangement differ from the floor arrangement?
Function (use)	"We are moving furniture into a new house. We have to	Make a floor plan and arrange labeled blocks representing	How were the items arranged for each activity?

(continues)

TABLE 5.1. *Continued*

Organizational Schema (means for attaining the goal)	***Task and Goal***	***Activity***	***Reflection***[a]
	arrange the living room for TV watching and conversation."	the furniture. Then rearrange them for special occasions, such as a cocktail party, Tupperware party, etc.	Why did you have to change them? How is this different from a department store arrangement?
Main idea and detail	"We will present today's news to the orientation group." (Watch a videotaped news item or listen to an audiotaped news item.)	Listen to the tape. Fill in a form, first identifying the main idea, then answering Who, What, When, Where, Why, and What happened questions. Relate the news item to another person using the diagram as notes.	How did the form help you remember? When wouldn't the form help? How did you stay so organized and coherent when you related the news item?
Story schema	"We will share a short story or TV show with ( ) who was unable to see or hear it."	Watch the videotape of a TV show or listen to an audiotape of a radio show. Fill out a schema diagram, including characters, setting, and episodes. Retell the story using the organizational diagram as a cue.	How did this form help you remember? How is the information arranged? Why is this arrangement good for a story? Would it be good for a math book? Why not?
General life scripts (abstracted common life events)	"We will write our autobiographies and present a 'this is your life' program."	Fill out a form with labeled boxes of common life events (birth, school, marriage, job) and uncommon significant events (e.g., head injury). Using the form as a guide, write the autobiography and then present it formally in a radio program format.	How did the form make writing more organized? How could the form help reconstruct the past? How is your autobiography organized (e.g., chronologically)? How did the written preparation help the oral presentation?

(*continues*)

TABLE 5.1. *Continued*

Organizational Schema (means for attaining the goal)	***Task and Goal***	***Activity***	***Reflection***[a]
Specific event scripts (e.g., going to a restaurant, going to the dentist)	"We will explain to (*a small child*) what it will be like when he has to go to the dentist."	Fill in a form with relevant information about the situation to prepare what you are going to say to the child: • Who will be there. • Equipment. • Sequence of expected events and actions. • Expected layout of the room and some variations. Then, using the guide, explain to a child or explain in a role-playing situation.	How did this form help you? Why wouldn't a general life script help you? How is your explanation to the child organized? Why would this help you remember what has happened to you?

[a]Possible probe questions to develop metacognition, understanding, and awareness.

From "Topics in Cognitive Rehabilitation Therapy" by M. Ylvisaker, S. Szekeres, K. Henry, D. Sullivan, and P. Wheeler, in *Community Re-Entry for Head Injured Adults* (pp. 166–169) by M. Ylvisaker and E. M. Gobble (Eds.), 1987, Austin, TX: PRO-ED. Reproduced with permission.

tion to other types; that is, when information is presented in the context of real-life functional relationships, scripts, or stories, it is easier for preschoolers to remember (Ceci & Howe, 1978; Szekeres, 1988). These thematic or "script"-oriented organizational schemes may be idiosyncratic to the individual child, based on that child's specific experiences. For example, when asked to associate ideas freely, a young child might associate "pie" with "grandma," because in his experience those things have gone together. A child in the early grades is more likely to give an association such as "pie–eat" (syntagmatic association). By the middle grades (approximately age 7 or 8), the association is increasingly likely to be based on an adult-like hierarchical set of categories, such as "pie–cake," "pie–cherry," or "pie–food" (paradigmatic association) (Ervin, 1961).

Children of all ages associate things and ideas in a variety of ways. This hierarchy represents development in *preferred* modes of organizing. An understanding of these developmental trends helps clinicians and teachers design tasks that form a best fit with the processing abilities of the child.

Therefore, when preschoolers emerge from brain injury with evidence of substantial conceptual and behavioral disorganization, there is value in helping them reestablish organized thinking by recreating the organizing scripts that were central to their experience before the injury. This is in contrast to the common therapy practice of using available curricular materials, which typically focus on semantic categories or perceptual attributes (e.g., color, shape, and size) as the primary form of organization. Structuring the preschooler's organizing activity around familiar themes or scripts has two advantages. First, the learning is old learning (recovering what had been learned before the injury), which tends to be easier than new learning following brain injury. Second, the organizational schemes that are presented fit with the child's level of cognitive development. Later in recovery, children may need help learning *new* organizing scripts as well as other forms of organizational schemata (see Table 5.1). In Case Study 5.2, we describe techniques used to help a kindergartner regain organizational abilities following TBI.

A similar focus in intervention might be considered for older children and adolescents who are relatively early in their process of cognitive recovery and whose thinking continues to be characterized by disorganization, concreteness, and egocentrism. Although severe brain injury does not produce a systematic developmental regression in all aspects of cognitive functioning, clinicians and family members consistently include many developmentally early features of cognition in their descriptions of older individuals with significant cognitive weakness following TBI. Therefore, using approaches that combine procedures that are known to promote cognitive growth in preschoolers with appropriate and respectful content is a reasonable starting point for addressing issues in organization and memory with older children.

CASE STUDY 5.2

Organizational Deficits

BT was injured in an automobile accident in the fall of his kindergarten year, shortly after his fifth birthday. He was minimally responsive for a week and did not interact purposefully with the environment for 2 weeks. When he became responsive, he did not use the left side of his body and neglected things in his left visual field. He was fiercely distractible, with an attention span of a few seconds. When he began to speak, he repeated what others said or he said things that did not fit the context. He frequently rhymed words, presumably based on the rhyming exercises that had been part of his kindergarten curriculum. He used simple sentences that were grammatically correct, but he seemed unable to connect more than one thought about a subject.

This difficulty organizing ideas was also evident in BT's play. He did not organize representational toys into meaningful scripts, connect ideas in his drawing, or organize building toys (e.g., Tinker Toys) in a meaningful way. A similar problem was evident in activities of daily living. BT seemed to get lost in the middle of apparently simple tasks such as brushing his teeth or putting on his shoes and socks. His behavior was a source of considerable frustration for nursing staff and therapists, because his excellent speech and language recovery, as well as his general level of alertness and apparent intelligence, suggested that he should be capable of a much higher level of performance of these basic tasks.

BT appeared at this time to have unusual memory functioning. Certain events, sometimes apparently meaningless events, were recalled in great detail. However, BT's recall of information that was explicitly taught to him was extremely weak. Similar results were obtained when BT's memory was probed in a structured way. When presented with nine animals and told that his job was to remember them and say back as many as possible after presentation (deliberate learning), he freely recalled only three. However, when asked to sort the same animals into groups for purposes of playing a game with them, he subsequently recalled seven without cues (involuntary or incidental learning).

The hypothesis used to explain BT's uniformly weak performance on organizational tasks and varied performance on memory tasks was that he had very inefficient access to the specific organizational schemes that he had relied on before his injury to organize his play, activities of daily living, expressive language, and recall of information. Furthermore, because of his developmental level and specific organizational weakness, telling him that his job was to learn something (deliberate learning) predictably caused significant deterioration in his performance relative to simply engaging him in interesting tasks that made sense to him and then presenting the to-be-learned information in that meaningful context (involuntary or incidental learning).

Therapy sessions and carry-over activities on the nursing unit and with family, therefore, focused on reestablishing his basic organizational schemes in the context of meaningful activities in which *his* goal was something other than learning organizational schemes. BT's mother gave staff detailed descriptions of the scripts and routines that were common to his experience (e.g., getting up and going to school, going to church, visiting his aunt, helping his father with chores, going camping). These were recreated in dramatic play or drawing. BT would then be asked to describe the event that was drawn or acted out. These descriptions or stories were written and BT carried them with him throughout the day; staff and family frequently reviewed these written scripts with BT so that he had a large number of reviews every day. New organizational scripts were added when BT evidenced adequate ability to describe the previous script without cues. In addition, pictures were taken of him completing his daily living routines (e.g., getting dressed, washing up) and placed in order on a ring that he carried with him to the task. He was cued to use these pictures to guide himself through his activities of daily living in an organized manner.

The features of BT's therapy program that are important for young children recovering from brain injury (or older children with significant cognitive impairment) are the following:

1. BT was taught using involuntary (incidental) versus deliberate learning procedures; that is, he was never told that his job was to learn something or to remember or to be better organized. Young children and cognitively impaired older children tend to learn far more effectively when they are engaged in tasks that are meaningful and enjoyable, and have a goal that is intrinsic to the task (e.g., creating some kind of product), than when they are told that their goal is to learn.

2. Initially, the organizational schemes that were taught were real-event scripts. The developmental literature suggests that this

type of organization is natural to preschoolers and is helpful in facilitating improved memory.

3. At the outset, the focus was on pretraumatically familiar scripts. Recovery of old learning is often easier for children with TBI than learning new information. Subsequently, new organizational schemes were introduced.
4. Putting BT's scripts on paper served the purpose of giving him a concrete goal in telling his stories, but also made possible a large number of reviews over the course of the day.
5. Having BT guide himself through activities of daily living using pictures of himself allowed him to be independently successful at these tasks without nagging. It also served as another form of practice of functional real-event scripts.

Feature analysis as an organized retrieval strategy

Many children with TBI have difficulty retrieving information from memory. This difficulty may be a result of poorly controlled attention, disorganized thoughts, disorganized searches of memory, poor initiation or monitoring of memory searches, or other factors. Searches of memory are often terminated with the first piece of information retrieved. Furthermore, little or no evaluation of the adequacy, completeness, appropriateness, or relevance of the information may occur before a response is formulated. If information is missing, children often fail to initiate an external search (e.g., questioning others, looking in reference materials). Inadequate search-and-retrieval behavior may have far-reaching consequences for problem solving and judgment, because errors are often based on inadequate or irrelevant information rather than on deficits in reasoning or social attitude.

Feature analysis is an organizing procedure that is useful in facilitating (a) deliberate control of attention (selective attention and shifting attention); (b) self-monitoring of knowledge of a topic; (c) organized retrieval of information or words; (d) organized discourse (descriptions or narratives); and (e) practical use of information in problem solving (Haarbauer-Krupa, Moser, Smith, Sullivan, & Szekeres, 1985). During feature analysis activities, one or another of these goals can be highlighted through the teacher's specific task demands and feedback. For example, if the focus is on selective attention, children are challenged to give only information that is relevant to the feature in focus and are rewarded for doing so.

The goals and procedures of feature analysis are consistent with the psycholinguistic and neurolinguistic hypothesis that information is stored in networks. Individual facts or features are connected by "links" or associative connections that facilitate retrieval of connected information (Smith, 1978). The purpose of feature analysis in therapy is to activate or create these links in an organized manner and to practice retrieving information by means of these organizational cues in practical activities such as constructing narratives or solving problems.

The initial phase of treatment involves a guided analysis of meaningful basic-level concepts (e.g., *dog, baseball, book*) using the following categories for analysis: superordinate category (e.g., a dog is an animal), action (e.g., a dog runs, bites, fetches, barks), use (e.g., a dog is used for hunting, guarding the house, companion-

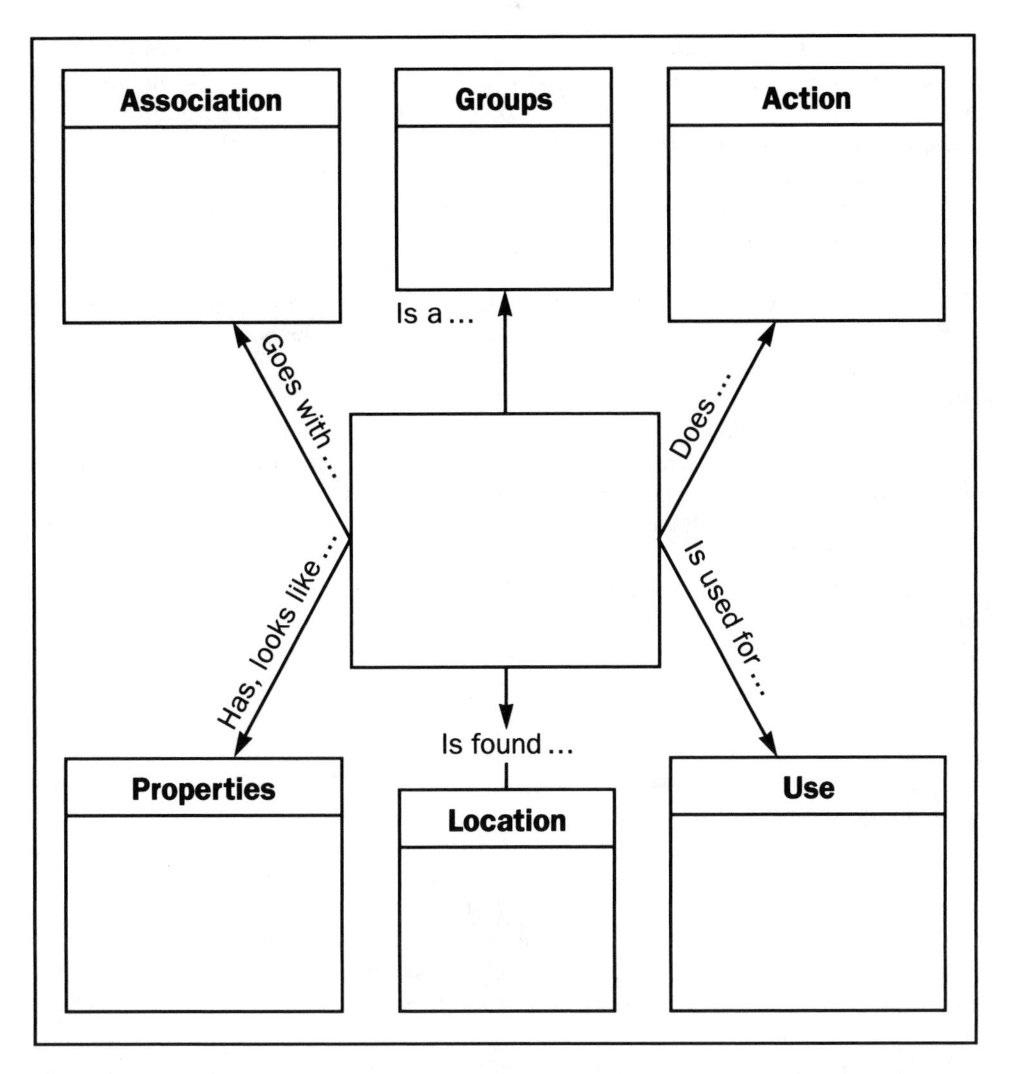

Figure 5.1. Feature analysis guide. From "Topics in Cognitive Rehabilitation Therapy" by M. Ylvisaker, S. Szekeres, K. Henry, D. Sullivan, and P. Wheeler, in *Community Re-Entry for Head Injured Adults* (p. 163) by M. Ylvisaker and E.M. Gobble (Eds.), 1987, Austin, TX: PRO-ED. Reproduced with permission.

ship), location (e.g., a dog can be found in a kennel, pet shop, doghouse), properties (e.g., a dog has body parts, good sense of smell, strong loyalty), and associations (e.g., "When I think of dogs, I think of bones, cats, shedding, licking my face, my uncle who hunted with dogs").

Figure 5.1 illustrates a feature analysis guide that can be used to structure the children's search through their knowledge base. Information is written in the appropriate boxes and evaluated for relevance, accuracy, and completeness. The sentence cues (e.g., ". . . is a . . . ," ". . . does . . .") can be used with younger children; older children are encouraged to think more abstractly by using the category cues (e.g., category, use, action, etc.) rather than the concrete sentence completion cues. If the children have completed their analysis and boxes are unfilled or sparsely filled, then the children are encouraged to *evaluate* their job (i.e., knowledge monitoring) and to *investigate* the concept further by asking good questions or by using reference materials.

In the early stages, the feature analysis activity (ideally done in groups) is designed to improve the children's selective and controlled attention, thoughtfulness about a topic, active search of memory, and evaluation of their contributions. Later, children are encouraged to learn the procedure itself; that is, they are expected to generate the diagram and the box labels, and to give reasons for this system of organizing information. In this way, they are encouraged to use the organizational scheme as a strategy for searching memory when information or words are needed.

As with all cognitive intervention activities, this thinking procedure must be connected explicitly with practical activities in which it might be used. For example, having generated information about an object using the guide, the children might use the information to write a clear description of the object, complete a similarities–differences exercise with some other concept, write a story in which the object figures prominently, or do a problem-solving exercise in which the information that had been generated about the object is needed to solve the problem. Table 5.2 presents lesson plans that incorporate the use of feature analysis procedures and their practical application.

The same type of activity could be used with adolescents, but with age-appropriate concepts and activities. Even relatively abstract concepts lend themselves to analysis using this procedure. A social skills group, for example, may wish to clarify their understanding of conversations by analyzing the concept *conversation*. A prevocational group may benefit from thoughtful analysis of concepts such as *interview, boss,* or *performance appraisal.* Analysis would be followed by various types of discussion, problem solving, or role playing, again making explicit use of the information generated through the feature analysis.

After the basic analysis procedure is well established and can be carried out independently, children are encouraged to use the procedure in describing things for which they are unable to retrieve the word. They are also encouraged to determine which features of a concept they do not know (e.g., where crocodiles are found) and to identify a way of finding that information (e.g., looking in an encyclopedia). Elaboration of knowledge is encouraged by asking additional questions, such as how, when, who, and why questions.

Feature analysis exercises can be used to encourage *divergent* thinking in children who have difficulty generating varied information about a topic or more than one or two features per category. Alternatively, they can be used to encourage *convergent* thinking in children who produce large numbers of features, many of which may be irrelevant or tangential; with these children, it is important to restrict contributions to the one or two *most important* features per category and discuss why these features are most important.

Finally, feature analysis exercises provide a useful context in which to encourage recovery of reading skills. The children's dictated contributions are written clearly in the boxes and, when complete, they review the analysis by reading the words that have been written. Reading is facilitated because the words are semantically connected in a highly structured way and because they are words that the children have recently dictated. Similarly, children can be asked to read the descriptive paragraph that they have dictated. The probability of success with reading is increased when the children read what they have just dictated. These exercises are easy for parents to use at home.

TABLE 5.2. Feature Analysis for Young Children: Sample Lesson Plans

Monday

1. Using the Feature Analysis Guide (Figure 5.1) and play objects, the group will generate information about dogs.
2. Using the information that they have retrieved, the group will write a descriptive paragraph about a dog. One of the members of the group will present the description in a "show-and-tell" manner.

Tuesday

1. The group will repeat Monday's activities, but focusing on the concept *cat*.

Wednesday

1. The group will retrieve the information from the two previous days.
2. The group will identify similarities and differences between dogs and cats.

Thursday

1. The group will write a short play or story in which a dog and a cat are prominent characters.
2. The group will act out the play, or a member of the group will tell the story to a listener.

Friday

1. The group will identify a practical problem that includes one or more of the week's concepts (e.g., a dog chased my cat up a tree).
2. Using the information that they had retrieved about dogs and cats, the group will generate a good solution to the problem.
3. In solving the problem, the group will use an organized problem-solving procedure:
   a. Identify the problem and the goal
   b. Identify the relevant information
   c. List possible solutions
   d. Evaluate the possible solutions
   e. Select the best solution
   f. Make a plan

Higher levels of organization

Organizational problems of adolescents may have subtle manifestations. For example, their comprehension of a multipage text may be surprisingly weak because they have not been able to see how all of the details relate to one another to create a central theme for the text. As a corollary, memory for the text is reduced by the inability to organize the information. Conversation may be tangential because of loose associations that create hard-to-follow twists and turns in the conversation. Essays may be incoherent because of the lack of an organizing theme. Vocational tasks may be incomplete or slow because of difficulty organizing the task.

Adolescents may profit from an organizing procedure that is designed to enhance organization within specific tasks. For example, if reading comprehension is weak because of weak organization of the information, then a procedure must be designed with the specific goal of facilitating improved organization of information in that type of text (see Case Study 5.3). If written essays are poorly organized, teachers should give the student helpful organizing or outlining procedures specific to the type of essay to be written.

Comprehension strategies include very general procedures (e.g., "Relate the information to other things with which you are familiar," "Ask questions about anything you do not understand") and traditional study guides (e.g., the SQ3R method—survey, question, read, recite, review). Teaching procedures that are more specific to the task are often useful. For example, timelines may be the most appropriate organizational strategy for a history text. Appendixes 5A and 5B include several examples of organizational strategies. Strategies for individual students should be selected on the basis of several considerations discussed in the next section of this chapter.

CASE STUDY 5.3

Organization and Deliberate Memory

MS was injured in an automobile accident in March of her sophomore year of high school. Prior to the injury, she was an above-average (A–B) student with above-average intelligence. She was essentially unresponsive for more than a month. She began to talk approximately 10 weeks postinjury and walked independently about a month later. Residual motor impairments included a mild left-sided hemiparesis and speech that was noticeably slurred, breathy, and monotonous.

Following resolution of significant confusion and disorientation (late August), her cognitive profile included adequate attentional skills; mildly disorganized perceptual functioning, with subtle signs of left visual field neglect; good receptive and expressive language skills at the level of vocabulary, syntax, and morphology; word-retrieval problems; disorganized narratives and other types of discourse; and concrete thinking. Her academic profile was very spotty. For example, she had recovered many higher-level ninth-grade skills (e.g., some of what she had learned in algebra), but had lost many lower-level skills (e.g., much of the multiplication tables). Her reading was excellent at the level of word recognition and phonics. Word and sentence comprehension tested within rough normal limits. However, both reading and listening comprehension of multiparagraph passages tested at a third-grade level, with particular difficulty isolating main ideas and drawing inferences. MS enjoyed reading and read chapters in a favorite novel in the evening; however, the next day, she routinely remembered nothing of what she had read the previous night.

Her memory profile included good episodic memory (i.e., memory for events in her life, both pretrauma and recent events) but very weak memory for new information that was taught to her. This weakness was evidenced by low scores on memory tests: −3 standard deviations on the Consistent Long Term Retrieval measure of the *Selective Reminding Test* (Buschke & Fuld, 1974) and an early first-grade–level score on the Visual–Auditory

Learning subtest of the *Woodcock–Johnson Psycho-Educational Test Battery* (Woodcock & Johnson, 1989). At this time, MS had no comprehension of her residual cognitive deficits and insisted that she was ready to return to her community school. She was highly motivated to succeed at school.

When passages were discussed with MS—with a focus on how the details were organized around meaningful themes—her memory improved dramatically. Therefore, therapy was initiated based on the assumption that, although her memory was significantly impaired, she would be able to learn and remember much more effectively if she actively organized the information to be remembered. The initial goals were (a) to help her see that there was a problem and that it was important for her to do something about it, and (b) to help her understand the notion of organizing information to make it more memorable.

Several sessions were devoted to clarifying the concept of organization, starting with concrete organization of things (e.g., how furniture, clothes, jewelry, and books were organized in her bedroom) and of people (e.g., the various ways in which the students in her class were grouped for different purposes). In each case, the purpose of the organization was highlighted. It was noted that, in some cases, the purpose of organization is to find things more easily (e.g., the organization of clothes in her room). This was then used as an analogy for organizing information in our heads so that it is easier to find later. MS then recalled that her eighth-grade English teacher had taught the class to use wh– questions for this purpose.

MS did not yet see the point of doing anything special when she read her novel. Therefore, an experiment was designed. She read a chapter with no special effort. The next day, she freely recalled nothing and was able to answer very few specific questions about the chapter. Then she read the next chapter with the therapist helping her to take notes using a specially adapted form (see Table 5.3). The next day, she remembered most of what she had read, given wh– questions. Without the question cues, she freely recalled a modest amount of the information.

With 3 week's practice with the form, MS achieved excellent *cued* recall of information from the novel (i.e., correct responses to wh– questions), suggesting that she was using the procedure as an *encoding* strategy. Because her free recall remained weak, she required subsequent encouragement to use the form as her own internal retrieval cue. With an additional 3 week's practice, her *free* recall for information from chapters that she had read the previous evening was good. On posttesting, she demonstrated minimal improvement on memory and verbal learning tests. She remained at an early first-grade level on the Visual–Auditory Learning subtest of the *Woodcock–Johnson* and scored $-2\frac{1}{2}$ standard deviations on the Consistent Long Term Retrieval measure of the *Selective Reminding Test*. However, she scored within normal limits on both listening and reading comprehension tasks, given ninth-grade–level multiparagraph passages. These results suggested that, whereas her general memory and verbal learning capacity had not improved (it was not a target of intervention and therefore served as a control procedure), her use of residual capacities to comprehend, retain, and retrieve information presented in narrative form had become much more effective.

The noteworthy features of this illustration are the following:

TABLE 5.3. Note-Taking Form for Comprehension of Fictional Narratives

Chapter Theme: ______________________

Episode #1 Theme: ______________________

Who: ______________________

Where: ______________________

When: ______________________

What Happened: ______________________

How Resolved: ______________________

Episode #2 Theme: ______________________

Who: ______________________

Where: ______________________

When: ______________________

What Happened: ______________________

How Resolved: ______________________

1. MS was actively engaged with the therapist in identifying her cognitive weakness and its impact on her functional goals, and in selecting a solution.
2. The concept of organizing ideas was explored and clarified in very concrete and meaningful terms.
3. The need to use a compensatory procedure was concretely demonstrated by means of a "product-monitoring" task; that is, a meaningful, functional task was attempted with and without the comprehension strategy and the results were compared.
4. The compensatory procedure was based in part on a suggestion that MS made on her own.
5. The use of the procedure as a retrieval strategy had to be trained separately after it had already come to be used as an encoding strategy.
6. Acquisition of the strategy required several weeks of practice.
7. The strategy effected significant improvement on the specific task for which it was designed without having a *generalized* impact on verbal learning.
8. To ensure generalization and maintenance, specialized note-taking forms were developed for other types of reading (e.g., so-

cial studies text), all staff were alerted to the need to support these procedures, and MS's mother was oriented to the procedures and their rationale and was asked to encourage these strategies at home.

Teaching Compensatory Strategies

Strategic procedures designed to compensate for residual cognitive weakness range from those that are simple and concrete (e.g., carrying a schedule card) to those that presuppose considerable cognitive skill. For example, teaching a child to learn more efficiently by deliberately using complex study procedures has a variety of prerequisites that make this mode of intervention inappropriate for young children or children who, following brain injury, are in the stage of recovery characterized by disorientation and shallow, egocentric thinking. However, because cognitive development and cognitive recovery both come in degrees and because strategies vary in their prerequisites, professionals would be misguided to seek clear criteria separating strategic from nonstrategic children and to restrict strategy intervention to those children who meet specific criteria. In fact, strategic behavior begins with simple, concrete, externally focused strategic activities observed in preschoolers (e.g., putting a favorite toy someplace where it will be easily found).

Cognitive strategies—procedures deliberately used to enhance performance on cognitively demanding tasks—may involve the use of external aids (e.g., printed schedule, memory book, printed task organizer, calculator), overt behavior (e.g., asking for information to be repeated, counting on fingers, repeating information out loud), or covert behavior (e.g., mentally rehearsing, elaborating, or organizing information; guiding oneself through a task with covert instructions). In normal development and also recovery from brain injury, strategic behavior progresses from prompted use of simple external aids to internally directed use of more elaborate mental procedures. An important fact to remember in this discussion is that *strategy* refers to what students do to help themselves, *not* what the teacher does to help the student (i.e., instructional strategies).

Research on strategy intervention has shown that children in the early grades and children with mild to moderate cognitive impairment profit from experimenter-prompted mnemonic strategies (Flavell, 1976). However, these children rarely transfer strategic behavior to other tasks. Only older and cognitively more intact children evidence transfer of strategic behavior to similar tasks, maintenance of the behavior over time, and effective use of strategic procedures without prompting (Brown & Barclay, 1976; Butterfield & Belmont, 1977; Keeney, Cannizzo, & Flavell, 1967; Pressley & Levin, 1983a, 1983b).

Selecting candidates for strategy intervention: Assessment

Unfortunately, no standardized procedures exist to determine if a given child is a candidate for learning and using cognitive strategies or to determine what type of strategy and what level of abstractness or concreteness of strategic behavior are appropriate. The large literature on procedures for teaching strategies (Alley & Deshler, 1979; Brown, 1974; Deshler, Alley, Warner, & Schumaker, 1981; Forrest-Pressley, MacKinnon, & Waller, 1985; Meichenbaum, 1977; Pressley, 1993; Pressley & Associates, 1990; Pressley, Borkowski, & Schneider, 1987; Pressley, Johnson, Symons, McGoldrick, & Kurita, 1989; Pressley & Levin, 1983a, 1983b) has not been paralleled by the development of techniques for assessing children's functioning in areas related to strategy use.

One of the obstacles to developing a "strategy readiness" test is that many factors have an impact on the acquisition and development of strategic behavior. Knowing the characteristics of mature, effective strategy users helps teachers and clinicians identify the areas that require careful assessment. Table 5.4 presents a list of characteristics of good strategy users, modified from the model described by Pressley, Goodchild, and colleagues (1989). These characteristics should suggest probes that clinicians can use to obtain a general picture of where a child is in relation to strategy use. Students who have all of the characteristics are not in need of strategy intervention because they are already adequately strategic. Students who fall short in most of the areas will at least need to have prerequisites addressed before strategies are introduced. Most students are somewhere between these two extremes and may require a period of diagnostic teaching of strategies to determine their level of readiness. The list of characteristics of good strategy users can also be considered a list of potential goals for strategy intervention.

Weak functioning in any of these areas jeopardizes the success of strategy intervention. For example, students who lack goals or are unaware of their cognitive limitations are unlikely to put effort into acquiring strategies. Because TBI is commonly associated with weak awareness of residual deficits, this is a particularly important consideration with these students. Similarly, if students are not vividly aware of the power of strategies to enhance performance or of their ability to use strategies, then they will lack interest in this intervention.

If students do not understand to what specific tasks a strategy applies, they may fail to use it when appropriate or may use it when not appropriate. In either case, they will not experience the success necessary to maintain strategic behavior. Similarly, if they use a strategy appropriately but fail to monitor its positive effect on their performance—or attribute improved performance to luck or some other factor—then their effort will not be reinforced and maintained.

Strategy intervention must be sufficiently intensive to make the behavior automatic. If special problem-solving effort is required every time the student faces a cognitively demanding task, the costs of this behavior may easily outweigh the benefits. The need for automaticity is particularly important for students who have restricted working memory (i.e., they cannot hold much information in mind at one time). These students may be unable to consider the problem at hand and at the same time think about a strategic procedure that will help deal with the problem. The same considerations support the use of strategic procedures that involve very few steps and are simple to master.

Students who are extremely impulsive are not good candidates for strategy intervention. Typically, they act long before it occurs to them that a strategy may have been helpful. However, because impulsiveness comes in degrees, caution must be exercised in making judgments about students' inability to use strategies. Severely impulsive students may profit from external reminders or other external aid strategies, whereas mildly impulsive students may benefit from simple "Wait!" strategies. Anxiety also interferes with strategy use, because anxious students may be so concerned with failure that they forget to use the procedures that could ensure success.

Environmental support is critical for the success of strategy intervention. For example, if a student is taught in a speech therapy session to ask for spoken instruc-

TABLE 5.4. Characteristics of Good Strategy Users

1. *Goals*	Good strategy users have goals to which strategies are relevant.
2. *Metacognitive knowledge*	Good strategy users know that their performance needs to be enhanced, that strategies enhance performance, and that they are capable of using strategies.
3. *Strategy-specific knowledge*	Good strategy users know when, where, how, and why to use specific strategies.
4. *Self-monitoring*	Good strategy users can monitor the effectiveness of their performance with strategies so that improved performance can be its own reward and ineffective performance can be changed.
5. *Flexibility*	Good strategy users know several strategic procedures and can select the procedure that is useful for a specific problem.
6. *Automaticity*	Good strategy users reach a point at which strategic procedures are automatic and require little effort or planning.
7. *Attentional space*	Good strategy users have adequate working memory so that they can think about the task at hand and strategic procedures at the same time.
8. *Impulsiveness*	Good strategy users are not so impulsive that they act before taking critical information into account and considering strategies.
9. *Anxiety*	Good strategy users are not so anxious about performance that they neglect strategies because of a dominant focus on fear of failure.
10. *Support*	Good strategy users receive support from teachers, parents, and others for the use of strategies.
11. *General knowledge*	Good strategy users know enough about a subject that they can meaningfully apply strategies to learn more.

Adapted from "The Challenges of Classroom Strategy Instruction" by M. Pressley, F. Goodchild, J. Fleet, R. Zajchowski, and E. D. Evans, 1989, *Elementary School Journal*, 89, 301–342.

tions to be written down and subsequently the teacher in the classroom refuses to do this because it would be unfair to the other students or take too much time, the student is unlikely to maintain this strategy. Similarly, parents can interfere with the success of strategy intervention if they believe that using strategic procedures is a sign of laziness or will interfere with the recovery of normal cognitive functioning. These considerations underscore the importance of an integrated approach to strategy intervention and of parent counseling.

Because of the number and complexity of the factors listed in Table 5.4, it is often difficult to know whether a student will profit from strategy intervention without a trial period of therapy. Students who are unable to master and internalize strategies may still be candidates for treatment that focuses on prerequisite skills. Because cognitive deficits make the use of strategies particularly important for these students, it is useful to begin focusing on the skills related to successful strategy use in the early grade school years.

Selecting strategies

Unfortunately, teachers and therapists commonly approach strategy intervention by identifying the student's need (e.g., inefficient comprehension of extended text), selecting a procedure that is designed to compensate for this deficit (e.g., a summarizing or note-taking strategy using wh– questions), and then proceeding to teach the student to use the strategy. What is critically missing from this approach is the student's active involvement in identifying the problem and the solution. Because strategic behavior is essentially active, problem-solving behavior, an approach that renders the student a passive recipient of this instruction is fundamentally flawed. If the student lacks an appreciation of the problem, lacks motivation to perform better, does not see the point of the strategy, or finds the strategy objectionable in some way, then the intervention has little chance to succeed. Therefore, selection of strategies for individual students should be considered a process of *negotiation* and shared problem solving between the student and the teacher or therapist. The process often begins with tasks designed to reveal the need for improved performance in areas of interest to the student ("product-monitoring" tasks, Haarbauer-Krupa, Henry, et al., 1985), followed by brainstorming on procedures that may promote success.

Table 5.5 lists factors that should be considered in selecting a strategy for a student who has already been determined to be a candidate for strategy intervention. Failure to consider these factors can jeopardize strategy intervention even if the student is a good candidate. For example, if a procedure is selected that successfully compensates for the student's cognitive deficit, but is novel, complex, and difficult, fails to capitalize on the student's strengths, and embarrasses the student, then it will not be used regardless of its potential to overcome an obstacle to successful performance.

Above all, the most critical component of strategy intervention is active student involvement in identifying the problem, selecting the procedure to compensate for the problem, and evaluating its effectiveness. There may be tension between the student's inclinations and the teacher's judgment. For example, a student with impaired fine motor functioning may find it natural to take notes, despite being a slow and ineffective note taker. Through a process of experimentation (including product monitoring) and negotiation, the most effective procedure should emerge. However, if the student's inclination is disregarded and the process is entirely driven by the teacher, generalized use of the strategy is unlikely.

Appendixes 5A and 5B present some of the cognitive problems with which students with TBI frequently struggle, along with a selection of strategies that can be explored for individual students. It is typically not difficult to find a strategy that could help a student overcome an obstacle posed by cognitive deficits. The difficulty—and it is a substantial difficulty—lies in matching the student with the strategy, engaging the

TABLE 5.5. Important Considerations in Selecting Specific Strategies for Specific Students

Consideration	Description
1. *Spontaneous use*	Other things being equal, procedures that a student uses spontaneously are preferable to essentially new procedures.
2. *Complexity and abstractness*	Simple, concrete, externally focused, and possibly externally cued procedures are preferable for young or significantly impaired students.
3. *Difficulty of use*	Difficult and time-consuming procedures are appropriate only if the payoff is substantial. Strategies should be as simple as possible.
4. *Domain of applicability*	Depending on the purpose of the strategy, either task-specific strategies (e.g., an outlining procedure for processing narrative text; mnemonics to remember people's names) or highly generalizable strategies (e.g., asking for clarification, checking one's work) may be selected.
5. *Neuropsychological strengths*	Strategies should capitalize on the student's strengths.
6. *Metacognitive requirements*	Strategies that require a high degree of self-insight or subtle situational discrimination and perception of task demands are not appropriate for young or significantly impaired students.
7. *Personality fit*	For example, strategies that involve social interactive behavior that is potentially stigmatizing (e.g., asking for help) are appropriate only for students who find this behavior emotionally acceptable.
8. *Negotiation*	The probability of generalized use of strategies is increased if the student is involved in selecting the procedure.

student's motivation and participation, and teaching the strategy in such a way that it becomes a functional part of the student's repertoire.

Selecting teaching procedures

Teaching strategies is in some ways like teaching any other skill, and therefore general principles and techniques of good teaching apply. These include (a) careful task analysis; (b) systematic progression from simple, easy-to-master components to more complex procedures; (c) gradual fading of cues and prompts that were designed specifically at each stage to ensure success; (d) limited goals, so the student can see the task as manageable and experience success; (e) reasonable criterion levels, again based on what the student can reasonably be expected to master; (f) a natural progression from describing the new behavior and modeling its use, to having the student verbally rehearse and practice, first with controlled materials and subsequently with classroom materials (Deshler et al., 1981); (g) some fun in the process.

Table 5.6 outlines a program of strategy intervention. The four phases of the program (general strategic thinking, selecting specific strategic procedures, teaching specific strategies, generalization and maintenance) are broadly sequential but can overlap. For example, the metacognitive awareness that is the goal of Phase I is important; however, it is not necessary that the student achieve a high level of general strategic awareness before proceeding with specific strategy instruction. Similarly, it is not necessary in every case to achieve a high level of mastery with the procedure before proceeding with activities designed to enhance generalization and maintenance. For example, some students are so concrete in their thinking that practicing a procedure in an artificial context actually interferes with its use in a functional context because the students may have come to associate the procedure with some aspect of the artificial context. Similarly, a student with limited motivation may lose interest in a strategic procedure if forced to practice it in a context in which it lacks real-world benefit. For these students, generalization activities are included from the beginning of instruction.

The acquisition phase of strategy intervention may tend more toward the self-discovery end or the direct instruction end of the teaching continuum. If required, direct instruction begins with a description of the procedure, including both what the student is expected to do and what purpose the strategy is supposed to serve. Teacher or peer modeling, with elicited imitation, adds a needed concrete element to the verbal description so that the behavior expected of the student is amply clear. During the modeling, it is useful to include planned thinking out loud to ensure that the student understands not only the specific overt behavior, but also the cognitive processes underlying the behavior and the purposes that this behavior serves. The student should be encouraged to ask questions during the modeling and then to rehearse the strategy.

The generalization and maintenance phase of strategy intervention deserves special attention. In most cases, the litmus test of good teaching is the student's generalization of the skill to varied settings and tasks, and maintenance of the skill over time. When attempts to teach a skill or change a behavior fail, it is most often *not* because the skill could not be acquired in a training context, but rather because it did not transfer to other tasks, generalize to other settings, or persist over time. Therefore, if the goal is to have the student use the procedure without cuing in a variety of tasks under varied conditions, then the generalization and maintenance procedures outlined in Table 5.6 are a critical component of the intervention.

An alternative approach to generalization, useful for individuals with significant cognitive impairment and limited potential to generalize new skills, is simply to give up the goal of generalization. In this case, students are taught a procedure that improves performance of a specific task in a specific context. The student is not expected to use the procedure in other tasks, and ongoing cuing is ensured by means of cue cards or teacher–supervisor prompting. This approach is illustrated by an adolescent's use of a task-organizing strategy in a vocational situation. The strategy may be very useful in promoting improved efficiency and on-task behavior in the absence of a realistic expectation that the student could generalize the behavior to other tasks or maintain its use without cues.

In light of the cognitive and psychosocial characteristics of many students with TBI, teachers and therapists must creatively use techniques designed to capture and

TABLE 5.6. Teaching Compensatory Strategies

Phase I: General Strategic Thinking

A. Metacognitive awareness

Goals: Students will discriminate effective from ineffective performance; become aware of their strengths and weaknesses; recognize implications of their deficits.

Rationale: Given the frequency of frontolimbic and right hemisphere damage in children with head injuries, self-awareness is frequently compromised. Individuals are unlikely to acquire and use procedures designed to compensate for problems that they do not recognize as problems.

Procedures:

1. *Objective:* Improve the student's perception of successful versus unsuccessful task performance. Illustrate successful and unsuccessful performance of a functional task through role play or on videotape. With the student, analyze the performances in sufficient detail that the student can identify the features that account for successful versus unsuccessful performance.
2. *Objective:* Improve the student's ability to perceive functional impairments. Individually, request that the student make note of specific deficits of other students in the program or of individuals observed on tape. Discuss these observations. Planned peer teaching is useful. Discuss the effects of head injury on cognitive and social functioning. If appropriate, read and discuss literature on the effects of head injury.
3. *Objective:* Improve the student's awareness of his or her own strengths and weaknesses. Videotape the student in activities designed to reveal strong and weak areas of functioning. (Alternatively, use role play.) Review the tapes (beginning with strong performance), first without commentary, and subsequently inviting comments about what was done well and what needs improvement. Gradually turn over to the student the responsibility for stopping the tape when problems are noted. **NOTE:** *Considerable desensitizing may be needed before video self-viewing is possible.*
4. *Objective:* Improve the student's understanding of the relation between deficits and long-term goals. Discuss in concrete detail the individual's long-term goals and expectations. Jointly create a list of specific skills and resources needed to achieve these goals. Jointly identify the skills that are present and those that are weak relative to this goal.

NOTE: *These metacognitive discoveries are facilitated if the activities are personally meaningful and intimately connected to the student's goals.*

B. Value of being strategic

Goal: Students will recognize the importance of being strategic and will identify the characteristics of strategic people.

Rationale: Because the ultimate goal of this intervention is to promote strategic thinking and strategic behavior in general—not simply to teach specific strategic behaviors as routines—it is important that the student understand what it is to be strategic and that these are valuable attributes.

(*continues*)

TABLE 5.6. *Continued*

Procedures:

1. *Objective:* Improve the student's understanding of strategy. Using games, sports, or other relevant model, clarify the concept of strategy as something that one does to achieve goals when there are obstacles.
2. *Objective:* Heighten the student's appreciation of strategic behavior. Together with the student, identify several individuals who are known to be very strategic (e.g., sports heroes, military heroes). Discuss why they are considered heroic. Clinicians should also clearly model their own strategic behavior and discuss the value of their own strategies.
3. *Objective:* Improve the student's understanding of the behaviors that are part of being strategic. Using models relevant to the student (e.g., military, sports, or business analogies), brainstorm about the characteristics of people who are known to be very strategic. Include the following: high level of motivation and initiative, ability to identify and clarify obstacles to goals; ability to plan procedures to overcome obstacles; ability to monitor and evaluate performance; willingness to engage in ongoing problem solving.

Phase II: Selecting Specific Strategic Procedures

Goal: Students will identify specific procedures useful in overcoming important personal obstacles.

Rationale: It is important that students participate in the selection of strategic procedures that they will use and that the procedures be truly useful in achieving their goals.

Procedures:

1. Use group brainstorming procedures to identify possible strategies.
2. Use "product monitoring" tasks to test the value of strategies: Have the student perform a task with and without the strategy or with a variety of different strategies. Objectively compare the results. (Video analysis may be useful here.)
3. Have advanced students demonstrate the value of certain procedures or offer testimonials.
4. Discuss the widespread use of compensatory procedures (lists, memos, tape recorders, etc.) by people who do not have brain injury.

Phase III: Teaching Specific Strategies

NOTE: *If the discovery procedures in Phase II (e.g., brainstorming and product monitoring) are effective, there may be little need for specific teaching procedures.*

Procedures:

A. *Modeling:* The steps in the strategy can be modeled by the therapist or by a peer, or by means of videotape or other media. Modeling is initially accompanied by overt ver-

(*continues*)

TABLE 5.6. *Continued*

balization of the strategy by the model. The student then rehearses the strategy with gradually decreasing cues and self-talk.

B. *Direct instruction:* The carefully programmed behavioral teaching procedures of direct instruction can be used to teach strategies. However, if this is the only approach used, the best result will likely be the acquisition of a learned sequence of behaviors (which may be a desireable outcome), without positive movement in the direction of becoming a strategic person.

C. *Functional practice:* However the strategy is acquired, it must be frequently rehearsed in natural settings using functional activities.

Phase IV: Generalization and Maintenance

Generalization of strategic behavior beyond the context of training is a combined consequence of the perceived utility of the strategy for the individual, the inherent generalizability and utility of the strategy, widespread environmental support for strategic behavior and thinking, and specific teaching procedures designed to enhance generalization.

Note 1: Generalization includes generalized use of specific strategies as well as strategic behavior in general.

Note 2: Generalization may not be a separate phase if the acquisition stage takes place in the context of functional activities and natural settings. This is particularly important for very concrete people.

Note 3: Generalization may be a relatively unimportant phase of intervention if the individual has acquired a strategic attitude and actively seeks occasions for transfer.

Note 4: Some individuals may need environmental reminders indefinitely to use their strategic procedures.

1. *Objective:* Improve the student's discrimination of situations that require or do not require a given strategy.
   - Use videotaped scenes or role play to illustrate the correct use of a strategy in an appropriate situation, inappropriate use of the strategy, and failure to use the strategy when appropriate. Discuss the conditions that require the strategy.
   - Use short videotaped scenes to train the student in efficient and accurate judgments as to whether a strategy is appropriate in a context.
2. *Objective:* Increase the student's spontaneous use of strategies in varied situations.
   - Include family members, work supervisors, and teachers in strategy intervention to (a) provide varied opportunities for the use of specific strategies and of strategic behavior in general, (b) reinforce the student's use of strategies, and (c) model strategic behavior themselves.
   - Ask students to keep a log in which they record their successes and failures in strategy use. Make generalization an explicit goal.

(*continues*)

TABLE 5.6. *Continued*

3. *Objective:* Increase the student's acceptance of strategic behavior.
   - Ensure that the student is successful using strategies.
   - Promote emotional acceptance of strategic behavior by using whatever motivating procedures work (e.g., personal images or metaphors, testimonials).

Note: These phases of intervention are not necessarily hierarchical or mutually exclusive.
Modified from "Cognitive Rehabilitation Therapy: Late Stages of Recovery" by J. Haarbauer-Krupa, K. Henry, S. F. Szekeres, and M. Ylvisaker, in *Head Injury Rehabilitation: Children and Adolescents* (pp. 318–319) by M. Ylvisaker (Ed.), 1985, Austin, TX: PRO-ED. Printed with permission.

retain the student's interest and engagement in the process. These include the following:

1. *Product-monitoring tasks:* The student performs a functional task with and without the use of the strategy, and then evaluates the performance ("monitors the product"). These tasks are designed to ensure that the student sees the point of the procedure and the benefit for him or her. Tasks must be selected that relate in some way to the student's goals or the strategy will have little perceived value. Therapists can use classroom tasks for this purpose because their utility is typically better understood by students than less familiar therapy tasks.
2. *Feedback:* As with all teaching, positive feedback on performance promotes learning. Strategy teaching should particularly highlight the *value* of the strategy in relation to the student's goals. Good teachers must be good "salesmen" when the skill they are teaching may be difficult to master or potentially embarrassing to use.
3. *Negotiation:* The student–teacher brainstorming, negotiating, and joint problem solving that are components of selecting a strategy should continue as strategies are modified over time. For example, a student may wish to give up a large memory book in exchange for a more discrete memo pad, or a student who no longer feels that taking elaborate notes is necessary may propose simply highlighting important points in the text.
4. *Overcoming resistance:* Students with limited understanding of their deficits or fear of doing anything that would identify them as "different" are likely to resist strategy intervention. Overcoming resistance may require counseling focused on adjustment to disability. Other techniques include helpful images and metaphors (e.g., "Doing this is like Joe Montana's wearing a back brace when he was hurt") and testimonials from trusted peers. Teachers should take advantage of opportunities to model and discuss their own strategies for overcoming functional obstacles.
5. *Limited goals:* It is easy to overwhelm students with too many goals, especially if the teachers and therapists do not actively inte-

grate their interventions and mutually identify a small number of priority areas for intervention. Students receiving services from several teachers and therapists must have a program coordinator whose job it is to ensure that the student's overall program is appropriately targeted and limited in scope. Often, intervention across the entire program must be limited to two or three critical goals with all staff focused on the same objectives.

6. *Support:* Considerable effort is required to become an effective strategy user and active problem solver. Support and encouragement from peers, teachers, and parents are therefore critical to the success of the program. MS, whose program of intervention was described in Case Study 5.3 as an illustration of intervention for higher-level organizational deficits, also illustrates many of the critical components of strategy instruction. Although she was not enthusiastic about approaching learning tasks in a way that was different from what she was comfortable with before her injury, she persevered with a great deal of support from a deeply committed and helpful mother and excellent teachers. Despite the severity of her challenges after the injury, she completed high school and enrolled in a state college program for students with learning disabilities.

Content, process, and strategy

When asked to focus increasing classroom attention on students' acquisition of cognitive–learning strategies or on improving cognitive processes, teachers often complain that the time required to teach academic content precludes this additional focus. This frustration is understandable. Teachers are evaluated primarily on the basis of their students' achievement of specific academic objectives or performance on standardized tests of academic content. Therefore, they are naturally resistant to classroom practices that are perceived as being in competition with teaching the core academic curriculum.

To a large degree, however, this reaction is based on a misunderstanding of the relation between teaching academic content on the one hand and improving cognitive processes and strategic behaviors on the other. Traditional methods for teaching arithmetic present a useful model for these relationships. Because multiple-digit adding, subtracting, and multiplying are cognitively demanding tasks, organized strategic procedures have been developed to make these tasks easier. These procedures include "carrying" and "borrowing" (i.e., "regrouping"). Teachers would not consider teaching arithmetic (academic content) without at the same time teaching these procedures (strategies). Indeed, the strategies are so commonly included in the curriculum that they are considered part of the academic content. Less customary but equally useful strategies used to facilitate performance in other areas—for example, comprehension and expression of language, efficient perceptual scanning, and selective attention—can similarly be taught as part of teaching curricular content. If understood in this way, the time devoted to teaching strategies is not in competition with time needed to teach content, but rather is time invested in increasing the ease with which students are able to master content. Furthermore, creative instructional practices can facilitate increases in the students' strategic thinking (versus rote learning of a strategic procedure) without adding to the demands on the teacher's instructional time.

Similarly, most arithmetic teachers use exercises in their teaching of academic *content* that are indistinguishable from exercises that may be used to improve underlying cognitive *processes*. For example, flash cards with math facts (e.g., the multiplication tables), using both speed and accuracy as measures of performance, are often used to help students internalize the "facts." The same exercises could equally be considered exercises in speed of processing or sustained attention or selective attention. In the same way, computerized reading exercises could be used as exercises designed to improve speed of processing or systematic left–right scanning. The specific instructions and feedback from the teacher can cause one and the same task to be a "cognitive process" activity or an "academic content" activity. Time is not lost, because the focus continues to be on the curricular content for which the teacher is held accountable. Rather, teaching time is used to serve a dual purpose that will ultimately improve the student's ability to succeed in school.

Using academic content as the context for improving cognitive processes or teaching compensatory strategies has the added benefit of addressing the troublesome issue of generalization. Students often fail to use strategies that are taught in contexts that are removed from the activities in which they are to be applied. Teaching strategies or sharpening cognitive processes in the appropriate "real-world" context (i.e., in the classroom with school materials and activities) goes a considerable distance toward solving the generalization problem.

Metacognitive and Executive Functions

Throughout our discussion of compensatory cognitive strategies, we have emphasized the metacognitive components of strategic behavior. As we have used the term, a strategy is not simply a procedure that improves performance. It is a procedure that one uses deliberately because of recognition that it will help to overcome obstacles to achieving one's goals. This implies a level of awareness that is often absent in individuals with TBI. In this section, we explicitly address the issue of helping students to improve their metacognitive functions and executive or self-regulatory skills (see also Case Study 5.4).

CASE STUDY 5.4

Metacognitive and Executive System Dysfunction

PD was a healthy 15-year-old when he was hit by a car and suffered a severe brain injury. Prior to the accident, he had been a low average student whose achievement was compromised by truancy and lack of effort. He had been arrested more than once, and had been removed from his home school and transferred to a nearby school in an attempt to give him a new beginning.

For several days after the accident, PD was unresponsive. CT scan revealed widespread contusions on the surface of the brain and evidence of intracerebral bleeding in several places. At 1 month postinjury, he was transferred to rehabilitation. He demonstrated growing alertness, but was nonverbal, nonambulatory, and continued to have a tracheostomy tube in place.

By 6 weeks postinjury, he spoke and inconsistently engaged in purposeful behavior. However, his speech was inappropriate and perseverative, attention was severely impaired, behavior was impulsive and random, and he was significantly disoriented. As confusion gradually cleared over the following 3 to 4 weeks, the most salient problems were in the areas of self-regulation (initiation and inhibition), loss of social and academic knowledge, disorganization in language and other behavior, and frustration and agitation in the face of failure. He appeared to be unable to evaluate the appropriateness of his own behavior, frequently asking questions such as "Is that right?" and "Is that what you want me to do?" Consistent routines, appropriate expectations, readily available orientation cues, and a great deal of patience and redirection from staff and family helped PD through this period of recovery.

After 2 months of rehabilitation, PD was generally oriented and goal directed. Specific cognitive and academic strengths and needs emerged, and strategies were designed by the rehabilitation team to address these issues. However, the dominant theme that affected all aspects of the program was that PD lacked awareness of the effects of his injury and insight into their implications for his return to home and school. Therefore, he saw no need for the procedures that the staff proposed as means for compensating for his deficits. As he became more independent, the demands on his cognitive and self-regulatory ability increased and breakdowns became more obvious and frustrating. He responded with anger and verbal outbursts.

Attempts to increase awareness of his deficits and active engagement in his rehabilitation included (a) using PD's own schoolbooks and materials in therapy despite his inability to perform at that level; (b) accompanying him on community outings that he insisted would prove that he was ready to leave, and allowing him to experience frustration in natural environments; (c) having him talk to a previously discharged patient of similar age and background who highlighted the difficulties that he had faced when he returned to home and school; and (d) using group support and peer feedback to increase awareness in a way that was as nonthreatening as possible. Peer teaching, brainstorming, peer testimonials, and group descriptions of individual strengths and weaknesses were all designed to heighten awareness of strengths and needs without confronting these newly injured individuals and threatening their fragile sense of self-worth and ability.

These efforts were only marginally successful. Predictably, PD placed great pressure on his family to remove him from the rehabilitation facility. Despite staff concerns that premature return to school would result in considerable failure and potentially unmanageable behavioral issues, PD was scheduled for discharge. School reentry programming included the following components:

1. Because of pretrauma academic weakness combined with considerable cognitive and academic loss, PD was scheduled for a self-contained special education classroom comprised primarily of students with learning disabilities.
2. Initially, PD's school day was shortened because he lacked the endurance required for a full day and because his physical rehabilitation needs dictated that his school program be complemented by ongoing clinic-based occupational and physical

therapy. School-based therapies all focused on functional school-related issues in consultation with the classroom teacher.

3. A classroom aide was a critical part of the school reentry package. The aide would ensure PD's orientation to task, prompt him to use the cognitive and academic strategies that he had not internalized in the rehabilitation program, and diffuse potential behavioral disruptions. It was made clear that, although the aide would assist as needed to ensure PD's academic success and facilitate social reintegration, she would fade her involvement as PD's orientation and independence increased.
4. Rehabilitation center staff visited the school and met at length with the teacher, counselor, classroom aide, and school principal. Individual therapists met with their counterparts in the school. This orientation session highlighted the classroom adaptations required by PD's current level of functioning. To ensure that the school staff would have appropriate expectations and not misinterpret PD's performance and behavior, the unusual profile of preserved strengths and severe impairment in other areas was explained, along with the complex issue of organically based unawareness combined with some degree of denial. Because of PD's academic and behavioral challenges before the injury, this orientation was critical to avoid the natural inference that resistance and disruptive behavior after the injury were nothing but a return to old ways and not related to the injury.
5. To deal effectively with PD's emerging awareness of deficit, it was agreed that the teacher would work closely with the school counselor to promote awareness in a way that was least likely to result in depression or acting out. In addition, the counselor was scheduled to meet with the parents to help them deal firmly and consistently with expected conflicts about homework, outside activities, and general limits on independence.
6. To promote metacognitive awareness, "product monitoring" tasks were recommended, to be followed by a routine expectation that PD would predict his performance on tests and assignments. Predictions, along with his plan to achieve the predicted level of success, would be recorded in his log and compared with actual performance. In the event of discrepancy, PD would be expected to prepare an explanation and a plan to improve the next time. This would become the functional context within which compensatory strategies would be discussed and promoted. Specific strategies would in all cases be a result of negotiation between PD and the teacher.
7. It was anticipated that PD's acting out would increase when it became clear to him that he could no longer distinguish himself in any of the activities that were important to him before the injury. As a preventive measure, the teacher agreed to put him in charge of a math study group in the class because his ability to

perform arithmetic calculations was superior to that of the other students in the room. The point of this plan was to give PD at least one activity in which he was important and in some way distinguished. Although he needed help in playing the role, the boost to his morale proved to be invaluable later when he became aware of the extent of his disability.

8. A presentation to PD's class was scheduled, but did not occur because he did not want his medical history and experiences discussed with his peers.

Follow-up occurred at regular intervals. As expected, the early weeks in school and at home included resistance, conflict, and acting out. However, the issues were no more severe than school staff and family had been led to expect. Given their preparation and understanding of the evolution of symptoms following PD's brain injury, issues that could easily have escalated were managed effectively.

Applied metacognitive research in developmental psychology has been motivated largely by the ineffectiveness of early attempts to teach cognitive strategies to students with cognitive impairment (Brown, 1981; Flavell, 1976; Meichenbaum & Asarnow, 1979; Wong, 1986). In these experiments, strategic behavior typically lacked durability and failed to transfer to nontraining tasks when the procedures were taught simply as specific isolated skills (Borkowski & Cavanaugh, 1979; Campione & Brown, 1977; Keeney et al., 1967). The suggestion was that, although the children's performance often improved with the use of the strategic procedure (e.g., rehearsal in memory tasks), the children lacked an awareness of the problem that the strategy was designed to solve, an appreciation of the relation between their cognitive deficits and their goals, recognition of the characteristics of the tasks that made them difficult, and an understanding that it was the strategic procedure that improved their performance. These types of knowledge and awareness are all included under the heading "metacognition."

In addition to this *static* component of metacognition (i.e., knowing about one's own cognitive processes, knowing which are weak and which are strong, and knowing that procedures can help in the performance of cognitively demanding tasks), there is a *dynamic* or *self-regulatory* dimension of metacognition, namely *using* strategies when they are helpful and *modifying* them to meet the demands of the task (Ylvisaker & Szekeres, 1989). Some children, for example, may have an adequate intellectual awareness of their cognitive strengths and weaknesses and an understanding that strategies improve performance, but they simply fail to use the procedures without prompts. Appreciation of the impact of both types of metacognitive functioning—static and dynamic—on receptiveness to cognitive instruction has led many educators and special educators to embrace a metacognitive approach to education (e.g., Butterfield & Belmont, 1977; Wittrock, 1978; Wong, 1986).

The term *executive functions* covers much of the same territory as metacognition, but is more widely used in discussions of adult rehabilitation. According to Lezak (1982), the executive system includes functions "necessary for formulating goals, planning how to achieve them, and carrying out the plans effectively" (p. 281). This includes awareness and appraisal of one's own strengths and weaknesses, goal setting, planning, self-directing and self-initiating, self-inhibiting, self-monitoring, self-evaluating, self-correcting, and flexible problem solving. Because the parts of the brain most closely associated with executive functions (prefrontal areas) are very vulnerable in closed head injury, rehabilitation for adults and children with TBI has increasingly come to focus on executive dysfunction (Ben-Yishay & Prigatano, 1990; Crosson et al., 1989; Prigatano, 1986; Ylvisaker & Szekeres, 1989).

Students returning to school following severe TBI often have unrealistic goals and expectations for themselves based on some combination of unawareness of deficits, insufficient experience with their new profile of strengths and weaknesses, and possibly psychoreactive denial. Furthermore, they may fail to (a) appreciate options open to them to improve performance, (b) use their cognitive skills without prompting (e.g., initiate searches of memory), (c) inhibit habitual but no longer functional approaches to tasks, (d) monitor and evaluate their performance in relation to their goals, (e) actively seek solutions to problems that arise in school, and (f) generalize skills and strategies from one task and setting to another. These manifestations of executive system weakness tend to be more debilitating in the long run than difficulties with specific cognitive processes or academic skills.

The traditional literature on adult rehabilitation is not optimistic about rehabilitative possibilities for individuals with significant frontal lobe damage and consequent executive system dysfunction (Lezak, 1987). For example, adults with severe initiation impairment are considered poor candidates for rehabilitation. More recently, clinicians and investigators have focused separately on components of executive functioning and degrees of dysfunction. This has yielded a more optimistic appraisal of possibilities in rehabilitation (Crosson et al., 1989; Prigatano, 1986; Ylvisaker & Szekeres, 1989) and in special education (Meichenbaum, 1977; Van Reusen, 1987).

Training the components of executive functioning

To be "strategic" or to be a good practical problem solver is a complex skill not readily grasped by those students most in need of improvement in this critical domain. Therefore, there is value in breaking the skill into components and illustrating their meaning and importance in concrete terms. The components worth highlighting are (a) self-appraisal of strengths and weaknesses, (b) setting goals or predicting performance based on the self-appraisal, (c) planning how to achieve the goals, (d) self-initiating, (e) self-monitoring, (f) self-evaluating, and (g) most importantly, problem solving when there is a mismatch between performance and prediction.

When these components are specifically targeted in the context of challenging academic or therapy activities, it is difficult for students with cognitive impairment to see the specific metacognitive or executive target and distinguish it from the content objective. Van Reusen's (1987) Goal Regulation Strategy Program, developed for adolescents with learning disabilities, emphasizes the importance of initially targeting executive skills in the context of enjoyable, concrete, and nonthreatening tasks (e.g., throwing balls into a basket). The rationale underlying this program applies with equal if not greater force to adolescents with TBI. Students are independently taught how to evaluate strengths, make predictions, plan achievement, monitor and evaluate progress, and make revisions in the plan in the event of an off-target prediction. Once mastered, these executive skills are then applied to challenging tasks in school or therapy.

The tasks chosen for initial demonstration of executive skills must have clear and readily quantifiable criteria for success. The student is asked to predict performance given a specified number of trials. If the student glibly predicts performance without asking to attempt the task, the teacher or clinician initiates discussion of the need to find out how well one can do something before setting goals or making predictions. The student then practices the task and makes a prediction (sets a goal). The prediction is recorded, and the teacher promises the student a meaningful reward *contingent on performance exactly matching the prediction.* It is critical that the student understand that the goal is accurate prediction of performance, not excellent performance of this concrete task.

The student then begins the actual trials. Periodically, the teacher interrupts to ask how he or she is doing (thereby promoting self-monitoring). The student is expected to describe accurately how current performance relates to the initial prediction (self-evaluating). An opportunity is then extended to do *something* that might facilitate performance matching prediction (problem solving). The teacher ensures that the student considers all meaningful categories of problem solving. These include the following:

1. *Change the prediction:* This corresponds to raising or lowering one's goals in real-world tasks if current performance is incompatible with the goal.
2. *Practice:* If he or she is doing badly in relation to the prediction, the student could choose to practice and thereby increase the likelihood of winning the reward.
3. *Change the task:* The student may wish to make the task easier (e.g., move closer to the basket in a shooting task). This corresponds to a variety of adaptations that can be made in academic tasks to facilitate success (e.g., additional time for tests, large-print books, shorter assignments).
4. *Change the manner of performing the task:* For example, the student may wish to try an alternative style of shooting the ball in a shooting task. Such changes correspond to using compensatory strategies in academic tasks (e.g., reading a text using advance organizers or recording important events in a memory book).
5. *Change the environment:* The student may choose to increase the lighting or ask other students to leave the room because they cause too much stress. These changes correspond to the multitude of ways in which school and study environments can be modified to enhance success.
6. *Ask for help:* The student may request suggestions, guidance, or coaching as a way of enhancing performance.
7. *Change the reward:* The student may demand a more substantial reward to make the effort worth his or her while.

Throughout these discussions, the teacher points out that these are the ways in which all people deal with the common situation of performance failing to match goals or expectations. The discussions should be rich in classroom analogies so that the student understands the connection between the executive skills being acquired in this training context and their real-world application. The purpose of these otherwise apparently silly tasks is to teach the components of executive functioning and the vocabulary that goes with these goals: What exactly do self-appraisal, realistic goal setting, planning, self-monitoring, self-evaluating, and problem solving amount to in real-world tasks, including the tasks with which the students are having difficulty in school?

Before transferring the skills to challenging academic or therapy tasks, it is useful to encapsulate all of the executive functions in the form of a meaningful image or metaphor. The "executive" part of executive functions identifies a metaphor that is useful, but not for most adolescents with TBI who have little sense for the roles of an executive. Because many of these students have some experience with team sports, the metaphor of a coach or the image of an internalized self-coach can cover the same territory in a way that makes the concept much more available to the student. We sometimes ask students to write a description of the roles of a coach (or other occupation with similar roles, but more meaningful to the students) and then promote the idea that these are the functions that they must assume for themselves.

When the student demonstrates mastery of the components of executive functioning in concrete and nonthreatening tasks, it is time to practice the same functions with academic or therapy tasks. Assuming that the tasks are quantifiable, as most are, the practice can proceed much as with the original concrete task. In math class, for example, the student can predict the number of problems he or she will solve correctly. In reading, the prediction can be of the number of questions that will be answered correctly. The teacher then proceeds with the activity, targeting the executive components rather than (or in addition to) math and reading mastery; that is, the goals are improved self-appraisal of skill levels, realistic goal setting, planning, active performance monitoring, accurate self-evaluating, and flexible brainstorming regarding how best to achieve one's goals—through practice, modifying the task, changing the way the task is done, changing the environment, requesting help, increasing the payoff, or changing the goal.

Like any other new skill, executive or metacognitive ("self-coaching") skills must be practiced in a variety of settings, in the context of a variety of tasks, with a variety of people, and with systematically decreasing cues to promote generalization and maintenance. Ideally, the educational program is designed to reward this type of growth and the environment is designed to promote improved self-regulatory functioning throughout the school day. We now turn to these two important topics. Whereas the structured executive system training program described in this section is not appropriate for children younger than adolescents, most of the classroom practices described in the following sections can be adapted for grade school–age children.

Classroom practices that promote metacognitive and executive functions

In the final analysis, children will likely develop and functionally use metacognitive and executive skills more as a product of general environmental expectations and models at home and school than of specific training as described in the previous section. Therefore, teachers and therapists need to implement a variety of classroom and therapy practices that contribute to this aspect of development. Several of these suggestions are outlined by Bondy (1989).

1. *Metacognitive IEP objectives:* Because of the need for IEP objectives to be behavioral and easily measured, they tend to focus on highly specific academic or closely related skills—for example,

"John will complete two-digit subtraction problems with regrouping with 90% accuracy on three consecutive days." Many teachers and therapists are skeptical about metacognitive goals in part because they do not fit this model of writing objectives. However, with some ingenuity, all metacognitive objectives can be described in measurable terms. For example, "John will correctly predict performance on math tests. If performance does not match prediction, he will write a plan of correction that includes some combination of the following: modified prediction; specific plan for increased study or practice; specific plan for changing the approach to taking math tests; specific plan for negotiating modifications in the test; request for additional tutoring. Prior to the next test, he will document all activity in relation to his plan." Alternatively, "John will select a strategy he feels will help him prepare for tests; he will record the strategy and the frequency of its use in his log book; after completing the test, he will record the effectiveness of the strategy and propose a modification if it was unsuccessful."

It is critical that metacognitive goals be taken seriously and therefore be included in IEPs. If not, they will inevitably become back-burner items when the teacher begins to feel pressure to meet specific academic content objectives.

2. *Annual self-evaluation of learning strengths and weaknesses:* Adolescent students should be expected to write a description of their own strengths and weaknesses in relation to school goals. These can be updated annually and should include plans for addressing weaknesses. Students can share their plans with one another.
3. *Daily learning log:* On a daily or less frequent basis, teachers should encourage students to make notes in their learning log including reflections, insights, reactions, and confusions regarding their performance in school.
4. *Teacher modeling:* The type of self-reflection encouraged in Items 2 and 3 should regularly be modeled by the teacher. This includes discussion of the teacher's own strengths and weaknesses and also frequent thinking out loud about strategies for tackling new and difficult problems. Teachers can highlight their own personal systems for organizing projects, maintaining orientation to their schedule, compensating for their weaknesses, and the like.
5. *Comprehension or performance rating:* Having completed a reading or other assignment, students should be expected to rate their own comprehension or performance. A simple system (e.g., "good," "ok," or "not ok" relative to their preestablished expectations and objectives) may be sufficient to institutionalize the expectation that students will continuously monitor and evaluate their own performance.
6. *Peer teaching:* Having students alternate playing the role of teacher helps them to gain appreciation of students' learning strengths and weaknesses and of strategies for approaching problems.

7. *Study guide:* The classroom as a whole can adopt a simple guide for approaching all academic tasks. For example, the expectation might be as follows: (a) Before the task, specify the job that needs to be done and identify the reasons for doing it. (b) During the task, monitor performance with questions such as, "Am I doing this correctly?" "Do I understand this information?" (c) After the task, ask "Did I achieve the goal?" "Did I make mistakes? If so, what can I do about it?" Daily repetition and review of these simple procedures and regular classroom modeling help to make metacognitive activity part of the normal school routine. It may be useful to have a section of the daily learning log for goal setting, planning, and goal achievement monitoring. In some cases, routines of this sort are internalized only after years of modeling and practice.
8. *Cognitive vocabulary:* Teachers should consistently use words (e.g., "think," "organize," "plan," "monitor–evaluate," "problem solve") that label and highlight the cognitive processes that are targeted in the classroom.

Environmental factors in the development of executive functions

Generalization of strategic and metacognitive behavior is facilitated in an environment in which strategic thinking and metacognitive insight are pervasive features. In a school setting, planned generalization includes the practices outlined in the previous section. It also includes "teacher talk" that highlights and promotes the value of metacognitive activity (Ylvisaker et al., 1992). Classrooms with a metacognitive focus are filled with comments such as the following:

- "Good question! How do you suppose you could find the answer?"
- "How do you think you will do on your math assignment? Why?"
- "How's the math going? Are you doing as well as expected?"
- "What was the hardest part of the assignment? What made it hard? What did you do? What went through your head? What did you learn from what you did?"
- "How long did it take you to finish? Could you cut that down by 5 minutes? How?"
- "What do you hope to accomplish by doing this assignment? How do you plan to achieve that goal?"
- "Would you like to get a higher grade? What could you do to accomplish that? Good idea!! Try it and let me know how it works out."
- "Be sure to check your work before you hand it in."
- "Before you hand in your essay, read it carefully and indicate all of the problems you had with spelling and grammar. I'll give you extra credit if you can find your own errors."

- "Why don't you pair up, find out how well your partner understands the social studies lesson, and figure out some way of ensuring that he will do well on the test. Has anybody found a good way of preparing for social studies tests?"
- "Is there anybody you know who is good at this sort of thing? Maybe you should talk to her and get some ideas about how to do it better."
- "What helps you to learn and remember? repetition? saying it out loud? making diagrams? outlining? teaching it to someone else?"

In normal cognitive development, most students do not begin to be reflective about their own learning strengths and weaknesses and acquire important academic strategies such as routinely checking their work for errors until the middle grade school years. Because children with cognitive problems have a greater need for strategic thinking than children whose automatic behavior generally serves them adequately and because children with TBI are often specifically impaired in this critical function, there is reason to begin this metacognitive and strategic focus earlier than would be expected based on normal development. Ironically, many teachers unconsciously deprive struggling students with weak executive functions of occasions to practice problem identification and problem solving by anticipating their problems and confusions and directively setting them straight before the student can act independently (Meichenbaum, 1993; Meichenbaum & Biemiller, 1990); that is, those students who need more practice than others to develop self-regulatory behaviors are actually given far fewer learning trials in functional classroom tasks. This is the classroom analogue of the vicious cycle of learned helplessness commonly observed in institutions for individuals with developmental disabilities.

Children as young as first graders (or younger) can learn the concept of "doing something special" to perform a demanding task. They learn this concept of special effort or clever tricks in the context of highly motivating and concrete tasks in which special effort has an obvious reward (e.g., using a sticker to mark the place in which a piece of candy was hidden so that it will be easy to find later). Teachers then work to transfer this concept of special effort to classroom tasks by modeling problem-solving thinking in relation to these tasks, encouraging students to find solutions, and encouraging students to use whatever resources are available to them (e.g., teachers, peers, reference materials) to achieve their goals. It may be years before the children have a mature grasp of strategic problem solving in cognitive tasks, but the foundation has been laid by these concrete activities and the child knows that strategic thinking and problem solving are valued because the culture is one in which these behaviors are modeled, prized, and rewarded.

Developing problem-solving skill in preschoolers

The home is the most likely environment for promotion of problem-solving skill in preschoolers. Unfortunately, many parents of children with TBI unconsciously assume problem-solving functions for the child. The underlying dynamics are undoubtedly complex. Understandably, parents of children who have been injured do not wish to see their children experience frustration. Furthermore, an environment that promotes independence and self-initiated problem solving in children may also be seen as an environment in which children take risks. Parents of injured preschoolers have a natural and very strong desire to protect their child from additional injury and, in the process, may create an environment in which there are no risks. Finally, consequences of the injury may result in time-consuming daily activities, thereby eliminating free time to allow the child to engage in trial-and-error problem solving.

However, because the development of problem-solving skill and strategic thinking is so critical for children with TBI, efforts must be made to help parents design an environment at home in which development of these skills is facilitated. Training parents of preschoolers includes the following components (Ylvisaker et al., 1992): (a) sensitizing them to the importance of metacognitive development and independent problem solving; (b) teaching them to identify natural problem-solving situations in the lives of young children (e.g., getting candy out of a jar with a tight lid, finding a lost toy, resolving a sibling conflict about which TV show to watch); (c) clarifying the difference between preschool problem solving that is mature (e.g., sequentially trying several possible solutions) and that which is immature (e.g., giving up, trying one unsuccessful solution and crying, trying the first unsuccessful solution over and over); (d) teaching them to model and explore alternative solutions with their child; (e) teaching them to encourage the child's trial-and-error experimentation without judgment; and (f) teaching them to give the child useful feedback that highlights the value of clever solutions and at the same time rewards the child for independent and creative thinking.

Clinicians can work with parents to create lists of everyday problem situations and possible solutions that can be explored in a way that is both safe and not overly time-consuming. This type of training has been shown to have a positive influence on the behavior of parents of young children with handicaps (Thompson & Hixson, 1984).

Developing problem-solving skill in older children

Training in problem solving is generally considered a critical component of cognitive rehabilitation for individuals with brain injury. In many cases, the training does not go beyond superficial workbook practice consisting of multitrial "What would you do if . . ." exercises. In this chapter and in Chapter 3, we have given many reasons to be skeptical of this type of training. Even when the exercises are enriched to include exploration of a variety of possible solutions to hypothetical problems and consideration of pros and cons for each possibility, there is little reason to believe that the exercises will result in generalizable skills that transfer to complex real-world situations.

The obvious challenge to retraining exercises of this sort is the transfer issue discussed in an earlier section of this chapter. An equally powerful challenge is based on the premises that mature problem solving is an extremely complex process and that the breakdown is often *not* at the stage of identifying a reasonable solution once the problem has been identified and clarified (the skill most frequently targeted in workbook problem-solving exercises). The critical issue for weak problem solvers is more likely to be (a) failure to identify or clarify the problem that one is facing, (b) failure to assume a problem-solving attitude once the problem is identified, (c) failure to consider relevant past experience in formulating a solution, (d) failure to move beyond "one-stop" thinking in choosing a solution, or (e) failure to act on the chosen solution and to profit from feedback. Improvement of functional problem-solving skill is more likely to occur as a result of the complex package of functional interventions that we have called compensatory strategies and metacognitive or executive functions than in

TABLE 5.7. Teaching Problem Solving to Young Children

Deficits: Disorganized problem solving; weak task organizing and planning

Goals: Improve problem solving, organizing, and planning

Procedures:

1. During the first phase, the therapist clearly models the following skills: (a) problem identification; (b) listing of relevant information; (c) listing and evaluating possible solutions; (d) creating a plan of action.
2. During the next phase, the children execute their own plans and solve their own problems, even if this involves obviously inefficient plans and solutions. The children receive feedback from the results of their activity or directly from the therapist. Ideally, segments of the activity are videotaped and jointly analyzed by the children and therapist to determine the efficiency of the plans and the efficiency of the problem-solving process.
3. The therapist then guides the children in the formulation of more useful (from the childrens' point of view) ways to solve problems.
4. Written or pictured reminders of the agreed-upon problem-solving procedure for a given activity are then posted in the room. As needed, the children's attention is called to these reminders as they face problems in their group activities.

Activities: Use a variety of interesting group projects that are loosely structured, requiring group planning and decision making, such as writing a play, making the props, and performing it, or creating a game (including rules and materials) and playing it (emphasizing social rules and cognitive strategies).

Modified from "Cognitive Rehabilitation Therapy: Late Stages of Recovery" by J. Haarbauer-Krupa, K. Henry, S. F. Szekeres, and M. Ylvisaker, in *Head Injury Rehabilitation: Children and Adolescents* (p. 331) by M. Ylvisaker (Ed.), 1985, Austin, TX: PRO-ED. Printed with permission.

response to isolated exercises targeting components of the total process of practical problem solving. Ylvisaker and colleagues (1987) discussed these themes in greater detail. Table 5.7 describes additional activities that can be used as a context for targeting problem-solving skills in grade school children. Table 5.8 describes activities that target social judgment and safety judgment in grade school children.

USE OF COMPUTERS IN COGNITIVE REHABILITATION

Personal computers play a variety of important roles in rehabilitation and education. A discussion of these roles would take us far beyond the limits of this chapter. However, it is important to place computer training in perspective, because many people unfortunately have come to associate cognitive "retraining" following brain injury with computer-based exercises. Many of the software packages that are explicitly identified as cognitive retraining programs focus on basic-level cognitive functions.

TABLE 5.8. Teaching Social Judgment and Safety Judgment to Young Children

DEFICITS: Poor safety and social judgment; decreased processing of environmental cues; poor organizational skills

GOALS: Improve the child's (a) physical safety, (b) social safety, (c) community mobility, and (d) use of community facilities

PROCEDURES:

Area	*Simulation (In Treatment)*	*Environment (Real World)*
Physical safety (street and playground)	Provide the children with repetitive drill to remember rules, such as the following: (a) stop, look, and listen; (b) wait for swings to be still before climbing on; (c) don't jump off the monkey bars. Provide the children with practice by means of role-playing and simulated situations.	Practice crossing real streets while reciting or using rules. Have group activities on the playground so that the therapist can coach and prompt the children in using the learned rules. Train families or staff members, or both, to cue the children in using the same rules.
Social safety	Provide the children with repetitive drill to remember rules such as the following: (a) don't talk to strangers; (b) check the weather before getting dressed; (c) don't take candy or presents from strangers. Provide the children with practice in using the rules by means of role-playing and simulated situations, along with discussions.	Simulate potentially dangerous social situations in a natural setting, with other staff members who are unknown to the children, using the rules previously taught. Train families or staff members, or both, to cue the children using the same rules.
Community mobility	Present a map of a familiar place on a gameboard. Encourage the children to determine what the map represents. Explain the concept of *landmarks* and have the children provide examples in verbal discussion. Have the children describe how to reach various locations on the map, using landmarks.	Have the children find landmarks to add to the map. Give the children directions to find specific locations using landmarks. Have the children take turns describing and finding places using the map. Take the children to an unfamiliar place and have them lead the group back.

(*continues*)

TABLE 5.8. *Continued*

Area	Simulation (In Treatment)	Environment (Real World)
		Ask families or staff members to prompt the children to look for landmarks in their daily environment.
Use of community facilities	Discuss a plan for using community facilities (e.g., stores, libraries, theaters, playgrounds). The discussion should include the following: (a) How do we use the facility? (b) What can we learn from it? (c) What kinds of questions should we ask in each place? (d) How should we ask permission to go to each place? As a group, devise a plan for a field trip to the facility using this information.	Actually visit the community facility and follow the children's plan for the visit. Ask family or staff members to provide time for the children to plan family outings or class field trips.

From "Cognitive Rehabilitation Therapy: Late Stages of Recovery" by J. Haarbauer-Krupa, K. Henry, S. F. Szekeres, and M. Ylvisaker, in *Head Injury Rehabilitation: Children and Adolescents* (pp. 311–340) by M. Ylvisaker (Ed.), 1985, Austin, TX: PRO-ED. Reproduced with permission.

Using a somewhat broader definition of cognitive rehabilitation software, programs can be grouped under the following categories (Ylvisaker et al., 1987):

- *Basic-level cognitive components:* Programs that address attentional functions (e.g., sustained–focused attention); speed of processing (e.g., reaction time); selective attention–impulse inhibition (e.g., reaction time with a distractor); visual perceptual components (e.g., attention to all visual fields, systematic scanning, visual discrimination, visual figure–ground relationships, visual–motor integration); time estimation; and working memory (e.g., memory span for digits and/or words).
- *Organizing processes:* Programs that address, using either verbal or nonverbal stimuli, categorizing, sequencing, part–whole relationships, and memory for meaningfully connected material.
- *Higher-level cognitive–language components:* Programs that address inferential reasoning, problem solving, linguistic abstractions, and multiple meaning.
- *Academic–integrative tasks:* Programs that address reading comprehension, composition, and curricular areas such as mathematics, science, social studies, and history.

Placing computers in perspective requires frank acknowledgment that they are simply a special *medium* for presenting or accomplishing tasks that in other forms have been part of traditional therapy and classroom instruction. Computerized activities may be helpful, but should be selected only after several challenging intervention questions have been answered: What are the appropriate *targets* of intervention? Should intervention be approached through *remediation* or *compensation* or some combination? Is there reason to believe that *exercising* the impaired function will result in significant and generalizable improvement in the function? Should intervention be *decontextualized* or rather take place within the context of *natural activities* in a *natural setting?*

The research literature on the effectiveness of attempts to remediate residual deficits in underlying cognitive areas through repetitive retraining exercises is not encouraging. Furthermore, because generalization is most commonly the source of failure in intervention, there is good reason to be skeptical about treatment activities that bear little resemblance to the activities in which performance needs to be improved. Finally, for many students with TBI, it is the *social* manifestations of cognitive weakness that prove to be most debilitating over the long run. Computer activities are not well suited to the task of improving social competence.

Despite these qualifications, computers possess a number of advantages in treatment and instruction.

- The tasks and environment can be highly structured and controlled, features that are important for many students with TBI.
- Computers make possible precision in presenting stimuli and systematically increasing difficulty levels.
- Performance can be objectively rated. If the program includes a record-keeping system, data can be stored and changes in performance clearly and objectively charted.
- The objective feedback provided by the computer is a more acceptable form of confrontation for many students than feedback from a teacher or therapist. Feedback can be immediate and consistent, but data can also be stored to show progress over time.
- Computers interest and motivate many students.
- Because computers have patience for endless drill and practice, they are useful to students who require more learning trials than most teachers are willing to give.
- With computers, many students can be independent in their cognitive or academic exercises without losing the precision of the task, carefully programmed sequence of tasks, or access to immediate feedback.
- Appropriately adapted computers can provide motorically handicapped students with access to a variety of cognitively challenging experiences and training tasks they might not otherwise have.
- Computer presentation of tasks frees the teacher or therapist to be observer and strategist. Computer activities are often a useful context for objectively illustrating a deficit, demonstrating the value of

a compensatory procedure, and practicing its use before transferring it to a more functional task.

A common feature of many "cognitive retraining" computer programs is that they are contentless; that is, they present cognitive challenges independent of any real-life content or context. For many students, particularly those who demonstrate little transfer of training, it is preferable to add academic or social content to the exercise, even if the goal is cognitive rather than academic. For example, students who need to improve sustained attention and speed of processing may profit from focusing on these goals in the context of math or reading exercises. In this case, the student practices attending to the type of stimuli to which he or she needs to attend, rather than practicing attending in the abstract. Similarly, practice organizing ideas for writing a letter or composing a theme for English class is more likely to have a generalizable impact on organizational functioning than practice organizing in the abstract (e.g., categorizing, sequencing, associating exercises), independent of the content to be organized. The "domain specificity" of cognitive skills is a theme that runs through current research and theory in cognitive science (Singley & Anderson, 1989) and must be taken seriously by educators and clinicians.

Among the most useful applications of computers in cognitive rehabilitation are those that, on the surface, have nothing to do with rehabilitation. For example, word processing is an excellent context in which to target various attentional and perceptual functions, language organizational skills, self-monitoring and correcting skills, and many more. Furthermore, it is a useful skill to possess for its own sake. Videogames can be used early in recovery to capture and focus attention at a time when little else may achieve these objectives. Programs such as PageMaker, Newsroom, and Print Shop can be used for projects that are as simple or complex as students want to make them, and they enable teachers to target planning, organizational, and problem-solving skills as well as group cooperation and interaction. Educational software is ideally suited for reacquisition of academic content early after the injury. Students can work independently and give themselves as many trials as needed to remaster skills or knowledge lost as a result of the injury.

Rehabilitation and education or special education catalogs describe a very large and growing number of software programs that are explicitly intended for use in cognitive rehabilitation or have been found to be useful for students with cognitive needs. In selecting computer programs and activities, professionals must remember several points:

1. *At best,* computers augment other forms of intervention following brain injury.

2. Matching students to computer exercises and activities requires the same careful judgments that are involved in any other instructional and curricular decisions.

3. Improving a skill using a computer exercise is only the first step in promoting improved performance of functional tasks. Generalization to functional tasks must be an explicit part of the instruction.

4. The aspects of cognitive dysfunction that are often most debilitating following brain injury—for example, impaired interpersonal

skills—may not lend themselves to computer-based remedial activities.

In addition to these considerations, specific characteristics of the software should be matched to specific needs of the student. For example, students with perceptual or attentional problems profit from simplified and highlighted stimuli, picture cues, directive arrows, and animation. Students with memory problems might need sound or color cues as memory aids and small steps with frequent responses and feedback. Impulsive students respond well to programs that frequently require them to press the return key to proceed. The National Council of Teachers of Mathematics publication, *Guidelines for Evaluating Computerized Instruction Materials* (National Council of Teachers of Mathematics, 1906 Association Dr., Reston, VA 22091), addresses the issue of software selection criteria.

COGNITIVE REHABILITATION IN PRESCHOOL CHILDREN

In the sections titled "Organization and Memory" and "Metacognitive and Executive Functions," we addressed selected issues in preschool cognitive rehabilitation. Although research on outcome following TBI in preschoolers is sparse, the available reports (e.g., Ewing-Cobbs, Miner, Fletcher, & Levin, 1989) combine with clinical experience to emphasize the frequency of cognitive problems in this group and their increasing impact on development over the years following the injury. Children who appear to recover well (as measured by developmental scales) in the early weeks after the injury often demonstrate increasing processing and learning problems when they face the demands of the early grades. This may be a combined result of the cumulative effects of new learning problems together with slow maturation of executive self-regulation produced by prefrontal injury. New learning problems and executive system weakness easily escape detection in the early months after TBI in a preschooler.

Careful examination of apparently well-recovered preschoolers often reveals deterioration of performance as a result of increased processing loads; disorganization in completing tasks and using language; word-retrieval difficulties, especially in confrontational contexts; poor behavioral self-control when compared with peers; and reduced ability to learn new information. Weakness in these areas interferes with the child's ability to attend, communicate, and organize play and daily living tasks.

A critical function of cognitive specialists is to follow the development of preschoolers after the injury to identify the possible emergence of issues that may require special attention. In the case of children whose families may not be alert to signs of developmental difficulty or who may disregard scheduled follow-up, it is useful to enroll the child in a Head Start or other preschool program to avoid the common phenomenon of significant problems emerging when the child reaches first grade.

Play is the most natural context for attention to cognitive dysfunction in preschoolers (see Table 5.9 for therapeutic play activities). Children with organizational weakness, for example, may need to increase systematically the number of representational toys that can be meaningfully integrated in play. Whereas normally developing children at 24 months of age are generally able to integrate at least three toys in familiar routines (e.g., feeding the baby, putting the baby to bed, putting a driver and objects in a truck and driving), 3- and 4-year-olds with organizational problems

TABLE 5.9. Sample Therapy Activities for Preschoolers

GOAL I: Improve organized representational and dramatic play

Features of therapeutic play activities:

1. The number of objects used can be systematically increased.
2. The activity has an obvious structure (beginning, middle, end).
3. The activity has a familiar theme.

Examples of play activities:

Less Complex		***More Complex***
Feed the baby a bottle.	Feed the baby food and a bottle.	Take care of baby; feed, bathe, and play.
Cars: Take one person for a ride.	*Cars:* Put two people in the car.	*Cars:* Build a road and take two people for a ride to the store.
Doctor's office: The child and the therapist play roles of doctor and patient, using two or three items in doctor's kit.	*Doctor's office:* The child and therapist use more items or switch roles.	*Doctor's office:* Add additional children and roles.
Store: The child tells the therapist what he or she wants from a set of pictured items.	*Store:* The "storekeeper" and the "customer" have play money. The child is a customer who comes to the store, buys, then goes home.	*Store:* Add other children and reverse roles.

GOAL II: Improve sequential organization and planning

Features of therapeutic activities:

1. The format is consistent: This includes a model of the finished product, organization of materials, demonstration of the process, and explicit instructions.
2. The activity should have a concrete product as its goal (e.g., cookies, macaroni necklace).

Process:

1. Divide the task into three clear and obviously sequential units (e.g., stir ingredients; put on cookie sheet; bake).
2. Take pictures using an instant camera of the children at each of the three phases as they complete the activity. Drawings may be used as a more advanced step.
3. Review the activity by ordering and discussing the pictures sequentially.

(*continues*)

TABLE 5.9. *Continued*

GOAL III: Improve turn-taking

Features of therapeutic activities:

1. An external feedback system (e.g., point card) is used.
2. The activity should offer obvious turn-taking cues (e.g., lotto games or simple card games).
3. The task structure can be gradually reduced (e.g., from board games with obvious turns to cooperative art projects with less obvious turns).

Process:

1. Identify the appropriate behavior for each child at every turn: "Johnny, it's your turn to talk." "Susan, it's your turn to look at Johnny and listen." Give the children obvious turn-taking cues by calling them by name and looking at them. Gradually withdraw these cues.
2. Give points for the target behavior (e.g., waiting quietly during the other child's turn).

From "Cognitive Rehabilitation Therapy: Late Stages of Recovery" by J. Haarbauer-Krupa, K. Henry, S. F. Szekeres, and M. Ylvisaker, in *Head Injury Rehabilitation: Children and Adolescents* (p. 336) by M. Ylvisaker (Ed.), 1985, Austin, TX: PRO-ED. Reproduced with permission.

following TBI may struggle with more than two toys. Treatment focuses on developing scripts and routines for organized play with gradually increasing numbers of props and systematically decreasing cues.

Play may also have as its treatment focus turn-taking, cooperative play, in-seat behavior, attending to picture book tasks, and other behaviors that are important in a school context. This treatment may be in part preventive, giving the child additional time to learn routines that are survival routines in grade school. Because of the child's developmental level, compensatory strategies and pedagogical teaching by means of deliberate learning tasks (in which the child's explicit goal is to learn) are inappropriate. However, organized playing and thinking as well as increasingly mature interaction with peers can be modeled and targeted in natural activities by means of incidental learning tasks.

Treating preschool word-retrieval difficulties illustrates many of these points (Haarbauer-Krupa, Henry, et al., 1985). Semantic feature analysis (described earlier) can be used during natural play activities to teach children how to understand various aspects of an object, event, or person, and to generate these descriptions when they cannot recall specific names in play (incidental learning context). Cuing by teachers, family, or therapists helps children to recall and express these ideas. Some children may be cued to pantomime the word, others to describe any feature of the item, and others to tell more specifically to what group it belongs. With daily practice in gamelike feature analysis of familiar concepts and cuing to use the information in communicating about the object, children may improve general communication and possibly even specific word retrieval, but without internalizing the procedure as a compensatory strategy.

CONCLUSION

Terms such as *cognitive rehabilitation* and *cognitive intervention* have a very wide scope. One of our goals in this chapter has been to describe and promote a functional approach to cognitive rehabilitation for children with TBI. Helping children to achieve goals that are blocked by cognitive deficits may include process-specific retraining activities, environmental compensations and task modifications, and the use of compensatory strategies. Such an approach most definitely includes helping students to understand what they can and cannot do well, and to become active problem solvers in the face of cognitive challenges.

Investigations of the effectiveness of intervention for children with TBI are only beginning. For this reason, confident pronouncements regarding what works and what does not work are premature. At this stage, educators and clinicians can merely draw cautious inferences from efficacy research with adults with TBI and children with other disabilities. In addition, a watchful eye on advances in cognitive science and developmental cognitive psychology, together with thoughtfully processed clinical experiences with these children, yields insights that help guide clinical decision making.

These sources of guidance have led us to be cautious about restoration of function through exercises that bear little resemblance to functional tasks that children face in school and in daily life. On the positive side, we are confident that a carefully designed, broad-based program of functional and integrative cognitive intervention can help children make optimal use of their residual cognitive functions, continue to master academic skills and information, and become actively engaged in practical problem solving, thereby avoiding the downward cycle of failure and behavioral deterioration.

APPENDIX 5A
*Examples of Compensatory Strategies for Students with Cognitive Impairments**

Attention and Concentration

A. *External aids*

1. Use a timer or alarm watch to focus attention for a specified period.
2. Organize the work environment and eliminate distractions.
3. Use a written or pictorial task plan with built-in rest periods and reinforcement; move a marker along to show progress.
4. Place a symbol or picture card in an obvious place in the work area as a reminder to maintain attention.

B. *Internal procedures*

1. Set increasingly demanding goals for self, including sustained work time.
2. Self-instruct (e.g., "Am I wandering? What am I supposed to do? What should I be doing now?"). (Written cue cards may be needed for these during training period.)

Orientation (to time, place, person, and event)

A. *External aids*

1. Use a log or journal book or tape recorder to record significant information and events of the day.
2. Refer to pictures of persons who are not readily identified (carry pictures attached to logbook).
3. Use appointment book or daily schedule sheet.
4. Use alarm watch set for regular intervals.
5. Refer to maps or pictures for spatial orientation; make maps with landmarks.

B. *Internal procedures*

1. Select anchor points or events during the week and then attempt to reconstruct either previous or subsequent points in time (e.g., "My birthday was on Wednesday and that was yesterday, so this must be Thursday").

---

*From "Cognitive Rehabilitation Therapy: Late Stages of Recovery" by J. Haarbauer-Krupa, K. Henry, S. F. Szekeres, and M. Ylvisaker, in *Head Injury Rehabilitation: Children and Adolescents* (pp. 317–319) by M. Ylvisaker (Ed.), 1985, Austin, TX: PRO-ED. Reproduced with permission.

2. Request time, date, and similar information from others, when necessary.
3. Scan environment for landmarks.

Input Control (amount, duration, complexity, rate, and interference)

A. *Auditory*
   1. Give feedback to speaker (e.g., "Please slow down; speed up; break information into smaller 'chunks'").
   2. Request repetition in another form (e.g., "Would you please write that down for me?").

B. *Visual*
   1. Request longer viewing time or repeated viewings; request extra time for reading.
   2. Cover parts of a page and look at exposed areas systematically, as in a "clockwise direction" or "left to right."
   3. Use finger or index card to assist scanning and to maintain place.
   4. Use symbol to mark right and left margins of written material or top and bottom segments as anchors in space.
   5. Use large-print books or talking books.
   6. Request a verbal description.
   7. Remove an object from its setting to examine it; then return it to the original setting and view it again.
   8. Place items in best visual field and eliminate visual distractors.
   9. Turn head to compensate for field cut.

Comprehension and Memory Processes

A. Use self-question (e.g., "Do I understand? Do I need to ask a question? How is this meaningful to me? How does this fit with what I know?"). Periodically look for gaps, misconceptions, or confusion by summarizing or explaining and checking back with speaker, a written source, or reference material.

B. Build "frames" or background for new information that is of particular significance or interest. Read summaries, general textbooks, and ask knowledgeable persons about topic of special interest (a procedure in building frames).

C. Use a study guide for extended discourse material (e.g., SQ3R procedure—survey, question, read, recite, review).

D. Make charts and graphs of important relationships in textual material.

E. Use external memory aids (e.g., tape recorder, logbook, notes, memos, written or pictured time lines).

F. Rehearse: Covert or overt; auditory-vocal or motor (pantomine).

G. Organization: Scan for or impose some order on incoming information.

H. Mnemonics: Method of loci, rhymes, imagery (meaningful and novel associations).

I. Use diagrams or forms that facilitate deeper encoding of information and its subsequent retrieval.

J. Relate the information to personal life experiences and current knowledge. Use semantic knowledge of basic scripts (e.g., going to a restaurant, buying groceries) to help reconstruct previous events.

K. Project and describe situation in which target information will be needed or used.

L. At retrieval, reconstruct environment in which information was received.

M. Verbalize visual–spatial information (e.g., "X is to the left of Y"). Visualize verbal information in graphs, pictures, cartoons, or action-based imagery.

N. Keep items in designated places.

Word Retrieval

A. Search lexical memory according to various categories and subcategories (e.g., person, family).

B. Describe the concept; circumlocute freely (talk about or around subject).

C. Use gestures or signs.

D. Attempt to generate a sentence or use a carrier phrase.

E. Search letters or sounds of the alphabet (more effective in retrieving members of a limited category, such as names).

F. Describe perceptual attributes and semantic features of the concept.

G. Draw the item.

H. Attempt to write the word.

I. Create an image of the object in a scene; then attempt to describe the scene.

J. Attempt to retrieve the overlearned opposite.

K. Free associate with image in mind.

L. Associate persons' names with physical characteristics or a known person of the same name.

Thought Organization and Verbal Expression

A. Use a structured thinking procedure (e.g., the feature analysis guide in Figure 5.1).

B. Use knowledge of scripts to generate real or imagined descriptions of experiences (narratives).

C. Construct a time line to maintain appropriate sequence of events.

D. Note topic in any conversation; self-question about the main point of expression; alert others before shifting a topic abruptly.

E. Watch others for feedback as to whether your words are confusing: Watch facial expression, and so forth, or directly ask listeners, "Am I being clear?"

F. Rehearse important comments or questions and listen to self.

G. Set limits of time or allowable number of sentences in any one turn.

Reasoning, Problem Solving, and Judgment

A. Use a problem-solving guide.

B. Use self-questioning for alternatives or consequences ("What else could I do?" "What would happen if I did that?").

C. Look at possible solutions from at least two different perspectives.

D. Scan environment for cues as to appropriateness or inappropriateness of a behavior (e.g., facial expression of others; signs such as "No Smoking"; formality vs. informality of setting).

E. Set specific times or places for behaviors that are appropriate only in specified situations.

F. Actively envision situations to which successful procedures can be generalized.

Self-Monitoring

A. Use symbols or signs, placed in obvious places, or alarms that mean "pause" or "stop" or "Am I doing what I should be doing?"

B. Use book or notebook with cards inserted at selected places with self-monitoring cues (e.g., "Summarize what you read").

C. Pair specific self-instruction with the associated emotion (e.g., "Calm down" when angry).

Task Organization

A. Use task organization checklist: materials, sequenced steps, time line, evaluation of results. Check each when completed.

B. Prepare work space and assign space as task demands.

APPENDIX 5B
*Compensatory Strategies for Cognitive Problems in a Classroom Setting**

Key: Strategies followed by the letter T are to be implemented by the teacher. Strategies followed by T/S can be used by the teacher or student. In the latter case, the teacher may initiate the use of the strategy and later require that the student use it independently.

PROBLEM: Attending. Students are unable to attend to auditory and visual information. They may do such things as talk out of turn or change the topic, be distracted by noise in the hall, fidget, or poke others. It is important to note that students may maintain eye contact and appear to be listening and actually not be attending.

Strategies

- Remove unnecessary distractions, such as pencils and books. Limit background noise at first and gradually increase it to more normal levels. (T)
- Provide visual cues to attend (e.g., have a sign on student's desk with the word or pictured symbol for behaviors, such as LOOK or LISTEN; point to the sign when students are off task). (T)
- Limit the amount of information on a page. (T/S)
- Adjust assignments to the length of students' attention span so that they can complete tasks successfully. (T)
- Focus students' attention on specific information: "I'm going to read a story and ask *who* is in the story." (T)

PROBLEM: Language Comprehension or Following Directions. Students have difficulty understanding language that is spoken rapidly, is complex, or is lengthy.

Strategies

- Limit amount of information presented—perhaps to one or two sentences. (T/S)
- Use more concrete language. (T)
- Teach students to ask for clarification or repetitions or for information to be given at a slower rate. (T/S)

---

*From "Educational Programming for Head Injured Students" by S. B. Cohen, C. M. Joyce, K. W. Rhoades, and D. M. Welks, in *Head Injury Rehabilitation: Children and Adolescents* (pp. 390–392) by M. Ylvisaker (Ed.), 1985, Austin, TX: PRO-ED. Reprinted with permission.

- Use pictures or written words to cue students: Use a picture of a chair and the written word *sit* if you want the students to exhibit that behavior. (T)
- Pair manual signs, gestures, or pictures with verbal information. (T/S)
- Act out directions: If the student is to collect papers and put them in a designated spot, demonstrate how this should be done. (T)
- Use cognitive mapping: Diagram ideas in order of importance or sequence to clarify content graphically. This also helps students to see part–whole relationships. (T/S)

Many of the strategies listed under Attending and Memory can also be used to improve language comprehension.

PROBLEM: Memory. Students are unable to retain information they have heard or read. They may not remember where to go or what materials to use.

Strategies

- Include pictures or visual cues with oral information, because multisensory input strengthens the information and provides various ways to recall it. (T/S)
- Use visual imagery. Have students form a mental picture of information that is presented orally. Retrieval of the visual images may trigger the recall of oral information. (T/S)
- Use verbal rehearsal. After the visual or auditory information is presented have the students "practice" it (repeat it) and *listen to themselves* before they act on it. (T/S)
- Limit the amount of information presented so that students can retain and retrieve it. (T/S)
- Provide a matrix for students to refer to if they have difficulty recalling information. (T/S)
- Have the student take notes or record information on tape. (T/S)
- Underline key words in a passage for emphasis. (T/S)
- Provide a log book to record assignments or daily events. (T/S)
- Provide a printed or pictured schedule of daily activities, locations, and materials needed. (T/S)
- Role-play or pantomine stories or procedures to strengthen the information to be remembered. (T/S)
- Write down key information to be remembered, such as who, what, when. (T/S)

PROBLEM: Retrieving Information that Has Been Stored in Memory.

Strategies

- Have students gesture or role-play. They may be able to act out a situation that has occurred but not have adequate verbal language to describe it. (T/S)
- Provide visual or auditory cues: "Is it _____ or _____?" or give the beginning sound of a word. (T)
- Include written multiple-choice cues or pictures in worksheets. (T)
- Teach students to compensate for word-finding problems by describing the function, size, or other attributes of items to be recalled. (T/S)

PROBLEM: Sequencing. Students have difficulty understanding, recognizing, displaying, or describing a sequence of events presented orally or visually.

Strategies

- Limit the number of steps in a task. (T/S)
- Present part of a sequence and have students finish it. (T)
- Show or discuss one step of the sequence (lesson) at a time. (T)
- Give general cues with each step: "What should you do first? second?" (T)
- Have students repeat multistep directions and listen to themselves before attempting a task. (T/S)
- Provide pictures or a written sequence of steps to remember: Tape a cue card to the desk with words or pictures of materials needed for a lesson, then expand original written directions. For example, if the direction was "Underline the words in each sentence in which *ou* or *ow* stands for the vowel sound. Then write the two words that have the same vowel sound," change it to "(1) Read the sentence; (2) underline *ou* and *ow* words; (3) read the underlined words; (4) find the two words that have the same vowel sounds; (5) write these two words on the lines below the sentence. (T)
- Tell students how many steps are in a task: "I'm going to tell you *three* things to do." (Hold up three fingers.) (T)
- Act out a sequence of events to clarify information. (T/S)
- Provide sample items describing how to proceed through parts of a worksheet. (T)
- Number the steps in a written direction and have the students cross off each step as it is completed. (T/S)
- Teach students to refer to directions if they are unsure of the task. (T/S)

PROBLEM: Thought Organization. Students have difficulty organizing thoughts in oral or written language. Students may not have adequate labels or vocabulary to convey a clear message; they may tend to ramble without getting to the point.

Strategies

- Attempt to limit impulsive responses by encouraging the students to take "thinking time" before they answer. (T/S)
- Have students organize information by using categories, such as who, what, when, where. (T/S) (Emphasize each of these separately if necessary.) This strategy can be used in an expanded form to write a story.
- Teach students a sequence of steps to aid in verbal organization: Have the students use cue cards with written pictured steps when formulating an answer. (T/S)
- Focus on one type of information at a time (e.g., the main idea). (T/S)
- Decrease rambling by having students express a thought "in one sentence." (T/S)

PROBLEM: Generalization. Students learn a skill or concept but have difficulty applying it to other situations (e.g., they may count a group of coins in a structured mathematics lesson but not be able to count their money for lunch).

Strategies

- Teach the structure or format of a task (e.g., *how* to complete a worksheet or mathematics problem). (T)
- Maintain a known format and change the content of a task to help students see a relationship: Two pictures are presented and students must say if they are in the same category, or have the same initial sound; a worksheet format requires filling in blanks with words or numbers. (T)
- Change the format of the task: Have students solve mathematics facts on a worksheet as well as on flash cards. (T)
- Have completed sample worksheets in a notebook serve as models indicating how to proceed. (T/S)
- Demonstrate how skills can be used throughout the day: Discuss how students rely on the clock or a schedule to get up in the morning, begin school, or catch a bus. (T)
- Role-play in situations that simulate those which students may encounter, emphasizing the generalization of specific skills taught; completing school assignments and going to the store may involve the same strategies (making a list or asking for help). (T)

REFERENCES

Alley, G. R., & Deshler, D. D. (1979). *Teaching the learning disabled adolescent strategies and methods.* Denver: Love.

Belmont, J., & Butterfield, E. (1977). The instructional approach to developmental cognitive research. In R. Kail & J. Hagen (Eds.), *Perspectives on the development of memory and cognition* (pp. 437–481). Hillsdale, NJ: Erlbaum.

Ben-Yishay, Y., & Prigatano, G. (1990). Cognitive remediation. In M. Rosenthal, E. R. Griffith, M. R. Bond, & J. D. Miller (Eds.), *Rehabilitation of the adult and child with traumatic brain injury* (2nd ed., pp. 393–409). Philadelphia: F. A. Davis.

Bondy, E. (1989). Thinking about thinking. *Childhood Education.*

Borkowski, J. G., & Cavanaugh, J. C. (1979). Maintenance and generalization of skills and strategies by the retarded. In N. R. Ellis (Ed.), *Handbook of mental deficiency: Psychological theory and research* (2nd ed., pp. 569–618). Hillsdale, NJ: Erlbaum.

Bower, G. (1972). A selective review of organizational factors in memory. In E. Tulving & W. Donaldson (Eds.), *Organization of memory* (pp. 93–137). New York: Academic Press.

Brown, A. L. (1974). The role of strategic behavior in retardate memory. In N. R. Ellis (Ed.), *International review of research in mental retardation* (Vol. 7, pp. 55–111). New York: Academic Press.

Brown, A. L. (1981). Learning to learn: On training students to learn from texts. *Educational Researcher, 10*(2), 14–21.

Brown, A. L., & Barclay, C. R. (1976). The effects of training specific mnemonics on the metamnemonic efficiency of retarded children. *Child Development, 47,* 71–80.

Brown, R. T., & Alford, M. (1984). Ameliorating attentional disorders and concomitant academic deficiencies in learning disabled children through cognitive training. *Journal of Learning Disabilities, 17,* 20–26.

Buschke, H., & Fuld, P. A. (1974). Evaluating storage, retention, and retrieval in disordered memory and learning. *Neurology, 24,* 1019–1025.

Butterfield, E., & Belmont, J. (1977). Assessing and improving the executive cognitive functions of mentally retarded people. In I. Bialer & M. Sternlicht (Eds.), *The psychology of mental retardation: Issues and approaches* (pp. 277–315). New York: Psychological Dimensions.

Campione, J. C., & Brown, A. L. (1977). Memory and metamemory development in educable retarded children. In R. V. Kail, Jr. & J. W. Hagen (Eds.), *Perspectives on the development of memory and cognition* (pp. 367–406). Hillsdale, NJ: Erlbaum.

Ceci, S. J., & Howe, M. J. (1978). Age-related differences in free recall as a function of retrieval flexibility. *Journal of Experimental Child Psychology, 26,* 432–442.

Cohen, S. B., Joyce, C. M., Rhoades, K. W., & Welks, D. M. (1985). Educational programming for head injured students. In M. Ylvisaker (Ed.), *Head injury rehabilitation: Children and adolescents* (pp. 383–409). Austin, TX: PRO-ED.

Crosson, B., Barco, P. P., Velozo, C. A., Bolesta, M. M., Cooper, P. V., Werts, D., & Brodbeck, T. C. (1989). Awareness and compensation in post-acute rehabilitation. *Journal of Head Trauma Rehabilitation, 4*(3), 46–54.

Deshler, D. D., Alley, G. R., Warner, M. M., & Schumaker, J. B. (1981). Instructional practices for promoting skill acquisition and generalization in severely learning disabled adolescents. *Learning Disability Quarterly, 4,* 415–421.

Douglas, V. I., Parry, P., Marton, P., & Garson, C. (1976). Assessment of cognitive training programs for hyperactive children. *Journal of Learning Disabilities, 4,* 389–410.

Ervin, S. (1961). Changes with age in the verbal determinants of word-association. *American Journal of Psychology, 74,* 361–372.
Ewing-Cobbs, L., Miner, M. S., Fletcher, J. M., & Levin, H. S. (1989). Intellectual, motor and language sequelae following closed head injury in infants and preschoolers. *Journal of Pediatric Psychology, 14,* 531–547.
Flavell, J. (1976). Metacognitive aspects of problem solving. In L. B. Resnick (Ed.), *The nature of intelligence* (pp. 231–235). Hillsdale, NJ: Erlbaum.
Forrest-Pressley, D. L., MacKinnon, G. E., & Waller, T. G. (Eds.). (1985). *Metacognition, cognition, and human performance: Vol. 1. Theoretical perspectives.* Orlando, FL: Academic Press.
Haarbauer-Krupa, J., Henry, K., Szekeres, S. F., & Ylvisaker, M. (1985). Cognitive rehabilitation therapy: Late stages of recovery. In M. Ylvisaker (Ed.), *Head injury rehabilitation: Children and adolescents* (pp. 311–343). Austin, TX: PRO-ED.
Haarbauer-Krupa, J., Moser, L., Smith, G., Sullivan, D. M., & Szekeres, S. F. (1985). Cognitive rehabilitation therapy: Middle stages of recovery. In M. Ylvisaker (Ed.), *Head injury rehabilitation: Children and adolescents* (pp. 288–310). Austin, TX: PRO-ED.
Hallahan, D. P., & Reeve, R. E. (1980). Selective attention and distractibility. In B. K. Keogh (Ed.), *Advances in special education: Vol. 1. Basic constructs and theoretical orientations* (pp. 141–181). Greenwich, CT: JAI Press.
Kavale, K., & Mattson, P. (1983). "One jumped off the balance beam": Meta-analysis of perceptual–motor training. *Journal of Learning Disabilities, 16,* 165–173.
Keeney, T., Cannizzo, S., & Flavell, J. (1967). Spontaneous and induced verbal rehearsal in a recall task. *Child Development, 38,* 953–966.
Kendall, P. C., & Finch, A. J. (1979). Developing nonimpulsive behavior in children: Cognitive–behavioral strategies for self-control. In P. C. Kendall & S. D. Hollon (Eds.), *Cognitive–behavioral interventions: Theory, research, and procedures* (pp. 37–79). New York: Academic Press.
Lezak, M. (1982). The problem of assessing executive functions. *International Journal of Psychology, 17,* 281–297.
Lezak, M. (1987). Assessment for rehabilitation planning. In M. Meier, A. L. Benton, & L. Diller (Eds.), *Neuropsychological rehabilitation* (pp. 41–58). New York: Guilford Press.
Meichenbaum, D. (1977). *Cognitive behavior modification: An integrative approach.* New York: Plenum Press.
Meichenbaum, D. (1993). The "potential" contributions of cognitive behavior modification to the rehabilitation of individuals with traumatic brain injury. *Seminars in Speech and Language, 14,* 18–30.
Meichenbaum, D., & Asarnow, J. (1979). Cognitive–behavioral modification and metacognitive development: Implications for the classroom. In P. C. Kendall & S. D. Hollon (Eds.), *Cognitive–behavioral interventions: Theory, research, and procedures* (pp. 11–35). New York: Academic Press.
Meichenbaum, D., & Biemiller, A. (1990, May). *In search of student expertise in the classroom: A metacognitive analysis.* Paper presented at the Conference on Cognitive Research for Instructional Innovation, University of Maryland, College Park.
Moffat, N. (1984). Strategies of memory therapy. In B. Wilson & N. Moffat (Eds.), *Clinical management of memory problems* (pp. 63–88). Rockville, MD: Aspen Systems.
Pellegrino, J., & Ingram, A. (1978). *Processes, products and measures of memory organization.* Learning Research Development Center Report. University of Pittsburgh, Pittsburgh, PA.
Pressley, M. (1993). Teaching cognitive strategies to brain-injured clients: The good information processing perspective. *Seminars in Speech and Language, 14,* 1–16.

Pressley, M., & Associates (1990). *Cognitive strategy instruction that really improves children's academic performance.* Cambridge, MA: Brookline Press.

Pressley, M., Borkowski, J. G., & Schneider, W. (1987). Cognitive strategies: Good strategy users coordinate metacognition and knowledge. In R. Vasta & G. Whitehurst (Eds.), *Annals of child development* (Vol. 4, pp. 89–129). Greenwich, CT: JAI Press.

Pressley, M., Goodchild, F., Fleet, J., Zajchowski, R., & Evans, E. D. (1989). The challenges of classroom strategy instruction. *Elementary School Journal, 89,* 301–342.

Pressley, M., Johnson, C. J., Symons, S., McGoldrick, J. A., & Kurita, J. A. (1989). Strategies that improve children's memory and comprehension of text. *Elementary School Journal, 90,* 3–32.

Pressley, M., & Levin, J. R. (Eds.). (1983a). *Cognitive strategy training: Educational applications.* New York: Springer Verlag.

Pressley, M., & Levin, J. R. (Eds.). (1983b). *Cognitive strategy training: Psychological foundations.* New York: Springer Verlag.

Prigatano, G. (1986). *Neuropsychological rehabilitation after brain injury.* Baltimore: Johns Hopkins University Press.

Schacter, D. L., & Glisky, E. L. (1986). Memory remediation: Restoration, alleviation, and the acquisition of domain-specific knowledge. In B. Uzzell & Y. Gross (Eds.), *Clinical neuropsychology of intervention* (pp. 257–282). Boston: Martinus Nijhoff.

Singley, M. K., & Anderson, J. R. (1989). *The transfer of cognitive skill.* Cambridge, MA: Harvard University Press.

Smith, E. E. (1978). Theories of semantic memory. In W. K. Estes (Ed.), *Handbook of learning and cognitive processes* (Vol. 6). Hillsdale, NJ: Erlbaum.

Sohlberg, M. M., & Mateer, C. (1989). *Introduction to cognitive rehabilitation.* New York: Guilford Press.

Szekeres, S. (1988). *Organization and recall in the young language impaired child.* Unpublished doctoral dissertation, University of Pittsburgh, Pittsburgh, PA.

Thompson, R. W., & Hixson, P. K. (1984). Teaching parents to encourage independent problem solving in preschool-age children. *Language, Speech, and Hearing Services in the Schools, 15,* 175–181.

Van Reusen, T. (1987, May). *Training learning disabled adolescents to use a goal regulation strategy.* Paper presented at the PRISE Conference on Cognition and Metacognition, Pittsburgh, PA.

Wittrock, M. C. (1978). The cognitive movement in instruction. *Educational Psychologist, 13,* 15–30.

Wong, B. (1986). Metacognition and special education: A review of a view. *Journal of Special Education, 20*(1), 9–29.

Woodcock, R., & Johnson, M. (1989). *Woodcock–Johnson Psycho-Educational Test Battery.* Allen Park, TX: DLM Teaching Resources.

Ylvisaker, M., & Szekeres, S. (1989). Metacognitive and executive impairments in head-injured children and adults. *Topics in Language Disorders, 9,* 34–49.

Ylvisaker, M., Szekeres, S., & Hartwick, P. (1992). Cognitive rehabilitation following traumatic brain injury in children. In M. Tramontana & S. Hooper (Eds.), *Advances in child neuropsychology: Vol. 1.* New York: Springer Verlag.

Ylvisaker, M., Szekeres, S., Henry, K., Sullivan, D., & Wheeler, P. (1987). Topics in cognitive rehabilitation therapy. In M. Ylvisaker & E. M. Gobble (Eds.), *Community re-entry for head injured adults* (pp. 137–220). Austin, TX: PRO-ED.

CHAPTER 6

Speech and Language Intervention

MARK YLVISAKER
SHIRLEY F. SZEKERES
JULIET HAARBAUER-KRUPA
BETH URBANCZYK
TIMOTHY J. FEENEY

A potential danger exists in separately addressing the concerns of a single profession, in this case speech-language pathology, in a book on school-based intervention for students with traumatic brain injury (TBI). Our intention is to promote an interdisciplinary and integrative approach to rehabilitation and education rather than one in which teachers and clinicians work in professional isolation. A fragmented approach is at best inefficient and in many cases subverts the goals of intervention and blocks the functional integration of newly acquired skills into the child's natural environments. This is particularly true of intervention for language and communication disorders which, in the case of students with TBI, characteristically lie in professional territory that speech-language pathologists share with classroom teachers, psychologists, social workers, school counselors, and occupational therapists.

However, because language and communication themes may be central to the student's program and because speech-language pathologists should play an important role in that program, we discuss in this chapter intervention themes that fall within the scope of practice of speech-language pathologists while at the same time highlighting the critical importance of interdisciplinary programming that includes a variety of professionals and often family members and friends as well. The purposes of the chapter are to review communication-related problems that frequently result from TBI; to highlight informal assessment strategies; to describe selected intervention guidelines, strategies, and procedures that are of special relevance to this group of students; and to discuss models of speech-language service delivery within schools and useful roles that can be played by speech-language pathologists.

This chapter should be read along with Chapters 3 through 5. Chapter 3 presents a framework for understanding and exploring cognitive functioning. In that many of the communication and language problems following TBI are grounded in cognitive dysfunction, such a framework is essential for language intervention with this population. Chapters 4 and 5 present many assessment and treatment procedures that could easily have been included in a chapter devoted to communication issues. However, because the themes are also relevant to the scope of practice of classroom teachers, psychologists, and others, they were included in explicitly interdisciplinary chapters on cognitive assessment and intervention.

Students with TBI comprise a very diverse group of individuals. Many with mild to moderate injuries recover well and have no need for the services of a speech-language pathologist. Others are left with residual motor, cognitive, psychosocial, linguistic, and academic needs that closely resemble those of students with other disabilities, including learning disabilities, mental retardation, behavioral disorder, cerebral palsy, and others. Furthermore, a disproportionate number of students with TBI have a pretrauma history of learning problems or delayed speech and language. Therefore, assessment and treatment strategies developed for other children may be an important component of services for students with TBI. However, there are also critical differences between central tendencies in the group of students with TBI and central tendencies in other special education populations. Some of these differences were listed in Chapter 3. With these population "central tendencies" in mind, we present selected assessment and treatment strategies in this chapter.

COMMUNICATION PROBLEMS AFTER TBI

Any function can be spared or impaired following TBI. However, students with mild and even severe injuries often recover basic speech and language skills (Ylvisaker, 1986). Profiles similar to those of students with developmental speech and language problems are not common, unless the problems predated the injury. Acquired brain injuries resulting from causes other than trauma (e.g., unilateral left hemisphere stroke) may produce aphasia-like symptoms that persist, but are of lesser magnitude than symptoms in adults with comparable injuries (Aram, 1988; Aram, Ekelman, Rose, & Whitaker, 1985). The summaries that follow highlight common patterns of outcome in pediatric TBI, based on available research as well as clinical experience. Communication challenges resulting from cognitive and psychosocial weakness merit greatest attention (Ylvisaker, in press).

Speech

Although the recovery of speech may be slow in children with prolonged coma (several days or more) following closed head injury, children rarely lack serviceable speech indefinitely after reasonable return of intellectual functioning (Levin et al., 1983; Ylvisaker, 1986). Oral and/or verbal apraxia (difficulty coordinating and executing the movements of speech structures) is often present initially, but typically resolves. A relatively small number of children with severe injuries remain incapable of functional speech indefinitely, despite the return of cognitive and language skills sufficient to support verbal interaction. Neuromuscular dysfunction producing significant dysarthria is more common following injury in infants and very young children and in older adolescents and adults than in preschoolers and grade school–aged children (Levin, Benton, & Grossman, 1982; Raimondi & Hirschauer, 1984).

A larger number of severely injured children, although still a minority, recover serviceable but noticeably altered speech. Symptoms often include some combination of the following:

- Articulatory imprecision, related to muscle weakness or spasticity, or to weak self-monitoring of speech production
- Phonatory weakness, often related to unilateral vocal fold paralysis possibly combined with upper trunk muscle tightness
- Hypernasality, related to inadequate velopharyngeal closure or incoordination
- Impaired prosody, including inadequate pitch variation
- Slow rate of speech
- Rapid rate of speech and cluttering, related to reduced self-monitoring of speech production or general disinhibition (frontal lobe syndrome)

Most children with TBI recover motor speech abilities that equal or closely approximate their pretrauma levels. Therefore children—including many with very severe injuries—commonly return to school looking and sounding much as they did before their injury. This appearance of full recovery contributes to the identification, diagnosis, and service acquisition problems faced by school personnel, including speech-language pathologists.

Language

Understood most narrowly, *language* refers to the *form* of verbal behavior, including phonologic, morphologic, and syntactic components. Investigators who have used aphasia screening tests to examine language outcome following TBI in children have found few clear-cut deficiencies or abnormalities in language functioning in children with good cognitive recovery (e.g., Klonoff, Low, & Clark, 1977; Winogren, Knights, & Bawden, 1984). With rare exceptions, children who had normal language before their injury eventually produce grammatically acceptable sentences and have little difficulty comprehending everyday language. This adds to the appearance of full recovery mentioned earlier. It also contributes mightily to identification and service acquisition problems, because standardized language tests routinely used by school-based speech-language pathologists often focus narrowly on exactly those areas of language functioning that are least vulnerable to the effects of TBI.

The semantic dimensions of language are more commonly problematic. Although receptive vocabulary as measured by the *Peabody Picture Vocabulary Test–Revised* (Dunn & Dunn, 1981) often returns to normal limits in the early weeks after the injury, standard scores on this test may *deteriorate* in subsequent years because the student fails to acquire *new* concepts and vocabulary at an age-appropriate rate (Cooper & Flowers, 1987); that is, the easy incidental acquisition of information, concepts, and vocabulary characteristic of normal child development may no longer be available to these children. This language consequence of new learning problems (see Chapters 3 and 4) requires careful attention to vocabulary learning even in cases in which this appears initially not to be an area of concern. The section that follows on cognitive–communicative functioning highlights a variety of additional dimensions of semantic knowledge and language comprehension deserving of attention following TBI.

Although errors in expressive syntax and morphology may occur under stress (Campbell & Dollaghan, 1990), most students with TBI produce language that is grammatically acceptable. However, impairments of confrontation naming and word retrieval (verbal fluency) are frequent findings in pediatric head injury (Chadwick, Rutter, Shaffer, & Shrout, 1981; Ewing-Cobbs, Fletcher, & Levin, 1985; Ewing-Cobbs, Levin, Eisenberg, & Fletcher, 1987; Levin & Eisenberg, 1979a, 1979b; Winogren et al., 1984). Difficulty retrieving the desired word may be most pronounced under stress, such as in classroom recitation or stressful social encounters. Consequences of word-finding problems in spontaneous language may be of two very different sorts: (a) limited verbal output and incomplete statements and (b) normal amount of output characterized by repetitions, reformulations, and word substitutions (German, 1987). Older students may become verbose and verbally tangential as a consequence of difficulty retrieving higher-level lexical items. Many children describe great frustration that accompanies knowing an answer but being unable to think of the correct word when called on in class. Fried-Oken (1987) described procedures for distinguishing between expressive vocabulary deficits and word-finding problems.

Fletcher, Miner, and Ewing-Cobbs (1987) suggested that, following TBI, skills in a rapid phase of development are particularly vulnerable to the injury. For example, writing has been found to be relatively impaired following TBI in the middle grades and expressive language in children injured before 31 months of age (Ewing-Cobbs, Miner, Fletcher, & Levin, 1989). Other aspects of language comprehension and expression are discussed in the following section.

Cognitive–Communicative Functioning

Many students with TBI score well on standardized tests of language knowledge and skill, and perform adequately with language in nonstressful social contexts. However, with added cognitive, academic, social, or communicative stress, language performance often deteriorates much more than would normally be expected. Cognitive stress may take the form of demands for speeded performance, a need to organize substantial quantities of information, increasingly abstract language, environmental interference, or new learning demands.

Demands for speeded performance

Because of a generalized slowness in information processing (Bawden, Knights, & Winogren, 1985), students with TBI may understand language when spoken at a deliberate rate, but fail to understand when the rate is increased. Teachers commonly observe that the student requires extra processing time to comprehend spoken language and formulate a response. Similarly, word-retrieval and organizational problems may be exacerbated when the student is required to respond rapidly. Teachers have also observed that many students with TBI read slowly and require extra time to complete writing assignments (Ylvisaker, 1986). This slowness in taking in language and formulating a response may not be evident on formal speech and language testing, because few language tests are timed. Generalized slowness may be demonstrated on timed reading tests and on nonverbal performance tests, such as the Performance Scale subtests of the *Wechsler Intelligence Scale for Children–Third Edition* (Wechsler, 1991), suggesting that the student may also be slow in language processing. Furthermore, we have worked with students who complained that all aspects of their thinking and academic performance seemed very slow to them after their injury even though a comprehensive neuropsychological battery did not confirm slowed processing. Children's thinking and responding may be slow for weeks or even months following apparently mild head injuries (Gulbrandsen, 1984).

Organizational demands

Impairments of language organization have been documented in controlled investigations of adults with TBI (Hartley & Jenson, 1991; Liles, Coelho, Duffy, & Zalagens, 1989; Mentis & Prutting, 1987; Milton, Prutting, & Binder, 1984; Prigatano, Roueche, & Fordyce, 1985; Wycoff, 1984) and in clinical descriptions of children with TBI (Haarbauer-Krupa, Moser, Smith, Sullivan, & Szekeres, 1985; Szekeres, Ylvisaker, & Holland, 1985). Recently, Chapman and colleagues (1992) found significant differences between children with severe closed head injury (at least 1 year postinjury) and control children on several measures of discourse (based on a story retelling task). Unfortunately, tests of language comprehension (auditory comprehension or reading) and expression (spoken or written language) rarely go beyond sentences or short paragraphs. Because the organizational demands of these tasks are minimal, students with TBI often score within normal limits. However, when organizational demands are high (e.g., reading a long chapter, producing a coherent spoken narrative or description, or writing an essay), performance often deteriorates rapidly. This relatively severe difficulty with comprehending and producing extended language was noted by teachers of students with TBI (Ylvisaker, 1986). Furthermore, these teachers rated expressive language problems (including disorganized expression in speech and writing) as contributing most to academic failure, compared with 15 academic and academic-related areas of functioning. Because most of the children in question had little difficulty with the mechanics of reading, writing, speaking, and understanding spoken language, the likely interpretation of this finding is that the teachers recognized breakdowns with larger units of language and believed that these breakdowns played a significant role in the child's academic difficulties.

The pattern of teacher questionnaire response was dramatic in the case of reading competence. Only 25% of the teachers reported that the students with TBI in their classrooms had difficulty (relative to classroom expectations) with reading individual words (word recognition or decoding). Fifty percent of these teachers said that the students with TBI read slowly; 70% reported that these students had relative difficulty with higher levels of comprehension (e.g., detecting main ideas, drawing inferences); 90% of the teachers indicated that these students experienced relatively severe deterioration in comprehension as the amount of material to be read increased. Comparable teacher responses were obtained in the areas of auditory comprehension, oral expression, and written expression. The emerging theme is that many students recover sufficient language competence to perform adequately on tasks that involve minimal cognitive or psychosocial stress, but have great difficulty organizing significant amounts of information for comprehension or expression.

One of the consequences of this pattern of abilities is that children may perform adequately on currently available tests administered by psychologists, educational diagnosticians, and speech-language pathologists alike, yet be unable to maintain the level of academic performance that their test results predict. This organizational problem may also explain the rambling, tangential conversations and narratives observed in many of these children. Alternatively, reduced verbal output and extremely short and uninformative written assignments may be a consequence of this organizational deficit.

Demands of increasing abstractness

Like many students with learning disabilities or general intellectual impairment, students with TBI are often "concrete" thinkers; that is, they have disproportionate difficulty comprehending abstract meaning (Dennis & Barnes, 1990). This may reveal itself in failure to grasp indirect meaning (e.g., "I'm chilly" meaning "Please close the window"), subtle humor, figures of speech (e.g., "He was climbing the walls"), and metaphors (e.g., "He is a Rock of Gibraltar"). In addition, as children age, the increasingly abstract nature of the academic content in subjects such as math, science, social studies, and English may present unexpectedly severe challenges. This problem may not be evident until years after the injury. For example, children injured in the early grade school years may recover a level of language and cognitive proficiency sufficient to handle all age-appropriate language tasks, but later be unable to negotiate the level of abstractness required when they approach adolescence and the middle school years. This phenomenon may explain deteriorating performance in math, science, social studies, or English that parents understandably interpret as regression.

Environmental interference

In a questionnaire survey, 60% of teachers of students with TBI indicated that, compared with peers, the students with TBI had relatively substantial difficulty performing in the presence of classroom distractions. Only 30% of the same students were identified by trained educational evaluators as evidencing distractibility during testing (Ylvisaker, 1981), suggesting that many children may be able to control attentional focus under optimal conditions, but experience considerable difficulty in natural classroom and social environments. Successful language performance (comprehension and production) is one possible casualty of this attentional difficulty. In the early weeks after a severe injury, distractibility is often more extreme than teachers and therapists are accustomed to in a special education setting. Later, students with TBI may more closely resemble children with attention deficit disorder from birth.

New learning demands

Children commonly regain much of the knowledge and skill acquired before their injury, but subsequently experience difficulty learning new information and skill at an age-appropriate rate. Standard scores on tests of vocabulary and academic knowledge may, therefore, deteriorate over the years following the injury. The problem in this case is not specific to language learning, but rather represents a general impairment of new learning (Fuld & Fisher, 1977; Levin & Eisenberg, 1979a; Levin, Eisenberg, Wigg, & Kobayashi, 1982). A consequence of this phenomenon is that diagnostic teaching of essentially new material, including vocabulary, should be a critical component of the assessment of children following head injury, particularly young children who may "look good" on general developmental scales shortly after the injury (see Chapter 4).

Social–Cognitive–Communicative Functioning

Given the vulnerable areas of the brain in closed head injury (see Chapter 2), the difficulty that students have adjusting to the many losses that may result from the injury, and the psychosocial challenges of normal development, effective and satisfying social interaction is often difficult to reestablish after the injury. This may be a result of impulsive, disinhibited, socially aggressive, and socially inappropriate behavior that is directly associated with anterior frontal lobe or anterior and medial temporal lobe damage. Alternatively, it may result from a lack of initiation, possibly combined with depression and social withdrawal associated with loss of friends and emerging awareness of deficits. Social and behavioral challenges are often in part a consequence of impaired social cognition (including reduced knowledge of social rules and roles, weak perception of social cues, difficulty interpreting social situations and the intentions of communication partners, and reduced perspective taking). Furthermore, many children and adolescents with TBI have documented pretraumatic behavioral problems that placed them at risk for their head injury, or they may have learned maladaptive behaviors as a result of mismanagement after the injury. Finally, they may be struggling socially in a new environment with new peers. Whatever the cause, socially ineffective behavior is a common finding in studies of children with TBI (Blau, 1936; Brown, Chadwick, Shaffer, Rutter, & Traub, 1981; Fletcher, Ewing-Cobbs, Miner, & Levin, 1990; Jacobson et al., 1986; Kasanan, 1929; Perrott, Taylor, & Montes, 1991; Petterson, 1988; Ylvisaker, in press).

It is difficult to overestimate the significance of impaired social skills. In the case of adults with head injury, family members rate changes in social behavior as more stressful than changes in cognitive or physical ability (Brooks & McKinlay, 1983). Furthermore, poorly regulated interpersonal behavior has been found to have the greatest negative impact on the ability of adults with TBI to maintain employment and family integrity (Lezak, 1987). In the case of children, quality of life depends heavily on possessing those skills that enable the child to have friends. Furthermore, there is reason to believe that a connection exists between social awkwardness in childhood and psychological maladjustment later in life (Bandura, 1973; Dowrick, 1986; Foster & Ritchley, 1979). Several studies have demonstrated that children with disability often do not acquire the social skills needed for effective social interaction or peer acceptance without specific instruction (Gresham, 1982).

Petterson (1988) found, as expected, that children and adolescents with TBI were impaired in social behavior relative to a control group of hospitalized children without brain injury. Of particular interest, she found that the children with TBI had difficulty interpreting social–emotional cues and that this cognitive impairment independently explained a significant portion of the impaired social behavior. This supports the view that specific weakness in social cognition (separate from general IQ) contributes to the ineffective social interaction of these children.

Figure 6.1 schematically represents relationships among verbal, cognitive, and psychosocial aspects of functioning. Whereas speech-language pathologists are trained most thoroughly to address issues in Area 1 (specific linguistic concerns), the areas that receive disproportionate attention in this chapter are Area 4, the intersection of cogni-

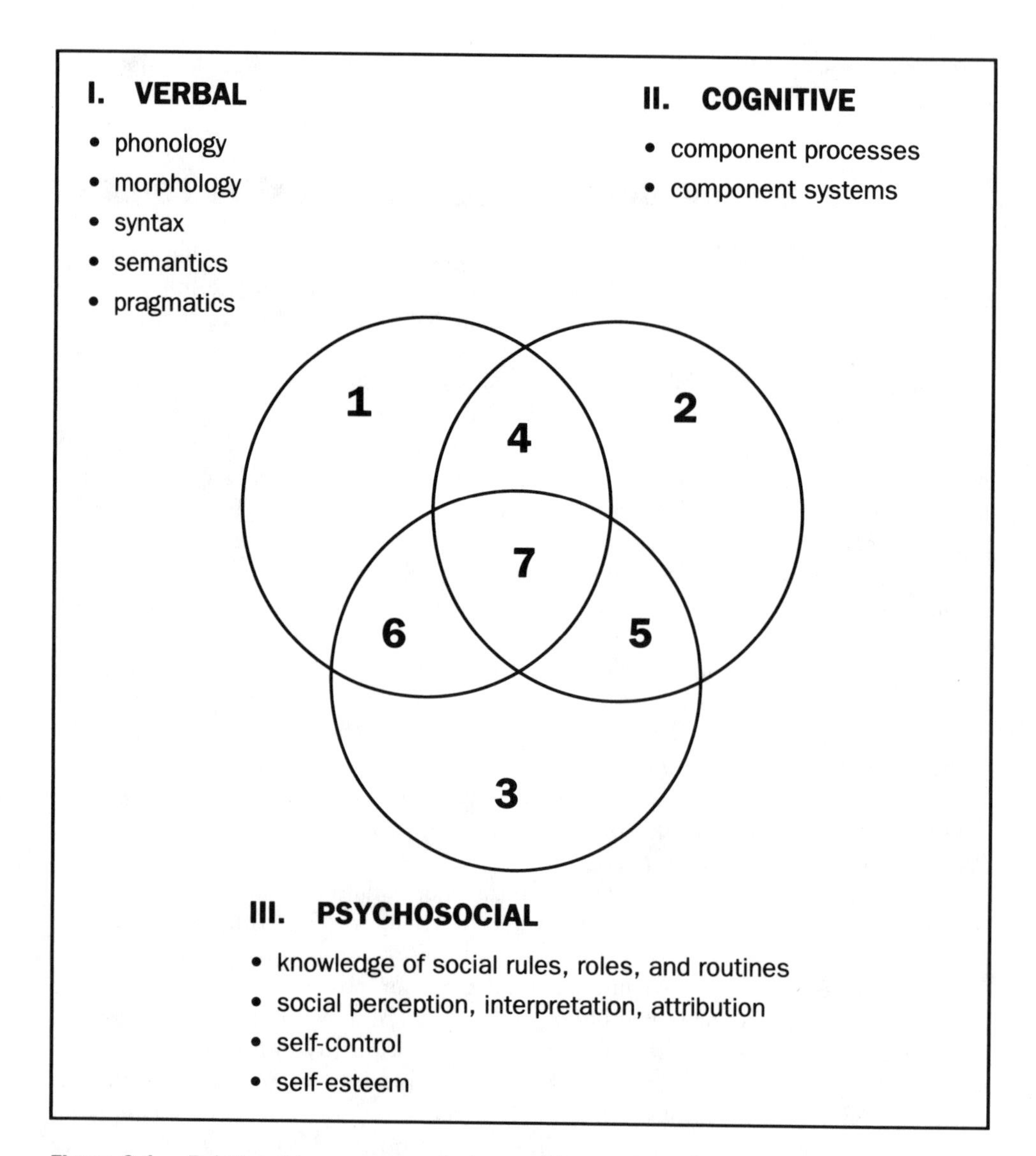

Figure 6.1. Relationships among verbal, cognitive, and psychosocial domains.

tive and verbal skills, and Area 7, the intersection of cognitive, verbal, and psychosocial skills.

ASSESSMENT

Speech Assessment

Assessment of dysarthria and related neuromuscular dysfunction following TBI is generally the same as assessment in the case of children with other causes of impairment. It includes evaluation of all speech-related motor systems (respiration, phonation, resonance, and articulation) and should be coordinated with physical and occupational therapy assessments. An otolaryngologist is generally consulted in the event of phonatory dysfunction (e.g., hoarse or breathy voice, inconsistent phonation), which may be due to laryngeal apraxia, unilateral vocal fold paralysis, subglottal stenosis, or granuloma.

The speech-language pathologist's assessment generally includes careful description of the perceptual features of speech (e.g., articulatory precision, loudness, rate, voice quality, variation in pitch and loudness, nasality) under a variety of instructions (speech and nonspeech tasks) and in a variety of settings. Diagnostic intervention is required to identify features of speech that can be modified with exercises or compensatory procedures. Because recovery in motor components of speech can continue for years following severe injuries, follow-up should be considered a long-term project, using periodic audiotape recordings to document change objectively.

The dysarthric student's general level of intelligibility should be determined in a variety of speaking contexts. Factors that impact on intelligibility include neuromuscular functioning, familiarity of the listener, demands of the speaking task, distractions in the environment, and the state of the speaker, including level of medication, fatigue, stress, and depression. In addition, confusion and tangentiality depress intelligibility by reducing the semantic support for listener interpretation. Fatigue levels and affective states (e.g., stress, anxiety, depression) have been found to be critical variables in relation to intelligibility of speech after head injury in adults (Sapir & Aronson, 1985, 1990).

Because cognitive and self-monitoring impairment can contribute to speech that is monotonous, overly loud or soft, or overly fast or slow, cognitive assessment is a critical component of speech evaluation in students with TBI. Furthermore, level of cognitive recovery dictates whether new learning, feedback, and self-monitoring techniques can be effectively used in speech intervention.

In addition to speech impairment related to the brain injury, young children may evidence developmental articulation errors. Standard procedures are used to identify the delay in speech development and to determine the usefulness of intervention.

Language Assessment

Table 4.2 in Chapter 4 presents questions that typically need to be asked about the language and communicative competence of children with TBI, together with suggestions of formal and informal procedures for answering the questions. Most of these assessment procedures are familiar to speech-language pathologists and are in common use with other populations of children. Of greatest importance in Table 4.2 are the Key Questions, which pinpoint critical aspects of the *process* of assessment rather than the specific tools to be used. Systematically answering these questions helps to reveal the language and communication profiles of children with TBI. Many of the other assessment themes discussed in Chapter 4, including the cognitive probes listed in Appendix 4A, apply to speech-language assessment as well as other assessments and should, therefore, be reviewed by speech-language pathologists.

In Chapter 4, we highlight selected assessment procedures that address the cognitive–communicative and cognitive–social–communicative dimensions that are often at center stage after head injury in children and adolescents. Many of the tasks that we recommend are not standardized and have no norms associated with them; therefore, they must be interpreted with great caution. Often only extreme results have interpretable clinical significance and interpretation is best accomplished by a clinician familiar with the performance of normally developing children in these areas. Despite these serious shortcomings, carefully selected informal assessment tasks often yield the most ecologically valid and clinically useful information.

Assessment of Language Deficits Associated with Cognitive Impairments

Speeded performance

Auditory comprehension tasks (e.g., the *Children's Token Test,* DiSimoni, 1978) can be administered at both a deliberate rate of speech and a relatively rapid rate of speech to determine the effects of increased rate of verbal input. Timed scores on reading tests should be compared with untimed scores to estimate the impact of time demands on reading comprehension. On the expressive side, clinicians should compare timed with untimed performance on word retrieval, naming, and narrative (spoken and written) tasks. For example, it is useful to document performance on the timed *Word Fluency* test (pediatric norms in Gaddes & Crocket, 1975) and subsequently compare with untimed performance. Classroom observation of children's language performance under time pressure is critical in developing a complete profile of the child's skills. Teachers are generally able to identify delayed responses to language and otherwise slow language performance. Furthermore, involving teachers in the assessment of language skills is a means of helping them to understand the classroom consequences of the student's injury.

Organization

In both auditory and reading comprehension, performance on word versus sentence versus paragraph versus multiparagraph tasks should be compared. Particular attention should be paid to the student's ability to grasp and clearly state the main idea from multiparagraph passages. As part of the initial assessment of well-recovered students, it is useful to assign them a chapter in one of their texts and request an outline and brief summary of the chapter. Students should be asked to time themselves, monitor the number of readings needed to acquire the information and write the summary, and finally evaluate the summary for organization and completeness. These self-monitoring tasks can become the first steps to self-awareness of the consequences of the injury.

Both spoken and written narratives should be analyzed for organization, coherence, elaboration, and completeness. An increasingly popular technique is to evaluate the organization of a narrative by analyzing its cohesive ties (Mentis & Prutting, 1987). Cohesive ties are the devices used to connect the meaning of one sentence to that of another, for example, pronominalization (using a pronoun to refer to something that was referred to by a noun in a previous sentence) and ellipsis (eliminating part of a sentence because the meaning is apparent from information stated in a previous sentence). It is important to remember, however, that *cohesion* refers solely to the *linguistic encoding* of narrative organization, not to the underlying *conceptual organization.* A narrative may be at the same time perfectly cohesive yet conceptually incoherent. Because cohesive markers, like other aspects of linguistic form, may return following head injury despite significant organizational problems, analysis of a narrative's *coherence* is more revealing than analysis of its *cohesion.*

Nonfictional discourse tasks (e.g., descriptive or procedural discourse) that lack an obvious and overlearned form of organization are often more useful for this analysis than storytelling or retelling. Because the organization or "grammar" of stories is often well rehearsed before the injury, storytelling tasks may be relatively insensitive to organizational weakness. Asking the child to describe a favorite game to a person with no knowledge of the game is useful for this purpose. Because children without brain damage have a wide range of performance on tasks of this sort, only obviously strong or weak descriptions have interpretable significance. Mentis and Prutting (1991) described interesting procedures for analyzing coherence in discourse.

Table 6.1 includes two descriptions of a complex rule-governed game, football. The first is linguistically unimpeachable and includes a variety of cohesive ties, but is incoherent. These are characteristics that one might anticipate in an adolescent with TBI whose language is disorganized and tangential. The second is well organized conceptually, but lacks the linguistic markers of organization. This description is more likely to be produced by an adolescent with specific language difficulties following left hemisphere stroke.

Young children can be asked to tell a story about an actual event following a demonstration by the clinician. On subsequent trials, the child should be asked to use the same format, but with different content. This reveals insight about the child's ability to learn verbal organization with practice. Barrier games (e.g., the child tells the clinician how to arrange toys so they are organized like the child's when the two sets of toys are separated by an opaque barrier) are also useful in evaluating and teaching verbal organization to young children. Young preschoolers can be asked to verbally direct the clinician to draw a face. Explicit instructions (e.g., "Put two eyes inside the circle," "Draw a line under the nose for the mouth") give evidence of the ability to organize language around an organizational task.

Environmental interference

Comprehension and production tasks, including conversation, should be sampled in distracting and nondistracting environments. In particular, the clinician should compare language performance in a quiet room with performance of the same task in a busy classroom. Effects of interference may be revealed in difficulty conversing in a busy hallway versus in a quiet therapy room. Teacher and parent reports are essential for understanding the impact of various types of interference on the child's language and interactive ability.

New learning

Appendix 4A in Chapter 4 includes a number of assessment probes related to memory and learning. Particularly with young children, the speech-language pathologist should identify a domain of vocabulary that is entirely new to the child (based on conversations with the parents and teacher) and teach it, carefully documenting the child's rate of learning.

Social–communicative competence

Standardized pragmatic inventories or rating scales, like that presented by Prutting and Kirchner (1987), are very useful in cataloging conversational strengths and

TABLE 6.1. Cohesion Versus Coherence in Written Descriptions of Football

Illustration 1: A description that is cohesive but not coherent

The ball is usually made out of leather, but sometimes it is rubber. They are the cheaper ones. We had a leather one when I was little, but it was real old. Football is played on big grass fields; you can find the players there. Actually, sometimes they are made out of artificial turf, which is pretty, but hard and so it causes injuries. My brother once tore his knee up real good on the artificial stuff. Then he was in the hospital for a week with that one. It's hard to figure, isn't it? Making people play like that so they injure themselves. Indoor stadiums need the artificial turf, but that's a pretty weird story in its own right, indoor football!! You think it's weird? Indoor? I do!

Football players on different teams wear different colors so they can tell each other apart. The referees and umpires and so forth wear stripes. Looks kind of like convicts. You hear jokes about refs, especially when the home team is losing. The fans drink alot, which may explain the bad humor. I don't think it should be allowed. When fans drink and get disruptive like that, the officials should just throw them out. But that wouldn't make them real popular, would it? Maybe the smart ones think about those things; I guess I would.

I'm not sure why half time is as long as it is. You can't believe the stuff that goes on. Bands, shows, presentations, people crowding every which way. And then you stand in line for hours for food. It's a madhouse. And besides that, I think the games are usually fixed anyway. It's probably all the mob, you know, since they seem to control most things these days, don't they? Even garbage collection, they say. I never could quite understand that one. Maybe that's what they deserve—trash.

Illustration 2: A description that is coherent but has few cohesive ties

Football is a rough game. Two teams—11 players on a team—play on a large grass field. The players try to score points. The team that has the most points at the end of the game wins. You get a touchdown—6 points—by carrying or catching the ball over the end line. You get a field goal—three points—by kicking the ball through large upright bars. After a touchdown, you get 1 point for kicking the ball through the upright bars.

The game starts when one team kicks the ball to the other team. The team with the ball has four plays to move the ball 10 yards. After 10 yards the team gets 4 more plays. If the team does not make 10 yards, they will probably kick the ball to the other team. The ball is advanced by running and avoiding being tackled, or by throwing and catching the ball. There is a great deal of physical contact. Players will do anything legal to tackle the ball carrier or protect the ball carrier. The game ends after two 30 minute halves. The team with the most points wins.

weaknesses. Given the typical effects of TBI, the pragmatic categories deserving special attention in Prutting and Kirchner's taxonomy include *topic* (selection, introduction, maintenance, change), *turn-taking* (initiation, response, contingency, conciseness), *lexical selection* (specificity, accuracy, cohesion), and *stylistic variation* (context and partner appropriateness). Erlich and Barry (1989) adapted Prutting and Kirchner's *Pragmatic Protocol* specifically for use with adults with head injury. Their *Communication Performance Scale* rates six behaviors: intelligibility, eye gaze, sentence formulation, coherence of narrative, topic, and initiation of communication. Rice, Sell, and Hadley (1990) described a social interaction assessment tool for use with preschool children.

Because many variables affect interactive competence, it is important to observe the student interacting in a variety of settings (e.g., clinic room, classroom, lunch room, social event) and with a variety of conversation partners. Parents and teachers are an important source of information. "Formal" pragmatic assessment in a clinical setting is often insufficient because the student may have learned the relevant pragmatic behaviors before the injury and may demonstrate use of the pragmatic skills with appropriate cues in a clinical setting, yet may be unable to interact appropriately in other settings or under additional stress.

Interviewing students about reasons for their apparently inappropriate interaction may be the most useful means of discovering gaps in social cognition. For example, students who are rude or overly familiar with teachers or other adults may have lost their understanding of the relevant social rules that are associated with conventional social roles, or students who respond emotionally to their peers may routinely misinterpret the intent of their peers' communication, for example, interpreting good-natured teasing as a serious insult. Students whose behavior is inappropriate relative to the context (e.g., speaking loudly in a study room) may fail to perceive or correctly interpret contextual cues. Because intervention for students with impaired social cognition differs from intervention for students with learned (conditioned) patterns of inappropriate behavior, it is important to gain insight into the student's perception of social cues, interpretation of the intent of communication partners, and general knowledge of social rules and roles. Teachers are often good sources of insight regarding students' skills in these areas. It may be useful to sample recognition and interpretation of emotional situations more formally, using procedures developed by Cicone, Wapner, and Gardner (1980) and Odom and Lemond (1972).

In the case of students with evident behavior problems, a joint assessment with a behavioral psychologist is useful. Often, the undesirable behaviors are a component of the student's communication system; that is, behaviors such as inattention or resistance in class, aggression toward peers, and withdrawal from social interaction may be the child's way of communicating feelings or thoughts that could be communicated much more effectively in some other way. This component of the child's functioning should, therefore, be evaluated and treated jointly by the language specialist and the behavioral specialist. In addition, communication frustration and/or inappropriate responses from partners may contribute to the student's behavior problem. In these cases, the communication–behavior matrix should be addressed jointly by the behavioral psychologist and the speech-language pathologist.

Consultation with the child's social worker or psychologist is useful for purposes of distinguishing social–emotional reactions, such as depression and social withdrawal, from communicative weakness grounded in impaired social cognition or in learned maladaptive behavior patterns. A combination of emotional reactions, behavioral responses, and associated social interaction problems may emerge several months after the student returns to school, when it becomes clear that academic and social life has been significantly changed.

Acquiring Appropriate Services

Speech-language pathologists sensitive to the needs of students with TBI often complain that state or school district criteria for speech-language therapy services prevent many children from receiving the services and support that they need. This is a combined consequence of three overlapping issues. First, many children with TBI recover adequate levels of knowledge and skill in the areas probed by the officially sanctioned assessment instruments, which are generally focused on motor speech, phonologic, morphologic, and syntactic functioning. Second, criteria for services were developed largely for children with *developmental* delays or disorders. Because children with acquired brain injury often recover much of what they had acquired before the injury, their profiles predictably vary from those of other children with speech or language therapy needs. Third, students and their families may initially resist special services because of an overly optimistic hope for full spontaneous recovery.

School districts vary with respect to adherence to formal criteria for services. Some speech-language pathologists have little difficulty serving students with TBI whose legitimate language or communication needs are not revealed by accepted standardized tests. Services may be consultative in nature, classroom based, or traditional "pull-out" therapy (discussed later in this chapter). With the addition in 1990 of TBI as an educational disability under PL 101-476, it is reasonable to expect that valid assessments and appropriate criteria for services will be increasingly used for this group of children.

Other districts resist providing services to students who fail to meet the letter of established criteria for those services. At the present time, justification for speech-language therapy for children with TBI may require the use of two strategies: (a) documenting the student's needs by completing a creative assessment, guided by the assessment questions in Table 4.2 and the assessment probes listed in this chapter and in Appendix 4A in Chapter 4, and (b) pointing out to the relevant decision makers that service decisions must be based on *valid* assessments and that the language tests generally accepted by school authorities have not been validated for use with this population. In some cases, the children may need every minute of available time for classroom learning. Under these circumstances, the speech-language pathologist may be able to contribute to the student's program through classroom-based therapy or by serving as a resource to the classroom teacher. Some children profit from additional after-school therapy that must be carefully coordinated with the school program.

SPEECH-LANGUAGE INTERVENTION

Students with TBI, like other students, should receive services based on their individual needs rather than on presumed needs related to a label that they happen to wear. In many cases, the needs of a student with TBI resemble those of students who fall under other diagnostic categories. Therefore, components of the vast literature on speech and language intervention for students with speech, language, or general communication disorders from birth are relevant to most students with TBI. Recognizing the importance of a new disability category should not entail reinventing valuable clinical wheels. The goals of this discussion of treatment options are to highlight special considerations for children with TBI and to emphasize in some detail the social communication themes that are frequently most critical for these students.

Speech Intervention

Experienced speech-language pathologists are familiar with intervention procedures designed for students with developmental articulation and phonologic disorders and for those with neuromuscular speech disorders (dysarthria and apraxia). Children with severe neuromuscular disorders secondary to TBI are treated much like students with cerebral palsy. Neurodevelopmental treatment procedures are particularly useful and should be coordinated with occupational and physical therapy intervention.

There are, however, important therapy qualifications for children with TBI. First, it is typically not recommended that clinicians directly target mild to moderate articulation problems or symptoms of dysarthria or apraxia during the early phases of confusion and rapid recovery following the injury. The speech symptoms often resolve without intervention. Furthermore, children in this phase of recovery are not good candidates for the type of drill and practice associated with speech intervention.

Second, many children with TBI have impaired phonation secondary to unilateral vocal fold paresis and hypernasal speech secondary to flaccid velopharyngeal musculature. In extreme cases, surgical intervention (e.g., vocal fold injection) or prosthetics (e.g., palatal lift) should be considered, but not before at least a year of recovery time and vigorous therapy have failed to resolve the problem. We have worked with several children with significantly impaired phonation and resonance several months postinjury, who have recovered near-normal speech, given considerable effort and time. Furthermore, velopharyngeal incompetence may be a result of incoordination and therefore not responsive to prosthetic intervention. Candidates for surgical or prosthetic management should be carefully selected using nasal endoscopy or videofluoroscopy procedures to clearly specify the problem.

Third, sensory systems must be evaluated and the contribution of impaired sensation or distorted interpretation of sensory feedback carefully considered. If natural feedback mechanisms are weak, which they often are in TBI, greater than normal concentration on video and audio feedback in therapy should be explored. In the event of significant frontal lobe damage and consequent impairment of self-monitoring, pacing boards may be useful in speech therapy.

Augmentative Communication Intervention

Augmentative communication options for students with severe speech impairment after TBI are the same as those for other nonspeaking students. Clinicians should be familiar with the growing literature on this important subject. Again, however, there are important qualifications and points of emphasis for students with TBI.

During the early stages of recovery when children gradually emerge from coma and begin to interact with the environment, it is reasonable first to promote natural and developmentally early types of communication, such as expressing desires and feelings by means of natural gestures and eye gaze. Typically, children move through this stage of recovery in a hospital where the clinical temptation is to teach them a system for expressing "yes" and "no" long before they have achieved the level of orientation and cognitive recovery that would support this achievement. In normal development, "yes" and "no" in the sense of affirmation and denial are relatively late acquisitions and appear months after children are actively expressing other communicative intentions, such as wants, demands, and rejection. When the child is at a stage of recovery that supports the learning of a yes–no system, it is important to choose interpretable gestures (e.g., thumbs up–down) rather than signals that are ambiguous because they are also reflexive behaviors (e.g., eye blinking or hand squeezing). Ease of movement is also a critical factor because children at this stage of recovery tire easily and will not consistently use a gesture that requires substantial effort.

During the stages of recovery characterized by confusion, severely impaired learning, and in many cases fairly rapid recovery, augmentative options should be chosen that are simple to use, easy to understand, and readily modified (e.g., homemade picture, symbol, word, or letter boards); that do not tax new learning skill (as sign language or a complex symbol system would); and that are not expensive (because the child's needs are likely to change rapidly). Pictures, words, or symbols can be added as recovery permits.

It is unreasonable at this stage to expect the child to initiate use of the augmentative system or to generalize its use from a training setting to an application setting. However, even if use of a communication board requires constant cuing, it still may serve valuable purposes. First, its presence on the child's lap tray tells potential communication partners that the child is capable of communicating, and the board offers possible topics. This may increase the number of positive interactions over the course of a day, which by itself is therapeutic. Second, even if a communication act is cued, it is still a communication act and gives the child the important opportunity to express desires and feelings. Finally, searching for pictures, symbols, or words on the board is a useful and functional visual–perceptual and perceptual–motor exercise that can be performed many times a day. At this stage, parents may need to be reassured that the use of a nonspeech communication system has no negative impact on the recovery of speech.

Communication boards are limited with respect to the content that a nonspelling child is capable of expressing. Inevitably, parents and staff make use of a 20-questions–type guessing game to enable the child to express additional thoughts and feelings. This game potentially holds great frustration for both parties. One way to reduce, though certainly not eliminate, the frustrations is to structure the game according to an agreed-upon set of categories and frequently used messages. The parents may be in the best position to negotiate such a set of categories (e.g., a person? food or drink? a feeling? something to do? something about home?) and messages with the child. With this system in place, communication partners are not left to guess in a vacuum, but rather proceed systematically through the set of categories until the correct category is selected and then through a set of frequently occurring preselected messages under that category. This does not solve the communication problem of the child who cannot speak, but may help.

If children remain nonspeaking following return of adequate cognitive functioning, a new set of considerations comes into focus. More sophisticated systems, such as computer-based speech output devices, are then worth considering. Consultation with a specialized rehabilitation technology center is useful in light of the complexity of the issues and rapid changes in this field. Regional centers of this sort generally conduct interdisciplinary team evaluations (involving physical, occupational, and speech therapy; psychology; special education; and rehabilitation engineering) and work together with the individual and family to select the most effective and appropriate communication system. Unless there is extremely persuasive pathophysiologic evidence that speech is not a reasonable goal, expensive devices should not be recommended until well over a year postinjury. We have worked with several children and adolescents who lacked serviceable speech 1 year after the injury, but who subsequently became quite intelligible, often with great effort and intensive therapy. In one such case, a girl injured at age 14, the neurosurgeon had earlier insisted that she would never regain functional speech because he had removed the speech center of her brain during the initial debridement following an extremely severe injury. In addition to the difficulty making a confident prediction regarding the recovery of speech, families are unlikely to be emotionally ready for consideration of a speech device in the early months after the injury.

Clinicians must also be sensitive to the likelihood of severe frustration in a child with TBI who becomes an augmentative communication user. Whereas a child with cerebral palsy has no experience with effortless and fast verbal communication, and may therefore be more than willing to work laboriously to produce a spoken message with a device, the child with TBI is accustomed to communicating quickly and easily. The effort required and the desperately slow pace of the device may be intolerable. Furthermore, the child knows what he or she should sound like, and even the best synthesized voice is not that familiar voice. Ironically, frustration tolerance is one of the likely victims of the brain injury; therefore, the child's possible resistance to nonspeech communication must be anticipated and addressed with great sensitivity.

The resistance may also represent the child's conscious or subconscious conviction that learning a nonspeech method of communicating is in effect giving up on speech. The student and family may require ongoing reassurance that augmentative communication does not interfere with and may facilitate the reacquisition of speech. Furthermore, if intelligible speech is recovered, a backup system for communicating may continue to be necessary in the event of fatigue or communication partners who cannot understand the individual's speech. Finally, in the face of frustration and resistance, the student is well advised to practice using the device in a nonthreatening, noninteractive context rather than in the context of actual communication exchanges. This progression may be inconsistent with the goal of generalization, but serves the purpose of giving the student time to adjust to the device and to gain adequate mastery before using it functionally. Engaging students in decisions about the device, about the amount and type of practice, and about the transition to functional use helps to reduce the behavioral and emotional threats.

Despite apparently good cognitive recovery, the student's efficiency of new learning and effectiveness of executive functions may continue to be weak. Therefore, the considerations discussed in relation to students in the confused stages of recovery may continue to be relevant.

Specific Language Intervention

Students with specific language impairments in the phonologic, morphologic, or syntactic domains of language may be candidates for types of intervention well known to speech-language pathologists who work with children with congenital language delays. In the case of students with specific language impairments and also cognitive–

communicative and cognitive–social–communicative problems, careful decisions must be made about clinical priorities. The easiest but not necessarily the wisest course may be to focus on language targets familiar to the clinician when other issues are more important in the life of the student.

Cognitive–Language Intervention

Several of the treatment discussions in Chapter 5 belong equally in this chapter, including the large section on therapies for impaired organizational functioning: teaching specific event scripts to young or very impaired children and using the scripts to facilitate improved receptive and expressive language; teaching other organizational schemes; using feature analysis activities to promote greater efficiency in language comprehension and expression, including word retrieval; and teaching higher levels of language organization for improving comprehension of text and organization of written narratives. Case Study 6.1 illustrates some of the cognitive themes discussed in Chapter 5, with a particular emphasis on the language dimensions of cognitive dysfunction. The extended discussions in Chapter 5 of compensatory strategies and metacognitive skills could also have appeared in this chapter. All of the considerations reviewed in those sections of Chapter 5 apply to the teaching of compensatory language and communication strategies. In addition, many of the specific procedures presented in the appendixes to Chapter 5 are language or communication strategies. The placement of these discussions in a chapter on cognitive rehabilitation should highlight the interdisciplinary nature of these important themes. In summary, Chapters 5 and 6 should be read together as a discussion of language intervention following TBI.

CASE STUDY 6.1

Feature Analysis, Word Retrieval, and Reading

At age 7, KW presented with above-average IQ together with a history of delayed language, significant naming and word-retrieval problems, and very slow acquisition of reading and writing skills. Scores on tests of language comprehension were below levels predicted by his IQ, but were generally within normal limits. Expressive difficulty resulting from his word-finding problems had led KW to develop excellent pantomime skills, which he freely used in the event of difficulty expressing his thoughts with language.

KW's thinking was fast paced and very creative. His associations were often unusual, sometimes very clever. The large number of loose associations seemed to be partially responsible for his frustration in not finding the correct word to express his thoughts. During the initial language evaluation, KW drew a picture that indicated great insight into his language processing (Figure 6.2). Searching for words in his head was like flying a jet airplane from cloud to cloud hoping that the cloud would be there when he arrived and that the correct word would be on the cloud. This image nicely captured the pace of KW's thinking and also the frustration of looking for words in an environment as disorderly, unpredictable, and changeable as clouds in the sky.

Figure 6.2. Drawing of a 7-year-old boy with word-retrieval problems. His description: "This is me flying around looking for the names."

On the assumption that KW's semantic system was rich in concepts and loose associations but poor in organization, a therapy program was developed that centered around the Feature Analysis Guide (Figure 5.1 in Chapter 5). KW quickly learned the guide. However, unlike children with weak vocabularies and poor divergent thinking, he was restricted to giving one or two of the most important features per feature category; that is, each analysis of a concept using the guide was at the same time an exercise in convergent thinking (e.g., "Tell me only the most important use for this, the most likely place to find this, etc.") and an effort to inject structure and organization into his lexicon and semantic knowledge base. Capitalizing on his own image of the process of finding words, he drove a toy plane from box to box on the Feature Analysis Guide as he filled them with appropriate features.

KW's typical feature analysis exercise consisted of the following steps:

1. He completed the analysis with only the most important words in each box. The words were printed clearly on the guide by the clinician.

2. KW reviewed his completed analysis by reading the words in the boxes. This served a rehearsal purpose and also gave him a successful reading experience. He was nearly always able to read the words, in part because he had just dictated them and in part because the semantic structure that generated the word initially was still present to guide his reading.

3. KW then used the information that he had produced on the Feature Analysis Guide to dictate an organized descriptive paragraph about the item that he had analyzed. It was important that this was a structured descriptive paragraph rather than a story because of KW's need to harness his associations and flights of fancy when necessary. The dictated paragraph was clearly printed by the clinician.

4. KW then read the paragraph that he had just dictated. For the reasons cited in Item 2 above, he was generally successful in reading this paragraph. He then evaluated the paragraph for accuracy and completeness (relative to the information on the Feature Analysis Guide) and for organization and importance of the information that was included.

Although initially uncomfortable with the structure and organization that the guide and associated rules imposed on his thinking, KW came to enjoy the exercises, no doubt largely because they facilitated relatively fluent and easy reading in contrast to his struggles and lack of success with a phonetic approach to reading at school. KW's success in reading his own dictations is reminiscent of the whole language approach to reading and writing. In contrast to that approach, however, KW's dictation, reading, and writing were highly organized from without, consistent with his need to create greater semantic organization as a basis for improved expressive language and reading skills. His mother clearly understood the rationale underlying the therapy program and appreciated the effect that it appeared to have on KW's reading and ability to describe things in words without resorting to pantomime. Several times each week she devoted 20 to 30 minutes at home to completing one of these exercises with KW.

KW's second-grade teacher was not interested in departing from her preferred approach to teaching reading. In other cases, however, speech-language pathologists and classroom teachers have collaboratively used approaches similar to KW's as a basis for semantically organized and enriched vocabulary learning and as a basis for reading and writing exercises.

Social–Cognitive–Communicative Intervention

The pragmatic focus in speech-language pathology that has grown in momentum over the past decade has positively influenced professional practice in at least two fundamental ways. First, clinicians now recognize that their job is not done when a student acquires a speech or language skill in a treatment setting. Unless the new skill becomes part of the individual's functional communication repertoire and is put to use in functional settings, little has been accomplished. Second, speech-language pathologists now consider pragmatic aspects of communication (including conversational skills, effective expression of varied communicative intentions, and general social skills) to be critical areas for their professional intervention. This focus is particularly important in serving students with TBI, given the multiple sources of vulnerability of social communication and social skills (Rustin & Kuhr, 1989).

Social skills include general competencies and specific behaviors that enable an individual to initiate and maintain positive and effective social interaction, to achieve acceptance by peers and others, and to successfully meet the demands of the social environment in school, on the job, at home, and in the community (Cartledge & Milburn, 1978; Walker, 1988). The two most critical categories of social skill in school are those involving teacher relations and those involving peer relations. For example, to be successful in the eyes of teachers, students must be skilled at compliance (e.g., following directions, completing assignments) and appropriately making their needs known. To be accepted by peers, students must be skilled at cooperating, sharing, conversing, compromising, disagreeing, and more (Walker, McConnell, & Clark, 1984).

In their review of the literature on social skills in grade school–aged children, La Greca and Mesibov (1979) identified nine areas of social behavior that contribute most to positive relationships and acceptance by peers:

1. Showing enjoyment in social situations (e.g., smiling and laughing)
2. Greeting others
3. Joining ongoing peer activities
4. Inviting peers to join activities
5. Conversing (e.g., taking turns, setting topics, asking questions)
6. Sharing and cooperating
7. Complimenting peers
8. Playing effectively
9. Maintaining hygiene and physical appearance

It is clear from this and many similar lists that "social skills" is a generic category that subsumes "pragmatic skills" as that term is currently used by speech-language pathologists. Greeting, inviting, conversing, and complimenting are among the skills commonly targeted in pragmatics training. The value of bringing these aspects of language under the broader umbrella of social skills is that all of these skills relate directly to effective social interaction and acceptance by others. Dealing with the linguistic components of social skills separately from the nonlinguistic (e.g., maintaining hygiene, playing cooperatively) fragments what should be a highly integrated and intensive effort to increase the individual's chances for satisfying social relationships and peer acceptance.

Approaches to intervention for students with impaired social interaction vary according to the student's age, setting, and nature of the impairment. We have found it useful to group these varied approaches into four roughly distinguishable categories: behavioral, social cognition and metacognitive, social–emotional, and atheoretic specific skills approaches. Considerable overlap exists among these categories and in many cases it is possible and even desirable to address an individual student's needs in more than one way. In other cases (discussed below), the approaches are incompatible. Medication may be a useful complement to any of the approaches.

Social skills training had attracted creative clinicians and educators long before the "pragmatic revolution" brought these themes to center stage in speech-language pathology. Behavioral and clinical psychologists, social workers, child development specialists, special educators, and others have developed a variety of programs and procedures that target social skills, including social communication. Program development in this area was stimulated in the 1970s by the deinstitutionalization of adults with developmental disabilities and by efforts to educate children with disabilities in a regular education environment (Phillips, 1985). Our goal in this section is to provide a framework for thinking about social skills training and then to summarize several intervention programs selected because of their relevance to the needs of students with TBI and because they may not be familiar to practicing speech-language pathologists.

Behavioral approaches

In their purest form, behavioral or operant approaches are based on the following assumptions: (a) a child's interactive behavior, like other aspects of behavior, is a combined consequence of the antecedent stimulus conditions present at the time of the behavior and the child's history of reinforcement; (b) the likelihood that the child will behave in a specific way is increased when that response is followed by some reinforcing event and decreased in the absence of such a consequence; (c) therefore, the options for modifying social behavior are to change the environment or antecedent conditions within which the child interacts with others or to change the child's history of reinforcement by systematically rewarding positive social behaviors and ignoring undesirable behaviors.

Various procedures, including modeling and direct instruction, may be used to stimulate positive social behaviors that are subsequently shaped and reinforced. Direct teaching of this sort is a component of traditional social skills training. Negative behavioral approaches include punishment as a procedure for decreasing undesirable behavior. However, the use of negative approaches has decreased because of legal and ethical considerations regarding punishment as a behavioral technique and because these approaches have in many cases been shown to be less successful than positive approaches (LaVigna & Donnellan, 1986). Countless refinements and detailed procedures exist within this general framework. Specific behavioral treatment procedures are listed later in this section.

For those children and adolescents with TBI who are proceeding through the stages of recovery characterized by severe confusion, disorientation, disinhibition, and possibly agitation, a behavioral approach, possibly combined with carefully selected and monitored medication, is generally the treatment of choice. The focus during this stage is on environmental manipulation (or "antecedent control") to decrease the occurrence of maladaptive behavior by eliminating its "triggers," and on contingency management (rewarding desirable behavior and ignoring or redirecting undesirable behavior) to prevent the evolution of learned maladaptive behavior. The techniques available to staff include *prevention* (e.g., controlling environmental events to eliminate behavioral triggers, keeping the child productively occupied, having reasonable performance expectations to minimize frustration, ensuring that active children have adequate physical exercise) and *redirection* (carefully shifting the individual's attention away from the stimulus that triggered the behavioral response without at the same time rewarding the undesirable behavior). Generally, undesirable behaviors during this stage of recovery are a consequence of confusion, extreme impulsiveness, or perseveration and are not learned or manipulative behaviors. However, it requires careful behavioral programming to prevent these behaviors from becoming learned maladaptive behavior patterns (Jacobs, 1993). This stage of recovery typically occurs in a hospital or rehabilitation facility, but may be observed in a child returned prematurely to school.

Other candidates for systematic and intensive behavioral programming (both contingency management and antecedent control) are students who had significant behavioral problems before the injury, students who acquired a set of learned maladaptive behaviors because of mismanagement during the acute phases of recovery, students whose behaviors (e.g., aggressive, self-injurious, or highly disruptive behaviors) are so serious that they require immediate management, and students with substantial cognitive impairment for the long term postinjury. Consistently managed behavioral programming is also often a component of the overall program for students receiving counseling, training in specific social skills, and intervention designed to improve social cognition.

Cohen, Joyce, Rhoades, and Welks (1985) argued that students with TBI may not be considered candidates for traditional behavior modification approaches because they may not remember why they are being rewarded, punished, or timed out; may fail to identify the causal connection between their behavior and its consequence; or may lack the neurologic wherewithal to control their impulsive responses. In extreme cases, these are very important considerations; however, most students with TBI who are in a school setting are able to profit from creative and flexible use of the principles of applied behavior analysis. Antecedent control procedures make few assumptions about cognitive functions.

Procedures designed to establish a repertoire of specific, concrete, observable positive social behaviors within a behavioral framework include the following:

1. *Reinforcing:* Critical to operant approaches to intervention is a systematic procedure for rewarding target behavior, beginning with consistently given powerful reinforcers (possibly tangible rewards) and progressing to an intermittent and variable schedule of more natural reinforcers (e.g., peer approval, accomplishment of a social goal), to promote maintenance of the social behavior in a natural environment.
2. *Ignoring or redirecting:* Redirecting (without reinforcing) is used to interrupt a negative behavioral set and help the child to resume positive behavior. If the undesirable behavior is perseverative or extremely disruptive, redirection is preferable to ignoring (which may have no effect whatsoever on the behavior).
3. *Modeling:* Demonstration of positive interaction is often done by peers who are then rewarded for their behavior. The goal is to stimulate the trainee to imitate the behavioral model and to experience its positive consequences.
4. *Direct instructing, prompting, shaping, cuing, and fading:* Many students require more than modeling to produce the desired behavior. In these cases, options include direct instructing, prompting, shaping (stimulating components of the target behavior and gradu-

ally increasing the complexity of the response), cuing (reminding the child of what is expected of him), and fading (gradually reducing the prompts and cues).

5. *Practicing:* Typically new skills are practiced until they are relatively automatic.
6. *Role playing:* Role playing is a critical component of most approaches to social skills training. The context should be as natural as possible.
7. *Scripting:* Learning scripts for negotiating specific social situations is a component of several approaches to social skills training.

Within a behavioral framework, training generally follows a traditional treatment hierarchy: acquisition, stabilization, and generalization. Procedures designed to promote generalization of newly learned positive social skills include the following:

1. *Overlearning* (stimulus control): This entails sufficient practice that a new behavior becomes habitual.
2. *Stimulus similarity* (functional equivalence): If possible, the context of training should include features of the application context so that the likelihood of transfer from training to real-life application is increased. For example, if the goal is appropriate classroom interaction, the actual classroom or at least a simulated classroom is the most reasonable place for the intervention to occur. Many school clinicians use the lunch room as the setting for social skills intervention.
3. *Stimulus variability:* Systematically varying the setting, activities, materials, and people during the training program should increase the likelihood of transfer to real-life settings. Having at least three staff members involved in the training (e.g., teacher, speech-language pathologist, and psychologist), each in a different setting with somewhat different activities, may increase the likelihood of generalization (Koegel & Koegel, 1988). In the absence of such variation, new social behaviors may be so strongly associated with some aspect of the training context that generalization has no chance of occurring. This is particularly true of individuals who have significant limitations and are "stimulus bound."
4. *Coaching:* Training programs often encourage the clinician to accompany the student into challenging situations and provide suggestions and feedback as indicated. In schools, teachers and paraprofessionals are in the best position to play this coaching role.
5. *Natural reinforcement:* Once behaviors are established, they should have consequences that are as similar as possible to consequences in the natural environment, including both reinforcing events and real-world consequences of unskilled social behavior (Favell & Reid, 1988). This argues against extended use of highly

artificial reinforcers (e.g., food, stickers) during training. One possibility, generally advocated more actively by professionals working within a metacognitive framework, is to encourage students to reinforce themselves for successful social behavior.

6. *Involvement of natural environment people:* Ideally, teachers, parents, and possibly peers are well oriented to the program so that the student has consistent responses to behavior between the training and natural environments.
7. *Homework assignments:* Higher level students can be asked to experiment with new social skills in their real-life environment and keep records of successes and failures.

Social skills training programs that embody these principles are described in the section entitled "Social Skills Training Programs: Selected Illustrations."

Social-cognition and metacognitive approaches

The primary assumption underlying a social cognition or metacognitive approach to social skills training is that social behavior is not simply a consequence of external factors, that is, the existing stimulus conditions together with the individual's history of reinforcement. In addition to these factors (which are undoubtedly very important), consideration must be given to the individual's (a) perception and interpretation of the social situation within which he or she acts, including potentially subtle social cues; (b) interpretation of the behavior of others; (c) knowledge of conventional social rules, roles, and routines; (d) goals; (e) ability to consider alternative responses and predict the consequences of proposed actions (including potential rewards); and (f) ability to self-direct, self-monitor, self-evaluate, and self-correct. Social information is processed through a complex filter that may yield a response that is consistent with the situation *as it was perceived and interpreted,* but is judged by others to be inappropriate or in some way awkward or unskilled (Dodge, 1985). Many children with TBI have difficulty perceiving social cues and interpreting social situations (Petterson, 1988) and may have lost basic knowledge of social roles and the rules that are conventionally associated with them.

Advocates of a social-cognition or metacognitive approach often begin with the conviction that traditional behavioral methods, although possibly effective in improving behavior in training contexts, have demonstrated limited capacity to extend newly acquired skills beyond the training setting and to ensure maintenance over time (Baer, 1981; Chandler, Lubeck, & Fowler, 1992; Collet-Klingenberg & Chadsey-Rusch, 1991; Hansen, Watson-Perczel, & Christopher, 1989; Meichenbaum, 1983; Vaughn, McIntosh, & Zaragoza, 1991; Zaragoza, Vaughn, & McIntosh, 1991). Furthermore, even if generalized from training to application setting, a limited repertoire of specific behavioral skills is insufficient to enable an individual to successfully negotiate the infinitely varied social situations and demands that life presents (Stokes, 1992). Successful graduates of strict behavioral programs often appear stiff and awkward in natural social environments because the demands of the situations in which they must act inevitably vary to some extent from those of their training context. Flexibility and adaptability are difficult to train as specific behaviors. For these reasons, the traditional behavioral model of social skills training (i.e., trainer model the behavior;

learner imitate and practice the behavior with feedback; trainer shape the behavior until it is used correctly) has been judged by many to be inadequate.

Because metacognitive approaches are designed in large part to ensure generalization and flexibility by focusing on internal control (i.e., self-direction—*how to decide* vs. *what to do*) from the early stages of training, there is less reason to distinguish in this approach between procedures designed to establish new social skills and procedures designed to promote generalization. Children inevitably will fail from time to time in their social interactions, but ideally they will have acquired the ability to learn from failure and to adapt their social behaviors in response to natural social feedback (Rose-Krasnor, 1985). Within this framework, procedures for both establishing new positive social skills and generalizing them to the natural environment include the following:

1. *Building the social knowledge base:* (a) *Knowledge of self*—To be autonomous and effective social agents, students need to understand themselves as decision makers, people who are capable of choices that may be positive or negative and who are ultimately responsible for the choices they make. Furthermore, they need to be aware of their strengths and weaknesses as social agents. (b) *Knowledge of social roles*—Students need to understand the different roles played by authority figures (e.g., parents, teachers, employers), peers (friends, acquaintances, strangers), and others. (c) *Knowledge of social rules, conventions, and expectations*—Students need to be aware of generally accepted rules governing interaction in varied social situations and with individuals occupying different roles (e.g., teachers, parents, friends, acquaintances). (d) *Knowledge of social routines*—Over the course of normal development, a large number of routines and their attendant rules of appropriate behavior are learned, much as one would learn scripts. As with any other component of the knowledge base, one should not assume that pretraumatically acquired social knowledge in any of these four areas has survived the injury. Reteaching may be necessary. Sheinker and Sheinker's (1988) metacognitive social skills training program describes a variety of procedures designed to build or rebuild aspects of the social knowledge base.

2. *Developing awareness of social situations and others' intent:* See Table 6.2 for examples of procedures to improve social interaction.

3. *Brainstorming about alternative actions:* One of the advantages of group intervention is that groups are typically much better than individuals at divergent thinking, that is, generating a variety of possible courses of action in a situation and considering a variety of possible outcomes. Brainstorming is used concretely to produce alternatives to be explored. It is also used more generally to encourage flexible thinking about behavioral choices. Metacognitive questioning (Item 4) is used to evaluate options once they are generated.

TABLE 6.2. A Program for Improving Conversational Interaction

GOAL: Develop awareness of the characteristics of conversation, including conversational rules and conventions

Procedures:

1. Identify the features of conversation (e.g., opening and closing, topics and topic control [setting, maintaining, and shifting], turn-taking, speech acts, uses of conversation, appropriate locations and behaviors involved). The Feature Analysis Guide (Figure 5.1) can be used to structure this analysis.
2. Using video- or audio-taped conversations, identify and evaluate the features of conversations. Discuss the rules and social conventions that apply to the conversation and explore why those rules may have evolved (e.g., without turn-taking, information would not be transmitted).
3. Role-play conversations with varied patterns (e.g., balanced vs. unequal turn-taking patterns). Explore situations in which different patterns may be appropriate.

GOAL: Develop awareness of speaker intent and improve ability to interpret speaker intent

Procedures:

1. Using video- or audio-taped conversations, discuss the speaker's intent. Consider possible interpretations of the speaker's intent, identifying and evaluating the evidence that supports each interpretation or inference (e.g., "I think that was an insult because of the tone of voice"; "I doubt it, because I know that he wouldn't do that and because he was smiling—I think it was good-natured teasing"). Discussions should be sufficiently deep to sensitize students to the complexity of interpretations and the ease with which distorted interpretations are generated. Repeated why questions are useful to force deeper analysis. If there are patterns to a given student's distorted interpretations (e.g., regularly inferring negative intent when none was present), this should be pointed out.
2. Role-play conversations with a variety of speaker intents (e.g., to console, scare, insult, encourage, threaten, entertain, punish). Identify signals of intent.

GOAL: Develop awareness of conversational topics; conventions for setting, maintaining, extending, shifting, or abruptly changing a topic; and methods of conversational control

Procedures:

1. Identify the topic and trace the topic flow in taped TV programs or in group conversation.
2. Practice maintaining the topic in conversation. Write a topic on the board, then analyze a taped conversation to determine the relevance of each contribution.
3. Practice shifting the conversational topic. Determine if the shifts were logical and easy to follow, or might confuse the listener.
4. Practice extending the topic by adding relevant information and seeking information from other interactants by using open-ended questions (e.g., "What do you like about the game?").
5. Practice controlling conversations by using specific techniques for opening, interrupting, shifting topic (e.g., marking abrupt shifts with "Oh, that reminds me"), and clos-

(*continues*)

TABLE 6.2. *Continued*

ing conversations. Practice using assertions to convey conviction; questions to get more information, confirm information, or transfer a turn; indirect requests to give polite commands (e.g., "Could you please open the window for me?"); and markers such as "Yes, go on" to show that one is listening to the speaker.

6. Make a chart of appropriate topics in relation to situations and conversation partners. This could be individualized for each student or identify generic social conventions.

GOAL: Develop effective use of varied speech acts

Procedure:

1. Practice techniques for such communicative intents as giving information, requesting information, directing, demanding, asserting, refusing, warning, threatening, promising, complimenting, criticizing, teasing, joking, and comforting.

GOAL: Develop awareness of one's listener

Procedures:

1. Practice "taking readings" and making inferences about the listener's interest in and knowledge of a topic, comprehension of what has been said, emotional reaction to what has been said, and feelings about the speaker. Discuss how best to present information to various types of listener.
2. Role-play communication situations with listeners of varying status, age, comprehension abilities, and familiarity. Determine appropriate vocabulary, speech acts, and intonation patterns for each listener.

GOAL: Develop effective speaking and listening skills, including compensatory strategies

Procedures:

1. Practice strategies for repairing comprehension or production breakdowns (e.g., "Could you repeat that, please?" "I don't think I'm making myself clear.").
2. Practice strategies for improving speech intelligibility (e.g., self-pacing, using a portable microphone).
3. Practice eye contact, interest postures, and continuation signals.
4. Discuss and rehearse specific rules and social conventions (e.g., use polite phrases, don't say certain things in public, don't talk with your mouth full).
5. Role-play conversations that focus on informativeness, truthfulness, relevance, and clarity.

---

4. *Metacognitive questioning:* The clinician repeatedly asks "how" and "why" questions centered around the following internal control themes: "(1) Why would you choose that alternative? (2) How is this alternative a better choice at this time and in this situation? (3) How did you go about making that decision?" (Sheinker & Sheinker, 1988, p. 3).
5. *Product monitoring:* Clinicians encourage students to try two or more alternative behaviors in a social situation and concretely compare the results in relation to their goals. For example, non-

compliant students can document the consequences of refusing to complete an assignment and later of completing an assignment. These consequences are then compared. In this way, students are encouraged to make good decisions because of their own clear assessment of the positive consequences.

6. *Out-loud thinking:* This procedure is used by the clinician or teacher to model internal problem-solving and decision-making processes, as opposed to modeling the prescribed external behavior. Out-loud thinking can include talk about the model's perceptions of the social situation, evaluations of the intentions of others, consideration of alternative responses, final decision making, and evaluation of the results. Out-loud thinking is a useful modeling procedure for young children as well as older children and adolescents.
7. *Self-talk:* In some metacognitive approaches, students are taught to talk to themselves (out loud or subvocally) for purposes of (a) self-motivation before they attempt a difficult behavior, (b) self-direction as they act, and (c) self-reinforcement if they are successful.
8. *Verbal rehearsal and visual rehearsal:* Students may be asked to talk through a new behavior or visually rehearse the new behavior before carrying it out (Meichenbaum & Burland, 1979).
9. *Self-monitoring:* Several techniques can be used to improve the student's self-monitoring. Informational feedback from the clinician is a type of modeling of self-monitoring. Students may be expected to keep records of their own performance in some area of social interaction that they take to be important. Video feedback can be used as a more objective means of improving the student's ability to monitor performance and its effects on others (Helffenstein & Wechsler, 1982). Cue cards may be necessary to remind students of their rules (e.g., "Raise your hand before talking") and of the need to monitor (e.g., "Record today's successes and failures").
10. *Self-evaluating:* In their record keeping, students may be expected to track the results and success of their choices, not merely the choices they made. Customized charts or notebooks are useful for this purpose.
11. *Self-rewarding:* Teaching students to congratulate themselves or give themselves a reward when they act in a manner that they have decided is appropriate is a way to deal with the reality that few real-life social situations include a person responsible for rewarding the student's positive behavior. As part of the program plan, students should specify what they will use as a reward.
12. *Role playing and scripting:* Most social skills training programs, regardless of their philosophical orientation, include role playing as a critical procedure. This enables students to practice new social behaviors in a situation that involves little risk. Students may

also choose to prepare and practice scripts that can guide them through difficult social interactions (e.g., asking a girl for a date; picking her up).

13. *Video therapy:* Video feedback is the central component of some social skills training programs, for example, Interpersonal Process Recall (discussed in the later section on social skills training programs). From a metacognitive perspective, video feedback, used creatively and sensitively, can help students understand their own interactive strengths and weaknesses and their own reasons for reacting as they do. Given the pervasiveness in TBI in self-awareness deficits and difficulty profiting from subtle feedback, direct and dramatic video feedback can play a positive role. From a cognitive perspective, video-assisted therapy can also be used to heighten awareness of social situations, of speakers' intentions, and of alternative social choices and their consequences. We have worked with groups of adolescents who have enjoyed producing video models of exaggeratedly inappropriate interactive behaviors. These serve as useful negative models during training. In addition, the process of producing the videos results in substantially increased understanding of the targeted social interaction. Hosford and Mills (1983) presented a useful six-step program of video-based social skills training.

14. *Negotiating goals:* Because the goal of cognitive and metacognitive approaches is ultimately improved social decision making and internal control rather than simply the acquisition of a set of appropriate social behaviors, rigidly progressing through a clinician-determined sequence of social skills may be inconsistent with the spirit of the intervention. Negotiating with the students regarding which social situations and skills are most critical for them individually helps to capture motivation and commitment. Ideally, treatment priorities are set by the students. This procedure is particularly critical in working with students with TBI. Their patchwork of skills and gaps, weak awareness of deficits, and understandable resistance to working on skills that they may feel they already possess invalidate a rigid adherence to a predesigned curriculum.

15. *Peer teaching:* Having students play the role of group leader in social skills training sessions helps to give them insight into the importance of the skills and the effort that must go into acquiring them.

16. *Response–cost reinforcement system:* This is a controversial behavior management procedure that involves taking away something desirable (e.g., a point or token) whenever a rule is violated. Because it involves attending to the student immediately after he or she violates the rule, it is an inappropriate system for individuals whose behavior is manipulative or attention seeking. However, it may be used with individuals who are very impulsive and who need to have their attention called immediately to the

effects of their impulsive acts and to the alternative behavior that is being taught (Nelson, Finch, & Hooke, 1975).

In addition to these procedures, direct instructing, prompting, cuing, rehearsing, systematically varying settings, and other behavioral techniques may be employed as needed to establish a social skill. Throughout the training, however, the focus is on the individual student's decision making and self-direction rather than the direction or manipulation of the clinician.

For some students, certain aspects of a cognitive approach are incompatible with a behavioral approach. This is illustrated by an instructive mistake made by one of the authors in managing a social skills training group. The group participants were three boys, ages 10 to 12, all between 6 and 18 months postinjury. None of the boys had a significant history of behavioral problems before the injury. All were impulsive, disinhibited, disruptive in class, and frequently in conflict with peers because of their poorly regulated behavior. The boys were intellectually within normal limits and had language skills adequate for normal social interaction.

The group had two general goals: (a) to equip the boys with specific social and interactive skills (appropriate techniques for gaining attention or interrupting, acceptable teasing and joking that would not be objectionable to peers, etc.) and (b) to give the boys general strategies for controlling their impulsive reactions. A component of group management was a response–cost reward system; that is, the boys started each session with 5 points and lost a point each time they violated one of their rules. The purpose of this system was to interrupt interaction on the occasion of a rule violation so that the boys could consider the consequences of not using their targeted skills and could discuss and practice alternatives when it was most meaningful to do so. Because their behavior was not primarily attention seeking and the goal was to help them to acquire greater self-control, this procedure was considered useful and the boys were making progress.

Response–cost behavior management systems are extremely dangerous, however, when used with individuals whose undesirable behavior is largely attention seeking or deliberately disruptive. Interrupting the group and focusing on the disruptive child on the occasion of a rule violation may well be what the child intends and therefore predictably increases the frequency of such behavior. This is exactly what happened when a fourth child was introduced to this group. The child had a long history of behavior problems before his injury and had extremely well-learned manipulative behaviors. Within 2 days, the group had disintegrated to near-total chaos because the disruptiveness of the fourth child, inadvertently encouraged by the behavior management system, spread to the other three impulsive and easily influenced boys, and control was lost.

This unfortunate clinical anecdote illustrates a very important point: Decisions about approaches for individual students must be made with great care. Although mixing procedures that are associated with different global approaches is often possible and useful, there are cases of important incompatibility between specific intervention procedures.

Social–emotional approaches

Students with serious emotional problems after their injury require referral to a trained counselor. Problems may include some combination of the following: sadness, depression, social withdrawal, fearfulness, anxiety, suicidal thoughts, anger, aggressiveness, hostility, moodiness, denial, serious family conflicts, and others. These students may at the same time be receiving social skills training. On the assumption that their lack of social adjustment and acceptance is largely grounded in their emotional reactions, intervention may occur within the counseling context. Alternatively, their social skills training may be independent of counseling and have either a behavioral or a metacognitive focus.

It is critical that the speech-language pathologist, teacher, or whoever is delivering the social skills training consult regularly with the counselor. Certain training techniques may be inappropriate in light of the student's emotional status. For example, video feedback or frank peer feedback may be dangerous for a student who is seriously anxious or depressed, because this type of feedback can easily intensify the emotional problem (Trower & Kiely, 1983). Furthermore, a counselor knowledgeable about the student's social skills training program is in a position to promote the goals of that program. We have experience with successful social skills group intervention jointly led by a social worker (or psychologist) and a speech-language pathologist. In some cases, teachers and therapists are in the best position to promote counseling goals (e.g., the acquisition of an increasingly realistic appreciation of limitations), but they should do so in coordination with a professional equipped to deal with what may be emotionally explosive consequences.

Dealing with a student's emotional reactions to the injury and the losses that it has caused by means of counseling may be useful, but must be combined with creative efforts to ensure that the student experiences success in important domains of life, including social life. Because the student's criteria for success are most likely based on pretrauma standards, creating experiences in which he or she feels successful and distinguished is hard work. It is nonetheless critical. Counseling intervention is further discussed in Chapter 11.

Specific skills approaches

Some social skills and pragmatics training programs focus primarily on the discrete skills to be acquired. These programs make few theoretic assumptions about the nature of human behavior and decision making, or about the most effective procedures for promoting acquisition of social skills. Such a program may suggest activities and teaching techniques, possibly including both behavioral and cognitive and/or metacognitive procedures. However, the emphasis is on the content to be mastered (the specific skills), not on *how* it is to be mastered. Many speech-language pathologists, for example, lead pragmatics groups that are designed to equip the members with discrete communication skills in the absence of a more general focus on social decision making or systematic behavior management.

The advantage of this approach is that it makes the target skills very clear to students. Many children need this level of concreteness in the development of social and interactive competence. With good instruction and sufficient practice, important skills may be acquired. The disadvantage, discussed above, is that specific skills may be acquired that either fail to generalize to application settings or are insufficient in variety to address the important social challenges that the student is likely to face.

Application to TBI

Given the variety of personalities and needs of children prior to TBI and the variety of outcomes following the injury, social skills intervention for these students must be approached in a flexible and individualized manner. Some students, for example, are not and may never be cognitively capable of benefitting from a metacognitive approach. For other students, enhanced awareness of their current strengths, weaknesses, and impact on others may be the key to interactive competence and acceptance by peers, teachers, and others.

For most students with TBI who have significant residual social skills needs, some combination of behavioral, metacognitive, and counseling interventions is appropriate. The goal of the interdisciplinary educational team is not to choose a specific approach and stick to it, but rather to meet the complex needs of individual students in a way that is integrated, coherent, and consistent for that student. In the comments that follow, we attempt to highlight issues that are critical in social skills intervention for many students with TBI.

Noncurricular, nonhierarchical approach

Unlike many children with developmental disabilities, students with TBI may once have been skilled socially, popular with peers, and well liked by teachers. After the injury, some high-level social skills may remain (e.g., the ability to tell a good joke or negotiate a deal) while more basic skills are lacking (e.g., the ability to inhibit sexually offensive remarks). This patchwork of social skills mirrors a more general patchwork of cognitive and academic skills and is reason to avoid a rigid progression through a programmed social skills curriculum.

Student engagement

Many students with TBI have a poor grasp of their needs, in part because their self-concept is based on pretrauma skills and in part because they may still possess some degree of organically based unawareness of deficits. Therefore, they may strongly resist training unless they have a hand in identifying the need and choosing the goals and procedures for achieving the goals. The discussion in Chapter 5 of engaging students in the process of identifying their own cognitive weaknesses and selecting their own strategies to compensate for the weaknesses applies equally to the identification of social interactive weakness and strategies to acquire more serviceable skills. It is also important to remember that the skills and skill sequences in existing curricula are generally the product of research into what social behaviors are most critical for a specific population (e.g., learning disabled students in a regular education setting) (Mesibov & La Greca, 1981); however, these may not be the skills most needed by a particular student with TBI.

Focus on strengths

Because of a natural desire to hold onto a self-concept that may be inconsistent with current levels of performance and to resist treatment that may be associated with the slow learners in school, students with TBI may respond well to intervention that capitalizes on their strengths and self-concept. For example, students may enjoy (and profit from) producing videos illustrating positive and negative models of selected social skills. The ostensible purpose may be to generate training materials that would be helpful for others; in the process, students gain both insight into and practice with the skills in question. Peer teaching similarly achieves therapeutic objectives for the peer teacher while allowing the individual to play a role that offers dignity and a sense of distinction.

Integrated cognitive and social focus

Many students with TBI have general cognitive challenges (e.g., impaired attention, memory, organization) that interfere with effective social interaction. In addition, they may have specific challenges in the area of social cognition (e.g., difficulty reading social cues, interpreting facial expression, understanding complex social situations). These are common consequences of closed head injury, regardless of site of impact (Petterson, 1988). In such cases, teachers and therapists must carefully integrate intervention for cognitive deficits with functional social skills practice.

Change over time

Following severe TBI, students may continue to undergo neurologic recovery—at a decelerating rate—for a considerable period of time. Combined with normal development and maturation, changes in friends and in family interaction, and possibly unpredictable emotional responses to life after the injury, these changes necessitate periodic review and flexible reorientation of intervention programs, including social skills intervention. For example, in the early weeks and months following return to school, every effort should be made to prevent academic and social failure. However, if unawareness and denial combined with unrealistic goals are a major issue years after the injury, staff and family may choose to ensure that real-world experiences of frustration and failure are a component of the student's total package of social skills services.

Context

It is a great irony that pragmatics—"language in context"—is often addressed in treatment contexts that bear little resemblance to the individual's real-world communication contexts. This is particularly ironic and unproductive in the case of individuals who have difficulty transferring learned skills from context to context. This important observation challenges teachers and clinicians to do whatever is necessary to make training contexts—including people, places, activities, and styles of interaction—as much like real-world contexts as possible. It is well known from work with other disabilities that, when social skills intervention fails, which it often does, the primary source of failure is lack of generalization (Vaughn et al., 1991; Zaragoza et al., 1991). This old lesson must be remembered in working with individuals with TBI.

Limits

Certain types of brain injury severely limit an individual's ability to achieve adequate levels of social and behavioral maturity. For example, individuals with substantial prefrontal injury may lack the neurologic substrate required for self-awareness, self-direction, and self-control beyond the level of a young child. It is critical for staff and family to appreciate these limits so that they maintain an appropriate balance of "childproofing" and expectations of self-control in their management of the student, and so that they do not yield to extreme frustration. At the same time, staff and family must guard against an unproductive overprotectiveness and overindulgence that may interfere with genuine potential for growth and maturation. These balances are not easy to strike and require close communication among the significant individuals in the student's life.

Peers

Because friendships play a powerful role in maintaining and developing social skills, an important component of school reentry often involves orienting peers to ways in which the child with TBI may have been affected by the injury and dispel any myths or fantasies that they have about brain injury. Adults can do nothing to guarantee that peers will be understanding and continue to befriend the injured student; however, certain questions and concerns can be anticipated and addressed in an effort to create a social environment that is as receptive as possible. Preparation for school reentry is discussed in Chapter 15 of this book. Often the most useful outlet and support for an adolescent with TBI is contact with another student who has had a similar experience.

Communication training for family and teachers

Because an individual's patterns of social interaction are often determined in large part by the interactive style of important people in that person's world, a social skills training program should target not only the student's behavior, but also that of family and staff. For example, young children with disabilities whose caregivers communicate in an assertive, demanding, and unresponsive manner tend to develop passive or indirect and manipulative communication styles. We have observed similar dynamics following brain injury in a child. Therefore, attention must be given to the partner side of the communication equation (Ylvisaker, Feeney, & Urbanczyk, 1993).

Importance

Based on studies of adults with TBI, social interactive competence is the most critical factor in successful reintegration into family, social, and vocational life and independent living. Research with other populations of children with disabilities indicates that social skills are most critical in social success and emotional development. Because children and adolescents with TBI are likely to have major challenges in this area, this domain of intervention deserves intensive and creative efforts from the educational team.

Social Skills Training Programs: Selected Illustrations

In this section, we describe seven intervention programs for children or adolescents with social interaction problems. The first three fall loosely within the social cognition and metacognition framework. The remaining four are best described as representing a combination of behavioral and specific skills approaches, although in application, lines are more blurred than these categories would suggest. For example, regardless of theoretical orientation, social skills training usually involves modeling, coaching, and behavioral rehearsal with feedback (La Greca & Mesibov, 1979). Most of the programs were developed for use with populations other than students with TBI. For example, Sheinker and Sheinker's program and those developed by Walker were designed to facilitate the mainstreaming of students with learning disabilities or mild mental retardation by means of systematic social skills training. This interest has spawned several social skills training programs. Careful decisions must be made about the applicability of any of these approaches or programs to individual students with TBI. The variety within this population is one reason for being familiar with a variety of training programs.

Metacognitive Approach to Social Skills Training

General focus

The goal of the Metacognitive Approach to Social Skills Training (MATSST) (Sheinker & Sheinker, 1988) is to help students behave in a socially appropriate manner by means of training designed to improve self-direction and decision making. At the most general level, this requires an understanding of oneself as an autonomous decision maker. More specifically, it requires a set of executive skills that enable one to act autonomously and effectively. This program is a clear illustration of a social-cognition approach to social skills training.

Targeted skills

Skills targeted by this program include accurate interpretation of social situations, self-directing, self-monitoring, self-evaluating, and self-correcting in order to produce appropriate social behaviors.

Appropriate students

The approach is said to be useful for students from 4th through 12th grades, including gifted, normal, and handicapped students. Severity of social–emotional and behavioral disturbance can range from mild to severe, but all students must at least have the intellectual, linguistic, and behavioral skills to participate in group sessions.

Context and duration

Sessions should last at least 40 minutes and should occur at least twice weekly. Training is in groups to capitalize on group interaction. Total duration of the training can range from several weeks to several months, depending on the number of lessons selected and the learning ability of the students.

Procedures

Metacognitive procedures include group brainstorming about the nature of social situations, possible alternative actions, and the consequences and value of each. Role playing, videotaping, scripting interactions, and peer interviewing contribute to the indirect learning process. Ample opportunity is given to formulate plans, evaluate the plans, practice new behaviors, monitor the effectiveness of social behaviors both within and outside of the training setting, and correct and improve plans.

Role of the teacher or clinician

Given the goals of this approach, the clinician's role is not to teach students what to do or think. Rather, the clinician engages in metacognitive questioning (e.g., "Why would you do that?" "What would you gain by doing that?" "How could you accomplish that goal?") and out-loud thinking (verbal models), both of which are designed to encourage and facilitate the student's self-observation, self-evaluation, and self-direction. The manual provides scripts for the early lessons to facilitate the clinician's use of these techniques. In addition, the clinician creates a nonjudgmental atmosphere in which risk taking and exploratory learning can take place, introduces topics for discussion, and designs group activities related to the topic.

Improving Conversational Competence

General focus

The overall goal of the suggestions offered by Ylvisaker, Szekeres, Henry, Sullivan, and Wheeler (1987) is to improve conversational competence by targeting its cognitive foundations as well as specific component skills. The intervention program has a social cognition focus.

Targeted skills

Three of the six goals are cognitive: (a) developing an awareness of conversational components, rules, and conventions; (b) improving the ability to interpret speaker intent; and (c) developing an awareness of one's listener. The remaining three relate more directly to specific conversational skills: (d) improving techniques for conversational control; (e) developing varied communication acts; and (f) developing related speaking and listening skills.

Appropriate students

The intervention program was developed for adolescents and young adults with TBI.

Context and duration

Intervention is administered with groups of students with similar communication needs and adequate cognitive, verbal, and behavioral skills to participate in groups.

Procedures

Table 6.2 presents a summary of the program.

Interpersonal Process Recall

General focus

Interpersonal Process Recall (IPR) was first described in 1969 by Kagan, Schauble, and Resnikoff. As applied by Helffenstein and Wechsler (1982) to the training of young adults with brain injury, the primary goal is to improve interactive skills by providing immediate objective feedback (videotape) and practice in more effective communication alternatives. In a controlled experiment, Helffenstein and Wechsler found that the method produced generalized improvements in a variety of interactive skills in their subjects with TBI.

Targeted skills

Intervention is designed to improve specific interpersonal and communication skills as well as to reduce anxiety and increase positive self-concept.

Appropriate students

IPR was initially developed for adults with psychiatric disturbances. Its head injury application has largely been with young adults and other adolescents. The student must be emotionally ready for detailed self-analysis using video feedback, and must have the cognitive and verbal skills to profit from feedback, coaching, and practice.

Context and duration

In its experimental form, 20 one-hour individual therapy sessions were administered by two staff members: an inquirer–coach and an interaction partner. It is possible to use only one staff person. The duration can vary.

Procedures

The session begins with 10 to 15 minutes of videotaped interaction between the client and a staff person. This interaction can be unstructured, or specific skills can be targeted. Approximately 45 minutes are then spent reviewing and processing the tape. Interactive weaknesses are identified, ideally by the client. Discussion ensues and a more positive alternative is agreed upon, modeled by the therapist, and practiced by the client.

Role of the teacher or clinician

The clinician's primary roles are to facilitate the client's discovery, through video analysis, or areas of interaction that could be improved and to brainstorm with the client about positive alternatives.

The Walker Social Skills Curriculum: The ACCEPTS Program

General focus

The primary goal of the Walker Social Skills Curriculum: The ACCEPTS Program (Walker, McConnell, et al., 1988) is to equip students with the skills needed to meet the behavioral demands of a regular education setting. The anticipated consequence of successful instruction is greater social acceptance of handicapped children by their nonhandicapped peers. This curriculum illustrates the intersection between specific skills and behavioral approaches. It is based on the behavioral principles of Direct Instruction (Englemann & Carnine, 1982).

Targeted skills

The student–teacher and peer–peer social behavioral competencies targeted by this program include *classroom skills* (e.g., listening to the teacher, following rules); *basic interaction skills* (e.g., eye contact, initiating interaction, listening, answering, taking turns); *getting along skills* (e.g., sharing, following rules, assisting others);

making friends skills (e.g., good grooming, complimenting); and *coping skills* (e.g., how to respond to teasing, how to respond to aggression).

Appropriate students

The program is designed for mildly and moderately handicapped children, as well as nonhandicapped children in grades K through 6 who are deficient in either classroom behavior or peer–peer social skills. The students must be able to listen to instructions, follow directions, imitate behavior, and learn skills through behavioral rehearsal procedures.

Context and duration

Five to 10 weeks of daily 40- to 45-minute sessions are required to complete the curriculum. Ideally, instruction takes place in a group setting (possibly the entire class) that includes several nonhandicapped peers, but individual instruction is also possible. One ACCEPTS skill is to be taught and mastered daily.

Procedures

The ACCEPTS manual specifies clear behavioral procedures for direct instruction of the competencies. The skills are sequenced and a large number and variety of practice activities are built into the training. Traditional behavioral procedures are prescribed for generalization to nontraining settings.

Role of the teacher or clinician

This program can be used by a variety of professionals, including regular education teachers, special education teachers, mental health personnel, school counselors, psychologists, social workers, and speech-language pathologists. The teacher's role is very directive. The manual includes specific scripts for teaching the behavioral competencies.

The Walker Social Skills Curriculum: The ACCESS Program: Adolescent Curriculum for Communication and Effective Social Skills

General focus

The ACCESS Program (Walker, Todis, Holmes, & Horton, 1988) is an upward extension of the previously discussed ACCEPTS program. Its main goal is to equip adolescents with the social skills needed to survive in the least restrictive educational environment and to successfully negotiate the transition to postschool environments. Like its companion program, the ACCESS program combines behavioral and specific skills approaches, and is based on principles of Direct Instruction (Englemann & Carnine, 1982).

Targeted skills

The student–adult and peer–peer social skills targeted by this program include *adult-related skills* (e.g., disagreeing, responding to requests, developing work habits); *peer-related skills* (e.g., greeting, listening, maintaining conversations, complimenting, expressing anger); and *self-related skills* (e.g., using self-control, coping with being upset).

Appropriate students

The program is intended for mildly to moderately handicapped adolescent students (e.g., students with learning disabilities, mild mental retardation, and/or behavioral disorders) who are capable of reading at a fourth- or fifth-grade level. The students must be capable of participating in group instruction, including role playing and behavioral rehearsal.

Context and duration

Groups of five students or fewer are considered optimal, although the curriculum can also be used with larger or smaller groups or in individual therapy sessions. The students need not be at the same level of functioning. Two to 4 months of daily 1-hour sessions are required to complete the program.

Procedures

The program includes a placement test and detailed procedures (including behavior management procedures) for direct instruction of the skills. Student study guides, role-play cards, and homework assignments are included. Each lesson contains the following 10 mandatory steps: review of the previous lesson; introduction to the new skill; role play of negative example; role play of positive example; discussion of critical skill features; presentation of central message; practice exercises; situational role plays; discussion of application in natural settings; and agreement by students to try the skill in an applied setting.

Role of the teacher or clinician

As with the companion ACCEPTS program, the teacher's role is very directive. Social skills are to be taught as specific behavioral competencies in a behaviorally prescribed manner. Scripts are provided to guide the teacher through the presentation of each lesson.

The Waksman Social Skills Curriculum: An Assertive Behavior Program for Adolescents

General focus

The goal of the Waksman Social Skills Curriculum (Waksman, Messmer, & Waksman, 1989) is to teach interpersonal social behaviors, with a particular focus on assertive behaviors. Assertive behaviors (or social competence) comprise those productive interactions that allow a child or adolescent to attain his or her goals in a manner that yields positive benefits for both the individual and other people in the environment (Waksman et al., 1989).

Targeted skills

Discrimination skills—Early lessons focus on the ability to distinguish among passive, aggressive, and assertive statements; refusals; requests; and nonverbal behavior. *Conversation skills*—Students are taught assertive components of conversation, including conversation openers and closers, topic initiation, and appropriate distance. *Affective communication skills*—Students are taught assertive ways to express feelings, listen to others' expression of feelings, give and receive feedback about personal attributes, give and receive compliments, receive criticism, calm down when angry, avoid fights, and demonstrate self-confidence.

Appropriate students

The program is designed specifically for use with handicapped and nonhandicapped middle school–age students. Because of the program's focus, students who are particularly aggressive or passive are ideal candidates. With modifications, it could be used with younger and with older children. *The Waksman Social Skills Rating Scale* (Waksman, 1984) is used to select students in need of social skills training.

Context and duration

Activities are designed for relatively large groups (6 to 9 members) of children and adolescents. Group size should vary with the level of passivity or aggressiveness of the students. Each lesson is designed for a 45- to 60-minute session. Groups are to meet twice per week for 9 weeks. Ideally, the groups are varied with respect to the presence or absence of handicap and skilled positive models are in the group.

Procedures

Each lesson includes a general goal, specific behavioral objectives, worksheets, and instructions for discussion and practice activities. Group activities are primarily discussions and role plays. Behavioral techniques, including reinforcement for demonstrating a new skill, are to be used liberally.

Role of the teacher or clinician

The program is intended to be used by counselors, school psychologists, or special education teachers. The group leader introduces skills to be learned, explains new skills, leads discussion, assigns worksheet activities, and orchestrates the role plays.

Skillstreaming the Adolescent: A Structured Learning Approach to Teaching Prosocial Skills

General focus

The goal of Skillstreaming the Adolescent (Goldstein, Sprafkin, Gershaw, & Klein, 1980) is to teach adolescents specific social skills in addition to a variety of general skills related to social competence. The orientation and instructional methodologies are largely behavioral.

Targeted skills

Interactive skills that are targeted include listening, starting a conversation, asking questions, saying thank you, introducing oneself, giving a compliment, apologizing, and asking for help. Other social skills are included under the following headings: skills for dealing with feelings, skill alternatives to aggression, skills for dealing with stress, and planning skills. Each of the skills is presented in clear behavioral steps.

Appropriate students

The target population is adolescents with behavior disorders. As with most social skills programs, students must have sufficient cognitive, linguistic, and behavioral skills to benefit from group instruction and role playing. Ideally, students are grouped according to the degree of their behavioral needs. (A Structured Learning Skill Checklist is included for assessment.) In other respects, variety within the group is an advantage because it promotes generalization.

Context and duration

Instruction occurs in groups of five to eight trainees and two trainers. One skill is addressed per session. The recommendation is that groups meet one to two times per week and that sessions last 60 minutes (shorter sessions are possible). Because there are 50 skills to be mastered, completing the program requires several months. The context of training should be as much like the context of application as possible.

Procedures

Procedures include most of those listed above under "Behavioral Approaches." Peer modeling, role playing, reinforcing, and using systematic transfer procedures are all central to the program. Homework is also emphasized.

Role of the teacher or clinician

The trainers could be classroom teachers or any other appropriate school personnel. Given that this is a structured learning approach, the clinician is very directive in instructing, providing feedback, and reinforcing.

We have devoted much of this chapter to a discussion of social skills training for several reasons. In TBI, social interaction is often the most vulnerable communication-related function. The "pragmatic revolution" has resulted in a growing interest in this area among speech-language pathologists. To enter this important clinical arena, clinicians need an adequate understanding of language pragmatics, but also of the cognitive, metacognitive, behavioral, and social–emotional realities that are inseparably tied to interactive success. This entails coordinating intervention with other professionals and gaining familiarity with relevant intervention programs that have been developed in other disciplines.

For the same reasons that social interaction is multiply vulnerable in TBI, intervention is multiply complex and time-consuming. No "quick fix"—whether behavioral, cognitive, social–emotional, or pharmacologic—exists for students with impaired social interaction following brain injury. However, the challenges of this intervention are certainly matched by its importance. Social, educational, and vocational success hangs in the balance.

Research reports provide some support for the effectiveness of social skills or pragmatics training with adults with TBI (Braunling-McMorrow, Lloyd, & Fralish, 1986; Brotherton, Thomas, Wisotzek, & Milan, 1988; Eames & Wood, 1985; Erlich & Sipes, 1985; Giles, Fussey, & Burgess, 1988; Helffenstein & Wechsler, 1982; Lewis, Nelson, Nelson, & Reusink, 1988). In addition, Gajar and colleagues described an effective intervention for impaired conversation and social skills in young people with head injury (Gajar, Schloss, Schloss, & Thompson, 1984; Schloss, Thompson, Gajar, & Schloss, 1985). However, because the number of individuals treated is small in most of these studies, control procedures are often weak, and there is considerable variation in the individuals treated and in the methods of intervention, this literature should not create a false sense of security. Teachers and clinicians must make careful decisions about the marriage of individual student and treatment approach, and should carefully track the effectiveness of intervention.

ROLES OF SCHOOL SPEECH-LANGUAGE PATHOLOGISTS WITH STUDENTS WITH TBI

Models of Service Delivery

In progressive school districts, the traditional model of pull-out individual or group speech-language therapy sessions has increasingly given ground to other means of delivering communication services (Nelson, 1989). For example, many districts offer a self-contained language classroom for children whose primary impairment is a language learning disability. There is a language focus throughout the instructional day, and new aspects of language are learned in a highly functional context. These classrooms, which often have a speech-language pathologist as teacher or co-teacher, have generally been developed for preschool or young school-aged children and may be appropriate for a young child with serious deficits following TBI.

Students with less intensive needs may be served in a regular education classroom, with the speech-language pathologist serving as a resource person or actually teaming with the teacher in the classroom to teach language or social communication lessons. This joint intervention supports a language and communication focus throughout the instructional day that may otherwise be absent. A combination of pull-out and classroom-based services may be appropriate for selected students. The pull-out services may be needed for specialized motor speech intervention, initial development of an augmentative communication system, or exploration of compensatory comprehension or expression strategies. In addition, the speech-language pathologist may play a role similar to that of a tutor in relation to language-intensive tasks such as writing themes and reading novels. In this case, the goal is not simply to help the student with a difficult classroom assignment, but also to use the assignment as a context for promoting improved (and generalizable) language strategies.

Classroom-based language and communication services have many advantages. First, systematic classroom observations and regular interaction with classroom teachers greatly enhance the validity and completeness of the speech-language evaluation. Second, regular presence in the classroom allows the clinician to evaluate the language and communication challenges of classroom discourse and academic materials, and to help the teacher to adjust these challenges to be consistent with the student's ability. Third, if teachers are well oriented to language and communication goals, they are in a position to integrate these goals with instruction throughout the day, thereby maximizing the effects of intervention. The undesirable possibility of teachers and therapists working at cross-purposes on shared language and communication goals is thereby also avoided. Fourth, a confusing schedule that includes several pull-out sessions can contribute to the student's disorientation. Finally, because generalization to functional settings and tasks is the touchstone of success for speech and language therapy, there is a profound advantage in providing the intervention in one of the settings and with tasks in which functional application is desired.

In addition to these advantages of classroom-based speech and language services that apply to most students with communication disorders, another advantage applies with particular vividness to students with TBI: maximizing the time that the student can stay in the classroom and receive needed academic instruction. Students often return to school from a rehabilitation setting with recommendations for intensive services in several areas, possibly including speech-language therapy, occupational therapy, physical therapy, and counseling. Compounding the scheduling problem, fatigue may rule out a full day of school for several weeks. The result may be that the child spends little time in the classroom receiving desperately needed academic instruction. This problem with the organization of services only exacerbates the new learning problems that by themselves impede academic progress.

Particularly needy students may, however, require intensive individual services in addition to a full day in the classroom. In such cases, after-school therapy may be recommended. To ensure integration of the services, communication must remain open between the two speech-language pathologists.

Program Coordination

Perhaps the most critical component of a successful school reentry program for a child with severe TBI is that there be a single person responsible for coordinating the program, maximizing the available school services, ensuring integration of services and communication among staff and between staff and family, monitoring the program so that it keeps pace with changes in the student over time, and facilitating communication between school and outside professionals involved in the child's program (Ylvisaker, Hartwick, & Stevens, 1991). Ironically, this case management component is not likely to be available in most school districts. This unfortunate fact helps to explain why many children with TBI experience failure and frustration on their return to school and respond with increasing levels of behavioral maladjustment (Ylvisaker, 1989).

Currently, no one professional is best positioned to play this important role. We have seen the role played by staff from the child's rehabilitation hospital, the rehabilitation nurse assigned by the insurance company, the special education resource room teacher, the school guidance counselor, psychologists and speech-language pathologists from the community or the school, and even parents. Some states are currently in the process of organizing and training teams of professionals who should be prepared to play this role following their training. In some settings, speech-language pathologists are good candidates for this role because their scope of practice ranges from physical rehabilitation to cognitive, academic, and psychosocial intervention, and because their training generally gives them familiarity with both hospital-based and school-based services. The essential point, however, is that the program coordination/case management function is served, not that it is served by a specific professional.

CONCLUSION

Following TBI, virtually any type of outcome is possible, ranging from full recovery to severe impairment in all areas of functioning. Therefore, speech-language therapy services can easily span the entire scope of practice with these students. In this chapter, together with Chapters 3 through 5, we have highlighted aspects of communication assessment and treatment that are particularly critical in serving students with TBI. These include dimensions of language comprehension and expression that are frequently compromised by the cognitive challenges associated with TBI and especially social communication skills that in the final analysis are probably most critical in relation to social, academic, and vocational success. We also have underscored the creativity that must go into designing language and communication assessment for students who may score well on available tests of language knowledge yet lack adequate facility with language in real-world tasks.

At this early stage in the development of services for this group of students, it is perhaps most important that clinicians approach their task creatively and flexibly, evaluating more like detectives than like technicians and treating more like problem-solving engineers than like deliverers of therapy programs. The field has much to learn and, if professionals are open and alert, the most important lessons will be learned from the students served.

REFERENCES

Aram, D. (1988). Language sequelae of unilateral brain lesions in children. In F. Plum (Ed.), *Language, communication, and the brain.* New York: Raven Press.

Aram, D. M., Ekelman, B. L., Rose, D. F., & Whitaker, H. A. (1985). Verbal and cognitive sequelae following unilateral lesions acquired in early childhood. *Journal of Clinical and Experimental Neuropsychology, 7,* 55–78.

Baer, D. (1981). *How to plan for generalization.* Manhattan, KS: H&H Enterprises.

Bandura, A. (1973). *Aggression: A social learning analysis.* Englewood Cliffs, NJ: Prentice-Hall.

Bawden, H. N., Knights, R. M., & Winogren, H. W. (1985). Speeded performance following head injury in children. *Journal of Clinical and Experimental Neuropsychology, 7,* 39–54.

Blau, A. (1936). Mental changes following head trauma in children. *Archives of Neurology and Psychiatry, 35,* 723–769.

Braunling-McMorrow, D., Lloyd, K., & Fralish, K. (1986). Teaching social skills to head injured adults. *Journal of Rehabilitation, 52,* 39–44.

Brooks, D. N., & McKinlay, W. (1983). Personality and behavioral change after severe blunt head injury—A relative's view. *Journal of Neurology, Neurosurgery, and Psychiatry, 46,* 336–344.

Brotherton, F. A., Thomas, L. L., Wisotzek, I. E., & Milan, M. A. (1988). Social skills training in the rehabilitation of patients with traumatic closed head injury. *Archives of Physical Medicine and Rehabilitation, 69,* 827–832.

Brown, G., Chadwick, O., Shaffer, D., Rutter, M., & Traub, M. (1981). A prospective study of children with head injuries: III. Psychiatric sequelae. *Psychological Medicine, 11,* 63–78.

Campbell, T., & Dollaghan, C. (1990). Expressive language recovery in severely brain-injured children and adolescents. *Journal of Speech and Hearing Disorders, 55,* 567–581.

Cartledge, G., & Milburn, J. F. (1978). The case for teaching social skills in the classroom: A review. *Review of Educational Research, 1,* 133–156.

Chadwick, O., Rutter, M., Shaffer, D., & Shrout, P. E. (1981). A prospective study of children with head injuries: IV. Specific cognitive deficits. *Journal of Clinical Neuropsychology, 3,* 101–120.

Chandler, L. K., Lubeck, R. C., & Fowler, S. A. (1992). Generalization and maintenance of preschool children's social skills: A critical review and analysis. *Journal of Applied Behavior Analysis, 25,* 415–428.

Chapman, S. B., Culhane, K. A., Levin, H. S., Harward, H., Mendelsohn, D., Ewing-Cobbs, L., Fletcher, J. M., & Bruce, D. (1992). Narrative discourse after closed head injury in children and adolescents. *Brain and Language, 43,* 42–65.

Cicone, M., Wapner, W., & Gardner, H. (1980). Sensitivity to emotional expressions and situations in organic patients. *Cortex, 16,* 145–158.

Cohen, S. B., Joyce, C. M., Rhoades, K. W., & Welks, D. M. (1985). Educational programming for head injured students. In M. Ylvisaker (Ed.), *Head injury rehabilitation: Children and adolescents* (pp. 383–409). San Diego: College-Hill.

Collet-Klingenberg, L., & Chadsey-Rusch, J. (1991). Using a cognitive-process approach to teach social skills. *Education and Training in Mental Retardation, 26,* 258–270.

Cooper, J. A., & Flowers, C. R. (1987). Children with a history of acquired aphasia: Residual language and academic impairments. *Journal of Speech and Hearing Disorders, 52,* 251–262.

Dennis, M., & Barnes, M. A. (1990). Knowing the meaning, getting the point, bridging the gap, and carrying the message: Aspects of discourse following closed head injury in childhood and adolescence. *Brain and Language, 39,* 428–446.

DiSimoni, F. (1978). *The Token Test for Children.* Allen, TX: DLM Teaching Resources.

Dodge, A. (1985). Facets of social interaction and the assessment of social competence in children. In B. H. Schneider, K. H. Rubin, & J. E. Ledingham (Eds.), *Children's peer relations: Issues in assessment and intervention.* New York: Springer Verlag.

Dowrick, P. W. (Ed.). (1986). *Social survival for children: A trainer's resource book.* New York: Brunner/Mazel.

Dunn, L., & Dunn, L. (1981). *Peabody Picture Vocabulary Test–Revised.* Minneapolis, MN: American Guidance Service.

Eames, P., & Wood, R. I. (1985). Rehabilitation after severe brain injury: A follow-up study of a behaviour modification approach. *Journal of Neurology, Neurosurgery, and Psychiatry, 48,* 613–617.

Englemann, S., & Carnine, D. (1982). *Theory of instruction: Principles and applications.* New York: Irvington.

Erlich, J., & Barry, P. (1989). Rating communication behaviors in the head injured adult. *Brain Injury, 3,* 193–198.

Erlich, J. S., & Sipes, A. L. (1985). Group treatment of communication skills for head trauma patients. *Cognitive Rehabilitation, 3,* 32–37.

Ewing-Cobbs, L., Fletcher, J., & Levin, H. S. (1985). Neuropsychological sequelae following pediatric head injury. In M. Ylvisaker (Ed.), *Head injury rehabilitation: Children and adolescents.* Austin, TX: PRO-ED.

Ewing-Cobbs, L., Levin, H., Eisenberg, H. M., & Fletcher, J. (1987). Language functioning following closed head injury in children and adolescents. *Journal of Experimental Neuropsychology, 9,* 575–592.

Ewing-Cobbs, L., Miner, M. E., Fletcher, J. M., & Levin, H. S. (1989). Intellectual, motor, and language sequelae following closed head injury in infants and preschoolers. *Journal of Pediatric Psychology, 14,* 531–547.

Favell, J. E., & Reid, D. (1988). Generalizing and maintaining improvement in problem behavior. In R. H. Horner, G. Dunlap, & R. L. Koegel (Eds.), *Generalization and maintenance: Life style changes in applied settings.* Baltimore: Brookes.

Fletcher, J. M., Ewing-Cobbs, L., Miner, M., & Levin, H. S. (1990). Behavioral changes after closed head injury in children. *Journal of Consulting and Clinical Psychology, 58,* 93–98.

Fletcher, J. M., Miner, M. E., & Ewing-Cobbs, L. (1987). Age and recovery from head injury in children: Developmental issues. In H. S. Levin, H. M. Eisenberg, & J. Grafman (Eds.), *Neurobehavioral recovery from head injury* (pp. 279–291). New York: Oxford University Press.

Foster, S. L., & Ritchley, W. L. (1979). Issues in the assessment of social competence in children. *Journal of Applied Behavior Analysis, 12,* 625–638.

Fried-Oken, M. L. (1987). Qualitative examination of children's naming skills through test adaptations. *Language, Speech, and Hearing Services in the Schools, 18,* 206–216.

Fuld, P. A., & Fisher, H. M. (1977). Recovery of intellectual ability after closed head injury. *Developmental Medicine and Child Neurology, 19,* 495–502.

Gaddes, W. H., & Crocket, D. J. (1975). The Spreen–Benton Aphasia Tests: Normative data as a measure of normal language development. *Brain and Language, 2,* 257–280.

Gajar, A., Schloss, P. J., Schloss, C. N., & Thompson, C. K. (1984). Effects of feedback and self-monitoring on head trauma youths' conversation skills. *Journal of Applied Behavior Analysis, 17,* 353–358.

German, D. J. (1987). Spontaneous language profiles of children with word-finding problems. *Language, Speech, and Hearing Services in the Schools, 18,* 217–230.

Giles, G. M., Fussey, I., & Burgess, P. (1988). The behavioral treatment of verbal interaction skills following severe head injury: A single case study. *Brain Injury, 2,* 75–79.

Goldstein, A. P., Sprafkin, R. P., Gershaw, N. J., & Klein, P. (1980). *Skillstreaming the adolescent: A structured learning approach to teaching prosocial skills.* Champaign, IL: Research Press.

Gresham, F. M. (1982). Misguided mainstreaming: The case for social skills training with handicapped children. *Exceptional Children, 48,* 422–433.

Gulbrandsen, G. B. (1984). Neuropsychological sequelae of light head injuries in older children six months after trauma. *Journal of Clinical Neuropsychology, 6,* 257–268.

Haarbauer-Krupa, J., Moser, L., Smith, G., Sullivan, D., & Szekeres, S. (1985). Cognitive rehabilitation therapy: Middle stages of recovery. In M. Ylvisaker (Ed.), *Head injury rehabilitation: Children and adolescents.* Austin, TX: PRO-ED.

Hansen, D. J., Watson-Perczel, M., & Christopher, J. S. (1989). Clinical issues in social-skills training with adolescents. *Clinical Psychology Review, 9,* 365–391.

Hartley, L., & Jensen, P. J. (1991). Narrative and procedural discourse after closed head injury. *Brain Injury, 8,* 267–285.

Helffenstein, D., & Wechsler, F. (1982). The use of interpersonal process recall (IPR) in the remediation of interpersonal and communication skill deficits in the newly brain injured. *Clinical Neuropsychology, 4,* 139–143.

Hosford, R. E., & Mills, M. E. (1983). Video in social skills training. In P. W. Dowrick & S. J. Biggs (Eds.), *Using video: Psychological and social applications* (pp. 123–150). New York: Wiley.

Jacobs, H. (1993). *Behavior analysis guidelines and brain injury rehabilitation.* Gaithersburg, MD: Aspen.

Jacobson, M. S., Rubenstein, E. M., Bohannon, W. E., Sondheimer, D. L., Cicci, R., Toner, J., Gong, E., & Heald, F. P. (1986). Follow-up of adolescent trauma victims: A new model of care. *Pediatrics, 77,* 236–241.

Kagan, N., Schauble, P., & Resnikoff, D. (1969). Interpersonal process recall. *Journal of Nervous and Mental Diseases, 148,* 365–374.

Kasanan, J. (1929). Personality changes in children following cerebral trauma. *Journal of Nervous and Mental Disease, 69,* 385–406.

Klonoff, H., Low, M. D., & Clark, C. (1977). Head injuries in children: A prospective five year follow-up. *Journal of Neurology, Neurosurgery, and Psychiatry, 40,* 1211–1219.

Koegel, R., & Koegel, L. (1988). Generalized responsivity and pivotal behaviors. In R. H. Horner, G. Dunlap, & R. L. Koegel (Eds.), *Generalization and maintenance: Life style changes in applied settings.* Baltimore: Brookes.

La Greca, A. M., & Mesibov, G. B. (1979). Social skills intervention with learning disabled children: Selecting skills and implementing training. *Journal of Clinical Child Psychology, 8,* 234–241.

LaVigna, G. W., & Donnellan, A. M. (1986). *Alternatives to punishment: Solving behavior problems with non-aversive strategies.* New York: Irvington.

Levin, H. S., Benton, A., & Grossman, R. (1982). *Neurobehavioral consequences of closed head injury.* New York: Oxford University Press.

Levin, H. S., & Eisenberg, H. M. (1979a). Neuropsychological impairment after closed head injury in children and adolescents. *Journal of Pediatric Psychology, 4,* 389–402.

Levin, H. S., & Eisenberg, H. M. (1979b). Neuropsychological outcome of closed head injury in children and adolescents. *Child's Brain, 5,* 281–292.

Levin, H. S., Eisenberg, H. M., Wigg, N. R., & Kobayashi, K. (1982). Memory and intellectual ability after head injury in children and adolescents. *Neurosurgery, 11,* 668–672.

Levin, H. S., Madison, C. F., Bailey, C. B., Meyers, C. A., Eisenberg, H. M., & Guinto, F. C. (1983). Mutism after closed head injury. *Archives of Neurology, 40,* 601–606.

Lewis, F. D., Nelson, J., Nelson, C., & Reusink, P. (1988). Effects of three feedback contingencies on the socially inappropriate talk of a brain-injured adult. *Behavior Therapy, 19,* 203–211.

Lezak, M. D. (1987). Relationships between personality disorders, social disturbances, and physical disability following traumatic brain injury. *Journal of Head Trauma Rehabilitation, 2,* 57–69.

Liles, B. Z., Coelho, C. A., Duffy, R. J., & Zalagens, M. R. (1989). Effects of elicitation procedures on the narratives of normal and closed head-injured adults. *Journal of Speech and Hearing Disorders, 54,* 356–366.

Meichenbaum, D. (1983). Teaching thinking: A cognitive–behavioral approach. In Society for Learning Disabilities and Remedial Education (Ed.), *Interdisciplinary voices in learning disabilities and remedial education* (pp. 127–150). Austin, TX: PRO-ED.

Meichenbaum, D., & Burland, S. (1979). Cognitive behavior modification with children. *School Psychology Digest, 8,* 426–433.

Mentis, M., & Prutting, C. (1987). Cohesion in the discourse of head injured and normal adults. *Journal of Speech and Hearing Research, 30,* 88–98.

Mentis, M., & Prutting, C. (1991). Analysis of topic in a head-injured and a normal adult. *Journal of Speech and Hearing Research, 34,* 583–595.

Mesibov, G. B., & La Greca, A. M. (1981). A social skills instructional module. *The Directive Teacher, 3,* 6–7.

Milton, S. B., Prutting, C. A., & Binder, G. M. (1984). Appraisal of communicative competence in head injured adults. In R. Brookshire (Ed.), *Clinical aphasiology conference proceedings.* Minneapolis: BRK Publishers.

Nelson, N. W. (1989). Language intervention in school settings. In D. K. Bernstein & E. Tiegerman (Eds.), *Language and communication disorders in children* (2nd ed., pp. 417–468). Columbus: Merrill.

Nelson, W. M., III, Finch, A. J., Jr., & Hooke, J. F. (1975). Effects of reinforcement and response-cost on the cognitive style of emotionally disturbed boys. *Journal of Abnormal Psychology, 84,* 426–428.

Odom, R. D., & Lemond, C. M. (1972). Developmental differences in the perception and production of facial expression. *Child Development, 43,* 359–369.

Perrott, S. B., Taylor, H. G., & Montes, J. L. (1991). Neuropsychological sequelae, familial stress, and environmental adaptation following pediatric head injury. *Developmental Neuropsychology, 7,* 69–86.

Petterson, L. (1988). *Sensitivity to emotional cues and social behavior in children and adolescents after head injury.* Unpublished manuscript.

Phillips, E. (1985). Social skills: History and prospect. In L. L'Abate & M. Milan (Eds.), *Handbook of social skills training and research* (pp. 3–22). New York: Wiley.

Prigatano, G. P., Roueche, J. R., & Fordyce, D. J. (1985). Nonaphasic language disturbances after closed head injury. *Language Sciences, 1,* 217–229.

Prutting, C. A., & Kirchner, D. M. (1987). A clinical appraisal of the pragmatic aspects of language. *Journal of Speech and Hearing Disorders, 52,* 105–119.

Raimondi, A. J., & Hirschauer, J. (1984). Head injury in the infant and toddler. *Child's Brain, 11,* 12–35.

Rice, M. L., Sell, M. A., & Hadley, P. A. (1990). The Social Interactive Coding System (SICS): An on-line, clinically relevant descriptive tool. *Language, Speech, and Hearing Services in the Schools, 21,* 2–14.

Rose-Krasnor, L. (1985). Observational assessment of social problem solving. In B. H. Schneider, K. H. Rubin, & J. E. Ledingham (Eds.), *Children's peer relations: Issues in assessment and intervention.* New York: Springer Verlag.

Rustin, L., & Kuhr, A. (1989). Social skills training for the speech and language handicapped. In L. Rustin & A. Kuhr (Eds.), *Social skills and the speech impaired.* London: Taylor & Francis.

Sapir, S., & Aronson, A. R. (1985). Aphonia after closed head injury: Aetiologic considerations. *British Journal of Disorders of Communication, 20,* 289–296.

Sapir, S., & Aronson, A. R. (1990). The relationship between psychopathology and speech and language disorders in neurologic patients. *Journal of Speech and Hearing Disorders, 55,* 503–509.

Schloss, P. J., Thompson, C. K., Gajar, A. H., & Schloss, C. N. (1985). Influence of self-monitoring on heterosexual conversational behaviors of head trauma youth. *Applied Research in Mental Retardation, 6,* 269–282.

Sheinker, J., & Sheinker, A. (1988). *Metacognitive approach to social skills training.* Rockville, MD: Aspen.

Stokes, T. (1992). Discrimination and generalization. *Journal of Applied Behavior Analysis, 25,* 429–432.

Szekeres, S. F., Ylvisaker, M., & Holland, A. (1985). Cognitive rehabilitation therapy: A framework for intervention. In M. Ylvisaker (Ed.), *Head injury rehabilitation: Children and adolescents* (pp. 219–246). Austin, TX: PRO-ED.

Trower, P., & Kiely, B. (1983). Video feedback: Help or hindrance? A review and analysis. In P. W. Dowrick & S. J. Biggs (Eds.), *Using video: Psychological and social applications.* New York: Wiley.

Vaughn, S., McIntosh, R., & Zaragoza, N. (1991). Social interventions for students with learning disabilities. Toward a broader perspective. In S. A. Vogel (Ed.), *Educational alternatives for students with learning disabilities.* New York: Springer Verlag.

Waksman, S. (1984). *The Waksman Social Skills Rating Scale Test and Training Manual.* Portland, OR: Asiep Education.

Waksman, S., Messmer, C. L., & Waksman, D. D. (1989). *The Waksman Social Skills Curriculum: An assertive behavior program for adolescents.* Austin, TX: PRO-ED.

Walker, H. (1988). Special education curriculum and instruction: Social skills. In T. Husen & N. Postlethwaite (Eds.), *International encyclopedia of education* (1988 Supplement). Oxford, England: Pergamon Books.

Walker, H. M., McConnell, S. M., & Clark, J. (1984). Social skills training in school settings: A model for the social integration of handicapped children into less restrictive settings. In R. McMahon & R. Peters (Eds.), *Childhood disorders: Behavioral–developmental approaches* (pp. 215–276). New York: Brunner/Mazel.

Walker, H. M., McConnell, S. M., Holmes, D., Todis, B., Walker, J., & Golden, N. (1988). *The Walker Social Skills Curriculum: The Accepts Program.* Austin, TX: PRO-ED.

Walker, H. M., Todis, B., Holmes, D., & Horton, G. (1988). *The Walker Social Skills Program: The ACCESS Program: Adolescent Curriculum for Communication and Effective Social Skills.* Austin, TX: PRO-ED.

Wechsler, D. (1991). *Wechsler Intelligence Scale for Children–Third Edition.* San Antonio, TX: Psychological Corp.

Winogren, H. W., Knights, R. M., & Bawden, H. N. (1984). Neuropsychological deficits following head injury in children. *Journal of Clinical Neuropsychology, 6,* 269–286.

Wycoff, L. H. (1984). *Narrative and procedural discourse following closed head injury.* Unpublished doctoral dissertation, University of Florida.

Ylvisaker, M. (1981, October). *Cognitive and behavioral outcome in head injured children.* Presented at the International Symposium on the Traumatic Brain Injured Adult and Child, Boston.

Ylvisaker, M. (1986). Language and communication disorders following pediatric head injury. *Journal of Head Trauma Rehabilitation, 1,* 48–56.

Ylvisaker, M. (1989). Cognitive and psychosocial outcome following head injury in children. In J. T. Hoff, T. E. Anderson, & T. M. Cole (Eds.), *Mild to moderate head injury.* London: Blackwell Scientific Publications.

Ylvisaker, M. (in press). Communication outcome in children and adolescents with traumatic brain injury. *Neuropsychological Rehabilitation.*

Ylvisaker, M., Feeney, T., & Urbanczyk, B. (1993). Developing a positive communication culture for rehabilitation. In C. J. Durgin, J. Fryer, & N. Schmidt (Eds.), *Staff development and clinical intervention in brain injury rehabilitation* (pp. 57–74). Gaithersburg, MD: Aspen.

Ylvisaker, M., Hartwick, P., & Stevens, M. B. (1991). School re-entry following head injury: Managing the transition from hospital to school. *Journal of Head Trauma Rehabilitation, 6,* 10–22.

Ylvisaker, M., Szekeres, S., Henry, K., Sullivan, D., & Wheeler, P. (1987). Topics in cognitive rehabilitation therapy. In M. Ylvisaker (Ed.). *Community re-entry for head injured adults* (pp. 137–220). Austin, TX: PRO-ED.

Zaragoza, N., Vaughn, S., & McIntosh, R. (1991). Social skills interventions and children with behavior problems: A review. *Behavioral Disorders, 16,* 260–275.

SECTION III

Psychosocial–Behavioral Dimensions

CHAPTER 7

Psychosocial Effects of Acquired Brain Injury

ANN V. DEATON
PAMELA WAALAND

The trauma of an acquired brain injury is limited neither to its physical pain nor to its visible effects on speech, appearance, and motor skills. The less obvious effects of brain injury are on the emotions, behavior, self-concept, and social interactions of the child who is injured. These so-called psychosocial effects are likely to be more enduring than the injury's physical effects, as well as more disturbing to the student, family, and classroom environment. Psychosocial problems appear to occur following most brain injuries to some degree. They include difficulties that are a direct result of the injury, those that reflect a worsening of preinjury personality or behavioral tendencies, and problems that occur in reaction to the injury and the changes it has brought about (e.g., Lehr, 1990; Prigatano, 1986; Rutter, Chadwick, & Shaffer, 1983). Psychosocial problems vary with the individual child, depending upon the nature and the circumstances of his or her injury, preinjury adjustment, developmental stage, and circumstances following the injury. They appear to be more persistent than many of the physical and cognitive problems following injury, and may even get worse instead of better with time. In this chapter, we describe the psychosocial effects of brain injury and some ways in which they impact the child's recovery and reintegration into the school and community. Subsequent chapters in this section address in more detail specific types of problems and appropriate interventions.

The term *psychosocial,* as used in this chapter, refers globally to the social, emotional, behavioral, and psychological effects of traumatic brain injury (TBI) on the student. These effects can include "social disinhibition or acting in socially inappropriate ways, irritability, increased emotionality, reduced judgment and motivation, perseveration, lowered tolerance for frustration, and egocentricity seen through insensitivity to others, unawareness of their impact on others, and an increase in demanding behavior" (Lehr, 1990, p. 160). In one study, 73% of those with severe TBIs and 67% of those with mild TBIs had behavior problems that were new since the injury (Asarnow, Satz, Light, Lewis, & Neumann, 1991). Moreover, one in four students has been described as impulsive following severe brain injury (Edwards, 1987). Obviously, the prevalence of these problems necessitates that they be addressed.

In addition to the changes in the child's abilities and behaviors, the environment to which the child returns following TBI may be substantially different. Only 8% of severely injured children in one study returned to a regular education program by 1 year after the injury and only 14% by 3 years (Boyer & Edwards, 1991). Less severely injured children may be more "fortunate" with respect to the proportion who return to regular classrooms, but they are frequently burdened by the unrealistic expectation that they are fully recovered by only a few months after the injury. These expectations can do additional psychological damage to the child who is no longer able to be successful in a traditional school setting.

WHAT CAUSES PSYCHOSOCIAL DIFFICULTIES POSTINJURY?

One of the most confusing aspects of TBI is the complex interplay between a variety of injury-specific, environmental, and child-specific factors and the vast array of resulting difficulties. Frequent mood changes, physical aggression, and social withdrawal can all follow a student's brain injury and may be due to a variety of causes. Asarnow et al. (1991) described at least six possibilities regarding behavior problems that follow a brain injury: (a) the behavior existed before the injury and may have even contributed to the injury's occurring; (b) the behavior existed before the injury but was worsened by the injury; (c) the behavior is a direct result of the injury; (d) the behavior is an immediate but indirect effect of the injury; (e) the behavior is a delayed effect of the injury; and (f) the behavior is unrelated to the injury. Understanding which of these possibilities is most likely can help with developing effective interventions and can limit the frustration inherent in dealing with the psychosocial effects of an injury.

Injury-Specific Factors

Behavior problems are common in childhood and may occur with or without a brain injury. In many cases, behavior problems such as impulsivity and short attention span may have existed before the injury and the injury may even have occurred because of them (e.g., the child acted impulsively by running out in front of a car). However, attentional difficulties, impulsivity, depression, and other problems (see Table 7.1) are also common effects of a brain injury, and thus may be caused by or worsened by the injury. So-called organic sequelae of TBI are those that are directly linked to the damage to the brain, thereby resulting in altered behavior. These direct effects of brain injury can include behavioral and social–emotional changes, such as an increase in social inappropriateness, aggressiveness, or frequent mood changes (Lehr, 1990). For example, poor self-awareness can be a direct physiological result of brain injury manifested by unrealistic expectations or appraisals of one's abilities as well as denial of others' observations regarding one's performance (Falvo, 1991).

Precocious puberty is an infrequently discussed but not infrequent consequence of brain injury in children. As the term suggests, precocious puberty is the premature development of secondary sex characteristics (e.g., body hair, breast development) by

TABLE 7.1. Common Psychosocial Problems Following Brain Injury

Acts immature for age
Has inappropriate manners and mannerisms
Cannot understand humor or "size up" situations
Gets frustrated easily
Cannot inhibit inappropriate behaviors (disinhibition)
Is inappropriately affectionate toward others
Cannot see others' viewpoint (egocentricity)
Has limited insight into own abilities and behaviors
Cannot correct behavior after feedback
Gets stuck on one thought or behavior (perseveration)
Appears apathetic or poorly motivated
Takes too many risks and/or acts impulsively
Acts fearful
Gets angry out of proportion to cause
Is verbally and/or physically aggressive
Appears anxious or depressed
Changes mood rapidly or laughs or cries for no apparent reason (emotional lability)
Isolates self
Seeks attention, even with negative behaviors
Is demanding
Is irritable
Gets tired easily
Denies problems
Seems unmotivated and passive

Sources include *Psychological Management of Traumatic Brain Injuries in Children and Adolescents* by E. Lehr, 1990, Rockville, MD: Aspen; and *An Educator's Manual: What Educators Need to Know About Students with TBI* by R. C. Savage and G. F. Wolcott, 1988, Southborough, MA: National Head Injury Foundation.

children, occurring in girls at or before age $8\frac{1}{2}$ years and in boys younger than 10 years. Although little research has been done on this sequela of TBI, the existing research suggests that this may be a relatively common phenomenon, occurring more commonly in girls, perhaps in as many as 21% of girls who have severe TBIs (Sockalosky, Kriel, Krach, & Sheehan, 1987). The cause of this condition is believed to be damage to the hypothalamic area of the brain, responsible in part for timing the release of hormones that trigger normal sexual development.

Precocious puberty brings, for any child and family, a host of concerns. These include practical concerns, such as the purchase of age-and size-appropriate clothing, anxiety about growing up too fast, fears about not fitting in with a peer group, and concerns about premature sexual activity. For the child who may already have worries about peer relationships and appearance subsequent to a brain injury, precocious puberty can be one additional burden.

Fortunately, treatments can be effective in arresting premature sexual development and limiting its psychosocial impact. These treatments are likely to take the form of analog therapy and need to be utilized before development is too far advanced. The keys to treatment of precocious puberty are recognizing the signs of its occurrence and prompt referral to a medical professional familiar with it, frequently a pediatric endocrinologist.

Injuries to certain parts of the brain may be more likely to result in specific behavioral patterns postinjury. However, no single pattern of disrupted behavior results from brain injury in children. For the most part, the nature of the psychosocial difficulties represents an interaction between the injury itself and the child-specific and environmental factors discussed in the following sections.

Child-Specific Factors

Preinjury factors

The direct effects of brain injury interact with other factors, such as what the child was like before the injury. Brain injury seldom "cures" preinjury problems but often worsens them. Frequently, the adolescent dabbling in substance abuse or sexual promiscuity before injury may develop significant problems in these areas afterward as he lacks the judgment to know when to stop. The self-conscious, quiet teen may become notably anxious and withdrawn, recognizing that she is now very different from her peers. A child who was often angry before his injury may become more angry and even aggressive afterward, as those parts of his brain that enabled him to exercise control over his angry impulses before the injury are now damaged. In contrast, the child who was easygoing before may not become more aggressive, even with damage to the same areas of the brain. Children who were very perfectionistic before injury often struggle with the notion that they can no longer do things perfectly but must find ways to adapt and to compensate for impaired abilities. Children who were more adaptable may find it easier to use their preinjury flexibility to find ways to get around the impairments caused by the injury.

Factors related to age and developmental level

The age at which the student incurs a brain injury has a tremendous impact on the individual's needs both at home and at school. In addition to differences in neuroanatomy and learning experiences (e.g., see Lehr, 1990, and Chapter 14 in this book), age will affect (a) developmental expectations of the person at the time of injury, (b) problems that might be anticipated as the student develops, and (c) experiences or perceptions of the student before the injury. As a child develops, abilities, societal expectations, and developmental tasks all evolve (see Table 7.2).

For the preschool child, injuries tend to be due to circumstances such as falls, child abuse, pedestrian–car accidents, and injury as an unrestrained passenger in a motor vehicle. Because parents assume primary responsibility for children of this age, the circumstances of the injury may lead to a tremendous amount of guilt on the part of the parents. Parental guilt may at times result in protective behavior on their part that interferes with the child's developing or redeveloping competencies following the injury.

TABLE 7.2. Developmental Stages and Changes

Eriksonian Stages

Age	*Stage*	*Task*
Infant–toddler	Trust vs. mistrust (0–2 years)	To develop a sense of trust through getting most of needs met
Preschool	Autonomy vs. shame and doubt (2–5 years)	To begin to develop a sense of self-control through successes
	Initiative vs. guilt (4–6 years)	To learn to take initiative by being rewarded for curiosity and exploration
Elementary	Industry vs. inferiority (7–12 years)	To develop a sense of competence and a desire to work hard through reinforcement of efforts; to develop social, physical, and academic skills
High school	Identity vs. role confusion (13–18 years)	To establish a sense of personal identity through seeing one's continuity with past and future and through reconciling diverse roles, abilities, and values

Piagetian Stages

Age	*Stage*	*Abilities*
Infant–toddler	Sensorimotor (0–2 years)	Child achieves concept of a stable physical world
Preschool	Preoperational (2–5 years)	Child can think of objects and events in their absence; child remains egocentric
Elementary	Concrete operations (6–11 years)	Child learns and can apply a system of rules bound to concrete reality
High school	Formal operations (12+ years)	Adolescent has abstract and symbolic modes of thought, allowing for abstract reasoning and conceptual judgment; adolescent can conceive of hypothetical possibilities

(*continues*)

TABLE 7.2. *Continued*

	Brain Development	
Age	***Brain Changes***	***Related Abilities***
Infant–toddler	By 2 years of age, brain weighs about 75% of its adult weight; basic sensory and motor areas of brain develop	Recognition and discrimination; motor abilities developed and refined; words understood as symbols for objects
Preschool *Elementary*	From 5 to 8 years, linkages between different perceptual areas develop; more efficient connections between the brain hemispheres	Academic learning possible because of integration of different types of sensory information; social skills development; mastery of gross motor skills
High school	Frontal lobes and complex connections to other areas of brain develop; process of myelination may continue into second decade	Ability to plan, initiate, self-monitor, and show cognitive flexibility become apparent

Sources include *Development of the Child* by D. Elkind and I. B. Weiner, 1978, New York: Wiley; *Psychology* by H. Gleitman, 1981, New York: Norton; *Psychological Management of Traumatic Brain Injuries in Children and Adolescents* by E. Lehr, 1990, Rockville, MD: Aspen; and "Neuropsychology of the Developing Brain: Implications for Neuropsychological Assessment" by A. H. Risser and D. Edgell, in *Assessment Issues in Child Neuropsychology* (pp. 41–65) by M. G. Tramontana and S. R. Hooper (Eds.), 1988, New York: Plenum Press.

The ages from birth to 5 are associated with an enormous amount of change as the totally dependent infant develops into an assertive toddler and an independent-minded preschooler. During this time, the child initially learns how to perceive the environment, how to act on it, and how to differentiate himself from others and to develop a basic sense of trust. He then moves on to learning how to control his own body and his environment and how to interact with others in a more emphatic (but still egocentric) fashion. Sustaining a brain injury at any point in this developmental continuum interrupts mastery of the skills that serve as building blocks for later development. Depending upon the type of injury and the child's communication abilities, temperament, and developmental stage, the child may react to these changes with constant irritability and crying, withdrawal, or frustration and temper tantrums. Older preschoolers may become anxious and fearful, feeling that the injury was a punishment for "being bad." Some children may remain mute, even after the cognitive and physiologic factors enabling them to speak have been restored.

Because of differing developmental expectations, the young child may appear to fare better following injury than older children. However, the younger child also is at much greater risk of "growing into" new problems over the course of neuroanatomical development. For example, the child who is injured at 4 years of age is not expected to problem solve effectively. She has neither the experience base nor the development of relevant brain areas (particularly the frontal lobes) to be able to do so. However, by the time this child is 16, she is expected to be able to recognize potentially dangerous or problematic situations, to generate some possible solutions, and to choose appropriately from among these solutions by anticipating their consequences. If the "problem-solving" parts of her brain were injured, the child may seem to be doing fine at 4 years old but appear significantly impaired at 16 years. The effect of brain injury may not be apparent until a later age because more complex reasoning skills and self-monitoring are not expected of the younger child.

By the time children reach school age, injuries are less often due to falls and more often to motor vehicle accidents (as passengers or pedestrians) and to sports-related injuries. Parents are less likely to blame themselves for the injury than when a younger child is injured. School-aged children are involved in mastery of the world at large, in particular social relationships, academic achievements, and cooperative and competitive activities. Development of secondary association areas of the cortex typically occurs between ages 5 and 8 (see Table 7.2). Damage to these areas, which mediate cross-modal skills (those involving more than one ability or sense), may impair the growing child's ability to learn to read, to write, or to adapt to the psychosocial demands of school. Because mastery in these areas contributes to the development of self-esteem and feelings of belongingness, school-aged children are likely to be frustrated by the differences between their achievements before an injury and their abilities after. Social disinhibition and the sense of being different are common, often leading to problems in feeling a part of the social group. Peers also tend to be quite sensitive to these differences, and teasing by peers is common.

Maturation of the frontal or "executive" lobes does not occur until prepuberty, with much of this development completed by about 12 years of age. The frontal lobes, which are very vulnerable in head injury, direct the ability to think conceptually, to organize complex tasks, and to make mature judgments expected of the young adult. Whether the brain injury is sustained in adolescence or years earlier, the damage may interfere with social judgment, the ability to learn from experience, and cognitive flexibility. These impairments leave the adolescent ill prepared to meet the expectations of society. The adolescent is in the process of establishing a sense of personal identity and taking on new responsibilities and new privileges; these important milestones often are stripped from the individual following brain injury. Previous social, athletic, and vocational pursuits often are thwarted following brain injury. Decision making regarding use of alcohol and drugs as well as engagement in sexual activity may also be impaired (see Case Study 7.1).

CASE STUDY 7.1

Alcohol and Drug Abuse Post–Traumatic Brain Injury

Seventeen-year-old RO has problems typical of those faced by many adolescents who do not receive adequate intervention after a brain injury. RO, who sustained an injury in a car accident, was comatose for a day and disoriented for several weeks. His family, feeling that RO was "like his old self," opted for RO to return to his rural community rather than to prolong his stay at a rehabilitation hospital. Nevertheless, RO's neuropsychological evaluation indicated significantly impaired visual perceptual, reasoning, and motor skills. At the time therapy was initiated for RO, his parents complained that he had become rebellious, aggressive, and antisocial. He began socializing with a different group of peers who stayed out late and used both drugs and alcohol. RO, who was a good student and athlete before his injury, was unable to be successful in either of these areas postinjury. As a consequence of his change in educational tracking, inability to play sports, and communication problems, RO was alienated from his previous friends. Although he had his driver's license, his mother adhered to hospital staff recommendations that he no longer drive. With little left of his "old self," RO reestablished his identity with less than desirable peers from his new classes. Drugs and alcohol helped to ease the pain of his losses but caused even further social problems for RO, who was even more vulnerable than his peers to the effects of drugs and alcohol. By the time he entered therapy, RO was failing most of his classes and was alienated from any potentially positive support system.

Changes in motor coordination, physical appearance, academic placement, and social status often tax the adolescent's already compromised coping skills. Changes in romantic relationships, driving abilities, and school and career plans can be devastating. The loss of independence, self-confidence, and the comforting sense of invulnerability may result in the adolescent's becoming withdrawn and depressed or rebellious and antisocial due to overwhelming feelings of despair or anger. Some adolescents attempt to incorporate the injury into their sense of identity by discovering the "meaning" of the injury (e.g., "I shouldn't have been drinking and driving") and incorporating it into their sense of self and beliefs about the future (e.g., "I need to get on a better path if I want to succeed"). Still other adolescents deny the effects of the injury on their functioning and engage in risk-taking behaviors (e.g., use of alcohol and/or drugs, increased sexual activity) in an attempt to prove that they still belong and can still do the things other adolescents do.

Environmental Factors

Family factors

Many of the effects of brain injury are due also to the injured person's reactions and to his or her postinjury environment. Children and families react in a myriad of ways to a traumatic injury and the changes it brings about. These reactions are affected by the recency of the child's injury, as well as each family's unique way of coping with crisis. Initially following injury, family members may downplay the child's problems, challenge professionals' "pessimistic" predictions, and become angered by suggestions by educators or therapists that special programs may be required. Other families become overprotective after a traumatic injury (see Case Study 7.2). Recognizing that the child might not have survived this injury, they make every effort to protect him or her from situations in which another injury could occur. They may restrict the child from participating in sports, outdoor activities, parties, and so forth, resulting in the child's having fewer opportunities for learning, social interactions, demonstrating competence, and redevelopment of self-esteem. Guides have been written to help family members better understand the injury's effects (e.g., Deaton, 1987; Lash, 1991).

CASE STUDY 7.2

Overprotection of Injured Child

AW was 2 years old when he wandered into the street after his ball and was struck by a car, sustaining a severe traumatic brain injury. Now 1 year postinjury, AW is unable to walk but can crawl. He can say four- to five-word sentences and follow one- and often two-step commands. AW is hypersensitive to noise and has a short attention span. When in a noisy environment, AW tends to startle and cry in response to loud noises and appears irritable and easily frustrated. He has five or six temper tantrums on the average day, usually in response to not getting a need or a want met immediately (request for juice, toy, etc.). His parents blame themselves for his injury and thus try to meet all of AW's demands. Because of this constellation of characteristics, AW has received only one-on-one interventions in the past year, seeing individual therapists and being seen in the home by a home tutor. An only child, he is seldom around other children close to his age.

Although AW's parents are concerned and devoted, their decision to protect AW from frustration and to isolate him from peers does not appear to be in his best interests. At 3 years of age, children are beginning to acquire social skills that include sharing with peers and delaying gratification. AW will not have an opportunity to learn these skills unless provided with peer interactions and unless the expectations for his behavior at home are gradually increased. Therefore, the treatment team recommended that AW attend an early childhood development center. His parents were provided with a structured behavioral program to implement at home and received frequent observation, support, and praise as they were able to do so. The most potent reward for them, however, was the obvious improvement in AW's behavior and independence following implementation of these changes.

Other family members may demonstrate different patterns of reaction. Sibling reactions may be particularly important to consider. In the initial days after a child has a brain injury, the attention of everyone is typically focused on the injured child: Will she live? Will she walk? Will she ever be the same? For the child with a minor or moderate brain injury, this focused attention may be short lived and the family may quickly resume normal routines. However, for the severely injured child, the severity of postinjury sequelae may dictate that the family continue to focus attention on the child's recovery and rehabilitation for long periods of time. In such cases, many siblings may feel responsible for the injury or wish they had been injured rather than their sibling. Some take on the role of the injured sibling, trying to fill her shoes so that the family's grief will be less pronounced. Others may be resentful, blaming the brain-injured child for irrevocably altering the family's life and their own sense of security and predictability.

Although it is often easy to overlook the difficulties siblings have in adjusting to a brother's or sister's injury, their needs must be recognized also. Monitoring their school performance and their overall development are important ways of ensuring that the child's brain injury does not prevent the siblings from continuing to achieve developmental milestones. With older children, it may be appropriate for parents to share their concerns about the injured child and to problem solve as a family about ways to help. Parents also should try to provide some quality time without the injured child present and listen actively to their other children. These efforts may prove valuable as supports to the child who is coping with a loss that differs from, but is no less significant than, that felt by the rest of the family. Also valuable is the provision of written information for siblings, such as *Understanding Brain Injury: For Kids Only* (Raines & Waaland, 1992). This is a guide for the siblings of children with brain injury to help them understand the injury's effects, to facilitate their own coping, and to help them assist the injured child to cope and to recover.

The quality of family life and available resources also significantly affect the child's psychosocial adjustment following the injury (Brown, Chadwick, Shaffer, Rutter, & Traub, 1981). Families with fewer resources often have greater difficulty facilitating successful community reentry. These families may lack an understanding of the injury, as well as the financial resources and social supports that help to promote successful adjustment of the child (Waaland, Burns, & Cockrell, 1993). The single parent who does not have insurance, money, or a car may be so stressed by the injury that he or she is forced to focus on the family's survival and daily needs rather than the child's recovery. Rehabilitation therapies, extracurricular activities, and respite for parent and child may be unaffordable luxuries. These limitations also tend to limit the family's contact with therapists, educators, and other families who have gone through similar experiences. As a consequence, the family members may not gain the knowledge and support needed to facilitate good home adjustment of the child.

School setting

When the transition back to school is made too rapidly or when educators do not understand the special needs of children with brain injury, programs may often be beyond the abilities of the recently injured child. Children who have sustained mild injuries may appear to be fine and, due to limited self-awareness, believe themselves to be fine. Thus, the problems that arise may be quite unexpected (see Case Study 7.3). The damage done by inadequate planning for school reentry is incalculable. Early failures after school reentry may make the child increasingly reluctant to persist in efforts to achieve and succeed. Later, when cognitive abilities have improved and the child could be successful academically, he or she may be unwilling to jeopardize self-esteem by trying. Examples of the positive effects of a good school reentry plan and the potentially disastrous effects of not planning are described in Case Studies 7.4 and 7.5, respectively.

CASE STUDY 7.3

Mild Head Injury

LA was unconscious for several hours and disoriented for several days following her involvement in a motor vehicle accident. After 3 weeks of homebound instruction, LA returned to school. She required only minimal educational support and did not have visible reminders of her injury. She was even able to resume driving. However, she at times "spaced out," did not understand jokes, and became "tongue-tied" during conversations with peers. Her boyfriend's typical response was an irritated "oh, sure" when she was too tired to go out by 8:30 PM. LA, who had been socially adept and popular before her injury, avoided parties after the wreck because she developed headaches and could not attend to a conversation with all the distracting background noise.

CASE STUDY 7.4

Successful School Reentry Plan

IC is a 9-year-old girl who sustained a severe traumatic brain injury in a fall from her horse 7 months ago. Although in a coma for 2 weeks, IC made a quick recovery following her injury. However, she continued to be easily fatigued and irritable, was quick to give up on difficult tasks, and was unable to see others' points of view. On neuropsychological testing, deficits were noted in attention span and selective attention, new learning, cognitive flexibility, and problem solving. On standard intellectual testing (the *Wechsler Intelligence Scale for Children–Revised*), IC has an above-average verbal IQ (118) and a below-average performance IQ (87). IC wanted to return to school immediately after she was discharged from the hospital 1 month postinjury. Her parents, having met with the neuropsychologist and other members of the hospital-based treatment team, recognized that IC was likely to have some problems when she returned to school. They requested a meeting with school personnel and were able to negotiate a plan such that IC would attend school in the mornings, return home for lunch and a rest period at noon, and then have a homebound teacher in the afternoon for an hour. Because her injury had occurred 10 weeks before the end of the school year, it was agreed that this arrangement would continue through the remainder of the year. On the home front, IC was eager to resume riding her horse, having no recollection that this was how she had sustained her injury. Her physician had stated that she could not ride for at least a year and that, at that point, he would reevaluate whether to let her ride with a helmet. Thus, IC was thwarted in her desire to return to her premorbid activities both at school and at home.

To meet some of IC's needs for peer interaction and mastery, her parents agreed to allow IC to participate in the 4-H club, something they had been reluctant to allow before because of their time and energy required to transport her to the many activities sponsored by the 4-H. This involvement exposed IC to new peers who had no preconceptions of who she was or what her abilities were. She was able to follow through on her love of horses through involvement in grooming activities and showing horses at the state fair. IC also attended a small group with a counselor and three other children (aged 9–12 years) who had endured similar injuries and were in various stages of returning to school. Many of the group activities were game or activity oriented, but the games also provided opportunities to compare experiences with one another and to express feelings.

IC continued her 4-H involvement, group therapy, and individual home tutoring through the summer. When school resumed, she was able to successfully rejoin her peers in a regular classroom, with a teacher who had received information about how to monitor IC's performance and provide prompt referral for services should the need arise. At time of reevaluation, IC had been back in school for 2 months and had been successful in her school performance, although she noted that she still fatigued more easily than her peers.

CASE STUDY 7.5

Unplanned School Reentry

ZT is a 15-year-old adolescent who was struck by a bus while riding his skateboard 9 months ago. ZT had made an excellent physical recovery from his injury and remained an attractive and active adolescent. Unfortunately, he was far more impulsive than he had been prior to his injury and often made poor decisions, taking unnecessary risks to prove he was "cool." ZT returned to his regular classroom 2 months after his injury. His school had no specific plan for his reentry and little information on the effects of brain injury. Due to the effects of his injury on his cognitive abilities, ZT was unable to understand what was expected of him in the classroom and to work independently on assignments. ZT reacted to these changes by refusing to do his work, clowning with his peers, and skipping classes. His behaviors seemed designed to avoid situations in which he might fail, thereby preserving his self-esteem.

Testing by the school psychologist revealed that ZT had low average intellectual functioning and performed in the average range compared with peers on measures of academic achievement. This finding is not uncommon for children soon after an injury before they have had a chance to fall behind peers in achievement (because of difficulties with new learning). An Individualized Education Program was developed, and school staff determined that ZT's needs would best be met in a behavior disordered (BD) classroom. His parents agreed with this plan but remained bewildered by the sudden deterioration in ZT's behavior. ZT viewed the placement as a punishment and was angry to be separated from his old friends and primary sources of support and self-esteem. He decided to be the "best at being bad" in his classroom.

This behavior caused concern for ZT's parents and the school. They asked for help from a neuropsychological consultant, who assessed the situation. It appeared that ZT had returned to school fully expecting to resume his normal routine, perhaps a bit of a hero after all he had been through. Both he and his school were ill prepared for the cognitive effects of his injury that made it difficult for him to complete his work adequately. This resulted in feelings of frustration on ZT's part as he began to perceive himself as a failure. Because ZT denied his cognitive problems and perhaps was even unaware of them himself, ZT's parents and teachers initially attributed some of these difficulties to normal adolescent rebellion. However, the striking contrast between his preinjury and postinjury development convinced them that he needed special assistance. The consultant's recommendations included the following: (a) neuropsychological evaluation to identify injury-related cognitive impairments and to recommend an approach for remediation; (b) individual and family counseling to improve ZT's and his family's understanding of brain injury and to assist them in negotiating a plan whereby ZT could earn more independence and privileges by demonstrating agreed-upon behaviors; and (c) social skills group, to enhance ZT's pragmatic skills (e.g., turn-taking, interruptions, response to criticism) and improve his competence and confidence in social situations. Additional recommendations were to be made pending the results of these interventions.

Social factors

Societal reactions can have a significant impact on the child's adjustment, depending upon how the child is viewed and accepted or rejected by strangers, peers, potential employers, and so forth. The effects of the injury itself interact with social factors as they do with the other environmental factors. For example, Pettersen (1991) noted that, following a brain injury, children are less able to interpret others' emotions and the meanings of subtle nonverbal cues, and thus are less appropriate in their social behaviors. The impact of this change in empathy and social savvy is often severe when it comes to interactions with friends, as they no longer experience the injured child as the same person they knew before the injury. Friendships can also be affected by cognitive impairments; the child who no longer remembers the significant events in his friends' lives may not seem like much of a friend.

In other social settings, the obvious effects of the brain injury, such as speech and motor difficulties, may have the immediate effect of causing people to stare or to avoid the child who has been injured. Other people's behaviors naturally have an impact on the child's self-esteem and may lead to social isolation as he or she increasingly avoids public settings. More subtle impairments in self-awareness and communication skills also affect casual social interactions, as the child who has been injured may miss conversational cues or may not process new information quickly enough to respond to the environment. If the child's self-esteem and awareness are intact, he or she may be able to cope adaptively with these situations, perhaps by asking someone to slow down, by explaining the injury, or by using a standard phrase (e.g., "Can you give me a minute?") to give themselves more time to react. The child's self-esteem is seldom intact, however, unless he or she has received adequate support in important settings such as the home and the school. Increasing societal knowledge and understanding of the effects of brain injury may also assist this situation.

POSTINJURY INTERVENTIONS WITH CHILDREN AND ADOLESCENTS

Evaluation and treatment of the psychosocial impact of TBIs are closely intertwined. Assessing psychosocial effects of TBI requires a team effort, including input from the child, parent(s) and other family members, teacher(s), and appropriate other professionals (pediatric neuropsychologist, school psychologist, recreation therapist, social worker, etc.). Each of these team members has unique expertise in what constitutes normal development and what difficulties the child is experiencing postinjury. The ideal assessment includes formal evaluative measures as well as systematic observations in the environments in which the child spends most of his or her time. This combination of measures is necessary because test results obtained in a structured one-on-one session between child and professional may differ from those obtained in more naturalistic settings (e.g., the classroom, the home).

Formal testing may include such instruments as self-esteem measures, depression inventories, projective figure drawing, and so forth. Observational measures include standardized rating scales, such as those that have been developed for assessing other populations (e.g., *Child Behavior Checklist,* Achenbach, 1981; *Personality Inventory for Children,* Wirt, Lachar, Klinedinst, & Seat, 1977, and Wirt, Seat, & Brown, 1977; *Conner's Teacher and Parent Rating Scales,* Goyette, Conners, & Ulrich, 1978), as well as individualized observational protocols designed to assess this specific child's strengths and deficits. The choice of a particular scale should be dictated by the type of information needed and the time constraints of the rater. *The ACTERS* (Ullman, Sleador, & Sprague, 1988), for example, includes scales that tap many problematic behaviors for youth with TBI. This scale has the advantages of ease of completion and comparison of input from many sources. These advantages make it particularly useful at the middle school or high school level when students may have seven or more teachers providing instruction. The *Child Behavior Checklist* provides much more detailed information, including scales assessing social withdrawal, depression, anxiety, hyperactivity, and physical or somatic complaints common following TBI. A most useful aspect of this scale is the availability of parallel forms for teacher, parent, and youth self-report (ages 11–18). These comparisons provide the educator with important information. For example, are there differences between classroom and home behavior due to the unique stresses at school? Does the parent fail to see or acknowledge problematic behaviors? Does the student show poor self-awareness and deny social or emotional problems that clearly interfere with school adjustment? In addition to its clinical scales, the *Child Behavior Checklist* also includes a social rating scale that helps the educator to assess the quality of the student's relationships, extracurricular activities, and leisure interests. These structured reports are best supplemented by talking to family, friends, school personnel, and particularly the student. It is important to find out how the student feels the injury has changed his or her life and what his or her perceptions of social, academic, and physical self are.

Although helpful, checklists cannot substitute for systematic, "real-life" observations. The child should be observed in different settings (e.g., the classroom, cafeteria, hall, playground), in different activities (e.g., physical education, music, art, social studies, class presentations), with different people (e.g., peers, younger children, family, authority figures), and at different times of the day. The effects of these different situations on social behavior should be carefully evaluated to develop a behavior plan based on the behaviors that appear most problematic and the situations in which they occur. For example, does the child fall asleep or become more irritable as the day progresses? In the classroom, does the child blurt out inappropriate comments or stare blankly when questions are asked? Does he display mannerisms (e.g., nose picking, immodesty) that cause a negative social reaction from others? Does she do well in the structured classroom but eat alone (or take food off other people's trays) in the cafeteria? Contrived situations also may help better understand the child's abilities and impairments. For example, when asked to plan a party, does he take the interests of classmates into account? When problems are called to his attention, is he able to alter the original plans accordingly?

Assessment of psychosocial functioning provides a baseline that allows for the development of appropriate interventions and the evaluation of the effectiveness of these interventions over time. Incorporating developmental expectations into interventions is essential. Parents of children at the toddler or preschool level need to experience a feeling of competence in their role as caretakers; thus, they may require help in providing a "safe" environment for the child to explore through "babyproofing" and other environmental strategies (e.g., see Case Study 7.2). Parents need information on what is expected and how to intervene appropriately. They may benefit from psychotherapy if their guilt prevents appropriate intervention. Many parents will require support and instruction in structured behavior management strategies (e.g., contingent rewards, time-out) that decrease physical punishment and negative parenting behaviors. Respite care may prevent caretaker "burnout," common among parents of disabled preschoolers, and neglect of other family members' needs. Preschool children with disabilities are vulnerable targets for parent abuse. Children at this age may also profit from involvement in a structured, center-based remedial program or nursery school program as appropriate. Long hospital stays are not usually recommended as these may disrupt the bonding process and the child's sense of security and trust. Parental rooming-in at the hospital may be a viable alternative, however, to home-based nursing intervention and outpatient therapies.

For the child functioning at the school-age level, the focus of intervention gradually shifts from home and family to school and peers. Cognitive intervention strategies (e.g., self-monitoring and reward, social skills training, problem-solving approaches) and logical consequences begin to replace structured behavioral approaches in the home. It is particularly important for parents and teachers to learn to break down tasks and modify expectations at this stage to promote successful mastery and to work on carryover between the home and the school. Areas of nonacademic strength, such as music, sports, crafts, and so forth, should be developed to foster social skills and self-identity. These types of interventions can also help the child avoid overidentification with the "sick role." Children who fail to develop their own unique strengths may use symptomatic behavior as a source of attention and identity.

Adolescence often precipitates significant adjustment problems for both the injured child and family members. The adolescent experiences dramatic hormonal changes, growth spurts, social stressors, and academic demands. These stresses often intensify home management problems and stressful parent–child interactions. The behavior management strategies effective with the younger school-aged child often precipitate rebellion when the child reaches adolescence. Many adolescents engage in inappropriate risk-taking, experimentation with drugs and alcohol, and other acting-out behaviors in an attempt to fit in socially. Due to disinhibition and emerging sexual feelings, sexual promiscuity is particularly problematic for adolescents with brain injuries. Typical adolescent management problems often precipitate family crises. It is particularly important to reduce parental overprotection and anxiety while at the same time helping the adolescent to accept responsibility and recognize personal limitations. Group interventions may be particularly effective, as they give the adolescent the opportunity to learn from his or her peers rather than accepting an authority figure's suggestions. Groups may take the form of support groups for adolescents with chronic medical problems (e.g., diabetes, asthma, brain injury, orthopedic injury) or may be skills focused (e.g., social skills or problem-solving groups). Hospitalization may occasionally be necessary to reduce parent–adolescent conflict and to protect the acting-out adolescent. At this stage, vocational and independent living skills become primary. Integration of academic and vocational services is the responsibility of the school, but families may have to request this service. For the student who is ultimately unable to function autonomously or in a supervised group home setting, the family will need assistance in formulating long-range plans.

CONCLUSION

The psychosocial difficulties that frequently follow brain injury can be as devastating or more so than the cognitive and physical effects that commonly occur. In this chapter, we have identified the range of psychosocial difficulties that occur and how these interact with developmental stage and the needs of the individual child. Several case studies were included so that the reader can identify more closely with the unique challenges involved. Although psychosocial sequelae are often difficult to quantify, they significantly affect the quality of life for the child who sustains a brain injury. We hope that this chapter provides some guidance to educators as they rise to meet the challenge.

REFERENCES

Achenbach, T. M. (1981). *The Child Behavior Checklist.* Burlington: University Associates in Psychiatry, University of Vermont.

Asarnow, R. F., Satz, P., Light, R., Lewis, R., & Neumann, E. (1991). Behavior problems and adaptive functioning in children with mild and severe closed head injury. *Journal of Pediatric Psychology, 16,* 543–555.

Boyer, M. G., & Edwards, P. (1991). Outcome 1 to 3 years after severe traumatic brain injury in children and adolescents. *Injury: The British Journal of Accident Surgery, 22,* 315–320.

Brown, G., Chadwick, O., Shaffer, D., Rutter, M., & Traub, M. (1981). A prospective study of children with head injuries: III. Psychiatric sequelae. *Psychological Medicine, 11,* 63–78.

Deaton, A. V. (1987). *Pediatric head trauma: A guide for families.* Austin, TX: Healthcare International.

Edwards, P. A. (1987). Rehabilitation outcomes in children with brain injury. *Rehabilitation Nursing, 12*(3), 125–127.

Elkind, D., & Weiner, I. B. (1978). *Development of the child.* New York: Wiley.

Falvo, D. R. (1991). *Medical and psychosocial aspects of chronic illness and disability.* Gaithersburg, MD: Aspen.

Gleitman, H. (1981). *Psychology.* New York: Norton.

Goyette, C. H., Conners, C. K., & Ulrich, R. F. (1978). Normative data for Revised Conners Parents and Teacher Rating Scales. *Journal of Abnormal Child Psychology, 6,* 221–236.

Lash, M. (1991). *When your child goes to school after an injury.* Boston: Tufts University/New England Medical Center: Research and Training Center in Rehabilitation and Childhood Trauma.

Lehr, E. (1990). *Psychological management of traumatic brain injuries in children and adolescents.* Rockville, MD: Aspen.

Pettersen, L. (1991). Sensitivity to emotional cues and social behavior in children and adolescents after head injury. *Perceptual and Motor Skills, 73*(3, Pt. 2), 1139–1150.

Prigatano, G. P. (1986). *Neuropsychological rehabilitation after brain injury.* Baltimore: Johns Hopkins University Press.

Raines, S. R., & Waaland, P. (1992). *Understanding traumatic brain injury: For kids only.* Richmond: Medical College of Virginia RRTC Press.

Risser, A. H., & Edgell, D. (1988). Neuropsychology of the developing brain: Implications for neuropsychological assessment. In M. G. Tramontana & S. R. Hooper (Eds), *Assessment issues in child neuropsychology* (pp. 41–65). New York: Plenum Press.

Rutter, M., Chadwick, O., & Shaffer, D. (1983). Head injury. In M. Rutter (Ed.), *Developmental neuropsychiatry.* New York: Guilford Press.

Savage, R. C., & Wolcott, G. F. (1988). *An educator's manual: What educators need to know about students with TBI.* Southborough, MA: National Head Injury Foundation.

Sockalosky, J. J., Kriel, R. L., Krach, L. E., & Sheehan, M. (1987). Precocious puberty after traumatic brain injury. *Journal of Pediatrics, 110,* 373–377.

Ullman, R. T., Sleador, E. K., & Sprague, R. L. (1988). *The ACTERS.* Champaign, IL: MetriTech.

Waaland, P. K., Burns, C., & Cockrell, J. (1993). Evaluation of needs of high- and low-income families following pediatric traumatic brain injury. *Brain Injury, 7*(2), 135–146.

Wirt, R. D., Lachar, D., Klinedinst, J. D., & Seat, P. D. (1977). *Multidimensional description of child personality: A manual for the Personality Inventory for Children.* Los Angeles: Western Psychological Services.

Wirt, R. D., Seat, P. D., & Brown, W. (1977). *Personality Inventory for Children.* Los Angeles: Western Psychological Services.

CHAPTER 8

Changing the Behaviors of Students with Acquired Brain Injuries*

ANN V. DEATON

For many, the most enduring, and potentially most incapacitating, effects of a brain injury are changes in behavior. Although no two persons with brain injuries experience precisely the same behavioral sequelae, behavioral difficulties are common. As noted in previous chapters, the cognitive effects of brain injury, such as distractibility, failure to initiate activities, poor decision making, and failure to shift attention from one activity or subject to another, can make return to the school environment difficult. These deficits interfere with the student's ability to adapt to the smallest changes in routine (e.g., a school assembly that causes a class to be canceled) or to plan appropriately how to deal with changes. Adding to the difficulty are interpersonal skills deficits, such as poor anger control, attention-seeking behavior (e.g., self-injury, physical complaints), failure to respond appropriately to others' social cues, and failure to monitor one's own behavior for appropriateness. When these behaviors are displayed by the student with an acquired brain injury (ABI), they can lead to rejection by peers and helping professionals alike and to failures in many settings. In addition, these impaired abilities and problem behaviors can increase the risk of further injury as the child may demonstrate decreased judgment and difficulty accepting the injury-related changes, leading to an increase in risk-taking behavior (Barin, Hanchett, Jacob, & Scott, 1985). In this chapter, I describe behavioral change strategies that can be helpful in improving the functioning of the student with an acquired brain injury.

* This manuscript is an extension and revision of a previous article by the author entitled "Behavioral Change Strategies for Children and Adolescents with Traumatic Brain Injuries," published in 1987 in the *Journal of Learning Disabilities, 20*(8), 581–589.

BEHAVIORAL CHANGE STRATEGIES

No matter how bad a child's behavior seems, it is important to remember that most children are driven to succeed and that at any given time they are probably doing the best they can with the abilities they have. Programs of behavioral change seek to help shape behavior by developing positive, adaptive skills and decreasing problem behaviors. Their ultimate goal is to enable the student with ABI to function with the greatest degree of independence possible, with the best quality of life, and in the least restrictive environment. Improving adaptive skills is often central to the child's self-esteem, independence, and success. Decreasing maladaptive behaviors is typically necessary if the child is to remain in a normative environment, such as the home or the classroom.

Behavior modification theories and strategies have proliferated since the 1950s and have been used with children with a variety of diagnoses. The basic premise of behavioral approaches is that behavior has antecedents (events that elicit or precede behaviors) and consequences (events that follow behaviors). By changing these, one can change the behavior. Procedures have been developed to increase desired behaviors, to decrease maladaptive behaviors, and to shape existing behaviors into more complex or appropriate ones.

A frequent error made in attempting to change a behavior is to proceed too quickly to the implementation of a strategy before adequately (a) defining the behavior; (b) evaluating its function, etiology, and frequency; (c) identifying all the potential resources available; and (d) listing all the possible strategies for intervention. Knowing the underlying reason for a problem behavior makes it much easier to change it. The child may refuse schoolwork, for example, because the time limits imposed for completion ensure that he will fail. He is doing things as well as he knows how: Refusing to do the work protects his tenuous sense of self-esteem and control. Recognizing that the child is trying to succeed makes it easier to develop behavioral programs in collaboration with the child rather than unilaterally. The most effective intervention in the above case may be to increase the time allotted to do the work rather than punishing the child's refusal. Proceeding carefully through the sequential process of behavior analysis and change will facilitate the selection of a successful intervention. The following steps, described in detail below, are essential to any plan to change behavior:

1. Defining the problem behavior
2. Identifying the function, cause, and rate of the target behavior
3. Identifying resources for behavioral intervention
4. Identifying strategies for behavior change
5. Implementing and evaluating intervention
6. Maintenance and generalization

Defining the Problem Behavior

Setting the stage for effective behavior change with the student who has a brain injury requires a measurable and precise definition of the target behavior. A teacher may feel, for example, that a student with ABI who has recently returned to school "does not belong in a regular classroom." If the reasons for the child not fitting in are behavioral, one way of arriving at a more specific definition of the behaviors that need to be changed is to think of specific examples of when this student's behavior is a problem. The teacher may note that the student cannot take notes quickly enough and frequently asks questions or bursts into tears. These behaviors likely make teaching difficult for the teacher and also result in the student's being ostracized by peers. Thus, the targets for change might include tearfulness, slowness, and frequent interruptions. One way of ensuring that the target behavior has been adequately defined is to check that all those working with the child can agree about the behavior's occurrence and nonoccurrence. This is relatively straightforward for behaviors such as tearfulness or physical aggression but more difficult when the problem is so-called rudeness, uncooperativeness, or not fitting in. Behaviors should be observed in a variety of settings and with a variety of people (Braunling-McMorrow, 1988) to ascertain whether they are situation specific. Frequently, problem behavior occurs only in certain settings. Looking at the settings in which it does *not* occur may suggest some avenues for changing the behavior. In addition, behavior that occurs in a variety of settings may be appropriate in some of them but inappropriate in others. For example, kissing family members is often acceptable behavior for a 14-year-old boy; kissing friends in class is not.

Additionally, the appropriate characteristic (i.e., duration, frequency, intensity) of the target behavior needs to be specified (Gelfand & Hartmann, 1984). The most important characteristic of attention, for example, may be its duration or span. The goal for a student who can attend to an activity for only 20 seconds may be to increase attention span to 5 minutes. In contrast, the changes desired in an aggressive child may be decreased frequency of aggressive episodes, decreased severity or intensity of the aggression, or increased speed in returning to a task following an aggressive outburst.

Identifying the Function, Cause, and Rate of the Target Behavior

Once the target behavior is known, an initial assessment, or baseline period, is useful to evaluate the function of the behavior, its underlying cause or immediate precipitants, and its salient characteristics (frequency, intensity, duration, etc.). A hallmark of brain injury is that the student's behavior after brain injury can be extremely variable from one day or time of day to another, making this initial assessment time-consuming but valuable. When possible, the baseline measure should include time of occurrence, a description of the behavior, and the exact events preceding and following the behavior. A sample baseline assessment is shown in Figure 8.1.

The data sheet could be supplemented by asking the student to explain his or her behavior in each circumstance. This single day of data collection shown in Figure 8.1 suggests a pattern to Jerry's physical aggression toward others. In each case, he was in a social situation and felt threatened in some way. When he hit Sara, he was reacting to her taking his ball and thereby preventing him from playing with the other boys. His self-esteem was threatened by a girl taking a ball from him. He regained his self-esteem by hitting her and reclaiming the ball. When he hit Paul, he was reacting to his own embarrassment at having dropped his tray. By hitting Paul, he caused Paul to drop his tray as well. He also was removed from the embarrassing situation. Finally, when he hit Ed, he was embarrassed by Ed's calling him stupid. Again, Jerry was successful in getting himself removed from the embarrassing situation.

Student: *Jerry* **Behavior:** *Hitting*

Day & Date: *Thursday, Jan. 4, 1993*

Time	***Place***	***What happened?***	***What happened before?***	***What happened after?***
10:12	playground	Jerry hit Sara.	Sara took his ball.	Jerry got to keep the ball.
12:05	lunchroom	Jerry hit Paul.	Paul accidentally bumped Jerry in line and Jerry dropped his tray.	Paul dropped his tray too and hit Jerry. Both boys taken to principal's office and made to sit in hall for rest of lunch period.
2:49	classroom	Jerry hit Ed.	Ed told Jerry he was stupid.	Ed was scolded for teasing. Classroom aide walked Jerry to the bus.

Figure 8.1. Sample data collection for baseline of behavior.

Although Jerry was probably not planning to hit these other students, his behavior was a response that turned out to be adaptive for him in those situations. An effective behavioral program to address Jerry's hitting would help him to develop other skills so that he no longer responded automatically with aggression. Such a program might include any or all of the following components: (a) social skills training including role playing to develop alternate strategies for dealing with problem situations; (b) a focus by both school and family on helping Jerry to identify his strengths and develop more positive feelings about himself so that he is less easily threatened; (c) use of rewards for each class period that Jerry makes it through without hitting anyone; and (d) use of brief time-out after hitting, followed by counseling about alternative ways of reacting and then return to the situation.

In addition to dealing with specific behaviors, Mateer and Williams (1991) noted the importance of behavioral patterns. Recognizing the pattern of behavior not only allows specific interventions in response to the behavior but also allows predictions as to when it might occur and intervention before it occurs. In the example above, it might be predicted that a variety of situations in which Jerry's deficits are apparent will precipitate aggressive acting out. Knowing this enables teachers, counselors, family, and the student to anticipate and prepare for those situations so that they can be managed successfully.

Identifying Resources for Behavioral Intervention

Implementing an effective intervention for changing behavior draws on many resources, including those of the injured individual, the staff who work directly with the individual, the family, and other students. Some behavioral interventions can require significant resources in terms of time, effort, and monetary expenditures. Identifying the available resources before selecting an intervention strategy should facilitate choosing a strategy that is consistent with the available resources and therefore feasible to implement. Resources may include (a) the student's assets, including memory, motivation, ability to learn, and so forth; (b) the professionals, including staff to student ratio, staff training, individual traits (e.g., patience, perseverance), and so on; (c) the family, including ability to consistently carry out programs at home, provision of relevant information for selecting reinforcers, and so forth; and (d) the setting, including natural reinforcers, peers, financial resources, and availability of time-out rooms (Deaton, 1987).

Resources are constantly changing as the individual student and situation change. As time passes after an injury, all involved tend to become increasingly valuable as resources. The student's overall abilities and perhaps awareness are improving with recovery. The family is becoming more knowledgeable about the effects of the brain injury and better connected with support systems. The teachers and other professionals are learning more about brain injury in general and this student's brain injury in particular. To understand this development of resources, one needs only to consider the limited initial resources during the initial period after the injury. At this time, the student's ability to learn and carry out any new behavior will likely be poor. Moreover, she will probably be unmotivated to work at developing new compensatory skills because she cannot yet recognize her deficits or the need for compensation. As her memory improves, more active self-monitoring becomes possible and, in many cases, the student can be actively involved in the behavioral change process. Families, professionals, and the student herself may also receive specific training that enables them to become resources. For example, training in the use of an augmentative communication device, such as IntroTalker (Prentke–Romich Co.), may provide the student with a means of communication that reduces her frustration. When teachers are trained to handle aggression in a manner that minimizes the risk of physical injury without rewarding the behavior, they can prevent the aggression from being inadvertently reinforced (e.g., by giving in to a student's demands) and thereby prevent its increasing in frequency. Training in behavioral management strategies, such as the use of token economies and appropriate reinforcers, may provide additional resources.

Being realistic about resources is important. Even with limited resources (e.g., little control over how peers behave, inadequate personnel or funds), it is usually possible to select a strategy that is effective in changing the student's behavior and enabling him or her to be successful. Relying on resources that do not exist or over which the teacher has no control usually yields an ineffective intervention, and failure to change a behavior may further reduce available resources (e.g., the student's self-esteem, the parents' willingness to cooperate, the teacher's motivation and energy).

Identifying Strategies for Behavior Change

How can one identify potential strategies for changing the behavior? Obviously, the strategies will depend upon the nature of the behavior, its function, and the available resources. Developing strategies requires creativity and flexibility, as well as knowledge of the behavioral principles involved. For the injured child who refuses to respond to requests, for example, possible strategies include providing written task instructions, rewards for task completion, time-out, removal to a less stressful situation, ignoring the noncompliance, loss of privileges or attention, giving more attention to cooperative students in the immediate environment, avoidance of frustrating situations, and many other possibilities. Depending upon the function of the behavior, its cause, and other characteristics of the student (e.g., ability to pick up on subtle social cues such as the teacher reinforcing more appropriate peers nearby), any of these strategies (and others) may be appropriate. The best behavioral management strategy for the student is that which uses as few resources as possible, but as many as needed to achieve the goals (Jacobs, 1987).

One rule of thumb in the selection of a strategy is to choose the least intrusive procedure that will be effective. In general, this means that altering antecedent conditions (e.g., the setting) and providing reinforcement are preferable to punishment. At least two reasons support this recommendation. First, reinforcement and/or changes in antecedent conditions are more likely than punishment alone to lead to lasting changes in the behavior of the child who has sustained a brain injury (Eames & Wood, 1985) and to generalize to other settings (Zencius, Wesolowski, Burke, & McQuade, 1989). Second, punishment may lead to depression, decreased initiative, and lower self-esteem in the student who may already be experiencing these problems and viewing himself or herself in a negative light (Malec, 1984). In the case of dangerous behaviors, such as self-abuse, physical restraint may be necessary and may be the least intrusive intervention that is effective in preventing bodily damage. However, this intervention alone is unlikely to produce any lasting change unless coupled with teaching alternative behaviors and providing rewards for positive, appropriate behavior. Sand, Trieschmann, Fordyce, and Fowler (1970) described the use of this two-faceted approach to decrease the tantrums of a 7-year-old boy who had sustained a traumatic brain injury. In this case, time-outs were given contingent on tantrum behavior. Other appropriate behaviors were rewarded with tokens that could be exchanged for rewards. When receiving attention was made contingent on positive behaviors instead of negative ones, this child quickly became more compliant. In other cases, alternative positive behaviors may be lacking and may have to be specifically taught.

Implementing and Evaluating Intervention

Once a strategy or strategies have been selected, they must be implemented consistently and their effectiveness evaluated. This requires ongoing collection of data about the behavior's occurrence. Because many students with brain injury have impairments in the area of attention and memory (Auerbach, 1986; Mateer & Williams, 1991), providing concrete feedback in the form of graphs or charts is often useful to remind them of gains. Particularly if progress is slow, videotaping at various intervals may provide for concrete comparisons between previous and current levels of functioning. Finally, changing antecedent conditions (e.g., providing a schedule or written instructions; using study carrels) can be extremely effective in changing the student's behavior because the antecedents provide a continuous prompt and do not require intact memory to be effective.

Not all programs will be effective, regardless of how well planned they are. If a behavioral program is not effective, it is useful to assess whether the program is being consistently implemented. Inconsistency in implementation often results in a program's failure (Divack, Herrie, & Scott, 1985). Moreover, inconsistency between the parents and the school may result in the maintenance of maladaptive behaviors and the student's failing to learn new, appropriate, and effective alternate behaviors (see Case Study 8.1).

CASE STUDY 8.1

Inconsistency in Program Implementation

SH is a 12-year-old who sustained a severe brain injury in a bicycle–car collision 4 years ago. She has been in school for the past 3 years but refuses to do assigned tasks she does not like. SH's school and her family tend to blame each other for SH's problems. Her school notes that her family brings her to school late each morning, in time for a preferred activity (art) but missing disliked classes (math and social sciences). Her school also notes the family's failure to carry out behavior programs, particularly regarding eating and homework completion, in the home.

SH's parents still blame themselves for their daughter's injury because they did not require her to wear a bike helmet. They feel that SH has special needs and that the school does not recognize SH's needs and is too strict. They note that they do not have behavioral problems at home; they simply allow SH to do what she enjoys doing. Due to the school's and family's blaming one another, little cooperation or collaboration exists between them. SH continues to refuse activities, have tantrums, and steal food at school, and the school staff acknowledges that they often end up punishing her, which is against the program developed for her. The family is able to avoid her demonstrating these behaviors in the home by not allowing her to be frustrated–or to be challenged.

A second cause for program failure is that additional resources may be required. An adolescent may be getting into trouble with alcohol and drugs because he lacks the ability to generate better alternatives. If he does not have the capacity to self-monitor his own behavior and work toward long-term objectives, he may need to be provided with external resources, such as supervised after-school activities (e.g., weight lifting at the YMCA), to limit his opportunities for involvement with alcohol and drugs and to provide him with another mechanism for socialization and the development of self-esteem.

Third, a program may not work because the strategy selected was inappropriate or not powerful enough. Most commonly, this is a result of the chosen reinforcement's not being truly reinforcing to a particular student. For example, free time may be rewarding to most students but may be anxiety provoking to the child with a brain injury who now functions best with a high degree of structure. It is particularly

TABLE 8.1. Possible Solutions to Failed Interventions

Explanation for Failure	***Possible Solutions***
1. Program inconsistently implemented	• Reeducate everyone about program • Identify barriers to implementation • Implement consistently
2. Lack of resources	• Identify more resources • Develop some resources
3. Inappropriate program	• Change the target behavior • Change the program
4. Poorly defined target behavior	• Additional behavioral baseline • Agreement on concrete definition
5. Behavior has existed for long time	• Lengthy intervention period • Start with easier behavior to change
6. Student cannot perform desired behavior	• Shape gradually or teach behavior • Change target behavior

difficult to identify effective reinforcers for the student who lacks motivation and initiative as a result of frontal lobe damage (Grimm & Bleiberg, 1986). Difficulties can sometimes be remedied by choosing a different reinforcer, decreasing the time it takes to earn a reward, or providing more structure and cues in the environment. Table 8.1 provides possible solutions to failed interventions.

An intervention may appear ineffective because the target behavior was poorly defined and the criteria for adequate performance shifted as the student's skills increased (e.g., because "uncooperativeness" was defined initially as refusal but later as grumbling when asked to complete a task). This gradual shifting of the definition of the problem behavior may well be appropriate in shaping more and more desirable behaviors as long as the shift is explicit and everyone is aware that the rules are changing.

Some target behaviors are difficult to change because they have been occurring for a long time with considerable reinforcement. In this case, they may require a lengthy intervention period. For example, when a child's refusal to eat has led to his receiving preferred foods such as ice cream, she may refuse other foods for a long period in order to obtain her preferred food. Acceptance of other foods may need to be shaped gradually (e.g., alternating bites of a sandwich with bites of ice cream, then progressing to two bites of a sandwich to every one bite of ice cream, etc.), even though the ultimate goal is resumption of a normal eating pattern.

The target behavior may have been inappropriate because the child is unable to perform the desired behavior. This can occur when the student has neurologically based limitations in cognitive, physical, or other abilities. An example might be attempting a self-monitoring program with a child who has difficulty writing and therefore cannot record his progress. If the target behavior is inappropriate, effective approaches include further defining the target behavior, selecting a new behavior that may be more readily changed, or gradually shaping the development of increasingly complex behaviors.

Maintenance and Generalization

Once desirable behaviors have been demonstrated in one setting, this change needs to be maintained in the original setting as well as generalized to other settings, such as other classrooms, the school bus, the home, and the community. The process of maintenance and generalization often involves shifting the control for the behavior back to the student and away from external sources and behavioral programs. Maintenance of a behavior when external reinforcers and/or controls are eliminated is facilitated by gradual rather than abrupt changes in the environmental contingencies, particularly in the case of brain injury. The basic process is that of moving from primary (concrete) to secondary reinforcers, from artificial to natural rewards, from immediate to delayed feedback, and from continuous to intermittent reinforcement. In short, the movement is toward a type of reinforcement more often found in natural environments (Braunling-McMorrow, 1988; Divack et al., 1985). The student who was initially rewarded with a token every time she participated in class may gradually move toward receiving tokens for each class period in which she participates and then eventually to receiving praise instead of tokens and finally to being able to reinforce herself through positive self-talk (i.e., "I did a good job").

Some relapses should be expected as attempts are made to decrease the levels of reinforcement. However, if the relapse is severe or prolonged, it may be necessary to reestablish control over the behavior before again attempting to phase out the external controls, this time more gradually. Fading out antecedent conditions may not be necessary unless they are unduly restrictive or intrusive. Use of a schedule, for example, is an acceptable strategy in a variety of settings and can usually be generalized to other settings without difficulty.

Even when a behavior can be successfully maintained in a given situation with decreased reinforcement, it may not generalize to other settings. Once again, because of the cognitive impairments often accompanying a brain injury, generalization may not occur and newly learned skills need to be specifically taught in the context of other settings. Plans for generalization must take into account the environments in which the injured person will be expected to function and the characteristics of those settings. The likelihood of generalization can be enhanced by modifying the target behavior in a variety of settings and with a variety of people. Because social situations are unpredictable, maladaptive behaviors may be inadvertently reinforced by some people and this occasional, intermittent reinforcement may serve to maintain the behavior. By training with a number of people and settings, it becomes more likely that a new situation will share some characteristics with situations in which appropriate behavior has been practiced and reinforced. In cases where generalization does not occur, the emphasis should move to teaching functional skills in each of the settings to which they are appropriate. Another strategy is to provide consistent cues in all environments (e.g., a note attached to the wheelchair that reads "Stop and think first").

BEHAVIORAL CHANGE STRATEGIES SPECIFIC TO BRAIN INJURY

Although the principles and methods discussed above have been applied to the behavioral difficulties of a number of different populations, little of the work has been carried out with children and adolescents with acquired brain injuries. This population is unique with respect to the suddenness of their injuries and the catastrophic changes and discontinuity brought about in their lives. Moreover, they differ from the populations of previously studied individuals (children and adolescents with mental retardation, conduct disorders, hyperactivity, etc.) with regard to their learning histories (pre- and postinjury), cognitive abilities, and dramatically altered self-perceptions. These unique characteristics require that the effectiveness of behavioral change strategies be evaluated anew and modified to suit the needs of this population.

The process of applying and evaluating the efficacy of behavioral change with children and adolescents with brain injury is rather recent. Although few published guidelines are available, clinical experience and anecdotal evidence are accumulating quickly as the need and potential value of behavioral approaches with this population are recognized (e.g., Eames & Wood, 1985; Zencius et al., 1989). An aspect of brain injury impacting the use and effectiveness of behavioral change strategies is the student's frequent inability to learn quickly from experience, necessitating more repetitions, more explicit expectations and contingencies, increased structure and cues, and specific programs to generalize behavioral change to new settings. The abrupt losses in self-esteem and the need to establish a new sense of self also impact behavioral programs. Increased support and reinforcement may be required. Goals need to be concrete and achievable in a short amount of time. Self-management skills may be learned or relearned if programs are implemented to help the student compensate for or overcome cognitive or neuropsychological deficits. Maladaptive behaviors that are inappropriately reinforced and thereby learned may persist even when the underlying cognitive deficits are no longer present (Malec, 1984).

Behavioral Change Strategies Gone Awry

When a behavior serves a purpose for the student, it is difficult to change, no matter how maladaptive it appears to others. The inadvertent application of behavioral contingencies to reinforce maladaptive behaviors frequently occurs due to the lack of adequate experience and education on the part of parents, teachers, and sometimes rehabilitation professionals.

Maladaptive behaviors are inadvertently reinforced for several reasons. First, the behavior may not be recognized as undesirable or problematic. Passivity, the absence of desirable initiative and activity, may be attributed to fatigue or the passive child may even be labeled as "quiet and well behaved." Diminished behaviors are often not labeled as problems because the absence of a behavior is frequently more difficult to recognize than the presence of a problem behavior.

Second, a maladaptive behavior may be recognized as a problem but not responded to appropriately because of others' feelings of overprotectiveness, guilt, or pity. ABI is a tragedy for those who experience it and strong feelings are to be expected; however, these feelings can interfere with the child's recovery and optimal functioning if not held in check. Feelings of guilt, sadness, and anger can result in the failure of families and schools to work together for the ABI student's benefit. Rather than supporting each other, they may act out their frustration and blame each other instead. Families and teachers who receive adequate information soon after the injury may be able to avoid such pitfalls by working to prevent maladaptive behaviors from becoming established.

In other cases, maladaptive behavior is eventually reinforced because others have become worn out and find it easier simply to do what the child or adolescent wants rather than what they recognize is best. This is the "third-time-is-the-charm" phenomenon in which the student with ABI learns that if he continues to behave in a maladaptive way or to make repetitive requests, he will eventually get what he wants. Obviously, when this occurs, the child does not learn how to act appropriately; rather, he learns that he should continue or escalate the behavior until his needs are met. Case Study 8.2 is an example of this occurring.

CASE STUDY 8.2

Giving in to Maladaptive Behavior

ER is a 17-year-old who sustained a brain injury in a motor vehicle accident 2 years ago. ER's cognitive abilities have been less affected by his injury than his motor abilities (severe tremor, inability to walk). In the 2 years since his accident, ER and his single mother have endured many changes in their relationship and experienced many failures in their efforts to adapt to ER's injury. During the acute stages of recovery, ER quickly learned that he could interrupt a conversation and get the immediate attention of those around him. Because of the obvious effects of his injury (being in a wheelchair; tremor), he was often able to get what he wanted quickly as others attempted to be polite and to pacify him rather than to identify and reward more appropriate behaviors. When he returned to school, ER found the work very difficult due to his physical and speech impairments. He disliked school, feeling that he was a failure and did not belong. ER's teacher recognized that she should not reward him for interrupting so she tried to ignore his inappropriate behavior. However, ER became louder and, if still ignored, often threw something or attempted to hit or kick someone. This behavior could not be ignored, so the teacher inadvertently reinforced even more severe behavior problems by excusing ER from class when he escalated his behavior. Being excused from class served as a reward to ER because he felt like such a failure when he was in the classroom.

ER was finally referred to a structured inpatient rehabilitation setting, where he did well and developed more appropriate behaviors. He also did well with individualized homebound instruction. Each attempt to return him to a school setting, however, met with failure as ER became frustrated and aggressive, resulting in his dismissal. After being dismissed, he would again receive individualized home tutoring in his home environment, where he was less subject to the frustrations of school and teasing by his peers. ER had learned that hitting someone was a foolproof way to get what he wanted, that is, to be out of the school environment.

Behavioral Change Strategies that Work

When behavioral intervention works, it is usually because the program has been well thought out, all participants are well educated, the student is an active participant, and there are both short-range and long-range goals. A behavioral intervention does not take place in isolation, but rather is incorporated into the student's daily activities and includes a consideration of developmental needs as well as recognition of social expectations and rules. Case Study 8.3 illustrates an effective program with an adolescent who sustained a mild brain injury and is fully capable of participating actively in improving his own behavioral functioning.

CASE STUDY 8.3

Effective Behavioral Change Program

CJ is a 15-year-old who sustained a mild brain injury 6 months ago when he fell from a skateboard. CJ had already been doing some adolescent experimentation with drugs, alcohol, and sexual activity prior to his injury, but his parents and teachers were unaware of these activities. Following his injury, CJ has become less able to effectively problem solve or to inhibit inappropriate behaviors or comments. Others are more protective and vigilant than before his injury and he is allowed less freedom and independence. To increase CJ's available resources, the school provides him with training, including instruction and practice in problem-solving skills and social skills in a group situation with lots of repetition. The school also provides him with sex, alcohol, and drug education as a normal part of the curriculum. CJ's course load was reduced to decrease his frustration and increase available resource room time for studying, tutoring, and completing work. Goals were negotiated and a stepwise approach to CJ's goals was written down and graphed over time so that he could see his progress and know concretely what he needed to do to become more independent. Short-term goals included the absence of inappropriate sexual remarks and impulsive actions. An intermediate goal was that of being able to ask a girl to a movie. On his doctor's advice, CJ also contracted to refrain from use of drugs or alcohol. His long-term goal of driver's ed class (at age 16) was made contingent on his progress toward and achievement of these short-term goals.

As Case Study 8.3 demonstrates, an effective behavioral change program can include goals set by the child or adolescent as well as by the school and family. Students who have brain injuries are as similar to other students as they are different: They are likely to share age-appropriate goals as well as the desire to fit in with their peers. These motivations can be one of the primary reasons for a program's effectiveness.

For the severely injured and those in the early stages of recovery, a structured environment may be the treatment of choice for reducing or preventing behavior problems (Grimm & Bleiberg, 1986). Environments and programs can be designed to minimize behavior difficulties and to maximize performance. Environmental modifications may reduce the need for new learning on the part of the student (Grimm & Bleiberg, 1986; Zencius et al., 1989). Having a routine daily schedule or having all classes in the same room, for example, can significantly reduce the amount of information a student has to remember, as well as confusion and anxiety about what to expect, thereby improving overall behavior and performance (Cohen, Joyce, Rhoades, & Welks, 1985). In some settings, providing written lists and cues can also facilitate independent functioning, even if the child or adolescent has severe memory problems or difficulty continuing tasks to completion. Case Study 8.4 suggests how a combination of social, behavioral, and physiological problems can be addressed effectively in a prevocational school setting through environmental modifications and careful selection of prevocational tasks (Deaton, Poole, & Long, 1987).

CASE STUDY 8.4

Effective Environmental Modifications

AN, a 16-year-old, sustained a brain injury as a result of a brain tumor and the subsequent surgery required to remove it. She had extensive brain damage as a result. Although AN was very verbal and performed in the borderline range on intelligence measures, she learned new information with difficulty and only after much repetition. AN had ongoing problems with sudden sleep onset and severe visual deficits. She tended to give up at the first sign of difficulty and was easily sidetracked. Resources included AN's responsiveness to praise and her willingness to attempt new tasks. To minimize the impact of her sleep disorder on work performance, AN was assigned a paper recycling job that was active in nature, requiring her to go from office to office to collect paper rather than staying in one place and, inevitably, falling asleep. The job was difficult for AN, however, because she was easily distracted and her visual limitations made finding the offices difficult. To deal with these problems, AN's route was the same each day so that she could establish a visual scanning routine as well as an internal "map" of where she needed to go. When the effectiveness of these interventions was evaluated, AN was found to perform well in her daily tasks but did not generalize her compensatory skills to novel tasks, indicating the need for changes in her routine to facilitate generalization. With these changes, AN's irritability and frustration returned, as did the episodes of sudden sleep onset. She was returned to her original route to reestablish an acceptable level of functioning. Recommendations were made for highly structured sheltered school and work settings with established routines for work completion.

ALTERNATIVE INTERVENTIONS

Although most of this chapter has dealt with more traditional behavioral change strategies, other interventions may be effective in addressing some of the more common behaviors occurring in students following brain injury. Some possible interventions include individual and family therapy, group interventions, cognitive remediation, and medication. These strategies may also be more appropriate in cases where available resources for consistent behavioral intervention are limited.

Individual and Family Therapy

When behavioral problems may be a manifestation of emotional reactions to a brain injury and its effects, individual and family therapy may be appropriate for dealing with the root cause of the behaviors. This is most appropriate for the student with a brain injury whose memory and insight are at least somewhat spared. However, written summaries or videotapes of sessions may be helpful in circumventing cognitive deficits. Because this type of counseling can differ greatly from traditional psychotherapy, families should seek out a practitioner who is accustomed to working with children and adolescents who have sustained brain injuries.

Family therapy as well as family support and information groups, such as local chapters of the National Head Injury Foundation, can be invaluable in helping families to view behaviors as manifestations of the brain injury and to manage feelings of anger, resentment, guilt, and sadness. Moreover, these resources may help families to gain perspective and to advocate effectively for their children within the limitations of the school system, thereby enabling them to act as partners in the child's long-term recovery.

Group Interventions

Group interventions have the advantages of providing peer support, feedback, and modeling and may therefore be particularly appropriate for children and adolescents seeking acceptance by their peer group when they return to school. Group interventions allow the child who has had a brain injury to feel less isolated and provide an opportunity for demonstrating competencies and successfully helping others, thereby increasing self-esteem. Group interventions may also facilitate social competence and comfort by providing practice in social settings and some degree of inoculation against teasing, peer insensitivity, and other stresses (Barin et al., 1985). Groups in school settings also allow for interactions and feedback among group members outside of the group itself in the natural school environment. This is an important advantage because the ultimate goal of group interventions, as with any behavioral management strategy, is to promote generalization.

Some examples of focused groups include anger control, social skills, self-assessment, and problem solving. Model formats for addressing these skills with adolescents and young adults have been developed (e.g., Ben-Yishay, 1980; Braunling-McMorrow, 1988; Deaton, 1986; Helffenstein & Wechsler, 1982; Prigatano, 1986). The individuals in the group, the setting, and the available resources also help determine the format. Initial studies indicate the effectiveness of groups in improving communication and social skills (Ben-Yishay, 1980; Helffenstein & Wechsler, 1982) and awareness of injury-related deficits and residual assets (Deaton, 1986). Unfortunately, there are few documented applications of group interventions with younger children after brain injury.

Cognitive Interventions

When problem behaviors are the result of cognitive impairments, cognitive remediation is often an effective route for addressing the cognitive deficits that cause or contribute to the behaviors. Many of the group interventions outlined above involve a cognitive–behavioral approach. In addition, individualized cognitive interventions can be useful in improving on deficit areas, capitalizing on strengths, and teaching compensation. These interventions allow the child to be less frustrated by the changes in his or her abilities and also enable the child to become more of a resource in his or her own academic program and overall recovery (Brown & Morgan, 1987). Cognitive remediation and neuropsychological evaluations can also be of value in ensuring that the student's expectations are realistic and that behavioral problems are not a result of the student's being asked to do tasks that are not within his or her capabilities.

Pharmacologic Interventions

Wood (1984) suggested that psychopharmacologic interventions can sometimes be a useful adjunct to behavioral management. The reported success of such interventions as aids to behavioral control has been variable and professional and family attitudes are mixed. Some authors have discussed the detrimental effects of medications on cognition, leading to a decrease in the student's ability to learn (Barin et al., 1985; Dean, 1986; Savage & Wolcott, 1988). However, some of these same authors have also noted instances in which medications can be helpful in increasing attention (Dean, 1986) and decreasing agitation (Barin et al., 1985), thereby facilitating learning and behavioral change. These issues are more completely addressed in Chapter 9.

ETHICAL AND LEGAL ISSUES

"The assumption that someone using behavioral procedures can directly control another individual against his/her will is frequently inaccurate, and always unethical" (Jacobs, 1988, p. 342). Behavioral intervention is sometimes thought of as something that is "done to" or "carried out on" the identified patient. The ethics of using behavioral change strategies, especially with individuals who have cognitive impairments, thus needs to be addressed. Ethics in behavioral change requires at a minimum that the injured individual and/or the guardian must have a complete understanding of the procedure being implemented; the right to decide to accept or reject this strategy; and the opportunity, when possible, to participate in the development and monitoring of the program (Jacobs, 1988). In general, the process of behavioral change, much like the development of an Individualized Education Program (IEP), should reflect collaboration, cooperation, and negotiation. All participants should agree on the behaviors that need to be changed and the methods used to change them (Gelfand & Hartmann, 1984).

Informed Consent

The ideal in behavioral change is to have a situation in which the planned changes are perceived as beneficial by both the person who has been injured and those who have initiated the change. An approach that ignores the need for all participants to have a say is unlikely to meet the student's needs or to ensure his or her cooperation and, as a consequence, is less likely to be successful (Vredevoogd, 1986). Tynan, Pearce, and Royall (1986) addressed the issue of informed consent following brain injury in an adolescent with relatively intact cognitive functioning. The essentially nonverbal adolescent used self-abusive behavior (biting his wrist) to communicate frustration and fatigue. In this case, the patient was told that an alternate behavior (communication via a letter board) could serve the same essential function. Contingent physical restraint (holding his wrist to keep him from biting it) was combined with teaching the use of the alternative communication device. These strategies eventually allowed near-elimination of the self-abuse. These strategies probably would not have been equally effective without the informed consent and active cooperation of the adolescent himself. His cooperation was required to learn and use the communication board. Obviously, in this example, it would not have been ethical to ignore this adolescent's inappropriate behavior and allow him to continue to bite himself. Similarly, it would have been wrong to physically restrain him without providing a way in which he could get his needs met. Given his relatively good cognitive abilities and his ability to understand the behavioral intervention, it would also have been unethical to proceed with the plan without getting his informed consent.

Attitudinal Barriers

Another ethical issue that arises in considering how to maintain the ABI student within the school system is that of negative attitudes of some educators regarding the medically involved child's returning to school. Teachers are often overworked and are concerned that they may not be able to meet the many needs of the child following brain injury. In response to this concern, Senator Randolph made the following remarks in Senate Report 94-168 (1975): "The integration requirement . . . [of Senate Bill 6] requires inservice training of general and special personnel in dealing with the general problem of attitudinal barriers" (cited in Martin, 1985, p. 14). Getting past these attitudinal barriers is both desirable and mandatory.

Aversive Procedures

As noted in the section on behavioral change strategies, interventions should begin with the least intrusive method that can be effective in changing the behavior. At times, however, the methods that seem most acceptable (e.g., environmental cues, reinforcement) may not be effective in changing a behavior. In these cases, strategies that seem extreme should be considered, including aversive procedures such as physical restraint, seclusion, and punishment. Factors that should be weighed in considering these alternatives include (a) how severe the problem behavior is, (b) what interventions have already been tried, (c) whether the injured person and the family are accepting of the intervention, (d) what will happen if the behavior is not changed, and (e) whether adequate resources are available to implement these strategies. Schools seldom have access to safe seclusion rooms in which the child can be kept. Similarly, school systems that infrequently deal with children with severe problem behaviors may be unable to provide their staff with adequate training to safely restrain a student who is severely aggressive or self-injurious. Mechanical cloth restraints may keep such children from hurting themselves or someone else, but also may interfere with socialization, self-esteem, and completion of tasks requiring free movement (e.g., writing, eating).

These issues cannot be decided on a global basis; there are no easy answers. Rather, each case requires individual consideration and review. It should be noted, however, that if a noxious procedure can be effective in eliminating a highly dangerous or disruptive behavior, and thereby allowing the child to remain in the school environment, use of the procedure may be far more ethical than the alternatives of institutionalization or pharmacologic intervention that leaves the child sedate but unable to effectively learn.

CONCLUSION

A traumatic brain injury suddenly and radically disrupts the life of a child, his or her family, and their community, including the school. Unlike any other type of injury, a brain injury can affect virtually any area of functioning, from those functions required to sustain life (breathing) to mobility, thought processes, language, emotions, and behavior. Anticipating and preventing maladaptive behaviors and encouraging and reinforcing the development of appropriate compensations are essential to helping the student with ABI return to school and function effectively, both in school and in society.

Traditional behavioral change strategies can be modified to be effective with children and adolescents with brain injuries as long as the strategies address the unique strengths and impairments of this population. These techniques can decrease specific problem behaviors, teach strategies for compensation, and help to increase adaptive skills such as initiation or socialization. Behavioral difficulties can often be prevented by structuring the student's environment to ensure success, which may, in turn, contribute to the redevelopment of self-esteem following a brain injury. Finally, when the child's behavior is acceptable and effective in one situation, it is often possible to facilitate gradual generalization to other settings or to provide the cues and structure in other settings that allow the student with ABI to function effectively. The challenge is clear, and the goals are achievable.

REFERENCES

Auerbach, S. H. (1986). Neuroanatomical correlates of attention and memory disorders in traumatic brain injury: An application of neurobehavioral subtypes. *The Journal of Head Trauma Rehabilitation, 1,* 1–12.

Barin, J. J., Hanchett, J. M., Jacob, W. L., & Scott, M. B. (1985). Counseling the head injured patient. In M. Ylvisaker (Ed.), *Head injury rehabilitation: Children and adolescents* (pp. 361–379). Austin, TX: PRO-ED.

Ben-Yishay, Y. (Ed.). (1980). *Working approaches to remediation of cognitive deficits in brain damaged* (Supplement to the 8th Annual Workshop for Rehabilitation Professionals). New York: New York University.

Braunling-McMorrow, D. (1988). Behavioral rehabilitation. In P. M. Deutsch & K. B. Fralish (Eds.), *Innovations in head injury rehabilitation* (pp. 8-1 to 8-52). New York: Matthew Bender.

Brown, T. L., & Morgan, S. B. (1987). Cognitive training with brain-injured children: General issues and approaches. In J. M. Williams & C. J. Long (Eds.), *The rehabilitation of cognitive disabilities* (pp. 217–231). New York: Plenum Press.

Cohen, S. B., Joyce, C. M., Rhoades, K. W., & Welks, D. M. (1985). Educational programming for head injured students. In M. Ylvisaker (Ed.), *Head injury rehabilitation: Children and adolescents* (pp. 383–410). Austin, TX: PRO-ED.

Dean, R. S. (1986). Neuropsychological aspects of psychiatric disorders. In J. Obrzut & G. W. Hynd (Eds.), *Child neuropsychology* (Vol. 2, pp. 83–112). New York: Academic Press.

Deaton, A. V. (1986, August). *Self assessment group: An intervention strategy for head injured adolescents.* Paper presented at the Annual Meeting of the American Psychological Association, Washington, DC.

Deaton, A. V. (1987). Behavioral change strategies for children and adolescents with traumatic brain injuries. *Journal of Learning Disabilities, 20*(8), 581–589.

Deaton, A. V., Poole, C. P., & Long, D. (1987). Improving the work potential of brain-injured adolescents and young adults: A model for evaluation and individualized training. *Occupational Therapy in Health Care, 4,* 147–159.

Divack, J. A., Herrie, J., & Scott, M. B. (1985). Behavior management. In M. Ylvisaker (Ed.), *Head injury rehabilitation: Children and adolescents* (pp. 347–360). Austin, TX: PRO-ED.

Eames, P., & Wood, R. (1985). Rehabilitation after severe brain injury: A special unit approach. *International Rehabilitation Medicine, 7*(3), 130–133.

Gelfand, D. M., & Hartmann, D. P. (1984). *Child behavior analysis and therapy.* New York: Pergamon Press.

Grimm, B. H., & Bleiberg, J. (1986). Psychological rehabilitation in traumatic brain injury. In S. Filskov & T. Boll (Eds.), *Handbook of clinical neuropsychology* (pp. 495–560). New York: Wiley.

Helffenstein, D. A., & Wechsler, F. (1982). The use of Interpersonal Process Recall (IPR) in the remediation of interpersonal and communication skill deficits in the newly brain injured. *Clinical Neuropsychology, 4*(3), 139–143.

Jacobs, H. (1987, March). *Behavior problems.* Workshop presented at the National Head Injury Foundation Annual Conference, Crystal City, VA.

Jacobs, H. (1988). Yes, behavior analysis can help, but do you know how to harness it? *Brain Injury, 2,* 339–346.

Malec, J. (1984). Training the brain-injured client in behavioral self-management skills. In B. A. Edelstein & E. T. Couture (Eds.), *Behavioral assessment and rehabilitation of the traumatically brain damaged* (pp. 121–150). New York: Plenum Press.

Martin, R. C. (1985). Legal issues and interpretation of P.L. 94–142. *Coalition Quarterly, 4*(2 & 3), 12–15. (Published by the Federation for Children with Special Needs, 312 Stuart St., 2nd Floor, Boston, MA 02116.)

Mateer, C. A., & Williams, D. (1991). Management of psychosocial and behavior problems in cognitive rehabilitation. In J. S. Kreutzer & P. H. Wehman (Eds.), *Cognitive rehabilitation for persons with traumatic brain injury* (pp. 117–126). Baltimore: Brookes.

Prigatano, G. P. (1986). *Neuropsychological rehabilitation after brain injury.* Baltimore: Johns Hopkins University Press.

Sand, P. L., Trieschmann, R. B., Fordyce, W. E., & Fowler, R. S. (1970). Behavior modification in the medical rehabilitation setting. *Rehabilitation Research and Practice Review, 1,* 11–24.

Savage, R., & Wolcott, G. (Eds.). (1988). *An educator's manual: What educators need to know about students with traumatic brain injury.* Southborough, MA: National Head Injury Foundation.

Tynan, W. D., Pearce, B. A., & Royall, K. W. (1986, November). *Comprehensive behavioral treatment of self injurious behavior in a head injured adolescent.* Presented at the 20th Annual Convention of the Association for the Advancement of Behavior Therapy, Chicago.

Vredevoogd, M. J. (1986, August/September). Suggestions for working with the difficult to handle closed head injured person. In *A Newsletter/Updater.* (Available from Ditty, Lynch, and Associates, Inc., Bloomfield Medical Village, 6405 Telegraph Rd., Suite K, Birmingham, MI 48010.)

Wood, R. L. (1984). Behavior disorders following severe brain injury: Their presentation and psychological management. In D. N. Brooks (Ed.), *Closed head injury: Psychological, social, and family consequences* (pp. 195–219). New York: Oxford University Press.

Zencius, A. H., Wesolowski, M. D., Burke, W. H., & McQuade, P. (1989). Antecedent control in the treatment of brain injured clients. *Brain Injury, 3*(2), 199–205.

CHAPTER 9

Behavior as Communication

TIMOTHY J. FEENEY
BETH URBANCZYK

A significant number of children and adolescents recovering from acquired brain injury (ABI) demonstrate problem behaviors beyond the confused and agitated state of recovery associated with *Ranchos Los Amigos Scale* Levels IV and V (Fletcher, Ewing-Cobbs, Miner, Levin, & Eisenberg, 1990; Goethe & Levin, 1984; McGuire, 1986). Behaviors such as self-injury, property destruction, and assault create a myriad of challenges to educators and educational systems (Feeney, Urbanczyk, Savage, & Blaustein, 1991). When these behavioral sequelae arise while the child is in the acute phase of recovery, behavioral interventions are developed by rehabilitation specialists in the hospital or rehabilitation center. Unfortunately, the interventions are bound to the controlled environment of the "clinic," with little emphasis given to the translation of the methods to the classroom. In a class of 20 or more students, the most gifted teacher would be pressed to implement any clinic-based behavioral plan. Put simply, most plans developed in specialized care centers are not functional in the real life of a classroom.

Another difficulty for educators is created by delays in the onset of behavioral challenges, especially when rehabilitation specialists have provided little (or no) indication of the potential for problems to emerge later in life. Delays in the emergence of problem behaviors are a likely consequence of the overwhelming combination of a number of factors, often masked by the structure of rehabilitation environments: (a) neurologically based deficits in cognitive, metacognitive, and executive functioning (Ylvisaker & Szekeres, 1989); (b) normal cognitive pressures associated with increasingly difficult curricular demands encountered as the student advances through the school years (Aram & Ekelman, 1986; Eslinger & Grattan, 1991; Holmes Bernstein & Waber, 1990); and (c) gradual and imperceptible fading of school and family support systems (Frye, 1987; Savage & Carter, 1984, 1991). These factors often reach "critical mass" during periods of transition, as in the promotion from one grade level to the next. Students who were able to manage behaviorally, academically, and socially at one grade level may be unable to negotiate the transition to increased behavioral, academic, and social demands and begin to demonstrate problem behaviors following advancement. Too often, the student's trauma fades to a memory, the intensity of involvement of persons who understand the sequelae of brain injury dwindles, and educators faced with unexpected behavioral crises are left to interpret the problems within the conventions they best understand—that is, as manifestations of some psychogenic emotional or behavioral disorder.

The hard-held belief that behavioral challenges are the consequence of disordered thought or some underlying psychological or psychiatric disturbance compels educators to develop Individualized Education Programs (IEPs) with a focus on the *elimination of "maladaptive" behaviors* (Reiher, 1992; Smith & Simpson, 1989). Consequently, educational services are provided in specialized and separate classrooms designed to control and contain problem behaviors (Steinberg & Knitzer, 1992; Weinberg & Weinberg, 1990) while providing consistent consequences to suppress problem behaviors (The Peacock Hill Working Group, 1991). External control is the norm (Eames & Wood, 1985; Wood & Burgess, 1988), and the student, the family, and the school personnel who provide direct services to the student, are often stripped of active involvement in programmatic decisions. Students lose their individualism and are forced to depend upon others to make the simplest choices. Basic human rights are lost.

In contrast, communication-based strategies focus on developing functional behavioral alternatives that can be used across all environments (Bird, Dores, Moniz, & Robinson, 1989; Durand & Carr, 1991; Knapczyk, 1988, 1992; LaVigna & Donnellan, 1986; Wacker et al., 1990). At the core of such strategies lies the principle that behaviors that appear maladaptive to others are in fact adaptive or functional to the individual who engages in them (Donnellan, Mirenda, Mesaros, & Fassbender, 1984; Ylvisaker, Feeney, & Urbanczyk, 1993a, 1993b). Problem behavior is more than the manifestation of a neurological or psychological disorder; it is *communication* (Burke, 1990; Carr & Durand, 1985a; Durand, 1986, 1990; Gordon, 1991; Schuler, 1980). In the most basic terms, a student with ABI who demonstrates behavioral challenges is saying, "I don't like this," "I don't understand," "I don't want to," or "Listen to me" (Feeney et al., 1991). We do not presume to declare all challenging behaviors as *intentionally communicative,* although some are (e.g., refusal behaviors); in many cases, the *unintentional communicative* functions of problem behaviors emerge only after the behaviors are examined in the context in which they occur (e.g., self-injurious behavior). The understanding of communicative functions of problem behaviors facilitates the development of effective educational–behavioral approaches (Durand, 1990), and the elimination of challenging behaviors follows (Horner & Budd, 1985). Interventions are designed to assist the student to develop a repertoire of socially and culturally acceptable, functionally communicative behaviors to use as an alternative to those that are traditionally identified as maladaptive.

Using this approach demands more than following rigid plans developed by a psychologist or behavioral specialist. The development of effective educationally based behavioral programming transcends the exclusive use of an applied behavior analytic approach and behavioral specialists. Communication-based treatment is a synthesized approach to functional capacity building, which requires the concerted efforts of school psychologists and speech pathologists, teachers and students, and families and school systems. In this context, communication is all-encompassing, more than daily interactions between people. The strategies focus on the nature, form, and course of the interactions between all the persons and systems who have a stake in the life of the student. It is a person-centered approach (Mount & Patterson, 1986) to educational–behavioral program development. The student with head injury, his or her family, and members of the school system join to determine the function of challenging behaviors, develop comprehensive–functional educational strategies, and construct long-term systems of support. The program comprises five interactive segments: stakeholders and collaborative communication, history, functional analysis of behaviors, functional analysis of communication, and the synthesized intervention plan.

SEGMENT I: STAKEHOLDERS AND COLLABORATIVE COMMUNICATION

The term *stakeholders* (O'Brien, 1985; O'Brien & Mount, 1985) can be applied to those persons who have a "stake" in the life of the student with an acquired brain injury. They are the people most intimately connected to the student and most invested in his or her success at home and in school. The group of stakeholders includes the student and any other people committed to the daily work required to foster the student's long-range educational success (family members, friends, teachers, ancillary educational staff, etc.). A number of researchers have found that a *collaborative relationship* among stakeholders is critical to the development of a unified team approach necessary to the development of successful, least restrictive educational (and behavioral) programs for students with special needs (Ford et al., 1989; Forest & Lusthaus, 1989, 1990; Forest & Snow, 1987; Giangreco, Cloninger, & Salce Iverson, 1990; Schnorr, Ford, Davern, Park-Lee, & Meyer, 1989; Thousand & Villa, 1990). All stakeholders share responsibility for educating students with ABI who demonstrate behavioral challenges.

Regular communication among stakeholders is essential to the development of collaborative relationships and can be established at face-to-face meetings (Thousand & Villa, 1990). Collaborative team meetings are used to clarify the student's personal history, develop long-term educational goals, develop short-range objectives, and share information on progress or problems (see Case Study 9.1). The team must also designate an "educational synthesizer" (Bicker, 1976; Savage & Carter, 1984, 1988) or "keeper of information," whose responsibilities include coordinating and disseminating information about the student's educational and behavioral plan to each stakeholder, leading team meetings, and facilitating program revisions when needed (Schnorr et al., 1989). Coordinated effort is crucial to cooperative teamwork (Forest & Snow, 1987; Johnson & Johnson, 1982). The flow of communication can be coordinated in a number of ways: a communication log or notebook for educational staff, the student, or his or her family to write anecdotal observations of behaviors, and pass on basic logistical information; a phone directory for each stakeholder listing all persons involved with treatment; and a monthly schedule of contact between family and staff to delineate specific dates, times, and types of contact (e.g., phone, meeting, therapy observation).

CASE STUDY 9.1

Stakeholders and Communication

OV is a 13-year-old boy who sustained a severe brain injury at the age of 10, when hit by a car while crossing the street on his bike. OV entered his first acute rehabilitation program 1 month after his injury, and remained there for approximately 1 year. In the last 2 months of his rehabilitation stay, OV began to demonstrate severe self-injurious behaviors (e.g., slapping and hitting his head with a closed fist). His parents disagreed with the rehabilitation providers over treatment issues and subsequently removed OV from the rehabilitation center. While at home, OV was introduced to more than three different educational settings and was subsequently removed from each one of them due to behavioral difficulties. His self-injury continued unabated at home with increased frequency and intensity. His family, concerned about further neurological damage, placed OV in another acute rehabilitation setting.

The rehabilitation team joined with OV's parents to delineate their thoughts and goals and generated a preliminary list of stakeholders, which included the home school system. Upon admission, a communication system was defined. Together, the family, school, and rehabilitation stakeholders continued to develop and update long-range goals, which included the reduction of self-injury and success in school. Together, the stakeholders made treatment decisions and established time frames for return to school. Six months after admission to his second acute rehabilitation, OV returned to home and school with a synthesized behavior plan, a problem-resolution agreement as part of the communication system, and an array of stakeholders.

A person-centered, individualized approach to competency building is an effective means to teach stakeholders who are active participants in the student's educational program. The focus of a person-centered approach is "inservice" or in vivo teaching of communication-based behavioral skills in the environments in which they will be used—at home and in school (Ylvisaker et al., 1993a, 1993b). The most commonly used method of in vivo teaching is coaching by an individual who has demonstrated competence in communication-based behavioral interventions. The coach guides the observations of others to help them discern the positive and negative effects of the environment and people in the environment on the student's behaviors. Observed interactions between the student and the stakeholder follow, and the coach and stakeholder then review tapes of the interactions and make adjustments in their behavior as needed (Wetzel & Hoschouer, 1984; Ylvisaker et al., 1993a, 1993b). Video feedback or guided self-critique of videotaped interactions is another method of guiding observations that is useful in establishing behaviorally competent stakeholders (Kern-Dunlap et al., 1992) (see Case Study 9.2). Video analysis is also useful to evaluate the efficacy of the communication and behavioral interventions (Wetzel & Taylor, 1991; Wetzel, Taylor, & Lachowicz, 1991). Formal "outservice" or classroom training can also be provided to impart basic programmatic information.

CASE STUDY 9.2

Capacities

WS, the 13-year-old son of divorced parents, had sustained a severe brain injury at the age of 2. As a result, WS demonstrated a number of significant attentional deficits and hyperactive behaviors. His parents spent much of their time in search of strategies and schools to control WS's behavior. In consultation with an educator and behavioral psychologist, WS's parents identified the environmental factors that impacted WS's behaviors (e.g., lack of structure, loud noises, demanding activities), and a videotape was made to demonstrate specific proactive behaviors that they could use to teach WS positive alternatives to challenging behaviors. WS's parents were periodically videotaped interacting with WS, and the success of their interactions was evaluated using video feedback.

SEGMENT II: HISTORY

Learning and Communication History

Although frequently overlooked, a systematic review of premorbid learning history, learning style, interpersonal interactional style, and motivational assessment is required. This review is developed in an attempt to examine brain injury in the continuum of an individual's life. Although personality and behavioral changes are often lasting, especially following a severe injury (Brooks, 1984; Brooks, McKinley, Symington, Beattie, & Campsie, 1987; Fletcher & Levin, 1988; Lezak, 1987), understanding premorbid learning history can help guide the development of effective behavioral interventions (Fletcher et al., 1990; McGuire, 1986). Because much of the information gathered is anecdotal, uniformity of information is unlikely. However, we have used disagreement in report and the extent of disagreement to evaluate the functionality of the system of stakeholders gathered around an individual for baseline impressions of the course and detail of training needs of the stakeholders. Family members, friends, and school staff who interacted with the individual on a regular basis can provide a starting point for evaluating changes and/or commonalities in behavior, cognition, learning style (Kolb, 1985; Renzulli & Smith, 1978), interactional style (Jacobs & Fuhrmann, 1980), and motivators (e.g., what the person liked to do preinjury). Objective evaluations, such as standardized psychometric examinations (e.g., *Wechsler Intelligence Scale for Children–Third Edition,* Wechsler, 1991; *Wide Range Achievement Test–Revised,* Jastak & Wilkinson, 1984), psychiatric and personality measures (e.g., *Personality Inventory for Children,* Wirt, Lachar, Kinedinst, & Seat, 1984), reading and math comprehension, class placement, and post hoc adaptive behavior evaluations (e.g., *Vineland Adaptive Behavior Scales,* Sparrow, Balla, & Cicchetti, 1984; *Child Behavior Checklist,* Achenbach & Edelbrock, 1983), further strengthen a learning history–learning style evaluation. This information is then synthesized to provide a framework for treatment choices and training needs.

Medical–Rehabilitation History

The neurological parameters of metacognitive and executive system functioning and language ability are best established by means of a complete medical history. Information about the person's age at the time of injury or onset of illness, the length of time since the injury occurred, lesion sites, medical treatments both to the brain and to other areas, length of coma, and course of emergence from coma are critical elements of a complete assessment (Dennis, 1988). Such information is most easily obtained when the individual enters a rehabilitation site directly from an acute care hospital. Because the availability of details decreases in proportion to the length of time since discharge from an acute care hospital or rehabilitation center, investigative work is often needed to secure a detailed medical history. If the student has experienced more than one rehabilitation or educational program, or is many years post-injury, a history of the course and type of programs that have been attempted is equally important. Such a history should include information about school and/or vocational placement, previous behavioral interventions, and medications.

Pharmacologic Status

A number of rehabilitation researchers have found that psychopharmacologic interventions often have positive impacts on the reduction of problem behaviors in adults with acquired brain injury (Gaultieri, 1988; Glenn, 1987a, 1987b, 1987c; O'Shanick & Zasler, 1990; Sutton, Weaver, & Feeney, 1987; Yudofsky, Silver, & Schneider, 1987). Despite a paucity of clinical data to indicate comparable efficacy in children and adolescents (Biederman & Jellinek, 1984; Parmelee & O'Shanick, 1987), medications are often used to control problem behaviors in these populations as well. Many of the medications used to control behaviors, however, also create negative side effects (Cockrell, 1991; O'Shanick, 1987).

Pharmacologic agents are often used at the request of stakeholders who have attempted a number of behavioral interventions with little benefit and who are understandably desperate for some positive change. We have frequently observed that the most active and committed stakeholders relinquish any involvement in determining medication plans almost immediately upon their plea for medications. This is unacceptable; a medication plan is a single, albeit important, part of the student's larger behavioral–educational plan, and the physician who administers the medication plan is only one member of the team. As a result, stakeholders should participate in medication decisions with intensity similar to that given to other program decisions. This does not mean that persons with limited or no medical training should direct medication plans; however, stakeholders need to have a good understanding of basic pharmacologic issues and a working knowledge of the potential costs and benefits of pharmacotherapy. This will enable the collaborative team to provide trained medical staff with meaningful data to make treatment decisions and to provide informed consent when changes in medications are recommended. In Appendix 9A, we list medications commonly used in children with challenging behaviors following ABI.

SEGMENT III: FUNCTIONAL ANALYSIS OF CHALLENGING BEHAVIORS

A functional analysis of behavior is a means of identifying the circumstances that impact presence or absence of challenging behaviors (Bailey, 1987; Carr & Durand, 1985a, 1985b; Donnellan et al., 1984; Evans & Meyer, 1985; Hayes & O'Brien, 1990;

Iwata, Dorsey, Slifer, Bauman, & Richman, 1982; LaVigna & Donnellan, 1986; Meyer & Evans, 1989; Repp, Felce, & Batton, 1988; Sulzer-Azaroff & Mayer, 1977). A completed functional analysis constitutes an objectification of the challenging behaviors and the environmental, cognitive, and neurological factors that elicit the behaviors (Fernandez-Ballesteros & Staats, 1992). Five categories of analysis are used in this approach:

1. *Description of behaviors and operational definitions:* This category consists of describing the behaviors in enough detail that they can be objectively measured. It includes onset and offset criterion (i.e., when the behaviors are determined to begin and end); specific topographies or behaviors; and the frequency, rate, and duration of the behaviors.
2. *Antecedent analysis:* This category includes actions of others, places, therapies, and other events that trigger the presence of challenging behaviors. This category also includes information about the premorbid antecedents (in situations where challenging behaviors were evident preinjury). In children with ABI, neurophysiological information is also an important element of an antecedent analysis. It is well established that the severity and type of injury, the sites and size of lesions, and the age of the person at the time of injury correlate to discrete categories of behavioral challenges (Brazis, Masdeu, & Biller, 1989; Brooks, 1984; Dennis, 1988; Fletcher, Ewing-Cobbs, McLaughlin, & Levin; 1985; Goethe & Levin, 1984; Stuss & Benson, 1986).
3. *Consequence analysis:* This category refers to circumstances that occur in the individual's environment that maintain the presence of the challenging behaviors. It includes the effects of the targeted behaviors on the immediate interpersonal and physical environment, the long-term environmental effects, and the frequency of occurrence of specific consequences. The two most frequently occurring consequences are object or activity acquisition (e.g., the student's getting what he or she wants) and demand avoidance.
4. *Motivational analysis* (Durand, 1990; Durand, Crimmins, Caulfield, & Taylor, 1989): This category refers to those elements available in the environment that will likely increase the presence of behaviors. Put simply, they are the reinforcers. A complete motivational analysis includes an objective evaluation of objects or activities that the individual has gained as a result of both negative and positive behaviors. It also includes objects or activities that the individual has indicated he or she likes or would like, and objects or activities that were identified as preferred preinjury.
5. *The personal "language" of behavior:* This category requires a synthesis of the functional analysis of behavior, the functional communication evaluation, and the learning history in an effort to interpret the "language" of problem behaviors. The strictest behavioral impressions are described to define reinforcement contingencies of the specific classes of behaviors (positive contingencies

serve to access things that the individual wants; negative contingencies serve to avoid or to escape unwanted events). These classes of consequences are instrumental to the development of problem behaviors as communicative. As stated earlier, these behaviors often appear maladaptive or nonfunctional; in fact, they are often a shorthand, nonstandardized, functional language. Put simply, this is the language of behavior. Using challenging behaviors, the student can communicate an array of feelings or needs, which may include "I don't like this," "I don't understand," "I want to . . . ," and "I don't want to . . . ," and those who provide care communicate "You don't have to . . ." and "I'll give you what you want." Challenging behaviors are typically utilized as a result of not having successfully learned or relearned what is generally recognized as functional communication. In other words, the individual may not have the ability to recognize or utilize universally recognized communication skills that are functionally related or equivalent to challenging behaviors.

SEGMENT IV: FUNCTIONAL ANALYSIS OF COMMUNICATION

Communication is the sum total of language skills, metacognitive abilities, and executive system functioning. Following an acquired brain injury, this assembly is distinctively, and often irrevocably, reorganized. The individual combination of these abilities, modified by neurological damage and learning history, influences the presence of challenging behaviors. The functional analysis of language objectifies strengths and weaknesses in language skills, metacognitive abilities, and executive functioning, enhancing the functional analysis of challenging behaviors. To maximize the functional validity of the assessment, information should be gleaned from repeated interactions across all environments (Ylvisaker & Holland, 1985), observation and interaction with the stakeholders, and formal testing in a quiet room away from all activity. Five levels of analysis are used in this approach:

1. *Operational description of language skills:* This process has two steps (Baxter, Cohen, & Ylvisaker, 1985): formal speech-language assessment and ongoing functional communication assessments (Milton & Wertz, 1986). Objective measures of auditory and reading comprehension, oral and written expression, and cognitive abilities demonstrated in communication skills merge to form an analysis of the idiosyncratic means of communication.

2. *Standardized language assessment:* Included in this level are the results of formal speech and language assessments (e.g., *Boston Diagnostic Aphasia Examination,* Goodglass & Kaplan, 1972; *Revised Token Test,* McNeil & Prescott, 1978; *Preschool Language Assessment Instrument,* Blank, Rose, & Berlin, 1978; *Test of Language Competence–Expanded Edition,* Wiig & Secord, 1988). The outcomes of these assessments reflect optimal performance. The

testing is individualized, expectations are clearly defined, and testing is typically terminated prior to reaching the demand threshold. The structure of the testing supplants the metacognitive and executive functions that are needed to successfully communicate in functional environments (Ylvisaker & Szekeres, 1989). The results are then interpreted within the context of a functional language assessment.

3. *Functional assessment of communication and language:* This level of assessment provides a practical analysis of the individual's functional communication and language skills (Goetz, Schuller, & Sailor, 1979, 1981, 1983). The communication assessment encompasses continuous observations of the individual interacting with various persons in diverse environments with differential demands. It also includes a description of the communication competencies demonstrated by the individual, an analysis of communicative demands (Hartley, 1990), and an evaluation of the percentage of times an individual makes his or her wants, needs, thoughts, and ideas known successfully via his or her most effective means of communication (e.g., spoken language, written language, gestures, challenging behaviors). An operational description of language details the methods of communication in a hierarchy of effectiveness, the ability to communicate successfully via socially recognized methods of communication, and methods of communication in circumstances that elicit challenging behaviors (see Case Study 9.3). The differentiation of communication abilities can then be utilized to establish a foundation for language-based interventions.

CASE STUDY 9.3

Behavior and Communication

LR, a 19-year-old male, sustained a severe brain injury subsequent to a motor vehicle accident. He demonstrated mild cognitive impairments and severe dysarthria, which resulted in reduced oral communication abilities. LR's limited ability to communicate orally increased his frustration. As a result, he engaged in a number of challenging behaviors, which included hitting others, breaking objects, and attempting to ingest noxious substances. Over time, LR learned that the use of these behaviors carried communicative content. He successfully communicated his frustration and had his needs met subsequent to engaging in a challenging behavior. A functional alternative coping plan was devised by LR and his stakeholders. The plan included identifying sources of his frustration, teaching functionally equivalent ways of communicating frustration (e.g., use of universally recognized gestures), continued oral–motor exercises to improve his dysarthria, and cued relaxation. As LR integrated these skills into his repertoire of behaviors, and he was able to communicate his frustration in ways that were effective, and functional to him, the problem behaviors were gradually eliminated.

4. *Analysis of interaction ability of stakeholders:* This category, related to the communication and language assessment, is an objective measure of the ecology that supports the communication of the individual, best evidenced in stakeholders' interactional abilities and including a detailed description of the stakeholders' abilities to comprehend communicative intent and the impact of environmental factors on the communication ability of the individual with an ABI. This analysis of interaction ability leads to a description of the characteristic style of communication and listening skills of the individual with an ABI and the stakeholders. Ideally, stakeholders consistently modify their means of interaction (McGee, Menolascino, Hobbs, & Menousek, 1987) as the student develops improved communication abilities.

5. *Impressions and analysis of executive functioning and problem-solving abilities* (Meichenbaum, Burland, & Gruson, 1985; Wong, 1987; Ylvisaker & Szekeres, 1989): The description of the personal communicative function(s) of challenging behaviors is concluded here. Impressions and analysis of metacognitive and problem-solving abilities are inferred from the objective information provided in the analysis of behavior and the analysis of language and communication. Behavior, language, and communication are integrated in this process, which encompasses an analysis of the behaviors the student has demonstrated in his or her current repertoire that are recognized as attempts to analyze problems, determine and implement solutions, and evaluate outcomes. The absence of these abilities increases the probability that the individual will use challenging behaviors to communicate a want or need.

SEGMENT V: SYNTHESIZED INTERVENTION PLAN

After the stakeholder competencies have been evaluated, the functional analysis of challenging behaviors completed, and the language–communication abilities demonstrated by the individual determined, a synthesized individualized intervention plan is generated. The methods that follow are designed to provide stakeholders with a systematic approach to develop functional and socially acceptable alternative student behaviors. The suggestions are not meant to be exhaustive, but to serve merely as a point of departure. We do not suggest that every strategy listed is indispensable to programmatic success; however, we strongly recommend that any plan developed by stakeholders should focus on instruction of *natural antecedents* to improve the student's problem-solving abilities and practical communication, essential to the replacement of the communicative functions of challenging behaviors.

Proactive Approaches to Antecedent Instruction

In this section, we list guidelines to follow in using proactive approaches to antecedent instruction. Then we discuss several proactive approaches: establishing instructional control, changing the environment, establishing a concrete daily routine of general living skills, and building functionally related capacity using discrete trial shaping.

Commonsense guidelines for proactive interaction

1. *Always make your expectations clear.* Tell the student
   a. Where you are going to take him.
   b. How much you want him to do.
   c. How long you want him to work.

   Break down each activity or task into smaller components. Give the individual the criterion to know that he has completed a task (how many minutes, how many math problems, etc.) and *stick to it.*
2. *Keep focused on the task at hand.*
3. *Praise effort, not outcome.* After a student has demonstrated that she has tried her best to complete a task, lavish her with praise. Students often work for long periods of time when praised every few minutes.
4. *Do not force confrontations.* Let disagreements about little things slide. Before beginning to confront a person, ask yourself, "Is this worth a fight?"
5. *Do not say "No"; say "Try again."* When giving an instruction or when the student is making a choice that you do not like, avoid emotional words (e.g., "No," "Bad," "Wrong"). Try to use positive statements (e.g., "Try again," "Try this . . .").
6. *Ask questions and give choices.* When you ask a question, you avoid confrontation. You are asking the student to own the problem and come up with his own solution. Examples of questions to ask include "What did I say?" "Do you remember?" "What should you do now?" "Is this going to help you?" "How do you want me to help you?" and "What do you want?"
7. *Speak with respect.*
   a. *Do not* give orders; *do* give clear choices.
   b. *Do not* yell; *do* speak calmly and firmly.
   c. *Do not* "teach lessons"; *do* things to help the student learn.
8. *Make a plan* prior to every activity.
   a. Identify exactly what the student will do.
   b. Stay focused on what you want.

c. Identify the general behaviors she should remember to follow (e.g., "Listen," "Follow directions," "Ask for help," "Take turns").

9. *Describe and model behaviors that you want.*

Establishing instructional control

Instructional control is established when the stimulus that elicits the behavior is regulated by the teacher and when the student responds in a desired manner after the presentation of a direction or request. The method works as follows:

1. At least once during each daily activity when the student is participating fully (e.g., is displaying no negative behaviors), the teacher uses a prearranged, consistent sign or verbal cue that indicates "stop," and has the individual pause for a short time (5–10 seconds).
2. After successfully discontinuing the activity, the student is provided with a positive reinforcer immediately and then is prompted to reengage in the activity.
3. The teacher uses the prearranged communication method to indicate "stop" when each activity is completed and immediately removes the activity materials.

Instructional control also can be used as a reactive control strategy:

1. At any time the student begins to demonstrate challenging behavior, the teacher approaches, makes eye contact, and indicates "stop." When the targeted behavior is terminated, the teacher gives positive reinforcement and verbally and gesturally prompts the individual to complete the specific activity.
2. Upon completion of the prescribed activity, the student is provided the opportunity to engage in a preferred activity.

Changing the environment

The environment may be altered (Jones, Lattimore, Ulicny, & Risley, 1986) to decrease the presence of cues for negative behavior. This manipulation also increases the student's control of the surroundings, thereby reducing the level of stress experienced prior to engaging in any activity. This strategy can also be used in a reactive manner, as a way of removing the cues for negative behavior. Environmental changes may include the following:

1. Teaching new skills (e.g., math, reading, augmented communication) in quiet, undisturbed settings.
2. Establishing an avenue of escape. Prior to the start of any activity, an avenue of escape should be established with the student to permit her to leave the area after indicating she needs to escape or "stop" an activity.

3. Removing objects or people from the environment. People or objects that have been identified as cues for challenging behavior are relocated prior to the initiation of any activity.

Establishing a concrete daily routine of general living skills

Most people learn best within the context of a daily routine (Wetzel & Hoschouer, 1984). The ability to predict the course of one's day sustains positive behaviors and reduces confusion and frustration (Olley, 1988). A consistent daily routine also provides a concrete framework in which to analyze problems, determine and implement solutions, and evaluate outcomes. It consists of an untimed succession of real-life activities, rather than a theoretically realistic but inflexible chronological structure. The elements of the routine should be selected from the naturally occurring teaching curriculum and then task analyzed into a sequence of component parts. As the student demonstrates the ability to successfully function throughout the course of the day, the concreteness of the routine is reduced, and the demands on the student to manage his or her daily routine are increased.

The daily routine can be implemented as follows:

1. Stakeholders develop a one-page checklist that includes each activity of the daily routine.
2. The checklist is placed in a folder or some other portable carrier and toted everywhere.
3. Prior to each activity, stakeholders verbally review the routine with the student and point to the prescribed activity on the checklist. This includes clearly identifying when the task is to begin and end. Review occurs prior to every activity.
4. Upon completion of an activity, stakeholders make an "X" through the word that represents the activity and indicate "stop." The student is then prompted to indicate "stop," after which the next activity on the checklist is presented. This procedure is followed until bedtime.
5. When the student has demonstrated the ability to follow the daily routine consistently (e.g., participates to criterion 90% of the time), the number of elements are reduced and the abstractness of the cues is increased.

Building functionally related capacity using discrete trial shaping

Using discrete trial shaping to build functionally related capacity involves teaching positive skills that are functionally related alternatives to negative behaviors (Gold, 1980; LaVigna & Donnellan, 1986). The primary targeted capacities are intended to supplant the communicative functions of negative behaviors and increase the individual's ability to problem solve. The shaping procedure consists of shifting the criteria (a) for success in approximation of the targeted positive behavior and (b) for termination of activities toward increased levels of stringency. This strategy is used across each activity of the daily routine, and can be implemented with the following methodologies (among others):

1. *Choice making:* This technique can be implemented in the following sequence:
   a. The student is given the opportunity to choose an activity item or an activity.
   b. Stakeholders provide two choices; make the sign, say the word, or point to the symbol for each one of them; and prompt the student to point to his choice.
   c. After the student has pointed to a choice, the other option is removed, and the student is prompted to make an approximation of the sign, say the word, or point to the vicinity of the symbol to indicate his choice.
   d. Upon completion of the sign approximation, the student is given the object he wanted or is engaged in an activity.
2. *Escape communication training* (Durand, 1990): This training involves teaching a specific method that a student can use as an alternative to negative behaviors to communicate "I don't want to . . ." or "I want to leave" a particular area or activity. The following sequence can be implemented:
   a. Identify a sign, phrase, or symbol that the student can use to communicate the general concept "stop."
   b. At the completion of each activity, prompt the student to make the sign, verbalize the phrase, or use the symbol, and then allow her to leave the activity.
   c. When the student appears to be upset, angry, or frustrated in an activity, and she is at a point in which the activity can be terminated, stakeholders use the prearranged communication behavior to signal "stop" and prompt a model of the sign. Upon modeling the behavior, the student leaves the activity.
3. *Relaxation training:* Relaxation training has a number of variations (Benson, 1975; Cautela & Groden, 1978; Forman & Myers, 1987; Jacobson, 1964). These approaches involve teaching the student a positive method of responding when confronted with anger-provoking situations. Relaxation training is functionally related to the instructional control strategy previously described; however, instructional control is designed as an externally directed strategy to maintain behavioral control in specific learning situations, whereas relaxation training is designed to teach a long-term, *internally controlled,* and generalizable coping behavior.
4. *Greeting training:* This strategy is designed to teach an individual an inherently reinforcing manner of initiating positive social interactions. Stakeholders model how to greet people in a socially acceptable manner (e.g., approach a person, shake his or her hand, and say hello in a tone of voice equal to a normal conversational tone). This simple means of initiating an interaction in an inher-

ently positive manner also serves as a cue of positive feedback from others.

Reactive Approaches

Nonaversive teaching strategies take time to work. Meanwhile, a number of planned reactive methods should be in place to assure continuity of interventions and comfort of stakeholders while the nonaversive methods become increasingly effective. These strategies are designed as a means of communicating with an individual in a nonthreatening manner, diffusing verbal or physical confrontation or agitation, and may include the following:

1. *Redirection:* This strategy entails shifting the focus of attention or concentration to a neutral topic or to the prescribed task that is identified on the daily routine. The source of anxiety or anger is not ignored; it is merely deferred until the student is better able to problem solve (i.e., as soon as possible).
2. *Active listening and supportive questioning:* Actively listening to an individual when he is beginning to demonstrate signs of agitation can often deescalate negative behaviors. This class of reactive communication strategies requires nonthreatening interaction with the individual; the only demand placed on the individual is that of responding to simple, concrete questions. No judgment is made regarding the individual's behavior or emotion. Question content is based on the responses given by the individual. All questions should promote problem solving and demonstrate active listening. This element of reactive strategy comprises four steps:
    a. *Identification:* The first step is to identify the actual emotion the person is experiencing (e.g., fear, anxiety, anger, frustration) as well as the source of the emotion.
    b. *Reflection:* The second step is to label the emotion with the person. This step is designed to teach the individual to differentiate her emotions and begin to label feelings in order to effectively communicate them to others.
    c. *Empathy:* This step is designed to demonstrate that *you* understand what the person is feeling. An effective empathic strategy is giving a concrete example of something equivalent in your life. Use of this strategy buys time, is a form of redirection, and demonstrates understanding. A caution: If your example is not similar, escalation of negative behavior will likely result.
    d. *Problem solving:* This final step is designed to direct the individual to the most positive solution possible. The individual identifies his emotions or feelings and their sources and then considers "if–then" scenarios in an effort to determine the most effective method of resolving the problem.
3. *The stoneface:* This strategy is designed as a reminder that the behavior of the individual with ABI is affected by the stakeholder's

behavior. Rapid movement and increased voice tone can cue the escalation of negative behavior. Slow movement and normal voice tone can deescalate negative behavior. Using the stoneface means adopting a facial expression and body movements that communicate self-control and calmness. Effective use of this strategy requires practice.

CONCLUSION

In this chapter, we have presented a process of communication-based assessments and interventions for educators and other stakeholders working with students with ABI who demonstrate challenging behaviors. At the heart of this process lies the premise that (a) problem behaviors are communicative and adaptive to the student who uses them and (b) collaborative communication among stakeholders is essential to effective assessment and intervention. The student is at the center of the process, and each approach used is designed to facilitate self-control in a manner that is meaningful to the student. Within this framework, all interventions focus on developing a repertoire of functionally equivalent communicative behaviors. The stakeholders join as a team to clarify the student's personal history and to analyze the functions of the behaviors and the communication abilities of the student and the stakeholders. These analyses are then synthesized by the collaborative team to develop an intervention plan. This is a time-consuming approach; there are no quick fixes to challenging behaviors that are rooted in complex personal histories and compromised neuropsychological functioning. However, we have found a profound reflection to guide us in the endeavour: "Would this be good enough for me?"

APPENDIX 9A
Medications Used with Children with Challenging Behaviors Following Acquired Brain Injury

In this appendix, we list some of the medications commonly used with children who demonstrate challenging behaviors following acquired brain injury. We describe the drugs from a layman's perspective to help stakeholders in considering pharmacologic treatment.

Antidepressants

Some antidepressants are thought to influence the effects of neurotransmitters in the limbic system and to blunt emotional responses to stressful situations. Most of the examples listed here represent the category of tricyclic antidepressants; another category of antidepressants, monoamine oxidase inhibitors, is not represented because they are rarely used to assist children with acquired brain injury.

- **Amitriptyline** (Elavil or Endep). The method of action is unknown. It is not a CNS stimulant. It is used for the relief of symptoms of depression. *Not recommended for children under 12.*
- **Chlordiazepoxide** and **amitriptyline** (Limbitrol). This compound has limbic system action and interferes with the reuptake of norepinephrine into adrenergic nerve endings. It is used to treat depression and anxiety.
- **Doxepin** (Sinequan or Adapin). Doxepin influences adrenergic activity at synapses where deactivation of norepinephrine is blocked by reuptake into nerve terminals. It is used primarily with depression and/or anxiety associated with organic disease, psychoneurotic persons, depression associated with alcohol abuse, and psychotic depressive disorders with anxiety.
- **Fluoxetine** (Prozac). This drug inhibits CNS uptake of serotonin. It is used for the treatment of depression. *Designed for short-term usage.*
- **Imipramine** (Tofranil). The method of action is unknown. It is believed to potentiate adrenergic synapses by blocking norepinephrine at nerve endings. It is used to treat mental depression.
- **Nortriptyline** (Aventyl or Pamelor). The method of action is unknown. Nortriptyline has both central nervous system (CNS) stimulant and depressant properties. It is used for the relief of symptoms of depression. *Not recommended for children under 12.*
- **Perphenazine** and **amitriptyline** (Triavil). The method of action is unknown. It is not a CNS stimulant. The compound is used with severe anxiety and/or agitation, depression with increased anxiety

and agitation, and depression associated with chronic physical disease.

- **Trazodone** (Deseryl). This drug is not a tricyclic. The method of action is unknown. It is not a CNS stimulant. It is used for the relief of symptoms of depression. *Not recommended for children under 12.*

Lithium carbonate

Lithium carbonate is an antimonic that alters sodium transport in nerve and muscle cells and effects shift toward interneuronal metabolism of catecholemines. Lithium is used in manic episodes of bipolar disorders.

Beta blockers

Beta blockers have been used to treat a rage behavior in individuals who have frontal lobe lesions.

- **Pindolol** (Visken). This agent affects behavior through the reduction of sympathetic stimulation by blocking autonomic nervous system activity. It is used less frequently than propranolol.
- **Propranolol** (Inderal). This agent affects behavior through the reduction of sympathetic stimulation by blocking autonomic nervous system activity.

Alpha agonist

Although alpha agonists are used less often than beta blockers, they have similar effects on persons with frontal lobe lesions.

- **Clonidine.**

Anticonvulsants

Anticonvulsants require a baseline electroencephalogram. It often takes 3–4 weeks to see any effects. These medications frequently have a *cognitive blunting effect,* increasing confusion and reducing the ability to effectively interpret environmental cues and verbal directions.

- **Carbamazepine** (Tegretol). This medication blocks a number of synaptic connections in the bulbar region. Carbamazepine is used frequently for behavior control, especially with individuals with frontal lobe damage, and to control partial seizures (psychomotor and temporal lobe) that are sometimes associated with challenging behaviors.
- **Clonazepam** (Klonopin). This is a CNS depressant that has historically been used to control petit mal seizures. A growing body of literature supports the use of clonazepam for behavioral control.

- **Dilantin** (Dilantin). This medication inhibits the spread of seizure activity at the motor cortex.
- **Phenobarbital** (Phenobarbital). This barbiturate is typically used in combination with other medications.

Psychostimulants

Psychostimulants have immediate effects and have a short half-life. These are often used with children who have profiles similar to children with attention deficit and hyperactivity disorders. However, some literature indicates that children who respond to psychostimulants following injury were children who would have responded prior to injury (i.e., children who were hyperactive before injury). Some possible side effects include anorexia, insomnia, headaches, irritability, and behavioral "rebound" (i.e., an increase in hyperactive behaviors after the medications lose their effects). These medications can also become addictive and require close monitoring by physicians.

- **Methamphetamine** (Desoxyn). This is a sympathomimetic amine, a CNS stimulant that is absorbed through the liver. It is used with nonlocalizing (soft) neurological signs, learning disabilities, moderate to severe distractibility, short attention span, hyperactivity, emotional lability, and impulsiveness.
- **Methylphenidate** (Ritalin). This central nervous system stimulant activates the brain stem arousal system and cortex. It is used for situations similar to those listed for methamphetamine. This medication is *not* intended for children who exhibit symptoms secondary to environmental factors and/or primary psychiatric disorders.
- **Pemoline** (Cylert). This CNS stimulant of dopaminergic mechanisms is used in situations similar to those listed for methamphetamine.

Neuroleptics

Neuroleptics are commonly used with children who display severe challenging behaviors. There are five categories of neuroleptics: phenothiazines, thioxanthenes, butyrophenones, dibenzoxazepines, and dihydroindolones. These medications frequently have a *cognitive blunting effect,* increasing confusion and reducing the ability to effectively interpret environmental cues and verbal directions. Other possible adverse side effects include Reye's syndrome, neuroleptic malignant syndrome, tardive dyskinesia (i.e., sucking, lipsmacking, and jaw movements), phototoxicity (i.e., extreme sensitivity to sunlight), blurred vision, lowered seizure thresholds, motor restlessness, Parkinsonism, sexual dysfunction, acute dystonia, and other extrapyramidal symptoms.

- **Haloperidol** (Haldol). It is not known how this medication affects neurochemistry. Haloperidol is most frequently used for management of psychotic disorders, severe behavior problems in children who display combativeness and explosive behaviors, and short-term treatment of hyperactivity. It has been used to control the behavioral manifestations of Tourette's syndrome.

- **Molindone** (Moban). This compound suppresses the activity of the ascending reticular activating system. It is used for the management of bizarre stereotypic behaviors, psychotic disorders, and severe behavior problems in children.
- **Perphenazine** (Trilafon or Triavil). This compound acts on the CNS as a tranquilizer; it also has antidepressant properties. It is used for persons who experience severe anxiety, agitation, or depression. *It is not recommended for usage in children.*
- **Prochlorperazine** (Compazine). The method of action of this compound is unknown. It has been used for treatment of nonpsychotic anxiety, and the management of behavior problems in developmentally disabled populations.
- **Thioridazine** (Mellaril). It is not known how this medication affects neurochemistry. Thioridazine reduces excitement, hypermotility, abnormal initiative, and affective tension through the inhibition of psychomotor functions. It is used for management of psychotic disorders, short-term treatment of depression with anxiety, and severe behavior problems in children who display combativeness and explosive behavior. Thioridazine also has some effect in the short-term treatment of hyperactivity.
- **Thiothixene** (Navane). It is not known how this medication affects neurochemistry. This medication is a thioxanthene, which is used for treatment of psychotic disorders and behavioral control in developmentally disabled populations.

Antianxiety agents

Antianxiety agents are used in the treatment of nonpsychotic personality problems and are used infrequently in children and adolescents who demonstrate agitation and restless gross motor movements secondary to ABI. Three categories of medication are represented in this sample: sedatives, hypnotics, and anxiolytics. All three are CNS depressants. These medications frequently have a *cognitive blunting effect,* increasing lethargy and confusion, exacerbating memory problems, and reducing the ability to effectively interpret environmental cues and verbal directions.

- **Alprazolam** (Xanax). This compound binds to the stereo-specific receptors at several sites within the CNS, making it a CNS depressant. Alprazolam is used in anxiety disorders or for short-term relief of anxiety associated with depression.
- **Chlorazepate** (Tranxene). This CNS depressant is used in anxiety disorders and for persons who demonstrate partial seizures.
- **Lorazepam** (Ativan). This CNS tranquilizer is used in anxiety disorders or for short-term relief of anxiety, anxiety associated with depression, and motor agitation secondary to TBI.

REFERENCES

Achenbach, T., & Edelbrock, C. (1983). *Manual for the Child Behavior Checklist and Revised Child Behavior Profile.* Burlington: University of Vermont.

Aram, D., & Ekelman, B. L. (1986). Cognitive profiles of children with early onset of unilateral lesions. *Developmental Neuropsychology, 2,* 147–154.

Bailey, J. S. (1987). *Functional analysis.* Paper presented at Applied Behavior Analysis Symposium, Nashville, TN.

Baxter, R., Cohen, S. B., & Ylvisaker, M. (1985). Comprehensive cognitive assessment. In M. Ylvisaker (Ed.), *Head injury rehabilitation: Children and adolescents* (pp. 275–286). Austin, TX: PRO-ED.

Benson, H. (1975). *The relaxation response.* New York: Morrow.

Bicker, D. (1976). The educational synthesizer. In M. Thomas (Ed.), *Hey, don't forget about me! Education's investment in the severely, profoundly, and multiply handicapped* (pp. 152–158). Reston, VA: Council for Exceptional Children.

Biederman, D. X., & Jellinek, M. S. (1984). Psychopharmacology in children. *New England Journal of Medicine, 310,* 938–972.

Bird, F., Dores, P. A., Moniz, D., & Robinson, J. (1989). Reducing severe aggressive and self-injurious behaviors with functional communication training: Direct, collateral, and generalized results. *American Journal of Mental Retardation, 94,* 37–48.

Blank, M., Rose, S. A., & Berlin, L. J. (1978). *Preschool Language Assessment Instrument.* San Antonio, TX: Psychological Corp.

Brazis, P. W., Masdeu, J. C., & Biller, J. (1989). *Localization in clinical neurology* (2nd ed.). Boston: Little, Brown.

Brooks, N. (Ed.). (1984). *Closed head injury: Psychological, social, and family consequences.* New York: Oxford University Press.

Brooks, N., McKinley, W., Symington, C., Beattie, A., & Campsie, L. (1987). Return to work within the first seven years of severe closed head injury. *Brain Injury, 1,* 5–19.

Burke, G. M. (1990). Unconventional behavior: A communicative interpretation in individuals with severe disabilities. *Topics in Language Disorders, 10,* 75–85.

Carr, E. G., & Durand, V. M. (1985a). Reducing behavior problems through functional communication training. *Journal of Applied Behavior Analysis, 18,* 111–126.

Carr, E. G., & Durand, V. M. (1985b). The social–communicative basis of severe behavior problems in children. In S. Reis, & R. Bootzin (Eds.), *Theoretical issues in behavior therapy.* New York: Academic Press.

Cautela, J. R., & Groden, J. (1978). *Relaxation: A comprehensive manual for adults, children, and children with special needs.* Champaign, IL: Research Press.

Cockrell, J. L. (1991). Pharmacologic treatment in pediatric rehabilitation: Potential adverse effects. *Neuro-Rehabilitation, 1,* 7–11.

Dennis, M. (1988). Language and the young damaged brain. In T. Boll & B. K. Bryant (Eds.), *Clinical neuropsychology and brain function: Research, measurement and practice* (pp. 87–123). Washington, DC: American Psychological Association.

Donnellan, A. M., Mirenda, P. L., Mesaros, R. A., & Fassbender, L. L. (1984). Analyzing the communicative functions of aberrant behavior. *Journal of the Association for Persons with Severe Handicaps, 9,* 201–212.

Durand, V. M. (1986). Self injurious behavior as intentional communication. In K. G. Gadow (Ed.), *Advances in learning and behavioral disabilities* (vol. 5, pp. 141–155). Greenwich, CT: JAI.

Durand, V. M. (1990). *Severe behavior problems: A functional communication training approach.* New York: Guilford Press.

Durand, V. M., & Carr, E. G. (1991). Functional communication training to reduce challenging behavior: Maintenance and application in new settings. *Journal of Applied Behavior Analysis, 24,* 251–264.

Durand, V. M., Crimmins, D. B., Caulfield, M., & Taylor, J. (1989). Reinforcer assessment: I. Using problem behavior to select reinforcers. *Journal of the Association for Persons with Severe Handicaps, 14,* 113–126.

Eames, D., & Wood, R. (1985). Rehabilitation after severe brain injury: A special unit approach. *International Rehabilitation Medicine, 7,* 130–133.

Eslinger, P. J., & Grattan, L. M. (1991). Perspectives on the developmental consequences of early frontal lobe damage: Introduction. *Developmental Neuropsychology, 7,* 257–260.

Evans, I. M., & Meyer, L. H. (1985). *An educative approach to behavior problems: A practical decision model for interventions with severely handicapped learners.* Baltimore: Brooks.

Feeney, T. J., Urbanczyk, B., Savage, R. C., & Blaustein, P. (1991). *School re-entry of children with TBI and challenging behaviors: Case studies of language-based, behavior interventions.* Blue Ribbon Paper Presented at International Brain Injury Symposium, New Orleans.

Fernandez-Ballesteros, R., & Staats, A. W. (1992). Paradigmatic behavioral assessment, treatment, and evaluation: Answering the crisis in behavioral assessment. *Advances in Behavioral Research and Therapy, 14,* 1–27.

Fletcher, J. M., Ewing-Cobbs, L., McLaughlin, E. J., & Levin, H. S. (1985). *Cognitive and psychosocial sequelae of head injury in children: Implications for assessment and management.* Austin: University of Texas Press.

Fletcher, J. M., Ewing-Cobbs, L., Miner, M. E., Levin, H. S., & Eisenberg, H. M. (1990). Behavioral changes after closed head injury in children. *Journal of Consulting and Clinical Psychology, 58,* 93–98.

Fletcher, J. M., & Levin, H. S. (1988). Neurobehavioral effects of brain injury in children. In D. Routh (Ed.), *Handbook of pediatric psychology* (pp. 258–295). New York: Academic Press.

Ford, A., Schnorr, R., Meyer, L., Davern, L., Black, S., & Dempsey, L. (1989). *The Syracuse curriculum revision manual.* Baltimore: Brookes.

Forest, M., & Lusthaus, E. (1989). Promoting educational equality for all students: Circles and maps. In S. Stainback, W. Stainback, & M. Forest (Eds.), *Educating all students in the mainstream of regular education* (pp. 43–57). Baltimore: Brookes.

Forest, M., & Lusthaus, E. (1990, Winter). Everyone belongs with the MAPS action planning system. *TEACHING Exceptional Children,* pp. 32–35.

Forest, M., & Snow, J. (1987). *More educational integration.* Toronto: G. Allan Rocher Institute.

Forman, J. W., & Myers, D. (1987). *The personal stress reduction program.* Englewood Cliffs, NJ: Prentice-Hall.

Frye, B. (1987). Head injury and the family-related literature. *Rehabilitation Nursing, 12,* 135–136.

Gaultieri, C. T. (1988). Pharmacotherapy and the neurobehavioral sequelae of traumatic brain injury. *Brain Injury, 2,* 101–129.

Giangreco, M. F., Cloninger, C. J., & Salce Iverson, V. (1990). *C.O.A.C.H.: Cayuga–Onondaga Assessment for Children with Handicaps.* Stillwater, OK: National Clearinghouse of Rehabilitation Training Materials.

Glenn, M. (1987a). A pharmacologic approach to aggressive and disruptive behavior after traumatic brain injury: Part 1. *Journal of Head Trauma Rehabilitation, 2,* 71–73.

Glenn, M. (1987b). A pharmacologic approach to aggressive and disruptive behavior after traumatic brain injury: Part 2. *Journal of Head Trauma Rehabilitation, 2,* 80–81.

Glenn, M. (1987c). A pharmacologic approach to aggressive and disruptive behavior after traumatic brain injury: Part 3. *Journal of Head Trauma Rehabilitation, 2,* 85–87.

Goethe, K. E., & Levin, H. S. (1984). Behavioral manifestations during the early and long term stages of recovery after closed head injury. *Psychiatric Annals, 14,* 540–546.

Goetz, L., Schuller, A., & Sailor, W. (1979). Teaching functional speech to severely handicapped: Current issues. *Journal of Autism and Developmental Disabilities, 9,* 325–343.

Goetz, L., Schuller, A., & Sailor, W. (1981). Functional competence as a factor in communication instruction. *Exceptional Education Quarterly, 2,* 51–61.

Goetz, L., Schuller, A., & Sailor, W. (1983). Motivational considerations in teaching language to severely handicapped students. In M. Henen, V. vanHasseut, & J. Watson (Eds.), *Behavior therapy for the developmentally and physically disabled: A handbook* (pp. 57–77). New York: Academic Press.

Gold, M. W. (1980). *Try another way: Training manual.* Champaign, IL: Research Press.

Goodglass, H., & Kaplan, E. (1972). *Boston Diagnostic Aphasia Examination.* Philadelphia: Lea & Febiger.

Gordon, N. (1991). The relationship between language and behavior. *Developmental Medicine and Child Neurology, 33,* 86–89.

Hartley, L. L. (1990). Assessment of functional communication. In D. E. Tupper & K. D. Cicerone (Eds.), *The neuropsychology of everyday life: Assessment and basic competencies* (pp. 125–168). Boston: Kluwer Academic Publishers.

Hayes, S. N., & O'Brien, W. H. (1990). Functional analysis in behavior therapy. *Clinical Psychology Review, 10,* 659–669.

Holmes Bernstein, J., & Waber, D. P. (1990). Developmental neuropsychological assessment: The systemic approach. In A. A. Boulton, G. B. Baker, & M. Hiscock (Eds.), *Neuromethods 17: Neuropsychology* (pp. 311–371). Clifton, NJ: Humana Press.

Horner, R. H., & Budd, C. M. (1985). Acquisition of manual sign use: Collateral reduction on maladaptive behaviors and factors limiting generalization. *Education and Training in Mental Retardation, 20,* 39–47.

Iwata, B. A., Dorsey, M. F., Slifer, K. J., Bauman, K. E., & Richman, G. S. (1982). Toward a functional analysis of self injury. *Analysis and Intervention in Developmental Disabilities, 2,* 3–20.

Jacobs, R., & Fuhrmann, B. (1980). *Learning interaction inventory.* Richmond, VA: Ronne Jacobs.

Jacobson, E. (1964). *Anxiety and tension control.* Philadelphia: Lippincott.

Jastak, J. F., & Wilkinson, G. (1984). *The Wide Range Achievement Test–Revised.* Wilmington, DE: Jastak Associates.

Johnson, D. W., & Johnson, F. P. (1982). *Joining together.* Englewood Cliffs, NJ: Prentice-Hall.

Jones, M. L., Lattimore, J., Ulicny, G. G., & Risley, T. R. (1986). Ecobehavioral design: A program for engagement. In R. P. Barrett (Ed.), *Severe behavior disorders in the mentally retarded.* New York: Plenum Press.

Kern-Dunlap, L., Dunlap, G., Clarke, S., Childs, K. E., White, R. L., & Stewart, M. P. (1992). Effects of a videotape feedback package on the peer interactions of children with serious behavioral and emotional challenges. *Journal of Applied Behavior Analysis, 25,* 355–364.

Knapczyk, D. R. (1988). Reducing aggressive behaviors in special and regular class settings by training alternative social responses. *Behavioral Disorders, 14,* 27–39.

Knapczyk, D. R. (1992). Effects of developing alternative responses on the aggressive behavior of adolescents. *Behavior Disorders, 17,* 247–263.

Kolb, D. A. (1985). *Learning style inventory.* Boston: McBer and Co.

LaVigna, G. W. (1983). The Jay Nolan Center: A community-based program. In E. Schapler & G. B. Mesibor (Eds.), *Autism in adolescents and adults* (pp. 381–410). New York: Plenum.

LaVigna, G. W., & Donnellan, A. M. (1986). *Alternatives to punishment: Solving behavior problems with non-aversive strategies.* New York: Irvington.

Lezak, M. D. (1987). Relationships between personality disorder, social disturbances, and physical disability following traumatic brain injury. *Journal of Head Trauma Rehabilitation, 2,* 57–69.

McGee, J. J., Menolascino, F. J., Hobbs, D. C., & Menousek, P. E. (1987). *Gentle teaching: A non-aversive approach to helping persons with mental retardation.* New York: Human Sciences Press.

McGuire, T. (1986). Behavioral and psychosocial sequelae of pediatric head injury. *Journal of Head Trauma Rehabilitation, 1,* 1–6.

McNeil, M., & Prescott, T. (1978). *Revised Token Test.* Austin, TX: PRO-ED.

Meichenbaum, D., Burland, S., & Gruson, L. (1985). Metacognitive assessment. In S. Yussen (Ed.), *The growth of reflection in children* (pp. 3–30). New York: Academic Press.

Meyer, L. H., & Evans, I. M. (1989). *Nonaversive intervention for behavior problems: A manual for home and community.* Baltimore: Brookes.

Milton, S. B., & Wertz, R. T. (1986). Management of persisting communication deficits in patients with traumatic brain injury. In B. P. Uzzell & Y. Gross (Eds.), *Clinical neuropsychology of intervention.* Boston: Martinus Nijhoff.

Mount, B., & Patterson, J. (1986, May). *Positive futures project.* Report to the Commissioner of the Connecticut Department of Mental Retardation.

O'Brien, J. (1985). *Design for accomplishment.* Cheshire, CT: Graphic Futures.

O'Brien, J., & Mount, B. (1985). *Design for accomplishment.* Lithonia, GA: Responsive Systems Associates.

Olley, J. G. (1988). Environmental structure for optimal learning in autistic children. In D. Cohen & A. M. Donnellan (Eds.), *Handbook on autism.* New York: Wiley.

O'Shanick, G. J. (1987). Clinical aspects of psychopharmacologic treatment in head-injured patients. *Journal of Head Trauma Rehabilitation, 2,* 59–67.

O'Shanick, G. J., & Zasler, N. D. (1990). Neuropsychopharmacological approaches to traumatic brain injury. In J. S. Kreutzer & P. Wehman (Eds.), *Community integration following traumatic brain injury.* Baltimore: Brookes.

Parmelee, D. X., & O'Shanick, G. S. (1987). Neuropsychiatric interventions with head injured children. *Brain Injury, 1,* 41–47.

Peacock Hill Working Group, The. (1991). Problems and promises in special education and related services for children and youth with emotional or behavioral disorders. *Behavioral Disorders, 16,* 299–313.

Reiher, T. C. (1992). Identified deficits and their congruence to the IEP for behaviorally disordered students. *Behavioral Disorders, 17,* 167–177.

Renzulli, J. S., & Smith, L. H. (1978). *Learning style inventory: A measure of student preference for instructional techniques.* Mansfield Center, CT: Creative Learning Press.

Repp, A., Felce, D., & Batton, L. (1988). Basing the treatment of stereotypic and self-injurious behaviors on hypotheses of their causes. *Journal of Applied Behavior Analysis, 23,* 11–27.

Savage, R. C., & Carter, R. R. (1988). Transitioning pediatric patients into educational systems: Guidelines for rehabilitation professionals. *Cognitive Rehabilitation,* 6(4), 10–14.

Savage, R. C., & Carter, R. R. (1984). Re-entry: The head-injured student returns to school. *Cognitive Rehabilitation, 2,* 28–33.

Savage, R. C., & Carter, R. R. (1991). Family and return to school. In J. M. Williams & T. Kay (Eds.), *Head injury: A family matter.* Baltimore: Brookes.

Schnorr, R., Ford, A., Davern, L., Park-Lee, S., & Meyer, L. (1989). *The Syracuse community referenced curriculum guide for students with moderate and severe disabilities.* Baltimore: Brookes.

Schuler, A. L. (1980, August). *Communicative intent and aberrant behavior.* Paper presented at Counsel on Exceptional Children Topical Conference on the Severely Emotionally Disturbed, Minneapolis, MN.

Smith, S. W., & Simpson, R. L. (1989). An analysis of individual educational programs (IEPs) for students with behavioral disorders. *Behavioral Disorders, 14,* 107–116.

Sparrow, S., Balla, D., & Cicchetti, D. (1984). *Vineland Adaptive Behavior Scales.* Circle Pines, MN: American Guidance Service.

Steinberg, Z., & Knitzer, J. (1992). Classrooms for emotionally and behaviorally disturbed students: Facing the challenge. *Behavioral Disorders, 17,* 145–156.

Stuss, D. T., & Benson, D. F. (1986). *The frontal lobes.* New York: Raven Press.

Sulzer-Azaroff, B., & Mayer, G. R. (1977). *Applying behavior-analysis procedures with children and youth.* New York: Holt, Rinehart and Winston.

Sutton, R. L., Weaver, M. S., & Feeney, D. M. (1987). Drug induced modifications of behavioral recovery following cortical trauma. *Journal of Head Trauma Rehabilitation, 2,* 50–58.

Thousand, J. S., & Villa, R. A. (1990). Strategies for educating learners with severe disabilities within their local home schools and communities. *Focus on Exceptional Children, 23,* 1–27.

Wacker, D. P., Steege, M. W., Northrup, J., Sasso, G., Berg, W., Reimers, T., Cooper, L., Cigrand, K., & Donn, L. (1990). A component analysis of functional communication training across three topographies of severe behavior problems. *Journal of Applied Behavior Analysis, 23,* 417–429.

Wechsler, D. (1991). *Wechsler Intelligence Scale for Children–Third Edition.* San Antonio, TX: Psychological Corp.

Weinberg, L. A., & Weinberg, C. (1990). Seriously emotionally disturbed or socially maladjusted? A critique of interpretations. *Behavioral Disorders, 15,* 149–158.

Wetzel, M. C., & Taylor, M. J. (1991). Ecological functions of staff interventions in a workday training program. *Education and Training in Mental Retardation, 23,* 232–242.

Wetzel, M. C., Taylor, M. J., & Lachowicz, J. M. (1991). Ecological assessment of disabling stereotyped behavior in a workday training program. *Education and Training in Mental Retardation, 26,* 223–231.

Wetzel, R. J., & Hoschouer, R. L. (1984). *Residential teaching communities: Program development and staff training for developmentally disabled persons.* Dallas: Scott, Foresman.

Wiig, E. H., & Secord, W. (1988). *Test of Language Competence–Expanded Edition.* San Antonio, TX: Psychological Corp.

Wong, B. Y. L. (1987). How do the results of metacognitive research impact on the learning disabled individual? *Learning Disability Quarterly, 10,* 189–195.

Wood, R. L., & Burgess, P. W. (1988). The psychological management of behaviour disorders following brain injury. In I. Fussey & G. Muir Giles (Eds.), *Rehabilitation of the severely brain-injured adult.* London: Croom Helms.

Ylvisaker, M., Feeney, T., & Urbanczyk, B. (1993a). Developing a positive communication culture for rehabilitation: Communication training for staff and family members. In C. Durgin, J. Freyer, & N. Schmidt (Eds.), *Brain injury rehabilitation: Clinical intervention and staff development techniques.* Gaithersburg, MD: Aspen.

Ylvisaker, M., Feeney, T., & Urbanczyk, B. (1993b). A social–environmental approach to communication and behavior after traumatic brain injury. *Seminars in Speech and Language, 14*(1), 74–87.

Ylvisaker, M., & Holland, A. (1985). Coaching, self-coaching, and rehabilitation of head injury. In D. Johns (Ed.), *Clinical management of neurogenic communicative disorders* (2nd ed., pp. 243–257). Boston: Little, Brown.

Ylvisaker, M., & Szekeres, S. (1989). Metacognitive and executive impairments in head-injured children and adults. *Topics in Language Disorders, 9,* 34–49.

Yudofsky, S. C., Silver, J. M., & Schneider, S. E. (1987). Pharmacologic treatment of aggression. *Psychiatric Annals, 17,* 397–407.

CHAPTER 10

Reestablishing an Acceptable Sense of Self

IRWIN W. POLLACK

The brain is a bewilderingly complex and wholly unique body organ. Unlike the other organs of the human body, such as the heart which pumps blood, the lungs which exchange carbon dioxide and oxygen, and the liver which detoxifies the waste products of metabolism, the brain has no such "pedestrian" functions. Rather, the "regal" brain controls, organizes, and integrates the operations of all the other organs that constitute the internal milieu. Because of this, whenever the brain is injured, a number of bodily functions are disturbed. Every brain injury causes a multisystem disorder and, as any physician will tell you, the effects of a multisystem disorder are difficult to understand and to treat successfully.

The uniqueness of the brain's activities, however, is not limited to internal functions. In addition, through the several sense organs, the brain receives, organizes, and integrates information about the world that exists outside of the body, and then uses that information to further regulate the elements of the internal milieu so that the person will respond appropriately to changes in the external environment. Furthermore, using information from both sources—the body and the external environment—the brain can set in motion actions on the part of the person that change the outside world of people and things in ways that benefit the person.

Perhaps most astonishing is the fact that the brain's activities are not limited to the present moment, for it also can use information about past events, both internal and external, and can make predictions about the nature of future events, using both internal and external sources to ensure that the person's responses are appropriate, not only for the present situation, but also for those that are anticipated for the future. The brain, thereby, functions as the body organ responsible for sociability and, from this, it follows that every significant brain injury causes social dysfunction on the part of both the injured person and those individuals who are most closely affiliated with that injured person. In effect, brain injury causes a true social disease.

Notwithstanding the significant progress that has been made in the treatment of acquired brain injuries, no generally agreed-upon overriding principle or concept adequately describes what a person experiences as a result of an acquired brain injury (ABI). No single concept incorporates and represents the composite effects of ABI (i.e., physical, intellectual, emotional, and social); encompasses the often-temporary residuals of a minor insult to the brain, as well as the usually permanent deficits that are the result of extensive brain damage; and is as viable for comprehending the impact of ABI in children as it is for comprehending the effects of ABI in the elderly.

Unless such a concept is agreed upon, there will continue to be no good way to determine whether a person's "progress" in therapy has any relevance to him or her or, for that matter, to anyone else. There also will be no meaningful way to compare the progress made by several individuals in a particular rehabilitation program or to weigh the effectiveness of the several different approaches to the rehabilitation of children, adolescents, and adults with ABIs.[1]

The existing lack of clarity about what kinds of change in a person's behavior, attitude, and mood are sufficient to show that meaningful progress has been made in treatment has caused many third-party payers to question the efficacy of any and all brain injury rehabilitation programs. For example, it would not be unreasonable to assume that progress has been made if a person formerly confined to a wheelchair is now able to walk a distance of 20 feet without assistance; however, does that conclusion hold if the nearest bathroom is 40 feet from that person's room or if the person's persisting spatial disorientation precludes the possibility of his or her ever leaving the house unaccompanied?

LONG-TERM GOALS: UNFORMED, UNCLEAR, AND IRRELEVANT

The confusion over what constitutes sufficient evidence of progress is related, in large part, to the lack of agreement over what constitutes appropriate long-term goals, that is, goals that reasonably define a successful ending to the rehabilitation process. Even for a single client, two different rehabilitation programs may well disagree about which long-term goals are most appropriate. The most frequently promulgated long-term goals are (a) reaching one's maximal potential, (b) achieving independence in activities of daily living, and (c) community reentry. Each of these goals has significant limitations.

First, it is impossible to know whether an individual has reached his or her maximal potential before the fact. Therefore, the determination that an individual has been rehabilitated successfully depends on a more or less arbitrary decision by the treatment team rather than a valid appraisal of what that individual can or cannot do. In this case, the person's progress is likely to be assessed in terms of each therapist's own field of interest.

The second frequently promulgated long-term goal, independence in activities of daily living, includes the ability to wash, dress, toilet oneself, shop and prepare simple meals, manage routine housekeeping chores, and use the telephone and public transportation, all with no or very minimal assistance from others. The assessment of therapeutic success or failure, in this case, is not arbitrary. Because the criteria are

[1] The reader, if he or she desires, can substitute "child or adolescent" for "person" or "individual," "teacher" or "educator" for "therapist," and "special education" for "rehabilitation." I chose not to do so in order to emphasize the general applicability of the concepts that are developed in the chapter.

directly observable, therapists are more likely to agree about the amount and kind of progress made by a particular individual. However, because success in achieving this long-term goal requires, by definition, that the person carry out the necessary activities without assistance, persons with significant physical and/or cognitive impairments, young children who have not yet matured sufficiently to operate without assistance, and the very elderly who, even before their injuries, required help to carry out routine daily activities successfully can never hope to be remediated.

Community reentry is the third frequently promulgated long-term goal for persons who have experienced ABI. Successful community reentry assumes that the person is able to manage activities of daily living at a level that meets the standards of the particular community to which he or she is returning. This goal may require the "rehabilitated" person to manage without assistance from others. To successfully meet this goal, the person of working age must be employed, preferably in gainful work activities or, if that is not possible, at least in a protected work situation or as a volunteer. In addition, the person must be able to take advantage of the opportunities for recreation and leisure pursuits available in the immediate community. Because each community has different offerings and expectations, the abilities that are necessary for successful community reentry also differ. For example, a school-aged child returning home may not be expected to manage all the necessary activities of daily living without assistance, and an elderly person living in a retirement community may be provided with opportunities for social interactions without being required to exert any initiative.

The goal of community reentry, then, provides a directly observable measure of success or failure that takes into account not only the injured person's abilities, but also the demands of the specific community to which he or she is expected to return. Essentially, the abilities that are required to achieve successful community reentry are physical and/or cognitive in nature. At the very least, the person must be able to move about in the community without becoming lost and must be able to recall where he or she is going and why.

Unfortunately, the quality of life that a person who is recovering from ABI attains in the community and the level of satisfaction gained from work and social experiences often are given "short shrift" in evaluations of whether the goal of community reentry has been achieved successfully. Nevertheless, according to several studies (Brooks & McKinlay, 1983; McKinlay, Brooks, & Bond, 1981; Thomsen, 1984), the most frequent persisting long-term effect of ABI is the person's inability to reestablish rewarding human relationships, a condition that inevitably leads to social isolation and loneliness. This unhappy state of affairs is prevalent after the occurrence of significant brain injuries, even for persons who are regularly employed and who by every other criterion have successfully reentered the world.

A NEW PERSPECTIVE ON THE CONDITION OF INDEPENDENCE

Over the past several years, the generally accepted interpretation of *independence* as the ability to function without assistance from others has been challenged by several investigators (Banja, 1988; Condeluci & Gretz-Lasky, 1987; Prigatano, 1989). Banja (1988), in his commentary in *The Archives of Physical Medicine and Rehabilitation,* maintained that independence in the form of self-reliance may not necessarily be a satisfactory or even a desirable experience for everyone. He decried the natural but disturbing tendency of many therapists to impose their values on their "clients," and he reminded the reader that independence for a given rehabilitation consumer is not necessarily what the service provider defines it to be. In fact, outside of the rehabilitation community, most people would agree that "enlightened interdependency"—that is, relationships in which, for the most part, only reasonable demands are made on the time, effort, and psyche of the related persons and in which any benefits that accrue are shared by all—is the ideal arrangement to ensure success in marriage, family relations, friendships, business, and so forth.

The belief that independence constitutes the most inclusive and meaningful long-term goal of rehabilitation need not be abandoned, however, provided that the concept is defined in a way that is universally applicable to people with ABI regardless of their age, sex, degree and type of injury, cultural background, and personal system of values. In his commentary, Banja proposed a definition of independence that meets these criteria: "Independence is a situation wherein an individual is capable of and is encouraged to determine his or her best interests, and then can assume available measures in society to secure the satisfaction of those interests" (Banja, 1988, p. 382). In Banja's view, achieving "authentic independence" requires that the achiever have an intact sense of self:

> An authentically independent person possesses the mental powers to weigh significant life options and to choose and refuse from among these options in accordance with his or her short term and long term needs and goals. Therefore . . . the ability to formulate a concept of self that is congruent with one's abilities, needs and interests, i.e. one that is based on a realistic self assessment, is a necessary condition for functioning independently. (Banja, 1988, p. 382)

Thus, just as developing an integrated sense of self was the *sine qua non* for a child's establishing independence during early development, it also is the essential condition for a person's reestablishing independence after an ABI.

THE SELF

The concept of *self* is defined as the entire person; the union of elements including body, thoughts, sensations, emotions, and desires; and the incorporation of the lived past, the experienced present, and the anticipated future. In the words of one young woman who had experienced a moderately severe brain injury, "the self is that which makes me unique, different from you or any one else." Although the concept of self is the realization of an abstraction, it is possible to delineate its properties. In *Pattern and Growth in Personality,* Allport (1961) proposed seven properties or elements that together effectively characterize the composite "self":

1. *Bodily self:* The earliest awareness of one's body, of its mass, of the dynamic interrelationship of its component parts, and of its movements through space with and against the force of gravity, provides the cornerstone that supports the further development of a sense of self. Throughout life, the body is the reference point to which a person returns as he or she strives to comprehend whom he or she is.

2. *Self-esteem:* Awareness of power and competence begins when the child acts in a way that brings about a change in the surrounding world (e.g., by moving things, throwing things, breaking things) (Csikszentmihalyi & Rochberg-Halton, 1981). These actions constitute the child's earliest transactions (i.e., actions that affect a change both in the environment and, through feedback, in the child). From these kinds of transactions stem the beginning discriminations of "self" as distinct from other people or things. This early awareness of one's power to effect change provides the foundation for later self-esteem.

3. *Continuity of self or self-identity:* Even though, over time, continuing and often striking changes occur in a person as well as in the surrounding world, one's sense of self is ongoing. For example, when a middle-aged woman thinks of herself as she was as a child, as an adolescent, and as a young adult, she recognizes no discontinuity; she is the same person in spite of all the changes. This sense of continuity is fortunate in that the ability to make meaningful decisions in life depends both on the integrity and the stability of a person's sense of self. If the sense of self was discontinuous, a person could neither learn from past experience nor plan for the future effectively. For all practical purposes, a person's life would be defined only by the present circumstances.

4. *Extended self:* As the ability to differentiate self from the surrounding world consolidates, a young child begins to develop simple relationships with other persons, as well as with animate and inanimate objects (e.g., his or her mommy, sister, dog, teddy bear, bed). At this point in a child's development, efforts to control his or her environment begin to be actualized symbolically through newly acquired language abilities (Gardner, 1976). Throughout their lives, the relationships that children form with other people and with significant things continue to contribute to their sense of self.

5. *Self-image:* The ability to relate to others through shared symbols or abstract concepts rather than solely through concrete experiences permits children not only to be aware of themselves as entities, but also, in a rudimentary fashion, to consider what others expect of them (Gardner, 1976). The comparison of the expectations of others with his or her actual behaviors provides information that can be used by a child to begin constructing an internalized system of values. With further elaboration, this elementary system of values develops into the young person's conscience or "superego," that aspect of self that, in later life, plays a major role in delimiting the choices that are acceptable and, therefore, available to the individual.

6. *Self as "rational coper" or problem solver:* When young children become able to relate to themselves much as they are able to relate to others and are motivated to evaluate the effects of their actions upon others, they are challenged to begin to reason—that is, to

think about the what and the why of their thoughts and actions in an effort to gain greater satisfaction from their transactions with other people and things. In this way, they further enhance their self-esteem.

7. *Self as "propriate striver" or planner and goal setter:* As children gradually accumulate information about themselves and about how they relate to the surrounding world, they become able to make reasonable predictions about the nature and outcome of future transactions, to set reasonable goals, and to develop plans that, if pursued successfully, will enable them to achieve those goals. The significance of the child's developing ability to guide his or her behavior by intention cannot be overemphasized. "The most basic fact about persons is that they are not only aware of their own existence but can assume control of that existence, directing it toward certain purposes" (M. B. Smith, cited in Csikszentmihalyi & Rochberg-Halton, 1981, p. 2).

In his description of the elements that together constitute the self, Allport (1961) put little emphasis on the importance of feelings (i.e., learned emotional responses to situations, people, objects, or events). Without a doubt, however, much of who a person is can be ascertained from his or her repertoire of unique and predictable emotional responses. The generation of a feeling in a situation that formerly did not call it forth or the absence of a familiar feeling in a situation that always provoked it in the past can result in the experience of differentness or estrangement from one's sense of self. Frequently, one responds to the threatened loss with significant anxiety and/or depression.

The Evolution of the Sense of Self: A Brief Review[2]

The fundamental task of childhood and adolescence is the development of an identity or self whose qualities are acceptable to the person as well as to the significant people around him or her.

> By its very nature, mind is a slow accumulation of increasingly differentiated representations of the self at different stages of development, affected and altered to some extent by each but never erasing altogether the traces of itself at a more primitive stage of evolution. (Gardner, 1976, p. 456)

The process begins with the efforts of the very young child to differentiate himself or herself from the rest of the world. Initially, this is accomplished by actions upon the world (Witkin, Dyk, Faterson, Goodenough, & Karp, 1962). These actions are not simply movements or motions, but rather are transactions in which the child is simultaneously organizing his or her inner component parts into a unity and forming a

[2]Two books, *Cognitive and Mental Development in the First Five Years of Life: A Review of Recent Research* by P. Lichtenberg and D. G. Norton (1970) and *The Meaning of Things: Domestic Symbols and the Self* by M. Csikszentmihalyi and E. Rochberg-Halton (1981), were the primary resources for this section. These books should be consulted for additional information on the subject.

systematic relationship with things and people in the outer world (Lichtenberg & Norton, 1970).

> A child proves his or her existence as an autonomous entity by forming intentions about actions that have a clear effect on the environment. . . . These gross actions provide the clearest evidence that there is an agent capable of having an effect. (Csikszentmihalyi & Rochberg-Halton, 1981, p. 117)

Seligman (1975, p. 141) observed that "the self grows as a function of environmental responses to intentions; it develops out of feedback to acts of control." For this reason, young children are most involved with toys and other objects that can be activated by them.

Experiences that are full of pleasure and pleasantness are central to the development of an acceptable sense of self. Children behave as if much of what they do is done chiefly because it is exciting, gratifying, or fun (Murphy et al., 1962). Murphy et al. (1962) reported that children who had a wide range of pleasurable experiences were better able to find or accept a substitute activity when they became frustrated. In general, when children are exposed to challenges that are within their ranges of competence, they will construct actions that are intended to meet those challenges (Hunt, 1967). Therefore, effective development of a sense of self also requires the availability of a range of opportunities that will ensure that the child's actions will have a tangible impact on his or her world. When deprived of such opportunities through impoverished socioeconomic conditions and/or uninformed, uninterested, or overly anxious parents, a child will not thrive cognitively or emotionally. If the elements in his or her world are not responsive to the child's intentions, the child will have no feedback to help to define his or her boundaries, capabilities, or limitations (Bruner, 1961).

Studies have demonstrated that young children with parents who encourage exploration and risk taking will tend to exert control over their own behaviors better than children whose activities were more restricted (Burton, Maccoby, & Allinsmith, 1961; Mussen & Distler, 1960). These research findings were viewed by Lichtenberg and Norton (1970, p. 63) as being "consistent with the general theme that children who are enabled to develop as actors are children who adopt greater internal controls over behavior when autonomy has been established." According to these authors, the most important facets of internal control for the young child are the ability to show self-restraint and the ability to be self-critical. Undoubtedly, the more effective the internal controls that are developed by a child, the more cooperative and socially acceptable he or she becomes.

In adolescence, a new set of tasks is added to the continuing, if now less energy-consuming, efforts to control one's environment and behavior. The most significant contribution to the adolescent's evolving sense of self comes through his or her successful attempts to exert control over impulses and feelings. Csikszentmihalyi and Rochberg-Halton (1981) emphasized that the young person who continues to be dominated by feelings and desires is not yet autonomous and, unless some additional "growth" occurs, will not develop a stable and acceptable sense of self. These investigators conjecture that interactions with television, stereos, musical instruments, and performing groups are important because they provide means for teenagers to modulate their emotions, whereas their involvement in "noble" causes and their participation in action-oriented groups permit them to express their impulses in socially acceptable ways.

As adulthood approaches, emphasis shifts once again, from the process of *differentiation,* in which active involvement with persons and things defines the boundaries of the self, to one of *integration,* in which participation with other people expands the boundaries of the self. In this latter process,the individual does not give up the efforts to satisfy his or her own needs, but rather modifies the measures that are taken to satisfy those needs in order to complement the needs and intentions of others (Csikszentmihalyi & Rochberg-Halton, 1981; Witkin et al., 1962). Indeed, the defining characteristic of adulthood is the recognition of the importance of considering the intentions of others in the course of meeting one's own needs. This is a necessary condition for all successful peer relationships.

In concluding this brief review of the development of the sense of self, it is essential that one keeps in mind Gardner's (1976, p. 456) admonition: "Our sense of self, in other words, is never wholly adult, never wholly mature, established and finished."

Traumatic Brain Injury and the Loss of the Sense of Self

Every traumatic brain injury, even those designated as minor, causes some disruption in the person's sense of self. The extent of disruption can range from a feeling of differentness or estrangement to a total disconnection from the person's past identity. Although the reasons for the change may escape them, most people who have experienced a brain injury are quite aware that something profoundly disturbing has occurred. One of the most frequent and plaintive of the complaints presented to a rehabilitation staff is, "I'm different; I can't explain how, but I'm not who I was before my injury." From the family, one hears, "She's just not my daughter; she's a different person since the accident."

From a narrow neuropsychological perspective, the problems that are experienced following a traumatic brain injury can be explained by the person's lowered level of arousal, increased distractibility, reduced ability to comprehend and to recall verbal information, impaired integration and use of information about personal and extrapersonal space, reduced ability to deal with abstract concepts and to control the expression of emotion, limited ability to anticipate future needs, and the impaired ability to recognize and to respond appropriately to the subtle signals involved in every human transaction. (See Chapters 3, 4, and 5 of this book for additional information.)

Although an in-depth knowledge of the neuropsychological ramifications of brain injury is necessary to comprehend the impact of such injuries on a person's sense of self, it is not sufficient. Perhaps the effects of a brain injury can be comprehended best in terms of the person's ongoing efforts to cope with his or her world: "The symptoms that follow brain damage do not stem from the missing or damaged part, but, rather from the organism's attempt to adapt, cope and survive" (Stein, 1988, p. 34). Stein (1988) emphasized the importance of recognizing the context in which the brain injury occurs and in which rehabilitation activities are undertaken. The "context" refers not only to environmental influences, both physical and social, but also to characteristics of the injured person, such as age at the time of injury, intelligence and educational levels, medical history, and present state of health. All of this information is important to understanding why people respond to their brain injuries in the way that they do.

Making matters more complicated, every brain injury in a child or adolescent occurs in a context of rapid development, a circumstance that must be taken into account if one is to comprehend the extent of the disturbance caused by the injury. The long-held belief that children are more resistant to the long-term effects of a brain injury is true only for certain abilities, and then only if the injury has occurred within a limited time period during the course of development. Even then, however, because an area of the brain is required to do more than it was designed to do, the functions ordinarily carried on in that area are compromised. For example, language functions may be spared after an early injury to the left hemisphere (up to 14 months of age) because of activation of potential language sites in the right hemisphere. However, as a side effect, certain other functions that normally depend on the integrity of the right hemisphere, such as visual spatial orientation and the ability to manage constructional tasks, usually suffer (Kennard, 1936; Levere, Gray-Silva, & Levere, 1988; Milner, 1974; Woods & Teuber, 1963). In addition, the true extent of the cognitive deficits and behavioral disturbances that can result from brain injuries in children may become apparent only in later years when the demands made on them by the outside world are more complex and stringent (Bowman, Blau, & Reich, 1974; Grattan & Eslinger, 1991).

THE FAMILY OF A PERSON WITH ABI

Although the presence of a supportive and understanding family generally adds significantly to an injured person's potential for successful rehabilitation, in the case of children and adolescents who, under the best of circumstances, still are dependent on others for much of their care, the influence of family is of unparalleled importance. Under the circumstances, persons with brain damage are very likely to conform to the expectations of family members on whom they depend:

> To the extent that his family treats the brain damaged individual as a functioning individual, he is likely to react as before; to the extent that he is treated as bizarre, unaware, stupid or half dead, he is all too likely to conform (perhaps literally) to their expectations. (Gardner, 1976, p. 439)

Unfortunately, family members rarely experience and communicate an attitude of calm rationality, especially when a child has been injured. In every case, the impact of a brain injury is "infectious," affecting not only the injured person, but also family members, close friends, teachers, and employers, disrupting each person's own sense of self as well as their relatedness to each other and, very often, to the community at large, thereby evoking the threat of social isolation with concomitant anxiety and depression (Brooks, 1991; Livingston, Brooks, & Bond, 1985; Thomsen, 1984). Any threat to the integrity of the family constellation is felt most intensely by its youngest members, especially a son or daughter who has had a brain injury. Several studies have shown that children whose parents have difficulty differentiating themselves from their injured offspring are faced with overwhelming obstacles as they strive to reassert their individuality and autonomy. In this situation, children with ABIs may have an increased risk of developing a psychiatric illness (G. Brown, 1982, cited in Rutter, 1982, p. 100; Rutter, Chadwick, & Shaffer, 1983).

THE LATE SEQUELAE OF BRAIN INJURY: IMPAIRED HUMAN RELATIONS

The short-term effects of brain injury stem from the physical and cognitive impairments, but the longer term effects, those that tend to be most disabling, are the result of personality changes and behavioral dyscontrol (Hpay, 1971, cited in Weddell, Oddy, & Jenkins, 1980). In a follow-up study of severe blunt head injury, McKinlay et al. (1981) learned from the reports of relatives that physical and language difficulties almost invariably declined in frequency over time, while over half of the descriptive items that referred to emotional distress were reported with increasing frequency at consecutive interviews. In a 2-year follow-up study, Weddell et al. (1980) found that people who had experienced severe brain injuries had fewer friends, made and received fewer visits, and dated less frequently than did a comparison group of persons without brain injuries. Indeed, it is not an exaggeration to state that the most frequent and most distressing long-term residue of ABI is loneliness.

The deficits in social effectiveness that become evident after brain injury can be understood best as the product of unconsummated or ineffectual transactions between the person with an ABI and many aspects of his or her physical and social worlds. Over time, without suitable interventions, the gulf separating the injured person from his or her community, family, and self grows so wide that it cannot be bridged (Pollack, 1989).

The process that culminates in social isolation begins immediately after the brain injury when the injured person is unconscious or, although conscious, has a significantly reduced level of arousal. During this time, no meaningful transactions with things or people occur. Later in the postinjury course, transactions are limited by the injured person's cognitive deficits, physical impairments, and emotional dyscontrol, as well as by the constraining environments first of the general hospital and later of the rehabilitation facility. Even after discharge from the rehabilitation hospital, a recovering person's opportunities for rewarding social transactions are limited by the "need" for frequent and time-consuming outpatient visits. During this time, often as long as 1 or 2 years, the gulf between the young person with a brain injury and his or her peers is ever widening. Friends are moving into the future, traveling along their respective developmental pathways, while those with brain injuries remain bogged down in their pasts, striving to move ahead to the present. Without a repertoire of shared social experiences, the usual transitions from one developmental stage to the next (e.g., graduating from school, obtaining employment, dating, marriage, parenthood) fail to occur, and the distance between the injured person and the rest of society grows until, if nothing is done to alter the course, that person finds himself or herself essentially alone and, lacking the necessary feedback, unable to reestablish his or her identity.

During their brief experience in neuropsychiatry, a group of second-year medical students felt the devastation brought about by a serious brain injury. One student, when asked to imagine what it must be like to have a traumatic brain injury, responded, "It must be like listening to the door on your past slam shut before the door to your future opens." Another student, asked to imagine what might go through the mind of a person who had been injured 10 years previously, wrote, "To most people loneliness is a word used to describe a transient feeling that one gets when he is the only familiar person in a crowded room; but, true loneliness is the feeling that one gets being in a room filled with people, not knowing one's self."

THE CHARACTERISTICS OF AN EFFECTIVE BRAIN INJURY REHABILITATION PROGRAM

Unlike brain injury in an adult, which fragments the person's more or less completely, though never finally, formed sense of self, brain injury in a child or adolescent not only disrupts the already existing self but also undermines its ongoing development. The child, then, has the twofold job of "catching up" to where he or she was before the injury while "keeping up" with the increasingly complex cognitive and psychosocial demands that are made on every maturing person.

Knowledge of the "normal" developmental processes can provide reference points for the brain injury rehabilitation team. This is not to advocate the slavish re–working through of each developmental stage, an approach to brain injury rehabilitation that appears to have few if any practical consequences, but rather to note those modifiable aspects of the physical and social universe that originally provided impetus, support, and guidance to the normally developing child so that those elements can be reproduced in the service of children and adolescents who have acquired brain injuries.

Primarily, an effective brain injury rehabilitation program is one that *enhances the injured person's potential for reestablishing an acceptable sense of self*. Some key points regarding the development and/or evaluation of a brain injury rehabilitation program for children or adolescents are listed below.

1. *The Program Must Be Responsive*. Most investigators who have followed the course of human psychosocial development agree that individuals cannot become "persons" if they are unable to cultivate their goals and therefore the shape that their selves will take (Banja, 1988; Lichtenberg & Norton, 1970). For this reason, a brain injury rehabilitation program must be responsive to the intentions of its clients: "An appropriate rehabilitation environment is one in which the individual's intentions can be fulfilled through appropriate actions which produce desired effects. These effects cannot be realized in an environment which provides little or no accommodation" (Banja, 1988, p. 382). A rehabilitation program that cannot or will not be modified or can be modified only to a limited degree in response to the intentions of its child and adolescent clients is not a program that promotes the reestablishing of a sense of self.

Growth in cognitive ability, which parallels the developing sense of self, is fostered by environments that offer and encourage a wide range of activities and challenges. Contrariwise, cognitive growth is restricted in an environment that presents limited challenges and few opportunities for consideration and choice (Hess & Shipman, 1965).

To further the injured child's efforts to reintegrate, treatment team members must interrelate closely and communicate effectively in order to work together toward the same overall goal. Splintering or dividing authority and responsibility for the several aspects of the rehabilitation process or for the several aspects of the injured child or adolescent (e.g., his or her physical self, social self, intellectual self, and emotional self) only supports continued disorganization in that child or adolescent client.

2. *The Rehabilitation Environment Should Be as Familiar and Natural as Possible*. Relearning occurs most effectively in a situation where the original motivation for that piece of learning can be reinstated.

> The brain damaged person is different. Though (often) able to deal with thoughts and ideas, he can do so only in a concrete way; he may, indeed, successfully exercise almost any skill but only if the need for that skill arises in a natural situation. Where he fails is in drawing voluntarily on his arsenal of skills, deliberately deciding what should be displayed, under what circumstances, and in what manner. (Gardner, 1976, p. 425)

To be most effective, rehabilitation activities should be embedded in meaningful, familiar tasks or projects. Engaging in rehabilitation activities that are disconnected from real life makes it difficult for the child or adolescent to see the relevance of the task to his or her life. It denies to the child a sense of personal accomplishment and the ability to evaluate the quality of his or her performance except as the evaluation is provided by another person, the therapist. One annoyed client put it this way: "I hate, 'It's in your best interest.'" Certainly for any child, brain injured or not, and indeed for many adolescents and adults, the ability to sustain attention is limited when they feel forced to attend to tasks against their present intentions in order to secure some future goal (Lichtenberg & Norton, 1970).

At this point, it is important to recall that, during normal development, cognition gradually emerged out of actions that were directed by the child at the people and things that made up his or her world. After brain injury, the growing independence of the child's cognitive processes from sensory and motor activities is compromised. Once again, cognition is closely interrelated with action, and pediatric brain injury rehabilitation programs must accommodate to this fact.

3. *The Rehabilitation Team Should Value and Utilize Group Activities.*

> The child is not only an actor, he is a person. One aspect of being a person is to have separateness, uniqueness, individuality or more generally speaking, autonomy. . . . A second aspect of being a person is to ever and always be socially related. Persons exist by their relations with other humans. (Lichtenberg & Norton, 1970, p. 40)

The fact is, people work and play in groups. To operate effectively within this natural state of human affairs, the child or adolescent who has sustained a brain injury must learn to communicate competently and must develop internal controls in areas of behavior such as resistance to impulse, moderation in the expression of emotion, and ability to delay gratification.

4. *Play and Pleasurable Social and Recreational Activities Are Essential.* In contrast to the enthusiastic emphasis placed on the value of health and educational activities in the rehabilitation program, the inclusion of recreational and social activities as essential elements has met with much resistance. However, as Lichtenberg and Norton (1970, p. 20) pointed out, "Pleasure and playfulness are central not only to normal growth, but equally to the reversal or correction of abnormality." The importance of pleasurable endeavors also was noted by Prigatano (1989, p. 430): "The experience of play helps patients reinstitute or reestablish a sense that whoever they were as human beings before their injury they continue to be despite the presence of brain damage."

Professionals who work with children often say, "The work of childhood is play," for this is the medium that provides children with the greatest opportunities to exert control over objects, situations, and persons. After a serious brain injury, persisting recreational interests and abilities may be the only surviving links to the injured person's preinjury self. A young man who was injured at the age of 16 could recall no details of his past life except that he had played a competent game of pool, an ability that had survived the ravages of brain injury well enough to enable him to defeat his therapist in a game despite moderate right hemiparesis. His obvious pleasure upon winning was as much a response to the recognition of a familiar part of himself as it was a response to his victory over his therapist.

5. *Family Members Must Be Involved in the Rehabilitation Process.* The therapeutic team must be concerned not only with fostering growth in the child or adolescent with ABI but also with encouraging an ongoing "healthy" affiliation by parents, siblings, and friends, not only in reference to the injured young person but also in respect to each other and to the community at large. It is crucial that parents, family members, and friends continue their active participation in the life of the injured child because, in large part, a child's sense of self is derived through successful transactions with these individuals. All too often, the parents of children or adolescents with ABI find themselves confronted by new needs and new demands from their offspring that they can neither comprehend nor fulfill (Doernberg, Rosen, & Walker, 1969). In these circumstances, parents may feel guilty and responsible for events over which they have little or no control. They may, then, direct their frustration inwardly and become self-punitive, insulating themselves from the support of sympathetic others, or they may direct their anger outwardly, seeking others to blame for their pain and attacking therapy staff for not being able to make their child whole again. If, for any of these reasons, parents are unable to interact productively with their children and with the members of the therapy team, all therapeutic efforts will fail (McNeill, 1966).

6. *Assets Rather than Liabilities Should Be Emphasized.* The philosophy of the rehabilitation program should emphasize the worth of the young person's preserved assets rather than concentrating on the residual deficits. In the process of rehabilitation, therapy should start from the central core of the most intact abilities and move outward to involve more complex and diverse experiences in a variety of environments. This process can be likened to tossing a pebble into a lake and watching the developing ripples form ever-widening concentric circles.

Everyone concerned with the rehabilitation process—client, family, friends, and therapists—needs to recognize that the work of reestablishing a sense of self is neverending and that, in the final analysis, the eventual success or failure of the effort lies far more in the hands of the client and of his or her family than it does in the hands of the staff.

7. *The Treatment Team Has Important Functions.* It is essential for therapists to recognize that, without the active involvement and cooperation of their young clients and their clients' families, nothing they can do will prevail. In the treatment situation, therapists are limited in their ability to "tune into" their clients with ABI because the brains of these clients function differently from those of other clients. For this reason, the therapy staff must depend on the client and members of the client's family to provide sufficient information, both verbal and nonverbal, so that the staff can come to truly know the injured child and can comprehend the awful situation into which he or she has been thrown. The personality that existed prior to the young person's injury plays a vital role in determining how postinjury problems will be expressed. According to Gardner (1976, p. 438), "It is this personality which must come to grips with and comprehend the nature of the brain damage."

It also is vital that therapists formulate goals, not only in terms of the client's anticipated levels of competence, but also in terms of the character of the environment, both physical and social, in which those competencies will be expressed. Therapists must accept the responsibility for poor treatment outcomes when the failures are caused by their inculcating new and inappropriate cultural and socioeconomic values and expectations in their child and adolescent clients. The potential for this therapist-led assault on a young person's already disrupted sense of self is very real, especially because the therapist is working with individuals who have experienced catastrophic injuries and who, as a result, are psychologically devastated and, consequently, exceptionally vulnerable.

Finally, therapists must be prepared to allow and to accept failures both by their clients and by themselves because the processes of recovery after ABI must include the dignity of risk, "for without the possibility of failure the injured person lacks true independence and the mark of his or her humanity, the right to choose for good or ill" (Dybwad, 1964).

CONCLUSION

Acquired brain injuries of any significance disrupt the injured person's sense of self. This is an especially difficult situation for children and adolescents who are in a period of rapid social development. To be successful, rehabilitation efforts, including special education, must be designed to assist the young person with an ABI to reestablish an acceptable identity.

REFERENCES

Allport, G. W. (1961). *Pattern and growth in personality.* New York: Holt, Reinhart and Winston.

Banja, J. D. (1988). Independence and rehabilitation: A philosophic perspective. *Archives of Physical Medicine and Rehabilitation, 69,* 381–422.

Bowman, K. M., Blau, A., & Reich, R. (1974). Psychiatric states following head injury in children. In G. H. Feiring (Ed.), *Brock's injuries of the brain and spinal cord and their coverings.* New York: Springer.

Brooks, D. N. (1991). The head injured family. *Journal of Clinical and Experimental Neuropsychology, 13,* 155–188.

Brooks, D. N., & McKinlay, W. (1983). Personality and behavioral change after severe blunt head injury—A relative's view. *Journal of Neurology, Neurosurgery and Psychiatry, 46,* 336–344.

Bruner, J. (1961). The cognitive consequences of early sensory deprivation. In P. Solomon (Ed.), *Sensory deprivation* (pp. 195–207). Cambridge, MA: Harvard University Press.

Burton, R. V., Maccoby, E. E., & Allinsmith, W. (1961). Antecedents of resistance to temptation in four year old children. *Child Development, 32,* 689–711.

Condeluci, A., & Gretz-Lasky, S. (1987). Social rule valorization: A model for community re-entry. *Journal of Head Trauma Rehabilitation, 2,* 49–56.

Csikszentmihalyi, M., & Rochberg-Halton, E. (1981). *The meaning of things: Domestic symbols and the self.* New York: Cambridge University Press.

Doernberg, N., Rosen, B., & Walker, R. T. (1969). *A home training program for young mentally ill children.* Brooklyn, NY: League School for Seriously Disturbed Children.

Dybwad, G. (1964). *Challenges in mental retardation.* New York: Columbia University Press.

Gardner, H. (1976). *The shattered mind: The person after brain damage.* New York: Knopf.

Grattan, L. M., & Eslinger, P. J. (1991). Frontal lobe damage in children and adults: A comparative review. *Developmental Neuropsychology, 7,* 283–326.

Hess, R. D., & Shipman, V. C. (1965). Early experience and the socialization of cognitive modes in children. *Child Development, 36,* 869–886.

Hunt, J. M. (1967). How children develop intellectually. In H. W. Bernard & W. C. Huckins (Eds.), *Readings in human development.* Boston: Allyn & Bacon.

Kennard, M. A. (1936). Age and other factors in motor recovery from precentral lesions in monkeys. *American Journal of Physiology, 1,* 138–146.

Levere, N. D., Gray-Silva, S., & Levere, T. E. (1988). Infant brain injury: The benefit of relocation and the cost of crowding. In S. Finger, T. E. Levere, C. R. Almi, & D. G. Stein (Eds.), *Brain injury and recovery: Theoretical and controversial issues.* New York: Plenum Press.

Lichtenberg, P., & Norton, D. G. (1970). *Cognitive and mental development in the first five years of life: A review of recent research.* Rockville, MD: National Institutes of Mental Health.

Livingston, M. G., Brooks, D. N., & Bond, M. R. (1985). Patient outcome in the year following severe head injury and relatives' psychiatric and social functioning. *Journal of Neurology, Neurosurgery and Psychiatry, 48,* 876–881.

McKinlay, W. W., Brooks, D. N., & Bond, M. R. (1981). The short term outcome of severe blunt head injury as reported by the relatives of the injured person. *Journal of Neurology, Neurosurgery and Psychiatry, 44,* 527–533.

McNeill, D. (1966). Developmental psycholinguistics. In F. Smith & G. A. Miller (Eds.), *The genesis of language* (pp. 15–84). Cambridge, MA: Massachusetts Institute of Technology Press.

Milner, B. (1974). Hemispheric specialization: Scope and limits. In F. O. Schmitt & F. G. Worden (Eds.), *The neurosciences: Third study program.* Cambridge, MA: MIT Press.

Murphy, L. B., & Collaborators. (1962). *The widening world of childhood: Paths toward mastery.* New York: Basic Books.

Mussen, P., & Distler, L. (1960). Child rearing antecedents of masculine identification in kindergarten boys. *Child Development, 31,* 89–100.

Pollack, I. W. (1989). Traumatic brain injury and the rehabilitation process: A psychiatric perspective. In D. W. Ellis & A. Christensen (Eds.), *Neuropsychological treatment after brain injury* (pp. 105–125). Boston: Kluwer Academic Publishers.

Prigatano, G. P. (1989). Work, love and play after brain injury. *Bulletin of the Menninger Clinic, 53,* 414–431.

Rutter, M. (Ed.). (1982). *Developmental neuropsychiatry:* New York: Guilford Press.

Rutter, M., Chadwick, O., & Shaffer, D. (1983). Head injury. In M. Rutter (Ed.), *Developmental neuropsychiatry* (pp. 83–111). New York: Guilford Press.

Seligman, M. E. P. (1975). *Helplessness: On depression, development and death.* New York: Freeman.

Stein, D. G. (1988). In pursuit of new strategies for understanding recovery from brain damage: Problems and perspectives. In T. Boll & B. Bryant (Eds.), *Clinical neuropsychology and brain function.* Washington, DC: American Psychological Association.

Thomsen, I. V. (1984). Late outcome of very severe head trauma: A 10–15 year second follow-up. *Journal of Neurology, Neurosurgery and Psychiatry, 47,* 260–268.

Weddell, M., Oddy, M., & Jenkins, D. (1980). Social adjustment after rehabilitation: A two year follow up of patients with severe brain injury. *Psychological Medicine, 10,* 257–263.

Witkin, H. A., Dyk, R. B., Faterson, H. F., Goodenough, D. R., & Karp, S. A. (1962). *Psychological differentiation: Studies of development.* New York: Wiley.

Woods, B. T., & Teuber, H. L. (1963). Early onset of complementary specialization of cerebral hemispheres in man. *Transactions of the American Neurological Association, 98,* 113–117.

CHAPTER 11

Psychotherapeutic Interventions for Mild Traumatic Brain Injury

WILLIAM F. FREY

The National Head Injury Foundation has taken over 12 years from its inception to clearly establish the necessity for treatment programs that specialize in treating acquired brain injury. Although the majority of this work has focused on prevention and programming for severe and moderately severe cases of traumatic brain injury (TBI), approximately 75% of reported TBIs fall in the mildly severe category (Kraus et al., 1984; Langfitt & Gennarelli, 1982). Clear distinctions among the TBI classifications on the acquired brain injury spectrum from mild to moderate to severe have not been established (see Chapter 1); however, the "major" TBIs, usually classified as severe, are at the far end of the TBI spectrum from the "mild" TBIs. Although a student who has experienced a "major" TBI is rarely placed in an educational setting without previous rehabilitation programming, once a child is placed in a school setting, an educator or allied professional, such as a counselor or psychologist, may be unable to determine the student's classification of TBI based on his or her current level of functioning. For example, a child classified at the time of injury as having experienced a moderate TBI may be experiencing difficulties in the classroom similar to those of children classified as having had a mild TBI. Usually, this discrepancy is due to the time that has elapsed since the child experienced the injury and the individual differences in each child's recovery curve. Educators knowledgeable about the classification range of TBIs may be better able than others to understand the nature of the initial injury and the general recovery expectations.

In this chapter, I focus on those students whose behavior, either at the time of injury or as a result of time elapsed, appears to have the characteristics of a mild TBI. At the time of injury, an individual is considered to have a mild TBI if he or she has experienced a trauma to the brain that is usually but not necessarily associated with a brief loss of consciousness (less than 1 hour) and/or amnesia and with little impairment of sensory processing. Mild TBI is most often associated with a concussion-type injury. The functional consequences of this injury are often both transient and long term and observed in physiological, cognitive, and behavioral spheres. As this definition implies, there is much room for variation in the experience of a mild TBI.

Healing interventions occur at both formal and informal levels during interpersonal interactions with students who have experienced a concussive injury, depending on the circumstances of the contact. The purpose of this chapter is to prepare educators and related service providers to be therapeutic in dealing with children, adolescents, and young adults who have experienced a mild traumatic brain injury.

Ample documentation supports the significant impact that mild TBIs may have on an individual's adaptation to life events in both the short and the long term (Alves, Colohan, O'Leary, Rimel, & Jane, 1986; Boll & Barth, 1983; Doronzo, 1990; Klonoff, 1971; Lehr & Savage, 1990; Rimel, Giordani, Barth, Boll, & Jane, 1981). These studies have reviewed problems related to cognitive functioning and development and school performance (Klonoff, 1971; Lehr, 1990; Lehr & Savage, 1990), difficulties in resuming daily activities and employment (Rimel et al., 1981), and posttraumatic symptoms that include headaches, dizziness, memory problems, weakness, nausea, numbness, double vision, and hearing difficulties (Alves et al., 1986). Persistent psychological problems have also been noted over the months following mild TBI. These emotional and motivational difficulties are expressed in terms of irritability, anxiety, depression, behavioral problems, apathy, easy fatigability, and distractibility (Binder, 1986; Rimel et al., 1981; Schoenhuber, Gentilini, & Orlando, 1988), and the extent to which they disrupt a child's or adult's life appears related to preexisting risk factors (Dikmen, McLean, & Temkin, 1986; Farmer, Singer, Mellits, Hall, & Charney, 1987; Fletcher, Ewing-Cobbs, Miner, Levin, & Eisenberg, 1990; Levin et al., 1987). Understanding the individual and social consequences of mild TBI provides an accurate perception of the acquired brain injury spectrum and underscores the impact these injuries have on public health. This understanding can be particularly valuable to the teacher who must be alert and sensitive to the demands that a mild TBI places on a student's ability to perform.

An irony exists in regard to the public's and, in many cases, the health care professionals' response to this type of traumatic brain injury. Although mild TBI is pandemic, it is not an obvious disorder. Herein lies the contradiction regarding the low intervention priority assigned to mild TBI. Boll (1983) highlighted this dilemma when he referred to mild TBI in children as a "quiet disorder" that is "out of sight but not out of mind" with the potential to cause serious long-term adjustment difficulties. Boll suggested that, until the risk factors associated with these injuries are clearly understood by pediatricians, educators, and significant others who have contact with these children, developmental problems may ensue that may never be traced to their source. Thus, psychological problems presenting in clinical and other settings that are manifestations of mild TBI sequelae (consequences or symptoms) are often treated without emphasis on programming that takes the unique nature of this injury into account (Bennett, 1989).

MEDICAL BACKGROUND

From the point of view of an educator as a healing facilitator, it is instructive to understand the events consequent to a mild TBI. This helps the teacher who has not experienced this type of injury relate to a child or adolescent with empathy and some empirical basis for the intervention efforts. The following composite case examples are provided to introduce a variety of the various experiences associated with mild TBIs as well as observations regarding intervention.

An adolescent comments that he could not make class the past few days because he experienced a "silly" or scary accident over the previous weekend. Inquiry reveals that the student was in a car accident in which no one was hurt "too badly—just a few scrapes and a bump on the head." Another student describes a window suddenly releasing and hitting her on the head with great force, causing her to "see stars" or "white dots" and to be "out of it" for a few minutes, which necessitated a visit to the hospital emergency room. Students also relate accident accounts in which they hit a tree while skiing, sledding, or snowmobiling and were "out" for a moment, felt "woozy," and their "head hurt." They report being released from the hospital feeling "okay" after a few hours of observation, but seem to have trouble remembering events surrounding the accident and specifics about the emergency visit. The dull headache and difficulty concentrating began a few hours or days after discharge from the hospital. Other common activities, such as riding a bicycle or horse, "fooling around," and contact sports, are often mentioned as reasons for head injury and the disruption of responsibilities associated with school.

In many cases of TBI, the following progression of events follows the accident: The parent or adult in charge is concerned that the injury may be serious and that the dizziness, the difficulty remembering the exact details of the accident, and the tender swelling on the head are not merely temporary and, according to the child, "nothing to worry about." Particular concern is expressed if the accident caused cuts and bruises and if the child had been unconscious. This concern quite appropriately leads the adult to take the child to the emergency medical care facility, where the adult seeks some comfort and reassurance. Obtaining this comfort, however, may be elusive. Results of studies by Casey, Ludwig, and McCormick (1986, 1987) indicated that parents' perception of the injury's severity or of their own inability to estimate the severity of the injury (parental anxiety) relates to functional problems for some children after the emergency room visit, even if the injury was considered mild and attempts at preventive education and direction were employed. The problems noted by these authors involved continued visits to medical personnel and a high rate of preschool, grade school, and middle school absenteeism.

Emergency medical facilities vary in how they assess TBIs, depending on the protocols of each facility (Colohan, Dacey, Alves, Rimel, & Jane, 1986). At present, many hospital protocols do not address the differences in a child's or adolescent's presentation after a mild TBI compared with that of an adult, and investigation is necessary to determine the sequence of symptom emergence. An important observation is that children often do not lose consciousness (Levine, 1988). In most cases, hospital protocols require the following information: what the injuries are, how they occurred, and how serious they are judged to be from a medical viewpoint. The hospital may require brief neurologic and mental status examinations, as well as the use of computerized tomography, electroencephalography, and other relevant medical interventions. In the most innovative settings, neurological, neuropsychological, and psychological evaluations designed specifically to assess mild TBI are completed (Ruff, Levin, & Marshall, 1986). Such settings recommend evaluation measures to address the frequent complaints of headaches, double vision, dizziness, and hearing problems, as well as the often encountered reluctant or measured speaking (Ruff et al., 1986). A good medical history is taken to assess vulnerability due to preexisting conditions that could have negatively disposed the child to a more serious condition than expected from the event reported.

Based on this data, the physician in charge makes a determination of the diagnosis and its apparent severity and formulates a treatment intervention. If the child or adolescent seems to have no medical complications present or expected, he or she is released to go home with precautionary instructions, which often include a list of postconcussion signs that may indicate possible complicating problems (see Figure 11.1). However, sending home instructions may be inadequate. Casey et al. (1987) found that instructions alone did not significantly diminish parents' anxiety regarding their child's vulnerability. Saunders, Cota, and Barton (1986) found that follow-up instructions were poorly remembered by those parents and guardians who attempted to follow the suggestions (only 38% recalled as many as half the items).

If the person has medical complications, such as lacerations and possible sprained or broken bones, these injuries are dealt with immediately. If the medical staff suspects or if the history or assessment techniques indicate that continued or more serious sequelae may present, the individual is hospitalized for continuing treatment, observation, and assessment. Following mild TBI, the child or adolescent may be in and out of consciousness and have difficulty remembering events or their chronology. These posttraumatic memory and orientation problems are of short duration, usually only a few minutes to an hour, although the amnesia of events immediately before and after the accident may remain. A number of the postconcussive physical symptoms, such as ringing in the ears, headaches, and double vision, also may occur for a day or two.

In-hospital screening for the severity of the TBI is performed. In ideal programs, this screening includes the periodic administration of the *Glascow Coma Scale* (GCS) or equivalent comparative measure of changes in consciousness or sensory processing. The GCS provides a score that aids professionals in determining the relative degree of severity of the TBI by evaluating the patient's eye opening, verbal, and motor responses over time (Teasdale & Jennett, 1974). An individual with a GCS of 13 to 15 (0–15 scale) would fall in the mild TBI range; the lower the score on this scale, the more severe the injury. In contrast, an average individual without prior history of an aquired brain injury and in good physical health would receive a 15 on the GCS.

When the injury to the brain is found not to be obviously medically severe and the data confirm a diagnosis of concussion or mild TBI, the patient's hospital stay is generally short (24–48 hours), and the patient is discharged to home, without specific programming in most instances. According to Gronwall (1986), however, patients do better if the hospital staff makes more effort to help them. In her review of the Auckland Hospital rehabilitation program in New Zealand, she found that, with early management of mild TBI cases, in which reassurance, education, support, and regular monitoring of progress were provided, patients' reports of "feeling better" were facilitated and appeared to aid in prevention of postconcussive psychological problems.

In the general hospital setting, however, the child, parents, and significant others must deal with the consequences of the mild TBI discharge situation in their unique ways. As noted in the study by Casey et al. (1987), even specific reassurance instructions provided limited help to anxious significant others. Confidence levels regarding prognosis vary, and the child with the injury, family, and significant others usually are armed with only a little healthy denial as the episode comes to a conclusion and all

Emergency Department Discharge Instructions for Head Injury

EXPLANATION:

Head injuries, as a rule, cause no permanent harm. However, a small possibility exists that bleeding may occur within the skull causing pressure on the brain. Signs that this may be happening are often subtle and are often noticed by those who know the patient well and can watch him or her closely. Skull X-rays are of little use in most cases in predicting which patients will have this bleeding. In addition, they are expensive and involve some radiation exposure. Therefore, the doctor may decide that they are not indicated, and elect not to take them.

Recommendations:

1. Headache with occasional vomiting (once or twice) may occur, particularly with young children. However, headache of increasing severity and frequent forceful vomiting should prompt a return to the emergency department.
2. Also return to the emergency department if the patient becomes confused (dizzy and unsteady on feet), shows weakness of facial muscles and/or arms and legs, or has a change in personality or a convulsion.
3. The patient may be allowed to sleep; however, he or she should be awakened every 2 hours and asked who and where he or she is. If the person cannot be awakened or cannot answer these questions correctly, he or she should be brought back to the emergency department to be rechecked.
4. Keep the patient's diet light; no heavy meals should be given. Try liquids at first, then gradually increase the diet over the next 24 hours.
5. Do not give any pain medication stronger than aspirin or Tylenol as they may cover up those symptoms listed above. An ice bag may help the pain.
6. If X-rays are taken, they will be interpreted by the doctor on duty. A radiologist will review these films within 24 hours, and any discrepancy will be reported to you. Please leave a phone number by which you can be reached.
7. Follow up with Dr. ______________________ in ___________ days.
8. Give medication as directed on the prescription.
9. I anticipate the patient should be able to return to work on _____________ with the following restrictions: ______________________________.
   If the patient is unable to return on that date, he or she should be rechecked by the private physician to extend the authorized disability.

I understand my instructions for medications and follow-up care.

______________________	______________________
Caregiver's Signature	*Physician Treating Patient*
______________________	______________________
Date and Time	*Nurse*

Figure 11.1. Typical discharge instructions for patients with traumatic brain injuries.

parties attempt to return to normal. At this point in time, the child resumes educational pursuits and the therapeutic interventions of a teacher often begin.

THE NATURE OF A MILD TRAUMATIC BRAIN INJURY

As noted at the beginning of this chapter and in Chapter 1, a consistent diagnostic classification of a person's degree or type of traumatic brain injury is not available. Even current neurological assessment measures, such as electroencephalography, computerized tomography, and magnetic resonance imaging, do not enable physicians to determine a precise categorization of the extent of the brain injury. This is particularly true of the concussive injuries, because of the technological limitations of these measures' sensitivity to the microscopic damage associated with mild brain injury. As a result of this serious limitation, researchers have proposed working definitions of mild TBI based on cases similar to those in the examples above that differ in detail regarding loss of consciousness or the length of time of unconsciousness and the posttraumatic amnesia period (Binder, 1986; Doronzo, 1990; Hugenholtz, Stuss, Stethem, & Richard, 1988). In practice, the research definitions may be distilled to adequately describe a mild TBI for an educator's purposes as long as the limitations discussed along with the definition stated early in the chapter are noted. Equally important to understanding the events surrounding a mild TBI is an understanding of what actually happens to the brain as a result of the injury.

This type of trauma to the brain is best explained as an "acceleration or deceleration" injury associated with a concussion that is mild (transient neurologic changes without a loss of consciousness) or classic (temporary neurologic dysfunction with a short-duration coma of less than 6 hours) (Gennarelli, 1986). The "seeing stars" phenomenon and the "ding" experiences associated with athletic injuries are examples of mild concussions (Gennarelli, 1986). Accidents involving transportation activities often account for the more severe mild TBIs and are typical of Gennarelli's (1986) definition of a classic concussion.

In mild and classic concussions, the damage to the brain may be focal (localized) or diffuse (spread across areas of the brain) or both, and subsequent dysfunction appears related to the type of damage incurred (Kay, 1986). In a focal concussion in which the individual "sees stars," the damage may be localized to the visual cortex and the transient symptom experience is minimal (Gennarelli, 1986). In a classic concussion, as a result of a motor vehicle accident, the damage to the brain is often both focal, involving the frontal and temporal lobes, and diffuse, initiating strain or stretching forces on neurons across the brain. Kay (1986) noted that these frontotemporal lesions are due to the acceleration of the brain into the bony surfaces of the skull in areas of the brain that appear to be involved in executive functions, such as the process of planning and organizing activities, as well as memory and learning, attention and concentration, and emotional self-monitoring.

Diffuse axonal damage to the cerebral cortex and to the lower and upper brain stem areas (see Chapter 2), as a result of the mechanical strains incurred in the vehicular accident, has been hypothesized as the underlying neurological explanation of the nonspecific physical, behavioral, and cognitive deficits associated with mild TBI (Gennarelli, 1986; Ommaya & Gennarelli, 1974; Oppenheimer, 1968). Gennarelli

(1986) suggested that the shear and strain damage caused by acceleration-type injuries to the axons in the brain is minimal structurally; however, changes in the electrical properties of the neurons affected may account for the transient concussive symptoms. Other researchers have suggested that, while the axonal damage is minimal, it is still significant and may be cumulative, placing individuals at risk of poor recovery from future brain injuries (Binder, 1986; Hugenholtz et al., 1988). Most interesting in this regard is the study of the effects of mild TBI in sports, in which it becomes clear that a series of injuries to the brain, even if slight individually, place an athlete at risk for significant consequences (see Barth et al., 1989, for review).

The diffuse damage that occurs in individuals following mild TBI appears to underlie the general cognitive deficits evident in their execution of tasks requiring efficient information processing (Hugenholtz et al., 1988). Examples of these deficits include an inability to attend to large amounts of detailed information in timed situations, concrete and inflexible thinking, and difficulties in making multiple simultaneous decisions (Kay, 1986). Kay (1986) cautioned that it is difficult to determine the type of brain damage involved in a specific mild TBI because both diffuse and focal damage are often present and the nature of the observable deficits reflects this interaction. Recognition of the extent of actual brain damage in mild TBIs is never easy, so the educator must be cautious in accepting estimates from professionals in either direction. In this regard, diagnosis of a concussion may take on many different meanings to different professionals. Because most concussive injuries are not life threatening, a physician may tell a teacher an injury is really nothing to worry about; however, the teacher may be concerned when a major shift occurs in a child's performance or attendance. The potential exists for miscommunication between professionals when it comes to using and interpreting diagnostic labels.

Even in an educational setting, a child with a mild TBI may be given a diagnostic label as a result of the medical interventions received. This can be a psychiatric diagnosis of a symptom complex or mild TBI syndrome established for the *Diagnostic and Statistical Manual of Mental Disorders, Third Edition–Revised* (DSM-III-R) (American Psychiatric Association, 1987). Most teachers are familiar with this coding system because mental health providers rely upon the DSM-III-R to label a child's disorder so that treatment planning can be developed. Usually in the case of mild TBI, the diagnosis sounds ominous: organic personality syndrome (change of personality due to brain trauma) or organic mental syndrome not otherwise stated (maladaptive symptoms without specific organic evidence). Educators need to remember that a diagnosis is simply descriptive language used by the medical community and is not intended to suggest severity or prognosis. In addition, some children may be labeled as having a conduct disorder or a dysthymic disorder (low-grade depression for the purposes of this text) because the impact of their mild TBI is undervalued. Such a diagnosis reflects the lack of awareness of the psychological impact of mild TBI by the medical and mental health fields. Inappropriate diagnoses may also be a reflection of the scientific controversy surrounding the distinction between the primary physiological and cognitive deficits associated with mild TBI and the secondary "personality" and affective symptoms noted. Educators also need to remember that labels (especially psychiatric diagnoses) are not always reliably determined (see Kirk & Kutchins, 1992).

As stated earlier, the primary sequelae of postconcussive brain injury—headaches, weakness, dizziness, vision and hearing problems, and memory difficulties—are well documented (Alves et al., 1986). These deficits are generally considered the result of direct damage to the brain and, thus, organic in origin. The secondary sequelae of mild TBI are also observed in many individuals, as those close to a head injury victim often report that the person is "just not the same since the injury." In addition to this anecdotal data, emotional volatility, anxiety responses to life events, and depression are the most frequently reported symptoms noted in research settings (Alves et al., 1986; Boll & Barth, 1983; Rimel et al., 1981; Schoenhuber & Gentilini, 1988). These personality changes and affective symptoms are not easily related to the direct physical damage to the brain and can occur in situations where there is no presumed head injury. Without the specific organic evidence to support the psychological morbidity noted after a mild TBI, the secondary sequelae are often attributed to a "mental disorder" unrelated to the injury. That is why some children seen in the classroom setting are labeled as having behavioral disorders with no consideration that the effects may be due to an earlier mild TBI. This mental disorder frame of reference biases motivational expectations, carries a further social stigma, and fosters etiologic assumptions that confound research, understanding, and treatment of mild TBI. It is understandable that the teaching professional is left with little guidance as to intervention techniques with students who have experienced TBI.

The difficulties that this lack of diagnostic precision in the DSM-III-R creates for an individual's recovery from a mild TBI are also well documented clinically (Bennett, 1989; Boll & Barth, 1983; O'Hara, 1988). O'Hara (1988) observed that many individuals are treated for problems related to the mild TBI with non–brain injury etiologic assumptions that misdirect intervention strategies. Often these interventions disregard the physiological and cognitive limitations inherent in concussive brain injury that may exacerbate the mild TBI symptoms or, in the worst case, create adjustment problems to the treatment itself (Bennett, 1989; O'Hara, 1988).

In the future, as the neuropathology of mild TBI is established, neurological and neuropsychological assessment techniques can be fine-tuned and aid in the discrimination of which symptoms of mild TBI are directly related to brain damage and which symptoms are consequential adjustment strategies based on an individual's preinjury organizational makeup (i.e., personality). The information accumulated from these conceptualizations and research technologies will provide the foundation necessary to understand the nuances of behavior change noted in a child or adolescent who has sustained a mild TBI.

THE PSYCHOLOGICAL FRAMEWORK

Therapeutic psychological intervention with children and adolescents who have experienced a mild traumatic brain injury can be conceptualized as an experience in which the communication of information occurs in a safe setting that fosters the child's ability to be healthy as he or she adjusts to the injury. A critical aspect of this intervention effort is the understanding that children and adolescents must be viewed in an evolving life span or developmental context. This developmental perspective presupposes a past set of given characteristics and behavior patterns and a future based upon the present interaction of life events with this history. In addition, as Valsiner (1989) stressed, the social system or culture maintains as the primary shaping mechanism of the child's personality. Thus, a child's awareness (necessarily incomplete) of the physiological, cognitive, and behavioral underpinnings and expressions of his or her organizational makeup or personality is represented in the child's "sense of self" (Kay, 1986). A person's sense of self is basically who the person thinks he or she is, and what he or she feels capable of doing. Based on this sense of self, the child adapts to (or negotiates, in an ecological sense) his or her sensory and social world.

Because children and adolescents are dynamic and changing as they go through rapid physical and psychological growth, the impact of a mild TBI has the potential to significantly modify and shape the child's sense of self. In contrast, an adult's matured awareness of the factors that make up his or her sense of self is expected to be more complete, which would suggest that adjustment to a mild TBI requires modification to a more elaborate and coalesced organizational makeup. In children, deficits from a mild TBI in regard to key developmental milestones have no comparative basis but are simply incorporated for better or worse into the child's self-perception. As a result, children's resiliency to life's events may be affected and place them at risk as they develop at a primary structural level. In addition, a child's "self-organization" patterns (Sroufe, 1988), dependent upon primary child–caregiver relationships, may be altered, which could in turn modify future development and attachment experiences and possibly place the child at risk socially. Substantial arguments are espoused by Bowlby (1988) and Ainsworth (1989) in regard to developmental vulnerability in children due to difficult or poor early attachment experiences.

As Kay (1986) suggested, this sense of self is a constant feedback construct or self-impression that is both shaped by and shaping a person's adaptive existence. Psychological intervention using the sense of self construct appears warranted. Pollack (see Chapter 10 of this text) emphasizes the unifying nature that addressing this sense of self has in the treatment of TBI victims of all ages and across the spectrum of severity. For an adult with a mild TBI, this means treatment is focused on the individual's awareness of the subtle changes in his or her functioning after the injury to address the disorientation of the sense of self. In a child with a mild TBI, the treatment must be prospective. Intervention must anticipate and prepare for developmental events to assist the child's integration of sensory and cognitive information and to provide a "secure base" (as noted by Ainsworth, 1973, in regard to infant–mother attachments and used in this context to include caregiver relationships) for a positive orientation of his or her sense of self. A key to successful adjustment appears to be the facilitation of an individual's orientation regarding his or her sense of self by providing to the individual and significant others basic information about the specific consequences of the mild TBI (Bennett, 1989; Kay, 1986; O'Hara, 1988).

The need for general educational and specific intervention strategies that address the developmental consequences of mild TBI in children and adolescents has been well documented (Lehr & Savage, 1990). Based on the understanding of children's developmental needs, programs can be designed to improve the resiliency of children who have experienced a minor brain injury. However, caution and careful analysis are required to ensure that the progression from the historic stance that presupposes no significant impact of mild TBI does not quickly lead to tacit acceptance that such an injury is always a core explanation of subsequent behaviors. In this regard, studies that have addressed this concern have screened children and adults for preexisting (premorbid) behavioral characteristics, such as prior psychiatric diagnosis, child abuse, and previous head injury, before inclusion in head injury recovery programs (Fletcher et al., 1990; Levin et al., 1987). These studies indicate that prognosis from the primary sequelae of mild TBI in the less at-risk subjects is good. Therefore, education regarding mild TBI sequelae appears critical for prevention and rehabilitation programs; however, care must be taken to ensure that the myth of "nothing is wrong" is not replaced by the myth of a "mild traumatic brain injury label" that becomes a self-fulfilling limit.

Whereas the determination of the impact of a mild TBI or posttraumatic syndrome is established in adults (Alves et al., 1986; Binder, 1986; Davidoff, Laibstain, Kessler, & Mark, 1988; Kay, 1986), much additional information is required to clarify the impact for children and adolescents. In particular, the psychological consequences of adjustment to mild TBI must be studied to assess qualitatively what happens over time to a child's or adolescent's structural world.

With this in mind, psychological intervention by the educator must be sensitive to the possible posttraumatic syndrome of mild TBI in the cases that present, as well as alert to the clues that may aid in the child's eventual adjustment. When a child's or adolescent's head injury is accompanied by a more physically obvious injury, such as lacerations or broken bones, the concerned observer (teacher or significant other) may "sense" changes in behavior and allow a "grace" period. If the head injury has no noticeable physical signs, then any behavior change may be incorporated into a modified "premorbid" synthesis and the injured person is judged accordingly. In the absence of a diagnostic screening device, this bias in one observer may conflict with that of another significant observer, often dependent upon the context. This noncongruence often results in referral of the person to specialized services, which in themselves have a potential for impact on adjustment. Thus, screening at the time of a concussive injury at the emergency care facility or doctor's office should include a routine follow-up visit with the family physician. A perfunctory follow-up examination is required for many minor illnesses of childhood. For example, in the case of an ear infection, in which an antibiotic is usually prescribed in an emergency context, a follow-up screening is arranged to ensure that the consequences of the infection have not damaged a child's hearing apparatus. This follow-up examination is a natural expectable precautionary procedure and, as a result, is considered part of "having had the illness." A standardized follow-up routine would maintain the primary care physician's alertness to possible sequelae of the mild TBI in a sequential and documentable fashion. This follow-up, in turn, could result in immediate psychological intervention in appropriate cases (Farmer et al., 1987) and facilitate the notification of teaching personnel so they can respond in a helpful fashion.

Furthermore, screening efforts for mild TBI consequences in the school, home, and eventually the clinical setting need to be operationalized. At present, the spectrum of assessment and treatment for a mild TBI appears variable (Levine, 1988). In addition, treatment strategies and their value are typically individual. Most comprehensive programs, such as the program outlined by Ruff et al. (1986), support the need for a multidiscipline team assessment procedure. The team approach to assessment can ensure that the physiological (medical symptoms), behavioral, and cognitive–affective components, as well as the social or support network (systems) factors, are addressed.

Although the scientific process adds to the understanding of mild TBI across dimensions, the "front-line" caregivers—parents or significant others, teachers, and medical and allied professionals—must deal with each case with scientific creativity. As in most therapy or rehabilitation endeavors, guesses must be made that can be tested to determine their positive, neutral, or negative impact. Again, accurate assessment over time is critical diagnostically, but also is not as readily available to the front-line caregivers in as many areas as hoped. Regardless of the difficulty, emphasis must be placed on grounding treatment or programming on solid medical, neuropsychological, and other objective assessments. In this context, a teacher who requests readministration of standard assessment tools (e.g., a reading skills test) is demonstrating scientific creativity that may provide excellent pre- and postinjury data for comparison. The distinctions between the reaction to a physical trauma with significant neural or structural damage and the reaction to the threat of damage or affective interaction with a life event may be moot in terms of recovery, but are the essence of sensitive, educated strategy building. Teachers especially appreciate having a benchmark on which to ground programming.

Because of the uncharted areas of intervention and understanding of mild TBI, frustration in the support network either at home or at school may impair recovery efforts. Therefore, educators need some structure to rely upon when being scientifically creative about helping a child in the classroom. Novack, Roth, and Boll (1988) proposed a scientifically creative, practical, and commonsense set of strategies for immediate intervention with cases of mild TBI. The key elements of their program include (a) education regarding mild TBI to all concerned parties, (b) thinking exercises using graded cognitive stimulation for the TBI patient, (c) individual stress management training, (d) individual counseling in more complicated cases of secondary sequelae, (e) group discussions for TBI patients, and (f) an individual physical activity schedule. This clearly defined program leaves room for flexible application of services based on individual differences and setting or support opportunities. The application of an extension of this program to the social system (school, home, job, or recreational setting) of a child with a mild TBI may help members of the support network find and define their place in the recovery effort. It also ensures a coordinated application of creative planning by each member in the support network. As noted earlier in this chapter and elsewhere in this book, the severe head injuries demand such organization in their programming. Equally important is an understanding that the potential for success using such a program in response to mild TBI may be significant (Novack et al., 1988).

With a general treatment strategy for mild TBI outlined (e.g., that provided by Novack et al., 1988), the individual parts of the support network can establish their goals regarding recovery and stay within the comfort of their expertise and responsibility. Clearly, the intervention provided by each support service element will improve as public awareness regarding mild TBI is raised and the response to the immediate injury is taken into account in an informed and standardized manner. Emergency protocols that are educational, are comforting, and provide follow-up expectations for routine medical evaluation, symptom focus, or specialized neurological assessment, start the recovery program as a directed process. From this point, significant caregivers and the child or adolescent with the mild TBI can develop an integrated support network.

HANDLING THE PRESENTING PROBLEMS

Teachers, parents, coaches, school psychologists, school nurses, counselors, the psychotherapist or primary care physician, and other significant persons in the child's or adolescent's support network may each become a resource for treating an individual with a mild TBI. In many cases, each resource person must gather information that will be useful in future contacts with this student; however, each person also needs to understand the limits of what he or she can offer the individual. The responsibility for recovery is the individual's, and support efforts, which vary in degree based on the person's age, are designed primarily to facilitate this recovery.

In all cases, some basic listening skills and interview techniques can help educators interact confidently with a student and make decisions about referral or level of involvement (Misenti, 1992). Rogers (1961, 1965) outlined the basic elements of a good counseling interview, which I have adapted for this chapter. The person-centered elements include a genuineness about interest in the student, acceptance of the student's problem, and an accurate understanding of his or her experience of the problem. Clearly, these interpersonal elements are standard for most student–teacher encounters, but they have particular relevance to children or adolescents with mild TBI. Because their complaints have often been dismissed as trivial or bothersome, the teacher's efforts may be the first step to getting the child validation for their difficulties.

Educators can apply these person-centered skills by following this checklist:

1. Be confident in your ability to help.
2. Be alert to the symptoms of a mild TBI.
3. Be structured and clear in your student contact.
4. Be genuine.
5. Be a good listener.
6. Be empathetic.
7. Be aware of boundaries.

Each of these items is discussed more fully in the following paragraphs.

Be confident in your ability to help. Your basic teaching skills can transfer to this situation and help you respond effectively to the student that has experienced a mild traumatic brain injury. By reviewing the beginning of this chapter, you will be familiar with the experiences a student and family has been through and will find relating reasonably easy. This is enough to get you started in your intervention and can be a reference for your subsequent interactions. You need to be a sensitive educator, not an expert on mild TBI.

Be alert to the symptoms of a mild traumatic brain injury. Review Table 11.1, which outlines the primary and secondary sequelae of mild TBI, so you can compare your observations of a student and bring this information to a principal, supervisor, or school counselor for an informed discussion of the situation.

Be structured and clear in your student contact. For example, set aside a specific time to talk with the student who may have a problem or complaint that may be related to mild TBI. This scheduling structure frames a positive and predictable relationship and demonstrates your genuineness or concern. If the student approaches you at an inconvenient time, as often happens, use your standard salutatory response, briefly acknowledge his or her need, and reference the symptom reflectively, but find a convenient time to follow up on the student's difficulty.

Example:

Student: Excuse me, Ms. Wright, but I can't seem to concentrate in lab because of all the noise. It makes my headache worse.

Teacher: Elizabeth, I wasn't aware you were having difficulty with the noise. Let's set up a time to talk about this. Can you see me at 12:15 today?

TABLE 11.1. Mild Traumatic Brain Injury Symptoms

SUBJECTIVE (individual self-reports)	***OBJECTIVE observer)***
Physical or Sensory*	**Physical or Sensory***
Headache	Physical signs of an accident or injury
Hypersensitivity to noise	• Scrapes
Dizziness	• Bruises
Blurred vision	• Lacerations
Double vision	
Ringing or hissing in the ears	
Hearing problems	
Numbness	
Weakness	
Cognitive–Affective	**Cognitive–Affective–Behavioral**
Memory problems*	Memory difficulties
Concentration difficulty*	Inability to follow chained or complex directions
Anxiety†	Shift in learning curve (academic performance)
Depression†	Attention difficulties
Concern regarding symptoms†	Mood shifts
Frustration†	Abstract reasoning difficulties
	Poor judgment
	Complaints about physical and/or sensory symptoms
Behavioral	**Behavioral**
Loss of interest in activities†	Irritability
Sleep difficulties*	Fatigability
Reaction time slowed*	Apathetic behavior
	Communication difficulties (speech and nonverbal)
	Absenteeism (school, job)
	Performance difficulties in work setting, home, or school responsibilities

*Primary sequela.
†Secondary sequela.

To ensure clarity and avoid any memory difficulties, write down the time and place for the student.

Be genuine. This simply means that you need to be sure you want to be helpful. The key to being genuine is to know yourself as you interact with the student. No one benefits if you are grudgingly giving your time, or if you feel overworked, or if you frankly never liked this student. If you do not want to be helpful, be responsible and have the student see someone else. You will have done better by this student by being honest with yourself. Knowing your limits is healthy, not inadequate. If you do choose to be helpful and possibly therapeutic, then do some genuine self-monitoring. Aid your interactions by being aware of your time constraints, responsibilities, and feelings about spending time with this student.

Be a good listener. This requires being open to listen. Let the student tell you what is on his or her mind before you assume you know. Work on the nonverbal aspects of listening, such as good eye contact, appropriate posture, and congruent facial expression. Do not smile if you are not happy and try not to look angry if you are only concerned. In addition, remember that listening to a student's problems may elicit a helping response that makes you want to attempt to "fix" whatever you suspect is wrong. Although solution-offering may work well at a later time in your interaction with a student, it is not appropriate early in the interaction. The child or adolescent with a mild TBI needs to let you know some very "disruptive" personal experiences and perceptions, and your job is to aid him or her in expressing these concerns within whatever limits he or she is comfortable. Some students may have experienced psychologically traumatic events in addition to their injury, and catharsis or encouragement to express details about their experience may help you know what happened but be negatively painful to the students. Using the example from above, as Elizabeth relates her sensitivity to noise and notes she has had a continual dull headache since her accident, the teacher needs to listen and ask whether she experiences any other difficulties in the class. If Elizabeth describes other problems, the teacher should mentally note these to help in assessing her needs. If other students or the teacher has problems with the noise in the lab, the teacher may be tempted to deal with this issue directly; however, in the case of mild TBI, hypersensitivity to such stimuli is diagnostic, so it helps to be patient and continue the inquiry. Nevertheless, the teacher needs to be sure not to dismiss the student prematurely.

Be empathetic. Making a reflective statement to the student exhibits accurate understanding. For example, Elizabeth's teacher might say, "I have trouble concentrating in that lab sometimes, but I sense the noise is really bothersome for you. What's it like for you in the lab?" Although many people have mild TBI symptoms, the quality or degree, or better the phenomenological experience, is not easily comparable.

Be aware of boundaries. If a student shares details of his "silly" accident and the responses he has gotten, you may be angry at the insensitivity or ignorance of friends, physicians, or other teachers. It is important that you refrain from judgment and stay focused on the student. You can educate the other professionals in a more effective context. If the student discusses personal problems that involve matters outside your classroom, remember that you are his teacher, not his therapist, so do not go further than your good judgment dictates. The best way to know if the student is stretching your boundaries is to monitor how you are feeling. If the student's problems seem overwhelming, they probably are and they cannot be solved by you in a meeting with the student. If you are unsure of what you should do to help a student, ask your principal or supervisor for advice. If you learn that Joseph needs a ride to the doctor's office and no one is picking him up, should you give him a ride? There is no clear answer to this question because it depends upon many factors specific to your situation. Have you talked to the parents about this situation? Is this an acceptable procedure at your school? Might this help set up the expectation that you will always be there to bail him out?

In summary, the checklist allows you to get to know your student better and helps rebuild the foundation for this student's recovery of his or her sense of self. This sharing depends on a thread of trust you build by listening carefully. If you are successful, the student may feel pleased that someone is taking his or her injury experience seriously. From this point, you can proceed to the next level of intervention.

As you become aware that a student demonstrates the characteristic pattern of mild TBI (see Table 11.1), it would be helpful to learn who has given the student information regarding her symptoms. Often a very direct approach works best: "Li-Shing, it sounds as if you have had these problems since you had that accident when you hit your head. Has anyone else talked to you about this injury?" Again, listen attentively and refrain from providing too much helpful information before you know who has talked to Li-Shing and what they may have told her. If the information provided indicates little or no knowledge of the possible effects of mild TBI, it is best to Go Back To Start. This means contacting the family to get the student evaluated medically, provide education to the student and significant caregivers, organize the support network, and develop a treatment plan that includes all concerned parties. Referral to a primary care physician can begin the medical evaluation and education about mild TBI. The basic education about the physical symptoms of mild TBI should come from a primary care physician, and a parent or significant other should be with the student when he or she receives information about the injury. If you must Go Back To Start with this student, you might say, "Li-Shing, I think you would be wise to check with your parents because some of the problems you are experiencing may be related to the concussion you had. Although this sounds like a mild injury, your doctor can make sure that is what you are dealing with. If you like, I'll speak to your parents about my concerns."

At this point in time, information about mild TBI is just beginning to filter to many professionals (Gade & Young, 1984; McSherry, 1989). You should be prepared to explain your understanding of mild TBI to a medical practitioner so that he or she may feel comfortable asking you about your knowledge if he or she is not familiar with current data. Your presentation may reinforce the medical practitioner's knowledge and result in a useful interchange between professionals. If you experience resistance, however, contact the National Head Injury Foundation for the number of your local chapter of this organization. The foundation can provide information about mild TBI to the physician or suggest professionals in your area who are familiar with this type of brain injury.

Provided the primary physician is knowledgeable of mild TBI and the diagnosis is accurate, the student should be given the essential information about the prognosis and treatment strategies. If referrals are necessary, the physician can assist this process. In addition, the support team at school can be mobilized to assess the student's needs and develop programming in a similar fashion to that described for other individuals who have experienced a TBI (see Lehr, 1990, for review). Here again, there is room for creative and flexible programming that is sensitive to the subtleties of mild TBI. Li-Shing's presentation was a worst case situation in which little initial education and treatment had been offered. In other cases, a student may have had sufficient education about the injury and you can use your creativity to develop planning that helps the student adjust while he or she recovers. Review the six suggested intervention strategies of Novack et al. (1988) listed near the end of the previous section and consider what you and your contacts might be able to do. Here are some examples: Your creative intervention efforts might include education of the support network, such as other teachers. You might suggest that the student follow an involved recipe for a pastry or dinner as part of a graded cognitive exercise. Training in deep muscle relaxation and a deep breathing exercise (diaphragmatic breathing) for stress reduction may be helpful. A doctor-approved exercise program may be devised to improve cardiovascular efficiency and overall health maintenance. In cases that you suspect present secondary sequelae to the mild TBI, such as depression and/or anxiety symptoms, your listening interviews with the student should make a referral to a mental health specialist clear. In such cases, a consultation with the guidance department or equivalent personnel director can aid your efforts. Be specific about your suspicions of mild TBI symptoms and let the referral source evaluate your observations and make a diagnosis. In summary, this interpersonal process—the basic ability to know your student—is both helpful in making an appropriate referral choice and useful in determining how you will implement compensatory planning.

In more complex cases, a referral for individual therapy may be necessary. Individual therapy is often helpful and necessary for those children and adolescents who are at risk. These are students with a history of school difficulties prior to the accident or a support system that has its own serious problems (e.g., parents who abuse alcohol). Although individual therapy may be helpful for students who have developed difficulties (secondary sequelae) because their support system lacked knowledge of mild TBI consequences, they are not considered at risk. In these cases, the Go Back To Start instructions apply, and supportive work with parents or significant others by a psychotherapist may be most helpful (Bennett, 1989; Novack et al., 1988; O'Hara, 1988). The Go Back To Start suggestion is equally applicable in the at-risk cases, but often does not work because a significant other or caregiver may not follow through with the recommendations.

The more complicated cases of adjustment to mild TBI involve the presentation of secondary sequelae unresponsive to the Go Back To Start formula. In these cases, affective dysfunction and/or behavioral acting out has become the primary focus. As stated above, these cases should be referred for individual or family psychotherapy. At this point in time, the child or adolescent has not profitted sufficiently from information sharing and the basic support efforts provided. "Something more" is needed but not easily ascertained. In addition, the symptoms are now psychiatric and must be considered significantly impairing and possibly life threatening. Understanding how the mental health professional approaches this type of referral may help school personnel and other support team members to tailor their efforts to complement treatment.

Establishing trust and rapport with the client is a given in psychotherapy; however, in cases where many months or years have passed since TBI, this first step is often difficult. In these cases, the therapy relationship usually develops tentatively because the injury itself seems to have lost significance and become overshadowed by the difficulties the child's support system has experienced. In spite of resistance issues, the therapist works to align with the child or adolescent and the support system. As this occurs, risk factors present and diagnostic alternatives are considered. Baseline behavioral and cognitive measures are obtained to aid in diagnosis and guide the direction of therapy.

Psychotherapists are categorized according to their theoretical bias (psychodynamic, Gestalt, existential, behavioral, eclectic [combined theoretical approaches], and numerous others). It is critical that the child or adolescent who has experienced a mild TBI be seen by a therapist who evaluates the person across the physiological, behavioral, and cognitive dimensions and in a social or system context. Most psychotherapists are integrative, regardless of their orientation, and may be helpful; however, those therapists with experience in dealing with acquired brain injury are often most aware of the physiological and psychosocial issues that must be addressed in conjunction with the secondary sequelae of mild TBI.

Evaluation of the physiological, behavioral, and cognitive deficits of mild TBI can best be accomplished using measures that are attentive to the subtle performance shifts in an individual's functioning in daily activities. Psychotherapists often have this assessment completed adjunctively, which provides the therapist with an objective and specialized evaluation by personnel from convergent disciplines (as recommended by Ruff et al., 1986). As noted, the primary care physician and other medical specialists help provide the initial assessment of primary mild TBI symptoms. A neuropsychological evaluation designed to tap mild TBI sequelae can provide the baseline of an individual's functional and cognitive abilities (Barth et al., 1983). The assessment information can be used to formulate treatment plans that can address specific problems in the school and other settings. In addition, the evaluation may be repeated over time (from 6 months to many years postbaseline) to provide progress estimates.

Inasmuch as evaluation of mild TBI requires attention to the subtle differences in an individual's functioning in daily activities, the neuropsychological data regarding reaction time, memory capabilities, and information processing efficiency provide only the assessment foundation. Behavioral data that can be related to the individual's pre- and postinjury organizational and interpersonal style must be gathered by the therapist and interpreted in the context of the current presenting problems. Interviews with significant others and those individuals working with a child may be helpful in providing this information. Quite specific questions regarding behavior tendencies are answered by using in vivo (real-life) trials focused on social skills and physical abilities. In Chapter 8, Ann Deaton outlines clearly the contributions of the behavioral focus. This information can help ground neuropsychological findings and become the basis for coordinated case management and therapy intervention.

The psychotherapist's focus in working with a child or adolescent is split between tracking outcome and monitoring the process of the interpersonal relationship. The assessment and goal setting are key to the outcome emphasis and are reflected in developmental progress and deficit remediation in the individual or symptoms, respectively. The process factors are nonspecific and involve motivational and emotional issues inherent in the therapist–child or therapist–support system relationships. Both the outcome and the process emphases in psychotherapy provide the balance required to deal with the issues associated with secondary sequelae to the mild traumatic brain injury.

Throughout the therapy experience, the therapist is addressing the "something more" that is required to help this child or adolescent recover or gain an oriented sense of self. In some cases, this may mean dealing with the variations of the child's resistance to a support team's recovery plans. Often, an at-risk individual requires an understanding of the complexity of his or her organizational approach to interpersonal relationships (Sroufe, 1988). A therapeutic stance must be maintained to utilize this person's style of interacting and work within its limits if the support team's efforts and recommendations are to be carried out. In other cases, depressive or anxiety symptoms (with no apparent physiological cause) must be interpreted to determine their meaningfulness to the individual in his or her social world. Compulsive or impulsive habits and addictive behaviors often interfere with recovery planning in adolescents and should be addressed independently. In many cases, these difficulties may be sufficient reasons for the emergence of secondary sequelae after the mild TBI.

Bennett (1989) stressed that therapy with individuals who are diagnosed with mild TBI must be accomplished with an understanding that neurological etiology is sufficient to account for presenting symptoms. The therapist must be sensitive to the intervention modality (e.g., a behavioral or cognitive emphasis) chosen with an individual who has experienced a mild TBI. This intervention decision is similar to that required in cases of severe and more easily documented brain injury. An example cited by Bennett (1989) that highlights the importance of the correct choice of therapy modality involves the "mis"-application of insight-oriented therapy. In certain situations, insight-oriented therapy for even a mild TBI may cause distress in the therapy encounter (on the part of both the therapist and the individual) because the basic cognitive structures necessary to process such abstract information are not available (Bennett, 1989). The frustration resulting in not assuming a neurological limiting factor has been hypothesized to precipitate secondary sequelae symptoms (Davidoff et al., 1988).

In mild TBI therapy cases, family, friends, and school personnel may find the assumption of neurological limitations to be unacceptable or unrecognizable because the child or adolescent appears fine (Boll, 1983). This dilemma is not new to the therapist or to the treatment of any disorder of the mind. Creditability for one's symptoms appears to obtain only after a physiological cause has been demonstrated. To complicate matters, controversy continues to exist in the professional community in regard to the cause of secondary sequelae of mild TBI. The question remains unanswered as to whether the injury itself may have such a psychologically perturbing influence on an individual's functional ability without the presence of prior risk factors (Davidoff et al., 1988). It is helpful to consider that at-risk children also have symtomatology associated with attention deficit hyperactivity disorder (ADHD), substance abuse, anxiety, and depression, all of which may have biological or neurophysiological substrates that are not entirely documented. Again, these at-risk individuals may have characteristics similar to those of persons with mild TBI except in motivational or emotional output. However, both the mild TBI victim and the at-risk person are assumed to have willful control over life choices because their psychological difficulties cannot be clearly traced to some acceptable "sickness." The implicit assumption is that the individuals are using an average "intact" biological system in a nonadaptive fashion. This assumption leads family and friends to the conclusion that nothing is really "wrong" with the individual other than the frustrating style of behavior, a paradox not easily explained. This denial by friends and family may prompt healthy defensive strategies on the part of the individual with a mild TBI (or even ADHD), but is just as likely to exacerbate problems (Slater, 1989). Clearly, understanding the physiological, behavioral, cognitive–affective, and social strengths and limitations of each individual, regardless of the inability to assuredly determine his or her brain's or system's "intactness," seems basic to creative and scientific application of treatment.

A psychotherapist must work with an understanding that change must represent an internal organizational realignment on the individual's part. The change may be conceptualized as cognitive restructuring or compensatory neurological change or both. In this way, the therapist can sensitize the family and friends to the nature of the injury and the healthy role they can play in the recovering process.

The process of psychotherapy with children and adolescents designated as at risk who also have sustained a mild TBI with secondary sequelae anticipates generalization of relationship building from therapy session to the child's social world. Each child can be seen as actively pursuing an organizational style in reference to his or her world that continues the development of self (Sroufe, 1988) while accommodating mild TBI sequelae. Individual psychotherapy must be aimed at facilitating this accommodation with realistic and sensitive feedback about the injury and recovery potential (Kay, 1986; Slater, 1989).

An example of dealing sensitively with feedback in the therapy process, and in the educational setting as well, involves communication within the child's support system. Often-asked questions in family sessions are "Is Ray's avoidance of his close friends due to the injury or merely a stage he's going through?" and "Where do the brain injury problems and the old personality traits begin and end?" In reference to both questions, if neuropsychological data are available, a professional can compare the child's performance levels with standard norms and get an idea of what impact a similar impairment might have on the average child. Thus, a cognitive deficit may inhibit Ray's ability to be around his close friends because his sense of self in reference to tracking a conversation is shaken. An educator might use Ray's previous schoolwork and the results of readministered tests for similar comparisons. As a rule, the symptoms present can be used to make logical deductions. For example, if Ray complains of double vision and no longer wants to play baseball, which he used to love, it is sensible to assume with reasonable probability that the double vision is the reason for his seeming avoidance of his friends rather than a "deep" psychological problem. He merely needs to be asked if this is the case. In reference to the second question, a teacher may be in a much better position to see a change in a child's approach to situations than is a therapist new to the case. When most people use the term *personality,* they are actually referring to *temperament* (more enduring qualities with less specific definitions, such as "He is shy," "She is aggressive"). When an individual is under stress, which includes having a TBI, temperament characteristics may be exaggerated. Ray, for instance, may use his coping traits or defensive styles or habits to a greater degree than is comfortable for those around him. Thus, he may be his usual avoidant self, but the injury is making these characteristics stand out. Ray, however, may not feel that he is exaggerating his behaviors, which is the distressing result of the mild TBI. Ray may be aware that his sense of self is not right, but not see the relationship to his behavior.

Because these questions cannot be answered easily, therapy must focus on "here-and-now" issues. The history of Ray's friendships is not as critical as the meaningfulness of his behavior to the family system at present. Therapy addresses this issue as a dynamic within Ray's interpersonal system and allows the development of solutions that encourage healthy development of his sense of self. Family members are encouraged to discuss and relate how they would like to interact with Ray and then engage in those activities. Follow-up discussion of the experiences is incorporated into the next set of interactions. In a school setting, work with peers in group interactions, such as social activities or team sports, might be helpful to the child's here-and-now therapy. This work should translate into improved peer relationships and allow for outcome strategies using social skills training if necessary. Experience with mild TBI cases suggests that therapy must focus on the child as emerging and in transition. An integrative approach, as proposed by Thorne (1968), which uses a multifactorial, psychodynamic, and developmental understanding of the core ego organization as the building block for successful interpersonal functioning, may assist the child's adjustment strategies. The child with a mild TBI may remain at risk if reactions to his or her deficits reflect a negation of "who" the child is or, more basically, disrupt the attachment feedback. This then presents a vulnerability–resiliency imbalance in which the major shaping relationships, including peers and institutions, decrease the probability of the healthy development of self.

In summary, quality of life may be a valuable objective in the most severe head injuries, but the expectation for children and adolescents after mild TBI is a return to perceived preinjury levels of functioning. There are few guarantees in this regard, however, and changes in the child after any injury, and mild head injury specifically, disrupt the family or support system (Farmer et al., 1987). The psychotherapy encounter is designed to compensate for this disruption when the stress on the system and child have exceeded their adaptive limits. Finally, the psychotherapist and boundaries of psychotherapy represent a potentially powerful ongoing relationship with a constant support figure (the therapist) over many years of the child's development. The number of sessions may be spaced according to the needs of the child or support system, but the bond transcends the time intervals. This relationship is not unique to therapy and often occurs in educational settings as the result of intervention with sensitive, knowledgeable, and caring teachers.

The outcome of all therapeutically inspired psychological intervention must necessarily be measured by success in deficit reduction or goal achievement, with the value of the interpersonal constancy provided by the process of treatment related to outcome but noted in the child's comfort with his or her sense of self. The educator has been therapeutic when the student has that sense of self and can focus on his or her academic and social life for the rest of the semester or year.

CONCLUSION

Educators must realize that mild TBIs have the potential to be disruptive and have sequelae that must be addressed (Boll, 1983). These injuries have been overshadowed by more severe injuries because mild TBIs are difficult to document medically, they show good improvement over time, and their classification as "mild" is often misinterpreted to mean of passing consequence. How fortunate a student is in adjusting to the consequences of a mild TBI depends on the nature and number of previous TBIs, as well as factors related to the type of support network available. The purpose of this chapter has been to help educators and allied school personnel understand the important therapeutic role they can play in helping a student regain his or her sense of self after a mild traumatic brain injury. By understanding the symptoms of a mild TBI, the use of basic interpersonal skills, and the creative application of intervention strategies, the educator can mimic the work of the professional therapist and play a significant role in minimizing the impact of this type of brain injury.

REFERENCES

Ainsworth, M. D. S. (1973). The development of infant–mother attachment. In B. Caldwell & H. Ricciuti (Eds.), *Review of child development research* (Vol. 3). Chicago: University of Chicago Press.

Ainsworth, M. D. S. (1989). Attachments beyond infancy. *American Psychologist, 44,* 709–716.

Alves, W. M., Colohan, A. R. T., O'Leary, T. J., Rimel, R. W., & Jane, J. A. (1986).

Understanding post-traumatic symptoms after minor head injury. *Journal of Head Trauma Rehabilitation, 1*(2), 1–12.
American Psychiatric Association. (1987). *Diagnostic and statistical manual of mental disorders* (3rd. ed., rev.). Washington, DC: Author.
Barth, J. T., Alves, W. M., Ryan, T. V., Macciocchi, S. N., Rimel, R. W., Jane, J. A., & Nelson, W. E. (1989). Mild head injury in sports: Neuropsychological sequelae and recovery of function. In H. S. Levin, H. M. Eisenberg, & A. L. Benton (Eds.), *Mild head injury* (pp. 257–275). New York: Oxford University Press.
Barth, J. T., Macciocchi, S. N., Giordani, B., Rimel, R., Jane, J. A., & Boll, T. J. (1983). Neuropsychological sequelae of minor head injury. *Neurosurgery, 13,* 529–533.
Bennett, T. L. (1989). Individual psychotherapy and minor head injury. *Cognitive Rehabilitation, 7*(5), 20–25.
Binder, L. M. (1986). Persisting symptoms after mild head injury: A review of the postconcussive syndrome. *Journal of Clinical and Experimental Neuropsychology, 8,* 323–346.
Boll, T. J. (1983). Mild traumatic brain injury in children—Out of sight but not out of mind. *Journal of Clinical Child Psychology, 12*(1), 74–80.
Boll, T. J., & Barth, J. (1983). Mild head injury. *Psychiatric Developments, 3,* 263–275.
Bowlby, J. (1988). Developmental psychiatry comes of age. *The American Journal of Psychiatry, 145*(1), 1–10.
Casey, R., Ludwig, S., & McCormick, M. C. (1986). Morbidity following minor head trauma in children. *Pediatrics, 78,* 497–502.
Casey, R., Ludwig, S., & McCormick, M. C. (1987). Minor head trauma in children: An intervention to decrease functional morbidity. *Pediatrics, 80,* 159–164.
Colohan, A. R. T., Dacey, R. G., Jr., Alves, W. M., Rimel, R. W., & Jane, J. A. (1986). Neurologic and neurosurgical implications of mild head injury. *Journal of Head Trauma Rehabilitation, 1*(2), 13–21.
Davidoff, D. A., Laibstain, D. F., Kessler, H. R., & Mark, V. H. (1988, March/April). Neurobehavioral sequelae of minor head injury: A consideration of post-concussive syndrome versus post-traumatic stress disorder. *Cognitive Rehabilitation,* pp. 8–13.
Dikmen, S., McLean, A., & Temkin, N. (1986). Neuropsychological and psychosocial consequences of minor head injury. *Journal of Neurology, Neurosurgery, and Psychiatry, 49,* 1227–1232.
Doronzo, J. F. (1990). Mild head injury. In E. Lehr (Ed.), *Psychological management of traumatic brain injuries in children and adolescents* (pp. 207–224). Rockville, MD: Aspen.
Farmer, M. Y., Singer, H. S., Mellits, E. D., Hall, D., & Charney, E. (1987). Neurobehavioral sequelae of minor head injuries in children. *Pediatric Neuroscience, 13,* 304–308.
Fletcher, J. M., Ewing-Cobbs, L., Miner, M. E., Levin, H. S., & Eisenberg, H. M. (1990). Behavioral changes after closed head injury in children. *Journal of Consulting and Clinical Psychology, 58*(1), 93–98.
Gade, G. F., & Young, R. F. (1984). Minor head injury. *Primary Care, 11,* 667–679.
Gennarelli, T. A. (1986). Mechanism and pathophysiology of cerebral concussion. *Journal of Head Trauma Rehabilitation, 1*(2), 23–29.
Gronwall, D. (1986). Rehabilitation programs for patients with mild head injury: Components, problems, and evaluation. *Journal of Head Trauma Rehabilitation, 1*(2), 53–62.
Hugenholtz, H., Stuss, D. T., Stethem, L. L., & Richard, M. T. (1988). How long does it take to recover from a mild concussion? *Neurosurgery, 22,* 853–858.
Kay, T. (1986). Minor head injury: An introduction for professionals. In *The unseen injury.* Southboro, MA: National Head Injury Foundation.

Kirk, S. A., & Kutchins, H. (1992). *The selling of DSM.* New York: Aldine DeGruyer.

Klonoff, H. (1971). Head injuries in children: Predisposing factors, accident conditions, accident proneness and sequelae. *American Journal of Public Health, 61,* 2405–2417.

Kraus, J. F., Black, M. A., Hessol, N., Ley, P., Rokaw, W., Sullivan, C., Bowers, S., Knowlton, S., & Marshall, L. (1984). The incidence of acute brain injury and serious impairment in a defined population. *American Journal of Epidemiology, 119,* 186–201.

Langfitt, T. W., & Gennarelli, T. A. (1982). Can the outcome from head injury be improved? *Journal of Neurosurgery, 56,* 19–25.

Lehr, E. (1990). *Psychological management of traumatic brain injuries in children and adolescents.* Rockville, MD: Aspen.

Lehr, E., & Savage, R. C. (1990). Community and school integration from a developmental perspective. In J. S. Kreutzer & P. H. Wehman (Eds.), *Community integration following traumatic brain injury.* Baltimore: Brookes.

Levin, H. S., Mattis, S., Ruff, R. M., Eisenberg, H. M., Marshall, L. F., Tabaddor, K., High, W. M., Jr., & Frankowski, R. F. (1987). Neurobehavioral outcome following minor head injury: A three-center study. *Journal of Neurosurgery, 66,* 234–243.

Levine, M. J. (1988, March/April). Issues in neurobehavioral assessment of mild head injury. *Cognitive Rehabilitation,* pp. 14–20.

McSherry, J. A. (1989). Cognitive impairment after head injury. *American Family Physician, 40*(4), 186–190.

Misenti, M. (1992, March/April). Have you ever had a head injury? *Headlines,* pp. 12–13.

Novack, T. A., Roth, D. L., & Boll, T. J. (1988). Treatment alternatives following mild head injury. *Rehabilitation Counseling Bulletin, 31,* 313–324.

O'Hara, C. (1988, March/April). Emotional adjustment following minor head injury. *Cognitive Rehabilitation,* pp. 26–33.

Ommaya, A. K., & Gennarelli, T. A. (1974). Cerebral concussion and traumatic unconsciousness: Correlation of experimental and clinical observations on blunt head injuries. *Brain, 97,* 633–654.

Oppenheimer, D. R. (1968). Microscopic lesions in the brain following head injury. *Journal of Neurology, Neurosurgery, and Psychiatry, 31,* 299–306.

Rimel, R. W., Giordani, B., Barth, J. T., Boll, T. J., & Jane, J. A. (1981). Disability caused by minor head injury. *Neurosurgery, 9,* 221–228.

Rogers, C. R. (1961). *On becoming a person.* Boston, MA: Houghton Mifflin.

Rogers, C. R. (1965). Client centered therapy: Part I. In E. Shostrom (Ed.), *Three approaches to psychotherapy* [Film]. Santa Ana, CA: Psychological Films.

Ruff, R. M., Levin, H. S., & Marshall, L. F. (1986). Neurobehavioral methods of assessment and the study of outcome in minor head injury. *Journal of Head Trauma Rehabilitation, 1*(2), 43–52.

Saunders, C. E., Cota, R., & Barton, C. A. (1986). Reliability of home observation for victims of mild closed-head injury. *Annals of Emergency Medicine, 15,* 160–163.

Schoenhuber, R., & Gentilini, M. (1988). Anxiety and depression after minor head injury: A case control study. *Journal of Neurology, Neurosurgery, and Psychiatry, 51,* 722–724.

Schoenhuber, R., Gentilini, M., & Orlando, A. (1988). Prognostic value of auditory brain-stem responses for late post-concussion symptoms following minor head injury. *Journal of Neurosurgery, 68,* 742–744.

Slater, E. J. (1989). Does mild mean minor? Recovery after closed head injury. *Journal of Adolescent Health Care, 10,* 237–240.

Sroufe, L. A. (1988). An organizational perspective on the self. In L. A. Sroufe & R.

Cooper (Eds.), *Child development: Its nature and course.* New York: McGraw-Hill.

Teasdale, G., & Jennett, B. (1974). Assessment of coma and impaired consciousness: A practical scale. *The Lancet, 2,* 81–83.

Thorne, F. C. (1968). *Psychological case handling: Volume Two—Specialized methods of counseling and psychotherapy.* Brandon, VT: Clinical Psychology Publishing.

Valsiner, J. (1989). *Human development and culture: The social nature of personality and its study.* Lexington, MA: Lexington Books.

SECTION IV

Neuromotor Dimensions

CHAPTER 12

Physical Assessment

JAMES L. DEPAEPE
ERNEST K. LANGE

All living things coexist in an ecosystem surrounded by radiant, mechanical, and thermal forces. According to Barsch (1965), "survival in such an energy surround is contingent on movement. If movement cannot be initiated independently, the organism is at the mercy of energy forces or is dependent on others for survival" (p. 5). There is little argument that children and adolescents with traumatic brain injury (TBI) are dependent on others to contend with these energy sources. If a movement deficiency exists in a child with TBI, it is crucial that a school-based physical and motor program be initiated immediately following outpatient treatment. The critical element is where to begin in establishing a program of intervention. Physical assessment is the key that unlocks the door to least restrictive movement programming for children and adolescents with TBI. An appropriate diagnosis of physical functioning has always been a necessary prerequisite to intervention. Unfortunately, there is little consensus in the literature relative to a physical or motor assessment instrument for children and adolescents with TBI. After reviewing the literature, including Bobath (1985), Bond (1976), Evans (1981), and Ylvisaker (1985), Freivogel and Piorreck (1990) were unable to locate "any assessment scale which records motor disability after head injury in a differentiated and objective way" (p. 407).

This chapter is intended to be used as a resource for educators interested in the physical assessment of children and adolescents with TBI. The chapter focuses on physical assessment from a kinesiological perspective, which is defined by motor behavior and physiological parameters. We provide a model as reference to this kinesiological perspective and examples of tests with which to measure each designated parameter. The parameters are discussed in order of administration and include reflexes, neuromuscular integrity, range of motion, fundamental motor ability, muscular strength, muscular endurance, and cardiorespiratory endurance. In each of these parameter sections, we illustrate test options and suggest where to find additional information. In addition, we illustrate and discuss a second assessment phase relative to functional skill analysis. The material and information found in this chapter is not all-inclusive. The intention of this chapter is not to provide a cookbook on assessment, but to serve as a resource for teachers, therapists, and parents interested in the physical assessment of children and adolescents with TBI.

Professionals in special physical education, physical therapy, and occupational therapy use a variety of physical and motor assessments for referred children. According to Miles, Nierengarten, and Nearing (1988), special physical educators typically use about 11 different assessment instruments. The *Bruininks–Oseretsky Test of Motor Proficiency* is the instrument selected 90% of the time, whereas the *Denver Developmental Screening Test* is used least, about 12% of the time (Miles et al., 1989). It seems there are almost as many assessments as there are programs for children and adolescents with disabilities. Many school districts devise their own instruments for the diagnosis of movement problems to fit specific ecological need. Some of these teacher-made instruments are better suited than many standardized tests. All of the standardized instruments have shortcomings, and few are appropriately normed for specific populations with disabilities. The only assessment instrument that reports validity and reliability for individuals with TBI is the *Motor Function Assessment Scale* (MFAS), designed by Freivogel and Piorreck (1990). These authors, however, failed to describe TBI subjects to any great extent, and even excluded the age range they studied. In addition, the 44-item instrument, although easily administered and economical, left many questions unanswered regarding physical and motor function. The MFAS has been criticized by physical therapists as being too general.

To measure existent levels of function of the child with TBI, one must determine the child's functional kinesiology using several established testing procedures. In this chapter, we review those physiological parameters, as well as those elements of motor behavior rudimentary to movement acquisition, which are of particular concern to teachers of students who have suffered from TBI. As a model, we describe the *Functional Kinesiological Analysis* (FKA) used in the Kinesiotherapy Clinic at the University of New Mexico. The FKA is an assessment methodology using content-, criterion-, and norm-referenced tests to detect intraindividual abilities and deficiencies of individuals with TBI. An integral feature of FKA is its reliability in evaluating the level and degree of functioning already acquired by individuals with TBI.

Before administering the FKA, one must be familiar with all of the characteristics associated with children and adolescents with TBI as discussed in this chapter. Some physical characteristics have been studied recently and are critical to the FKA's successful administration. For example, it is important to know that recovery of activities of daily living (ADL) is independent of trauma site, but that complications associated with the upper extremities following contralateral left hemispheric trauma are of greater magnitude and longer duration than those following right hemispheric trauma (Smutok et al., 1989). Additionally, most of the TBI literature is based on the affective and cognitive domains. Therefore, characteristics relative to these domains, including problem solving, attention, memory, distractibility, irritability, concentration, and general intellectual functioning, are necessary background data to consider before successfully administering the FKA.

The FKA is divided into three phases, with intervention as the third phase. For the purposes of this chapter, only the first two phases are discussed. It should be noted that the FKA is a method of assessing and not an assessment instrument. A variety of evaluative techniques and instruments are used in Phase I, which contains all of the technical kinesiological analyses (see Figure 12.1). Phase II contains a discrepancy analysis, and its underlying premise is functional skill acquisition (see Figure 12.2). For children and youth with TBI to function independently in their respective environments, movement problems must be addressed first at a rudimentary functional level. The FKA was designed to detect rudimentary movement deficiencies that would im-

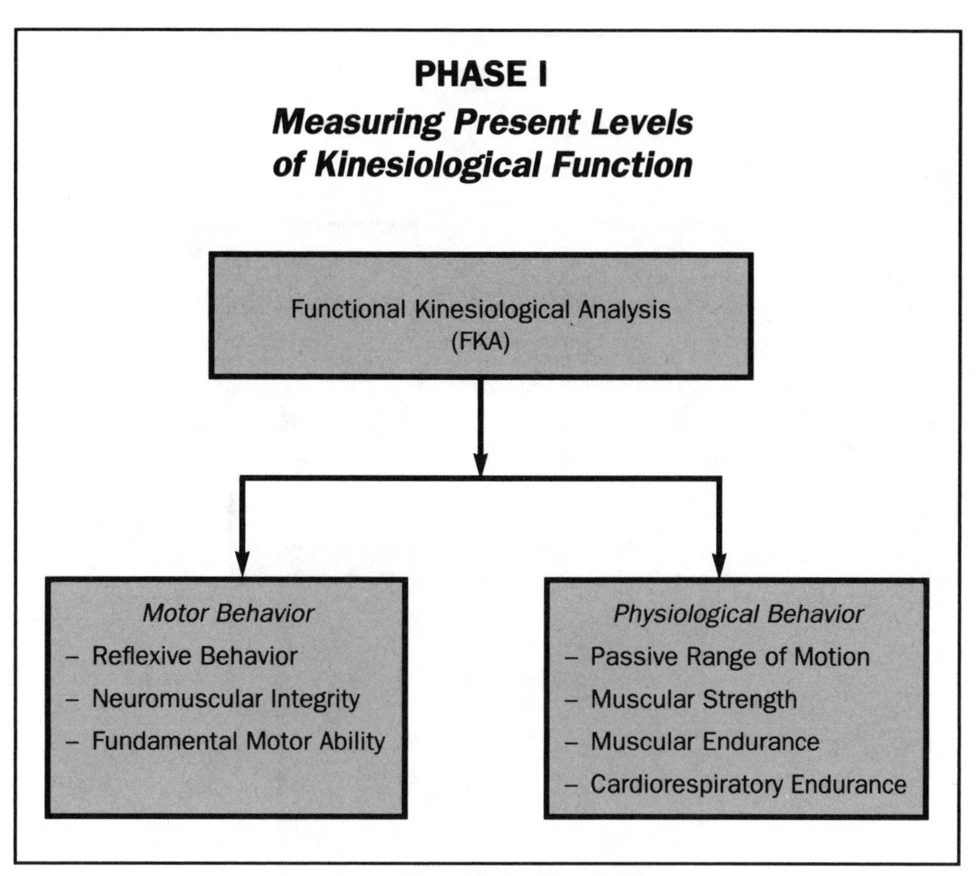

Figure 12.1. Phase I of Functional Kinesiological Analysis.

pede functional skill development. After a present level of kinesiological functioning is diagnosed, Phase II is initiated by analyzing appropriate functional skills to be relearned. A comparison is made between selected functional skills and the individual's FKA results. This reduces the problems of frustration, motivation, and irritability encountered in intervention programming. Next, an initial functional level is determined and intervention is prescribed.

PHASE I: MEASURING PRESENT LEVELS OF KINESIOLOGICAL FUNCTION

The following sections are organized by motor and physiological parameters as illustrated in Phase I of the functional kinesiological analysis. Each parameter is discussed in terms of its utility for children and adolescents with TBI. Optional testing measures are also provided in each section, but a detailed procedure is not included.

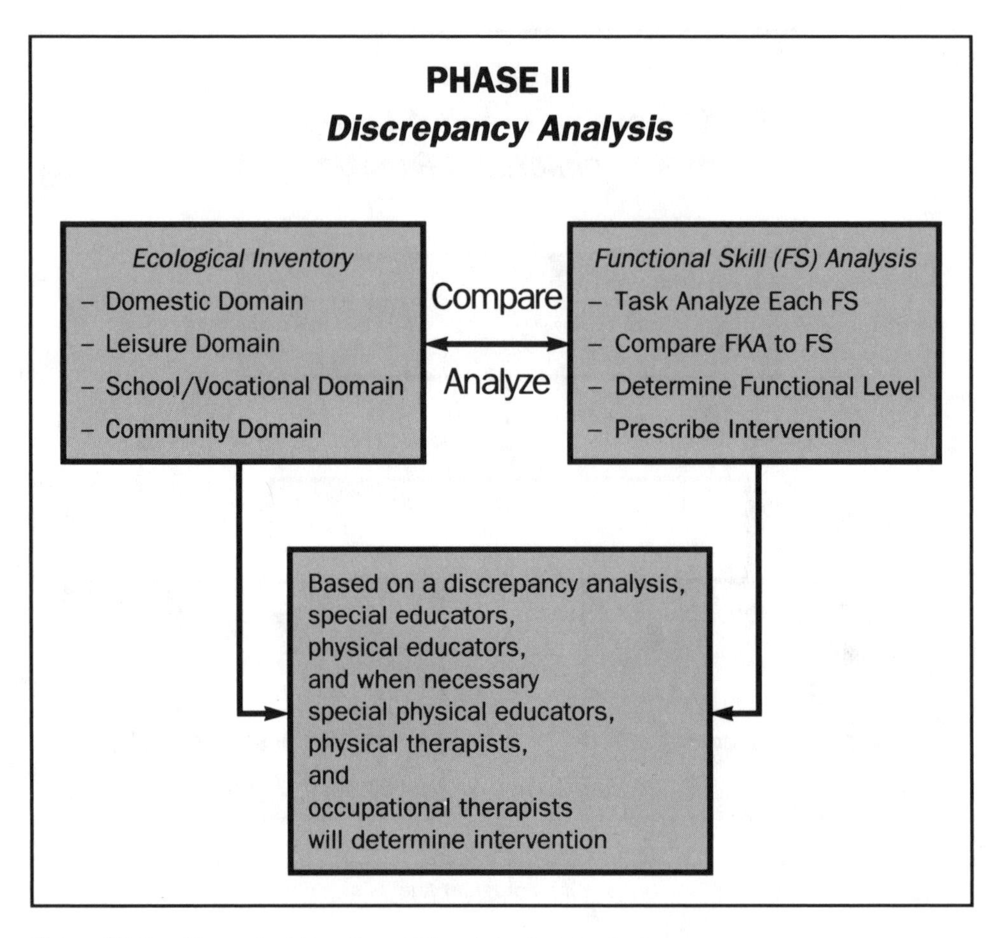

Figure 12.2. Phase II of Functional Kinesiological Analysis.

Motor Behavior Parameters

In goal setting for recovery of patients with TBI, physicians often identify motor loss from trauma as being the most important component in the recovery process (Rao, Jellinek, Harberg, & Fryback, 1988). With this in mind, the reestablishment of functional motor behavior becomes critical. The long-term needs of persons with severe TBI must be addressed (Jacobs, 1988). When children suffer severe brain trauma from accidents, ultimately the schools may need to provide intervention in recovery and adjustment through application of exercise activities.

Accurate assessment of the child with TBI, to determine the extent of reflexive behavior, neuromuscular integrity, and fundamental motor ability, will not result from the use of differential diagnoses purported as appropriate for such purposes. Application of information for intervention is determined by individual case, extent of damage, and other factors peculiar to the individual.

Assessing reflexes

Because of the tendency for primitive and especially postural reflexes (those reflexive actions necessary to maintain proper body postures prior to independent control) to reappear after trauma, the first item tested is reflexive movement. If extensive reflexive movement is present, any subsequent testing could yield inaccurate results. If minimal reflexive movement is present, it should be noted and further testing must account for effects due to these involuntary actions.

One of the available practical procedures is the *Rancho Los Amigos Scale of Cognitive Levels* (Baggerly, 1986). Patients are classified by one of the eight levels associated with descriptive characteristics. Level II, generalized response, considers postural and reflex responses. However, assessment of reflexive actions of the human body is accomplished with various procedures. Innate reflexive behavior is often considered a nonrecoverable ability in individuals with brain injuries. However, compensatory activity may result in exhibition of reflexes previously thought to be lost due to the brain trauma. If this is the case, then reflexive abilities should be constantly monitored throughout the individual's recovery and adjustment periods. Generally, the person who is less than 18 years of age has stronger prognosis for recovery than the person older than 18 years, assuming the extent of brain injury is the same (DePompolo, 1987). Considering such a possibility, it is logical to assume that recovery and gains of former abilities in the motor domain may be of greater magnitude for children and adolescents than for adults. Consequently, there may be progressive recovery in reflexive action as well as other aspects of motor behavior.

The following descriptive list of selected primitive and postural reflexes can aid in assessing the extent to which trauma has affected neuromuscular control. If several of these reflexive patterns test positive, many of the other physiological and motor behavior tests of the FKA model will yield inaccurate results. We recommend that, if extensive reflexive patterning exists, then intervention in the form of active range of motion stimulation begin immediately. Testing for reflexive action can be done by physical therapists, occupational therapists, special physical educators, and special educators who have specific concentrated training.

Primitive Reflexes

- *Moro reflex:* Place the child in a supine position. Tap the child's abdomen or produce a feeling of insecurity of support. The reflex is characterized by a sudden extension of the arms and legs, followed by recovery to the normal flexed position. An asymmetrical response may indicate some limb problem due to contractures.

- *Palmar grasp reflex:* Stimulate the palm of the child's hand. The reflex is present if the stimulation causes the hand to close tightly around the stimulating implement. Using your own finger for stimulating this response will permit you to detect any bilateral discrepancy. In infants, the left-hand grip in normally stronger than the right.

- *Plantar grasp reflex:* Stimulate by pressing against the ball of the child's foot. The reflex is present if the toes flex around the implement used for stimulation.

- *Asymmetrical tonic neck reflex:* Place the child in a supine position and turn the head to either side. If the reflex is present, the arm and the leg ipsilateral to the head will extend and the contralateral arm and leg will assume a flexed position.

- *Symmetrical tonic neck reflex:* Support the child in a sitting position. If the reflex is present, arms and legs will extend when the child is gradually tipped backward so the head and neck fall into extension. It is also present if the arms and legs flex when the child's head and neck are tipped forward.

Postural Reflexes

- *Labyrinthine righting reflex:* Support the child in a standing position. Tip the child to the right, left, forward, and backward. If the reflex is present, the child's head will always remain upright by moving in the opposite direction of the tipping.
- *Pull-up reflex:* Support the child in a sitting position by holding hands. If the reflex is present, the arms will flex and seem to pull to maintain an upright posture as you tip the child backward.
- *Neck righting reflex:* Place the child in the supine position and turn the head to one side. The reflex is present if the hips, legs, and trunk move in the same direction as the head to keep the body aligned.
- *Body righting reflex:* Place the child in a prone position and turn the hips to a side-lying position. If the reflex is present, the child will react by turning the head in the same direction.

Tendon reflexes can provide further neuromuscular information for assessing the functional kinesiological capacity of a child with TBI. Methods of tendon reflex palpation follow:

- *Patellar reflex:* This reflex, commonly known as the knee jerk, is probably the best known and most widely tested of the reflexes. In testing, provide percussive stimulation to the subject's patellar tendon by use of a small rubber hammer.
- *Achilles reflex:* In testing this reflex, tap the subject's calcaneous tendon (tendon of the Achilles), which should cause the foot to plantar flex or extend.
- *Biceps and triceps reflexes:* The biceps and triceps muscles are located anterior and posterior to the upper arm, respectively. Tapping these muscles causes the forearm to flex and extend, respectively.
- *Plantar reflex:* To measure plantar flexion or extension, run the handle of a percussion hammer along the lateral border of the sole of the foot.

For additional information regarding the many reflexes found in the human body, one may consult any contemporary textbook on human anatomy and physiology or a motor development text. Many of these reflex actions are observable by the care provider when working with a child who has a brain injury. Constant monitoring will enhance possibilities of detection of improvement as the child progresses in the posttrauma process.

Finally, muscle stretch reflexes, which include the jaw, biceps, brachioradialis (forearm), triceps, quadriceps, hamstrings, and gastrocnemius-soleus (calf) reflexes should also be examined. Stimulation of nerve response will suggest integrity of the nervous system associated with the reflexive action and specific spinal nerves. Ability to respond on an involuntary basis suggests that the child is regaining complete or partial use of neuromuscular function associated with particular movements.

Related to reflexes and their manifestation are postural control, coordination, and rapid alternating movements, which are listed below. Such movements are indicative of a child's ability to demonstrate balance, coordinate muscular function, and change body position rapidly.

- *Sitting balance:* Is the child able to assume correct posture while seated, and maintain that posture for a relatively appropriate period of time?
- *Standing balance:* Is standing balance assumed, when requested, on a voluntary basis? While the child is standing, is there any weaving, adjustment of foot position for compensation of instability, or lifting of arms in an attempt to maintain position? What is the response of the child in an upright stance when his or her eyes are closed? Is there lean toward one direction? Does the child compensate easily, or is there loss of balance requiring shifting of weight to maintain position?
- *Rapid alternating movements:* Can actions of manual dexterity be performed (e.g., touching fingertips as rapidly as possible to the thumb pad in a sequential and repetitive fashion) to large and overt body movements (e.g., standing as fast as possible, following a signal, from a back-lying position on the floor or a mat)?
- *Finger–nose–finger movements:* With arms extended horizontally to the sides and the child in an upright position, either standing or sitting, is the child able to bring first the index finger of the right hand to the nose and return to the starting position, with the eyes closed? Can he or she repeat the action with the left arm and hand? In the same upright position with arms extended, can the child slowly flex the fingers with the index fingers extended, and bring the tips of the two index fingers together while the eyes are closed, and return to the start position?
- *Heel–toe–movements:* Is the child able to walk in a straight line with the heel of the lead foot directly in front of and touching the trailing foot? Does alternate foot placement and heel–toe contact result in straight-line progression? Does the child sway the upper body or shift a foot to the side to compensate for loss of balance?

Assessing neuromuscular integrity

In assessing neuromuscular integrity, the goal is to determine whether the child has normal motor control. Assessment should include whether the child has the ability to receive sensory input, establish a motor plan, and successfully respond in an appropriate manner. Several tests are necessary to adequately assess motor control function.

Visual perceptual behavior is one important element found in the motor control function. Even in newborns, a considerable amount of ocular activity is present. Most of this initial visual behavior can be classified as visual regard and tracking. When children and adolescents suffer TBI, significant differences may be detected when the child's visual capabilities are evaluated and compared with charts that suggest normal or expected age-related functions. Table 12.1 illustrates age-appropriate visual perceptual behaviors of young children (Cratty, 1979). This chart is useful when assessing the level of visual sensory information input. Children will have little success motor planning or responding to a motor plan if sensory information is not being received.

Auditory, kinesthetic, and haptic sensory information can be assessed in a similar manner. Haptic sensory information is acquired through simultaneous stimulation of tactile (skin sense) and kinesthetic (muscle sense) sources. In practice, separating the elements of these two senses is very difficult; thus, they are often combined with the haptic sense. Texts of perceptual motor development provide similar charts illustrating normal function.

Subsequent to sensory input is motor planning, an important feature that emerges slowly in developing children. When a child receives information from the

TABLE 12.1. Age-Appropriate Visual Perceptual Behaviors of Children

Time of Occurrence (Approximate)	***Selected Visual Perceptual Behaviors***
Birth	Rudimentary fixation; brief periods of reflexive tracking.
3 months	Accommodation more flexible. Head and eyes coordinated.
6 months	Visual tracking through 90 degrees in horizontal and vertical planes. Visually alert about 50% of time. Depth awareness in visual cliff studies.
1 year	Appearance of mature pupil fibrillation.
2 years	Distinguishes vertical from horizontal lines.
5 years	Distinguishes lateral, vertical, horizontal lines.
7 years	b, p, d, q inversions and reversals resolved.
9 years	
10 years	Intercepts ball thrown from a distance.

environment (e.g., a verbal request, a demonstration, or a problem to be solved through movement), the child formulates a performance scheme for the purpose of responding to the stimulus or cue. This cognitive behavior is referred to as a motor plan or schema. When the child is confronted with a new object or situation, he or she makes a decision pertaining to a particular response. Related literature includes discussion of how the child responds, and for what purposes (Croce & DePaepe, 1989). One way to analyze the mechanical capabilities of human response or performance is through filmed analysis (i.e, videotape), which provides the professional with sufficient observational opportunity to critically analyze the child's performance. Also, through use of stop-action and rapid-access replay, observational traits can be specified and distinguished as unique to the child. Whatever the means of interpreting performance following the initiation of a stimulus, the ability to respond correctly to verbal description of a movement or movements necessitates the use of motor planning by the child. Use of a motor plan enables the child to demonstrate actions that include varying degrees of complexity.

Expectations pertaining to age-related behavior can be found in various books, guides, and pamphlets. When children are unable to plan a complex movement, such as may be the case with children who have TBI, they are demonstrating *apraxia* (Cratty, 1986). Similarly, when children display inadequate motor planning, they are classified as *dyspraxic.*

Because the ability to function in motor planning is a cognitive ability, and the child with TBI has suffered insult resulting in central nervous system dysfunction, he or she may demonstrate reduced ability to function in expected age-appropriate motor actions when compared with non-TBI peers. Tests to measure motor planning generate data relative to verbal commands and demonstration (Kools & Tweedie, 1975). These tests should use verbal directions, which consist of a sliding (0–3, 0–5, etc.) scale as a measure of the child's ability to follow such commands as "clap your hands," "wave good-bye," and "walk forward looking at me." To assess the neuromuscular integrity of motor planning, an active range of motion (ROM) test is used. For children with TBI, the best choices are rudimentary movements of limited complexity (e.g., bilateral raising of extended arms from the side to an overhead position, resulting in touching of hands overhead with the arms extended). Generally, ROM actions are good indexes of neuromuscular integrity. Range of motion (ROM) tests usually suggest integrity of joint function, degree of muscle strength, and flexibility in movement. Active ROM occurs as the individual voluntarily moves a body part through a range of motion without assistance from another person or through the use of a machine. In the case of the child with TBI, movement is provided through a range of motion on request. The discussion and suggested activities in this section of the text are provided with the assumption that the ROM actions tested are considered important for assessing motor ability and control rather than for determining the integrity or physiological ability of the joint. In other words, emphasis is placed on observation of the ROM movement rather than on evaluation of joint flexibility.

An anatomical joint is an articulation. The joint occurs where two bony articulating surfaces meet. Movement is permissible because neuromuscular facilitation occurs as a result of perceptual interpretations of sensory input and motor planning. In assessing this function, according to the Kools and Tweedie (1975) protocol, the administrator asks the child to respond to simple anatomical movements. The movements consist of all possible actions, which are generally described below. The intent is to distinguish whether the child is capable of controlling the simplest movements in an active range of motion; therefore, the following movements and their concomitant descriptions are provided in general kinesiological terms.

Angular Movements: Angular movements result in an increase or decrease in the angle between adjacent bones.

- *Flexion:* A part is bent so the anterior surfaces become closer and the angle between the two bones is decreased.
- *Dorsiflexion:* The ventral surface of the foot is brought closer to the anterior surface of the lower leg, decreasing the angle.
- *Extension:* A part is straightened and movement occurs in the direction opposite to flexion movements. The angle between two articulating parts is increased.
- *Hyperextension:* A part moves past the normal anatomical joint position that occurs in extension.
- *Abduction:* A part is moved away from the midline of the body or body part.
- *Adduction:* A part is moved toward the midline of the body or body part.

Rotary Movements: Rotary movements usually occur around a longitudinal or vertical axis of the body.

- *Internal rotation:* The anterior surface of a body part is turned toward the midline of the body.
- *External rotation:* The anterior surface of a body part is turned away from the midline of the body.
- *Neck or trunk rotation:* The neck or trunk is turned around a vertical axis to either the right side or the left side.
- *Circumduction:* The movements of flexion, extension, abduction, and adduction are combined.

Assessing passive range of motion

Because prevention of contractures is an ultimate concern for individuals with TBI, ROM testing is done to evaluate the integrity of each joint, especially those typically affected. Contractions are a concern because the onset of the condition results in the loss of range of motion of the involved limb. Contracture is fixed resistance to a passive stretch of a muscle. As the muscle loses opportunity for extension through movement, the muscle also gradually loses ability to produce full movement. According to MacKay-Lyons (1989), those joints found to be most affected in patients with TBI are hips (86%), shoulders (76%), ankles (76%), and elbows (44%). ROM testing requires the use of a measuring instrument. The most common instrument used is a universal goniometer, which is a large protractor with two arms, an extended stationary arm and a fulcrum-mounted moveable arm. The universal goniometer is nothing more than an oversized caliper, which is relatively inexpensive and easily attainable for use by a trained classroom teacher, physical educator, or therapist. The goniometer's stationary arm is held along the fixed limb side of the joint and the fulcrum end is placed nearest the axis of the joint. Then the moveable end of the goniometer is held longitudinally along the person's moveable limb while that limb is passively moved. After the limb is moved through its range, the fulcrum is read to find the extent to which, by degree, the joint can articulate. Clarkson and Gilewich (1989) wrote an excellent, illustrated procedure of ROM assessment. Although all suspected joints should be tested, we agree with MacKay-Lyons (1989) that hips, shoulders, ankles, and elbows are the most critical, because they are most susceptible to contractures. Table 12.2 is a sample hip region record.

Fluid-based goniometers also are available. These instruments are filled with fluid and work much like a carpenter's level. Advantages in the use of a fluid-based goniometer are measurement consistency and reliability among different evaluators. Although the instrument is reliable and valid (Rheault, Miller, Nothnagel, Straessle, & Urban, 1988), it cannot measure movements of rotation. Recently, however, an OB goniometer was developed that uses a compass needle for measuring joint motion. The OB goniometer is strapped on a limb much like a blood pressure cuff and takes less training to read. It is capable of providing measurements of rotation movements, as well as extensions and flexions. Its only disadvantage is its expense; whereas a universal goniometer costs under $25, an OB costs closer to $100.

Assessing fundamental motor ability

Much of a person's functional independence obviously depends on movement. When the child with brain trauma begins the recovery process, and evaluation is needed to determine changes in the instructional process, knowledge of various motor development trends can be useful. Some of these trends are age related, but the ages are

TABLE 12.2. Sample Range of Motion (ROM) Record for Hip Region

	Hip ROM to Each Side		
Motion	***Left***	***Right***	***Normal ROM for Hip***
Flexion	110°	98°	0–12°
Extension	28°	15°	0–30°
Abduction	40°	22°	0–45°
Adduction	23°	18°	0–30°
Internal rotation	43°	28°	0–45°
External rotation	40°	23°	0–45°

only approximations. For example, locomotor ability (being able to move independently about one's space by self-propulsion) is a steadily increasing characteristic as the child gains maturity and experience. Various techniques become available to the child as refinement of specific abilities occurs. Variations in locomotion, for instance, occur within the various activities used by the child. Once the child has learned to walk, he or she may attempt to alter the way of walking in response to perceived stimulation. Sometime around the second year, the child will be able to walk backward and/or sideways, and will display these abilities on occasion. Such actions are related to expectations deemed age appropriate. As Eckert (1987) discussed, trends can include qualitative and quantitative measures:

- *Walking:* Once walking is achieved, the child's gait becomes narrower and more rhythmic. The lead food is placed straight ahead with the heel directly in line with the toes of the trailing foot. Children of 2 years demonstrate a rhythmic pattern of about 170 steps per minute. The length of steps is about half that of adults.
- *Running:* Most children exhibit a true run at about 2 to 3 years of age, although ability to efficiently start and stop quickly is generally lacking at this age. By age 4½ to 5, children display remarkable improvement, and good reciprocal arm action is noted. By age 5, the child develops reasonable speed in running; the average is approximately 11.5 feet per second.
- *Jumping:* Children initially retain contact with the ground with one foot while jumping. At about 18 months of age, they begin to step off with one foot and are suspended momentarily before regaining support. When a momentary period occurs during which the child is not supported in progress from a higher to a lower level, a downward leap is completed.

When assessing the ability of children with TBI to function in locomotor activities, reference to grade and age expectations may assist in determining intervention. Familiarity with normal approximations, and comparison of performance by TBI children who deviate from the normal trends, will allow the teacher or clinician to understand the differences caused by TBI. The literature contains quantitative movement characteristics as they relate to age approximations. Table 12.3, for example, shows approximate age of achievement for several jumping tasks. Child development books often contain examples of age approximation charts that illustrate trends. Additionally, motor development texts include qualitative content-referenced task analyses of motor patterns (Cratty, 1986; Gallahue, 1989; Haywood, 1986; Payne & Isaacs, 1987; Wickstrom, 1983). A content-referenced qualitative assessment is recommended for estimating fundamental motor ability. A test of fundamental motor patterns should be sensitive enough to detect both strengths and weaknesses in children with TBI. Moreover, the motor patterns assessed should represent movements that are of absolute functional necessity.

In this section, the FKA is used to assess fundamental motor patterns based on functional patterns found in activities of daily living. These patterns are content referenced by task and have been validated by means of biomechanical kinematic analysis (BKA). The BKA system uses observation as the basis for detecting movement qualities, and uses correct human movement behavior as a reference for analysis (e.g.,

TABLE 12.3. Level of Achievement for Several Jumping Tasks

Task	***Age***
From a 12″ step, jump a distance of	
4″–14″	37 months
14″–24″	39 months
24″–33″	48 months
Standing long jump on the ground	
mean = 20″	3 years
27″	4 years
38″	5 years
43″	6 years
Jump over string at 32″ height	41 months
Hurdle jump (standing long jump over a bar)	
mean = 14″	5 years
17″	6 years

Adapted from *Movement Skill Development* by J. Keough and D. Sugden, 1985, New York: Macmillan.

the age-appropriate trends described above for walking, running, and jumping). Each pattern has three schematic stages, represented by the terms initial, elementary, and mature, which represent the level of motor pattern response as observed through live recordings. There are no age-related norms, because only approximations of age-related performances exist in the literature. Therefore, this content referencing system uses qualitative criteria for detecting present levels of fundamental motor ability. The movements to be assessed are arranged by order of development and are separated by function. Locomotor function includes rolling, crawling, creeping, walking, running, jumping, sliding, and leaping, whereas manual control function includes reaching and grasping, throwing, catching, kicking, and striking.

The initial stage of walking, for instance, includes difficulty maintaining upright posture, unpredictable loss of balance, rigid and halting leg action, short truncated steps, a flat-footed surface contact, outward-turned foot placements, a wide base of support, flexion of the knee at surface contact followed by a quick leg extension, and arms held high and away from the body for balance. Development is evident in the elementary stage: gradual smoothness in the increased gait, increased heel–toe pattern, reduced base of support within the lateral dimensions relative to the torso, increased pelvic tilt, an apparent vertical lift, and the arms held lower and closer to the side with little swing evident. The mature stage is represented by contralateral arm action, narrow base of support, relaxed and longer gait, little vertical lifting, and a defined heel–toe surface contact.

The initial stage of catching, to take one of the manual control functions as an example, is represented by the following: the child exhibits a defined avoidance reaction to a thrown object; fingers are extended and held tense; palms are facing upward and together; only arms are used in the catching action; and no movement of the fully extended arms occurs until contact is made with the thrown object, then an attempt is made to scoop the object and trap it with the arms against the body. During the elementary stage, the child demonstrates a decreased avoidance reaction: Eyes may close, but the head does not move; arms show more flexion and are held wider apart; hands are in more opposition, with palms now facing each other; and during contact, the hands attempt to catch the ball but the maneuver is usually poorly timed, and there is still a trapping against the body. By the mature stage, however, the child shows no sign of avoidance reaction. The thumbs of each hand are held very near to each other and the fingers point upward and slightly toward the thrower. Timing is coordinated with a hand grasping response; as the object enters the hands, the arms, which are relaxed, absorb the impact by giving way to the oncoming object.

Qualitative content-referenced task analyses of motor patterns such as those described above appear in many motor development texts. See Wickstrom (1983) and Gallahue (1989) for excellent descriptions of these qualitative movement criteria.

In assessing fundamental motor ability, one needs to keep in mind the wide range of performance levels demonstrated by children and select from among various evaluation devices. The primary intent is to establish a point of reference for children who are brain injured. Understanding the qualitative measures of performance relative to normal stages will allow the observer to arrange activities with the intent of anticipating progress while still maintaining performance expectations that are within the child's range.

Physiological Parameters

As is the case for motor behavior, physiological behavior is integral to the long-term functional needs of persons with severe TBI. When muscular strength, muscular endurance, and cardiorespiratory endurance are deficient, retraining becomes imperative. Poor levels of physiological function will exaccerbate relative affect of residual dysfunction. Conversely, dysfunction may be reduced by increasing levels of muscular strength, muscular endurance, and cardiorespiratory endurance, which are all necessary elements of functional skill acquisition.

Assessing muscular strength

Following testing of active and passive range of motion, one must examine muscular strength of specific muscle groups. It is extremely difficult to isolate muscle actions, because most muscles work in concert and should be tested together for functional synergy (ability of the muscle to coordinate with other muscles effectively and efficiently in performance of specific movements). One should examine an individual both in a gravity-eliminated position and against gravity. Clarkson and Gilewich (1989) provided detailed, illustrated step-by-step procedures. Before attempting either muscle testing or ROM testing, one should be knowledgeable about kinesiological principles. Critical prerequisite knowledge includes the origin and insertion of muscles, their agonists and antagonists, their fixation and substitution, and neuromuscular physiology. Most physical therapists, kinesiotherapists, and some special physical educators have sound kinesiological knowledge and have received specific training in ROM and muscle testing and are capable of conducting this type of testing and

TABLE 12.4. Criteria for Grading Strength and Weakness in Muscle Integrity

Test Performance	***By Percent***	***By Word***	***By Numerals***
Movement to test position and hold against gravity and maximum resistance	100/95	normal/normal−	5/5−
Movement to test position and hold against gravity and moderate resistance	90/80	good+/good	4+/4
Movement to test position and hold against gravity and minimum resistance	70/60	good−/fair+	4−/3+
Movement to test position and hold against gravity only	50	fair	3
Movement to test position and hold against gravity with slight assistance	40	fair−	3−
Movement to test position with moderate/more assistance	30/20	poor+/poor	2+/2
Movement is not visible, but a tendon is observed during contraction	10/5	poor−/trace	2−/1
Contraction is not felt in the muscle when palpated	0	zero	0

training. They may also act as resource personnel. Example criteria for grading strength and weakness in muscle integrity are shown in Table 12.4.

Validity and reliability of manual muscle testing relies on the skill and experience of the test administrator. The method in and of itself does not produce objective measures. Over the years, however, several researchers have attempted to design a more objective measurement instrument. One such instrument is the myometer, which was developed and marketed in 1982. The myometer is a pressure-sensitive hand-held device that detects and records muscle movement in its smallest unit of measurement. The testing procedure uses the same positions and sequences used in manual muscle testing. As the individual with TBI moves in the instructed direction, the test administrator offers resistance with the measuring head of the myometer. The best value of three attempts is recorded. The myometer has been found to be a highly objective, reliable, and valid tool for measuring muscle strength (Hyde, Goodard, & Scott, 1983). A school can purchase the myometer for under $1,000 and connect it to an existing personal computer.

Many functional skills require muscular strength beyond what is diagnosed during a manual muscle test. If it is obvious that the child being assessed has a normal range of strength, then use alternative measures to assess functional strength. Most assessments use hand dynamometers to estimate strength because they have been shown to correlate highly with general muscular strength; however, because of neuromuscular anomalies characteristic of children with TBI, a hand dynamometer may not yield an accurate estimate of this parameter. Therefore, a more systematic and individualized method is suggested. To determine a child's strength, the administrator starts the child with a light weight and works up to the heaviest weight that the child can possibly move. Using the positions and movements that are tested in an active ROM test, the administrator gradually increases a weighted resistance against each movement to find the child's maximal muscular strength capacity. When the child has reached maximum potential, the administrator records the type of movement and level of resistance achieved. These data are valuable for selecting intervention procedures and appropriate functional skills. This method may slightly underestimate maximum capacity, but a slight underestimate is psychologically beneficial when intervention is initiated.

For these tests, weighted bags that wrap around a limb and close with Velcro are most adaptable, but any method of measurable resistance is appropriate. Cable tensiometry (used to measure muscular strength in resistance to tension by a cable device) provides accurate clinical data, but the equipment is too cumbersome for field testing. Cable tensiometers can be made at the school site, but are difficult to move.

Assessing muscular endurance

Muscular endurance (ME) is defined in two ways, depending on the type of contraction. An *isotonic* ME contraction is an ability to maintain a muscular contraction against a given resistance with repeated repetitions in moving the resistance, whereas an *isometric* ME contraction is an ability to maintain a muscular contraction against an immovable object over an extended period of time. It is important for individuals to achieve endurance functionality in each of these types of contractions. Isometric contractions are important for movement stabilization, which is used in balance and postural control, whereas isotonic contractions allow the individual to move repetitively, which is used in the manual manipulation of objects and in locomotion.

Assessing the integrity of each type of contraction is relatively easy. For isotonic contractions, the administrator uses the data for maximum muscular strength, which varies for each movement measured. The individual is asked to move the calculated weight (60% of maximum strength capacity) repeatedly, and the administrator makes sure that the lifting is done according to the movement protocol established in the manual muscle testing guide and through the fullest range of motion possible. (Many children try to compensate for weaknesses through body position adjustments and inappropriate muscle recruitment.) The administrator merely counts and records the number of repetitions accomplished accurately.

Isometric contractions are assessed using the same movement starting positions, but the administrator records the time contractions are sustained while immovable resistance is provided. Children with known cardiac problems should never be given an isometric assessment. Also, isometric and isotonic assessments should be scheduled on separate days. Fatigue and muscle soreness may negatively affect results should both assessments be administered on the same day.

Assessing cardiorespiratory endurance

Traumatic brain injury often produces side effects due to a loss of functional capacity, which results in a marked hypoactivity and eventual risk of cardiovascular disease. Because of these concerns, it is imperative that cardiorespiratory endurance (CRE) be assessed. Cardiorespiratory endurance falls directly within the purview and training of any physical educator. A special educator and physical educator team or a special physical educator alone can easily develop this testing and manage an effective program of CRE exercise.

As functional capacity returns, the child's CRE must be developed to meet demands required of each functional movement attempted. When designing an assessment for persons with TBI, one should be aware of the differences in CRE response. Children and youth respond differently to CRE demands than do adults. For instance, an average 8-year-old boy's oxygen consumption is half of that needed when he becomes 18, but little or no increase in CRE occurs in girls beyond the age of 14. When oxygen consumption (VO_2 max) is defined in relative as opposed to absolute terms (i.e., per kilogram of body weight), however, there is little difference among the ages of boys, and girls tend to show decreases with age. Consequently, metabolic cost is higher in children than in adolescents or adults, but this may be due to an inefficient motor pattern exhibited by younger children (Croce & DePaepe, 1988). Distinctive from aerobic capacity, anaerobic power (the ability to function in cardiovascular activities beyond the stage of revitalizing sufficient oxygen stores) is markedly lower in children than in adolescents or adults, even in relative terms. Therefore, younger children are at a functional disadvantage while performing activities lasting 10 to 60 seconds. Although several tests for cardiorespiratory endurance exist, none seems appropriately designed for assessing basic levels needed for functional skill achievement or basic health requirements of persons with TBI.

According to Heyward (1984), assessing the functional aerobic capacity of individuals for appropriate exercise intervention is not always practical in a field setting. Because direct measurements of valid maximum oxygen consumption require expensive and heavy equipment, it is desirable to select a submaximum exercise test as an alternative to estimate cardiorespiratory baselines. Heart rate, oxygen consumption, and exercise intensity are assumed to be linearly related when exercise intensity remains moderate to light.

We prefer to use a submaximum bicycle ergometer test for children and adolescents with TBI because the mechanical efficiency is most similar when comparing children, youth, and adults. (When children are compared with adults in walking or running, their oxygen [O_2] costs are greater.) Most children with TBI who have returned to the classroom can sit on a stationary bicycle with assistance, even if the stabilizing muscles of the abdomen and back exhibit residual neuromotor deficiency. Many TBI persons confined to wheelchairs are able to peddle an adapted cycle ergometer or use an arm ergometer. To estimate functional aerobic capacity in the University of New Mexico Kinesiotherapy Clinic, Schwinn Air Dyne Exercycles are used. One can be purchased from a Schwinn dealer for $300 to $700. A submaximum aerobic test has been developed by Dr. Fran Nagle of the Biodynamics Laboratory at the University of Wisconsin. (For detailed information regarding the complete testing protocols, contact Ms. Vaunda Carter, Director of Program Development, 217 North Jefferson St., Chicago, IL 60606.) The Initial Aerobic Fitness Test (IAFT) is the recom-

TABLE 12.5. Aerobic Fitness Ratings for Adolescents Aged 14 to 17 (in Mets)

Rating	Boys	Girls
Poor	<12.0	<9.4
Fair	12.3–13.7	9.7–10.6
Good	14.4–17.1	10.9–12.9
Excellent	>17.1	>13.1

mended level for adolescents with TBI. The aerobic fitness ratings for adolescents aged 14 to 17 are provided in Table 12.5 in terms of Mets (predicted maximum aerobic power), which means that energy demands are measured in units of O_2 used. In other words, a 12 Met translates into an aerobic level equivalent to O_2 intensity requirements for running an 8-minute mile pace. To calculate Mets, we use the IAFT (8-minute duration). The highest aerobic demand is equal to a brisk walk. The formulas for calculation are clearly illustrated in the Schwinn Air Dyne Aerobic Fitness Appraisal Kit.

For those in the field with limited or no equipment budget, ergometers with incremental resistance in either kpm or Watts will suffice. The National Handicapped Sports and Recreation Association (NHSRA) Fitness Assessment Procedures is an excellent field-based assessment. The procedures of the NHSRA fitness assessment and normative data can be obtained by writing NHSRA, 451 Hungerford Drive, Suite 100, Rockville, MD 20850. No submaximum estimates are available for children under the age of 15. Currently, however, researchers are investigating the target heart rate criteria for estimating oxygen consumption in pediatrics. Because there are issues relative to validity, tests using run–walk endurance protocols and norm-referenced standards of specific populations are questionable at best. We do not recommend spending the time to assess cardiorespiratory endurance invalidly.

PHASE II: DISCREPANCY ANALYSIS

Without Phase II of the Functional Kinesiological Analysis (see Figure 12.1), assessment of the physical domain has little relevance for appropriate programming and least restrictive placement. An examination of domains is necessary to determine which functional skills are integral to each child's independent performance within those domains. After appropriate functional skills are selected, each skill should be task analyzed with respect to motor and physiological demands. Then a comparison can be made with the child's present level of kinesiological functioning and those demands required for performing each skill. Once the comparison is complete, a level of intervention can be prescribed. In schools with a variety of support services, it is best for a team to administer the FKA system. Team members may share, in a transdisciplinary manner, testing responsibilities as well as domain analyses. Prescription, however, should include the special education teacher as the process manager and all of the team members in making a decision relative to appropriate intervention.

The comprehensive delivery of appropriate services for children and adolescents with TBI is far beyond the scope of any single individual, regardless of professional preparation. Literature perusal supports the need for interdisciplinary, multidisciplinary, and transdisciplinary approaches in the provision of services to any person with a disability (Masters, Mori, & Lange, 1983).

CONCLUSION

Because this textbook is intended to fill a resource void for teachers, therapists, clinicians, and parents, a word of conclusion seems appropriate. Frequently, service personnel find professional expertise overlapping when considering the domains involved with fulfillment of various needs and services for individuals who are incapacitated in some way. This is especially true for professionals working with children who are traumatically brain injured. An essential ingredient in holistic philosophy pertaining

TABLE 12.6. Role Responsibility for the Multidisciplinary Team

Therapist	***Physical Educator***	
Basic biological proficiency	*Advanced biological proficiency*	
Strength	Muscular strength	
Endurance	Muscular endurance	
Range of Motion	Flexibility	
Flexibility	Cardiorespiratory endurance	
	Speed and power	
Basic perceptual–motor proficiency	*Advanced perceptual–motor proficiency*	
Infant reflexes	Reaction time	
Sensory stimulation	Movement time	
Conditioned reflexes	Directionality	
Static balance	Laterality	
Figure–ground relationships	Spatial awareness	
Kinesthesis	Kinesthesis	
Basic locomotor proficiency	*Advanced locomotor and manual control proficiency*	
Rolling	Running	Throwing
Crawling	Hopping	Catching
Creeping	Galloping	Kicking
Walking	Jumping	Striking

to service for persons with TBI is cooperation between and among various professional individuals. A multidisciplinary organizational effort is essential for most effective interaction in meeting the needs of the student. Such an approach is most obviously necessary when considering the close and often overlapping services in physical education and therapy. The most important ingredient in the activity–therapy program is effective communication between the teacher and the therapist. In an attempt to promote better communication, we provide Table 12.6 to illustrate a suggested breakdown of role responsibilities (Eichstaedt & Kalakian, 1987). This table is a menu of proficiencies illustrated by professional role; it is not to be considered all-inclusive. Additionally, if a school has the advantage of having a qualified special physical educator on staff, this person should have at least a masters degree and the capability to assess and prescribe basic as well as advanced forms of physical and motor proficiency, as listed on each side of the table.

REFERENCES

Astrand, P.-O., & Rodhl, K. (1986). *Textbook of work physiology: Physiological bases of exercise.* New York: McGraw-Hill.

Baggerly, J. (1986). Rehabilitation of adults with head trauma. *Nursing Clinics of North America, 21,* 577–587.

Bar-Or, O. (1987). The importance of differences between children and adults for exercise testing and exercise prescription. In *Exercise Testing and Exercise Prescription for Special Cases* (pp. 49–65) by J. S. Skinner (Ed.). Philadelphia: Lea & Febiger.

Barsch, R. A. (1965). *Movegenic curriculum.* Madison, WI: Bureau for Handicapped Children.

Bobath, B. (1985). *Hemiplegia: Examination, assessment and treatment.* Stuttgart, West Germany: Thieme.

Bond, M. R. (1976). Assessment of the psychological outcome of severe head injury. *ACTA Neurochirurgica,* (Wien), *4,* 57–70.

Clarkson, H. M., & Gilewich, G. B. (1989). *Musculoskeletal assessment.* Baltimore: Williams and Wilkins.

Cratty, B. (1979). *Perceptual and motor development in infants and children* (3rd ed.). Englewood Cliffs, NJ: Prentice-Hall.

Cratty, B. (1986). *Perceptual and motor development in infants and children.* Englewood Cliffs, NJ: Prentice-Hall.

Croce, R., & DePaepe, J. (1988). Exercise as a therapeutic modality for children with pediatric diseases. In *Proceedings 17th Physical Activity for Exceptional Children* (pp. 47–51). Oakland, CA.

Croce, R., & DePaepe, J. (1989). A critique of therapeutic intervention programming with reference to an alternative approach based on motor learning theory. *Physical and Occupational Therapy in Pediatrics,* 9(3), 5–33.

DePompolo, R. (1987). Traumatic brain injury. In M. Sinaki (Ed.), *Basic clinical rehabilitation medicine.* Philadelphia: Decker.

Eckert, H. (1987). *Motor development.* Indianapolis, IN: Benchmark Press.

Eichstaedt, C., & Kalakian, L. (1987). *Developmental/adapted physical education.* New York: Macmillan.

Evans, C. D. (1981). *Rehabilitation after severe head injury.* Edinburgh, Scotland: Churchill.

Freivogel, S., & Piorreck, S. (1990). Motor Function Assessment Scale. In G. Doll-Tepper, C. Dahms, B. Doll, & H. von Selzam (Eds.), *Adapted physical activity.* Berlin: Springer Verlag.

Gallahue, D. (1989). *Understanding motor development.* Carmel, IN: Benchmark Press.
Haywood, K. M. (1986). *Life span motor development.* Champaign, IL: Human Kinetics.
Heyward, V. (1984). *Designs for fitness.* Minneapolis: Burgess.
Hyde, S. A., Goodard, C. M., & Scott, O. M. (1983). The Myometer: The development of a clinical tool. *Physiotherapy, 69*(12), 424–427.
Jacobs, H. E. (1988). The Los Angeles Head Injury Survey: Procedures and initial findings. *Archives of Physical Medicine Rehabilitation, 69,* 425–431.
Keough, J., & Sugden, D. (1985). *Movement skill development.* New York: Macmillan.
Kools, J., Tweedie, D. (1975). Development of praxis in children. *Perceptual and Motor Skills, 40,* 11–19.
MacKay-Lyons, M. (1989). Low-load, prolonged stretch in treatment of elbow flexion contractures secondary to head trauma: A case report. *Physical Therapy, 69*(4), 292–296.
Masters, L. F., Mori, A. A., & Lange, E. K. (1983). *Adapted physical education: A practitioner's guide.* Austin, TX: PRO-ED.
Miles, B. H., Nierengarten, M. A., & Nearing, R. J. (1988). A review of the eleven most often cited assessment instruments used in adapted physical education. *Clinical Kinesiology, 42*(4), 33–40.
Payne, G. P., & Isaacs, L. D. (1987). *Human motor development: A lifespan approach.* Mountain View, CA: Mayfield.
Rao, N., Jellinek, H. M., Harberg, J. K., & Fryback, D. G. (1988). The art of medicine: Subjective measures as predictors of outcomes in stroke and traumatic brain injury. *Archives of Physical Medicine Rehabilitation, 69,* 179–182.
Reheault, W., Miller, M., Nothnagel, P., Straessle, J., & Urban, D. (1988). Intertester reliability and concurrent validity of fluid-based and universal goniometers for active knee flexion. *Physical Therapy, 68,* 1676–1678.
Smutock, M. A., Grafman, J., Salazar, A. M., Sweeney, J. K., Jonas, B. S., & DiRocco, P. J. (1989). Effects of unilateral brain damage on contralateral and ipsilateral upper extremity function in hemiplesia. *Physical Therapy, 69,* 195–203.
Wickstrom, R. L. (1983). *Fundamental motor patterns.* Philadelphia: Lea & Febiger.
Ylvisaker, M. (Ed.). (1985). *Head injury rehabilitation: Children and adolescents.* Austin, TX: PRO-ED.

CHAPTER 13

Physical Interventions and Accommodations

JOHN J. FEENICK
DENNIS JUDD

Physical educational programming for individuals who have suffered a traumatic brain injury (TBI) can present challenging problems unique from those found in other segments of the educational system. Students who have suffered a brain injury frequently have physical, sensory, cognitive, and social–behavioral problems. Results of TBI can range from mild motor impairment to severe paralysis with a complete loss of motor function. It has been reported that 10% of severely injured school-aged students showed no significant sensorimotor problems, 10% were partially physically dependent, 17% were totally dependent, and 73% achieved motoric independence (Savage & Wolcott, 1988). Students who are experiencing sensorimotor problems should be monitored by a school-based physical education (PE) teacher who has some training in adapted physical education and sensorimotor development (Savage & Wolcott, 1988). Some of the identified problems may be familiar to the teacher, whereas others pose situations that require special consideration and innovation. When a child returns to school following a TBI, the teacher cannot assume that the child is able to fully participate in physical education. Professionals such as physical and occupational therapists should be consulted, and the school should obtain a written statement from the supervising physician stating that participation in physical activities is permissible. In this chapter, we concentrate on providing information that has proven helpful in developing programming for the situations that require unique strategies.

To this point, little literature is available on reintegrating the student with TBI into the PE program. Common motor deficits, affective disorders, and cognitive problems are well documented, and solutions for reintegrating these students into the traditional classroom have received attention. Because the issue of returning students with TBI to playing fields, gymnasiums, and recreational activities has not received much attention, teachers seeking assistance need to enlist help from physical education teachers, physical and occupational therapists, recreational therapists, and special education teachers who have experience in dealing with these students.

The majority of students who experience TBI were not enrolled in special education prior to their injury. Martin (1988) stated that the parents of most students with TBI are much less likely than those of children born with disabilities to understand special education needs or to realize that these services are available. Section 504 of the Rehabilitation Act and Public Law 101-476 mandate that the public schools must evaluate the student sufficiently to be able to program educationally. This mandate includes medical diagnostic services, if necessary, at the school's expense (Martin, 1988). A school district that does not employ professionals who can write a specific individualized physical intervention educational program for a student with TBI, can often find services by contacting the National Head Injury Foundation. Most states have local chapters that could help the school find qualified professionals.

A look at the demographics of survivors of TBI is helpful in explaining that physical activities are important to this population. Survivors tend to be young, male, and lacking a strong predisposition for classroom activities (Vogenthaler, 1987). Prior to their injuries, many of this group were physically active and oriented toward risk taking activities. Performance in the physical education setting is often important in reestablishing the student's sense of self-esteem following return to school from a medical environment. The types of motor deficits vary with each situation, and students with brain injury who have difficulty dealing with residual deficits may have a greater problem adjusting to loss of physical skills than to loss of cognitive skills. Vocational goals for many people with serious brain injuries tend to be oriented toward technical or manual labor, with postsecondary education not a priority (Ben-Yishay, 1987). Thus, the development of motor skill becomes even more necessary to ensure future success.

INTERVENTION STRATEGIES

To develop strategies for attaining objectives related to a physical education curriculum, one needs a basic understanding of motor relearning. It is impossible to discuss every possible combination of deficits and their effect on physical education or reeducation; however, knowledge of the following concepts will help in the planning and implementation stages.

Open Versus Closed Skills

Activities can be divided into two general categories, open and closed skills (see Table 13.1). Closed activities can be described as static and require only limited perceptual skills. During the performance of closed skills, the individual relies primarily upon proprioceptive control (unconscious sensations from receptors in the skin and joints that allow conscious appreciation of the position of the body) and is usually not forced to make temporal or spatial adjustments (Oxendine, 1984). Developing closed skills requires the individual to work on repetitive and efficient movement patterns. Performing a closed skill, although it requires many physical and perceptual skills, is not as difficult as participating in a team sport that requires rapid responses to movements of teammates and opponents. Team sport, which is classified as an open skill, requires much more rapid decision making and presents a greater number of spatial or temporal decisions than does a closed skill. The student must make unpredictable

TABLE 13.1. Examples of Closed and Open Skills

Closed Skill	*Open Skill*
Unstructured walking	Competitive singles tennis
Catching a ball	Competitive doubles tennis
Tumbling activities	Competitive basketball
Partner tennis drills	Soccer
Golf	
Running broad jump	

decisions of when and how a response should be made in a team sport setting. Table 13.1 lists physical activities that require different levels of perceptual processing. The order of difficulty of these tasks will vary for each student, depending upon individual skills and prior experiences. In general, as the number of participants and the degree of competitiveness increase, so do the number and complexity of decisions involved.

Fatigue's Role on Learning

Fatigue has a significant influence on the learning of motor skills. Many family members report patient tiredness as one of the most common problems following head injury. A rapid decrease in ability to attend to difficult tasks and to perform even familiar activities is common following TBI. Incorporating endurance activities into the student's overall program plan should be a priority (Novack, Roth, & Boll, 1988).

Response to Feedback

Feedback is an important component of motor relearning. A student's ability to accurately perceive feedback, both internal and external, is often affected following TBI. The student with TBI often has difficulty with accurately understanding the reactions of other students or the instructor, and is unable to "feel" the difference between correct and incorrect motor performance. Information feedback is the provision of some signal to indicate the correctness, accuracy, or adequacy of a response or behavior (Oxendine, 1984). The student with brain injury often needs more feedback than most students to motivate him or her to continue to work. It is often necessary to change teaching techniques even for students with mild brain injury. Memory impairments and cognitive deficits that occur with brain injury affect the student's ability to use and integrate feedback as other students do. If no feedback is given as to how the performance compares with a desired response, the student has no point of reference. When the student is repetitiously working on a motor skill, concurrent feedback is most valuable. The teacher may give immediate feedback by praising the student's improvement or by pointing to errors in movement patterns during performance. This reduces delays in positive feedback and can motivate the student to continue working on the skill. Record keeping and competition against personal standards usually result in greater motivation, more serious practice, and continued efforts to improve movement patterns (Oxendine, 1984). Teachers should remember, however, that giving too much information could confuse the student because of his or her physical and cognitive deficits. Teachers should provide feedback for gradual improvement or small progressive steps using the type of reinforcement that works best for each particular student.

CLASSROOM STRATEGIES

Addressing teaching strategies in relation to groups of problems or syndromes is difficult due to the large number of possible combinations of deficits from which students with TBI could suffer (see Table 13.2 for a list of deficits that may need to be considered when developing a program). In the following sections, we briefly explain

TABLE 13.2. Physical and Motor Sequelae Following Traumatic Brain Injury

Dysfunction	*Definition*	*Implication*
Hemiplegia	Motor paralysis of one side of body	Inhibits movement of arm, face, and leg
Hemiparesis	Motor weakness of one side of body	Limits movement of arm, face, and leg
Hypotonicity	Low muscle tone of trunk or extremities	Prevents initiation of balanced muscle contraction for stability
Rigidity	Resistance to movement in any range	Prevents active movements and good positioning
Spasticity	Inappropriate sustained contraction of muscles	Limits full range of movement; can lead to contractures
Ataxia	Loss of ability to coordinate smooth movements or steady gait	Limits control of trunk, extremities, and ability to regain balance
Tremors	Involuntary movements from contractions of opposing muscles	May inhibit fine motor precision or gross motor ability
Apraxia	Problems in planning, organizing, and carrying out sequential movements on command	Prevents deliberate and spontaneous execution of motion or of speed

teaching strategies that have been effective in dealing with specific problems. Modifying these techniques to fit the structure of the existing PE program will create an environment that allows the student with TBI to meet with more success.

Goal Setting

A clear understanding of class expectations is critical to the student's success, especially in the early reintegration process. Development of goals and objectives appears to have greater importance for these students. Because of memory deficits and decreased internal motivation, the student needs to see visible evidence of improvement. In academic classes, this evidence comprises test scores, reviewed assignments, and so forth, but the physical educator has to use other methods.

It is useful to identify specific tasks that both the teacher and the student feel would be important to improve. Finding a way to measure improvement may be difficult as it is often necessary to break down the identified task into small pieces in order to record improvement frequently enough to maintain student interest and effort. Once this step is in place, the teacher should devise a schedule of reassessment and revision of goals and objectives. Although this may seem like more work than it is worth, once the student sees improvement, the remainder of the program will run smoothly. Case Study 13.1 describes a goal-setting program devised to help a student run.

CASE STUDY 13.1

A Goal-Setting Program

HA has coordination deficits and is unable to run due to increased influence of abnormal posture and decreased balance when performing faster paced activities. She has a strong desire to run and participate with her peers but does not do well when participating in group tasks. HA's family and academic teachers note her decreased endurance and would like to see her be able to participate in a more active education program.

After some discussion, HA and the teacher decided that endurance objectives would be most realistic and functional for HA at present. The measurement of her endurance indicates that she can walk $\frac{2}{3}$ of a mile in 30 minutes before asking to stop. The teacher and HA established objectives to focus on improving HA's performance on this task and developed a goal for completion of this task:

Objective 1: HA will walk $\frac{3}{4}$ of a mile in less than 30 minutes.

Goal 1: HA will walk $1\frac{1}{4}$ mile in less than 45 minutes.

Thus, HA knows her first level of achievement and the level of performance she will work to attain before moving to more difficult tasks. Upon obtaining the first objective, another will be established. The setting of goals and objectives does not preclude other activities in the physical education class or even other objectives in this skill area. As endurance improves and HA meets her goal in this area, additional goals are developed that focus on skills of balance and coordination. This will help HA reach her ultimate goal of returning to full participation in physical education with her peers.

Task Selection

Identifying appropriate tasks is difficult to separate from setting proper goals. Whenever possible, including the student with a TBI in the activities of the rest of the class is the optimal choice. Orthopedic, visual, behavioral, or other factors could interfere with this option, however. Then the student with TBI might withdraw from individual help because of a desire to integrate into the traditional classroom setting. Although the selection of activities is rarely clear-cut, the process of identifying good options can be similar from one case to the next. Work with and include the treatment team in any decisions (Carr & Shepherd, 1987).

Identifying Parameters of Safety

Students with TBI often demonstrate a lack of awareness of their deficits. This, along with the tendency of adolescents—especially males—to be risk takers, creates serious safety concerns. The teacher needs to establish acceptable safety guidelines, such as activities considered off limits. Not all injuries can be avoided, but a set of guidelines will help in establishing a reasonably safe program.

Matching Activities with Goals

Selected activities should include those that require balance, speed, visual tracking, rapid changes in direction, and other components of skilled motor tasks. It will frequently be necessary to break down activities into progressions. Breaking tasks into smaller components makes it easier for the student to reach his or her goal (Schmidt, 1988). For example, if a student has difficulty hopping on one foot, have him hop on two feet, or on one foot while holding onto a moving support such as a shopping or laundry cart. Activities should be mixed as much as possible, with the emphasis on specific skills to reach individual goals and objectives.

Modifying the Environment

In most instances, the student with TBI will not be able to succeed in the school setting without some assistance. The treatment team should determine how much assistance is enough and how much is excessive. The nature of most PE classes makes modifications difficult. Therefore, in the early stages of reintegration, the program often must allow for individual or small group activity (Savage & Wolcott, 1988). For example, a simple weight training and calisthenics program that the student can perform away from the rest of the class allows for consistency and does not require the student to make rapid conditional decisions that are frequent in large group activities.

When group activities are to be integrated, they can be modified such that the student performs the same role in each class or is positioned with or against the same students. Finding a student who demonstrates insight into and interest in the student with TBI can be helpful. This student can serve as an assistant and guide when possible. The assistant's support can motivate the student with TBI to complete tasks and feel confident about peer interaction. It is important to note, however, that too much modification can be counterproductive and have an impact on the student's self-esteem.

The most important modification in the PE setting is to educate the student's classmates to his or her deficits and strengths. The class should be taught how they can help in the reintegration process. Most literature regarding reintegration of students with brain injury into the classroom does not address how the student's peers can help in the rehabilitation process. Most teachers and students would be more helpful if they better understood common deficits that students face in the difficult process of moving back into the school environment following neurological injury.

PHYSICAL EDUCATION FOR THE STUDENT WITH TBI IN THE ELEMENTARY SCHOOL SETTING

Although developing educational plans for younger students following traumatic brain injury is similar to developing those in the secondary schools, several differences should be considered. Some of these differences are directly related to motor performance, whereas others fall into the categories of cognitive or emotional behaviors. The physical educator needs to consider all the differences discussed in the following sections when deciding on teaching strategies and goal selection (Savage, 1987).

Dependence Versus Independence

As children age, they naturally begin expressing some sense of autonomy from parents and stop depending on them for basic needs. When a child suffers an injury at an early age, family members tend to care for all of the child's needs without allowing the child to contribute. If the child had not begun the move toward independence prior to the injury, cognitive, emotional, and physical dependence often fostered in the hospital setting can contribute to the delay in the child's becoming more independent. Parents must undergo a reintegration process similar to that of the student and should allow the school environment to play a role as their child becomes progressively more independent.

Habilitation Versus Rehabilitation

Younger students generally have fewer life experiences to assist them in the recovery process. With long-term memory more intact following injury than short-term or immediate memory, the student with TBI often uses these preinjury experiences to build skills. Younger students without work experience, significant social interaction, or developed study skills have fewer tools to assist them in the formal education process. Thus, the teacher's goal is to allow the student to draw from previous experiences or create new exciting experiences.

Interrupted Motor Skill Development

When a TBI occurs during the early school years, the student has not had time enough to develop and refine basic motor skills. These skills, such as throwing, catching, running to kick a moving object, and performing difficult balance activities, are difficult to relearn after injury. If the student has never learned or mastered the task, it is even more difficult. The older student who has already mastered most basic motor patterns may be limited by orthopedic, perceptual, or other neurological problems but still have a mental image of what the task is and how it feels to perform the skill correctly. Because younger students do not have this image, they may be at a disadvantage. For example, if the student has performed a cartwheel with some success prior to the injury, the chances are better that the student can learn this skill. On the other hand, if the student was not familiar with this task and experienced a brain injury that resulted in balance and memory deficits, this skill would be more difficult to master.

Awareness of Deficits

Although most students who have suffered TBIs are aware of their deficits, this awareness is often confusing to the younger student. Children are less aware of their physical and cognitive deficits because they have had less opportunity to experience related abilities. Younger students have difficulty with dividing attention between several aspects of an activity. In large group, open skill activities, children must make many decisions within a very short period of time. If the skill is not familiar to the student, these decisions are difficult and the student becomes frustrated.

Motivation

Following brain injury, many students demonstrate changes in their desire to achieve success in the school environment (Savage & Wolcott, 1988). Because the younger student has not usually developed an appreciation of more abstract positive reinforcement by the time of the injury, his or her motivation level is frequently lower than that of the normal child. Often compounding this problem is the close personal attention and support the child received during hospitalization and rehabilitation prior to returning to school. The student often learns to expect this type of attention and grows accustomed to special treatment.

To be successful, the PE teacher must identify the type of environment that motivates the younger student and design the structure to limit or eliminate the dependent behavior. Often, this requires starting the student in very small classes or with a teacher's aid assisting the child in a large class. Feedback and the use of positive reinforcement need to be frequent initially and carefully diminished when possible.

SELECTION OF ACTIVITIES FOR YOUNG STUDENTS

When choosing classroom activities for young students, teachers must consider magnified attention deficits, inability to stay on task, and memory problems. Setting clear goals and modifying the class environment become increasingly important when working with young students who have suffered TBI. Based on the student's abilities, the range of activities can vary from remedial closed skill activities advocated by physical and occupational therapists to sports and games used in the traditional classroom (see Table 13.3).

Difficulties demonstrated by younger children in learning new motor skills are similar to those demonstrated by older students, except the younger children have fewer experiences from which to draw. The teacher should keep in mind that the sport or game to be learned is not as critical as the strategy for learning the skills (Sherrill, 1977).

Younger students with TBI present unique problems due to their limited educational and social development prior to injury. The lack of insight into cognitive and motor deficits by both these students and their peers creates a significant obstacle to reintegration into the mainstream classroom. The students' successful return to the regular PE classroom will require a concerted effort by the entire educational team, with the parents playing a major role. Each child's parents are encouraged to take an interest in the student's motor development and to work individually on the skills being developed in the PE classroom.

TABLE 13.3. Range of Activities for Students with Physical or Cognitive Deficits Following TBI

	Physical Deficits	***Cognitive Deficits***
Less demanding	Student remains stationary with large base of support	Student performs single activity with minimal options
	Student remains stationary with object to respond to	Student experiences variety of changes to objects or environment
	Student moves but has no secondary task to attend to	Student participates in one-on-one activities
More demanding	Student participates in ball game that requires running or rapid movement	Student responds to changes made by other students

PHYSICAL AND COGNITIVE DEFICITS AND THEIR IMPACT ON MOTOR PERFORMANCE

The deficits described in the following sections are often experienced by students following traumatic brain injury. Not all the deficits are strictly motor problems, but they all influence the ability to learn and perform physical skills. Each brief description is followed by discussion of how the problem can affect the student in the PE setting. Case Studies 13.2 through 13.5 describe students who have some of these deficits that affect their performance in physical education classes. Because each problem is rarely seen in isolation and usually occurs in combination with several others, many more combinations of problems present than can be discussed (Mercer & Boch, 1983).

CASE STUDY 13.2

A Plan to Solve Behavior Problems in Physical Education Following TBI

JY, a 16-year-old male, was involved in a motor vehicle accident in which he was thrown from a truck and received head injuries and a fractured femur. Computerized tomography indicated significant damage to the left frontal and partial areas of the cerebral cortex. Following completion of his acute rehabilitation program, JY returned home and reentered school.

Despite demonstrating physical skills appropriate for his age and development, JY had difficulty participating with his peers in a regular physical education program. Behaviors that were not evident prior to the accident, such as frequent verbal outbursts, refusal to participate in activities and occasional fighting, became problematic. He developed a pattern of avoiding class by skipping, forgetting to bring equipment, or managing to be assigned to in-school suspension during physical education class. Although JY's manipulative behaviors caused other teachers difficulty, they were more frequent during physical education class.

When JY was confronted with his behavior, he stated that he was not having problems except that his leg hurt during activity. After 6 weeks of gradually increasing problems in physical education and a corresponding decrease in other courses, a reassessment of JY's educational plan was suggested.

The first step was to assess the current program and try to determine what may have been causing the problems. His complaints of leg pain were ruled out by follow-up with his orthopedic physician and his mother, who stated that JY never complained of leg pain while he participated in physical activities at home. It was suggested that the difference in environment between the gymnasium and the classroom could be the root of the problem. The noise, confusion, and structure of most physical education classes can be contributing factors.

JY was scheduled into an alternative physical education class for three of his five weekly PE classes. These three classes were spent working with skill building drills related to activity being taught in the regular class.

The physical education teacher solicited a student with a career interest in medicine as a volunteer to help with JY's special program. The program emphasized staying on task, following instructions, and being able to complete activities with a minimum of instruction. Very little emphasis was placed on physical performance; instead, feedback was directed at JY's behavior. During the two other classes, JY participated with the regular physical education class. He was initially paired with the student volunteer, and later weaned from his support.

Although JY continued to have some behavioral problems in the large group for several weeks, a sharp decrease in absenteeism was noted immediately. As he became more comfortable in the class and demonstrated fewer outbursts, more effects of his cognitive deficits became evident. While able to perform all the basic skills required to participate in a volleyball game, he had trouble understanding simple strategies and responding to the flow of play. The inflexibility of his thought process, which was not evident in structured reading and writing tasks, became clear when he was asked to respond quickly to the reactions of others in an open skill environment. The model of 3 days per week in individual sessions and 2 days with the larger group was continued to help JY deal with the frustration and provide practice in making decisions in response to his environment.

Sixteen weeks following initiation of this program, JY was participating in the large class 5 days per week without significant behavioral problems and no unusual absenteeism. Although his ability to compete with his peers in open skills has not returned to the level he demonstrated prior to his accident, he has shown improvement. The model described in this case study allowed JY to gradually reintegrate into a structured physical education setting as he recovered his skills during the process of neurologic healing. The continuous assessment of his recovery and the insight into his deficits by other members of the educational team were two very important factors in the successful outcome of this program.

CASE STUDY 13.3

Encouraging Continued Interest in Physical Education Following TBI

RK, a 14-year-old male, was struck by a motor vehicle while riding his bicycle. The accident resulted in head injury, multiple rib fractures, and liver damage. A computerized tomography scan indicated bilateral and parietal lobe damage. He remained hospitalized due to medical complications for 3 weeks and participated in an inpatient rehabilitation program for 3 months prior to returning to the public schools.

RK's major deficits were identified by the rehabilitation team as distractibility, left hemiplegia, impaired short-term memory, and poor judgment. The majority of in-patient activities were provided in a one-to-one setting in order to focus his attention and compensate for short-term memory deficits. His behavior was also marked by a tendency to disrupt group activities and tease students who were easily angered by such behaviors.

Prior to his injury, RK enjoyed physical education (PE) and was very active in youth soccer and basketball programs. Upon his return to school, he requested to be involved in PE classes and indicated very little interest in other classes except math. His residual left hemiplegia disallowed any participation in team-related activities with his peers. The educational planning team believed, however, that involvement in the PE setting would be important in motivating RK to participate in other aspects of his education.

Based upon the recommendations of the physical therapist, RK's program included jogging (despite his poor control, the activity was deemed safe on level surfaces), throwing and catching activities, modified calisthenics, and kicking and punting. It was recommended that he not participate in activities that required sudden changes in direction or coordinated use of both arms. RK was scheduled into regular PE class (he refused participation in adapted PE class) with modifications in grading guidelines to reflect his expected levels of performance. According to the program, he would dress out for class (gym clothes were brought by his sister only if he forgot them) and would be ready to begin class with the rest of his classmates. He would participate in calisthenics using modifications as needed and would require no more than one cue to remember the appropriate exercise. He would participate in any drill of which he was physically capable and would sit out one daily activity of his choosing. During activities that required rapid changes in direction or coordinated use of both arms, RK was excused from direct participation but was required to record selected statistics of classmates' activities. This activity incorporates his interest in math and requires work on attention and concentration.

Due to the very controlled structure on specific aspects of his program, fewer decisions were required of RK and he was expected only to participate and follow directions. In RK's case, it was important that he was motivated to participate in PE or problems could surface due to his attention deficit. Frontal lobe damage similar to what RK experienced often is accompanied by decreased motivation to work toward abstract or intrinsic rewards. The emphasis of his PE program was aligned more with the general learning skills and the reinforcement of participation in other less motivating aspects of his program. Physical therapy was one area in which RK was never a willing participant due to the emphasis on his physical problems. By tying RK's participation in physical education with his performance in physical therapy, his motivation improved and, in time, so did his motor skills. By restructuring the typical objectives of the class, the desired goal of improved motor performance was attained.

CASE STUDY 13.4

Physical Education Program for Wheelchair-Bound Student

Following a motor vehicle accident, GN, aged 15, received multiple trauma, which included a left femoral fracture, multiple rib fractures, and a collapsed lung. His massive head injuries included left frontotemporal and cerebellar trauma. He remained in a coma for 6 weeks and required inpatient rehabilitation for 5 months. His physical problems included mild tremors of both arms, slow uncoordinated movement of both arms (affecting the right more than the left), and inability to stand without assistance due to poor balance. He used a wheelchair and was able to propel it slowly for only a short distance.

GN had a strong athletic background prior to his injury and was considered an average student in academic areas. Following his injury, he demonstrated decreased academic motivation, poor short-term memory, significant visual perceptual deficits (including altered depth perception), and difficulty tracking moving objects.

Typically, this type of student is not enrolled in physical education, but instead receives physical and occupational therapy. In GN's case, the treatment team discussed physical education as an option because it might motivate him in other areas of his education. Members of the team expressed concern that this type of student would require more attention in PE than was possible due to a shortage of staff. Concern was also raised that any PE activity that was too difficult could increase tightness in GN's muscles or fatigue him to the point that his participation in an important reading comprehension class would be affected. After much discussion, however, the team determined that participation in PE would play an important role in GN's overall educational plan.

His program consisted of working in the weight room 3 days per week using universal gym and hydra-fitness resistive exercise equipment. Free weights were not used because of GN's lack of coordination and the presence of tremors in his arms. With the assistance of the instructor, GN developed a structured list of activities consisting of basic use of the standard exercise stations. Upon the physical therapist's recommendation, the resistance was limited to a level at which GN could perform all repetitions with a symmetrical technique without straining. GN's initial program consisted of three sets of 10 repetitions of the following exercises: bench press, military press, leg press, rowing, and latissimus dorsi pull-down. The teacher stressed the importance of maintaining symmetry and of avoiding twisting of the trunk or leaning, as these activities could further increase GN's already exaggerated asymmetry. After GN became comfortable with this routine and could complete it without difficulty, stretching and wheelchair endurance exercises were added to his program.

To assure GN's concentration and to maximize his effort, his performance on tasks was recorded and monitored on a regular basis. Strength was measured by recording how much weight GN could lift or how much force he could generate without straining, using asymmetrical techniques. Flexibility was measured by recording the distance between his fingertips and a predetermined target, with the target and test position changing depending on the muscle group being tested. Wheelchair mobility skills were measured by timing GN in propelling his chair. With significant improvements in his performance, GN became invested in the program with only occasional setbacks due to frustration or depression. Because he enjoyed the classes, his therapists were able to correlate completion of his objectives in their class to participation in physical education. Although slow, several improvements resulted, including increased tolerance for physical activity and increased motivation to continue working on the long difficult process of physical rehabilitation. Gary's progress in physical education also allowed the physical therapist to concentrate on training functional skills rather than spending time on more time-consuming activities that are required to build strength, flexibility, and endurance.

CASE STUDY 13.5

Gradually Working Student with TBI into Large Group Activities

SB was 7 years old when she was hit by a car while riding her bicycle in front of her family's home. She returned to school after 5 months of hospitalization and 8 months of homebound instruction. Diagnostic tests performed shortly after the injury revealed significant damage to both frontal lobes and diffuse damage in the region of the cerebellum. SB was in a coma for 6 days and required tube feeding for 4 weeks before swallowing problems were resolved. Her homebound therapists reported continued problems with distractibility, poor immediate and short-term memory (although she knew the lyrics to all current top-40 hits), low frustration tolerance, and trouble with social interactions. Her homebound physical and occupational therapist placed emphasis on improving visual skills and coordination to allow SB to participate in age-appropriate games and activities.

In school physical education, SB was very disruptive when attempts were made to include her in large group activities. Her behaviors included wandering away from the group, not following teacher instructions, and screaming episodes when she did not want to participate. The PE instructor noted poor visual motor skills, "floppy posture," and poor endurance.

SB's behavior in the classroom setting was similar to that seen in physical education. She had difficulty sitting still for longer than 3 minutes and was easily distracted. Her teachers had success by adapting her work to short goal-directed activities that addressed her use of compensatory memory strategies and rewarding her on-task behavior.

In physical education class, SB was grouped with an older student and another student SB's age. Both students were educated about SB's injury and her physical, mental, and social deficits. For several weeks, the three students participated in separate activities from the rest of the class. Most of the activities were familiar and designed to be as fun as possible. Some activities included kicking skills, simple tumbling activities, scooter board, tag games, and rollerskating. Both younger students developed an attachment to the older student who, with the help of the teacher, tried to develop a bond between the students. Although the younger student did not develop a strong relationship with SB, the additional student was important in that she did not make SB feel singled out and she helped keep SB from becoming too dependent on the older student. The program continued for 16 weeks, with the frequency of the small group meetings decreasing to once per week after 8 weeks.

The older student attended the large group sessions not as a participant, but more as a "coach" figure. SB was able to participate in large class activities for 30 minutes without straying off task or having tantrums. SB completed 50% of the classes without difficulty other than minor redirection offered by her "coach." When the school year ended, SB was attending physical education once per week without the older student in attendance and completing 75% of these classes without any unusually disruptive behavior. Although she continued to have difficulty with social interactions with her peers, SB was able to demonstrate an ability to learn new motor skills and participate in group activities without apparent confusion or inability to follow game rules. The teacher noted improved posture and, along with SB's other teachers, found that her visual motor skill had developed significantly.

Fatigability

Endurance for performance of physical activities can be significantly impaired following TBI due to changes in cardiopulmonary control mechanisms. In combination with prolonged inactivity in the early stages of recovery, these changes can have a profound effect on the student's cardiovascular and muscular endurance capabilities (Novack et al., 1988).

Impact on function

The student may be lethargic and unable to fully participate in full class activities. The student may never attain normal endurance levels due to neurological damage. Activities may need to be adjusted to the student's endurance levels. The teacher must determine the student's present levels of endurance, establish goals and objectives, and then motivate the student.

Memory Deficits

An important cognitive aspect of motor learning is the ability to remember verbal, visual, or tactile cues to learn new skills. For the student with TBI, discrete portions of memory may be impaired while the remainder of memory functions remain intact.

Impact on function

The student may be unable to remember routines familiar to other students, may forget class rules, and may leave athletic gear at home. The teacher must develop a system to help the student compensate for gaps in memory skill.

Poor Attention

The student may be unable to attend to instruction within the framework of the typical class setting. Poor attention is usually a symptom of some other deficit, such as impaired selective attention, auditory perception problems, or fatigability. Factors that affect attention include (a) how much information the student can grasp at once, (b) whether processing speed is normal, (c) whether attention and concentration deteriorate rapidly as skills become more complex, and (d) how distractible the student is.

Impact on function

In combination with memory problems, the student will have significant problems learning new skills. Those activities that are most familiar and motivating to the student hold the greatest potential for success.

Irritability

The student may not respond to stressful situations as effectively as he or she did prior to the injury. This problem is related to the student's self-image, level of motivation, and level of fatigue.

Impact on function

Competitive activities can lead to irritability. The adolescent may want to give up on activities easily and refuse tasks in which he or she anticipates problems. If the teacher anticipates that a student may have a negative experience by participating in competitive activities, that student should be withheld from them. Some students can be selectively involved in competitive activities as a mechanism to help control their irritability.

Decreased Motor Speed

The student may be unable to move quickly enough to generate the force necessary to throw for distance, change direction quickly, or jump effectively. The teacher should determine if there is weakness of one or more limbs (usually only one side of the body is affected).

Impact on function

Decreased motor speed may influence the performance of motor skills that require a coordinated effort of the entire body. The student may display inadequate reactions to thrown objects, difficulty in balance for simple activities, and inability to stop and start quickly.

Apathy

The central catalyst for motor performance is motivation (Oxendine, 1984). Without the drive to succeed, the student's improvement and recovery are significantly reduced. Damage to the frontal lobe of the cerebral cortex and the limbic system often affects the motivation of the student with TBI.

Impact on function

Reducing apathy is very important when developing an educational plan for students with TBI. With carefully structured behavioral programming, extrinsic motivation can be used as a temporary substitute for internal motivation, with the hope that extrinsic motivation can be increasingly unnecessary.

Visual Perceptual Deficits

TBI can affect how the student sees and interprets visual information. Portions of the visual field may be blank, depth perception may be altered, and the student may be confused as to an object's shape. The occupational therapist can often identify when these and other visual problems exist and how to correct them.

Impact on function

The student may have a difficult time performing tasks that require foot–eye and hand–eye coordination, such as soccer, basketball, or tennis. These skills need to be modified (see section on open vs. closed activities) but should continue to be part of the active rehabilitation process.

Aphasia

Aphasia is a term that identifies loss of the ability to understand or use verbal communication. In the TBI student, aphasia can be a large but often overlooked problem. Deficits can range from the inability to make sounds to the inability to form words, or the student may be able to make sentences that are coherent but unrelated to the topic of conversation. This impairment is a common source of anger and confusion in students with TBI.

Impact on function

The student may have difficulty understanding rules, instructions, or cues. The student may have difficulty asking questions or communicating with peers and classmates. Often the student will pretend to understand rather than risk asking a question of the instructor. Alternate forms of communication should be considered and can be developed with the assistance of a speech pathologist.

Apraxia

Apraxia is defined as problems in planning, organizing, and carrying out sequential movements on command. Students who experience these problems may not demonstrate any observable physical problem. Despite clear verbal or visual cues, the individual may not be able to successfully complete a task or series of tasks routinely performed by his or her peers. The student also may be able to perform the task on his or her own, without cues or prompts, but unable to do so on request. Apraxia is often the most difficult problem to understand and identify.

Impact on function

The patient may be unable to perform structured group skills but able to participate in unstructured activities, such as shooting a basketball alone or hitting a tennis ball against a wall. The student may be able to play volleyball in a group situation but unable to participate in a simple but unfamiliar drill designed to teach a specific skill, such as setting or spiking.

Poor Balance

Balance problems, like most deficits identified in this section, are extremely variable. The student may require a wheelchair or walker for mobility. In the physical education setting, a student's poor balance may be evident only when performing difficult tasks. The student could be unsafe in many activities that require rapid movements.

Impact on function

Individuals with balance disorders often display two very different sets of behaviors. They either display poor judgment and participate in unsafe activities without taking precautions or are extremely fearful of movement and choose not to participate in any activities even if they are capable. Safety awareness is an important consideration with a student who exhibits poor balance. Safety goals can be established with the student while providing adequate protection. A student who falls frequently while jogging may initially be required to wear a protective helmet and knee and elbow pads. When the student can complete two consecutive laps without falls, the teacher should allow the student to remove the protective gear.

Mental Inflexibility

Some students with TBI are unable to change mental focus from one task to another. This skill is extremely important in fast-moving team sports that require, for instance, moving from defense to offense, from shooting a basketball to rebounding, or from trying to hit a ball to running to first base. These skills, which are important in open skill activities and sports strategies, are lost or delayed significantly in the student with TBI.

Impact on function

The student with TBI may have difficulty following even the most basic changes in strategies. This student should participate in more closed skill activities and, as improvements are seen, progress into more open skills.

Sensory Changes

Students with TBI may be extremely sensitive to pain of any type, may not feel portions of their extremities, or may be unable to differentiate one sensation from another.

Impact on function

Students with TBI may not tolerate activities such as stretching or may respond to gentle contact with agitation or complaints of injury. They may complain frequently of minor injury, headache, or nausea. These complaints are difficult to verify and should be monitored closely. The school nurse should be consulted when questions arise as to the validity of the complaints.

PHYSICAL OR OCCUPATIONAL THERAPIST'S ROLE IN REINTEGRATION

The physical educator is the member of the educational team who is primarily responsible for the development of motor skills, lifetime leisure interests, and physical fitness for the student with TBI. The easiest and most important step to take in developing a physical education plan for a student with TBI is to seek assistance. Members of the student's family and support group should be among the first resources contacted. These individuals, along with the student, will provide much of the information necessary to begin the planning process (Giangrico, 1989). Three specialists in particular also may be helpful in developing effective programs. The physical and occupational therapists specialize in retraining skills and making adaptations to the environments of individuals who have physical and perceptual impairments, whereas the recreational therapist (see next section) develops recreational and leisure programs.

Selecting consultants is often difficult if a school system does not employ a physical or occupational therapist. The family should be aware of and provide the name of specialists who were involved in the student's early rehabilitation. If this information is not available, the National Head Injury Foundation or a local chapter could offer information on local resources. If unable to locate a therapist with experience in working with patients with TBI, the next best choice is a therapist with experience working with pediatric populations, as this person will be familiar with the school setting and will have insight into effective approaches in dealing with disabled adolescents.

Determining which specialist to consult for specific deficits can often lead to confusion. Is the occupational therapist the best choice for insight into visual problems? Is the physical therapist the best source of information regarding an endurance problem? In general, a degree in either occupational or physical therapy is not as important as the postgraduate experience with evaluation and treatment of individuals with brain injuries. To provide effective treatment, the two disciplines must rely on each other's expertise to become familiar with aspects of both treatment philosophies.

The following list identifies some problem behaviors of students with TBI and interventions used by occupational and physical therapists to assist in providing physical education:

1. *The student consistently has difficulty learning new tasks.* The therapist should identify what motor tasks are most difficult and identify strategies to teach those tasks. He or she should look for key words and cues that effectively elicit a response.

2. *The student is unable to participate in an activity due to decreased control of one arm.* The therapist should instruct the student in exercise to improve hand function. Activities should be modified so the student can participate. The therapist may fabricate an assistive device to improve hand function.

3. *The student frequently complains of pain or injury.* The therapist should assess the range of motion, flexibility, and so forth. (The school nurse and physician may need to examine the student, as well.)

4. *The student exhibits poor hand–eye and foot–eye coordination.* The therapist can recommend enjoyable activities to build coordination; suggest equipment or task modifications to improve performance; and test to help identify any visual deficits.

5. *The student falls frequently.* The therapist can identify balance or perceptual problems, suggest alternative safe activities, and instruct the student in balance activities.

INCORPORATING THERAPEUTIC RECREATION INTO THE SCHOOL SETTING

The constructive and enjoyable use of leisure time is important to people's satisfaction and well-being. Although physical education and leisure skills are generally not considered similar, combining the two can often be beneficial. Many students are motivated to participate in physical education because of grades, peer pressure, parental encouragement, or intrinsic motivation, but these variables are absent in most children who have suffered a traumatic brain injury. To be effective, tasks usually must be enjoyable and result in immediate and concrete reinforcement. The specialist in therapeutic recreation (TR), often referred to as a recreation therapist, is a professional trained to assess the needs of students who have physical, emotional, perceptual, and cognitive problems (Peterson & Gunn, 1984).

Recreational activities provide the ideal setting for students with TBI to test their social skills (Fazio & Fralish, 1988). Determining the student's strengths and weaknesses in their use of leisure time can help the therapist develop a program to aid the student and instructor to enhance class participation. It is important to consult with TR specialists who have experience working with students with TBI. These specialists will help the classroom instructor anticipate the student's recovery process and the unique problems that might arise from the combinations of cognitive, physical, and emotional sequelae.

The following list demonstrates how the philosophy of the TR specialist can be used to assist the physical educator to successfully integrate the student with TBI into the PE environment:

1. *The student does not wish to participate in PE class and prefers vocational classes.* If the student prefers vocational tasks, many of these tasks should be designed to provide endurance and gross motor development.

2. *The student uses a variety of excuses to avoid participation in PE class.* The student may avoid competition due to motor problems. Tasks should be designed to eliminate competition or stress on performance. Emphasis should be placed on participation.

3. *The student does not do well working in large group activities, and prefers one-to-one or individual tasks.* Socialization skills should be built in a small group or one-on-one setting. Group

members should be changed frequently. The size of the group can be increased as the student feels comfortable.

4. *The student is unable to demonstrate skill development in the classroom due to cognitive and attention problems but enjoys and does well in the PE setting.* The student should be rewarded for performance in PE activities as he or she would be in other classes. Although the student may never completely master academic or vocational skills, it is important to have leisure skills to compensate.

These examples are not necessarily indicative of the programming ideas offered by a TR specialist in any given situation. They do suggest the importance of development of leisure skills to help the individual in the constructive use of spare-time activities and enhancement of self-image. The TR specialist can assist in determining the most appropriate environment for the development of socialization and leisure skills in students with TBI using the unique environment of the PE class to its full potential.

CONCUSSION IN SPORTS: GUIDELINES FOR ITS MANAGEMENT

Traumatic brain injuries are always a major concern while student athletes are participating in sports. Serious brain injuries in athletics, although infrequent, get most of the attention from the media and medical profession. The National Football Head and Neck Registry reported 33 football-related deaths from cerebral intracranial hematomas from 1980 to 1986 (Wilberger & Maroon, 1989). In high school football alone, an estimated 20% of players receive minor head injuries yearly, with a total of more than 250,000 injuries. In many instances, individuals who sustain minor head injuries do not seek medical attention. Brain injury in sports can result from any rotational (angular) or translational (linear) force applied to the head. Rotational forces are more commonly the cause of loss of consciousness associated with deep shearing injuries of nerve fibers, whereas translational forces are less likely to cause unconsciousness but more commonly lead to skull fractures, intracranial hematomas, and cerebral contusions (Colorado Medical Society, 1991). The recognition, immediate management, and institution of guidelines for return to competition become important considerations for coaches and school personnel.

The most prevalent head injury in a sports setting is the minor head injury or concussion. Wilberger and Maroon (1989) defined mild concussion as immediate and transient impairment of neural function, such as alteration of consciousness, disturbance of vision or equilibrium, and other similar symptoms. Many attempts have been made to classify mild concussions. Bruno and Gennarelli (1987) divided cerebral concussion into two major categories, the mild and the classic. In a mild cerebral concussion, consciousness is preserved, but the individual experiences some degree of neurologic disturbance. An athlete who experiences a Grade I mild concussion shows signs of temporary confusion and disorientation, and may exhibit mild unsteadiness of gait and a dazed facial expression. Posttraumatic amnesia (forgetting events from the moment of injury) and retrograde amnesia (loss of memory of events immediately preceding and including impact) are absent in a Grade I injury. Grade II mild concussion is characterized by confusion associated with retrograde amnesia that develops 5 to 10 minutes following injury. In a Grade III mild concussion, confusion and amnesia are present at the time of impact. The athlete's signs and confusion last for several minutes, but soon his or her level of consciousness returns to normal with some permanent retrograde and posttraumatic amnesia. Although no loss of consciousness is experienced in the three grades of mild cerebral concussion, some degree of cerebral dysfunction has occurred (Bruno & Gennarelli, 1987). Thus, these athletes require postinjury evaluation. They may develop postconcussion syndrome characterized by headache, inability to concentrate, and irritability.

The classic cerebral concussion involves loss of consciousness. This unconsciousness occurs at impact, and its duration generally correlates with the severity of injury. The individual usually recovers within a matter of seconds or minutes, then experiences phases of confusion, disorientation, and retrograde and posttraumatic amnesia before becoming fully alert. Athletes who have suffered a period of unconsciousness for any period of time should not be allowed to return to play the same day, and strong consideration should be given to physician evaluation (Cantu, 1986). These athletes will experience any number of postconcussion signs, such as headache, subtle changes in personality, inability to concentrate, and losses in memory (Bruno & Gennarelli, 1987). The educator and coaching staff must be aware of these problems, monitor them, and not allow the athlete to return to play until these signs return to normal. The athlete should be required to receive physician clearance before he or she returns to full participation.

Opinions of medical professionals vary as to when an athlete should return to competition following a mild cerebral concussion. Every case should be judged individually with the consultation of the team physician. Wilberger and Maroon (1989) reported that an athlete who has experienced a minor head injury will have a four times greater risk of sustaining another injury within a short period of time. Repeated concussions appear to impart cumulative damage, resulting in increasing severity and duration with each incident. Information processing ability can be reduced following concussion. Twenty-five percent of athletes with three minor head injuries, 33% of athletes with four minor head injuries, and 40% of athletes with five minor head injuries showed persistent abnormalities on neuropsychological testing at 6 months after injury (Colorado Medical Society, 1991). Not only does this have a profound effect on the return of the athlete to play following a brain injury, but educators should be concerned with the effects of minor brain injury on learning in the classroom in the immediate weeks following injury.

In a *Grade I* mild concussion, the athlete should be allowed to return to play after a period of 20 minutes only if all symptoms (headache, dizziness, impaired orientation, impaired concentration, memory dysfunction) are absent at rest and during exertion (Cantu, 1986). This 20-minute period allows observation of the athlete for any underlying sequela. Returning an athlete to play the same day as the injury should be a decision based on objective criteria rather than emotion. Computerized tomography (CT) or magnetic resonance imaging is recommended in all instances in which headache or other associated symptoms either worsen or persist longer than 1 week (Colorado Medical Society, 1991). If a second mild concussion is experienced in the same sports season, the student should be withheld from competition for at least 2 weeks and not allowed to participate until asymptomatic for 1 week. Three mild concussions should terminate the student's play for the season (Wilberger & Maroon, 1989).

Following a *Grade II* mild concussion, the athlete should discontinue play for at least 2 weeks and have a thorough neurological evaluation. A second incidence should eliminate the student from play for at least 1 month; the student should return only after a complete neurological evaluation has cleared the athlete. Three moderate concussions should require the athlete to discontinue participation for the season.

After a *Grade III* mild concussion, the student should not participate in athletics for at least 1 month. Return to play is dependent upon a feeling of no symptoms for 1 week after the month's rest. Two Grade III concussions in one sports season should conclude the student's participation for the season. This athlete should have a full neurological evaluation, including a CT scan, before a return to play is considered (Cantu, 1986). An athlete is often advised to avoid certain contact sports, although alternative sports activities may still be possible.

Athletes rendered unconscious (classic cerebral concussion) should be transported from the field to the nearest hospital by ambulance, with cervical immobilization if indicated. Neuroimaging of the brain should be performed on all athletes rendered unconscious and on all those who exhibit worsening postconcussion symptoms, focal neurological deficits, or persistent mental status alterations (Kelly et al., 1991). The athlete must rest for at least a month, and may return only after he or she exhibits no symptoms both at rest and during exertion. A student's season is terminated following two classic concussions, and return to any contact sports in the future should be discouraged in discussions with the athlete.

CONCLUSION

Students who suffer traumatic brain injury often experience significant sensory motor deficits that must be addressed. The majority of these students were young, healthy individuals who may have been physically active in school physical education and/or athletics. Reentry into a PE program can act to reestablish the student's self-esteem, especially if he or she was physically active prior to injury.

The student with TBI is dealing with many cognitive, emotional, and physical deficits. The educational team, which must work to reestablish the whole individual, must emphasize sensorimotor, cognitive, and social–behavior areas. The use of physical therapists, occupational therapists, physical educators, and recreational therapists can help in the physical intervention of the student with an acquired brain injury.

REFERENCES

Ben-Yishay, U. (1987). Relationship between employability and vocational outcome after intensive holistic cognitive rehabilitation. *Journal of Head Trauma Rehabilitation, 2*(1).

Bruno, L. A., & Gennarelli, T. A. (1987). Management guidelines for head injuries in athletics. *Clinics in Sports Medicine, 6,* 17–29.

Cantu, R. C. (1986). Guidelines for return to contact sports after a cerebral concussion. *The Physician and Sportsmedicine, 14,* 75–80.

Carr, J. H., & Shepherd, R. B. (1987). *Movement science: Foundations for physical therapy in rehabilitation.* Rockville, MD: Aspen.

Colorado Medical Society. (1991). *Guidelines for the management of concussion in sports.* Developed by the Colorado Sports Medicine Committee, Denver.

Fazio, M., & Fralish, K. (1988). A survey of leisure and recreation programs offered by agencies serving traumatic head injured adults. *Therapeutic Recreation Journal, 22,* 46–53.

Giangrico, M. F. (1989). *Providing related services to learners with severe handicaps in educational settings: Pursuing the least restrictive option.* Baltimore: Williams and Wilkins.

Kelly, J. P., Nichols, J. S., Filley, C. M., Lillehei, K. O., Rubinstein, D., & Kleinschmidt-Demasters, B. K. (1991, November 27). Concussion in sports: Guidelines for the prevention of catastrophic outcome. *Journal of the American Medical Association,* pp. 2867–2869.

Martin, R. (1988). Legal challenges in educating traumatic brain injured students. *Journal of Learning Disabilities, 21*(8).

Mercer, L., & Boch, M. (1983). Residual sensorimotor deficits in the adult head injured patient: A treatment approach. *Physical Therapy, 63,* 12.

Novack, T., Roth, D. L., & Boll, J. (1988). Treatment alternatives following mild head injury. *Rehabilitation Counseling Bulletin, 31,* 313–324.

Oxendine, J. B. (1984). *Psychology of motor learning* (2nd ed.). Englewood Cliffs, NJ: Prentice-Hall.

Peterson, C. A., & Gunn, S. L. (1984). *Therapeutic recreation program design: Principles and procedures.* Englewood Cliffs, NJ: Prentice-Hall.

Savage, R. (1987). Educational issues for the head injured adolescent and young adults. *The Journal of Head Injury Rehabilitation, 2,* 1–9.

Savage, R., & Wolcott, G. (1988). *An educators manual—What educators need to know about students with traumatic brain injury.* Washington, DC: National Head Injury Foundation.

Schmidt, R. A. (1988). *Motor control and learning* (2nd ed.). Champaign, IL: Human Kinetics.

Sherrill, C. (1977). *Adaptive physical education and recreation.* Dubuque, IA: W. C. Brown.

Vogenthaler, O. R. (1987). An overview of head injury: Its consequences and rehabilitation. *Brain Injury, 1.*

Wilberger, J. E., & Maroon, J. C. (1989). Head injuries in athletes. *Clinics in Sports Medicine, 8,* 1–9.

SECTION V

School and Community Dimensions

CHAPTER 14

A Neuroeducational Model for Teaching Students with Acquired Brain Injuries

RONALD C. SAVAGE
LOIS MISHKIN

The effect of an acquired brain injury (ABI) on a student is not merely a moment in time, but rather the initiation of a series of ever-widening circles of complexity. As other chapters have pointed out, an ABI for a child or adolescent creates an array of problems not yet entirely understood by physicians, psychologists, or educators. Thus, to truly do the best possible with these students, educators need to look carefully at the models used to guide this process. Can educators rely on past models that merely looked at the brain as a "black box"? or those models that likened the brain to a mere computer? or previous beliefs that the brain was merely a collection of experiences dictated by external cultural vestiges? Probably not. To work with students with acquired brain injuries, educators need a model that addresses three major questions:

1. How does the brain learn?
2. What happens to the brain when it is injured?
3. What do educators need to do to help students with ABI make progress over time?

An understanding of how the brain learns combined with knowledge of what happens to the brain when it is injured will help students meet the demands of the multiple life experiences they will face throughout their lives. Thus, educators need a model of learning and teaching that encompasses and respects the neurology of the brain. Educators have begun to recognize the need to increase their understanding of the brain in relationship to teaching and learning. A recent field called neuroeducation is taking steps that paralleled those of neurology and neuropsychology a few years back.

Neuroeducation is a model that supports brain-based teaching and learning for all students, especially those with neurologic (brain-based) problems. Learning resides in the brain, and to understand how to best teach students, educators need to know how the brain processes information, stores memories, connects new learnings with prior experiences, and mobilizes entire beings to make individuals who they are. The basic premise of a neuroeducation model is that the brain helps humans to accomplish three very important tasks: to think, to feel and act, and to move about the environment. Although it also is responsible for maintaining and operating all the other body systems (e.g., hearts beat, lungs take in and expel air), it is these three higher-level functions that make humans unique. Sadly, these three domains are what become disrupted when one sustains a brain injury; thinking, feelings and actions, and movements can become forever impaired within the blink of an eye.

HOW THE BRAIN LEARNS

The first step in learning about the brain requires a self-study. The brain needs to be asked a simple but elegant question: "How do you learn?" Whereas experts in cognitive psychology and neurology respond with models that become microscopic at genetic and biochemical levels, educators need to respond from a telescopic point of view and look more broadly at the three higher-level brain functions that propel lives.

First, we as humans cognitively respond (see Chapters 3–6) to our surroundings through all kinds of thinking efforts to make sense out of our world and to expand what we know. We "think" and we think about our own thinking—a process so neurologically complex that we may never really understand all that we are capable of accomplishing. Cognition involves awareness and judgment and knowing how to use what we have when we need to address new challenges. Our ability to think takes many forms; it is far beyond simple right and left hemisphere processing differences or frontal lobe functioning. Cognition is how we have defined the world through our ability (or inability) to think in ways that bring us the things we need to know, even when we did not choose to know them. Cognition is the way our brain understands the complexities of our internal and external cosmos. Thus, when a student sustains a brain injury, his or her ability to safely make sense of the world is grossly interrupted by the inability of the brain to think in those ways that had once been useful. A brain injury robs a person of the power to make sense out of his or her life in the world in which the person lives.

Second, the ability to feel and act upon those feelings (see Chapters 7–11) is also compromised by a brain injury. Our personalities, behaviors, beliefs, responses to others, love and caring, anger, self-perceptions—that is, our whole world—can become so traumatized by injury or disease that we actually lose who we are and who we were to become. Our behaviors—our actions onto ourselves and others—have long been the sole concern of behavioral psychology. Researchers are now learning that all things (genetics, language, culture, neurology, environments) affect how we behave and that many facets of behavior are much more complex than ever envisioned.

Third, our ability to move and explore our environment (see Chapters 12–13) within personal and ever-developing transportation systems has redefined our concept of place and time. We can move freely through once-restricted environments; we can change our movements or change where we want to move with the use of our brains. Once again, these are functions that become inhibited or eliminated after a brain injury. Our ability to be free-moving explorers of our universe is critically altered and inhibits our use of our world by limiting our ability to move ourselves where we want to go.

To think, to feel and act, and to move about are precisely the domains that neuroeducators need to address in a comprehensive, interdisciplinary model for students with ABI. It is the first step in understanding how the brain learns and how educators should best teach.

THE INJURED BRAIN

A crucial second step in understanding how the brain learns is increasing understanding of neuroanatomy to improve awareness of hemispheric processing similarities and differences, the functions and interrelationships among the four brain lobes (temporal, occipital, parietal, and frontal), the reticular activating system, the limbic system, and the executive system. By learning more about neurotransmitters, the hippocampus, hormones, seizures, neuropharmacology, and an array of other neurologic issues, educators will better understand how to reeducate the brain after injury.

Additionally, educators need to better understand the different kinds of brain injuries and their effects on individuals. Even though, as pointed out in Chapter 1, federal and state regulations and guidelines do not clearly define brain injury, educators can make an effort to learn the neurologic sequela of lack of oxygen to the brain, or the effect that neurotoxins have on students' intelligence. Many of the acquired brain injuries children sustain have very different effects depending on the individual child—prior history, age at injury, access to rehabilitation, and life circumstances. As pointed out in earlier chapters, these factors can tend to become more complex as the child continues to grow and develop over time. Unfortunately, the ever-widening ripples from an acquired brain injury may become greater as the student gets older.

What Educators Need to Do

To help children and adolescents with brain injuries to succeed, educators need to consider four factors in the neuroeducation model that can influence a student's outcome:

1. What environmental changes need to be made to help students with acquired brain injuries?
2. What are the critical transition issues in school reentry for students, parents, and the school?
3. What developmental factors impact on a student's recovery over time?
4. What type of teaching–learning framework best combines current knowledge of the brain and brain injury?

Although students who sustain brain injuries frequently are treated in medically dominated, *biophysical* environments (i.e., hospitals, rehabilitation centers) during

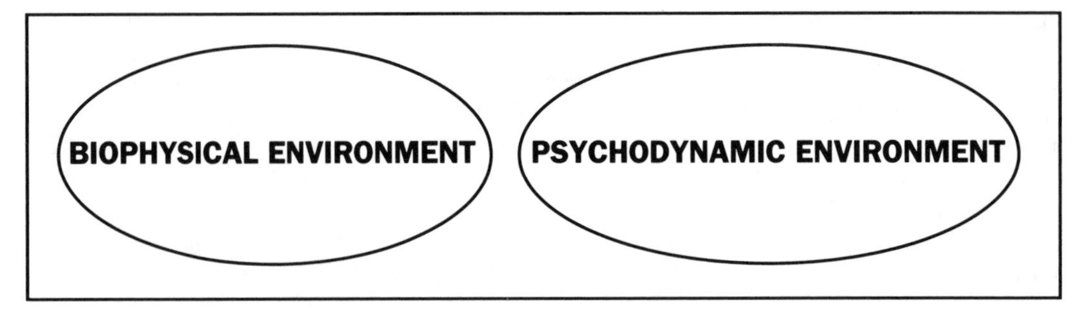

Figure 14.1. An individual's biophysical and psychodynamic environments, which rarely meet when students are treated solely in a medical model program.

their early recovery periods, these are rarely the *psychodynamic* environments that truly represent a child's life (see Figure 14.1). Often, children with serious brain injuries are likely to receive extensive physical, occupational, and speech therapies within a medical model program that is foreign and confusing to children (and adults). Children generally live, however, in a very psychodynamic world that centers around three critical and interlocking themes: their families and friends, school, and recreation. These driving forces in a student's life need to be recreated or brought into the biophysical environment as early as possible for better rehabilitation outcomes. In addition, the cracks that exist between the biophysical and the psychodynamic environments of the child often become the downfall of children as they transition from one model to another.

To eliminate these gaps between environments, the neuroeducation model proposes that these environments merge their resources and knowledge of students with ABI into one holistic model that allows children an array of services within a developmental continuum so that they are followed from the moment of injury throughout their lifetime (see Figure 14.2). Realistic efforts to bridge the gaps between hospitals, schools, insurance companies, families, and so on have demonstrated that children with ABI often end up forgotten, only to turn up somewhere else with more serious needs. Case Study 14.1 demonstrates this scenario.

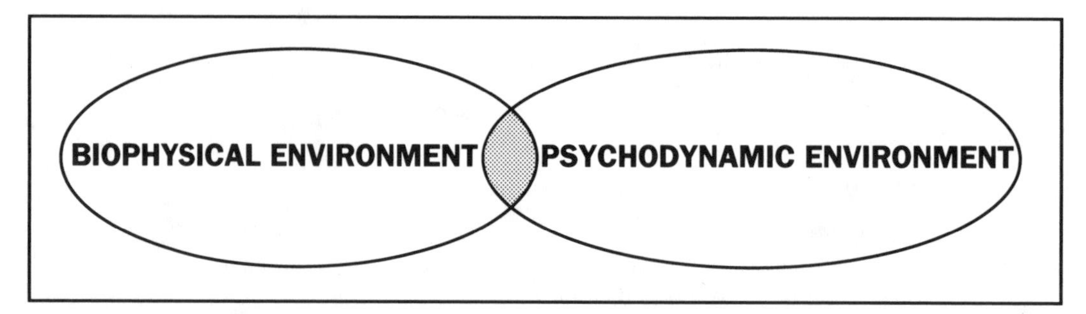

Figure 14.2. An individual's biophysical and psychodynamic environments, which are merged within a holistic neuroeducation model.

CASE STUDY 14.1

Forgotten Brain Injury

DW was 27 months old when he was riding in his parents' jeep while sitting on his mother's lap. A car abruptly stopped and DW's father hit the brakes, propelling his son and wife into the dash of the jeep. DW struck the hand grip bar on the dashboard with his forehead, receiving a moderate gash.

DW's parents immediately took him to the emergency room at the local medical center. On the way to the hospital, DW was vomiting and lost consciousness for 30 to 45 minutes. The physician who saw DW closed the laceration on his forehead and admitted him overnight. The next day, DW was very disoriented and confused. Testing revealed that DW had a small bleed in his left frontal lobe that needed to be removed by surgery. The operation was successful, and DW went home in 1 week.

Over the next 6 months, DW had uncontrollable crying spells, was very impulsive, and was inattentive. When he was 4 years old, his parents enrolled him in a preschool. His teacher reported that DW had five to six tantrums every day and that he needed to be isolated in a time-out area for his own safety and the safety of his schoolmates.

By the time DW started kindergarten, his impulsivity and outbursts were so severe that the teacher recommended counseling with the school psychologist. DW was retained in kindergarten and again retained in first grade. He spent most of his time outside the classroom in counseling or one-on-one tutoring sessions because of his distractibility and behavioral outbursts. At mid-year, his parents were asked to have DW evaluated by a child psychiatrist. Although a psychiatrist interviewed DW and his parents, nobody referenced DW's prior brain injury. The psychiatrist recommended that the parents receive counseling and behavior modification training in order to work with their child.

When DW turned 10 years old, he was hospitalized for severe behavioral outbursts and depression. He was placed in a private psychiatric facility for 2 years and has shown little if any progress to date. DW's medical records still do not note his traumatic brain injury.

Unfortunately for the student described in Case Study 14.1, he did not receive any therapeutic intervention, nor did the hospital or school interact regarding his immediate and ongoing needs. Students with lingering effects from ABI need the hospital and school to carefully coordinate services and information, and to follow the students over time. More specifically, early contact between the hospital and school would initiate early recognition of the student's needs prior to returning to school. In addition, the rehabilitation hospital should make every effort to document through videotape the student's progress and the various therapeutic interventions used in the student's rehabilitation. This videotape will later greatly benefit the classroom teacher when the student is transitioned into school, because teachers do not see the student until many weeks after the injury and often do not realize the tremendous progress the student has made to date. Hence, the videotape provides the teacher with a series of taped highlights that will provide the teacher with a better sense of the cognitive processes disrupted by the brain injury and problems that still exist, though possibly in a less prominent form.

It is also sound practice for the rehabilitation team to visit the school prior to the student's reentering. By walking around the school and observing instructional areas, the rehabilitation professionals who have worked with the student will be able to spot potential problem areas that could interfere with the student's continued progress. Rehabilitation staff need to be aware of potential movement problems for the student within the school's physical plant (i.e., classroom environments that may be overly stimulating and/or instructional components that may need to be adapted to eliminate frustration for the student). With many students, fatigue is a major factor in cognitive recovery, and the students may need a place to rest during the day. These situations and others can best be recognized by the rehabilitation professionals who have been working with the student since the injury.

Just prior to the student's reentering school, the rehabilitation team and the special education team should conduct an inservice training for all the teachers, school staff (teacher aides, secretaries and clerks, student support services), and, when applicable, the student's peers. At the inservice, the rehabilitation team needs to carefully present not only information on ABI and its effects on this particular student, but also a general overview of how the brain works from a neurologic perspective. Case Study 14.2 describes a student who returned to school without any prior communication between the hospital and the school.

CASE STUDY 14.2

Neglected Communication

Hi! My name is Carol J., "CJ" for short. I'm in the 10th grade and I had a head injury last year. This is my story. I hope it helps you understand what happens when you get a head trauma injury.

I was with my boyfriend in his three-wheeler. We were riding around the fields and didn't have any helmets on. Yes, I know how stupid that sounds. Anyway, we were trying to get "air" over some jumps when the three-wheeler I guess hit a rock and it bounced me off some other rocks. My boyfriend (except he is not my boyfriend now) flipped the bike and it came down on top of both of us. My boyfriend ended up okay but he had a concussion and lots of burns from the three-wheeler. I was knocked out.

My boyfriend went and got his father who put me in his truck and took me to the medical center. I guess my parents met us there but I don't remember because I ended up in a coma for 1 week. I remember my mom and dad being near me when I was in a coma. I know that sounds weird but I do. They say they tried to get me to squeeze their hand or to open my eyes but I didn't do it. I think I remember my friend Elaine singing to me and I remember my mom's perfume.

I was in the hospital for 1 month. I had to go over to another hospital after I got out of the medical center for some speech, some physical therapy, and occupational therapy. My therapists were really great and made me work hard. I owe them a lot. The trouble started when I got back to school.

When I got back to school (the 9th grade) my teachers had a meeting about me. My mom and dad went to the meeting and I went, too. I don't remember much of what was said but I sure remember all the work they piled on me to take home. I had a whole month of school work to make up and there were only 2 months of school left! I was sick to my stomach that night, but my dad said not to worry about it. Sure, he didn't have to do it.

Everything in school was hard. I kept forgetting my locker number. I went to some wrong classes. And my friends were saying I was trying to get attention with my head injury. I even had one teacher tell me that I had better get my work in soon or I would fail for the year. Pretty soon I started getting really depressed and didn't want to go to school or talk to my friends. I hated everything. I hated school, I hated my friends, I hated some of my teachers, and I hated having a traumatic brain injury. I really hated taking the Dilantin. It was like I was retarded or something. I don't mean that in a mean way I just felt horrible.

My biggest mistake was at the beginning of my 10th grade year. I had made it through 9th grade thanks to two teachers who helped me after school. But over the summer I started hanging around some different kids. We didn't do anything we just went around. I didn't see many of my old friends, not even Elaine. When school started again I was really different. My parents were fighting all the time and I heard them talk about divorce. My two younger brothers by my dad's first marriage were doing really great in school. And I still felt like I had a head injury. One day at school one of my friends from the summer gave me some liquor to drink from her hair brush. All of her friends had them. The rest of the day went by nice and easy.

Pretty soon I was taking my own "hair spray" to school every day. The teachers didn't know a thing. My grades were failures and none of my friends cared because they had the same grades. One day I stopped taking my Dilantin. I figured what the hell I'm not taking this crap any more nor am I going to take any other crap from anyone. My parents only yelled at me and the teachers didn't know I was alive. On the day before my third period study hall I went into the girls room. One of the girls in there had a bottle of vodka and was drinking from it with another girl. They said "here—want some" and I took the bottle and drank half of it down. I don't know what ever made me do it. The two girls started to laugh and said drink the rest so I did. Two hours later I was in the hospital.

After I drank the vodka I had a seizure. The two girls took off and somebody told the principal. He got the school nurse and she called an ambulance. I'm not sure what they did in the hospital and I really don't care to know. I guess I was violent and they had to drug me up.

I'm back in school again and I see my guidance counselor every day. She also helps me with some of my classes, especially algebra. I'm trying to stay calm and take my medication. My parents have separated and they think this is the best thing for right now. I still think I caused them to split up but my mom says "no." I am also trying to make some new friends. Elaine is still nice to me and I think that school is going better. I'm also getting some help two times a week from Dr. S. who is a head injury doctor. He says many of my problems were due to my head injury and not being able to handle things like I could before. I'm not sure but he says you've got nowhere to go but up.

I hope you or anyone you know never has a head injury.

Reentry and Educational Program Planning

Much work needs to be done by everyone during the process of a student's reentering school. Transition from the medical environment to the educational community is often mistakenly thought of as a 1-day activity. In fact, effective transition of the student into the mainstream of school may take several days, weeks, or even months. The student will most likely need a comprehensive educational plan that will need continual adjustment and flexibility in order to best meet the student's needs. Rehabilitation professionals need to keep in mind three very important questions in the transition process:

1. When is the child really ready to reenter school-based programs?
2. Where should the student initially be placed?
3. What comprises an Individualized Education Program (IEP) for a student with acquired brain injury?

As previously mentioned, many students reenter school without their teachers' having a firm understanding of acquired brain injury. Equally important, many students are placed back into school before they are ready. Rehabilitation professionals and educators have identified several factors that need to be considered before a student reenters school. To benefit from a school experience, students should be able to do the following (Cohen, 1986; Cohen, Joyce, Rhodes, & Welks, 1985):

1. Attend to a task for 10 to 15 minutes
2. Tolerate 20 to 30 minutes of general classroom stimulation (movement, distractions, noises)
3. Function within a group of two or more students
4. Engage in some type of meaningful communication
5. Follow simple directions
6. Give evidence of learning potential

Such factors greatly contribute to the success or failure of the transition process. In addition, the initial placement of the student needs to be carefully considered by the rehabilitation professionals and the school-based special educator. The student may initially be placed in one of the following educational options:

1. Regular class placement
2. Regular class placement with a range of support services that may include (a) classroom consultation with the teacher and special educator to services outside the classroom, such as cognitive rehabilitation, speech and language, occupational therapy, physical therapy, and/or adaptive physical/counseling services, and (b) tutoring in reading or mathematics.
3. Resource room services

4. Self-contained classes
5. Home instruction or residential programs

The educational placement decision must be based on the strengths and needs of each student, and as these needs change the placement of the student must also change. Students with acquired brain injuries often make rapid gains at the beginning of their recovery, but may need to have their placement in the school reevaluated more often than do other students receiving special education services. It would be preferable, of course, for each child to return to his or her original peer group; however, after being in a hospital environment for several weeks or months, the challenge of returning to a full academic program would be difficult for even the best of students. Hence, the initial placement and continual reevaluation of the student constitute major components in the successful transition of the student over time. Case Study 14.3 describes a student whose school did a poor job of considering his initial needs and evaluating his situation.

CASE STUDY 14.3

Misunderstood Brain Injury

JM was 15 years old when he sustained a closed head injury from a motorcycle accident. He was comatose for 6 days and suffered injury to the right frontal and temporal lobe areas of his brain. After 36 days in the regional medical center, JM returned home while still experiencing problems in attention, memory, impulsiveness, and appropriate social and personal behaviors.

Upon reentering school 44 days after his accident, JM, who had previously been a "C" to "B" student, was unable to keep up in his previous academic subjects, failed to complete homework assignments, and began to act out aggressively in class. His friends soon began to avoid him because of his "weird actions." After an extremely violent fight with a younger student, JM was suspended from school for 10 days. Following the suspension period, the special educator tested JM and found his academic skills to be 4 years below grade level and his emotional stability to be below the norm for his age group.

The school's basic staffing team, consisting of the special educator, his subject area teachers, and the assistant principal, decided to place JM in a classroom for "emotionally impaired" students within the school's special education program. However, JM continued his outbursts and aggressive acts to the point where residential placement in a school for emotionally disturbed adolescents with initiated. After only weeks in the residential school, JM attempted suicide with a drug overdose. At this point, a psychologist with experience in working with adolescents with acquired brain injuries was consulted to assist JM and his family.

Ideally, the IEP for the student should be written initially on a short-term basis (4–6 weeks) and reviewed every 6–8 weeks. Often, for other students with special needs, the IEP is written to cover an extended period of time, such as 6 months or longer. Many states even provide for the development of multi-year plans for some students. Regardless of the time frame, IEPs must be reviewed at least once a year. Because the student often makes rapid changes in the first year following a brain injury, it is important that the IEP be flexible enough not to restrict the changing needs of the child. Case Study 14.4 is about a student whose school helped her to achieve success in school by writing and periodically reevaluating her IEP.

CASE STUDY 14.4

Successful Individualized Education Program

NA was 16 years old when she sustained a head injury while snow skiing. She was comatose for 7 of the 33 days she spent in a medical center. While NA suffered diffuse head injury to her brain as the result of the impacting head-on collision with a tree, major damage was particularly noted in the frontal lobes and the left temporal lobe. When NA returned home, she had problems with remembering, following through with initiated plans, understanding the salient points in written and spoken language, age-appropriate behavior, and fatigue.

While NA was in the hospital, the speech-language pathologist worked with her and developed some cognitive strategies that NA could use to help organize her thoughts and actions. The school nurse, the special educator, and the speech therapist from NA's school visited her while she was in the hospital and met with NA's medical team to begin transition services prior to actual hospital discharge.

During the same time period, the school nurse and the special educator also set up three afternoon training sessions on traumatic brain injury for NA's teachers, guidance counselor, and the school administrators. A speaker from the state head injury chapter worked with the faculty and distributed print and videotape information on head injury to help them better understand what NA would be experiencing.

The basic staffing team for NA consisted of her subject area teachers, assistant principal, special educator, speech therapist, school nurse, a vocational rehabilitation counselor, a neuroeducator from the state head injury chapter, NA's parents, and her speech-language pathologist from the hospital. An educational plan was developed for NA as follows:

- NA would reenter school for morning sessions only until it was determined by her physician that she could physically handle a full school day.
- Prior to her accident, NA had been a "C" student. The decision was made that she should attend the morning classes in which she was enrolled before her accident (English, history, study hall, and algebra) with support services provided by the special educator during her third-period study hall.
- NA would check in with the special educator before each school day to make sure she had the right books and supplies for her

classes that day. Later she would check out with the special educator regarding homework assignments, upcoming tests, and any special needs.

- Three times each week, NA would meet with the special therapist and continue with the cognitive strategies program set up while in the hospital.
- NA would be guided to her next class by one of her friends and would be peer tutored in subject area assignments after school and on weekends as needed.
- NA's friends would also informally plan one social activity each weekend (athletic game, school dance, etc.) for NA to attend with her peers. They would also help NA monitor and relearn appropriate social behaviors.
- Academic strategies specified that NA would keep a daily journal with a calendar of "things to do"; her teachers would give NA a written structured overview of the main points for each of their lessons for her; NA would receive textbook study guides to use as she completed her homework with the help of the special educator and/or her peers; she would receive differentiated assignments to decrease the academic load without sacrificing the learning process.

One month after NA reentered school, she returned to a full school day, and another meeting was held. An IEP was written for the remainder of the year and a 5-year long-term plan was outlined that would include NA's future career goals. The vocational rehabilitation counselor helped plan NA's entrance into the area's new vocational-technical school in the fall and helped assess NA's present and potential work skills in regard to specific vocational training programs.

Two years later, NA was allowed to "graduate" with her peers; however, she was not formally awarded a high school diploma so that she could remain in school until age 21 to complete her vocational-technical school program in mechanical arts. Today NA works for a local ski resort repairing and renting ski equipment.

DEVELOPMENTAL ISSUES AND CONCERNS

Infants and Toddlers

The primary causes of acquired brain injuries in the infant and toddler years are falls, motor vehicle accidents (especially if the children are unrestrained or improperly restrained), and child abuse (DiScala, 1993). Almost all injuries occur either at home, in the immediate neighborhood, or with family members when away from home. As the infant begins to move around more independently, the possibility of injury becomes a daily, if not hourly, possibility. Toddlers are characterized by the ability to move independently and rapidly through the environment, sampling and exploring virtually everything in their path, but with little awareness of the possible hazards of doing so.

Developmentally, this is a period of very rapid changes as the infant progresses from complete dependence on others to understand and provide for his or her needs into a much more autonomous toddler who is capable of independent mobility, self-assertion, communication through spoken language, and social interaction. The specific facets of functioning (i.e., sensory, motor, language, emotional, behavioral, and social) are highly independent on each other during this period. Interruption of functioning or impairment in any one area is likely to have repercussions on other facets and can jeopardize the developmental course of the child during this period of growth. Brain injury can also interfere with the ability to learn from experience, to make connections between objects or actions, to attend and respond to demands, and to have the energy or ability to explore (Kaiser, Rideberg, Fankhauser, & Zumbohl, 1986). Although these kinds of alterations may be difficult to quantify, their impact on development can be pervasive and extensive.

Preschool-Aged Children

Preschool-aged children are at relatively high risk for injuries as this developmental period has the second highest incidence after adolescence (DiScala, 1993; Hendrick, Harwood-Hashe, & Hudson, 1964; Mannheimer, Dewey, & Melinger, 1966). Developmentally, preschool-aged children are increasingly involved in the larger social world. They are expected to learn to play and share with other children, to master and abide by basic social rules, to engage in most of their own immediate self-care, and to contain some of their emotional and behavioral expression. Although much of this development occurs within the family context, preschool-aged children are also expected to be able to separate comfortably and function for short periods of time without their parents. This is a also a period of rapid cognitive development with laying of the foundation for academic learning that will follow. The preschool child's exuberance and capacity for learning in all settings and practically at all times is probably unmatched. During this period, the child experiences an explosion in conceptualization, grappling with and mastering the basic concepts of time, size, and quantity, and developing an awareness of self, emotions, and relationships (Lehr & Savage, 1990).

Supporting and possibly driving this rapid development in learning is a "supercharged brain." Although the number of brain cells is no longer increasing, the connections between cells are rapidly expanding and are more numerous than in an adult brain (Huttenlocher, 1984). The developing brain is also using twice as much energy as the adult brain (Chugani, Phelps, & Mazziotta, 1987). The effect of injury on this brain that is in "high gear" is unknown because virtually no research studies have focused on injury sustained during the preschool-age period. The greater plasticity during this period may enhance recovery; however, severe injuries during this period are equally as likely to impair the long-term capacity for learning because the brain is not mature enough to develop adequate compensatory strategies.

Elementary- and Middle School–Aged Students

The years from 6 to 14 are lowest in terms of traumatic brain injury incidence (Annegers, Grabow, Kurland, & Laws, 1980; Kraus, Fife, Cox, Ramstein, & Conroy, 1986). Severe injuries at this age usually are related to motor vehicle accidents, with the child injured either as a passenger, bicycle rider, or pedestrian. Sports-related injuries also become more common during this period.

During the elementary and middle school–age years, the child's brain continues to be "supercharged," supporting the rapid development and learning that occurs during this period. The connections between the two hemispheres of the brain and between areas within each hemisphere become more efficient (Lehr & Savage, 1990). The interconnections between primary sensory, perceptual, motor, and association areas increase the ease in learning, such as that needed for academically related activities, including reading, spelling, writing, arithmetic, and reasoning.

Students during this period are immersed in learning; however, unlike during the preschool period, they are expected to do so in a group, away from home, and under the direction of adults other than family members. Despite the importance of mastery of academic skills, development of competence in social interaction (especially with other children) and of self-control and self-confidence is also essential. Acquired brain injury can interfere not only with academic learning, but also with psychosocial–emotional aspects of functioning during this developmental period. After a loss of consciousness greater than 24 hours, intellectual deficits can be serious and persistent (Klonoff, Clark, & Klonoff, 1993; Klonoff & Paris, 1974; Levin & Eisenberg, 1979). The effect of an ABI on academic skill learning may be most significant for younger children who have not yet mastered the basics of reading, writing, and arithmetic prior to injury (Chadwick, Rutter, Thompson, & Shaffer, 1981; Shaffer, Bijur, Chadwick, & Rutter, 1980). Controlled processes that underlie learning, such as attention, memory, and speed of information processing, may be impaired after a brain injury and can directly affect academic learning (Levin & Benton, 1986). In Case Study 14.5, an elementary student describes his experience following a head injury.

CASE STUDY 14.5

Elementary School Student's Experience Following Head Injury

I was 8 years old when I got my head injury. I was riding my bike on the sandpit road when a high school kid came around the corner and hit me. I don't remember anything about it. My brother Ian was with me and he saw the car smack me and me fly over the car into the bushes. My bike got run over cause the kid that hit me was drinking. And he didn't even stop until he saw my brother and his friends up the road. That's all stuff that Ian told me because I was unconscious.

I don't remember the hospital much. I remember my mom holding me and rubbing my head. My leg hurt the most cause it got broke in the accident. My mom says I was unconscious for 16 days and nights. She says they had to feed me with tubes and I had another tube to help me breathe. Mrs. R. had the kids in school send me cards. My mom read them to me over and over. I wanted to be back in school real bad. I missed our Halloween party.

After I got home a teacher worked with me. Then I went back to school. I only remember how happy I was to be back. I didn't remember where my desk was. I guess I cried the first day cause everything was so hard and the kids were way ahead of me. My mom says I cried all week. I had to take two medicines for my head injury. I don't know what they were.

Now I'm in the fifth grade and I am doing much better. I got two B's and three C's on my last report card. My mom says to say that it is still hard for me to read and think for a long time. As for me, I hate spelling. But I hated it before my head injury too. It takes me a while to get things and sometimes I have to bring work to my special teacher Mr. M. He helps me every afternoon for 45 minutes. When I first came back to school I saw him all afternoon. He says cause of me he is a head injury expert—ha, ha.

One thing I remember in Grade 3 is not being able to stay awake long. I was tired a lot. I even fell asleep in school. And I hated lunch, not the food. But I got mixed up cause everything was so loud. Mrs. R. used to let me eat lunch with her. This was good except she made me practice my math as we ate lunch.

I am suppose [sic] to tell you about my friends too. Ian, my brother, is still my best friend. He helps me with my homework and he is teaching me his computer. He said to say that I also have friends like Tommy, Jason, Franky, and Mica. We are on the same baseball team. We ride our bikes almost every day. I got a new bike after a year. My dad sent it from New York. My mom wasn't too happy about it. But I told her not to worry.

Right now I feel very good. I only take one medicine for my head injury. I think I am the same but sometimes it is still hard for me to learn stuff like reading for ideas and stuff. My teacher says I have come a long ways. Next year will be better, I hope.

Adolescent Students

During adolescence, the rate of traumatic brain injury increases dramatically, with the number of injuries sustained between ages 15 and 19 equal to that of all of the previous 14 years combined (Gross, Wolf, Kunitz, & Jane, 1985). Neurologically, the brain appears to be going through a major, and perhaps its last, reorganization. It has been known for many years that the frontal area of the brain is myelinated during adolescence; however, recent research has indicated that neurological changes may be more widespread. The increased number of nerve connections or synapses that characterized the earlier stages of development is reduced by as much as half in adolescence (Feinberg, 1982/1983). This appears to be the end of the "supercharged" childhood brain and the beginning of the efficient, stabilized adult brain. Both the changes in the frontal or "executive" part of the brain and the more efficient connections are likely to be related to the emerging ability to sustain logical thought in solving abstract and complex problems.

Adolescents are confronted with rapid psychological changes, including sexual and physical maturation. They are in the process of getting ready to become adults, but are not yet expected to grapple with the demands of adulthood (Savage & Allen, 1987). Along with the development of conceptual thought comes the ability to struggle with issues of self-identity and intimacy. Most adolescents confront the developmental tasks of this period with energy and with a burgeoning sense of independence, self-sufficiency, and self-confidence; however, they are also more aware of the fragility of life and the reality of death (Lehr, 1990; Lehr & Savage, 1990).

An acquired brain injury can alter the adolescent's sense of physical attractiveness, perception of invulnerability, self-confidence, social appropriateness, and cognitive capacities. Previously mastered academic skills appear to be more resistant to injury effects, and intellectual deficits may be less pronounced than in children (Brink, Garrett, Hale, Woo-Sam, & Nickel, 1970; Levin, Eisenberg, Wigg, & Kobayashi, 1982). Adolescents may resent the perception of being different subsequent to their injuries and may become quite resistant to the need to alter any part of their lives, despite the injury-related necessity. Any loss of school time can present significant difficulty in the high school years, both in terms of academic achievement and in psychosocial relationships. In the latter part of adolescence, the transition to adulthood in terms of vocational planning and training, as well as the development of intimate relationships, can be derailed by the effects of traumatic brain injury. The loss or postponement of future plans and dreams can trigger anger, depression, and possibly suicidal thoughts or behavior. In an attempt to blunt the personal impact of acquired brain injury effects, adolescents may resort to alcohol or drug use. Case Study 14.6 describes a high school student whose educators worked with her to achieve success.

CASE STUDY 14.6

High School Student's Reentry to Education Program

MD was an honor student who sustained a traumatic brain injury after being hit by a drunken driver during the spring vacation of her senior high school year. She spent 67 days in the hospital, 14 of which were in a coma. Following discharge from the hospital, MD continued to have problems with her memory, planning and organizational skills, and hearing. During the summer, she attended a special 2-week head injury program for young adults and received tutoring from two of her high school teachers so she could complete her graduation requirements.

MD had previously been accepted into a 4-year nursing program at the state university. She and her family decided to postpone her enrollment at the university for 1 year and opted for MD to take courses at the local community college. This would allow her to live at home, continue her outpatient therapy at the hospital, and rebuild her academic skills in English, mathematics, science, history, art, and music at the community college.

After enrolling in the community college, MD and her family met with the dean of students and each of her instructors to explain her injury and to offer the college information about traumatic brain injury. In addition to her courses, MD registered for a basic study skills course that offered academic tutoring and support services. Because the majority of students in this course were nontraditional students (people returning to school after raising a family), MD received much personal support from the other students and served as an inspiration to everyone else.

After a successful year at the community college, MD decided to stay an additional year and complete an associate's degree in liberal arts. She was successful in all of her academic courses except science. She found that the amount and type of memorization required in science were extremely frustrating for her. With the help of a neuroeducator, she rethought her original nursing goals, because scientific knowledge is a major requirement in such programs. Instead, she made plans to attend a state college within commuting distance from her home.

MD then transferred her associate's degree to that state college and selected a program leading to a bachelor's degree in education that would certify her as an early childhood teacher. With the help of her neuroeducator, MD registered for 9 to 13 credit hours of courses per semester and received peer tutoring and counseling provided by the college. She also became involved in the drama club and found that acting offered her an opportunity to role-play different characters, which, in turn, helped her to relearn subtle social skills. Three years later, she completed the requirements for her degree in education and is presently employed as a teacher's aide in a private preschool.

The careful planning and support services designed around MD's strengths and needs resulted in her successful integration into two postsecondary institutions. She not only received a bachelor's degree but, more important, she found an area of employment that she thoroughly enjoyed. Although she required an additional year of schooling and summer sessions, she was able to combine her rehabilitation therapy with her educational training and to begin living independently.

As one looks over the chapters in this book covering cognitive, psychosocial, and psychomotor issues, it is clear that, although students with brain injuries are individually different, they have overlapping similarities. Students with ABI frequently have difficulty attending to and concentrating on learning tasks; they need information carefully presented to them through their strengths and use of compensatory strategies; they need to practice through a number of modalities that which they are trying to learn; and they need to be able to personalize and generalize new learning so they can continue to grow. The neuroeducation model proposes that for many children with ABI to meet success, their program developers must consider answers to the following questions:

1. Do we know who this student was before the injury?
2. Do we know how this student has been changed by this injury?
3. Do we know this student's strengths, needs, and compensatory issues?
4. Do we know what environmental modifications we need to make for this student?

The neuroeducation model further proposes that, for many students, educators need to teach new information and strengthen previous learning through a five-step process that capitalizes on answers to these questions, as well as the common similarities seen in students with ABI (see Chapter 15 for an overview of specific teaching interventions). This five-step process is outlined below:

1. *Build the bridge from the old to the new.* Engage and focus the student's attention by introducing new information by either tying it to prior knowledge on the topic or tying it to the student's personal life experiences.

   EXAMPLE:

   "John, tell me what you already know about tigers." OR "John, have you ever seen a tiger in a zoo?"

   "Megan, what did we learn yesterday about fractions like $\frac{1}{2}$ and $\frac{1}{4}$?" OR "Megan, have you ever eaten just $\frac{1}{2}$ a candy bar? How much is that?"

2. *Create a framework for learning.* Teach the new information by using the student's strongest modalities and using compensatory strategies to reinforce particular learning needs.

   EXAMPLE:

   "John, here is a paragraph about tigers. Read it to yourself. Then use the color cues to help you answer the questions."

3. *Implement functional practice with a purpose.* Have the student practice the newly taught information to ensure learning and establish memory cues.

   EXAMPLE:

   "John, I have cut up your paragraph on tigers into sentences. Put the story back together so it makes sense. Then raise your hand."

4. *Generalize the learning to new situations.* Have the student extend the information to a new situation to help generalize learning.

   EXAMPLE:

   "John, write three sentences about tigers that you learned from your story. Draw a picture to go with your story."

5. *Move toward independence.* Use metacognitive strategies to help the student become more independent in his or her learning.

   EXAMPLE:

   "John, let's think of some ways to help you remember your facts about tigers. Can you think of one way?"

The neuroeducation model relies on teachers using a framework that focuses and personalizes attention by engaging the reticular activating system and the limbic system so that the student can tie new information to prior knowledge. Next, the information is taught through a multimodal process using all brain lobes (frontal, occipital, temporal, and parietal) with supported compensatory strategies. The student practices the information using an organizational framework and memory cues to enhance and store information. Then the newly learned information is looked at metacognitively to help the student generalize the learning and to discover how he or she can learn and/or remember best.

CONCLUSION

The major concepts addressed in this chapter through a neuroeducation model challenge educators' use of present models to adequately meet the needs of students with acquired brain injuries. Educators need to learn how to better identify these students and how to provide them with the educational services they deserve. As understanding increases about how the brain learns before and after injury and a brain-based teaching model is developed, educators will be able to develop educational programming options for students of all ages with different brain injuries.

REFERENCES

Annegers, J. F., Grabow, J. D., Kurland, L. T., & Laws, E. R. (1980). The epidemiology of head trauma in children. In K. Shapiro (Ed.). *Pediatric head trauma.* Mt. Kisco, NY: Futura.

Brink, J. D., Garrett, A. L., Hale, W. R., Woo-Sam, J., & Nickel, V. L. (1970). Recovery of motor and intellectual function in children sustaining severe head injuries. *Developmental Medicine and Child Neurology, 12,* 565–571.

Chadwick, O., Rutter, M., Thompson, J., & Shaffer, D. (1981). Intellectual performance and reading skills after localized head injury in childhood. *Journal of Child Psychology and Psychiatry, 22,* 117–139.

Chugani, H. T., Phelps, M. E., & Mazziotta, J. C. (1987). Positron emission tomography study of human brain functional development. *Annals of Neurology, 2,* 487–497.

Cohen, S. B. (1986). Educational reintegration and programming for children with head injuries. *Journal of Head Trauma Rehabilitation, 1,* 22–29.

Cohen, S. B., Joyce, C. M., Rhodes, K. W., & Welks, D. M. (1985). Educational programming for head injured students. In M. Ylvisaker (Ed.), *Head injury rehabilitation: Children and adolescents.* Austin, TX: PRO-ED.

DiScala, C. (1993). *Pediatric Trauma Registry biannual report.* Boston: Tufts University, Research and Training Center, National Pediatric Trauma Registry.

Feinberg, I. (1982/1983). Schizophrenia: Caused by a fault in programmed synaptic elimination during adolescence. *Journal of Psychiatric Research, 17,* 319–334.

Gross, C. R., Wolf, C., Kunitz, S. C., & Jane, J. A. (1985). Pilot traumatic coma data bank: A profile of head injuries in children. In R. G. Dacey, R. Winn, & R. Rimel (Eds.), *Trauma of the central nervous system.* New York: Raven Press.

Hendrick, E. B., Harwood-Hashe, D. C. F., & Hudson, A. R. (1964). Head injuries in children: A survey of 4465 consecutive cases at the Hospital for Sick Children, Toronto, Canada. *Clinical Neurosurgery, 11,* 46–65.

Huttenlocher, P. R. (1984). Synapse of elimination and plasticity in developing human cerebral cortex. *American Journal of Mental Deficiency, 88,* 488–496.

Kaiser, G., Rideberg, A., Fankhauser, I., & Zumbohl, C. (1986). Rehabilitation medicine following severe head injury in infants and children. In A. J. Raimondi, M. Choux, & C. DiRocco (Eds.), *Head injuries in newborn and infant.* New York: Springer-Verlag.

Klonoff, H., Clark, C., & Klonoff, P. (1993). Long-term outcome of head injuries: A 23 year follow-up study of children with head injuries. *Journal of Neurology, Neurosurgery, and Psychiatry, 56,* 410–415.

Klonoff, H., & Paris, R. (1974). Immediate, short-term and residual effects of acute head injuries in children: Neuropsychological and neurological correlates. In R.

Reitan & L. Davison (Eds.), *Clinical neuropsychology: Current status and applications*. New York: Wiley.

Kraus, J. F., Fife, D., Cox, P., Ramstein, K., & Conroy, C. (1986). Incidence, severity, and external causes of pediatric brain injury. *American Journal of Diseases of Childhood, 140,* 687–693.

Lehr, E., & Savage, R. C. (1990). Community and school integration from a developmental perspective. In *Community integration following traumatic brain injury.* Baltimore: Brookes.

Lehr, E. (1990). *Psychological management of traumatic brain injuries in children and adolescents.* Rockville, MD: Aspen.

Levin, H. S., & Benton, A. L. (1986). Developmental and acquired dyscalculia in children. In I. Fleming (Ed.), *Second European Symposium on Developmental Neurology.* Stuttgart, West Germany: Gustav Fisher Verlag.

Levin, H. S., & Eisenberg, H. M. (1979). Neuropsychological impairment after closed head injury in children and adolescents. *Journal of Pediatric Psychology, 4,* 389–402.

Levin, H. S., Eisenberg, H. M., Wigg, N. R., & Kobayashi, K. (1982). Memory and intellectual abilities after head injury in children and adolescents. *Neurosurgery, 11,* 668–673.

Mannheimer, D. I., Dewey, J., & Melinger, G. D. (1966). Fifty thousand child-years of accidental injuries. *Public Health Reports, 81,* 519.

Savage, R. C., & Allen, M. G. (1987). Educational issues for the traumatically brain injured early adolescent. *The Early Adolescent Magazine, 1,* 23–27.

Shaffer, D., Bijur, P., Chadwick, O. R. D., & Rutter, M. L. (1980). Head injury and later reading disability. *Journal of the American Academy of Child Psychiatry, 19,* 592–610.

CHAPTER 15

Creating an Effective Classroom Environment

JEAN L. BLOSSER
ROBERTA DEPOMPEI

Educating students with acquired brain injury (ABI) is a complex task requiring sensitivity to the behavioral and learning problems these students present as well as implementation of effective instructional strategies. Case studies and anecdotal summaries in the literature characterize students who do not possess the academic skills, the work or learning habits, or the cognitive strategies needed to succeed in the school setting. Because academic success is related to these capabilities, problems and weaknesses in these areas are of great concern to educators. Steps educators can take to consider each student's unique needs will have a positive impact on the student's performance and potential for success within the academic setting. In this chapter, we seek to help educators create an effective classroom environment. We propose a planning process for determining the educational needs of students with ABI; suggest classroom environments appropriate for providing educational instruction to these students; discuss the need for networking and collaboration among rehabilitation professionals, educators, and parents in order to plan effectively for school reintegration; provide promising instructional strategies that have been used successfully with a broad range of students with ABI from elementary school to high school; and provide examples of tools that can be used to facilitate discussion during the planning and education process.

Between 1989 and 1992, we surveyed over 750 general and special educators to determine their level of understanding of ABI and areas of concern to them with regard to working with students with ABI. In response to a question asking the type of information they needed, educators requested specific teaching and behavior management techniques appropriate to this population, ideas for arranging the teaching and learning environment, and strategies for adapting and altering the curriculum. In this chapter, we strive to respond to these requests.

The educational problems of these students may be related to the educational approaches being used. Therefore, if changes are made in the approach, the educational effort should become more productive. The educational experience can be more appropriate if educators take individual differences into account, analyze the learning tasks that must be accomplished, determine those student behaviors that contribute to success or nonsuccess, create a learning environment conducive to the student's needs, and selectively apply a variety of teaching techniques and strategies.

Intervention requires a multidimensional approach and the use of multiple strategies and resource materials. Several techniques and classroom adaptations can be implemented to help the student. All teachers who are working (or will be working) with the student should be encouraged to use as many of the techniques as possible during classroom and school interactions with the student. The family must also be apprised of the strategies and adaptations so they can promote successful practice within the home environment.

Rehabilitation and education professionals agree that good teaching strategies designed especially for students with ABI are necessary and essential. Although the literature about intervention for this population is growing rapidly, a definitive set of answers regarding the most effective teaching methods and strategies has not yet been generated. Because empirical evidence is lacking and research findings have not yet provided clear rules and guidelines, educators must be creative in finding workable teaching strategies. Several sources are available for obtaining the needed information. Some ideas can be derived from recommendations for effectively teaching other populations of children with disabilities who present similar problems and characteristics. Good insights can also be gained through experimentation, practice, and observation. The available literature in developmental psychology, special education, communicative disorders, and education also enables educators to derive teaching strategies suitable to this population's needs. Armed with a clear understanding of the student's acquired brain injury and residual strengths and weaknesses, the insightful teacher can make management decisions that will increase the potential for the student's success. By taking advantage of their existing repertoire of teaching strategies for children who present challenging needs, creative educators can meet the needs of the student with ABI. They need only to know how to identify which strategies are needed and when to apply them.

Knowledge of instructional strategies is essential; however, as with other areas of student–teacher interaction, the knowledge is useful only if acted upon. A definite relationship exists between the educator's attitudes, philosophies, and perceptions and the students' academic achievement and social behaviors. The educator must be responsive to the students' individual needs, interests, and abilities within the context of the educational and social expectations placed upon the students. This requires a unique person. The educators and educational programs that will be most effective with students with ABI are those that demonstrate positive attitudes toward children with disabilities and philosophies that demonstrate willingness to learn about ABI, willingness to personalize the curriculum and expectations for students, proven records of ability to focus on individual needs, and willingness to provide assistance as needed. Aside from these attitudinal qualities, teachers should be able to understand suggested methodologies and establish priorities.

DESIGNING INDIVIDUALIZED EDUCATION PROGRAMS THAT WORK

Educational programming for students with ABI can be thought of as a dynamic, ongoing four-step process consisting of *preplanning, planning, implementation,* and *evaluation* efforts. Preplanning involves laying the groundwork by increasing educators' understanding of ABI and its consequences in relation to the individual student (i.e., getting to know the student). Planning involves joint collaboration with family members, rehabilitation professionals, and educational team members to determine the student's strengths, needs, educational goals, and strategies for best serving the student's needs. Implementation includes establishing the educational climate, selecting the appropriate strategies, and structuring the learning experiences to meet the identified needs; it is putting the plan into action. Evaluation provides a framework for determining if the goal and strategy selections were successful and if they should be continued, modified, or abandoned. Figure 15.1 illustrates this four-step process.

Understanding this four-step process enables educators to be systematic in intervention. This is a circular, continuous process; it can be viewed as an endless loop.

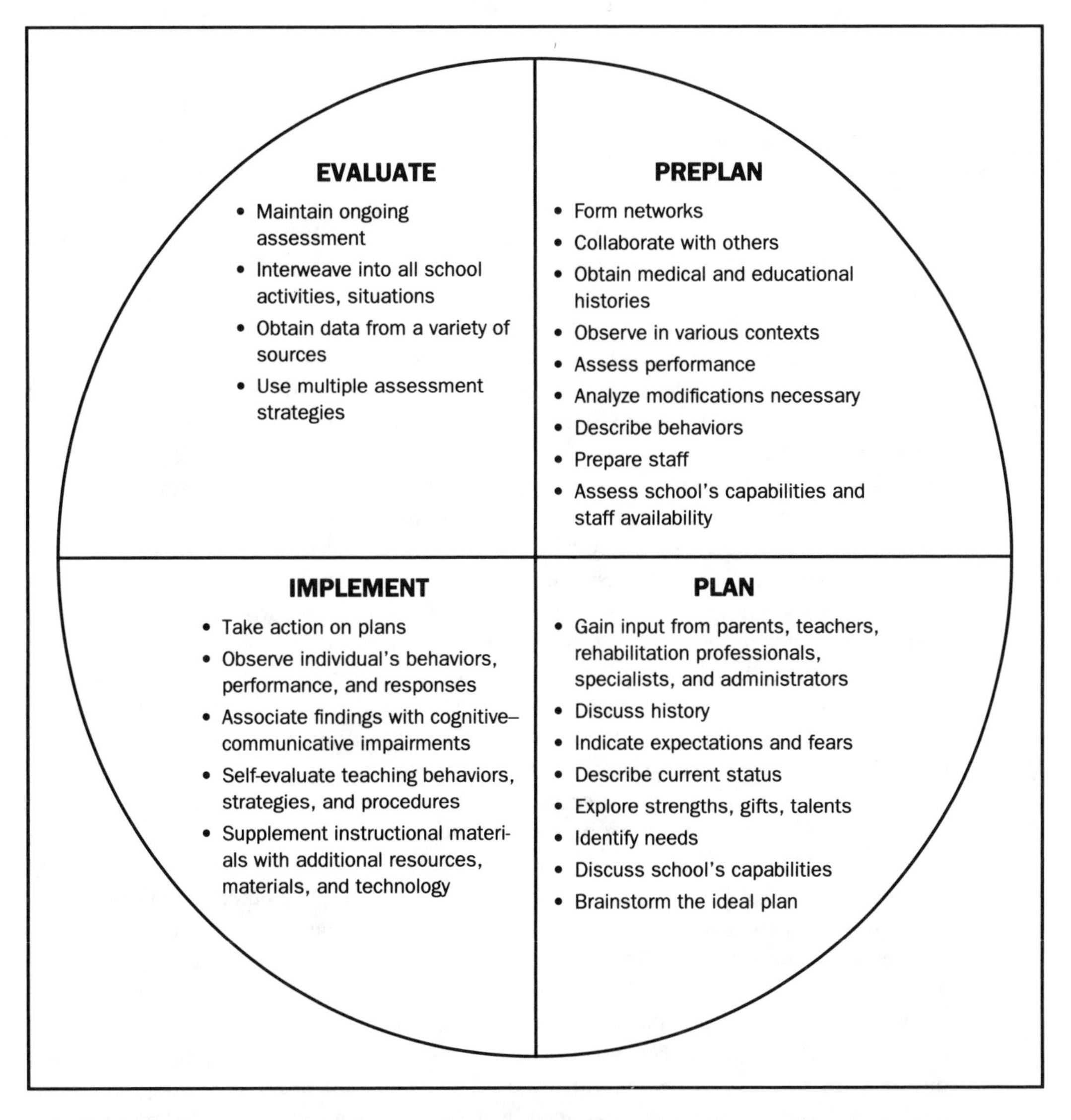

Figure 15.1. Dynamic planning procedure. Significant changes made by individuals with traumatic brain injury must be recognized and accommodated within the educational plan. From "A Proactive Model for Treating Communication Disorders in Children and Adolescents with Traumatic Brain Injury" by J. Blosser and R. DePompei, 1992, *Clinics in Communication Disorders, 2*(2), 52–65. Copyright 1992 by Andover Medical Publishers. Reprinted with permission.

After the initial school entry or reintegration, no single step represents the beginning or end of the cycle. All parts are related. Change in one component will produce related changes in another. As the student progresses through school, the process should continue. Too often, 1 to 3 years postinjury and postentry, the ABI and its resulting effects on the student's learning capabilities are no longer discussed and considered by educators. Therefore, teaching strategies matched to specific needs are not identified and employed. However, the process cannot be discontinued at the end of the first or the third year. Continuity is important as the student transitions into new classroom settings from grade to grade or placement to placement. With this four-step process, new teachers can always be introduced to the existence of a brain injury and to its consequences; this will enable ongoing program maintenance and improvement.

PREPLANNING

This book is devoted to increasing understanding of acquired brain injury and its impact on the student's educational performance. During the preplanning process, this information should be used to prepare the educational staff for the student's arrival and the family for interaction with school personnel.

The educator should use all available information and resources to learn about the individual student's learning deficiencies. This is a good time to form networks and collaborative relationships with rehabilitation professionals who have been involved with the student. These professionals can provide accurate history information regarding the injury, course of recovery, and learning difficulties. DePompei and Blosser (1987) described a process for networking between rehabilitation professionals and education professionals that demonstrates how to establish a basis for communication, understanding, and cooperative planning when school reentry is recommended.

The preplanning phase also includes assessment of the student's current status and performance in relation to those behaviors expected in the classroom setting. The results of testing, interviewing, and observation procedures can be used to focus later discussion on the behaviors and skills the student presents. Information obtained during this phase can provide early insights into modifications and adaptations needed. Analysis of results will enable team members to predict the effect of the injury on skills necessary for school success. The checklist presented in Figure 15.2 can be used to focus discussion during planning sessions.

The learning and social difficulties of students with ABI are well documented (Cohen, 1991; Rosen & Gerring, 1986; Savage, 1991; Ylvisaker, 1985). To teach effectively, educators must know how to determine the learning characteristics of the learner with brain injury. They must know the scope of similarities and differences in attitudes, learning styles, and cognitive processing styles that exist among groups of students with ABI and between students with ABI and students with other types of disabilities (DePompei & Blosser, 1987). Informal observational techniques in combination with formalized testing can be used to determine students' strengths, weaknesses, and needs. Assessment data can be derived from a variety of sources, including neuropsychological reports, medical reports, informal teachers' evaluations, parent comments, and observations within a variety of contexts within the school setting. Telzrow (1991) presented an excellent review on testing students to determine learning capabilities and school-related needs.

Social, Educational, and Language Behaviors of the Client with Acquired Brain Injury

Name ______________________ Parent's Name ______________________
Address ______________________________ Phone ________________
School District ______________ Last Grade Level ______ Birth Date __________
Diagnosis: ____
____

Social Behaviors	Did not assess	Severe	Marked	Moderate	Mild	Normal
1. Withdrawn	☐	☐	☐	☐	☐	☐
2. Ability to assume role in family	☐	☐	☐	☐	☐	☐
3. Ability to be accepted by:						
peers	☐	☐	☐	☐	☐	☐
family	☐	☐	☐	☐	☐	☐
4. Appropriate social responses to:						
peers	☐	☐	☐	☐	☐	☐
family	☐	☐	☐	☐	☐	☐
therapist	☐	☐	☐	☐	☐	☐
5. Ability to structure self in social activities	☐	☐	☐	☐	☐	☐
6. Ability to learn from social experience	☐	☐	☐	☐	☐	☐
7. Concern for others	☐	☐	☐	☐	☐	☐
8. Self-care skills	☐	☐	☐	☐	☐	☐
9. Drug, alcohol reported use	☐	☐	☐	☐	☐	☐
10. Turn-taking skills	☐	☐	☐	☐	☐	☐
Speech Behaviors						
1. Swallowing	☐	☐	☐	☐	☐	☐
2. Oral movements	☐	☐	☐	☐	☐	☐
3. Self-initiated speech	☐	☐	☐	☐	☐	☐
4. Intelligibility	☐	☐	☐	☐	☐	☐
5. Fluency	☐	☐	☐	☐	☐	☐
6. Voice	☐	☐	☐	☐	☐	☐
Emotional Behaviors						
1. Apathy	☐	☐	☐	☐	☐	☐
2. Impulsiveness	☐	☐	☐	☐	☐	☐
3. Irritability	☐	☐	☐	☐	☐	☐
4. Aggressiveness	☐	☐	☐	☐	☐	☐
5. Depression	☐	☐	☐	☐	☐	☐
6. Emotional lability	☐	☐	☐	☐	☐	☐
7. Silliness	☐	☐	☐	☐	☐	☐
8. Anxiety	☐	☐	☐	☐	☐	☐
9. Adequate self-image	☐	☐	☐	☐	☐	☐
10. Denial of disability	☐	☐	☐	☐	☐	☐

Educational Behaviors	Did not assess	Severe	Marked	Moderate	Mild	Normal
1. Disorientation	☐	☐	☐	☐	☐	☐
2. Ability to abstract	☐	☐	☐	☐	☐	☐
3. Memory deficits						
short term	☐	☐	☐	☐	☐	☐
long term	☐	☐	☐	☐	☐	☐
4. Ability to initiate	☐	☐	☐	☐	☐	☐
5. Logical thinking	☐	☐	☐	☐	☐	☐
6. Judgment	☐	☐	☐	☐	☐	☐
7. Verbal perseveration	☐	☐	☐	☐	☐	☐
8. Motor perseveration	☐	☐	☐	☐	☐	☐
9. Attention span	☐	☐	☐	☐	☐	☐
10. Distractibility	☐	☐	☐	☐	☐	☐
11. Fatigability	☐	☐	☐	☐	☐	☐
12. Confusion	☐	☐	☐	☐	☐	☐
Language Behaviors						
Receptive						
1. Understands yes–no questions	☐	☐	☐	☐	☐	☐
2. Follows directions	☐	☐	☐	☐	☐	☐
3. Immediate recall	☐	☐	☐	☐	☐	☐
4. Reads and comprehends appropriate grade-level sentences	☐	☐	☐	☐	☐	☐
5. Reads and comprehends appropriate grade-level paragraphs	☐	☐	☐	☐	☐	☐
6. Follows and comprehends conversational speech	☐	☐	☐	☐	☐	☐
Expressive						
1. Anomia (word finding)	☐	☐	☐	☐	☐	☐
2. Ability to define	☐	☐	☐	☐	☐	☐
3. Ability to use sentence	☐	☐	☐	☐	☐	☐
4. Ability to use conversational speech	☐	☐	☐	☐	☐	☐
5. Ability to use humor	☐	☐	☐	☐	☐	☐
6. Vocabulary usage	☐	☐	☐	☐	☐	☐
7. Written sentences appropriate to grade level	☐	☐	☐	☐	☐	☐
8. Written paragraphs appropriate to grade level	☐	☐	☐	☐	☐	☐

COMMENTS:

Date ______________ Clinician ______________________________

Figure 15.2. Checklist to focus planning sessions for student returning to school following acquired brain injury. From "Strategies for Helping Head-Injured Children Successfully Return to School" by R. DePompei and J. L. Blosser, 1987, *Language, Speech, and Hearing Services in the Schools, 18,* p. 292–300. Reprinted with permission.

School places great cognitive–communicative demands upon students (Blosser & Secord, 1989; Neidecker & Blosser, 1993). Experienced educators can provide extensive lists of skills and behaviors needed for academic success. For example, learning is largely a communication-based process. In addition, specific schoolwork-related behaviors enable students to perform successfully. These two areas are quite often affected by brain injury. Figure 15.3 is a form that lists communication and work-related behaviors needed for success in the academic setting. This summary is a compilation of skills derived from a variety of sources (Blosser, 1990; Gloeckler & Simpson, 1988; Solomon, Schaps, Watson, & Battistich, 1992). Unless these skill areas are addressed, academic failure will surely result. Education and health care professionals need to work to increase desired learning behaviors.

During the preplanning process, educators should identify areas of communication-based or school-related strengths or needs presented by the student. The findings are used to describe the student's characteristic patterns (i.e., observed behaviors) at that particular point in time. This description is used during the planning process either prior to school entry, after a period of school attendance, or for evaluating progress.

Educators' success in dealing with the student with ABI will depend on what they know about acquired brain injury (in general and in relation to the student in question) and how well they integrate what they know into developing an educational plan for the student and into their teaching. Flexibility is important. Flexibility can be increased by strengthening those factors that remove the mystery from ABI and providing educators with the understanding and tools they need to provide a high-quality educational experience. Flexibility can be increased through teacher inservice, provision of appropriate resource materials, and support services. Therefore, it is essential that the reintegration process incorporate inservice staff training for all persons who will work with the student (Blosser & DePompei, 1991). Furthermore, the staff training should be ongoing from year to year as the student passes through various grade levels and educational program placements. Through the inservice training format, educators can learn about ABI as well as how to talk to the student, how to observe and respond to his or her behaviors, how to reevaluate and reestablish goals, and how to respond to their own frustrations as educators.

PLANNING

When planning for the educational program, each involved rehabilitation professional, educator, and family member should be encouraged to contribute valuable information about the student from his or her perspective. The planning should yield an educational design that includes specification of the roles each team member will play, learning outcomes, teaching orientation, performance criteria, the learning environment, appropriate teaching activities and materials, and teaching procedures and strategies. These topics are discussed in the following sections. Student behaviors and performance strategies also need to be specified.

Forest and Lusthause (1990) described an excellent process for educational planning, which can be readily applied to students with ABI. Their approach, Map Action Planning System (MAPS), is a systems approach designed to help team members plan for the integration of students with challenging needs into regular age-appropriate

Skills Needed for Academic Success

During the preplanning process, identify areas of school-related strength or need presented by your student. Indicate strength with a plus (+) and need with a minus (−). Summarize your findings by describing your student's characteristic patterns at this point in time. Use your description during the planning process either prior to school entry, after a period of school attendance, or for evaluating progress. In your description, specify those areas that will facilitate success and those that will inhibit it. Plan to discuss these at the planning meeting.

AT THIS TIME, THIS STUDENT DOES (+) OR DOES NOT (−) DEMONSTRATE:

_____ **Active learning**
Participates in learning actively
Takes initiative
Demonstrates motivation

_____ **Awareness**
Recognizes critical information
Responds to directions

_____ **Communication efficiency**
Demonstrates oral and written communication skills that do not interfere with learning and interactions

_____ **Attention and concentration**
Tunes in and stays on task

_____ **Information processing**
Processes incoming information when average speed and amounts are presented

_____ **Internal locus of control**
In charge; responsible for what is accomplished
Inhibits actions that are inappropriate or impulsive

_____ **Interactive learning**
Engages in meaningful dialogue and interaction with teachers and peers
Gains information from textbooks, lectures, discussions
Answers questions
Gives reports, contributes to discussions

_____ **Field independence**
Works in spite of distractions in the environment

_____ **Persistence**
Stays on task until completed
Completes assignments

_____ **Problem solving**
Identifies problem situations and poses reasonable and appropriate solutions
Generalizes information from one situation to another

_____ **Organization**
Follows a specified routing
Organizes materials and self for learning
Transitions from one activity to another smoothly

_____ **Recall**
Displays accurate memory for information

_____ **Reflection**
Ponders and thinks
Evaluates situations

Figure 15.3. Communication and work-related behaviors needed for academic success.

classrooms. The MAPS approach focuses the planning team's discussion on seven key questions, which have been modified slightly for this discussion:

1. What is the student's history?
2. What are the family's dreams for the student?
3. What are their nightmares?
4. Who is student? (Characterize him or her.)
5. What are the student's strengths, gifts, and talents?
6. What are his or her needs?
7. What is the ideal school plan for the student? (Include discussions of environments, goals, objectives, and activities.)

It would be helpful to provide all participants, including the parents, with a list of the MAPS questions in advance of the planning meeting to enable discussion and consideration of important issues before anyone is placed "on the spot" during the meeting.

Team Members' Involvement

The family

The family is an important (but often forgotten) component of the planning process. Parents have a right to participate in planning their child's instructional program. The level of participation, however, is not stipulated. Unfortunately, the current level of family involvement in educational programs is limited to distant observation and minimal participation during the development of the Individualized Education Program (IEP). To be truly effective, educators should constantly solicit family concerns, encourage family members to make suggestions, determine their expectations and aspirations for the student, invite their participation in school-related activities, and show them how to create a home learning environment in which they can help their child. When family members are involved as partners in the entire educational process, positive consequences result. Specific mechanisms for increasing family involvement are discussed in Chapter 18 in this book.

A unique feature of MAPS is that parents (and the student if possible) are included as more than "observers" and "approvers." They are equal participants in the planning meetings. They bring valuable insights, information, and recommendations to the process.

To make the parent's role more meaningful, an exchange of ideas needs to occur among team members for the purposes of obtaining data, conveying information, or providing support. We offer the following practical suggestions that will facilitate meaningful interaction between the team and the student's parents. The team should

1. Consider the unique characteristics each family brings to the situation. Avoid prejudging the family's responses to discussion and/or recommendations.

2. Jointly establish the meeting agenda before beginning the meeting. Allow ample time for discussion and planning to take place.
3. Decide on relevant issues that must be discussed; encourage parents to do the same before coming. Ask them to prepare a written list of their concerns, questions, expectations, and ideas. Encourage them to verbally express this information during the meeting.
4. Incorporate positive and encouraging comments; discuss strengths as well as needs.
5. Fully explore issues and options before changing topics or adjourning the meeting.
6. Use lay terminology. Develop a nonverbal or verbal signal that parents can use to show other team members that they do not understand what is being discussed.
7. Be aware of emotions, frustrations, and fears about working with the parents.
8. Provide action steps for each participant, including the parents, to implement at home.
9. End the meeting on a positive note, summarizing the results of the discussion, recommendations, and respective responsibilities.
10. Schedule the next meeting date or format for future contacts. Follow the meeting with a note, phone call, or brief summary report.

Rehabilitation team members

Educational teams frequently resist having "outside personnel" participate in the planning process. This resistance may be due to barriers created by time constraints, misunderstanding, financial problems, "turf issues," and fear of interaction. However, rehabilitation team members have insights into the students' problems and capabilities. If afforded the opportunity to share these insights, greater potential exists for efficient and effective planning. DePompei and Blosser (1987) recommended a process for initiating and maintaining effective networks between personnel at the rehabilitation or hospital setting and the school setting.

Educational team members

Within the educational setting, numerous professionals should be involved in the planning process. These include administrators, teachers (special education and regular education), speech-language pathologists, audiologists, psychologists, guidance counselors, occupational therapists, physical therapists, and vision consultants. Selection of appropriate professionals for participation will depend on the student's presenting characteristics and data obtained prior to the meeting. Based on his or her expertise, each professional can contribute data and impressions collected about the student and make valuable suggestions for placement, teaching techniques, and remediation. As problems arise or new information is realized about the student's capabilities or needs, appropriate professionals should be brought into the planning and implementation processes. All of the professionals should maintain an open door for communication so that valuable information can be readily exchanged.

Learning Outcomes

The goals and expectations established for the student must be clearly defined. To determine appropriate outcomes, the team should seek answers to questions such as Is the student to accomplish a specific number of academic tasks? Is the goal to develop in the student a functional learning attitude and strategy to prepare him or her to succeed academically, emotionally, socially, and vocationally?

Because the student is likely to encounter difficulties for a long period of time following the ABI, teaching should emphasize life skills and coping strategies, including adaptations to physical and cognitive limitations as well as to surroundings. For other children who have physical or mental disabilities, Schellentrager (1987) recommended discussing topics such as peer relationships, resolving conflicts, solving problems, communicating with authority figures, making changes, handling frustrations, improving self-concept, improving mobility, grooming, participating in leisure time activities, and career awareness. These topics are applicable to ABI students as well.

Teaching Orientation

Perhaps one of the most important decisions the team has to make is whether the teaching orientation and learning goals should be process or product oriented. A process orientation emphasizes "how to do and learn," whereas a product orientation emphasizes "completion of instructional tasks," such as writing essays, doing workbook exercises, and calculating math problems. Literature on school integration and reintegration for students with ABI supports focusing on the processes of performance rather than the products of performance. These approaches are sometimes referred to in the literature as cognitive learning strategy interventions (Brown & Palincsar, 1982; Ryan, Short, & Weed, 1986; Wong, Wong, Perry, & Sawatsky, 1986). Regardless of the approach used, the educational program should be adapted to fit the student's needs.

A combined process–product approach may actually yield much more functional results. The underlying idea is that teaching should center simultaneously on products to be completed (class assignments and tasks) and the strategy needed for successful completion (organization skills, attention, direction following the assignments). This approach will help establish those behaviors that will lead to success, contribute to overall performance, and lead to higher task engagement. Rather than being concerned about the amount of work a student is to complete, teachers should consider the demand that a particular task presents and the skills necessary for successful completion. Teachers should answer the following questions: What behavior is required for successful performance? Is the student to formulate questions and/or answers at the end of a chapter? work cooperatively in a group? proofread and edit an essay? The educator needs to determine the skills needed for successful task performance and teach specific cognitive strategies so the child can perform those skills. For the child who has difficulty coping with the extensive amount of content information presented in the classroom, the teacher may need to teach the child to organize, summarize, and paraphrase that information. Teaching these adaptive skills with decontextualized bits of information will result in low task engagement and may not be productive. Rather, instruction should be geared to promote understanding of concepts as well as completion of products. Students can be taught cognitive strategies that will enable them to exercise some control over their learning and thinking (Gagne, 1990; Gleason, 1989; Hobbs, Moguin, & Troyler, 1980; Hoskisson & Tompkins, 1987; Meven, 1990; Uve & Bransford, 1981).

This approach may pose a problem for general education teachers who did not learn these types of teaching techniques as a part of their preservice training or who are confronted with a large class of students and little time to individualize work. They may have had limited exposure and experience with children who present challenging needs. Special education teachers, on the other hand, have knowledge and experience in teaching through a process orientation. They know how to analyze tasks, adapt curricula, and continuously measure student progress. They are comfortable individualizing work. Therefore, we suggest that general educators and special educators work together and exchange ideas. Collaboration will be a critical component to problem solving for educational success. Educators are encouraged to make use of all resources, including fellow teachers, specialists, and counselors. Graden (1989) supported teacher–teacher problem solving, teacher–special services problem solving, and prescribed use of teacher problem solving as essential to developing effective service delivery models to meet the complex problems experienced by students who have difficulties.

Performance Criteria

Decisions about evaluating the student's work (grading) must be made early so that the teacher, student, and family are confident about the procedures used and the interpretation. Evaluation alternatives used with children with other types of disabilities include the following:

1. The student may be provided with an opportunity to retake a test or quiz if the grade achieved independently is below average or failing. The second test can be administered by a tutor or special educator with restructuring provided as needed. The two test scores can be averaged for a grade.
2. The student's grade may be raised one level higher than actually achieved if the test performance is independent and the student shows effort. Grades that are raised should be indicated as such on the report card.
3. Failing grades should be given only if the student demonstrates an unwillingness or resistance to trying and no effort.

Learning Environment

The instructional environment is the context in which the teaching and learning take place. It should be designed so that learning can be enhanced and supported (Solomon et al., 1992). The school environment can be structured to encourage learning, to provide opportunities for student–student and student–teacher interactions, and to compensate for learning deficiencies. The ideal teaching environment should be diverse, flexible, functional, and appropriate to the student's abilities.

The learning environment is an often-overlooked element of the educational process, yet the environment can directly influence students' performance, behavior, and learning. Structuring the classroom environment can be described as controlling aspects of the classroom such as degree of structure, daily routine, requirements for participation, time allocation, space, and materials. Another important quality of school environment is relayed through the teacher's acceptance of and response to the student. When planning the educational program, the team should discuss and mutually agree upon these environmental elements.

Gloeckler and Simpson (1988) described three aspects of the educational environment that interact with one another: the physical environment, the social environment, and the psychological environment. Based on their comments, we derived the following suggestions with regard to the physical, social, and psychological environments most conducive to optimal learning for the student with ABI. Educators should

1. Identify aspects of the environment that will restrict a student's learning or pose barriers (physically, auditorially, visually).
2. Eliminate or modify barriers and decrease distractions.
3. Convey a sense of order by structuring and manipulating the classroom environment physically and visually to facilitate organization and identification of learning activities and materials (post due dates and schedules, using simple directions, codes, and numbers).
4. Consider the student's location in relation to the teacher's usual teaching position.
5. Permit ease of movement and promote clear movement of traffic patterns by carefully planning seating and furniture arrangements.
6. Make teaching resources and materials, such as calculators, tape recorders, and computers, available and accessible.

The classroom psychological environment is conveyed through the atmosphere created by the teacher. A teacher can establish a positive psychological environment by warmly accepting the students as individuals, clearly relaying expectations and goals to the students, responding fairly and consistently to the students' behaviors, and engaging the students in meaningful learning tasks.

The social environment is especially important for the student with ABI. Because of cognitive–communicative difficulties, this student may have difficulty establishing and maintaining relationships with peers. Therefore, teachers should promote a warm, friendly, sharing, and accepting social environment to benefit the student optimally.

Appropriate Teaching Activities and Materials

The more severe a student's presenting impairments are, the more the teacher needs to incorporate multisensory stimuli and demonstrate a high level of direct involvement. Materials selected should be appropriate for the student's developmental level, of high interest, and functional. Efforts should be made to maintain the student's interests through a variety of teaching activities, including discussions, role playing, brainstorming, interviewing, and audiovisual materials. Appendix 15A lists numerous materials that have been used successfully to enhance learning objectives for students with ABI.

Teaching Procedures and Strategies

Individualized Education Programs generally reflect selected teaching goals, targeted student behaviors, and evaluation criteria. *How* to teach the student (i.e., the educator's role and teaching strategies) is frequently not specified. However, teaching procedures and strategies can have a great impact on the overall program success. Decisions regarding teaching strategies should be based on knowledge of the student's strengths and capabilities and the purposes of the teaching. Teaching strategies need to reflect prevailing research and theory. Teacher behaviors that need to be incorporated into teaching and interaction with the students should be discussed and specified during the planning process. Furthermore, the techniques should be specified *in writing* on the IEP to ensure implementation. In this way, teachers can appraise their own performance and make changes where indicated.

Research has demonstrated that teachers' behaviors can and do influence students' learning behaviors. Teachers need to strive to stimulate students' thought processes and elicit student responses. The following lists of general teaching strategies have proven successful with students with ABI. Educators will find that these suggestions do not sound "new" or "unique." That is because most teachers have excellent techniques in their teaching repertoire; the key is knowing when and how to apply them to the population of students with ABI.

Educators can use the following teaching methods to encourage learning in students who present challenges:

1. Establish expectations for the student and make them known to the student and family.
2. Provide instructional feedback.
3. Assist the student with tools and methods for organizing information.
4. Furnish multiple opportunities for practice.
5. Deliver systematic incentives and consequences. Develop a system for having the student measure his or her individual progress toward accomplishing established goals.

Because students with ABI frequently exhibit problems initiating and maintaining social interactions, frequent classroom activities that promote quality student-to-student interactions should be arranged. This can be facilitated if the IEP plans require teachers to

1. Incorporate the student into small group activities to facilitate informal interactions and permit peer modeling.
2. Assign a "buddy" to assist with travel throughout the school if the student has problems with memory for places.

3. Select a classroom work partner to help keep the student aware of instructions, transitions, and assignments if his or her recall of details is impaired.
4. Plan extracurricular activities based on the student's physical and emotional capabilities as well as interests to encourage nonacademic experiences.

Student's cognitive–communicative impairments are often most evident when the student displays difficulty following the classroom discussion or maintaining effective conversations. Numerous communicative interaction strategies are successful in increasing the potential for understanding, direction following, and better communication. Teachers can employ these strategies to facilitate the student's communication skills (Blosser & DePompei, 1989, 1991). These strategies should be discussed and written directly into the IEP:

1. Present information at a slower rate.
2. Give explicit directions. Clarify verbal and written instructions in the following ways:
   a. Accompany verbal instructions with written instructions.
   b. Repeat instructions and redefine words and terms.
   c. Verbally explain written instructions.
   d. Alert the student to the important topic or concept being taught.
3. Use pauses when giving classroom instructions to permit time for processing information.
4. Avoid figurative, idiomatic, ambiguous, and sarcastic language when presenting lessons.
5. Privately ask the student to repeat information and/or answer a few key questions to be sure that important information presented has been understood.
6. Ask direct questions with caution.
7. Establish a system of verbal or nonverbal signals to cue the student to attend, respond, or alter behavior. Examples include calling the student's name; touching a hand, arm, or shoulder; and using written signs or hand signals.
8. Attend to and respond clearly to the student's questions and concerns.
9. Provide written and graphic cues to promote the understanding of new concepts and vocabulary.
10. Use gestures and visual cues to clarify communication as long as it does not become distracting to the student.
11. Use a slow rate and simplify oral reading presentations.
12. Present information in clusters, groups, and reduced sequences.

13. Respond to the student's unintelligible utterances by asking open-ended and directive questions.

14. Reinforce the student's communication attempts. Provide feedback to let the student know what was correct or incorrect about his or her productions. Clarify expectations.

Because students with ABI will be at a disadvantage due to their resulting impairments, supportive measures should be taken during all learning activities. The team should determine the resources and assistance that will be needed. As appropriate, teachers should

1. Permit the use of assistive devices, such as calculators, tape recorders, and computers (augmentative computer systems or amplification equipment).

2. Help the student formulate and use a system for maintaining organization (written log of activities, schedule of classes, assignment or record book).

3. Modify and individualize the student's assignments and tests to accommodate special needs (reduce the number of questions to be answered or the amount of material to be read, permit the student to record teacher's lectures, increase the print size, change the format of a task).

4. Develop resources to accompany text assignments. Use pictures and written cues to illustrate important information and concepts. Assign review questions at the end of chapters. Review errors made on class work to let the student know where and why errors occurred.

5. Be analytical: Analyze the demands made upon the student.

6. Measure student performance regularly and frequently. Use the analysis to suggest instructional and motivational strategies. Make necessary adjustments to facilitate learning. Prioritize learning activities and content.

7. Be systematic: Introduce information at the appropriate developmental level.

8. Work closely with other educators to promote understanding of the student in all learning and social environments within the school setting.

9. Provide opportunities for repeated attempts.

Reinforce appropriate social, emotional, and interactive behaviors by being supportive, accepting, and helpful. Teachers should

1. Schedule a specific time for rest and/or emotional release.

2. Encourage the student to share problems he or she may be experiencing.

3. Provide explanations for the student's inappropriate or unexpected behaviors and problems.
4. Help the student understand the relationship of his or her brain injury to problems being experienced.
5. Be observant of pressures placed upon the student by teachers, peers, family, and administrators.

IMPLEMENTATION

Assessment and planning are necessary to provide direction to the academic experience. Implementation of the instructional program means taking action on information derived during these two steps in the process. During classroom activities, educators are encouraged to manipulate and experiment with a variety of teaching behaviors and strategies to determine the ones that work best. Learning goals will most likely shift as the student attempts to learn new concepts and skills or is confronted by new situations. By documenting the student's performance and response to specific teaching strategies, successful ones can be refined, repeated, and expanded. Unsuccessful strategies can by analyzed, modified, and/or eliminated. This process will require an open mind and willingness to make modifications.

Appendix 15A was constructed to demonstrate representative cognitive–communicative skills that may need to be integrated into classroom teaching and interactions. No specific age or grade category is defined. Rather, the purpose for the appendix is to illustrate how behavioral observation and interpretation can serve as a guide for developing learning goals and teaching strategies, as well as determining resources. The skills illustrated were derived from the research in ABI as well as observations and analysis of students who experienced difficulty when they returned to the school setting. The appendix is separated into five categories: general behaviors, social behaviors, expressive language, receptive language, and written language. This breakdown is not meant to suggest that these skills should be observed or taught separately. Rather, dividing the behaviors into the five categories permitted us to organize similar information for purposes of illustration. Column 1 lists the cognitive–communicative impairments that may be associated with the classroom behaviors listed in Column 2. Column 3 presents skills to target and teaching strategies to facilitate success. Finally, Column 4 provides examples of resources that may be used to supplement instructional books and materials. (These resources are listed at the end of the appendix.) A blank form is provided at the end of each section for the reader's use. During a conference, teachers should discuss examples of classroom behaviors they have observed and relate those behaviors to cognitive–communicative impairments that have resulted from the ABI. They can then discuss teaching strategies that might be used to develop the student's skills or remediate problems.

Although attention has been given to strategies the educator can use, it is also important for the student to have responsibility for learning. Use of student communication–thinking strategies will facilitate learning (see Table 15.1). These strategies can also be incorporated into home-based programs to provide parents with suggestions for helping their child's organizational skills (DePompei & Blosser, 1992). Not all of the strategies will prove appropriate or useful for all students; therefore, some time should be spent experimenting with the strategies to determine which ones

TABLE 15.1. Communication–Thinking Techniques for Students

Read
Reread instructions
Repeat verbatim
Restate with different terminology
Review work, proofread
Self-evaluate, verbalize correct and incorrect aspects of work
Repeat assignments
Ask questions
Write instructions

yield better performance and the circumstances under which they are successful. Educators and parents should reinforce the student's use of these strategies with compliments describing the strategy the student used and why it worked. This will help transfer the control of the strategy from the teacher or parent to the student, enabling him or her to become independent and aware of strategies that can be applied when problems occur. After a period of time, the student can be asked to explain the strategy used, why it was selected, and why it worked. This will promote repeated practice for the student, thus increasing his or her self-control over the learning situation. To support students' use of the strategies listed in Table 15.1, teachers can try the following suggestions:

1. Encourage the student to *reread* instructions more than once, exercising care to underline, highlight, and note important elements.
2. Ask the student to *repeat instructions* verbatim before initiating an activity.
3. Verify the student's comprehension of directions by requesting that the instructions be *restated using different terminology.*
4. Have the student *review work* after completing it by *proofreading* assignments before submitting them, looking for completeness and accuracy.
5. Have the student *self-evaluate work* to see if it is appropriate and then *verbalize correct and incorrect aspects of the work.*

6. Provide the student with opportunities to *repeat* assignments at another time to see if performance can be improved.
7. Invite the student to *ask questions* and to clarify information not understood.
8. Have the student *write instructions* on a separate sheet of paper.

EVALUATION

Other sections of this book discuss evaluation of the student with ABI to determine the level of performance and address placement issues. Assessing the student with ABI is a sensitive issue. Because of individual differences between students, no single, accepted format exists for assessing capabilities, behavior, and learning.

Ongoing evaluation of the student's classroom and social performance and response to teaching goals and strategies must also be considered. This is an important problem-solving step in the school reintegration process. Evaluation must be interwoven into all school activities. It should serve as a guide for identifying problems with class placement and established goals, selecting new educational goals, and modifying teaching strategies dependent on the student's progress. Thus, the primary responsibility for organizing ongoing evaluation is placed on the classroom teacher. Information should also be collected and collated by a variety of persons (including the family and related professionals) and in a variety of situations. Observations and assessments should focus on the student as a learner, communicator, and interactor. In addition, changes in performance in different situations and contexts should be observed and analyzed.

The findings should guide the "what" and "how" of future instructional plans. The resulting information should be used to update and formulate priorities for future plans, a process that is not as easy as it sounds. The following key questions are applicable:

1. *What is the purpose of the ongoing evaluation?* Descriptive data about the student's performance is necessary to provide accurate input for altering teaching objectives, establishing new criteria for performance objectives, and determining effective teaching strategies. Questions that might be asked include What has the student learned? Was the learning related to the teacher's strategies? Should more have been accomplished?

2. *Who will conduct the evaluation?* The teacher is the primary person to observe and assess the student's classroom performance on a day-to-day basis to determine the student's progress toward established objectives. Consultation with other teachers, related professionals, family members, and specialists is necessary to create the complete picture.

3. *What behaviors are to be evaluated?* Unless specific behaviors are targeted for monitoring, the evaluation will yield unusable information. The following information might be evaluated: indications of progress; response to various teaching strategies; changes in behavior over time or associated with varying contents, persons, challenges, and situations; learning strategies utilized; degree of independence; and approximate levels of functioning.

4. *How will the evaluation be completed?* Systematic formal and informal procedures to determine the student's performance should be used. The usual standardized tests, developmental tests, nonstandardized tests, curriculum-based tests, and completion of assignments may be used. Behavioral observation techniques often yield the most useful information because the student's performance can be evaluated in relation to expectations that were established, unique circumstances that occurred, and modifications that were implemented. Information collected during observations should be recorded, documented, and presented in planning meetings.

5. *What decisions should be made?* As a result of the testing, the questions considered during the initial stages of planning should be reconsidered. Evaluation results should lead to increased communication among professionals, problem solving, and program improvement.

CONCLUSION

The issues and questions regarding educational programming for students with ABI are complex. The solutions are not simple because of the great diversity within this population, within school programs, and among educators. If the quality of instruction for students with ABI is to be improved, it is essential that educators (a) apply to this population what is known about successful strategies for teaching students with other types of disorders, (b) network with related professionals, (c) work with families, and (d) make educational decisions designed to increase the students' opportunities for success.

The potential for effective programming can be enhanced by using a systematic process during the preplanning, planning, implementation, and evaluation stages of the reintegration process. This chapter has described such a process. Strategies for success involve fostering a school environment in which creative problem solving and continuous evaluation are an integral part of the school plan. Modifying the structure of the school program to meet the needs of the student with ABI requires interaction with the family, a receptive and flexible educational philosophy, a commitment to preparing the student for future life demands, and a willingness to recognize when problems have occurred and make changes when indicated.

APPENDIX 15A
Strategies for Developing Cognitive–Communicative Skills

General Behaviors

Impairment	*Classroom Behaviors*	*Skills and Teaching Strategies*	*Resources*
Decreased judgment	Is easily persuaded by others (can be convinced by others to act inappropriately; abuse drugs and alcohol)	*DECISION MAKING:* Select a classroom buddy to keep the student aware of instructions, class rules, appropriate social conduct.	12, 13, 14, 32
	Is impulsive	Establish a system of verbal or nonverbal signals to cue the student to alter behavior (call the student's name, touch the student, use a written sign or hand signal).	
	Speaks out of turn in class; gets up and moves about the classroom	*SELF-MONITORING:* Schedule special time for freedom of movement and informal conversation	
	Is careless about safety (does not look before crossing streets; makes poor decisions about playing on the playground equipment or about activities in physical education class)	*DECISION MAKING:* Establish specific rules for behavior in certain places and times of the day; practice implementation frequently in controlled situations before allowing the child to do something independently.	
	Makes unreasonable demands to be unsupervised (wants to begin driving again too soon)	*SELF-AWARENESS:* Make the student aware of the need for supervision (e.g., motoric problem, safety, etc.). Establish small steps for progress toward greater independence.	

(*continues*)

General Behaviors (*Continued*)

Impairment	*Classroom Behaviors*	*Skills and Teaching Strategies*	*Resources*
Lack of self-insight	Does not understand the rationale behind another person's reaction to his or her behavior; is paranoid	*AWARENESS OF SELF AND OTHERS:* Explain the cause for the other person's reaction. Explain what would have been a better way to behave (use simplistic explanations; reasoning will not help).	44, 45, 46, 47
	Responds defensively to comments made or questions asked by teachers and fellow students	Do not react or respond as if you need to prove a point; avoid confrontation; avoid "buying into" the argument.	
Poor problem-solving skills	Does not carefully think through solutions to situations	*PROBLEM SOLVING:* Ask questions designed to help the student identify the problem; plan out and organize implementation of a solution.	5, 6, 7, 11, 12, 13, 18, 21, 22, 34, 48
Inability to plan for the future	Does not recognize own physical or cognitive problem or limitations to taking classes or performing tasks	*SELF-AWARENESS:* Plan activities that are similar to what other classmates are doing, but adjust the level of complexity to the student's limitations. Build on successes rather than making the student feel a failure.	10, 14, 41
Recognition	Is unaware of due dates or amount of time needed to complete a class project. Forgets to prepare for a field trip. Cannot predetermine materials needed for completing class projects (material, thread, pattern for home economics)	*ORGANIZATION AND PLANNING:* Help the student formulate and use a system for maintaining organization. Require the student to carry a written log of activities, schedule of classes, list of assignments and due dates, and map of room locations. Frequently monitor the student's use of the organization system.	
Decreased carry-over for new learning	Does not recall or generalize information presented in class several days earlier	*COMPENSATORY MEMORY STRATEGIES:* Teach the student to categorize, associate, rehearse, and chunk information. Require the student to write things. Assign a student buddy to monitor and check what has been written.	10, 33, 43

(*continues*)

General Behaviors (*Continued*)

Impairment	*Classroom Behaviors*	*Skills and Teaching Strategies*	*Resources*
Decreased ability to generalize learned information to new or different situations	Is unable to take tests that require newly learned information to be applied or generalized	*MEMORY AND RECALL STRATEGIES:* Provide the student with a variety of examples of the topic or information to be tested. (Recognize that this skill is not likely to improve; change may not occur.)	12, 13, 24, 29, 31, 32
Decreased ability to store and retrieve information upon demand	Pays little or no attention to details in deductive reasoning tasks Is unable to recall specific details of a history lesson or all of the critical elements of a science experiment	*IDENTIFYING DETAILS:* Use visual and auditory cues to draw attention to details (highlight, underline, use reference pictures).	5, 6, 10, 11, 12, 18, 21, 22, 24, 32, 48

General Behaviors Worksheet

Impairment	*Classroom Behaviors*	*Skills and Teaching Strategies*	*Resources*
Decreased judgment			12, 13, 14, 32
Lack of self-insight			44, 45, 46, 47
Poor problem-solving skills			5, 6, 7, 11, 12, 13, 18, 21, 22, 34, 48
Inability to plan for the future			10, 14, 41
Recognition			
Decreased carryover for new learning			10, 33, 43
Decreased ability to generalize learned information to new or different situations			12, 13, 24, 29, 31, 32
Decreased ability to store and retrieve information upon demand			5, 6, 10, 11, 12, 18, 21, 22, 24, 32, 48

Social Behaviors

Impairment	*Classroom Behaviors*	*Skills and Teaching Strategies*	*Resources*
Inability to perform well in competitive and stressful situations	Argues and fights with peers on the playground	*SHARING:* Select a classroom buddy with whom the child already gets along. Introduce sharing during small group activities; gradually include in full classroom activities; repeat the same procedure from individual to small group to large group on the playground.	43, 44, 45, 46, 47
Subtle noncompliance of classroom rules and activities	Is withdrawn and unwilling to participate in group activities (e.g., work on a science project, small group discussion) Refuses to recite in class even when called upon	*INITIATING SELF-CONCEPT:* Begin to elicit responses from the student during individual and seatwork activities when you can be assured that the student can be correct; gradually request occasional responses in front of the student's friends, then small groups; repeat until the student feels comfortable participating in a large group.	41
Rudeness, silliness, immaturity	Makes nasty and/or inappropriate comments to fellow students and teachers Laughs aloud during serious discussions or quiet seatwork	*JUDGMENT:* Present the student with "what if" situations and choices. Give the student opportunities to verbally express judgment and decision making regarding appropriate behavior as well as opportunities to role-play.	1, 41, 43, 44, 45, 47
Agressiveness (verbal)	Interrupts conversations between fellow classmates	*TURN-TAKING:* Teach the student to concentrate on the comments of others. Nonverbally cue the student to discontinue interruptive behaviors.	44, 45, 46, 47
Lacks initiative	Does not do, complete, or turn in homework	*MEMORY TASK-COMPLETION RESPONSIBILITY:* Develop, with the student, a daily written assignment sheet indicating dates and times assignments are due.	10, 15, 16, 17

(*continues*)

Social Behaviors (*Continued*)

Impairment	*Classroom Behaviors*	*Skills and Teaching Strategies*	*Resources*
Inability to stay on task	Is unable to begin and/or complete timed math tests Is unable to sit still in class while others are busy doing seatwork or taking notes Goes from one assignment to the next, unable to complete either one; skips around while doing an assignment, completing only parts of it	*ATTENTION–CONCENTRATION:* Remove distractions; verbally cue the student to begin a task; nonverbally regain the student's attention and direct it to the required task.	15, 16, 17, 19
Low frustration tolerance	Displays an outburst of temper when others would try a different approach or request help	*SELF-AWARENESS OF INTERNAL STRESS:* Do not attempt to punish the behavior using traditional behavior management approaches. Learn to detect behaviors leading up to the outburst and intervene prior to its happening (watch the student's body language). Allow time for the student to be away from the situation and get needed rest or emotional release. Provide an understanding person with whom the student can share feelings and frustrations.	
Inconsistent performance	Obtains perfect score on homework one day but does poorly the next Demonstrates model behavior one day and totally inappropriate behavior the next	*SELF-MONITORING:* Inform the student of errors made and why they were made. When giving an assignment, let the student know the similarities to previous work that has been completed successfully.	35, 36

Social Behaviors Worksheet

Impairment	*Classroom Behaviors*	*Skills and Teaching Strategies*	*Resources*
Inability to perform well in competitive and stressful situations			43, 44, 45, 46, 47
Subtle noncompliance of classroom rules and activities			41
Rudeness, silliness, immaturity			1, 41, 43, 44, 45, 47
Aggressiveness (verbal)			44, 45, 46, 47
Lack of initiative			10, 15, 16, 17
Inability to stay on task			15, 16, 17, 19
Low frustration tolerance			
Inconsistent performance			35, 36

Expressive Language

Impairment	*Classroom Behaviors*	*Skills and Teaching Strategies*	*Resources*
Difference between communication in informal situations and formal situations (e.g., the classroom)	Answers teacher's questions at a surface level; when pressed to explain or provide more detail, is unable to provide more information	*PROVIDING ADEQUATE AND SUBSTANTIAL INFORMATION:* Direct the amount and type of information provided by the student. Encourage conversations to develop by giving instructions such as "Tell me more"; "How many did you see?"	4, 13, 24, 43
Normal length of sentences and use of gestures, but below-normal depth of communication	Appears to do well conversationally during social situations, but classroom speaking lacks detail and depth	Role-play formal conversations in small groups. Direct the context of the student's responses with your own verbal models, cues, and leading questions. *STORAGE AND RETRIEVAL OF INFORMATION:* Teach memory strategies (rehearsal, chunking, visualization, association, etc.).	4, 13, 24, 43
Tangential (rambling) communication	Tends to ramble with no acknowledgment of the listener's interest or attention May discuss the appropriate topic, but not focus on the key to the discussion (e.g., when asked to name the major food groups, the student might begin a discussion about irrigation and growing crops)	*TOPIC MAINTENANCE:* When the student begins to deviate from the topic, either provide a nonverbal cue or stop the student from continuing in front of classmates. Teach the student to recognize nonverbal behaviors indicating lack of interest or desire to make a comment. (Work with this skill during private conversations with the student.) Teach about the beginning, middle, and ends of stories. Stop the student's response and restate the original question, focusing the student's attention on the key issues.	31, 32
Word retrieval errors	Answers using many vague terms ("this," "that," "those things," "whatchamacallits")	*WORD RECALL:* Teach the student to use association skills and to give definitions of words he cannot recall.	18, 33, 49

(*continues*)

Expressive Language *(Continued)*

Impairment	*Classroom Behaviors*	*Skills and Teaching Strategies*	*Resources*
	Has difficulty providing answers in fill-in-the-blank tests	Teach memory strategies (rehearsal, association, visualization, etc.).	
Reduced verbal reasoning and problem-solving skills	May arrive at a correct answer but be unable to recite the steps followed to solve the problem	*PROBLEM SOLVING:* Teach inductive and deductive reasoning at appropriate age levels.	2, 3, 12, 13, 15, 16, 17, 19, 20, 25, 26, 27, 28, 29
Poor reasoning skills		*REASONING:* Privately (not during classroom situations or in front of peers) ask the student to explain answers and provide reasons.	5, 6, 7, 11, 18, 21, 22, 48
Reduced ability to use abstractness in conversation (ambiguity, satire, inferences, drawing conclusions)	Says things that classmates interpret as satirical, funny, or bizarre although they were not intended that way	*SEMANTICS:* Teach the student common phrases used for satire, idioms, puns, etc.	12, 31, 32
Delayed responses	When called upon to give an answer, does not answer immediately, appearing not to know the answer	*PROCESSING:* Allow extra time for the student to discuss and explain. Avoid asking too many questions.	12, 31, 32
Inability to describe events in appropriate detail and sequence	When relating an experience, gets details out of order, confused, or overlapping Cannot explain to another student the directions for playing a game in physical education class	*SEQUENCING:* Teach sequencing skills. Direct the context of the student's responses.	8, 9, 10, 12, 13, 21, 30, 35, 36, 39, 40, 48
Inadequate labeling or vocabulary to convey clear messages	Inappropriately labels materials in class	*SEMANTICS:* Teach the student vocabulary associated with specific subject areas and classroom activities.	1, 4, 13, 14, 24, 31, 36, 41, 49

Expressive Language Worksheet

Impairment	*Classroom Behaviors*	*Skills and Teaching Strategies*	*Resources*
Difference between communication in informal situations and formal situations (e.g., the classroom)			4, 13, 24, 43
Normal length of sentences and use of gestures, but below-normal depth of communication			
Tangential (rambling) communication			31, 32
World retrieval errors			18, 33, 49
Reduced verbal reasoning and problem-solving ability			2, 3, 12, 13, 15, 16, 17, 19, 20, 25, 26, 27, 28, 29
Poor reasoning skills			5, 6, 7, 11, 18, 21, 22, 48
Reduced ability to use abstractness in conversation (ambiguity, satire, inferences, drawing conclusions)			12, 31, 32
Delayed responses			
Inability to describe events in appropriate detail and sequence			8, 9, 10, 12, 13, 21, 30, 35, 36, 39, 40, 48
Inadequate labeling or vocabulary to convey clear messages			1, 4, 13, 14, 24, 31, 36, 41, 49

Receptive Language

Impairment	*Classroom Behaviors*	*Skills and Teaching Strategies*	*Resources*
Inability to determine salient features of questions asked, information presented, or assignments read	Completes the wrong assignment (e.g., teacher requested that the class complete problems 9–12; this student completed problems 1–12)	*ORGANIZATION:* Encourage the student to write assignments in a daily log.	35, 36, 42, 49
Inability to determine specific aspects of questions	Gets the details confused when answering questions about the details of an academic lesson Provides related but not exact response when asked specific question Is unable to decipher long story problems	*FINDING THE FACTS:* Ask questions that will elicit the student's recall of important facts.	19
Inability to mentally organize information presented verbally or in written form	Performs steps of a project out of sequence, either fixating on one step or performing the most apparent step ("I know the other steps, I just didn't need to do them")	*SEQUENCING:* Provide the student with written three- and four-step sequences to sort and organize. Do not allow the student to skip steps in a demonstration even if the student claims to know what to do.	5, 6, 7, 10, 11, 12, 18, 21, 22, 25, 29, 48
Inability to analyze and integrate information received	Executes written directions in an unorganized and incomplete manner Goes to the gymnasium for a program although announcement stated that it would be held in the auditorium	*DIRECTION FOLLOWING:* Write directions as numbered steps rather than in paragraph form.	2, 3, 5, 6, 7, 11, 15, 18, 21, 22, 27, 34, 37, 38, 48

(*continues*)

Receptive Language (*Continued*)

Impairment	*Classroom Behaviors*	*Skills and Teaching Strategies*	*Resources*
Easily overloaded by large amounts of oral information presented during classroom instruction	Appears to be daydreaming and nonresponsive while the teacher is lecturing or giving instructions	*FOCUS ATTENTION:* Use pauses when giving classroom instructions to allow for processing information. Use short, simple sentences when explaining information	34, 35, 36, 37, 38
Inability to read nonverbal cues of others	Is unaware that the teacher or other classmates do not want to be bothered while they are working	*SOCIAL AWARENESS:* Use preestablished nonverbal cues to alert the student that behavior is inappropriate. Explain what was wrong with the behavior and what would have been appropriate.	44, 45, 46, 47
Difficulty comprehending spoken messages if presented in rapid manner or with abstract vocabulary	Exhibits poor notetaking skills; is unable to sort out and note the important parts of the teacher's discussion	*COMPREHENSION:* Use short, simple sentences emphasizing key points by voice variations, intonations, etc. Alert the student to the important topic being discussed.	4, 14, 24, 31
Difficulty understanding or recognizing a sequence of events	Even after being back at school for a while, still gets lost in the daily routine of the school day (knowing that spelling follows math, etc.)	*ORGANIZATION:* Provide the student with a written schedule of his or her school routine and a map of the daily route.	
Difficulty maintaining attention and concentration	Loses place while reading; is unable to relate information recently read; is easily distracted during reading assignments; is unable to complete silent reading and seatwork assignments at the same rate as classmates	*PROCESSING:* Provide the student additional time to complete classroom and homework tasks. *ATTENTION CONCENTRATION:* Because the student will most likely be processing at the best rate possible, provide with ample time for reading assignments. Reduce the amount of work to be read to summaries, etc.	3, 5, 7, 18, 19, 20, 27, 28, 48

(*continues*)

Receptive Language *(Continued)*

Impairment	*Classroom Behaviors*	*Skills and Teaching Strategies*	*Resources*
Inability to understand abstractness (satire, puns) in others' language	Misunderstands instructions and comments made; while classmates are responding to satire, jokes, pun, etc., appears to be unaware of what is funny	*SEMANTICS:* Avoid satire, jokes, and puns when presenting important information, teaching, or trying to correct the student's behavior. Teach the student the meaning of idioms, figurative language, ambiguous phrases, etc.	12, 29, 32

Receptive Language Worksheet

Impairment	*Classroom Behaviors*	*Skills and Teaching Strategies*	*Resources*
Inability to determine salient features			35, 36, 42, 49
Inability to determine specific aspects of questions			19
Inability to mentally organize information presented verbally or in written form			5, 6, 7, 10, 11, 12, 18, 21, 22, 25, 29, 48
Inability to analyze and integrate information received			2, 3, 5, 6, 7, 11, 15, 18, 21, 22, 27, 34, 37, 38, 48
Easily overloaded by large amounts of information presented during classroom instruction			34, 35, 36, 37, 38
Inability to read nonverbal cues of others			44, 45, 46, 47
Difficulty comprehending spoken messages if presented in rapid or lengthy manner or with abstract vocabulary			4, 14, 24, 31
Difficulty understanding or recognizing a sequence of events			
Difficulty maintaining attention and concentration			3, 5, 7, 18, 19, 20, 27, 28, 48
Inability to understand abstractness (satire, puns) in others' language			12, 29, 32

Written Language

Impairment	*Classroom Behaviors*	*Skills and Teaching Strategies*	*Resources*
Levels of writing structure and content that may differ from preinjury levels	Demonstrates grammatical, sentence structure, and organizational errors in answers to essay test	*SYNTACTIC COMPLEXITY:* Give the student time to go over written work with a partner or teaching aide to find and correct errors.	23, 24, 29, 32, 42, 43
Simplistic sentence structure and syntactic disorganization	Uses sentences and chooses topics that are simplistic compared with expectations for age and grade; writes themes that are short and dry	*PROOFREADING AND SEMANTICS:* Provide the student with worksheets that focus on teaching vocabulary, grammar, and proofreading skills.	23, 24, 29, 32, 42, 43
Content of writing that is very literal, is devoid of figurative language; and contains irrelevancies and unsubstantiated information	Provides nonessential details in written descriptions of projects Provides issue assertions with no supporting evidence Lacks preinjury flair and creativity in writing	*PROVIDING ADEQUATE AND SUBSTANTIAL INFORMATION, AND SEQUENCING AND EXPRESSING IDEAS THROUGH WRITING:* Allow the student to verbally state ideas, tape record, and write from dictation. Present the student with "question cards" indicating the specific issues that are to be addressed in an essay or discussed in a theme. Accept that the student will exhibit a difference in skill level pre- and postinjury. Work at the student's level and ability.	12, 18, 31, 32
Decreased speed and accuracy; poor legibility	Is slower on timed tests than classmates	*CHECK WORK FOR ACCURACY:* Accept that the student will take longer to complete assignments; reduce and alter the requirements.	
Poor planning of use of space on the paper	Is not concerned about appearance of work Sizes drawings disproportionately or locates them inappropriately on paper	*SPATIAL RELATIONSHIPS:* Use art teaching methodology to help the student identify and correct problems. Understand that physical capabilities may be limiting writing skills. Reteach if appropriate for age and grade.	31

Written Language Worksheet

Impairment	*Classroom Behaviors*	*Skills and Teaching Strategies*	*Resources*
Levels of writing structure and content that may differ from preinjury levels			23, 24, 29, 32, 42, 43
Simplistic sentence structure and syntactic disorganization			23, 24, 29, 32, 42, 43
Content of writing that is very literal, is devoid of figurative language; and contains irrelevancies and unsubstantiated information			12, 18, 31, 32
Decreased speed and accuracy; poor legibility			
Poor planning of use of space on paper			31

Resources to Supplement Classroom Materials

1. *Amazing adventures of Harvey Crumbaker: Skills for living.* (1983). Carson, CA: Lakeshore Curriculum Materials.
2. Baker, M. (1989). *Roller dog* [Computer program]. Pacific Grove, CA: Midwest Publications.
3. Baker, M. (1989). *What's my logic: Version 1.0* [Computer program]. Pacific Grove, CA: Midwest Publications.
4. Bender, M., & Valletutti, P. J. (1982). *Teaching functional academics: A curriculum guide for adolescents and adults with learning problems.* Austin, TX: PRO-ED.
5. Black, H., & Black, S. (1984). *Building thinking skills.* Pacific Grove, CA: Midwest Publications.
6. Black, H., & Black, S. (1985). *Figural building thinking skills.* Pacific Grove, CA: Midwest Publications.
7. Black, H., & Black, S. (1985). *Verbal building skills.* Pacific Grove, CA: Midwest Publications.
8. Blosser, J. (1984). *Let's talk about it! A calendar of daily activities for teaching language skills at home.* (Ages 4–8). Uniontown, OH: Author.
9. Blosser, J., & DePompei, R. (1985). *Let's listen today! A calendar of daily activities for teaching listening skills at home.* (Ages 4–8). Uniontown, OH: J. Blosser.
10. Blosser, J., & DePompei, R. (1992). *Let's organize today! A calendar of daily cognitive–communication activities.* Stow, OH: Interactive Therapeutics.
11. Bronniche, R. S. (1987). *Figural mind benders.* Pacific Grove, CA: Midwest Publications.
12. Brubaker, S. (1983). *Workbook for reasoning skills.* Detroit, MI: Wayne State University Press.
13. Carter, L., Caruso, M., Languirand, M., & Berard, M. A. (1987). *The thinking skills workbook: A cognitive skills remediation manual for adults.* Springfield, IL: Thomas.
14. Craine, J., & Gudeman, H. (1981). *The rehabilitation of brain functions.* Springfield, IL: Thomas.
15. Cwirko-Godycki, J. T. (1989). *Five in a row: Addition and subtraction* [Computer program]. Pacific Grove, CA: Midwest Publications.
16. Cwirko-Godycki, J. T. (1989). *Five in a row: Division* [Computer program]. Pacific Grove, CA: Midwest Publications.
17. Cwirko-Godycki, J. T. (1989). *Five in a row: Multiplication* [Computer program]. Pacific Grove, CA: Midwest Publications.
18. Doolittle, J. H. (1989). *Connectors vectors.* Pacific Grove, CA: Midwest Publications.

19. Doolittle, J. H. (1989). *Hangtown* [Computer program]. Pacific Grove, CA: Midwest Publications.

20. Edwards, R. (1989). *Target math* [Computer program]. Pacific Grove, CA: Midwest Publications.

21. Edwards, R., & Hill, W. (1987). *Primary building thinking skills.* Pacific Grove, CA: Midwest Publications.

22. Edwards, R., & Hill, W. (1988). *Mathematical reasoning through verbal analysis.* Pacific Grove, CA: Midwest Publications.

23. Greatsinger, C., & Waelder, P. (1987). *Practice in survival reading* (series of 7 books). Syracuse, NY: New Readers Press.

24. Gruenewald, L. J., & Pollack, S. A. (1984). *Language interaction in teaching and learning.* Austin, TX: PRO-ED.

25. Harnadek, A. (1976). *Critical thinking: Book one.* Pacific Grove, CA: Midwest Publications.

26. Harnadek, A. (1980). *Math mindbenders–A1* [Computer program]. Pacific Grove, CA: Midwest Publications.

27. Harnadek, A. (1988). *Mindbenders–A1* [Computer program]. Pacific Grove, CA: Midwest Publications.

28. Harnadek, A. (1988). *Mindbenders–B1* [Computer program]. Pacific Grove, CA: Midwest Publications.

29. Jaffe, C., & Roberts, B. (1984). *Thinkathon I.* Hawthorne, NJ: Educational Impressions.

30. Kahn, C., & Hanna, J. (1983). *Working makes sense* (2nd ed.) (practical arithmetic series). Belmont, CA: Fearon Education.

31. Kilpatrick, K. (1979). *Therapy guide for the adult with language and speech disorders. Volume I: A selection of stimulus materials.* Akron, OH: Visiting Nurse Service.

32. Kilpatrick, K. (1981). *Therapy guide for the adult with language and speech disorders. Volume 2: Advanced stimulus materials.* Akron, OH: Visiting Nurse Service.

33. Kilpatrick, K. (1983). *Working with words, Volume 3.* Akron, OH: Visiting Nurse Service.

34. Kilpatrick, K. (1985). *Putting the pieces together, Volume 4.* Akron, OH: Visiting Nurse Service.

35. Lazzari, A., & Peters, P. M. (1980). *HELP: Handbook of exercises for language processing. Volume 1: Auditory discrimination, auditory reception, auditory association, auditory memory.* Moline, IL: Lingui Systems.

36. Lazzari, A., & Peters, A. M. (1980). *HELP: Handbook of exercises for language processing. Volume 2: Specific word finding, categorization, wh– questions, grammar.* Moline, IL: Lingui Systems.

37. *Mindbenders: Deductive Thinking Skills* A-1 (easy) through C-3 (hard). (1978). Pacific Grove, CA: Midwest Publications.
38. Nash, G., & Nash, B. (1985). *Pundles*. New York: The Stone Song Press, 51 Madison Ave., New York, NY 10010.
39. Parsons, J. (1979). *Math A Riddle I (subtraction)*. Belmont, CA: Fearon Education.
40. Parsons, J. (1979). *Math A Riddle II (multiplication)*. Belmont, CA: Fearon Education.
41. Pelton, V. (1980). *Learning to live on our own* (series of 6 books). Cortland, OH: Professional Educational Services.
42. *Readers Workshop I and II*. Pleasantville, NY: Readers Digest Educational Division.
43. Schwartz, L., & McKenley, N. (1984). *Daily communication: Strategies for the language disordered adolescent*. Eau Claire, WI: Thinking Publications.
44. Wiig, E. (1982). *Let's talk: Asking for favors*. Columbus, OH: Merrill Publishing Co., A Bell and Howell Company.
45. Wiig, E. (1982). *Let's talk: Dating*. Columbus, OH: Merrill Publishing Co., A Bell and Howell Company.
46. Wiig, E. (1982). *Let's talk: Making dates*. Columbus, OH: Merrill Publishing Co., A Bell and Howell Company.
47. Wiig, E. (1982). *Let's talk: Sharing feelings*. Columbus, OH: Merrill Publishing Co., A Bell and Howell Company.
48. Wiseman, R. (1985). *Thinking about time*. Pacific Grove, CA: Midwest Publications.
49. Zachman, L., Jorgensen, C., Barrett, M., Huisingh, R., & Snedden, M. K. (1982). *Manual of exercises for expressive reasoning*. Molene, IL: Lingui Systems.

REFERENCES

Blosser, J. L. (1990). *Making your speech-language pathology program relevant to educational needs*. Scranton, PA: Luczerne County School Speech-Language Pathologists.

Blosser, J. L., & DePompei, R. (1989). The head-injured student returns to school: Recognizing and treating deficits. In J. L. Blosser & R. DePompei (Eds.), Cognitive–communicative impairments following head injury. *Topics in Language Disorders, 9*(2), 67–77.

Blosser, J. L., & DePompei, R. (1991). Preparing education professionals for meeting the needs of students with TBI. *Journal of Head Trauma Rehabilitation, 6*, 1.

Blosser, J. L., & Secord, W. (1989). *Curriculum referenced language assessment*. Miniseminar at The Ohio Speech and Hearing Association Annual Convention, Columbus.

Brown, A. L., & Palincsar, A. S. (1982). Inducing strategic learning from texts by means of informed self-control training. *Topics in Learning and Learning Disabilities, 2,* 1–17.

Cohen, S. B. (1991). Adapting educational programs for students with head injuries. *Journal of Head Trauma Rehabilitation, 6*(1), 56–63.

DePompei, R., & Blosser, J. L. (1987). Strategies for helping head-injured children successfully return to school. *Language, Speech, and Hearing Services in the Schools, 18,* 292–300.

DePompei, R., & Blosser, J. L. (1992). *Let's organize today! A calendar of daily cognitive–communication activities.* Stow, OH: Interactive Therapeutics.

Forest, M., & Lusthause, E. (1990). Everyone belongs with the MAPS action planning system. *Teaching Exceptional Children, 22*(2), 32–35.

Gagne, R. M. (1990). Learnable aspects of problem solving. *Educational Psychologists, 15,* 84–94.

Gleason, M. M. (1989, Spring). Teaching study skills. *Teaching Exceptional Children,* pp. 52–53.

Gloeckler, T., & Simpson, S. (1988). *Exceptional students in regular classrooms: Challenges, services, methods.* Mountain View, CA: Mayfield.

Graden, J. L. (1989, November). Redefining "prereferral" intervention as intervention assistance: Collaboration between general and special education. *Exceptional Children, 56,* 227–231.

Hobbs, S. A., Moguin, L. E., & Troyler, N. (1980). Cognitive behavioral therapy with children. *Catalogue of Selected Documents in Psychology, 10,* 62–63.

Hoskisson, K., & Tompkins, G. E. (1987). *Language arts: Content and teaching strategies.* Columbus, OH: Merrill.

Meven, E. (1990). Quality instruction for students with disabilities. *Teaching Exceptional Children, 22,* 12–13.

Neidecker, E., & Blosser, J. (1993). *School programs in speech-language: Organization and management.* Englewood Cliffs, NJ: Prentice-Hall.

Rosen, C. D., & Gerring, J. R. (1986). *Head trauma: Educational re-integration.* San Diego: College-Hill.

Ryan, E. B., Short, E., & Weed, K. A. (1986). The role of cognitive strategy training in improving the academic performance of learning disabled children. *Journal of Learning Disabilities, 19,* 521–529.

Savage, R. (1991). Identification, classification and placement issues for students with TBI. *Journal of Head Trauma Rehabilitation, 6*(1), 1–9.

Schellentrager, J. (1987). Those powerful peers! In C. Paolano & J. Hammond (Eds.), *Special Ideas Newsletter.* Akron, OH: Summit County Board of Education.

Solomon, D., Schaps, E., Watson, M., & Battistich, V. (1992). Creating caring school and classroom communities for all students. In R. A. Villa, J. S. Thousand, W. Stainback, & S. Stainback (Eds.), *Restructuring for caring and effective education.* Baltimore: Brookes.

Telzrow, C. (1991). The school psychologist's perspective on testing students with traumatic head injury. *Journal of Head Trauma Rehabilitation, 6*(1), 23–26.

Uve, N. J., & Bransford, J. D. (1981). Programs for teaching thinking. *Educational Leadership, 39*(1), 26–28.

Wong, B. Y. L., Wong, R., Perry, N., & Sawatsky, D. (1986). The efficacy of a self questioning, summarization strategy for use by underachievers and learning disabled adolescents in social studies. *Learning Disabilities Focus, 2,* 20–31.

Ylvisaker, M. (Ed.). (1985). *Head injury rehabilitation: Children and adolescents.* Austin, TX: PRO-ED.

CHAPTER 16

The Role of the School Psychologist

VIVIAN BEGALI

With the inclusion of traumatic brain injury (TBI) as one of 13 educational disabilities (*Federal Register,* 1991), school psychologists are expected to assume an ever-increasing role in the direct service, assessment, and educational program planning of students with such an injury. As uniquely qualified members of the educational team, school psychologists can make distinct contributions on behalf of students with acquired brain injuries (ABI). The generic backgrounds of school psychologists make them the logical team member to integrate the pertinent principles of psychology, education, neuropsychology, assessment, and counseling into a cohesive backdrop for school-based treatment planning. Specifically, school psychologists can (a) provide the leadership for hospital-to-school reintegration efforts; (b) collect, analyze, and interpret cognitive, psychological, neuropsychological, and behavioral information for school personnel in preparation for the child's reentry; (c) assist staff with eligibility and placement decisions; (d) provide ongoing consultation to staff regarding the development of appropriate treatment and behavioral management plans that reflect state-of-the-art technologies; (e) share responsibility for ongoing assessment and progress monitoring; (f) coordinate inservice activities that promote an understanding of ABI and its educational implications; (g) participate in program development; (h) provide individual, group, or family counseling; and (i) serve as referral agent and case manager. Clearly, school psychologists can serve children with ABI in a variety of direct and indirect roles, such as team leader, program and placement strategist, consultant, assessor, expert, counselor, and case manager.

SCHOOL PSYCHOLOGIST AS ABI TEAM LEADER

Plans for school reintegration following ABI should begin during the early stages of the child's hospitalization. School psychologists can promote a well-organized transition by serving as the designated school contact with whom the child's medical case manager will communicate progress updates and projected service needs. School psychologists can analyze and translate such information to school personnel in preparation for the student's return. The potential for student regression that often occurs when a child with ABI is transferred from a medical facility to a public school (or from any highly restrictive environment to a less restrictive one) may be minimized with advance preparation, transitional accommodations, and collaboration between hospital and school professionals. Plans for reciprocal on-site visits can be arranged. The inservice needs of school staff can be identified, and the responsibility for addressing these needs can be shared with rehabilitation specialists. Following reentry, the school psychologist can help fulfill the changing inservice needs of school staff, monitor and modify student program goals, and remain abreast of pertinent ABI research.

The transition from hospital to school is the first critical juncture at which assessment results play a significant role in educational program planning and service delivery. The answers to critical questions regarding placement, programming, ancillary services, and instructional goals depend on the ability of educational professionals to organize and transform the findings of medical discharge summaries into meaningful treatment strategies. Interdisciplinary assessment results following ABI provide the formal reference against which recovery is continually charted. Short- and long-term objectives are best developed on the basis of identifiable intact and deficit functions. Psychologists who have an understanding of brain injury and the implications of postinjury evaluation results can communicate a multidimensional view of the child and advocate for the kinds of services and instructional emphases that promote recovery and adjustment.

When reviewing interdisciplinary discharge summaries and preparing for a child's return to school, educational teams need to extract answers to a variety of preliminary questions. The answers to these questions not only provide the team with a multidimensional understanding of the child's injury and its educational implications but, more importantly, establish a sense of direction for purposes of program planning and service delivery. Table 16.1 is a guide for collecting and organizing multidisciplinary data. School psychologists may elect to use this format for structuring interviews with medical personnel or as a way of consolidating multidisciplinary data for formal presentation.

SCHOOL PSYCHOLOGIST AS ABI PROGRAM AND PLACEMENT STRATEGIST

The interdisciplinary evaluations and discharge summaries from the medical facility (hospital or rehabilitation center) are likely to serve as the basis for special education eligibility and placement decisions. The Individuals with Disabilities Education Act (IDEA) defines traumatic brain injury as

> an acquired injury to the brain caused by an external physical force, resulting in total or partial functional disability or psychosocial functioning, or both, that adversely affects a child's educational performance. The term applies to open or closed head injuries resulting in impairments in one or more areas, such as:

TABLE 16.1. Planning for Re-Entry: Twenty Questions for Educational Treatment Teams

1. What type of injury did the child sustain? (open or closed)
2. What was the extent of damage? (mild, moderate, severe)
3. What areas of the brain were compromised?
4. How long was the child unconscious?
5. When did the injury occur? How old was the child at the time?
6. What was the child's estimated cognitive and educational status before the injury?
7. How long after the injury was assessment conducted?
8. What notable sensory impairments does the child exhibit?
9. What motor impairments prevail and how will this impact the child's ability to function within the academic setting?
10. What are the child's predominant cognitive, physical, academic, and/or behavioral problems?
11. What are the child's strengths? Which functions remain intact?
12. How long is the child's attention span?
13. What specialized equipment will the child need?
14. What personal assistance will the child require?
15. Does the child require medication?
16. Is the child at risk for seizures?
17. What safety precautions need to be taken?
18. What special concerns do the child's parents have?
19. Can the child's needs be addressed within the regular classroom?
20. Does the child qualify for special education and ancillary services?

From *Head Injury in Children and Adolescents: A Resource and Review for School and Allied Professionals* (2nd ed., p. 176) by V. Begali, 1992, Brandon, VT: Clinical Psychology Publishing. Reprinted with permission.

> cognition; language; memory; attention; reasoning; abstract thinking; judgment; problem-solving; sensory, perceptual, and motor abilities; psychosocial behavior; physical functions; information processing; and speech. The term does not apply to brain injuries that are congenital or degenerative, or brain injuries induced by birth trauma. (*Federal Register,* 1992, p. 44802)

Degree of impairment is not a factor in determining eligibility for special education services. The critical elements for determining eligibility are (a) that the injury be *acquired;* (b) that it be caused by an *external force;* (c) that it result in *total or partial functional disability and/or psychosocial impairment;* (d) that the impairment *adversely affect educational performance;* and (e) that the need for special education and related services be *tied to the disability or impairment.*

Although special education services may not be required for all school-aged students with ABI, even those with the mildest injuries are likely to require some form of special consideration or assistance during the early stages of their return (Begali, 1992). For each child who does qualify, the team must decide upon the appropriate placement for the child and determine his or her related service needs (special transportation, specialized equipment, psychological services, physical or occupational therapy, speech-language therapy, social work services, transition services, rehabilitation counseling, etc.).

Students with ABI are not mentally retarded, learning disabled, or emotionally disturbed in the traditional sense. Unlike children whose educational dispositions can be directly tied to long-standing intellectual, cognitive, or emotional disorders, children with TBI, in particular, have sustained sudden impairment as a result of a physical agent (e.g., gunshot wound, acceleration–deceleration injury, or blow to the head). As such, these children are more likely to have experienced a relatively normal and uncompromised period of development prior to injury. Their potential for rapid and dramatic change and their fluctuating ability profiles further distinguish them from other, more familiar exceptional populations. These distinctions should, in turn, affect the way educational teams assess students with TBI, place and program, and monitor their progress. Multiple cognitive, emotional, behavioral, and physical complications can exist concurrently, making assessment following ABI more than the perfunctory administration of a standard battery of tests and educational programming and placement more than a simple match between student and classroom. The effects of each additional impairment are multiplicative. The complex and interactive sequelae that can result from ABI and the impact these consequences can have on a child's educational progress make it necessary for school professionals to cultivate a comprehensive and unbiased appreciation of ABI before the challenges associated with assessment, program planning, and placement are undertaken (Begali, 1987, 1992). Without the impending pressure of having to classify the student with ABI as mentally retarded, learning disabled, or seriously emotionally disturbed, educational programming and placement teams can instead govern their efforts based on a clear and pragmatic understanding of the very features that warrant attention.

To develop a suitable education program for the student with ABI, the team must determine not only how much the individual is lacking, but also what processes are missing, distorted, or exaggerated. Table 16.2 identifies a range of complications that may accompany TBI.

Because of the potential for rapid and dramatic change in the ability profiles of students with ABI, Individualized Education Programs (IEPs) need to be revised at frequent intervals to reflect recommended programmatic changes. Interim IEPs can be written for the purpose of evaluating the appropriateness of initial placements. Federal mandate requires, however, that temporary placements not become the final placement before the IEP is finalized. Therefore, interim IEPs should specify the specific conditions and timelines for trial placement and parents should agree to the interim placement before it is attempted (*Federal Register,* 1992, p. 44834). Placement alternatives following ABI can range from least restrictive (regular education with monitoring) to most restrictive (e.g., hospital, extended care facility). Most children with ABI require one or a combination of special placement alternatives, such as self-contained special education, resource, home-based, or outpatient services. Some may need to return to school on a half-day basis.

Students who return to school while in a critical stage of recovery may require extended school year services. Extended services may be offered to those for whom the

TABLE 16.2. Common Sequelae Following TBI: What Can Be Expected?

Cognitive consequences

A. Decrease in overall intellectual status

B. Highly specific cognitive deficits

C. Attention–concentration deficits

D. Complete or partial impairment of language functions

E. Highly specific or generalized memory problems

F. Problems in abstract reasoning or social judgment

G. Specific academic problems

Physical consequences

A. Sensory deficits
   1. Visual impairment (e.g., double vision, visual field loss, tracking problems, color blindness, perceptual disturbances)
   2. Impaired ability to taste or smell
   3. Hypersensitivity or hyposensitivity to sensory stimuli
   4. Reduced auditory acuity

B. Motor deficits
   1. Mild impairment of fine motor movement
   2. Complete loss of specific functional abilities
   3. Tremors
   4. Balance or coordination problems
   5. Specific motor weakness
   6. Speech disturbances
   7. Slowness of motor speed and reaction time

C. Neurological deficits
   1. Problems with bowel and bladder control
   2. Seizure disorder
   3. Hyperphagia (voracious food seeking, overeating)
   4. Perseveration
   5. Chronic fatigue
   6. Sleep disturbances
   7. Hydrocephalus

Affective consequences

A. Behavioral disturbances
   1. Impulsivity
   2. Social crudeness

(*continues*)

TABLE 16.2. *Continued*

3. Disinhibition
4. Hyperactivity

B. Psychological disturbances
1. Depression
2. Withdrawal
3. Anxiety
4. Emotional lability

C. Personality changes
1. Oppositionalism
2. Stubbornness
3. Dependency
4. Aggressiveness
5. Self-centeredness

traditional summer vacation would result in regression such that recoupment within a reasonable period of time would not be possible and for whom self-sufficiency would be significantly jeopardized (Slenkovich, 1987).

SCHOOL PSYCHOLOGIST AS ABI CONSULTANT

School-based consultation refers to the process of collaborative problem solving between school psychologist (consultant) and one or more significant adults (consultees) who are responsible for providing some form of intervention to the student (client). Unlike counseling–therapy and assessment, consultation is an indirect service delivery model whereby the consultant seeks to positively affect student outcome by modifying the behavior or attitudes of significant adults in the child's environment (Gutkin & Curtis, 1982). Consultation to administrators, teachers, aides, support staff, or parents is provided by the psychologist in the interest of promoting the student's educational success and adjustment. The relationships in consultation are formulated on the level of colleague to colleague. Both consultant and consultee are considered expert within their respective domains and as such have equal authority. Ultimately, the product of this collegial relationship is a rich mix of collaborative energy and resources that serves the student well.

Consultation to professionals working with children and adolescents who have sustained TBI is likely to be focused on residual deficits, curriculum and interventions, behavioral management, team functioning, attitudes toward the child and his or her injury, and/or associated stress. School-based consultation may take a variety of forms. School psychologists can use consultation as a means to increase the skills and knowledge of educational team members in order to promote greater program consistency and instructional effectiveness. The psychologist and teacher share responsibility for identifying problems, generating possible solutions, and evaluating the effectiveness of various interventions.

As discussed in earlier chapters, many children and adolescents who sustain TBI experience difficulty reading social cues, attending, understanding cause and effect, generalizing, processing information, and remembering. These deficits can influence the degree to which conventional behavioral techniques are effective. Hence, consultation is likely to become a much sought-after service, particularly by those who are unaccustomed to the behavioral nuances of ABI. School psychologists can collaborate with teachers to develop an orderly and structured plan for decreasing inappropriate behavior and increasing desirable behavior in ways that reflect best practices in brain injury rehabilitation (Begali, 1992; Bigler, 1990; Lehr, 1990; Sohlberg & Mateer, 1989; Wood, 1990). School psychologists and educators need to devise behavioral management plans that are adjusted to accommodate the student's specific neurobehavioral deficits (memory problems, distractibility, disinhibition, cognitive dulling, etc.). Classroom rules need to be restated regularly in direct and explicit terms. Behavioral treatments need to be simple and persistent, and consistently applied across settings.

SCHOOL PSYCHOLOGIST AS ABI ASSESSOR

Traumatic brain injury may produce (a) a general deterioration in many areas of functioning; (b) differential effects, depending upon such variables as age at injury and type, extent, and site of damage; (c) highly specific effects; or (d) no observable effects (Sattler, 1988). It follows, then, that formal assessment following injury should allow for these possibilities and account for the variables. Postinjury assessment should be multifactored. Specifically, it should provide for the examination of those areas of functioning that are most susceptible to disruption (see Table 16.3). No single index, such as IQ, should be used as the primary determinant of general status, educational placement, potential for change, or program needs. No standard battery of tests, for that matter, can be expected to adequately cover all of the functions susceptible to impairment by brain damage (Lezak, 1987). The purposes of assessment and the unique characteristics of the individual should dictate the choice of tests.

The formal assessment of children with ABI is likely to include measures of various cognitive and intellectual skills, sensory–perceptual functions, motor functions, problem-solving abilities, orientation, academic achievement, language and communication skills, emotional status, and adaptive behavior. (See Table 16.4 for a list of formal assessment procedures useful in the evaluation of children and adolescents with ABI.) Equal emphasis should be given to determining intervention techniques that will help promote the child's adjustment and continued recovery. Likewise, the identification of performance characteristics—namely, problem-solving strategies, test-taking attitudes, error patterns, self-monitoring behavior, attitudes toward failure, stamina, reinforcement preferences, and so on—has a prominent place in the assessment hierarchy and is of particular value when assessing the student with ABI (Lezak, 1987).

School-based evaluations allow for (a) a review of eligibility status; (b) the modification or reorganization of placements; (c) a measure of the success or failure of

TABLE 16.3. Functions to be Examined Following TBI

Intelligence
- *Verbal*
- *Nonverbal*

Attention–Concentration
- *Visual*
- *Auditory*

Communication
- *Spoken vs. written*
- *Receptive vs. expressive*
- *Speech vs. language*

Memory
- *Short term vs. written*
- *Verbal and nonverbal*
- *Episodic and semantic*
- *Visual and Auditory*

New learning ability

Abstract reasoning and judgment

Orientation
- *Personal*
- *Spatial*
- *Temporal*

Manual dexterity–laterality
- *Left vs. right*
- *Lateral dominance*

Academic achievement

Personality–adjustment

Perception
- *Sensory (visual, auditory, tactile functions)*
- *Visual–motor*

Behavior
- *Among peers, family, strangers*
- *Home, school, community*

From *Head Injury in Children and Adolescents: A Resource and Review for School and Allied Professionals* (2nd ed., p. 103) by V. Begali, 1992, Brandon, VT: Clinical Psychology Publishing Company. Reprinted with permission.

TABLE 16.4. Formal Assessment Techniques and Procedures for Children and Adolescents with ABI

Intelligence

British Ability Scales (Elliott, Murray, & Pearson, 1983)
Columbia Mental Maturity Scale (Burgemeister, Blum, & Lorge, 1972)
Differential Ability Scales (Elliot, 1990)
Kaufman Assessment Battery for Children (Kaufman & Kaufman, 1983)
Leiter International Performance Scale (Leiter, 1969)
Nonverbal Test of Cognitive Ability (Johnson & Boyd, 1981)
Pictorial Test of Intelligence (French, 1983)
Raven's Standard Progressive Matrices (Raven, 1989)
Stanford–Binet Intelligence Scale: Fourth Edition (Thorndike, Hagen, & Sattler, 1986)
Wechsler Adult Intelligence Scale–Revised (Wechsler, 1981)
Wechsler Intelligence Scale for Children–III (Wechsler, 1991)
Wechsler Preschool and Primary Scale of Intelligence–Revised (Wechsler, 1989)
Woodcock–Johnson Psycho-Educational Battery–Revised (WJPEB-R): *Tests of Cognitive Ability* (Woodcock & Johnson, 1989)

Attention–concentration

Freedom from Distractibility (Wechsler scales)
Matching Familiar Figures Test (Campbell, 1976)
Paced Auditory Serial Addition Test (Gronwall & Sampson, 1974)
Rhythm subtest (*Luria–Nebraska Neuropsychological Battery–Children's Revision*) (LNNB-C) (Golden, Purisch, & Hammeke, 1985)
Seashore Rhythm Test (*Halstead–Reitan Battery*) (Halstead, 1947)

Communication

Boston Diagnostic Aphasia Examination (Goodglass & Kaplan, 1972)
Communicative Abilities in Daily Living (Holland, 1980)
Controlled Oral Word Association (Benton, Hamsher, Varney, & Spreen, 1983)
Expressive One-Word Vocabulary Test–Revised (Gardner, 1990)
Multilingual Aphasia Examination (Benton & Hamsher, 1978)
Peabody Picture Vocabulary Test–Revised (Dunn, 1981)
Porch Index of Communicative Ability (Porch, 1967)
Selective Reminding Test (Buschke & Fuld, 1974)
Test of Adolescent Word Finding (German, 1990)
Test for Auditory Comprehension of Language (Carrow-Woolfolk, 1985)
Test of Written Language–Second Edition (Hammill & Larsen, 1988)
Token Test for Children (DeRenzi, 1980; DiSimoni, 1978)
Vocabulary subtest (Wechsler scales)

(*continues*)

TABLE 16.4. *Continued*

Memory

Benton Visual Retention Test (Benton, 1974)
Digit Span subtest (Wechsler scales)
Information subtest (Wechsler scales)
Rivermead Behavioral Memory Test–Revised (Wilson, Cockburn, & Braddeley, 1985)
Sentence Memory Test (Benton, 1965)
Short Term and Long Term Memory clusters (WJPEB-R)
Visual Aural Digit Span Test (Koppitz, 1977)
Wechsler Memory Scale–Revised (Wechsler, 1987)

New learning ability

Category Test (Reitan, 1959)
Performance Scale (Wechsler scales)
Reitan–Modified Halstead Category Test (Kimura, 1981)
Selective Reminding Test (Buschke & Fuld, 1974)
Serial Digit Learning (Benton, Hamsher, Varney, & Spreen, 1983)
Wisconsin Card Sorting Test (Grant & Berg, 1980)

Abstract reasoning–judgment

British Ability Scales (Elliott, Murray, & Pearson, 1983)
Category Test (Reitan, 1959)
Comprehension subtest (Wechsler scales)
Matrix Analogies Test (Naglieri, 1985)
Similarities subtest (Wechsler scales)
Wisconsin Card Sorting Test (Grant & Berg, 1980)

Orientation

Children's Orientation and Amnesia Test (Ewing-Cobbs et al., 1984)
Galveston Orientation and Amnesia Test (Levin, O'Donnell, & Grossman, 1979)
Personal Orientation Test (Benton et al., 1983)
Right–Left Orientation Test (Benton et al., 1983)
Spatial Orientation Memory Test (Wepman & Turaids, 1975)
Standardized Road Map Test of Direction Sense (Money, 1976)
Temporal Orientation Test (Benton et al., 1983)

Manual dexterity–laterality

Finger Tapping Test (Reitan & Davison, 1974)
Grooved Pegboard Test (Matthews & Klove, 1964)
Harris Test of Lateral Dominance (Harris, 1947)
Left/Right Hemisphere Scales (LNNB)

(*continues*)

TABLE 16.4. *Continued*

Purdue Pegboard (Purdue Research, 1948)
Purdue Perceptual–Motor Survey (Roach & Kephart, 1966)
Strength of Grip (Reitan & Davison, 1974)

Academic achievement

Diagnostic [reading] *Screening Procedure* (Boder, 1973)
Kaufman Test of Educational Achievement (Kaufman & Kaufman, 1985)
Peabody Individual Achievement Test (Dunn & Markwardt, 1970)
Reading/Everyday Activities in Life (Lichtman, 1972)
Wide Range Achievement Test–Revised (Jastak & Wilkinson, 1984)
WJPEB-R: Tests of Academic Achievement (Woodcock & Johnson, 1989)

Personality–adjustment

Brief Psychiatric Rating Scale (Overall & Gorham, 1962)
Children's Apperception Test (Bellak & Bellak, 1974)
Draw A Person Projective Technique (Machover, 1948)
Katz Adjustment Scale (Katz & Lyerly, 1963)
Personality Inventory for Children (Wirt, Lachar, Klinedinst, & Seat, 1977)
Portland Adaptability Inventory (Lezak, 1980)
Roberts Apperception Test (McArthur & Roberts, 1982)
Rorschach Technique (1945)

Perception

Auditory Discrimination Test (Reynolds, 1987)
Bender Visual Motor Gestalt (Bender, 1984)
Benton Visual Retention Test (Benton, 1974)
Block Design subtest (Wechsler scales)
Developmental Test of Visual Motor Integration (Beery, 1967)
Facial Recognition (Benton et al., 1983)
Fingertip Symbol Writing Recognition (Reitan & Davison, 1974)
Hooper Visual Organization Test (Hooper, 1983)
Map Localization Test (Benton, Levin, & Van Allen, 1974)
Minnesota Percepto-Diagnostic Test (Fuller, 1982)
Pantomime Recognition (Varney & Benton, 1982)
Speech Sounds Perception Test (Reitan & Davison, 1974)
Tactile Form Perception Test (Benton et al., 1983)
Tactual Performance Test (Reitan & Davison, 1974)
Trail Making Test (Reitan & Davison, 1974)
Underlining Test (Rourke & Gates, 1980)

(*continues*)

TABLE 16.4. *Continued*

Behavior

AAMD Adaptive Behavior Scale (Lambert, Windmiller, Tharinger, & Cole, 1981)
Adaptive Behavior Inventory for Children (Mercer & Lewis, 1978)
Boyd Developmental Progress Scale (Boyd, 1974)
Child Behavior Checklist (Achenback & Edelbrock, 1986)
Conners Parent Rating Scale (Conners, 1985)
Conners Teacher Rating Scale (Conners, 1985)
Devereux Child/Adolescent Rating Scale (Spivack & Spotts, 1966)
Revised Behavior Problem Checklist (Quay & Peterson, 1983)
Vineland Adaptive Behavior Scales (Sparrow, Balla, & Cicchetti, 1984)

Neuropsychological batteries and manuals

Benton Tests: A Clinical Manual (Benton et al., 1983)
Halstead–Reitan Battery (Reitan & Davison, 1974)
Halstead–Reitan Neuropsychological Test Battery for Children (Reitan & Davison, 1974)
Halstead–Reitan Test Battery: An Interpretive Guide (Jarvis & Barth)
Lafayette Clinic Repeatable Neuropsychological Test Battery (Lewis & Kupke, 1977)
Luria–Nebraska Neuropsychological Battery (Golden, Hammeke, & Purisch, 1980)
Luria–Nebraska Neuropsychological Battery–Form II (Golden, Purisch, & Hammeke, 1985)
Luria–Nebraska Neuropsychological Battery–Children's Revision (Golden, 1987)
Reitan–Indiana Neuropsychological Test Battery for Children (Reitan & Davison, 1974)
Wechsler Adult Intelligence Scale–Revised as a Neuropsychological Instrument (Kaplan, Fein, Morris, & Delis, 1991)
Wisconsin Neuropsychological Test Battery (Harley, Leuthold, Matthews, & Bergs, 1980)

Note: See original source for references for listed tests. From *Head Injury in Children and Adolescents: A Resource and Review for School and Allied Professionals* (2nd ed., pp. 104–107) by V. Begali, 1992, Brandon, VT: Clinical Psychology Publishing. Reprinted with permission.

various treatment strategies; (d) a reappraisal of relative strengths and weaknesses; (e) the opportunity to update short- and long-term instructional objectives; and (f) the occasion to redirect and revitalize team efforts. Periodic school-based evaluations make it possible to systematically monitor student progress and modify program goals and instructional strategies. The way is then paved for a total service plan that accommodates the immediate, ongoing, and often-changing needs of the child with ABI.

Preinjury standardized test results (when available), anecdotal entries, teacher observations, work samples, and so forth, that are available in a student's school records can be used to determine the extent to which brain damage has altered academic performance and as a collective mechanism by which to gauge progress (or deterioration). Adaptive behavior scales, behavioral checklists, and formal inventories can be administered retrospectively to parents and teachers, thus enabling multiple comparisons between a child's functioning before and after the injury, at home and at school, and across constructs. Specific instructional objectives can be generated on the basis of lost or altered functions. McFie (1975) recommended that, when premorbid IQ scores are not available for purposes of comparison, the highest postinjury score on either the Vocabulary or the Picture Completion subtest of a Wechsler intelligence scale serve as an estimate of premorbid functioning. As an alternative, Lezak (1983) suggested estimating premorbid ability by using the "best performance method"—that is, evidence of the student's best preinjury performance, such as the highest score or set of scores, observed behavior, or achievement. Because of their potential for dramatic change during the first 18 months following injury, students with TBI need to be reevaluated at regular 3- to 6-month intervals (Barth & Macciocchi, 1985) until recovery plateaus. Serial assessments may then be spaced farther apart (Levin & Goldstein, 1989).

When follow-up assessments use previously administered instruments, the effects of prior exposure (practice effects) should be taken into account because shorter intervals between testings produce greater practice effects (Sattler, 1988). Lehr (1990) determined that children and adolescents with TBI are less likely than noninjured peers to benefit from practice effects on initial testing but are more likely to show greater practice effects than noninjured children upon repeated assessment. Consequently, higher retest scores need to be qualified as reflective of intervention, recovery, error, or prior exposure to the task.

To offset the artificial effects of practice upon qualitative results, the psychologist can use any of several options. One possibility is to use alternate test forms. Routine samples of problem-solving strategies, criterion- or curriculum-based performance, and adaptive behavior taken informally may also serve as an alternative or supplement to repeated formal assessments. To offer balance to the inherent limitations of fixed or battery assessments, Kaplan (1988) advocated a *process approach*. The focus of the process approach is upon optimal rather than typical performance. The student's behavior and strategies en route to a solution become the focus of the examiner's attention rather than the child's ability to conform to rigid standards and time limits. In addition to providing a context by which to determine the examinee's problem-solving strategies, the assessment process becomes the means by which to identify performance enhancers and learning preferences. Thus, the questions to be answered by formal reassessment are likely to be qualitative and pragmatic in nature (e.g., To what extent has this child recovered? Which functions continue to show impairment and to what degree? What strategies enhance performance and promote recovery? How can assessment results be used to direct instructional efforts?). Table 16.5 offers a proposed format for collecting and reporting psychological assessment data following ABI.

SCHOOL PSYCHOLOGIST AS ABI EXPERT

School psychologists who develop an understanding of ABI can provide expertise based upon research, theory, and/or experience to promote greater effectiveness in other professionals by increasing their knowledge and skills. To make the most of the assessment process and to interpret results in a way that will yield educationally

TABLE 16.5. Psychological Evaluation Following ABI: A Format for Organizing and Reporting

I. *Identifying data*

II. *Reason for referral*

  A. Purpose of assessment

  B. Type of injury

  C. Time since injury

III. *Tests administered* (adaptations noted)

IV. *Background data*

  A. Relevant developmental–educational history

  B. Preinjury status
    1. Estimated preinjury intellectual–academic status
    2. Age and grade of child at injury
    3. Preinjury behavior

  C. Current status
    1. Description of current educational program and related services
    2. Notable cognitive, physical, personality, or behavioral changes and problems since injury
    3. Parent, teacher, and child perceptions of injury and its effects

V. *Behavioral impressions* (process analysis)

  A. Degree of alertness, orientation, motivation, attention

  B. Performance characteristics
    1. Problem-solving strategies
    2. Test-taking attitude
    3. Error patterns
    4. Self-monitoring behavior
    5. Ability to make conceptual shifts
    6. Attitude toward failure; frustration tolerance
    7. Degree of persistence; motivation; stamina
    8. Dexterity; hand preference
    9. Optimal performance characteristics (e.g., preference for verbal vs. visual input); need for structure or redirection; optimal response mode; task preferences
    10. Adjustment to injury

VI. *Test results*

  A. Intellectual status (contrast with previous test results and/or evidence of best premorbid performance)
    1. Statistically significant changes in cognitive subskills
    2. Relative strengths and weaknesses

(*continues*)

TABLE 16.5. *Continued*

- B. Academic achievement
  1. Standard score comparisons
  2. Compare with preinjury scores
  3. Specific strengths and weaknesses
- C. Communication skills
  1. Language abilities (reading, writing, listening, talking)
  2. Articulation; intelligibility; pragmatics
- D. Motor functions
  1. Hand preference (pre- and postinjury)
  2. Fine and gross motor coordination (adequate or impaired)
- E. Perceptual (visual, auditory, tactile)
- F. Memory processes
  1. Short term and long term
  2. Verbal and nonverbal
  3. Episodic and semantic
  4. Visual and auditory
- G. Functional living skills
- H. Emotional, behavioral, and personality functioning

VII. *Summary and recommendations*

- A. Overall impressions of strengths and weaknesses in relation to
  1. Preinjury status
  2. Current educational placement
  3. Vocational goals
- B. Compensatory strategies
  1. Strategies that optimize performance
  2. Strategies that interfere with performance
  3. Behavioral recommendations for school and home
  4. Recommendations for classroom instruction
- C. Specific treatment recommendations
  1. Retraining versus compensation
  2. Additional testing, referrals
  3. Ancillary services
  4. Projected date for reevaluation

VIII. *Data summary sheet*

Adapted from *Head Injury in Children and Adolescents: A Resource and Review for School and Allied Professionals* (2nd ed., pp. 108–109) by V. Begali, 1992, Brandon, VT: Clinical Psychology Publishing. Adapted with permission.

relevant information, professionals need to understand the complex nature of the student's brain injury and its ramifications. Such variables as the type, extent, and site of brain damage, age at injury, time since injury, preinjury status, and others, have a relative bearing upon a child's prognosis for recovery and are associated with various outcomes and probable sequelae. Efforts to conduct and interpret formal assessment, as well as develop IEPs, select teaching strategies, project long-term goals, and propose curricular foci are facilitated by the added insight into a child's condition that preliminary knowledge of the pertinent neuropsychological variables and their implications can provide. When educational professionals develop a sense of what to expect and why, programming efforts are more likely to take a proactive and calculated course. Moreover, the negative consequences associated with misplacement and counterproductive methodologies can be avoided.

With respect to the evaluative process per se, preliminary knowledge of the variables and their implications spotlights the logic of a multifactored assessment and defines the context within which interpretations should be made. For example, school psychologists can ensure that professional team members recognize that a child who has sustained a severe closed head injury (as opposed to a mild open head injury) will more than likely experience chronic disruption to a broad range of functions because of the diffuse and generalized impairment that typically follows. Professionals should be alerted to the probability of certain complications, including a general deterioration in many areas of function, an increased risk for psychiatric disorders, cognitive dysfunction, attention deficits, significant memory problems, and possible motor residua.

Psychologists can inform those working with students who have sustained TBI that the risk of epilepsy (seizure disorder) is much greater following an open head injury than a closed head injury (Jennett, 1979). Prolonged coma is the exception rather than the rule in open head injuries (Grafman & Salazar, 1987). Recovery following an open head injury is generally more rapid (Alexander, 1984); because the lesions are usually confined, the losses they produce are relatively circumscribed and predictable (Lezak, 1983). For example, focalized lesions to primary sensory areas of the brain are likely to produce rather specific sensory deficits, such as tactile insensitivity or hearing impairment. Hemiparesis and visual field loss are also relatively more common among those who sustain focalized lesions (Grafman & Salazar, 1987).

The pattern of cognitive consequences following TBI is related to the location of brain damage or the site of injury (Chadwick, Rutter, Thompson, & Shaffer, 1981). For example, left hemispheric lesions are generally associated with language and verbal impairments, whereas visual spatial abilities are generally the result of right hemispheric lesions (Rourke, Bakker, Fisk, & Strang, 1983; Rutter, 1981). Educators should be made aware that motor functions are disturbed according to a contralateral scheme; injury to one side of the motor area will affect the corresponding functions on the opposite side of the body (Kaufman et al., 1985). More perceptual errors will be made on the side opposite the damage. Widespread damage to the frontal lobe affects executive functions (i.e., abilities for initiation, planning, carrying out activities, and self-regulation) (Lezak, 1982). Bruising of the temporal lobe results in memory and learning deficits, as well as possible alterations in drive, emotional capacity, and appropriateness (Lehr, 1990; Lilly, Cummings, Benson, & Frankel, 1983; Miller, 1993).

Intellectual and educational status prior to TBI correlates positively with outcome. Bright well-educated individuals who sustain brain injury tend to fare better than others. Well-ingrained skills, as the products of overlearning, are more likely to be spared (Miller, 1984; Rutter, 1981). Brighter and better educated youngsters are more likely to retain "pockets of knowledge" that can help fuel the recovery process. These islands of memory, or *engrams* (Rourke et al., 1983), should not, however, be mistaken as evidence that precursor skills and related functions have been spared. Test performances, though suggestive of recovery, often fail to account for the subtle, yet potentially disruptive deficits that may remain. "Normal" test scores following TBI are neither proof that all has recovered nor indication that progress will continue in a linear fashion. A relationship also exists between premorbid status and postinjury behavioral sequelae. Premorbid personality traits are often exacerbated by brain injury (Lezak, 1983; Rosen & Gerring, 1986). Low IQ prior to injury has also been associated with an increased potential for emotional and behavioral problems (Seidel, Chadwick, & Rutter, 1975).

Brain damage sustained in childhood—that is, before the brain has fully matured—may not show its effects until the damaged area becomes operational (Lehr, 1990; Rourke et al., 1983). Because certain areas of the brain do not become fully active until late adolescence, early damage may not become evident for many years. For example, a young child who sustains physiological damage to the area of the brain destined to assume the function of abstract reasoning, may not show evidence of the impending impairment until adolescence. In children, the effects of brain damage may (a) initially surface and fade, (b) appear and persist, or (c) surface during a more advanced stage of development (Rudel, 1978).

Barth and Macciocchi (1985) established that the most important period of recovery is during the first 2 years of an injury. The accelerated rate at which improvement can occur during the early to middle stages of recovery has major educational implications. In a matter of days or weeks, changes can occur in a child's cognitive and behavioral status that are sufficient to warrant major modifications in his or her educational program (Begali, 1987). Children with TBI have been known to recoup as many as 30 IQ points during their first year of recovery (Chadwick, Rutter, Shaffer, & Shrout, 1981). The early period of accelerated recovery (first 18 months after coma) that follows the resolution of coma offers a unique window of opportunity, during which time remedial efforts will have a decisive effect. Hence, educational professionals cannot afford to expend this precious time casually (Begali, 1992).

SCHOOL PSYCHOLOGIST AS ABI COUNSELOR

School psychologists are in a position to provide posttrauma adjustment counseling for the child and family. Some students need help understanding the injury or devising ways to compensate for their acquired inadequacies. Music, art, literature, and storytelling can be used in counseling sessions as compensatory strategies for offsetting such neuropsychological deficits as poor memory, limited verbal ability, faulty abstract reasoning, distractibility, or impulsivity which would render traditional cognitive methods ineffective (Prigatano, 1991). Significant memory problems may be accommodated by increasing the frequency of sessions, limiting topics to one or two per session, or requiring counselees to summarize their perceptions at strategic intervals (Miller, 1993). The use of video in counseling or therapy with children and adolescents with ABI is recommended because of its concrete, visual, and repeatable proper-

TABLE 16.6. A Format for Individual Counseling or Psychotherapy with Children and Adolescents Following Acquired Brain Injury

Initial Stage (ongoing)

1. Develop therapeutic alliance with child or adolescent counselee.
2. Validate counselee's initial perceptions of the injury (i.e., come to understand his or her point of view).
3. Gradually reconcile discrepancy between perceptions, reality, and expectations with facts about the injury and the consequences the injury produced.
4. Mutually determine a manageable set of realistic goals.
5. Identify obstacles and advantages to achieving goals.

Middle Stage

6. Collaborate with counselee to develop and fortify residual skills and abilities that may be used to meet personal goals and/or circumvent weaknesses.
7. Teach counselee how to go about accomplishing goals (e.g., how to behave in certain circumstances, how to cope with specific neuropsychological deficits, how to seek assistance).
8. Increase capacity for renewed self-awareness using, for example, self-inventories, checklists, video, play, and drawings.
9. Develop therapeutic plan to modify body image and low self-esteem.

Late Stage

10. Continue to clarify reality rather than confront denial.
11. (Optional) Provide partial, tentative insights and interpretation, allowing for elaboration and acceptance.
12. Continue to help client reformulate and break down new or revised goals into manageable steps.
13. Teach generalization of rehabilitated or newly developed skills through modeling, role-play, practice, and guided application within real-life settings.
14. Begin to discuss and implement a gradual termination of services.

ties that help to counteract the cognitive and social problems associated with ABI (see Table 16.6 for a format for individual counseling or psychotherapy).

Parents need assistance coping with the changes the injury has brought to bear upon their child's educational performance. Family counseling efforts should (a) help family members set realistic expectations; (b) provide guidance in behavioral management and parent effectiveness; and (c) direct family members toward an awareness of their needs and responsibilities to one another.

SCHOOL PSYCHOLOGIST AS ABI CASE MANAGER

The complex nature of ABI generally requires an integration of various treatment modalities and the special services of many professionals. Some children require extended outpatient services and medical follow-up. Some require specialized treatments that go beyond what is typically viewed as educationally relevant. Others may require medication. As case managers, psychologists can promote collaboration among multiple service providers within the school and across settings. Outside consultation becomes necessary should evidence of possible regression surface (i.e., headaches, nausea, vomiting, increased distractibility, seizures, or a sudden deterioration in cognitive ability). Likewise, psychiatric consultation and possible psychopharmacologic intervention should be explored if a child exhibits extreme agitation and emotional lability, severe depression, extreme amotivation, psychotic reactions, or the reemergence of premorbid personality disorders or psychiatric problems. As case managers, school psychologists also may elect to participate in the development of postsecondary transition services, which are defined as

> a coordinated set of activities for a student, designed within an outcome-oriented process, that promotes movement from school to post-school activities, including post secondary education, vocational training, integrated employment (including supported employment), continuing and adult education, adult services, independent living, or community participation. (*Federal Register,* 1992, p. 44804)

CONCLUSION

As generalists, school psychologists are capable of integrating the pertinent aspects of psychology, education, neuropsychology, assessment, and counseling to provide a broad range of direct and indirect services to children and adolescents with ABI. School psychologists can facilitate hospital-to-school transition efforts. They can prepare staff for the reintegration of a student with ABI and can offer the supportive services of counseling, assessment, and consultation. As case managers, school psychologists can help to coordinate multidisciplinary services and treatment goals. Specifically, school psychologists can provide the leadership for hospital to school transition efforts; collect, analyze, and interpret cognitive, psychological, neuropsychological, and behavioral information to school personnel in preparation for student reentry; assist staff with eligibility and placement decisions; provide ongoing consultation to staff regarding the development of appropriate treatment and behavioral management plans that reflect state-of-the-art technologies; share responsibility for ongoing assessment and progress monitoring; coordinate inservice activities that promote an understanding of ABI and its educational implications; participate in program development; provide individual, group, or family counseling; and serve as referral agent and case manager.

REFERENCES

Alexander, M. P. (1984). Neurobehavioral consequences of closed head injury. *Neurology and Neurosurgery, 5*(20), 1–8.

Barth, J. T., & Macciocchi, S. N. (1985). The Halstead–Reitan Neuropsychological Test Battery. In C. Newmark (Ed.), *Major psychological assessment techniques* (pp. 381–414). Boston: Allyn & Bacon.

Begali, V. (1987). *Head injury in children and adolescents: A resource and review for school and allied professionals.* Brandon, VT: Clinical Psychology Publishing.

Begali, V. (1992). *Head injury in children and adolescents: A resource and review for school and allied professionals* (2nd ed.). Brandon, VT: Clinical Psychology Publishing.

Bigler, E. D. (1990). *Traumatic brain injury: Mechanisms of damage, assessment, intervention and outcome.* Austin, TX: PRO-ED.

Chadwick, O., Rutter, M., Shaffer, D., & Shrout, P. E. (1981). A prospective study of children with head injuries: IV. Specific cognitive deficits. *Journal of Clinical Neuropsychology, 3,* 101–120.

Chadwick, O., Rutter, M., Thompson, J., & Shaffer, D. (1981). Intellectual performance and reading ability after localized head injury in childhood. *Journal of Child Psychology and Psychiatry, 22,* 117–139.

Federal Register. (1991). Individuals with Disabilities Education Act Amendments. *56*(160), p. 41266.

Federal Register. (1992). Assistance to States for the Education of Children with Disabilities Program and Preschool Grants for Children with Disabilities; Final Rule. *57*(189), p. 44834.

Grafman, J., & Salazar, A. (1987). Methodological considerations relevent to the comparison of recovery from penetrating and closed head injuries. In H. S. Levin, J. Grafman, & H. M. Eisenberg (Eds.), *Neurobehavioral recovery from head injury* (pp. 43–54). New York: Oxford University Press.

Gutkin, T. B., & Curtis, M. J. (1982). School-based consultation: Theory and techniques. In C. Reynolds & E. T. Gutkin (Eds.), *The handbook of school psychology* (pp. 796–828). New York: Wiley.

Jennett, B. (1979). Severity of brain damage: Altered consciousness and other indicators. In G. L. Odom (Ed.), *Central nervous system trauma research status report.* Bethesda, MD: National Institutes of Health, National Institute of Neurological and Communicative Disorders and Stroke.

Kaplan, E. (1988). A process approach to neuropsychological assessment. In T. Boll & B. K. Bryant (Eds.), *Clinical neuropsychology and brain function* (pp. 125–167). Washington, DC: American Psychological Association.

Kaufman, H. H., Levin, H. S., High, W. M., Childs, T. L., Wagner, K. A., & Gildenberg, P. L. (1985). Neurobehavioral outcome after gunshot wounds to the head in adult civilians and children. *Neurosurgery, 16,* 754–758.

Lehr, E. (1990). *Psychological management of traumatic brain injuries in children and adolescents.* Rockville, MD: Aspen.

Levin, H. S., & Goldstein, F. C. (1989). Neurobehavioral aspects of traumatic head injury. In P. Bach-y-Rita (Ed.), *Comprehensive neurologic rehabilitation: Vol. 2. Traumatic brain injury* (pp. 53–72). New York: Demos.

Lezak, M. D. (1982). The problem of assessing executive functions. *International Journal of Psychology, 17,* 281–297.

Lezak, M. D. (1983). *Neuropsychological assessment.* New York: Oxford University Press.

Lezak, M. D. (1987). Making neuropsychological assessment relevant to head injury. In H. S. Levin, J. Grafman, & H. M. Eisenbery (Eds.), *Neurobehavioral recovery from head injury* (pp. 116–128). New York: Oxford Press.

Lilly, R., Cummings, J. L., Benson, D. F., & Frankel, M. (1983). The human Kluver–Bucy syndrome. *Neurology, 33,* 1141–1145.

McFie, J. (1975). *Assessment of organic intellectual impairment.* London: Academic Press.

Miller, E. (1984). *Recovery and management of neuropsychological impairments.* New York: Wiley.

Miller, L. (1993). *Psychotherapy of the brain-injured patient: Reclaiming the shattered self.* New York: Norton.
Prigatano, G. P. (1991). Disordered mind, wounded soul: The emerging role of psychotherapy in rehabilitation after brain injury. *Journal of Head Trauma Rehabilitation, 6*(4), 1–10.
Rosen, C. D., & Gerring, J. P. (1986). *Head trauma: Educational reintegration.* San Diego: College-Hill.
Rourke, B. P., Bakker, D. J., Fisk, J. L., & Strang, J. D. (1983). *Child neuropsychology: An introduction to theory, research, and clinical practice.* New York: Guilford Press.
Rudel, R. G. (1978). Neuroplasticity: Implications for development and education. In J. S. Chall & A. F. Mirsky (Eds.), *Education and the brain, Part II.* Chicago: University of Chicago Press.
Rutter, M. (1981). Psychological sequelae of brain damage in children. *American Journal of Psychiatry, 138,* 1533–1544.
Sattler, J. M. (1988). *Assessment of children* (3rd ed.). San Diego: Author.
Seidel, V. P., Chadwick, O., & Rutter, M. (1975). Psychological disorders in crippled children: A comparative study of children with and without brain damage. *Developmental Medicine and Child Neurology, 17,* 563–573.
Slenkovich, J. E. (1987, February). Extended school: When is it really required? *Schools Advocate,* pp. 65–71.
Sohlberg, M. M., & Mateer, C. A. (1989). *Introduction to cognitive rehabilitation: Theory and practice.* New York: Guilford Press.
Wood, R. L. (1990). *Neurobehavioral sequelae of traumatic brain injury.* New York: Taylor & Frances.

CHAPTER 17

The Role of School Administration

PATRICIA L. JANUS

The field of education has only recently begun to recognize the unique learning needs of students with acquired brain injury (ABI). Although medical and rehabilitation facilities have made notable strides in responding to the medical and physical needs of children with ABI, cognitive and social–emotional needs have been inadequately addressed in the majority of educational systems. Few state or local education administrators are aware that students with ABI exist within their systems. Even fewer have an adequate understanding of the causes and outcomes of brain injury. In a survey of state directors of special education, the primary issue identified in providing service to students with traumatic brain injury was inservice training at all levels, including administrators (Janus & Goldberg, 1991). Similarly, in a study to determine the special education inservice training needs of public school principals in Maryland, instruction of students with head injuries was ranked third of 15 areas for which training was desired (Hayden, 1989).

It is not surprising, then, that administrators may react with anxiety and frustration when first approached about providing and managing programs for students who have sustained brain injuries. They may be reluctant to assume ownership of an issue for which they are poorly informed or even unaware. The potential high cost of needed services may cause even further apprehension. However, if appropriate programs for students with ABI are to be effectively developed, administrative support at both state and local levels is a necessity.

State- and local-level officials play a key role in providing funding for staff training and program development while building-level principals play a critical role in determining the type and quality of education that is available in their individual schools (Begley, 1982; Lindsey & Gobert, 1986; Roth, 1986). All three levels of administration need accurate information to set goals and allocate resources aimed at developing appropriate, coordinated programs for students with ABI.

Administrators need to address several key issues to improve the services currently available to students with ABI. Among these issues, each of which is discussed in the following sections, are:

1. Awareness of ABI
2. Staff training
3. Identification of students with ABI
4. Evaluation and school placement
5. School reentry, which involves transitioning from a medical model to an educational model
6. Integrated programming
7. School environment modifications
8. Family and peer support
9. Funding
10. Prevention

With an adequate understanding of these issues, educators will be better equipped to provide needed services for the student with ABI.

AWARENESS

Promoting awareness of an issue requires acknowledgment of a need and a corresponding allocation of resources to address that need. To that end, support and leadership from legislators, community leaders, and state and local education administrators are essential to increasing recognition of ABI. These individuals must have a thorough understanding of the process and the resources involved in facilitating a student's successful reintegration into school and community life after an injury.

Several strategies can be used to increase awareness of ABI. Information and statistics on brain injury can be obtained from both the national and the state chapters of the National Head Injury Foundation. Local statistics may be available from state agencies, hospitals, and rehabilitation facilities providing services to individuals with ABI. Speakers, printed materials, and videotapes are often available from these same sources. Many individuals with ABI and family members are willing to share their stories with educational personnel and students in the school system. Awareness conferences are also effective ways to reach a large number of individuals. Agenda topics should include general information on causes and outcomes of brain injury, levels of treatment, implications for school planning, prevention, and sharing of personal experiences.

STAFF TRAINING

Most school systems are equipped with a variety of resources to provide special education programs and related services to students with educationally disabling conditions. These systems have developed a variety of placement options based on student needs; hired certified, multidisciplinary professionals to implement programs; and allocated materials, equipment, and other resources as necessary. Administrators should recognize that, with additional staff training, many of these same resources can be effectively used in meeting the needs of the student with ABI.

Professionals in both regular and special education, as well as parents and peers, need to be informed of the special learning needs of students with ABI. Pertinent areas to be addressed in training sessions include brain mechanics; causes and incidence of ABI; levels and goals of treatment (medical, rehabilitation, education); evaluation and assessment; physical, cognitive, and social–emotional outcomes; impact on family members; teaming; intervention models; learning strategies; program review; and prevention.

Administrators play a vital role in locating consultants who have the expertise to conduct the training sessions. As noted by Idol and West (1987), administrative support may be one of the most critical factors for consultation to be successful. Several points should be considered before choosing a consultant. Effective consultation requires an organized structure based on specific objectives and planned follow-up. Administrators need to have a clear picture of the issues before objectives for staff training can be accurately developed. With the issue defined, the search for a consultant who possesses the expertise to meet the training needs can be initiated. A variety of resources can be contacted when locating appropriate presenters, including national and state chapters of the National Head Injury Foundation, state education agencies, hospitals, rehabilitation facilities, and parents. Once identified, the consultant works with the school system to develop a strategy that addresses the identified issue.

There are basically two types of consultation, expert and collegial, both of which may be appropriate and effective at different times. In the expert model, the consultant serves as the expert and the consultee (school system) as the receiver of the knowledge. This model generally describes the services an outside consultant would provide at a workshop to a group of people and is clearly training based. It is often the model first used when a school system does not possess a subject matter expert within its ranks. As school-based personnel gain experience and expertise, avenues for collegial consultation become more readily available. In collegial models, peers join together to share experiences and expertise in problem solving.

Proponents for effective collegial consultation point to the need for true collaboration among multidisciplinary personnel (Brown, Wyne, Blackburn, & Powell, 1979; Curtis & Meyers, 1988; Idol, Paolucci-Whitcomb, & Nevin, 1986). This is especially relevant to those professionals providing services to students with ABI who often present with a wide variety of needs and require services from many disciplines. Educational leaders must develop ways to institute collaborative relationships in the school setting. Collaboration empowers professionals to help one another in solving problems that might otherwise seem insurmountable. Phillips and McCullough (1990) identified several major tenets of collaborative efforts: joint responsibility for problems; joint accountability and recognition for problem resolution; a belief that pooling resources is beneficial in increasing the range of solutions generated and in providing creativity and diversity in problem solving; belief that problem solving merits an expenditure of time, energy, and resources; and a belief that collaboration results in desirable correlates, such as motivation, group cohesion, and increased knowledge. Some states have found it effective to identify and train a multidisciplinary team from each educational region on ABI. These individuals, while maintaining other responsibilities in their systems, are called upon for technical assistance to a local school when a student with ABI is identified.

The development of appropriate programs for students with ABI depends on ongoing staff training and administrative support. Staff development is most influential when conducted over a period of time and often enough to assure gain in knowledge, skills, and confidence (Little, 1986). When staff members are regularly given the opportunity to use new information in addressing the needs of individual students, mastery and generalization of training are more likely to occur.

In addition to providing staff training on an inservice basis, administrative support for preservice training at the university level is needed in establishing accredited courses on ABI. Few colleges or universities currently address the needs and strategies for teaching students with ABI.

IDENTIFICATION

Although school systems are likely to be aware of those students who have experienced serious brain injuries, those who have experienced milder injuries, especially over the summer months, may never be identified to the school. Frequently, parents do not inform the school that an injury has occurred if their child appears to be intact physically. This position is often reinforced by physicians who lead parents to believe that all is well based on medical and physical recovery alone.

When students are not identified, problems may be exacerbated due to misdiagnosis. For example, it is not uncommon, even after a mild head injury, for a child to develop problems with impulsivity and poor judgment. School personnel may erroneously view these manifestations as discipline problems, identify the student as conduct disordered or emotionally disturbed, and program accordingly. With prior information on the nature of the student's brain injury, school systems can be better prepared to respond with appropriate services based on accurate interpretations of presenting problems.

Another area of difficulty in identifying and collecting data on the number of students with acquired brain injuries has been the lack of a universal definition of traumatic brain injury, although definitions existed in the law for other disabilities. With the passage of the Individuals with Disabilities Education Act (PL 101-476) in 1990, which added traumatic brain injury as a disability category (and defined it), accurate figures will become more readily available.

EVALUATION AND PLACEMENT

Although some students with ABI are able to return to regular education immediately after their injury, the majority returning to school require program modifications or some level of special education services (Klonoff, Low, & Clark, 1977; Mahoney et al., 1983). Special education services are federally mandated under PL 101-476, the Individuals with Disabilities Education Act, originally authorized as PL 94-142 in 1975. With the passage of this law, the role of the administrator increased to encompass a variety of activities that assured free, appropriate public education for every student, regardless of disability.

For a student to qualify for special education services, certain criteria must be met, including the establishment of a disability that adversely affects educational progress. This involves administering accurate, comprehensive evaluations to determine the student's strengths and needs. If the student with ABI has received evaluations and/or treatment at a medical facility, this information should be shared with school personnel. School personnel who complete additional testing to determine eligibility for special education and placement must understand the possible effects of a brain injury on student learning. The expertise of a neuropsychologist is helpful in pinpointing the areas of the brain and the learning processes affected by the injury. For those lacking knowledge of ABI, test data may be misinterpreted. Most standardized tests routinely used by school psychologists and other educational personnel evaluate mastery of previous learning and do not measure the student's capacity for acquiring new knowledge. Many students with ABI demonstrate memory for information mastered prior to their injury and therefore profile well on a standard psychoeducational battery. However, when presented with new information in the classroom, problems with processing may negatively affect these students' ability to effectively learn.

On the other hand, students with ABI may be underestimated in their cognitive ability. After a brain injury, some individuals with frontal lobe damage may have difficulty organizing themselves to begin a task, but possess the knowledge or cognitive skills to complete the task. Burke (1990) pointed out that these people are considered unmotivated or uncooperative when, in fact, they have lost the ability to initiate purposeful activity. Efforts must be made in the evaluation and teaching process to sort out what effects inability to initiate may have on the student's ability to demonstrate knowledge.

Once evaluation is completed, a multidisciplinary educational team must determine if the student has a disability that adversely affects his or her ability to benefit from an educational program. Although some variation exists in disability categories from state to state, federal regulations originally listed the following: deaf, deaf–blind, hard of hearing, mentally retarded, multihandicapped, orthopedically impaired, other health impaired, emotionally impaired, learning disabled, speech and language impaired, and visually handicapped. Two more categories, autism and traumatic brain injury (TBI), were added in 1990. Educational committees are just beginning to use the TBI code. Previously, when PL 94-142 was written, the needs of students with ABI were not considered as a separate category, largely due to the low number of survivors at the time. As a result, educational committees identified a disability from the original list for the student to receive special education services. This "labeling" process was further complicated by the fact that students with ABI often demonstrate characteristics of many disability categories. A large number of school systems coded students with ABI who require special education services as other health impaired or learning disabled. Mentally retarded, emotionally disturbed, and orthopedically disabled have also been frequently used.

After evaluation and identification of an educational disability, the team needs to develop goals and objectives to address assessed needs. These, in turn, are used to determine a student's school placement. Placement options in the school system include regular education classes (with or without modifications), part-time special education services, full-time special education classes, residential placements, and home instruction. An important realization is that, for the student with ABI, different settings and interventions may be needed at different levels of recovery. Additionally, educational administrators must be prepared to hold frequent review meetings of the student's progress. Recovery, especially during the first year after injury, may bring rapid changes that require modifications in the existing program.

Along with determining the student's placement, educational committees must determine if any related services are necessary for the student to benefit from his or her special education program. Related services include the following: transportation, speech, audiology, assistive technology, psychological services, physical therapy, occupational therapy, recreation, counseling, school health, social work, and parent counseling and training.

Parents should be aware that their child is eligible for special education services from birth through the age of 21 or until graduation from high school. It is sometimes advisable to defer graduation so that a child may obtain educational services that are still needed and appropriate.

SCHOOL REENTRY

Students who experience serious brain injuries are absent from school for a prolonged period of time. Before returning to school, they often progress through two levels of intervention: medical treatment in an acute care hospital and a rehabilitation program. The return to school is significant for both the student and his or her family. It signals a return to normal, to routine, to something all children do—attend school. However, the student who has experienced a brain injury undoubtedly returns to school with different strengths and needs than before the injury. The school system needs advance preparation to successfully plan for the changes in the student's learning profile.

Reentry to school from a rehabilitation facility must be viewed as a planned process, not a single event that occurs on the day of discharge. It involves transitioning from a medical model to an educational model and establishing communication networks between two settings that operate in different ways. To facilitate smooth reentry, several procedures should be followed. School systems should be contacted upon a student's admission to a medical or rehabilitation facility. If the contact is not established until time of discharge, a gap in service may result as educators scramble to contact former service providers and obtain medical records for review. The most effective avenue to linking the rehabilitation facility and the school system is the establishment of a contact person or service coordinator at each site. Service coordinators are instrumental in fostering a mutual understanding between personnel in both agencies.

Rehabilitation personnel must have an understanding of the school system to which the student is returning. Without this knowledge, they may be unrealistic about what a school can and should provide. By becoming familiar with the environment to which the student is returning, rehabilitation personnel can gradually incorporate more elements into treatment that will facilitate a smoother transition for the student. For example, treatment sessions in a rehabilitation hospital are traditionally individual in nature. As a student nears discharge, therapists can involve the student in small group sessions to prepare for classroom participation. Reinforcement and cuing can be provided less frequently to assess the student's ability to remain on task and self-confidence in problem-solving skills.

Likewise, school personnel should have the opportunity to meet with service providers at the rehabilitation facility to discuss the student's needs and corresponding strategies to address those needs. When feasible, school personnel should arrange to visit the facility to observe the student in treatment. This is not always possible if the facility is geographically distant from the school. In these instances, the use of videotapes, photographs, and diagrams can be helpful in demonstrating techniques and relaying information.

Rehabilitation personnel should be aware that school systems need lead time if they are going to be prepared for the student upon discharge. Processing the paperwork for special education services can often take months. If the school system is contacted while the student is in rehabilitation, it will be in a better position to implement an appropriate program for the student upon return.

Several major differences exist between the medical model used in the rehabilitation facility and the educational model in the school system. Nonetheless, these two systems must work together in sharing their expertise if a smooth transition is to occur. Medical personnel need to be able to share their results in educationally relevant terminology because the focus of the goals in school is educational in nature, not medical. With a return to school, the team leader shifts from a physician to an educator. Intervention is usually delivered in small to large group settings, not individually. Whereas medical goals are generally short term, educational goals are long term in nature. Additionally, whereas therapy in a rehabilitation setting is undertaken as an adjunct to medical treatment and holds a primary position, therapy goals in the school are considered secondary while educational goals hold a primary position. Therapy, if provided, is undertaken to support the educational goals.

INTEGRATION OF SERVICES

Students who have experienced brain injuries may require services from many disciplines, including speech-language therapy, occupational therapy, physical therapy, counseling, and school health. These individuals, while available in school systems, usually possess neither a working knowledge of brain injury nor experience working in a team model. Although the need for cooperative planning is well recognized, true interdisciplinary teaming does not routinely occur in school settings, largely due to size of caseloads and lack of time and planning. Insufficient time and inappropriate caseloads have been cited as critical problems to effective collaboration (Evans, 1980; Idol-Maestas & Ritter, 1985). Many systems operate in a fashion that results in general isolation of professionals, and sometimes misunderstandings of the roles of team members. An administrative framework needs to be established that facilitates cooperative team interaction and the development of integrated programs. Professionals need time to meet on a regular basis to evaluate intervention approaches and promote consistency in delivering services. Parents and the student, where appropriate, should be involved as team members in order for school and home to reinforce each other's efforts.

Some students, upon their return to school, may be receiving additional services from private therapists or outpatient rehabilitation services. A communication network should be established with these providers to exchange information and avoid disjointed intervention.

In the rehabilitation facility, therapy services generally are provided on an individual basis, are delivered daily, and are discipline specific. In the school setting, however, related services are closely linked to the student's instructional goals, necessitating that specialists serve as consultants to classroom personnel. Therapy, where appropriate, should be provided in the classroom so that the teacher can reinforce on a daily basis what the therapist is contributing to the student's program.

This integrated, transdisciplinary approach (vs. pull-out from classroom) is gaining wide popularity for students with disabilities as educational systems are faced with a growing number of pupils whose needs are inadequately met by existing delivery models. Removing a child from class for two periods a week does little to promote growth if not integrated with his or her overall program and reinforced by others in the course of the week. This is especially relevant to students with ABI who have difficulty with generalization. An integrated model facilitates the student's ability to transfer skills to other situations.

SCHOOL ENVIRONMENT

Appropriate, effective programming for students with ABI requires creativity and flexibility in a number of instructional components. One area in which the school principal can exhibit flexibility is in promoting modifications that make the school environment more receptive to the student with ABI.

Students who initially return to school after an injury may not be able to tolerate a full day of programming. Administrators can address this issue by arranging a half-day schedule or approving rest periods for the student throughout the day. For students with orientation difficulties, the location of classrooms and lockers needs to be carefully planned, especially if the student is new to the building. Students may need additional time and assistance to get from one room to the next. The use of maps, checklists, written schedules, and assignment books can assist students with orientation and memory problems. Peers can also be used in providing needed support to successfully maneuver through the school environment.

For students returning to school using a wheelchair, buildings must be assessed for accessibility. Many high schools are built with two or three levels, requiring the use of an elevator for students with significant motor needs. Lavatories and cafeteria lines may need to be adapted for wheelchair use. Ramps and curb cuts may need to be added for entrance and exit to the building. Backup plans for elevator breakdowns and emergency plans for fire drills should be developed with consultation from the fire marshall and provided to all personnel at the school.

FAMILY AND PEER SUPPORT

The lasting effects of brain trauma are not limited to the student alone, but usually have a major impact on the entire family structure. The interactions that normally take place within the family can be drastically altered, resulting in the inability to effectively communicate with one another or those outside of the family. When parents initially learn that their child is permanently disabled, they are vulnerable to many strong emotions. It is not uncommon for them to feel overwhelmed or unprepared to cope with a situation they did not choose. Common questions include Why did this happen to us? and How will our family and marriage survive this? Parents may exhibit a variety of needs, concerns, and emotions, including shock, mourning, denial, blame, guilt, anger, and depression.

It is important that school personnel meet regularly with parents to offer understanding, exchange information, and provide instruction on the special education process, if necessary. Because parents may be anxious and concerned at the time of school reentry and subsequent reviews, they may find it helpful to bring a friend to meetings and to receive written summaries of what was discussed. As with other children with special needs, methods and procedures to involve parents in the educational process must be fostered. Parents must be viewed as team members who can provide valuable information to decision making. They have usually gained a knowledge of brain injury during their child's recovery and understand how it has altered their child's behavior.

Some parents require in-depth counseling to adjust to the physical, cognitive, and emotional changes in their child and corresponding changes in the family. Educators may need to refer parents with intensive counseling needs to professionals and support groups outside of the school setting with experience in brain injury. Counseling needs, however, can often be decreased by giving parents opportunities to share information and training them in educational planning procedures.

Like parents, siblings also experience a variety of emotions. They, too, need support and information in adjusting to a new situation for which they are unprepared. Siblings may sometimes resent the attention and time that their recovering brother or sister may require. Support groups for both parents and siblings may be located by contacting state chapters of the National Head Injury Foundation, local hospitals, or pupil personnel workers in the schools.

When a child returns to school, much of his or her success is measured by the child's ability to reestablish social ties with peers. However, unless peers are given information that explains why there are changes in their friend, isolation and rejection may occur. This is especially true of the student returning to school with no obvious physical disabilities, but who exhibits impulsivity, poor judgment, or other behavioral changes.

FUNDING

For students with severe residual needs resulting from brain injury, the cost of providing appropriate services and equipment can be extremely high and require multiple funding sources. Students may require more speech, occupational, and physical therapy than is available or appropriate in the school system. Often, a student's therapy requirements need to be addressed through a joint effort of school-based and private medical-based resources, reimbursable through third-party billing or Medicaid.

Although most third-party and Medicaid reimbursements are made to private providers, some school systems are receiving funds from these sources for certain related services. A 1988 amendment to the Social Security Act authorizes Medicaid reimbursements for related services in the Individualized Education Programs of students with disabilities who are Medicaid eligible. Additionally, some parents have allowed school systems to bill their insurance companies for related services provided in the educational setting. School systems may use this avenue only when (a) parents voluntarily consent to billing their insurance company for related services, and (b) by doing so, the parents do not incur any financial loss, even short term. Some school systems, therefore, pay for the services and deductible in advance of third-party reimbursement.

Funding programs for students with ABI require creative, cooperative efforts on the part of numerous agencies working together. The many regulations and policies surrounding disability legislation, special education delivery, individual insurance companies, and Medicaid make this a difficult, but necessary challenge in an era of financial burden and shortages of related services personnel.

PREVENTION

The major cause of death and disability among children is traumatic brain injury. While impossible to totally eliminate, the number and severity of brain traumas that occur annually can be greatly decreased through prevention actions.

Current efforts within school systems deal primarily with staff training to remediate or compensate for residual problems after a brain injury. However, the scope of these intervention efforts needs to be enlarged to include the implementation of preventive actions. Administrators are increasingly under pressure to provide services in educational systems that are straining to meet needs with limited resources. Time spent on prevention can have a positive impact on reducing the need for specialized services.

Only recently has research in the area of prevention been recognized as a priority. To adequately plan appropriate prevention, accurate information on risk factors associated with TBI must be obtained. TBI may result from both accidental and nonaccidental causes. Accidental causes of TBI include motor vehicle accidents (which may involve drugs or alcohol), falls, and sports and recreation injuries, such as diving into shallow water. Prevention targeted at reducing accidental causes includes educating both the general public and students about vehicular safety and the effects of drugs and alcohol. Drug and alcohol education courses should be provided to all students. Alcohol use is involved in 50% to 70% of all head injuries in the United States. Not only does alcohol often precipitate the occurrence of the injury, but its presence in the body complicates the early recovery process. A growing number of states have passed mandatory seatbelt, carseat, and motorcycle helmet laws. Additionally, a few localities, such as Howard County and Montgomery County in Maryland, have recently passed legislation mandating the use of bicycle helmets by children.

Nonaccidental causes include brain injuries due to violence or physical abuse. Abuse leading to serious injury and impairment is most common in babies and small children. However, a history of mild head injuries can also cause significant problems. Repeated mild head injuries have cumulative effects, with a greater impairment being associated with more head injuries (Barth et al., 1983; Leinenger, Gramling, Fanell, Kreutzer, & Peck, 1990). Repeated injuries may occur when a parent's method of discipline involves strikes or blows to the face or head. Courses in effective parenting skills can help to reduce abuse and TBI.

Supports available to children outside of the school system have steadily declined in recent years. Schorr (1988) stated that employment training for jobless parents, housing support, infant nutrition programs, and social services that deal with child welfare and child abuse issues have all decreased substantially in the last 8 years. Our nation has witnessed an increase in the number of children living in poverty, single-parent homes, and children who are exposed to family violence and/or experience abuse (National Center for Clinical Infant Programs, 1986). These children are at substantial risk for developing problems related to brain trauma caused by ongoing abuse. Several research studies suggest a correlation between TBI and delinquent behaviors (Lewis, 1985; Robbins, Beck, Pries, Jacobs, & Smith, 1983). Youth involved with the legal system often have histories of child abuse and exhibit problems characteristic of learning disabilities, such as poor impulse control and judgment (Rosen & Gerring, 1986).

Knowing what protective measures can combat these causes needs to be translated into prevention programs. Preventive efforts to reduce the number of brain injuries can be pursued through several avenues: (a) legislative action, such as the passage of mandatory helmet and seatbelt laws; (b) environmental and design studies that examine areas such as traffic flow, intersections, and safety features of playground equipment; and (c) public awareness programs, such as the National Head Injury Foundation's (n.d.) Head Smart Schools for elementary students. Topics covered in Head Smart Schools include pedestrian safety, bicycle safety, use of safety belts and child safety seats, safety on the playground, and violence. Other examples of published educational prevention programs include *Head Injury Prevention Goes to School,* available from the New York State Head Injury Association (n.d.), and *TIPS: Traumatic Injury Prevention Strategies,* available from the Iowa Head Injury Association.

Developing school prevention programs requires that educational systems first identify the outcome(s) they wish to prevent. Other criteria to be established before implementation occurs include choosing the means by which the outcome is to be prevented, determining why the preventive intervention should work, specifying the target audience, and deciding upon a formal evaluation component (Cowen, 1980, 1983). Parent–teacher associations, school assemblies featuring students with ABI, videotapes, and events such as bicycle rodeos can be effectively used in prevention efforts.

ADMINISTRATIVE GUIDELINES

Administrative support and flexibility are critical to achieving appropriate educational programming for students with acquired brain injury. The passage of PL 94-142 in 1975 resulted in a widening of the administrator's responsibilities to ensure an appropriate educational program for all students. Although traumatic brain injury was not specifically considered in the drafting of the original law, its reauthorization, PL 101-476, ensures that the rights and assurances are applicable to those students surviving brain trauma today. As school systems work through the process of educational planning for students with ABI, the following administrative guidelines are helpful to keep in mind:

- Develop a plan of action for getting the information that is needed by your system. Contact state education agencies, universities, hospitals, rehabilitation centers, and state and national head injury foundations for advice and information.
- Provide opportunities and time for staff training.
- Stay current on litigation and initiatives pertaining to special education law, most specifically least restrictive environment, zero reject, related services, and the regular education initiative.
- Monitor and evaluate placement decisions frequently. As students progress through the sequence of recovery, changes may be rapid.

- Characterize the student by learning behaviors and individual needs, not by a definition and curriculum for a specific disability. Emphasize an integrated program model and data-based instruction.
- Facilitate access to needed materials and resources.
- Communicate with parents and peers. Use what is learned from them.
- Initiate and support local prevention efforts to reduce the incidence of ABI.
- Be available as a liaison and provide professional support to staff members.
- Set an example of acceptance and commitment to finding what works.

CONCLUSION

The majority of educational systems are only beginning to address the learning needs of students with acquired brain injury. Because state and local school administrators play a key role in staff training and allocation of resources, their understanding of issues related to ABI is critical. Informed leadership, working in cooperation with parents, is instrumental to increasing appropriate services to students with ABI. The information provided in this chapter should help administrators understand their roles.

REFERENCES

Barth, J. T., Macciocchi, S. N., Giordani, B., Rimel, R., Jane, J. A., & Boll, T. J. (1983). Neuropsychological sequelae of minor head injury. *Neurosurgery, 13,* 529–533.

Begley, D. (1982). *Burnout among special education administrators.* Paper presented at the International Convention of the Council for Exceptional Children, Houston. (ERIC Document Reproduction No. ED 219 902)

Brown, D., Wyne, M. D., Blackburn, J. E., & Powell, W. C. (1979). *Consultation: Strategy for improving education.* Boston: Allyn & Bacon.

Burke, W. (1990). Emotionally charged: Why do head injuries make some people seem out of control? *Headlines, 1*(1), 4.

Cowen, E. (1980). The Primary Mental Health Project: A summary. *Journal of Special Education, 14,* 133–154.

Cowen, E. (1983). Primary prevention in mental health: Past, present and future. In R. Felner, L. Jason, J. Moritsugu, & S. Farber (Eds.), *Preventive psychology* (pp. 11–25). New York: Pergamon Press.

Curtis, M. J., & Meyers, J. (1988). Consultation: A foundation for alternative services in the schools. In J. L. Graden, J. E. Zins, & M. J. Curtis (Eds.), *Alternative educational delivery systems: Enhancing instructional options for all students* (pp. 35–48). Washington, DC: National Association of School Psychologists.

Evans, S. (1980). The consultant role of the resource teacher. *Exceptional Children, 46,* 402–404.

Hayden, H. (1989). A study of Maryland public school principals' perception of their special education inservice training needs. (Doctoral dissertation, University of Maryland, 1989). *Dissertation Abstracts International, 50.*

Idol, L., Paolucci-Whitcomb, P., & Nevin, A. (1986). *Collaborative consultation.* Austin, TX: PRO-ED.

Idol, L., & West, J. F. (1987). Consultation in special education. Part II: Training and practice. *Journal of Learning Disabilities, 20*(8), 474–493.

Idol-Maestas, L., & Ritter, S. (1985). A follow-up study of resource/consulting teachers. *Teacher Education and Special Education, 8*(3), 121–131.

Iowa Head Injury Association. (n.d.). *TIPS: Traumatic injury prevention strategies.* Waterloo, IA: Author.

Janus, P., & Goldberg, A. (1991). [Survey of state directors of special education on traumatic brain injury]. Unpublished raw data.

Klonoff, H., Low, M. D., & Clark, C. (1977). Head injuries in children: A prospective five year follow-up. *Journal of Neurology, Neurosurgery, and Psychiatry, 40,* 1211–1219.

Leinenger, B. E., Gramling, S. E., Fanell, H. D., Kreutzer, J. S., & Peck, E. A. (1990). Neuropsychological deficits in symptomatic minor head injury patients after concussion and mild concussion. *Journal of Neurology, Neurosurgery, and Psychiatry, 53,* 293–296.

Lewis, D. O. (1985). Child delinquents who later commit murder have identifiable traits, study suggests. *Psychiatric News,* pp. 32–34.

Lindsey, B., & Gobert, C. (1986). *PRIDE: Principals, resources, information and direction for excellence in special education.* Paper presented at the 11th Annual Meeting of the National Council of States on Inservice Education, Nashville, TN. (ERIC Document Reproduction Service No. ED 277 123)

Little, J. W. (1986). Seductive images and organizational realities in professional development. In A. Lieberman, *Rethinking school improvement: Research, craft and concept* (pp. 26–44). New York: Teachers College Press.

Mahoney, W. J., D'Souza, B. J., Haller, J. A., Rogers, M. C., Epstein, M. H., & Freeman, J. M. (1983). Long-term outcome of children with severe head trauma and prolonged coma. *Pediatrics, 71,* 756–762.

National Center for Clinical Infant Programs. (1986). *Infants can't wait.* Washington, DC: Author.

National Head Injury Foundation. (n.d.). *Head smart schools.* Washington, DC: Author.

New York State Head Injury Association. (n.d.). *Head injury prevention goes to school.* Albany, NY: Author.

Phillips, V., & McCullough, L. (1990). Consultation-based programming: Instituting the collaborative ethic in schools. *Exceptional Children, 56,* 291–304.

P.L. 101-476. (1990). Individuals with Disabilities Education Act (originally authorized as P.L. 94-142), 20 U.S.C. S1400 *et seq.*

Robbins, D. M., Beck, J. C., Pries, R., Jacobs, D., & Smith, C. (1983). Learning disability and neuropsychological impairment in adjudicated unincarcerated male delinquents. *Journal of the American Academy of Child Psychiatry, 22,* 40–46.

Rosen, C. D., & Gerring, J. P. (1986). *Head trauma: Educational reintegration.* San Diego: College-Hill.

Roth, M. A. (Ed.). (1986). *Beyond special education compliance: Administrative challenges for reaching educational excellence.* Morgantown: West Virginia University. (ERIC Document Reproduction Service No. ED 274 027)

Schorr, L. B. (1988). *Within our reach: Breaking the cycle of disadvantage.* New York: Anchor/Doubleday.

CHAPTER 18

The Family as Collaborator for Effective School Reintegration

ROBERTA DePOMPEI
JEAN L. BLOSSER

Various authors (Berroll & Rosenthal, 1989; Blosser & DePompei, 1989, 1992; Brooks, 1984; Brooks, Campsie, Symington, Beattie, & McKinlay, 1986; DePompei & Blosser, 1991; DePompei & Zarski, 1989; Eames & Wood, 1985; Klonoff & Prigatano, 1987; McKinaly, Brooks, Bond, Martinage, & Marshall, 1987; Savage, 1991; Waaland, 1990; Williams & Kay, 1991; Ylvisaker, 1992; Zarski, DePompei, & Zook, 1989) consider the family an increasingly important factor in the rehabilitation of its member who has sustained a traumatic brain injury (TBI). Family members' participation in rehabilitation activities is important if treatment is to be functional and facilitate a return to the "real world," which for children and adolescents is school. The family should have an essential role in implementing that return.

Relationships formed among rehabilitation professionals, family, and educational personnel during the reintegration process can greatly affect the success of the student's reentry. All involved can interact positively to enhance the process of successful reintegration, or their responses and interactions can contribute to problems within the reintegration process. Therefore, both family members and school personnel may help set the tone and climate for planning the reintegration by participating as equal team members in the collaborative planning process. This should be done in the spirit of cooperation and collaboration rather than in an adversarial manner.

Understanding the family's potential to help and attitudes they may develop is important to the professional who is involved in school reintegration plans. Use of the family's strengths and anticipation of their concerns, needs, and weaknesses are essential in effecting a smooth transition into and maintaining the child within the educational system.

The purpose of this chapter is to aid professionals in understanding the impact of TBI on family and peers; establish expectations for the school return; suggest methods for empowering the family to aid in school reintegration and maintenance planning; provide a format for educating family and peers; recommend teaching techniques that can be used in educational situations with family and peers; explain a method for developing educational plans for family and peers; and outline the benefits of working with family and peers. In this chapter, we emphasize the meaningful involvement that families can have in school reintegration. We make specific recommendations for what families and professionals can do to prepare for their role in the planning and implementation process.

IMPACT OF THE INJURY ON PARENTS, SIBLINGS, AND PEERS

The family with a child or adolescent who has sustained a traumatic brain injury deals with a particular set of circumstances that differ somewhat from those faced by parents of children with other handicaps. In most cases, these children were normally achieving students within the regular classroom; they entered school in traditional ways and were involved in routine school activities.

A TBI is a sudden and unexpected intrusion in the family system. The family is unprepared to deal with the problem and often reacts with feelings of injustice and anger at what has occurred (DePompei, Zarski, & Hall, 1988). All responses should not be considered to be negative, however. Families respond with coping strategies that reflect the family functioning that is familiar to them. Family coping styles can either enhance or deter the child's or adolescent's adaptation to the injury (Maitz, 1991). In the following sections, we describe some of the various responses that parents, siblings, other relatives, and peers may exhibit.

Parents

The parents of a child or adolescent who has sustained a TBI have experienced that moment that all parents dread: hearing that their child has been critically injured. They may have watched as their child emerged from coma; learned to walk, eat, and talk again; and developed new behaviors following the accident. They have had to learn how to deal with an entire new world of hospitals, therapists, neurologists, psychologists, social workers, and nurses. They may have been overwhelmed with feelings of anger, denial, blame, dismay, and guilt (DePompei et al., 1988; Klonoff & Prigatano, 1987; Waaland, 1990; Waaland & Raines, 1991). They have been swept up in hope as their child began to speak again, only to plunge into despair as the words were unclear and thought patterns disorganized.

The realization that the child or adolescent who has sustained a TBI is not the same as prior to the injury is often an emotionally draining experience for parents. They may need months or years to understand that the physical, psychological, cognitive–communicative, and emotional behaviors resulting from the TBI are permanent and the child is significantly altered for life. Many parents have problems accommodating to the concept that their child cannot be like he or she was prior to the injury. They remember their child as he or she was and strive hard to make professionals understand who the child was, and whom they hope the child can be again.

Meanwhile, professional rehabilitation and educational teams know the child or adolescent only as he or she is behaving now, and they strive equally hard to make the parents understand the present test results and behavioral descriptions of impairments that can impact learning. Professionals often get caught up in trying to make the family "accept" the child's changes.

The term *denial* is often used to describe the parents' response to the injury. Denial may be considered a healthy response when parents are initially attempting to cope with the vast changes within their family system. Their behavior should be considered a problem only if they refuse treatments that are necessary for the child or adolescent to improve or if they continue to deny deficits over long periods of time. It is the impasse that some professionals and parents reach over "denial" and "acceptance" that rehabilitation and educational professionals may find difficult to understand in their relationships with parents. Understanding how parents are reacting and allowing time for development of accommodation to the problems is often beneficial.

The parents of a child with TBI are asked to deal with rehabilitation and education of their child, maintain a life for other children, keep working to provide an income for the family, cope with friends and relatives who have little understanding of the injury, and maintain a relationship as a couple. Brooks (1984) and Hock (1984) indicated that stresses on the couple can be severe and that many seek counseling for the problems that emerge in trying to cope with all of the changes in the family structure. The recommendation for counseling should be made with the understanding that it is a support to couples who need assistance and not that it is necessary because they cannot cope.

Siblings

Siblings also find it difficult to deal with their injured brother or sister. They may have lived in a family system in which no special educational or medical problems forced attention on one sibling over the others. When the injury occurred, the siblings may have been cared for by other family members, such as aunts and uncles or grandparents, while the parents' major time commitments were made to the sibling who sustained the TBI. In some families, teenage siblings have been left to care for themselves, as well as younger children, while parents (or a single parent) spent long hours at the hospital or rehabilitation center.

Although the sibling may understand the necessity of the loss of parental attention, he or she often feels a sense of abandonment, guilt over feeling that way, and need for special attention. Davis (1989) reported that, while he was overwhelmed by his brother's physical problems and understood the need for his parents to be at the hospital for long periods of time, he resented the loss of family activities and felt the desire to have his parents' attention. Many family outings and activities were abandoned, and his feelings of guilt about his resentment were of concern to him. Unfortunately, he had nobody with whom to discuss these feelings, so he chose to withdraw and not express his concerns. He felt that he was viewed by other family members as uncaring when exactly the opposite emotions were occurring internally.

Davis's experience may be the norm for many siblings who have been left out of the educational process of learning about a sibling who has sustained a TBI. Siblings often do not participate in conferences about their brother or sister. They learn secondhand, if at all, about the injury, and are unable to experience interactions with their injured sibling until he or she returns home. In this case, the siblings often assume that the returning sibling is "better" and that things will return to normal for the family. Unfortunately, behaviors that are embarrassing to or not understood by siblings often continue when the child or adolescent with TBI returns home.

When the impact of the injury affects the school performance or behavior of the child or adolescent with TBI, the sibling is often placed in a position of explaining and defending the injured brother or sister. Because the sibling may not have a firm understanding of the deficits and how they may appear at school, it is embarrassing and frustrating to be placed in such situations. The sibling also is asked by teachers and parents to deliver messages, such as "Tell your mother that Jim misbehaved on the bus again today" or "Tell Ms. Foster that Judy was too tired to complete her homework."

Siblings often react by withdrawing from the situation physically and emotionally. They may prefer to protect themselves from further pain by being less involved at home and by spending more time away from home. Unfortunately, parents may interpret this withdrawal as lack of love or concern on the part of the sibling. One young woman, who reported that she chose not to bring friends home to avoid the embarrassment of having to explain the behaviors of her 13-year-old brother, was viewed by her parents as uninterested and secretive.

Other Relatives

Immediate family members often gain some information about the injury, rehabilitation, and reintegration process because of the extensive amount of time they spend with the injured child or adolescent. Ideally, they would pass this information along to other relatives. However, due to their close involvement during the hospitalization, hectic schedules, unfamiliarity with TBI problems and treatment processes, and discomfort with the topic, immediate family are often reluctant to discuss the injury and resulting problems with others. This leaves relatives (grandparents, aunts, uncles, etc.) with a need and desire for information.

Peers

Peers are even more excluded than siblings and relatives in education about the TBI of their friend. They must rely on word of mouth, hospital visits, and information from school professionals or other adults to learn about their friend's condition. As a result, many peers are unprepared for the differences that are present when their friend returns to school. Friendships are difficult enough for children and adolescents to maintain in the best of circumstances. When a period of time in a hospital or rehabilitation center intervenes, and when a friend returns to school and demonstrates behavior that is not understood and that is embarrassing, friendships often are discontinued.

Peers, through lack of understanding, often withdraw to protect themselves from feelings of guilt, blame, or embarrassment. They often do not know what to do, so they choose to do nothing. This results in a loss of friends for the student with a TBI and further feelings of isolation and abandonment, which in turn create self-esteem and self-confidence problems. These secondary problems contribute to the existing physical, cognitive, and communicative deficits that the student with TBI may also be experiencing at school. The child's or adolescent's sense of loss of support from his or her friends is great.

When the recommendation is made that the child or adolescent who has sustained a TBI return to school, parents, siblings, relatives, and peers all feel relief. They all have experienced the world of school, which is not new like the hospital and rehabilitation facility may have been. They expect the school to provide what the child or adolescent needs because it always has for them.

EXPECTATIONS OF FAMILIES, PEERS, AND PROFESSIONALS

Professionals working with the family to bring about a student's positive school reentry and continued success in the placement must consider how family and peer units can influence this procedure. Families and professionals together should answer the following questions to provide the best possible reintegration planning for the child or adolescent.

1. *What does the family know about the child's or adolescent's educational needs?* Rehabilitation personnel have usually counseled the parents about the child's or adolescent's physical, emotional, or cognitive–communicative impairments. However, these discussions usually have centered around descriptions of the deficits and not around how the deficit may appear in the classroom. For example, although parents may be aware that their child has attention problems, they may be unaware that this attention problem may interfere with listening to a class lecture or with receiving directions so that homework can be completed. They may know that their child is disinhibited, but may be unaware that the classroom teacher may have difficulty in keeping the child from acting out inappropriately in class.

When asked, the majority of families will state that they assumed that a return to school signaled the return to regular classroom activities (even though, in some cases, special education was recommended). Families relate the return to school with a return to normalcy. They believe that the school will make the necessary adaptations and that "everything will be okay." They often base this belief on the school curriculum and procedures that they experienced themselves.

2. *What does the family know about policies and procedures for admission to special education programs, tutors, or homebound instruction?* Families generally understand school operational policies and procedures based on previous experiences. Because the majority of children with TBI had no prior history of special services, the families have no base of information with which to develop expectations for special education services. The families usually have had no prior involvement with tutors, special education, Individualized Education Programs (IEPs), or administrators. They are unaware of the special testing and planning that must take place prior to school reintegration. They have never considered what schools must provide versus what people think they ought to provide. As a result, and because they pay taxes, the family expects the school to provide services for the child to facilitate recovery.

Families often expect that, after completing the rehabilitation experience with their child, the recommendation for a school return will be efficiently and accurately completed. They gain a great deal of respect for the rehabilitation team that has brought their child to the point that a return to school is possible. They are comfortable with the concept that, whatever the rehabilitation experts have recommended, the school will provide.

3. *What are the expectations of rehabilitation personnel for the school?* Professionals in the hospital or rehabilitation facility often make recommendations for continued rehabilitation services without consulting with educational specialists. It is important to note that, although therapy may be deemed necessary by the rehabilitation team, the school may not be responsible for providing such services unless the relationship to educational need is evident. When the rehabilitation team has recommended that therapy continue and the educational team indicates that it is not possible in the educational setting, the parents feel trapped.

As a result, adversarial relationships between parents and schools can be developed and school reintegration can become a problem. Services can be limited due to financial or personnel constraints of the school district. This is an especially pressing issue in rural school districts where support personnel, such as physical therapists, speech-language pathologists, and occupational therapists, may be not available or are available on a limited basis.

The best way to obtain information about what a school can or must provide is to visit that school and talk with the appropriate personnel. Each state also has information about child and parental rights and due process procedures. Professionals in each rehabilitation facility should have these pamphlets from their own state's department of education, division of special education.

Creative solutions to the problem of the child's or adolescent's needing more special services than the school may be able to provide might include sharing of special staff among school districts; payment for therapy elsewhere, with the school, insurance company, and parents dividing the costs; development of special classrooms for provision of services with cooperative agreements among school districts; and retention of the child or adolescent in the rehabilitation facility for a longer period of time until therapeutic needs are decreased. Professionals can help families avoid false expectations by understanding how recommendations will affect the parents and educating them early about what is possible within the school setting.

4. *What do families and peers expect about the social aspects of school return?* Parents, siblings, and peers expect that the child or adolescent with TBI will return to old friends and activities. Peers who have not been prepared for a differently behaving friend are embarrassed and shocked by uninhibited, immature behaviors. They have no reason to believe that their friend will not be exactly as he or she was prior to the accident. When their expectations are not met, friendships are often abruptly ended.

A child's inability to participate in social activities, such as scouts, sports, shopping trips to the mall, or an art class at the museum, can become discouraging for parents who expected these activities to resume without a problem. They did not anticipate that even social events may have to be carefully arranged and accounted for within the family's busy schedules. What happened spontaneously before injury may now have to be planned. For example, a family with a daughter who has difficulty walking had to consider how to enable their daughter to sit with her friends at basketball games. Her friends always sat in the top row. The parents had to determine whether to leave very early for the game so that they could assist their daughter to the top row before everyone else arrived, or whether to encourage their daughter to ask her friends to sit on lower seats.

The family and school personnel often do not include planning for social experiences when discussing school reintegration. The impact of lost friendships on the child or adolescent and the need to assist in reestablishing contact are also rarely considered within planning sessions. When plans are developed for school return, provision should be made for inclusion of these social aspects wherever possible. For example, when the student's class plans a school trip to a museum, the family, teachers, and peers should be asked for ideas as to how the trip could be successful. Suggestions, such as developing a buddy system or discussing trip behavior and procedures ahead of time, may help the child or adolescent participate more fully. All means of encouraging reestablishment of relationships with peers should be supported.

EMPOWERING THE FAMILY

Professionals can help empower the family to be positive forces in planning and implementing a school reentry. The family should participate with the educational team in decision making about maintaining the child or adolescent within the educational setting. Ways to include the family follow.

1. *Begin networking early:* Obtain parental permission so that communication among the school, family, and hospital or rehabilitation facility can begin early in the rehabilitation process. Schools usually do not receive ample notification that a child or adolescent with TBI will be returning. Ideally, planning should begin as soon as the child or adolescent enters the hospital or during initial stages of rehabilitation so that school personnel can follow progress and make adequate preparations. Rehabilitation personnel also will benefit from integrating school-related materials into the treatment they are providing.

DePompei and Blosser (1987) made the following suggestions for fostering effective networks between school and rehabilitation personnel:

a. Learn about TBI and its implications for education.

b. Know the special services offered by school systems in your area.

c. Make a personal call (with family permission) to the school or rehabilitation center and establish individuals at each facility who will maintain contact for planning purposes.

d. Relate the student's deficit areas to his or her ability to perform successfully on specific curricular tasks.

e. Invite professionals from the rehabilitation center to participate in the school's IEP meeting.

f. Share information about progress in the rehabilitation center with school personnel for school planning.

g. Encourage ongoing communication among rehabilitation facility, school, and family.

2. *Seek family input in the planning process:* Although professionals know the deficit areas that the child or adolescent with TBI exhibits, there is no substitute for

gaining information from the family about their child. DePompei and Zarski (1991) suggested that professionals must understand the dynamics of the family to understand how the child will function once he or she returns home and is reentered in school.

Consideration of family ethnic and cultural background is also essential to understanding the family. Williams and Savage (1991) described a variety of situations that are impacted by ethnic or cultural differences and that will make a difference to the family and the professionals who interact with them. They pointed out that educational planning without considering various cultural backgrounds may be destined to fail, not because of inappropriate educational planning, but because of the professional's lack of accommodation to the ethnic background of the family. For example, a Mexican–American child was reentered into third grade with a strongly structured day, and his parents were expected to maintain the same type of structure at home; however, they were unable to plan their days because of the uncertain nature of their work as part-time cooks. Culturally, highly structured days are of minimal importance in their culture. The parents were perceived by school personnel as unwilling to cooperate with essential programming, and the child was eventually dropped from special education planning because of lack of parental participation and lack of progress on the child's part.

3. *Recognize the expertise of the family:* The best source of information about the child or adolescent is the family (DePompei & Blosser, 1991; Waaland, 1990; Ylvisaker, Szekeres, Henry, Sullivan, & Wheeler, 1987). Family members often provide insights about behaviors, ways to stimulate, and methods of challenging responses that professionals cannot know. They can provide information about the child or adolescent that can be employed as a means to reward desirable behaviors. For example, using a few minutes of a child's favorite music can serve to reward concentration on a math lesson.

A form similar to the one in Figure 18.1 may be helpful in obtaining information from the family about the likes and dislikes of the child or adolescent, as well as how he or she learns within the family setting. This information is valuable in planning intervention and establishing rewards for appropriate behavior.

4. *Educate the family about school procedures:* Families must understand the procedures that need to be followed for their child to receive special services from their school district. Prior to holding an IEP meeting, parents and other significant family members should attend a short informational meeting with rehabilitation and/or school personnel at which procedures for obtaining special services and the rights of the child and parents are outlined. The recommendations of the rehabilitation facility might also be outlined at this educational meeting. This meeting might form the basis for the scheduling of several psychoeducational meetings at which family and professionals work together to plan and implement educational goals.

PSYCHOEDUCATIONAL COUNSELING WITH THE FAMILY

Psychoeducational counseling is a mechanism through which the family can obtain educational information about all aspects of the injury and how it impacts on the

Informational Guide About Client

Client Name ____

Date of Birth ______________________ Age ____________________

Address ____

Parents' Name(s) ____

Parents' Address(es) _______________________________________

Type of Injury ____

Facility ____

School District ____

School ____

Please fill in all of the following information to the best of your ability. This information will help the staff plan appropriate intervention and education for your child.

1. List the names, ages, and relationships of all individuals living in the home with your child.

2. A. Has anything happened recently in your family that we should be aware of, such as marriages, deaths, or divorces?

   B. Is your child aware of these changes in the family and should this topic be avoided at this time?

3. A. What are your child's favorite foods?

   B. What does he or she dislike to eat?

(continues)

Figure 18.1. Questionnaire to derive information from family of child or adolescent with traumatic brain injury. Adapted from *Lifeline*, 1984, Akron, OH: Akron City Hospital, Department of Communicative Disorders.

4. How does your child like to dress (jeans, dressy clothes, hats)?

5. What type of music does your child prefer?

6. List some hobbies or activities your child enjoys.

7. Name some of your child's close friends and indicate the type of activities they share.

8. What are some typical activities that you engage in as a family?

9. A. Did your child have any learning problems prior to this accident?

   B. Was he or she in any special classes or receiving any special services (reading, speech therapy)?

10. A. Have you participated in Individualized Education Planning (IEP) meetings for this child?

    B. What is the name of the individual at the school with whom you had contact about these special problems?

11. A. List examples of the rules you have for your home.

    B. How do you enforce these rules?

(continues)

Figure 18.1. *Continued*

12. A. Was your child's injury drug or alcohol related?

    B. Is there a history of drug or alcohol abuse in your family?

13. Write a few sentences about your child and what he or she was like prior to the injury.

14. Is there any other information you would like us to have about your child or family?

Figure 18.1. *Continued*

individual and the family and friend systems. This type of counseling can provide the family with general information about TBI, as well as specific information about how the individual's problems and deficits will affect school performance, how to cope with particular behaviors, and how to provide assistance when needed. These sessions can also be employed to develop cooperative plans for working with the child or adolescent at school and at home.

Families vary in their need or readiness to be involved in psychoeducational sessions. Some are knowledgeable about the injury and need only additional information about the school's involvement. Others are having trouble coping with the injury and have been unable to absorb information they have been given previously. Still others are unwilling to participate in any educational counseling because they feel it is the professionals' responsibility to do what they are trained to do. They do not want to be involved in providing suggestions or in obtaining information about the injury or school reintegration process.

Families may give indications about their readiness for involvement by their comments and questions. Professionals know that the family is ready for information and sessions with educated team members when the family asks questions such as Will he return to all his accelerated classes? When will she be able to drive again? Will he have the will to get back into the school routine?

Educational and/or rehabilitation team members and family need to establish goals for these psychoeducational sessions because not all meetings are directed toward the same objectives. In fact, the focus may differ depending on the family members' knowledge, ethnicity, needs for information, availability, and willingness to participate. Goals for involving family and friends can be tailored to the unique needs presented. Psychoeducational goals for parents, siblings, and peers might include the following:

1. Fostering communication between the family or peers and the professional.
2. Providing information about the nature of TBI, its consequences, and the school reintegration process. This information should include information about special education programs, special services, and IEP procedures.
3. Developing an understanding of the individual's strengths and weaknesses and working with family and peers to establish realistic school-related goals and expectations.
4. Providing mind-setting experiences for those family members involved so they can view themselves as competent in their roles as case manager and facilitator of planning for their child.
5. Enabling family and friends to discover how the person has changed so that behavior at social activities and school can be anticipated and understood.
6. Encouraging interaction between the individual with TBI and family and peers.
7. Strengthening the professional's sensitivity and responsiveness to the individual's needs and helping the professional to become aware of family's and peers' priorities and concerns.
8. Developing the family's and peers' skills at using intervention techniques and identifying materials, resources, and activities that may be beneficial.
9. Facilitating understanding of the individual's impairments, their impact on learning, and the school rehabilitation process.
10. Assisting in alleviation of fearful or negative feelings and/or reactions to the person with TBI.

Psychoeducational counseling can be conducted in small or large group formats. *Intimate groups* involve only the immediate family or peers of the child or adolescent with TBI. These groups can be as small as two or three individuals. *Extended groups* involve a broader group of people from the individual's extended family (aunts, uncles, grandparents), acquaintances (schoolmates, work associates), or community (job setting, church, school). *Combined groups* involve a combination of the above.

PSYCHOEDUCATIONAL TEACHING TECHNIQUES

The psychoeducational teaching techniques used depend on educator-related factors, such as the professional's understanding of psychoeducational processes, time constraints, commitment, willingness to involve others, and competency. They are also affected by recipient-related factors, such as the person's capability of understanding difficult medical and educational concepts, relationship to the child or adolescent with TBI, willingness to try different strategies, and opportunities to become involved. After determining how much involvement is possible and the information to be relayed, the educator can select from a variety of psychoeducational teaching techniques, including the following:

1. *Lecture format:* The professional discusses specific information that family or peers need to know about TBI, school policies, and anticipated behaviors of the child or adolescent with TBI.
2. *Directed observation:* Family members observe a tape or live demonstration in the rehabilitation facility or classroom. A professional is present to point out behaviors and application of techniques by the teacher or therapist.
3. *Formal and informal technique demonstrations:* The professional demonstrates to family and friends a procedure or technique used to obtain a particular response from the person with TBI.
4. *Guided reading, and video- and audiotape reviews:* Materials that are available commercially or developed by the individual professional can be recommended for viewing or reading. They can also be used as a focal point for discussions with the group.
5. *Informal discussion formats:* The group is asked what they want or need to know, and the discussion centers on the group's stated concerns. This technique is particularly useful when working with teenage peers and siblings; they often can explain exactly what they need to know and are willing to listen because they have chosen the topic.
6. *Role playing:* After a particular response or technique has been explained, family or peers can rehearse the behavior and obtain feedback from the professional.
7. *Active involvement:* Family or peers are made a part of the student's rehabilitation or educational session. They can learn by active participation, or they can make suggestions about how to modify an activity so that it might be better suited to the interests of their loved one.

An Individualized Family–Peer Intervention Plan (IF-PIP), similar to an IEP, is useful for defining how each meeting with family or peers should be implemented. Figure 18.2 is a suggested model for such a plan. The plan should specify

- Family and/or peers to be involved
- Educational format to be employed
- Family characteristics and needs
- Goals

(list continues on p. 503)

Individualized Family–Peer Intervention Plan

School Year ______________

Child's Name ____________________ School District ____________________

Address ____________________ School ____________________

____________________ Grade ______________

Phone Number ____________________

Parent's Name ____________________

Parent's Address ____________________

I. *Family and/or peers to be involved*

II. *Staff to be involved*

III. *Estimated number of sessions*

IV. *Family or peer needs*

V. *Goals per session*

VI. *Topics to be covered*

VII. *Techniques/Resources*

VIII. *Evaluation*

Figure 18.2. Sample Individualized Family–Peer Intervention Plan.

- Topic(s) to be covered
- Techniques and resources to be used
- Method of evaluation of sessions and means to determine need for future sessions

Devising a plan to work with each family or group of peers may be challenging for several reasons. First, each plan must be individualized, much as the IEP is created for the individual child or adolescent. Second, resources such as professionals' time, energy, and financing for such planning and implementation are limited by the many other demands on their schedule and time. Professionals may have to select families and peers on a "needs" and "willingness to participate" basis until they can establish a full psychoeducational program. However, in some cases, only one or two sessions are necessary to establish family and peer information and cooperation. The time expended is well worth the effort.

Some families, however, are unwilling to participate in educational and planning sessions, regardless of the professional's attempts to involve them, and they are disinterested in the procedures for school readmission and continuation in school programming. When attempting to work with these family systems, the professional should keep in mind some of the following information:

1. *Family's rules and roles:* Some families have rules (how a family operates and communicates) and roles (what "job" each member of the family has, such as clown, troublemaker, peacemaker) that influence how they respond to requests for changes in their system to accommodate their member with TBI. Families whose structures are typically disengaged (those in which members do not feel responsibility for each other) have difficulty altering family responsibilities.

2. *Burn out:* Some families have expended so much energy at the hospital and rehabilitation facility that they are exhausted and prefer that the school simply take over the responsibility. They consider the school to be in charge of the education of the child or adolescent and are in need of time-out from the situation.

3. *Internal locus of control versus external locus of control families:* DePompei and Zarski (1991), Maitz (1991), and Rolland (1988) indicated that families can be responsive in two ways to the role of professionals. Some families operate from an internal locus of control and believe that they are in charge of all the decisions that need to be made. These families insist on much input from professionals, but they steadfastly maintain that all decisions are to be made by them as to what is best for family members. Other families operate from an external locus of control; they believe that what happens is essentially destiny or luck. They expect professionals to make all decisions and may feel resentful or abandoned if professionals place too much responsibility for decision making on the family.

4. *Ethnic and cultural differences:* Families come from varied cultural backgrounds. Differences in beliefs and behaviors must be considered when attempting to involve families in the planning procedure. McGoldrick, Pearce, and Geordano (1982) presented various family backgrounds and described how their cultural differences might be understood. This book is very helpful in learning how to relate to individuals from various ethnic and cultural backgrounds.

5. *Misinformed families:* On occasion, families have been supplied with incorrect information about the services that school can or will provide. Reviewing information and providing reading material about services is helpful to these families.

Unfortunately, some families do not choose to be involved, regardless of the attempts of educational teams to include them. Although this decision is regrettable, little can be done to force families to participate. Forcing would most likely result in further resentment and alienation. If all the information has been provided to these families about how they may obtain help and a sincere effort has been made to understand the family's perspective, the professional can do little else except be available if, at some time in the future, the family seeks help.

CONCLUSION

When families are provided the opportunity to be a part of the decision-making team, they often provide valuable information for the educational reentry and program maintenance of the child or adolescent with ABI. Advantages to involving family and peers in the planning and evaluation process include the following:

- *Prior information:* When individuals have information about how students with TBI might behave, they are better prepared to deal with the problems as they occur. Knowledge about why a certain behavior may happen makes the behavior easier to accept and handle.
- *School preparation:* If individuals know the school's procedures and provisions for the student with TBI, they are better prepared to accept what the school offers or make a decision to maintain their requests for more services. Although this communication does not eliminate an adversarial role completely, all parties' positions are clearer from the beginning.
- *Family's information:* When family and friends provide information on which planning and treatment can be based, a more cooperative relationship can be established. Families often have information that professionals do not have about the student with TBI and that is useful in the therapeutic and school environment.
- *Understanding of progress:* If family members are involved in frequent and regular staffings about the child or adolescent, and have helped to establish goals for IEP and monitoring programs, they can be more realistic in determining future needs and directions. They may also be more realistic in understanding failures and needs for reestablishing priorities and goals that are more stringent or are based in additional special programming.

By providing families with individualized information about the school reintegration process and establishing a means of monitoring the readmission beyond the first few months, the educational team helps them adapt to the possible changes within the school environment that may be necessary. When these lines of communication are maintained, the family becomes a powerful positive force in the student's return to school.

REFERENCES

Berroll, S., & Rosenthal, M. (Eds.). (1989). Families of the Brain Injured [special issue]. *Journal of Head Trauma Rehabilitation, 3*(4).

Blosser, J. L., & DePompei, R. (1989, November). *Counseling family and friends of TBI survivors: The path less traveled.* Paper presented at American Speech-Language-Hearing Association National Convention, St. Louis, MO.

Blosser, J. L., & DePompei, R. (1992). A proactive model for treating communication disorders in children and adolescents with traumatic brain injury. *Clinics in Communicative Disorders, 2*(2), 52–65.

Brooks, N. (1984). *Closed head injury: Psychological, social and family consequences.* Oxford, England: Oxford University Press.

Brooks, N., Campsie, L., Symington, C., Beattie, A., & McKinlay, W. (1986). The five year outcome of severe blunt head injury: A relative's view. *Journal of Neurology, Neurosurgery and Psychiatry, 49,* 764–770.

Davis, M. (1989, November). Lecture presented at West Virginia Head Injury Foundation Convention, Charleston, WV.

DePompei, R., & Blosser, J. L. (1987). Strategies for helping head injured children successfully return to school. *Language, Speech and Hearing Services in Schools, 18,* 292–300.

DePompei, R., & Blosser, J. (1991). Families of children with traumatic brain injury as advocates in school reentry. *Neurorehabilitation, 1*(2), 29–37.

DePompei, R., & Zarski, J. J. (1989). Families, head injury, and cognitive–communicative impairments: Issues for family counseling. *Topics in Language Disorders, 9*(2), 78–89.

DePompei, R., & Zarski, J. J. (1991). Assessment of the family. In J. Williams & T. Kay (Eds.), *Head injury: A family matter.* Baltimore: Brookes.

DePompei, R., Zarski, J. J., & Hall, D. E. (1988). Cognitive communicative impairments: A family focused viewpoint. *Journal of Head Trauma Rehabilitation, 3*(2), 13–22.

Eames, P., & Wood, R. (1985). Rehabilitation after severe brain injury: A follow up study of a behaviour modification approach. *Journal of Neurology, Neurosurgery and Psychiatry, 48,* 613–619.

Hock, R. A. (1984). *The rehabilitation of a child with a traumatic brain injury.* Springfield, IL: Thomas.

Klonoff, P., & Prigatano, G. (1987). Reactions of family members and clinical intervention after traumatic brain injury. In M. Ylvisaker & E. M. Gobble (Eds.), *Community reentry for head injured adults.* Austin, TX: PRO-ED.

Lifeline. (1984). Akron, OH: Akron City Hospital, Department of Communicative Disorders.

Maitz, E. (1991). Family systems theory applied to head injury. In J. Williams & T. Kay (Eds.), *Head injury: A family matter.* Baltimore: Brookes.

McGoldrick, M., Pearce, J., & Geordano, P. (1982). *Ethnicity and family therapy.* New York: Guilford Press.

McKinaly, W. W., Brooks, D. N., Bond, M. R., Martinage, D. P., & Marshall, M. M. (1987). The short term outcome of severe blunt head injury as reported by relatives of the injured persons. *Journal of Neurology, Neurosurgery and Psychiatry, 44,* 527–533.

Rolland, J. (1988). Chronic illness and the family life cycle. In B. Carter & M. McGoldrick (Eds.), *The changing family life cycle: A framework for family therapy.* New York: Gardner Press.

Savage, R. (1991, Fall). Pediatric brain injury and Public Law 94-142. *NeuroDevelopments Newsletter of the Pediatric Brain Injury Resource Center, 1*(2), 3.

Waaland, P. K. (1990). Family response to childhood traumatic brain injury. In J. Kreutzer & P. Wehman, *Community reintegration following traumatic brain injury.* Baltimore: Brookes.

Waaland, P., & Raines, S. R. (1991). Families coping with childhood neurological disability: Assessment and treatment. *Neurorehabilitation, 1*(2), 19–28.

Williams, J., & Kay, T. (Eds.). (1991). *Head injury: A family matter.* Baltimore: Brookes.

Williams, J., & Savage, R. (1991). Family, culture, and child development. *Head injury: A family matter.* Baltimore: Brookes.

Ylvisaker, M. (1992, Winter). What families can expect from schools after TBI. *NeuroDevelopments Newsletter of the Pediatric Brain Injury Resource Center, 1*(3), 1.

Ylvisaker, M., Szekeres, S. R., Henry, K., Sullivan, D., & Wheeler, P. (1987). Topics in cognitive rehabilitation therapy. In M. Ylvisaker & E. M. Gobbel (Eds.), *Community re-entry for head injured adults.* Austin, TX: PRO-ED.

Zarski, J. J., DePompei, R., & Zook, A. (1989). Traumatic head injury: Dimensions of family responsivity. *The Journal of Head Trauma Rehabilitation: Families of the Brain Injured, 3*(4), 31–41.

CHAPTER 19

Transition to Postsecondary Education

MARCIA R. NORDLUND

Every student beginning postsecondary education faces adjustments when dealing with the pressures and expectations of life-impacting decision making and newfound independence. Although this transition may be difficult for any student, it can be overwhelming for the student with acquired brain injury (ABI) (Holmes, 1988). This student, the family, and professionals must expend significant time and energy weighing the available options and determining the best placement. To help in that effort, I discuss in this chapter the viability of postsecondary education, ways to determine goals, evaluation of college services, investigation of college options, and timeline considerations.

VIABILITY OF POSTSECONDARY EDUCATION

Many variables must be considered in choosing appropriate postsecondary placement for students with ABI. The process of evaluating the factors that may determine the success of a placement requires careful self-examination by the student, as well as identification of the student's strengths and weaknesses relative to academic or vocational planning, programming, and placement. Only if this examination process is completed with open and sometimes painful honesty can the most appropriate placement be selected.

A critical factor in determining the viability of postsecondary education for a student is assessing the student's current level of functioning. That assessment involves the following important considerations: academic strengths and weaknesses, acceptance of disability, level of independence, and stage of rehabilitation.

Learning Strengths and Academic Weaknesses

Each person has relatively strong and weak processing modalities (Lerner, 1989). Some people learn best by watching, other people learn best by listening, and still others work well with their hands but find academic learning to be difficult. A full assessment of a student's learning strengths and weaknesses is necessary in determining a postsecondary placement (Elrod & Sorgenfrei, 1988). Information can be gathered from various sources. A psychologist or neurologist at the student's rehabilitation facility may have completed a case study, which may contain reports from the speech-language clinician, educational specialist, physical therapist, and occupational therapist. If the student returned to public high school after injury, a full case study may have been completed by the multidisciplinary team and evaluated at a special education staffing to determine placement at the secondary level; these findings are useful in determining a reasonable placement at the postsecondary level. In general, if a student has been receiving services through the special education department at the secondary level, this student will also require special assistance at the postsecondary level. If the student is reentering the postsecondary educational system directly from a rehabilitation institute, the educational recommendations from the rehabilitation case study may offer valuable insights into the student's special needs.

Acceptance of Disability

Another critical factor in determining placement is how well the student has accepted his or her current level of disability (Baron, Hanchett, Jacob, & Scott, 1985). If the student has not yet accepted the full impact of the new state of abilities, postsecondary education may not yet be appropriate. The student who is unable to admit that a problem exists is often unmotivated to accept problem-solving assistance, deficit compensation, or special services. If the brain injury has resulted in cognitive deficits, however, special services may be required for the student to realize success. If the student resists any form of help, certain failure may occur. Other options, such as part-time employment, may be more appropriate until further counseling can lead the student to more complete acceptance of the disability.

Alternatively, allowing the student the "right to fail" can often expedite his or her full acceptance of limitations due to the disability. If a student refuses any form of special services, the student should have the right to attempt classes without interference. After the student realizes that refusal of help has resulted in a failing grade, the student often returns requesting future assistance (see Case Study 19.1).

CASE STUDY 19.1

Student Allowed the "Right to Fail"

Eighteen-year-old TH had been in the top 5% of his high school graduating class and on his way to an Ivy League college when his accident occurred. After 2 years of rehabilitation, he was ready to begin his postsecondary education. He was sure that he could still attend the college that he had planned to attend before his injury, but his parents wanted him to spend a semester at the local community college, which would give him the opportunity to begin college without moving away from home. Although TH was openly hostile about the idea, he agreed to attend a "dummy college" for only one semester to prove to his parents that the curriculum was too easy for him. He refused all special assistance from the Office of Services for

Students with Disabilities. At the end of the semester, TH received very low or failing grades in each class. Through continued counseling, he realized the scope of his injuries and returned to the community college requesting support services.

Level of Independence

The student's current level of physical, cognitive, and emotional independence must be assessed to aid in the determination of placement. Most vocational schools and colleges do not provide physical assistance to students, who are generally responsible for transportation to and from home and all personal hygiene needs. Most programs without support services may be unable to meet the special cognitive needs of a student with ABI, such as impaired memory or psychosocial deficits. Thus, students must be medically stable and physically and emotionally independent before considering postsecondary education.

Stage of Rehabilitation

The student's stage of rehabilitation is another important consideration. Cognitive growth is greatest during the first year of rehabilitation, although significant growth may be seen during the second year as well. Thus, the educational program must be matched to the student's need for cognitive retraining. If specific cognitive intervention is warranted, an outpatient rehabilitation facility may offer a more advantageous program for the student initially so that the student may reap all possible benefits during the first 2 years postinjury (Rosen & Gerring, 1986; Vogenthaler, 1987). If a different form of postsecondary education is selected, an important determining factor may be the availability of a 12-month program for those all-important first 2 years. Colleges or vocational schools may offer programs only during the traditional school term (September through May). Thus, 3 months of critical learning time (June through August) during the first important year of cognitive retraining could be wasted. A 12-month, year-round program is crucial to maximize the student's learning.

DETERMINING GOALS

After a student has attempted to fully understand the viability of postsecondary education, he or she needs to determine both personal and professional goals (Sitlington, Brolin, Clark, & Vacanti, 1985). This step enables the student to determine which type of placement best accommodates the fulfillment of these goals.

Considerations

In determining goals, the student needs to consider his or her attributes, interests, and experiences.

Attributes

It is important that the student analyze those ares in which he or she demonstrates a strength (Brolin & West, 1985). Often, a vocational goal can be based on an ability or a skill in which the student excels. A student who demonstrates an aptitude for working with people might investigate a career that uses this skill. A student who is good at operating machines or working with tools might transfer this skill into a career. Conversely, an analysis of weaknesses can also aid in career choice. A student with memory problems would be foolish to pursue further education in a field that requires short-term memory skills.

Interests

A person's interests are formed through the enjoyment of activities in which he or she engages. If an individual can perform an activity well and enjoys performing this activity, the activity will become an interest. The more an individual practices this activity, the more aptitude the person will demonstrate. Thus, a career can often be based upon an interest that the student has pursued or desires to pursue in greater depth. A student who demonstrates a strong interest in gardening, for instance, might pursue a horticultural vocation. Further education or training would be necessary to turn this interest into a career.

Past experiences

The skills used in past experiences can often be transferred to career skills. By assessing personal work-related experiences, a student may help to identify occupations of interest. Summer jobs or part-time jobs can offer an insight into careers that may be pursued. The student who enjoys babysitting may transfer this skill into working in a child care career. The student who worked summers in an office may transfer those skills into a career.

Altered Goals

The process of professional goal selection should begin as soon as the student with ABI is stabilized cognitively. Hopefully, the student's academic abilities will continue to improve throughout postsecondary education; however, realistic educational and professional goals cannot be selected without a long-term indication of abilities.

Often, students with ABI need to change or alter preinjury goals. In some cases, a professional goal determined before injury can be altered to meet the educational restraints imposed by the injury (see Case Study 19.2). Careful analysis of the student's interests and abilities is necessary to ensure success while promoting job satisfaction.

CASE STUDY 19.2

Postinjury Alteration of Professional Goals

VL was 24 and enrolled in medical school when she sustained a moderate head injury. The sequelae resulting from the injury precluded her return to medical school; however, a careful vocational assessment revealed that training to become a paramedic was within her abilities. VL was able to pursue a profession in the medical field that was within the scope of her posttraumatic abilities.

Determination of Further Education

Many students are not aware of the vast selection of educational placements, including degree programs, vocational programs, and certificate programs, available at the postsecondary level. If a student has several broad career goals, these can be articulated into different educational placements depending on the student's abilities. Through careful and critical analysis of the student's academic strengths and weaknesses, an appropriate educational placement can be achieved.

Degree programs

Students whose abilities warrant the pursuit of a college education have the choice of either a 4-year institution or a 2-year community college. Community colleges offer a wide range of associate degree programs, which can either be used as a stepping stone to a 4-year college or offer career availability at the completion of the program. A requirement for most associate degrees is the successful completion of "general education courses," which include communications, science, math, behavioral sciences, social sciences, and humanities. If academic deficiencies are evident in the student, trouble completing general education courses may make attainment of an associate degree difficult. However, many community colleges offer academic assistance to special needs students that may enable the student to complete the necessary coursework. These services may include notetakers, test readers, untimed tests, scribes, or tutoring.

Vocational programs

Both community colleges and vocational schools offer vocational programs, which often can be completed in less than 2 years. Community colleges usually offer classes that teach job skills for relatively low tuition. Many community colleges also offer assistance to special needs students enrolled in vocational programs. Tuition is generally higher at private vocational schools, and few offer special services to disabled students. However, training in a specialized field may be attainable only through private vocational schools.

Certificate programs

Certificate programs are generally very short, lasting for as short a period as 8 weeks or as long as 2 years. At the completion of the program, the student receives a certificate that enables the pursuit of a career. Certificate programs are often available in such vocational areas as baking, automotive service, architectural drafting technology, or computer information systems.

Undetermined goals

The most streamlined method of entering postsecondary education is to have predetermined goals. This ability to establish entry goals is difficult for many non-disabled students, but even more so for students who have sustained a traumatic brain injury. Most students change their majors at least twice during their postsecondary education. College provides the time and opportunities for a student to explore interests and career options. Students often find that trying courses in several areas of interest can yield a new direction for professional and educational goals. College can also serve as a tool to develop support systems and to better understand one's independence level.

EVALUATING COLLEGE SERVICES

Different colleges throughout the United States offer different assistance options. A school's commitment to the education of students with disabilities will determine the involvement of the faculty and staff and their ability to meet the special needs of students with ABI. A prospective student must carefully investigate the realm of support services available from any college that the student is considering attending. Most college assistance plans can be grouped into three categories: accommodations, services, and programs.

Accommodations

Section 504 of the Rehabilitation Act of 1973 ensures that all colleges that are recipients of federal financial assistance from the Department of Education operate programs or activities readily accessible to individuals with handicaps. This regulation applies to all colleges, universities, and vocational schools that receive federal financial assistance. Colleges that offer *accommodations* offer the minimal services required by law. The law is specific as to which schools must offer these services; however, the regulation is vague as to implementation. The regulation states that students with disabilities must be afforded an equal opportunity to participate in programs, activities, and courses of study in the most integrated setting appropriate. This means that a student cannot be denied access to a class based solely on the student's disability. Additionally, Section 504 states that academic requirements must be modified on a case-by-case basis to afford qualified students with disabilities an equal educational opportunity. The key in this case is the word "qualified." The regulation enumerates that the student must meet the academic and technical standards requisite to admission. Therefore, once the student meets admission standards, accommodations must be made to help the student attain an education. These accommodations can include such things as a ramp for a wheelchair, untimed tests, and provision for tape recording lectures, having readers, or acquiring tape recorded textbooks. The college is given the flexibility of choosing the method of supplying the student with these auxiliary aids.

Services

Whereas accommodations are specified by law, the *services* that a college offers are not. Schools voluntarily decide the amount of involvement and the extent of special services they choose to offer; thus, the type and extent of special services vary greatly from college to college. Special services may include such assistance as tutoring in subject areas, support groups for students with ABI, diagnostic assessment, notetakers, or a special staff member assigned to work specifically with students with ABI. Some colleges charge an extra fee for such services, whereas others absorb the costs incurred.

Programs

A college that offers a special program is demonstrating a firm commitment to enabling special students to achieve as much as possible. Although few colleges offer a program specifically for students with ABI, several college programs have been developed for special needs students. These programs generally are based on the needs of learning disabled college students. The components may include an intensive summer school preceding the freshman year, remedial classes to improve basic skills, and special class sections so that subject matter can be taught at a slower pace. In addition, most schools offering a special program also offer intensive support services that enable a student to achieve success when otherwise impossible.

INVESTIGATING COLLEGE OPTIONS

As a student begins investigating available postsecondary options, a key to success may be the matching of college services to the needs of the student. One of the primary considerations is the emotional maturity level that the student demonstrates. If the student needs time to achieve a level of adult responsibility, perhaps the first option to investigate is the local community college or vocational school. This option would afford the student the opportunity of meeting the educational challenges of postsecondary education without dealing with the additional stress of living away from home. When the student feels more confident and is able to assume more responsibility, other options for further education may become available.

Other important considerations, which are discussed below, include educational support services, school size, school location, housing, availability of therapeutic services, and cost. After a school is selected that meets the necessary criteria, the student should meet with the school's special services office. At that time, the student can more fully investigate whether the available services match the student's needs. The student needs to arrange the appointment and develop questions before the meeting (see Figure 19.1 for list of critical topics); this offers the student a good first step in establishing independence. The parent may be tempted to take over this important step; however, it needs to be established early that postsecondary education is the student's responsibility. Parents can offer their support, but the student should learn independence and responsibility. If the student is unable to begin to take most of the responsibility at this point, further pursuit of postsecondary education may not be warranted at this time.

Educational Support Services

Students with ABI who were enrolled in special education classes in high school may be accustomed to working with educational professionals trained to work with

Topics to Discuss with College Office of Special Services

1. Availability of support
   - *Accommodations*
   - *Services*
   - *Program*
2. Eligibility requirements for support
   - *Individualized Education Program*
   - *Doctor's note*
   - *Psychological exam*
3. Cost of support to student
4. Availability of financial aid
5. Housing options
   - *Accessibility*
   - *Study floors*
   - *Proximity to campus*
6. Application deadlines
   - *Admission*
   - *Housing*
   - *Financial aid*
7. Availability of medical services (if needed)
   - *Occupational therapy*
   - *Physical therapy*
   - *Speech*
   - *Allied health services*
8. Recommended number of credit hours for returning student
9. Number of students on campus
10. Average number of students per class
11. Transportation options
    - *On campus*
    - *To/from campus*

Figure 19.1. Critical topics to consider in choosing an appropriate school.

students with special needs. However, the educational professionals at the college level are professors highly trained in the subject content, not in specialized methodology. Therefore, investigating the school's level of support is vital. On college campuses, this assistance generally comes from the Office of Services for Students with Disabilities or a comparably named department. Incoming students with ABI should carefully research the realm of services provided by this office and the relationship between professionals from this office and professors.

Size of School

If a student has been accustomed to a small high school, a small private college may be best suited to the student. Smaller colleges often offer smaller classes, which result in more personalized attention from instructors. If a wide range of extracurricular activities is a key component, however, a larger school may be preferable.

Location of School

A student needs to decide what issues of location are important. Some students prefer a school that is close to home, whereas others consider close proximity to large cities or specific activities to be a top priority. Regardless, easily accessible transportation should be a concern.

Housing

If the student is planning to live on campus, housing options should be investigated. This is particularly important if the student has any special needs for housing, such as accessibility. Some schools offer dormitory floors with enforced study hours and limited visitation; this may be helpful for the student who has difficulties with distractibility. The availability of counselors may also be of importance.

Availability of Therapeutic Support Services

Many students with ABI must continue with physical therapy, occupational therapy, speech therapy, or other allied health services while attending postsecondary institutions. Some schools offer such services or are able to refer students to agencies that can offer assistance. Some schools have established working relationships with rehabilitation facilities for students who are injured while attending school. In such an instance, the college may be contacted while the student is attending the rehabilitation facility. A member of the college staff may begin contact with the student in rehabilitation and begin the transition to postsecondary education well before the student is released from rehabilitation. The school's continued contact with the rehabilitation specialists ensures a smooth transition.

Cost Factors

The cost of special services and the availability of financial aid may significantly affect the college selection of a student with ABI. Some colleges charge additional fees for the special services that they offer; others increase the tuition charged for special programs. Students need to verify the cost of each necessary service and determine who will be responsible for paying the charge. Some services may be covered under the student's insurance, whereas other costs must be paid by the student.

Many financial assistance options are available for the student who qualifies. Some financial assistance programs are available through the federal or state government, and others are offered directly through the college. Possible financial aid sources include the following:

- Department of Rehabilitation Services, which may be able to offer financial assistance if the student qualifies with this state agency's criteria
- Social Security Disability Insurance, which may be available if the student was fully employed and paying Social Security taxes prior to trauma
- Pell Grants, which are based on financial need and are available to students who are enrolled at least half time
- Perkins Loans, which are low-interest loans based on need and are campus based
- Guaranteed Student Loans, which are also based on need and are available to students who are enrolled at least half time

Students should contact the financial aid office of any college to further investigate available funding.

TIMELINE CONSIDERATIONS

When any student is preparing to attend college, certain timelines must be strictly met. Deadlines are even more important for the student with ABI who may be requesting additional assistance.

Application Deadlines

Some colleges require additional time to process applications of students who are requesting special assistance. Application forms often ask whether the student has a disabling condition and, if so, what it is. Colleges need to determine whether they have adequate staff, equipment, and services to meet the student's needs. Special services that require additional time for the college to locate include taped texts (which usually require at least 8 weeks to process), notetakers, typists, readers, or scribes (students who will write from a dictaphone for a special needs student).

Financial Aid Deadlines

Because many financial aid options are at a premium, early application increases the student's chances for acceptance. If a student is considering requesting financial assistance from the Department of Rehabilitation Services (DORS), the application should be made well in advance. Becoming a DORS client may take several months, so a student should investigate this option early.

Housing

On many campuses, housing is sometimes difficult to obtain. Acquiring housing for a student needing special accommodations could be even more difficult. Students with any type of special needs for housing should apply as early as possible.

Class Registration

When a student with an acquired brain injury is returning to school for the first time, he or she should try to reduce stress as much as possible. Reducing the number of classes in which the student enrolls is an excellent way to alleviate pressure and offer an opportunity for adjustment (Rourke, Bakker, Fisk, & Strang, 1983). Even students who have returned to postsecondary education following ABI may not have the stamina to endure a full class load. They also should enroll in fewer classes during the first term back, giving themselves a better chance to achieve success. During subsequent terms, a student can increase the number of classes if desired. *Some insurance companies, however, require that dependents be full-time students to be covered by their parents' insurance policies.* Other insurance companies allow students with disabilities to take a reduced load and still be covered. Parents need to check with their individual companies before a student registers for classes.

PROCESS EVALUATION

After a student has investigated all available postsecondary options, it is time to determine which program best matches his or her special needs. The college or vocational program should fit into the student's career goals while providing the needed special services. Financial considerations should be appraised.

The first decision the student makes does not have to reflect a permanent commitment. Many students have achieved greater success by starting their postsecondary education close to home at a small school and later transferring to a larger school away from home as their capabilities improve. A student's educational options can be expanded as the student develops a clearer understanding of his or her disabilities and their implications as abilities improve, and as his or her sense of independence strengthens.

CONCLUSION

A well-planned postsecondary education can offer many exciting options to the student with an acquired brain injury. Although this selection process can be one of great turmoil, the end results warrant the effort.

REFERENCES

Baron, J., Hanchett, J., Jacob, W., & Scott, M. (1985). Counseling the head injured patient. In M. Ylvisaker (Ed.), *Head injury rehabilitation: Children and adolescents.* Austin, TX: PRO-ED.

Brolin, D., & West, L. (1985). Services for special needs learners in post-secondary educational programs. *Journal of Vocational Special Needs Education, 7,* 29–34.

Elrod, G., & Sorgenfrei, T. (1988). Toward an appropriate assessment model for adolescents who are mildly handicapped. *Career Development for Exceptional Individuals, 11,* 2.

Holmes, C. (1988). *The head injured college student.* Springfield, IL: Thomas.

Lerner, J. (1989). *Learning disabilities.* Boston: Houghton Mifflin.

Rosen, C., & Gerring, J. (1986). *Head trauma.* San Diego: College-Hill.

Rourke, B., Bakker, D., Fisk, J., & Strang, J. (1983). *Child neuropsychology: An introduction to theory, research, and clinical practice.* New York: Guilford Press.

Sitlington, P., Brolin, D., Clark, G., & Vacanti, J. (1985). Career/vocational assessment in the public school setting: The position of the Division on Career Development. *Career Development for Exceptional Individuals, 8*(1), 3–6.

Vogenthaler, D. (1987). An overview of head injury: Its consequences and rehabilitation. *Brain Injury, 1*(1), 113–127.

CHAPTER 20

Transition to Employment

AL CONDELUCI

In the United States, vocational pursuits are extremely important to both a person's economic stability and the person's self-image and feelings of self-worth. Indeed, for many people, the great measure of success is the status of vocational title and the amount of money earned. In a person's pursuit of this important quest, structured education is playing an increasingly vital role. For many people, employment attained is the implied outcome of the school systems (Wirth, 1983). If one can achieve a good job upon completion of formal education, then the school system has done its job. Indeed, many colleges "market their product" (education) based upon the number of graduates placed in desirable positions.

Nowhere is the concept of transition, the movement from being a student to being a worker and citizen, more important than in school systems that include students with disabilities. The fact that, as a group, people with disabilities remain the largest unemployed or underemployed minority in the United States is testimony to this point (Condeluci, 1991). Consequently, many educational systems have identified or developed disability-specific positions that specialize in transition from student to worker and citizen.

Given the importance of employment in the United States, the role of the educator dealing with vocational or transitional planning for students with disabilities is critical to a viable curriculum. This person must recognize that, along with being an educator, he or she is accountable to integrate participation of families and other human service professionals that understand disabilities. Interestingly enough, however, studies have shown that many educators do not feel that transition to employment is within their purview. Furthermore, those educators that do are not using the variety of players critical to the process. These concerns must be addressed.

In this chapter, I focus in detail on the concept of transitioning. I examine the basic philosophy of education and suggest alternative formats better suited to transitioning; review the importance of role formation and role experiences; inspect the critical notion of community and advance suggestions as to ways and means that the transition expert can weave community into the process; include the vital elements of the planning process; and overview the current system designed to support people with disabilities and make observations as to how these organizations might be helpful to the goals of transitioning.

THE NEED FOR TRANSITIONING

The vocational success of people with severe disabilities exiting special education programs is generally poor (Everson & Moon, 1987). The vocational outcomes for children with acquired brain injuries (ABIs) are particularly vexing (Prigatano, 1989; Kreutzer & Wehman, 1990). These findings make it critical to examine the efficacy of the structured educational process. Undoubtedly, not all elements of the average educational system are faulty; however, there is always room for change, adjustment, and improvement. Better ways need to be found to prepare and transition students with ABI to the world of work.

Over the years, researchers in special education and vocational rehabilitation have attempted to find better ways to prepare their students and clients. Indeed, over the past dozen years, a number of new initiatives, directives, and requests for proposals have been advanced by the Office of Special Education and Rehabilitation Services and the United States Department of Education. These actions have resulted in the funding and growth of research and demonstration projects, all designed to enhance vocational and citizen success for students with disabilities. Nevertheless, the poor outcomes continue. Thus, a deeper examination is needed as to why transitioning has not worked better. It is essential that the important foundations established in school cross over to the adult world of work and community. In fact, if they do not, one wonders why certain individuals should bother to be educated.

PHILOSOPHY OF SPECIAL EDUCATION

In examining why transitioning has not worked better, one needs to understand that service systems build from a basic premise or foundation. These foundations are referred to as *paradigms* (Barker, 1985; Kuhn, 1962) or *mental models* (Argyris, 1982; Gardner, 1984; Senge, 1990). These paradigms have a deep-rooted influence on the direction and action of the service. If transitioning is not working well, perhaps the educational paradigm needs to be changed.

Understanding the Existing Paradigm

Before reviewing prevailing paradigms, some definitions must be advanced. Kuhn (1962) popularized the term paradigm to mean a basic set of beliefs that allow for a coherent picture of the world and of how problems can be solved in that world. Kuhn, a physicist by trade, explored paradigms from a scientific perspective, and his writings refer to hard science examples.

More recently, Barker (1985) described paradigm as "a set of rules and regulations that: 1) defines boundaries; and 2) tells you what to do to be successful within these boundaries" (p. 14). Barker, who addressed the importance of paradigms primarily in a business perspective, suggested that businessmen who can anticipate shifting paradigms can be in a better position to profit from the shift.

In a controversial article, Skrtic (1986) concluded that, for any real progress to occur in special education, a new approach must be developed. In this article, he referred to the need for a paradigm shift from existing special–vocational education approaches to multidisciplinary approaches. Quite simply, what Skrtic advanced is that the rules of the game must change on the most foundational of levels if children with disabilities are to be successfully educated. This mandates that the philosophy behind education must be examined.

Skrtic (1986) defined a paradigm as "a set of explicit or implicit presuppositions or basic beliefs that scientists use to prove with essence their picture of the world and how it works" (p. 7). Although his interest was the nature of paradigms in special education, he believed that special education's disciplinary base is biology (medicine) and psychology. This perspective suggests, then, that the special education paradigm has roots in the basic medical model. Thus, the special education paradigm must be understood in relation to and compared with the medical paradigm.

The general consensus in all of these writings is that paradigms are powerful entities that are self-protective and self-serving. Those who are agents of paradigms must put in detailed time and schooling before their paradigms are accepted. Once a paradigm prevails within a field, however, critics often are quickly dismissed.

The special education paradigm is represented in the following questions and answers:

- *What is problem?* Student doesn't know
- *What is locus of problem?* Student's ability
- *What are actions?* Teacher assesses ability
Students sit and listen in class
Classes are homogeneous
Teacher teaches
- *Who is in charge?* Teacher
- *What is outcome?* Student acquires new information

In this approach, the focus is microscopic with emphasis on the deficits or incapabilities of the student. The key goal is to impart new information to the student, and often the sole judge of content and success of activity is the teacher. If the student does not learn according to some preset standard, his or her inability or lack of motivation is deemed the primary cause.

As Skrtic (1986) suggested, the special education paradigm also is driven from within the roots of the more dominant medical paradigm. A comparison of the medical and special education paradigms is as follows:

	Medical	**Special Education**
Focus	*Deficits*	*Deficits*
Problem	*Person*	*Student*
Actions	*Label* *Congregate* *Treat*	*Label* *Congregate* *Teach*
In charge	*Expert*	*Teacher*
Goal	*To fix*	*To impart new info*

In a review of the educational paradigm, Freire (1989) argued that Western education does not teach critical consciousness because it emphasizes the "banking approach." In his opinion, teacher-driven education stresses primarily the ingestion of information. It is non–critically productive because it promotes the following:

- Teacher teaches, the students are taught.
- Teacher knows everything, students know nothing.
- Teacher chooses, students comply.
- Teacher is the subject of the learning process, the pupils are mere objects. (p. 59)

These paradigms alone are not the cause of the problems experienced with transitioning students with disabilities to the community and world of work. Rather, problems occur when the educational and medical paradigms converge to create in the practitioner a mental model in which the student with a disability is viewed as *the* problem. At this point, the paradigm becomes damaging to the process. Any educator who is frustrated with the difficulties surrounding transitioning must examine and consider the influence of the prevailing paradigm.

Toward a New Paradigm

An important preset to change is that the special education paradigm considers the challenges students present from a *deficit approach*. In essence, students are often seen, placed, recorded, and taught with extreme attention placed on the things they cannot do. Furthermore, given the special education paradigm's propensity for labels and congregation, once these students' deficits are acknowledged, the students are quickly labeled and harnessed into "special classes" with like students. The actions of segregation, in the name of the paradigm, are legion.

Because my focus in this chapter is on the school–work transition, I must consider the prevailing paradigm and the part it plays in the challenge of improving the poor vocational outcomes experienced by students who have acquired brain injuries. Thus, I propose an approach to this challenge by making recommendations based on the interdependent paradigm (Condeluci, 1991). *Interdependence* is a term used to reframe the starting point for human service or education. It denotes a partnership and reciprocity between players—in this case, between the students with disabilities and the people to whom they relate, including the educator or transition expert.

The interdependent paradigm has been drawn and developed from a number of perspectives. Most notably, the basis for the paradigm comes from the independent living movement for people with disabilities (DeJong, 1979). It is also a counteraction to the dominant medical paradigm, in an effort to lessen the emphasis on "sickness" and empower the person with a disability (Condeluci, 1991; Illich, 1976).

One way to present the interdependent paradigm is to display it in the same format used earlier to represent the special education paradigm:

- *What is problem?* Dependence on teachers and relatives
- *What is locus of problem?* The school system, the community, the home
- *What are actions?* Relationships, connections, circles of support, understanding of system and network
- *Who is in charge?* Student
- *What is goal?* Interdependence and interrelationships

If educators hope to enhance transition outcomes, they must not totally rule out the existing special education paradigm. Clearly, however, some areas of that paradigm must change to support the concept of transitioning.

UNDERSTANDING THE IMPORTANCE OF SOCIAL ROLES

As the educator looks anew at the challenges of transition, it becomes critical to recognize the vital dimension of role formation along with the practical vocational skills currently addressed. Vocational rehabilitation research has discovered that often it is not job skill issues that lead to failure on the work site, but relationship and role issues (Gold, 1973; Rusch, 1979; Wehman, 1975). Quite simply, the way persons are perceived, placed, and treated has a powerful effect on how they see themselves and how they adapt and relate when in the world outside of school. Any examination of the importance of roles, however, must begin with an understanding of the concept of social role valorization.

Wolfensberger (1972) introduced the concept of normalization and its effect on role success and failure. He defined normalization as the "Utilization of means which are as culturally normative as possible, in order to establish and/or maintain personal behaviors and characteristics which are as culturally normative as possible" (p. 28). Through the 1970s the concept flourished and was integrated into all types of human services. In an effort to further promote a thorough understanding of his normalization principle, and to lessen perversion of the concept, Wolfensberger refined and retitled it as Normalization as Social Role Valorization (SRV) in 1983.

SRV is defined as a process of bringing value to the social roles that people with disabilities have in the community or workplace by promoting real, age-appropriate experiences and by changing societal perceptions, attitudes, and expectations. To this extent, SRV is both a micro (prepare the person) and a macro (prepare the community) challenge.

Condeluci and Gretz-Lasky (1987) explored the relationship of SRV to community reentry for people with traumatic brain injuries. Table 20.1 lists their proposed

TABLE 20.1. The Expression of the Social Role Valorization Principle

	Dimensions of Action	
Levels of Action	**INTERACTION**	**INTERPRETATION**
Person (micro)	Eliciting, shaping, and maintaining normative skills and habits in persons by means of direct physical and social interactions with them	Presenting, managing, addressing, labeling, and interpreting individual persons in a manner that emphasizes their similarities to rather than differences from others
Primary and intermediate social systems (macro)	Eliciting, shaping, and maintaining normative skills and habits in persons by working indirectly through their primary and intermediate social systems, such as family, classroom, school, work setting, service agency, and neighborhood	Shaping, presenting, and interpreting intermediate social systems surrounding a person or consisting of target persons so that these systems as well as the persons in them are perceived as being as culturally normative as possible
Societal systems (macro)	Eliciting, shaping, and maintaining normative behavior in persons by appropriate shaping of large societal social systems and structures such as entire school systems, laws, and government	Shaping cultural values, attitudes, and stereotypes so as to elicit maximal feasible cultural acceptance of differences

baselines for examining the micro and macro perspectives of SRV. Through the dimensions and levels of actions described in the table, SRV suggests a holistic approach to eliciting and maintaining viable role status for people with disabilities.

SRV Applied to Education

Education, in light of the challenge of transitioning, would do well to analyze its actions and practices via an SRV perspective. At the various levels and dimensions described in Table 20.1, key questions should be engaged:

Person–Integration: *This area deals with direct student activity.*

- Are attempts made to teach and prepare the student with an acquired brain injury in real adult–world settings?
- Is the student treated in a respectful way?

- Regardless of cognitive manifestation, are the materials used age appropriate?
- Is the student included with the regular student body?
- Is the student allowed as much self-direction as possible in sculpting and assessing his own plan?

Person–Interpretation: *This area relates to how the student is presented or imaged to others around her.*

- Are the labels used to target the student with an acquired brain injury known (either directly or indirectly) to other students?
- Do teaching activities call undue attention to the student, so as to imply her deviancy?

Primary Systems–Interaction: *This area moves toward the person's important social systems (family, church, friendships, etc.).*

- Is the family included in transition actions and plans?
- Does the person accompany the family in activities and outings?
- How is the person treated by the family?

Primary Systems–Interpretation: *This area involves the important social systems' perceptions and imaging of the student.*

- How do neighbors and relatives see and treat the person?
- Does the family react differently with the person in novel situations?
- How is the school's program perceived by the family and neighbors?
- Does the student's routines in school and community life match those of same-aged peers?

Societal Systems–Interaction: *This area deals with larger, direct systems' change efforts.*

- Does the school (and its members) actively work toward a community and societal understanding of inclusion?
- Does the school (and its members) actively participate in public actions to promote inclusion of people with disabilities?

Societal Systems–Interpretation: *This area concerns attempts to indirectly influence and impact the image and perception of people with disabilities.*

- To a large extent, this area deals with macroscopic impressions of disability. Clearly, advances such as the Americans with Disabilities Act (PL 101-336) should serve to promote a more inclusionary macroscopic agenda.

Role Formation

Given the importance of social roles and their relevance to the successful transition to work and adulthood, it is prudent to explore role formation. More importantly, the concept of role formation must be considered within the context of SRV and the interdependent paradigm previously reviewed. Key issues important to a person's role formation are discussed in the following sections.

Focus on capacity

All too often, human service systems are quick to label individuals based on their diagnosis. This practice has been found to promote serious negative perspectives regarding the individual with a disability (Condeluci, 1991). Furthermore, the practice of labeling tempts one to focus on deficits; that is, once the person is given a diagnosis, people assume he or she has all the textbook deficits attributed to that diagnosis. For example, once people are labeled "TBI" (traumatic brain injury), they are expected to demonstrate judgment impairment, impulsivity, poor memory, and so on. These expectations can and do lead to some elements of role behavior. In fact, merely the existence of the acronym TBI and its use in the literature perpetuate a preexisting stereotype that people might hold. To this point, Biklen, Knoll, and Taylor (1987) concluded,

> While a disability is but one of many personal qualities—such as stature, hair color, ethnic origin, race, and sex—it is frequently a basis for negative evaluation. People with disabilities find themselves given labels such as mentally retarded, brain injured, deaf, blind, emotionally disturbed, mentally ill, autistic, or learning disabled. Occasionally, these labels become epithets: "What are you, blind?" "It's like the blind leading the blind." "Retard." "What are you, deaf?" For severely disabled people, there is the term "vegetable." While professionals will sometimes make the case for the social utility of classifications and labeling—for example, to decide who needs special school or clinic services or economic subsidies—we cannot help wondering why such services cannot be provided without subjecting people to disability labels. (p. 5)

Furthermore, a deficit labeling orientation can offer a starting point for the cause–effect phenomenon. For example, if a deficit is expected to cause a particular effect, heightened awareness of that effect can cause the teacher to wait for the expected behavior. Even if the behavior is infrequent or rare, the teacher's accelerated expectation makes it seem more prominent, problematic, and regular.

Those involved in transition planning and role formation must start with and stay focused on the capacities, gifts, and contributions of the student with acquired brain injury. It is much easier for people to adopt appropriate roles when the people are involved in areas in which they excel and with which they are comfortable. To this extent, transition planners should work hard to identify and acknowledge capacities. One strategy is to conduct a capacity hunt (Mount & Zwernik, 1988). In this approach, people who surround the person with a disability identify and review all the capacities, gifts, and contributions that the individual has. These features can be as basic as a smile, as detailed as a skill, and as personal as a character trait. Knowledge of these capacities assists the transition support team in their efforts.

Choice of individual

Often a person with a disability label is typecast into a particular role. When this happens, other people often make decisions *for* rather than *with* the person with a disability. Theorists have suggested that this happens when educators tend to emphasize remediation and deficits. Choice may also be compromised by limited communication or perceived lack of maturation. Regardless of reason, this preset judgment has happened countless times, with certain features of the disability being stereotypically matched with a perceived role. For instance, a person with a traumatic brain injury may be encouraged to pursue jobs that require repetitive work to avoid the stress of decision making. Although some people with disabilities have successfully filled stereotypic roles, professionals must listen to the person with a disability define and describe the things he or she would like to do and then work to develop a viable support mechanism to make this happen. Although some people with disability labels may not be able to successfully fill the work roles of their choice, transition planners must be cautious to not fall prey to stereotypes and unconsciously guide people to roles assumed to be best for them.

Realism

All people have certain strengths, character aspects, and skills that make them better suited for certain roles than for others. Individuals also, however, may have desires that are unrealistic. Clearly, choice needs to be flavored with reality. To help students test reality in a constructive and instructive manner, educators must do viable research and observation of critical elements necessary to success in the student's desired work or community roles. It is important to remember that, although certain physical or cognitive requirements might affect a person's success in certain work roles, ancillary work roles may be satisfactory to the individual and better suited to his or her cognitive and physical capacities.

One method to achieve this type of job match is a concentric job search. First, the educator identifies the student's desired target work role. This role is then explored in realistic ways to ascertain the student's potential in the role. All creative technical and job supports should be considered before the targeted work role is ruled out. If that role is ruled out, however, energy moves to the next closest related work role. The same process of exploration is used for that secondary work role. If this role also is not a good fit, the next related work role is examined.

As shown in the example of a concentric job search in Figure 20.1, the individual wants to return to bus driving after a head injury. The person's capacities have changed, however, and he is no longer suited to drive a bus. After examining his potential to work as a dispatcher or office support personnel, he settled on becoming a maintenance worker in the bus station garage. This option was suited to his skills yet satisfying to his desire to remain in the same environment.

Adaptations to reality

Many people with disabilities in the past were directed away from targeted job roles due to lack of technical knowledge on the part of the teacher, guidance counselor, or vocational specialist. The professional sometimes ruled out a possibility, thinking that the student would be unable to do the job. Over the past 10 years, however, countless technological advances have created an entire specialty of rehabilitation

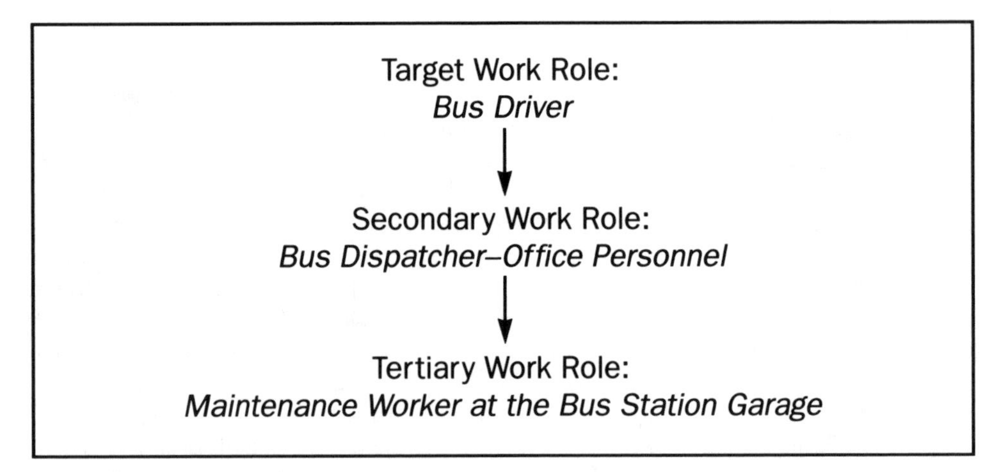

Figure 20.1. Example of concentric job search.

engineering. Engineers have developed machines, devices, and inventions (e.g., standing wheelchair, laser-activated devices, computers, communicators, word finders, calculators) that allow the person with a disability to compete successfully in the job market.

Modeling and observation opportunities

It is important to remember that most people understand and become successful in roles through observation, informal conversation, modeling of successful people in the role, or mentors. Ironically, most people with disabilities, children and adults alike, have fewer opportunities to observe and model activities that lead to role success. In fact, because most children with disabilities are congregated and taught in "special" classes or schools where observation of typical peers in any situation (work, play, formal, informal) is restricted or nonexistent, they have little chance for modeling. Some "integrated" curriculums link students with disabilities with typical peers only for gym and music class. Some people (e.g., Biklen, Knoll, & Taylor, 1987) argue that special education in segregated settings not only limits observations of typical peers, but in fact teaches inappropriate behaviors by heaping all the "special students" together.

To truly understand and be successful in work roles, students *must* have opportunity to observe, relate to, and interact with typical peers in their work roles. Although separate education, sheltered workshops, and congregated experiences may be helpful in some areas, they can never fully develop the labeled student's understanding and identity with targeted work roles. Furthermore, typical peers will never fully understand or appreciate the gifts and talents of labeled peers as long as they remain separated in education and activities. Quite simply, integrated presence leads to better acceptance between disabled and nondisabled peers.

In recent years, much attention has been placed on this concept of inclusion. Writings, workshops, and conferences have focused on the topic. In fact, in Canada, The Centre for Integrated Education and Community has been developed to advance the cause of inclusion in schools and communities (Pearpoint, Forest, & Snow, 1992). Given these trends, educators must make viable opportunities for students to experience possible work roles, and preferably in the actual settings.

Steps to Role Formation

A number of stages can assist in role formation for students with ABI (see Table 20.2). These stages are basic when compared with the typical ways that people forge a role identity. Each stage can be considered in transition activities, examples of which are provided in the right hand column of the table.

Although the role stages presented in Table 20.2 are suggested for transition to employment activities, they can apply to any role formation situation. Because the concept of inclusion is a constellational activity in which roles interrelate and success can be infectious, the educator might do well to explore and discuss a variety of roles that impact on life success. These roles include worker, friend, co-worker, consumer, neighbor, and citizen.

The concept of symbiosis (reviewed by Condeluci, 1990) is built from the premise that vocational failures are not related to lack of job skills, but to difficulties in personal relationships (Gold, 1973; Rusch, 1979; Wehman, 1975). This awareness should guide educators to identify and to help formulate a viable understanding of the key roles listed in the previous paragraph. Each of these roles can and does play a vital part in transitional success in job placement. Each has specific components that can be dissected and analyzed. These components can be studied and then played out in safe settings. A good starting point for educators is to conduct a nominal discussion with students about key aspects of each role. In a nominal process, the teacher might ask, "What makes a person a friend?" or "What is your definition of a friend?" or "Tell me what makes your best friend special?" For each question, the teacher might record all comments on the blackboard or a flipchart. All students should be encouraged to participate. The teacher should then tease out further elements that might have been missed by the students. As students identify specific features, the teacher should expand them to identify common themes. The nominal process can then be repeated for the common themes. As more information is revealed, the teacher should attempt to concretize responses and make sure the students understand the elements of the role.

The next step might be to have the students research or ask their family members what they think makes a good friend, and bring this information back to the class. Then the students can role-play how friends might act in certain situations. Some students can role-play while others observe. During this process, the teacher needs to provide supportive and constructive feedback.

Role formation is a vital element to transition success. The ideas presented above offer a starting point in the development of students' roles. They also provide a didactic dimension to a balanced transition activity that includes both classroom and community (in vivo) elements.

TRANSITION PLANNING MODEL

The key to success in any endeavor is closely related to good planning. This is certainly true for the challenge of transitioning.

Wehman (1975) defined transition as the process of seeking to establish and implement a plan for either employment or additional vocational training of students with disabilities. He suggested that the process must be multidisciplinary and include the work site and adult services system. With a focus on planning, Wehman recom-

TABLE 20.2. Role Transition Stages and Examples of Transition Activities

Stage	***Examples***
1. *General Observation:* The student is introduced to the role. This first stage can revolve around discussion and/or observation of the role.	• Role described by teacher. • Role described by guest speaker who has the role. • Role introduced via film. • Role introduced via readings. • Role observed where role typically occurs.
2. *Formal Observation:* The role is formally reviewed and analyzed. Important elements of the role are dissected for the student to critique or think about. The student is given real opportunity to think and learn about the role and what leads to role success.	• Student does on-site review of role. • Student reviews role details. • Student assigned to interview and research people who have the role. • Student observes the role over a period of time.
3. *Role Play:* The student is given opportunity to simulate the role as best as possible in a safe setting. In the role play, a person who has or understands the role offers gentle, yet instructive critiques.	• Student practices the role. • Role play is videotaped and discussed. • Student observes or requests feedback from the role-play activity.
4. *Volunteer/Placement Role Activity:* The student is presented in vivo opportunity to try out the role. Regular, gentle feedback is given to support the student in the role. If the role is active or real, a mentor might be assigned to accompany the student.	• Student is placed in volunteer role setting. • Student keeps a journal or has regular opportunity to think about and analyze the role. • Student has opportunities to exit from role for purposes of relief or review. • Student gets formal feedback on role via grade or report.
5. *Formal Entry to Role:* The student formally enters the role as a trainee, junior partner, or real member. Student is held accountable by the role standards and evaluation.	• Student is actively hired. • Student starts at part-time or sliding scale of wages.

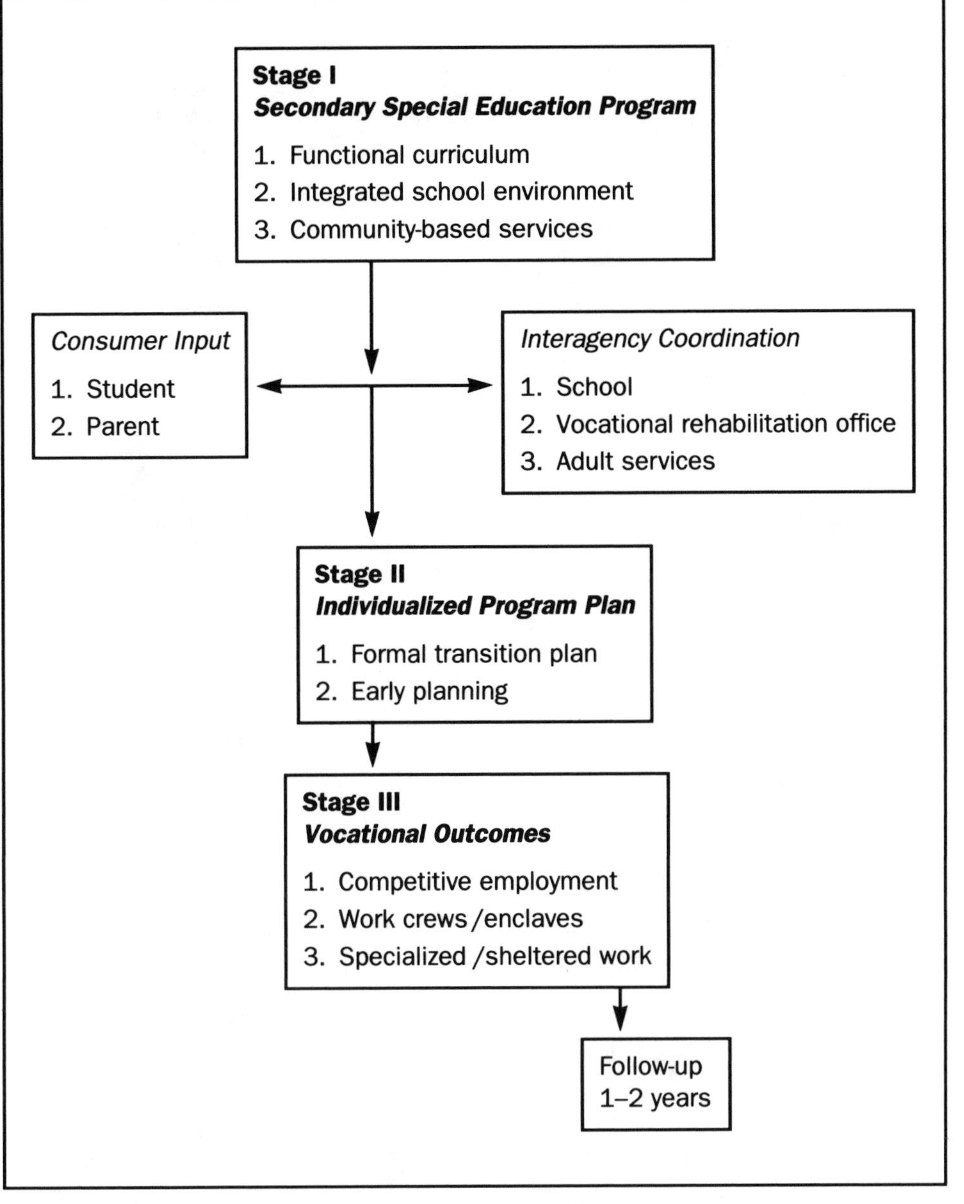

Figure 20.2. Three-stage model for vocational transition.

mended the three-stage model for vocational transition shown in Figure 20.2. This model starts with an emphasis on the secondary school program and curriculum. It also acknowledges the importance of community participation and inclusion activities within the school. With solid contribution from the student and his or her family, along with educational professionals, an individual program plan is developed and implemented. This plan is developed as early as possible and updated and adjusted as changes occur. All of this action, when initiated in concert, should lead the student to competitive employment opportunities.

During this systematic process, key questions must remain in focus:

- What are the student's vocational goals and desires?
- Is the student's educational program actively addressing these goals and desires?
- If not, why?
- What parallel activity program might get the student closer to his or her goals and desires?
- What are the existing adult vocational rehabilitation services in the community?
- Which ones will fit or link to the student's goals or desires?
- Are they accessible to the student?
- What are the entry criteria?

As the transition planner looks at transition, he or she must also factor in community living issues. For most young adults, graduation from high school marks a transition not only to a career or job path but to a new (and often autonomous) lifestyle change as well. To consider only vocational issues without equal attention to *community living* is an oversight. Thus, the following questions need to be considered in the transition plan:

- What are the student's community living goals and desires?
- Is the educational program activity addressing these goals and desires?
- If not, why?
- What parallel community living activity might get the student closer to those goals and desires?
- What are the existing community living services available?
- Which ones fit or link to the student's goals and desires?
- Are they accessible to the student?
- What are the entry criteria?

Additionally, attention must be paid to recreational activities, family issues, and general community concerns. In these areas, the transition expert must allow for relaxation, flexibility, and sensitivity to family activities, as well as the nature and form of the community. These dimensions can be the difference between a successful plan and one that fails to deliver. In the remainder of this chapter, I discuss important community-related issues.

TRANSITION ACTIVITIES AND COMMUNITY FACTORS

Transition, as used in this chapter, is an educational term that implies actions and efforts to effectively shift a student from the world of school to responsibilities of the adult world. This process should start early in the student's academic career and continue until well after the student has moved into adult roles. Adult roles include all those aforementioned symbiotic roles that are important to success in the world: worker, neighbor, co-worker, friend, citizen, and consumer. In traditional vocational rehabilitation terms, these are work roles and independent living roles.

The goal of transition is to offer viable and meaningful independent living and vocational activities and opportunities to students with disabilities (Everson & Moon, 1987; Wehman & Kregel, 1985). In fact, the goal of transition is the overall goal of all of special education—to ensure that the student makes it in the community.

Furthermore, given the intent of transition, the critical nature of community and vocational role formation, and the importance of seeing these roles carried out in vivo, a shift from transitional classroom-based education to community-based activities is in order. Such a shift, however, requires teachers to take a more active role in the community (Everson & Moon, 1987) and, thus, to think anew about community. Most special education preparation does not emphasize elements of community or the ways and means that teachers can incorporate community into their transition plans. Nevertheless, successful transition activity must blend and use community to color, fine-tune, and reality base the plan.

Community is common space, where people come together to solve problems and celebrate. It is the structured and unstructured setting in which give-and-take occurs toward a common good. O'Brien (1986) defined community as common experiences that lead people to mutually supportive relationships that are vital to living well. Community happens when personal relationships synergize with purposeful action and celebration.

Another way to review community is to explore key people factors (O'Connell, 1988). The following are some important tenets for people in community (Condeluci, 1991):

- People are known as individuals.
- People are as they are with opportunity to dream.
- Relationships are reciprocal.
- People are accepted as whole and viewed as part of whole society.
- People seek answers from their own experiences and wisdom of others.
- People can make honest efforts and acknowledge honest mistakes and fears.
- There is room for confusion, mystery, and recognition that some things are beyond human control.

For the transition planner, efforts must be made to discover and understand the ways and means to best use the community. In this effort, some general ideas or actions might be as follows:

- List community resources (i.e., businesses, services, government resources, formal and informal leaders).
- Discover places in the community where people gather.
- Identify places that may serve as role-formation sites.

- Find those people in the community who seem to be the most receptive to students with disabilities.
- Incorporate families in the ideas and plans of mapping and discovery.
- Link with community groups that have broad-based agendas (i.e., ecology groups, sports clubs, community festivals).
- Include key groups or institutions (e.g., churches, civic groups, boys and girls clubs, 4-H clubs, service groups, librarians).

In making all of these connections, the transition planner needs to initiate a linkage from a position of merely wanting to contribute. Remember, these groups have traditionally seen their place as "giving to" the disabled. This charity image is one that is difficult to break through, but the transition specialist must continue to emphasize the spirit of reconnection.

The following are some ways to advance a more interdependent approach:

- Individualize in the connection.
- Make sure that groups of students with disabilities are kept to a minimum.
- Avoid "formal" presentations about disability or your students. Try to make meetings with people informal.
- Have some students accompany you to meetings.
- Try to avoid old stereotypes. When community people tell you that you are wonderful or "special" for working with "them," find opportunity to reframe your role and the contributions that people with disabilities can and do make.
- Be clear that you are looking for ways and means for your students to observe, experience, and contribute to their community.
- Your goal should be to get students on committees, to observe situations, to find community mentors, and to enhance the overall participation in community activities and events.

Promoting community-based curriculum requires that the transition expert, administration, and school district adopt a creative and flexible approach to transitioning. Many community options and experiences happen at times other than the traditional classroom hours. Festivals and meetings are usually scheduled to accommodate working people; thus, most of these activities occur during weeknights and weekends. To enable transitioning supports during these time frames, the transition expert needs a flexible work schedule. If he or she is given the time and space to work in supported community activity, real transition experiences can happen.

Understanding Formal Services for People with Disabilities

An important part of the transition efforts is to connect or link the student with a variety of formal organizations that might play roles in promoting vocational or independent living success. Thus, the transition planner needs to know the agencies, services, and organizations that are specific to disability issues. Generally, most services for people with disabilities have emerged from the medical–expert focus of considering the person with a disability as having problems that need to be fixed. In this effort to fix, the system has developed articulate methods to measure deficits and has fine-tuned skills and specialties designed to eradicate or downplay the deficit.

For the most part, organizations fall into two major categories: topical organizations and diagnostic organizations. *Topical organizations* specialize in areas such as housing, counseling, family issues, recreation, transportation, skills training, and employment. A topical organization has emerged as the expert in understanding its topic and is recognized in the community for applying its specialty to people with disabilities. *Diagnostic organizations* specialize in some particular disability type, such as cerebral palsy, head injury, mental retardation, autism, homelessness, and epilepsy. Educators will find it helpful to know that some organizations are only topical serving all or most disability types, some are topical serving only one type of disability, some are diagnostic with a focus on a variety of topics, and others are diagnostic with only one specialty topic.

Additionally, organizations can be either private or public. *Private organizations* are nongovernmental and can be either nonprofit or for profit. *Public agencies* are mostly nonprofit and are related to either federal, state, or local government entities. Private, nonprofit organizations can be topical, diagnostic, or both and are usually governed with a board of directors. All nonprofit organizations have achieved charitable status from the Internal Revenue Service and are tax exempt. For profit organizations are usually topical, with a particular diagnostic specialization. They can be proprietary or stock owned, and their major goal is to achieve an annual profit margin.

Private profit and nonprofit organizations that relate to traumatic head injury are often part of a rehabilitation continuum that addresses services from prevention through trauma, acute and rehabilitation care through community reentry, and vocational and independent living services. Condeluci (1988) reviewed this continuum of services as follows:

1. *Trauma:* Trauma intervention often happens at the scene of the accident. In these cases, paramedics are equipped to offer life-saving supports and procedures, such as shunting that can reduce swelling and pressure to the injured brain. Quick transport, either via helicopter or ambulance, to strategically located trauma centers has resulted in the survival of thousands of people who would have died only 10 years ago. As the name implies, the trauma center devotes its entire attention to saving the person's life and lessening the long-term damage.
2. *Acute care:* Once the individual has survived the accident and is somewhat stabilized, he or she is transferred to an acute care facility. Often, these facilities are basic medical hospitals capable of offering or contracting some continued specialty service needs. Although the injured individual is still in serious condition, often in a coma or on a life-support respirator, he or she is usually out of critical condition and will probably survive.
3. *Rehabilitation care:* As the individual moves out of the critical and intensive medical care area, the next step is usually inpatient reha-

bilitation care. These rehabilitation hospitals or centers specialize in disability (usually physical) and have a mission to restore the individual as close to preinjury functioning as possible. Most rehabilitation centers have developed specific head injury programs.

4. *Transitional programs:* As the injured individual makes continued gains in the rehabilitation hospital or center, the discharge process begins. In many cases, however, the individual does not need the intensity of continued inpatient rehabilitation but also is not ready for home. This is particularly true for individuals who have sustained very severe injuries. As the need for intermediate care has grown, transitional rehabilitation programs have emerged. These programs, which can be either residential or nonresidential, continue to focus on the person's basic life skills, interpersonal relationships, and vocational areas. Like all other areas of rehabilitation, these transitional programs are goal oriented.

5. *Return to the community:* The final stage, indeed the ultimate goal of the rehabilitation process, is the individual's return to the community. In most cases, this means returning home. Initially, home appears to be the best setting. The family is happy to have the family member returned. In many cases, however, this return proves to be a real challenge to the family, especially after the honeymoon period. In these cases, as well as for the individuals who clearly cannot return home, there are very few options. Up to a few years ago, the only available long-term option was nursing homes. Today, other types of long-term options are becoming available.

Through legislation or governmental order, public organizations are mandated and authorized to provide services, support, funding, and technical or educational services. Some of the relevant legislation and public services and organizations for people with acquired head injuries are listed below.

Social Security Income Programs: Presently Social Security Income or Social Security Disability Income are programs that provide a baseline allotment to eligible recipients.

Title XX Programs: These programs are federally authorized social services that are structured through state government and carried out at the local level. They can include counseling, family supports, attendant care, and other services.

Title XIX Programs: These are federally authorized health care and pharmaceutical services that are state and/or locally administrated.

Education Programs: Under Public Law 101-476, the Individuals with Disabilities Education Act, every state must provide for the least restrictive, most individualized educational program possible for children who have disabilities.

Development Disabilities Assistance Act: This federal legislation has created and mandated Developmental Disabilities Planning Councils in each state. These councils, although outside of government, work closely with their state government to provide direct services or issue grants for innovative services to people with developmental disabilities. The federal act makes eligible any person 21 or under (some states have age 22 as the cutoff) who have difficulty in one of seven identified life skill areas.

Vocational Rehabilitation Act: This federal legislation mandates and creates a vocational rehabilitation program to be carried out by each state. Any person with a disability is eligible to receive vocational assessment, training, and placement services toward the goal of gainful employment. In 1978, this law was amended to include independent living services within the existing range of vocational services.

Protection and Advocacy Services: The Developmental Disabilities Assistance Act authorized each state to develop a protection and advocacy organization to ensure that eligible people have protection and due process under the law. This protection and advocacy service can provide citizen and protective advocacy, as well as legal services or representation, to eligible individuals.

Americans with Disabilities Act: In July 1990, President George Bush signed this civil rights bill, which is also a protection and advocacy bill that ensures accessibility, participation, and opportunities to all people with disabilities.

Urban Mass Transit Services: The Urban Mass Transit Services Act, passed in the mid 1970s, initiated provisions for urban transit to be both accessible and affordable. This act, with reinforcement from Section 504 of the Vocational Rehabilitation Act, led way to the development of accessible rapid transit (in some cities), accessible door-to-door paid transit (in other cities), and various types of fare subsidy programs. These actions have been culminated by the Americans with Disabilities Act, which mandates full accessible public transit within certain target dates.

Housing Assistance: Housing and Urban Development acts during the 1970s and early 1980s created a variety of housing initiations that have resulted in accessible public housing (often developed in conjunction with elderly high-rises); rental subsidy programs, such as Section 8 which keeps eligible persons' rents at no more than 30% of their income; and architectural improvement programs designed to provide loans or grants to allow for accessibility.

State Services: Many states have moved independently to legislate and mandate needed services. Although states vary, major industrial states have developed the following services that might apply to students with acquired brain injuries transitioning to the community:

- Mental health services
- Mental retardation programs
- Aging adult services
- State attendant care programs
- Food stamp programs

- Domicilliary/foster home programs
- State head injury programs
- State health programs
- State educational subsidies

Local Services: Every county, city, municipality, and township in the country has the authority to create programs funded with local tax-base revenues. In these cases, either direct programs or discretionary services can be or may have been developed.

Vocational Services: As previously mentioned, the Vocational Rehabilitation Act has mandated that a number of services be developed by each state. These services might be provided by public or private organizations. Furthermore, because vocational rehabilitation is of interest to many organizations, the funding and eligibility vary. Given the importance of work and the focus on transition planning, it is important for the educator to have some introduction to the typical vocational services available in most major communities:

- *Therapeutic activities:* For individuals with severe situations, therapeutic activities have been developed to focus on basic relationship and life skills. These centers are congregate in nature and often have some prevocational elements.
- *Work activities:* These centers are very similar to those offering only therapeutic activities, except they emphasize work activities and offer therapeutic activities as a secondary venture.
- *Sheltered workshops:* These settings are group-work oriented and usually function on contracts to carry out the provision of some product. Workers are paid for time in production on a sliding scale according to performance.
- *Supported employment:* This approach is designed as integrated, gainful work supported through a job coach or aide. The worker receives full pay, but the coach or aide is subsidized or funded through a public or private program. Usually, the job support is expected to last indefinitely.
- *Transitional employment:* In these programs, individuals with disabilities are placed in gainful jobs, often with initial supports. The plan, however, is to progressively fade supports until the individual is autonomously performing the job.
- *Gainful employment:* At this level, the individual is placed in a position with full job autonomy. Pay is at gainful levels and the individual is on his or her own.

This listing is only a broad overview. The transition expert needs to be a detective of sorts to find the many possible public and private services that might apply to his or her students. Most communities have listings of public services and, when all else fails, the local telephone directory may help. In large cities, the phone directory Blue Pages display all government and human services in the area.

Another way to identify formal disability services is to network with a professional from the rehabilitation community and seek his or her counsel. This contact will provide a starting point to uncovering many key services in an area. The transition expert might do well to keep a good card catalog of discoveries. Recorded information might include that shown in Figure 20.3.

Using Generic Community Services

Although the transition expert needs to have a working knowledge of the formal service system for people with disabilities, to consider only these options in a transition plan may be a serious mistake. Formal services for people with disabilities may have a place for some students with acquired brain injuries, but not for all. It is imperative that the transition planner understand that formal services should be dispatched only when linkages to the regular, "generic" world simply do not work. This point cannot be made strongly enough. The goal of transitioning is to shift the student with a disability to the world of regular work—not sheltered work or specialized work, but regular work. If this transition can be done right from school, the better. I do not mean to imply that the formal system is not helpful for people with disabilities. Rather, I suggest that, if the formal system can be bypassed, then the goal of regular employment can be achieved more quickly.

Name of Service ________________ Date of Contact ________________

Authorization ____

Types of Services Offered ________________________________

____

Eligible Constituents ____________________________________

____

Application Procedure ___________________________________

____

Key Contact Person _____________________________________

____

Other Information ______________________________________

____

Figure 20.3. Community contact log.

The transition expert should be cautious before referring a student with a disability to the formal service system for a number of reasons:

- Once a student is moved into a specialized, congregated service system (and most formal human service systems are), the person becomes more associated with the specialty of that service. For example, if a student is referred to a skill-building program run by the United Cerebral Palsy Association, the student becomes further identified as a person with "cerebral palsy." When this congregated approach is necessary, a conditioned effect is created; that is, the person starts to see himself or herself through the deficit or disability focus lens, as does the rest of the world. A vicious cycle is created. In fact, in exploration of the notion of prework skills, or sheltered employment, often associated with the formal specialty service agencies, Bellamy (1988) suggested that "pre" means "never."
- The congregated approach promotes a role formation that offers limited exposure. In other words, if students with disabilities are transitioned to spend the majority of their time with other people with similar situations, the net effect is limited diversity and role option exploration. Quite simply, the transitioned student simply does not have opportunity for exposure to varied people and roles.
- The congregated approach keeps the transitioned student in the charity–devaluation cycle. Most formal services for people with disabilities have grown from a charity model. The services are often austere, based on eligibility, and have long waiting lists. Many operate on tight budgets and resort to charitable gifts to keep them in operation. In fact, a number of major human service agencies have canister programs (canisters available at check-out areas of stores and restaurants). These practices often create in the minds of those being served and the public at large an image of poverty, instability, incapability, or lack of motivation. These images die hard.

Given this reality, some of the best practices in the formal service system for people with disabilities are those that represent a shift in this perspective. Sheltered workshops are converting to community employment sites with job coaches. Skill-building programs are looking to link participants with disabilities into community colleges and other typical services. Group homes are giving way to individual choice in residential arrangements with personal assistants available for support.

Nevertheless, old ways are deeply rooted, and the transition expert may often be tempted to "refer" students to the formal disability service system. Although for a few students, this may be a viable step, the message of this chapter is for the transition expert to do everything possible, to bend over backward, to facilitate the more direct path from school to the generic community. Consider involving the student in the following:

- Community colleges
- Local colleges and universities

- Theme-oriented clubs and associations (e.g., ski clubs, video clubs, computer clubs)
- Service-oriented groups (e.g., church groups, environmental groups, social-help groups)
- Local noncredit classes
- Local employment agencies
- YMCAs or YWCAs

If the transition planner does make contact with formal disability service agencies, he or she should stress that these special services are to be adjunct to the student's life and merely used as supportive to inclusion to the greater community. Too many students with disabilities who get referred to specialty agencies get lost and stigmatized in the process. Best practices have proven that this situation does not have to be.

CONCLUSION

My intent in this chapter has been to explore the concept of transitioning. Without question, transitioning and its component parts are critical to the ultimate goal of the education process: successful work and community participation. At first glance, transitioning seems a simple concept—a shift from classroom to the world of work and community. However, given the background and history of how people with disabilities have been distanced and disenfranchised, all in the name of specialty programs, this simple concept becomes much more complex. To fully understand transitioning, one must examine the critical themes of the prevailing paradigm, roles in community, role formation, the concept of community, and the formal service world for people with disabilities. Each of these parts not only improves understanding of transitioning, but is a key to achieving success in this effort.

Without question, the next century will witness changes to the role and position of people with disabilities in the United States. With passage of the Americans with Disabilities Act and efforts to reform the present health care system, a fundamental shift in the position of people with disabilities will occur in the United States. As laws mandate accessibility and participation, more Americans with disabilities will take part in the "mainstream." These trends can only promote a more active sense of inclusion. Thus, the component parts of transitioning become critical in the repertoire of the educator. The time is now to more actively work to understand and use transitioning concepts.

REFERENCES

Argyris, C. (1982). *Reasoning, learning and action.* San Francisco: Jossey-Bass.

Barker, J. (1985). *Discovering the future.* Minneapolis: ILI Press.

Bellamy, G. T. (1988). *Supported employment: A community implementation guide.* Baltimore: Brookes.

Biklin, D., Knoll, J., & Taylor (1987). The disabled minority. In Taylor, D. Biklin, & J. Knoll (Eds.), *Community integration for people with severe disabilities.* New York: Teachers College Press.

Condeluci, A. (1988). *Community residential supports for persons with head injuries.* Washington, DC: United Cerebral Palsy Association.

Condeluci, A. (1990). Community factors and successful work reentry. In P. Wehman & J. Kreutzer (Eds.), *Vocational rehabilitation for persons with traumatic brain injury.* Baltimore: Aspen Press.

Condeluci, A. (1991). *Interdependence: The route to community.* Orlando, FL: PMD Press.

Condeluci, A., & Gretz-Lasky, S. (1987). Social role valorization: A model for community re-entry. *Journal of Head Trauma Rehabilitation, 2*(1), 49–56.

DeJong, G. (1979). Independent living: From social movement to analytical paradigm. *Archives of Physical Medicine and Rehabilitation, 60,* 435–456.

Everson, J., & Moon, M. S. (1987). Transition services for young adults with severe disabilities: Defining professional and parental roles and responsibilities. *Journal of the Association for the Severely Handicapped, 12*(2), 15–33.

Ferguson, M. (1980). *The Aquarian conspiracy.* New York: Tarcher Press.

Freire, P. (1989). *Pedagogy of the oppressed.* New York: Continuum.

Gardner, H. (1984). *The mind's new science.* New York: Basic Books.

Gold, M. W. (1973). Vocational rehabilitation for the mentally retarded. In N. R. Ellis (Ed.), *International review of research in mental retardation* (Vol. 6). New York: Academic Press.

Illich, I. (1976). *Medical nemesis.* New York: Pantheon.

Kreutzer, J., & Wehman, P. (1990). *Community integration following traumatic brain injury.* Baltimore: Brookes.

Kuhn, T. (1962). *The structure of scientific revolution.* Chicago: University of Chicago Press.

Mount, B., & Zwernik, K. (1988). *It's never too early, it's never too late.* St. Paul, MN: Metropolitan Council.

O'Brien, J. (1986). *Discovering community.* Atlanta: Responsive Systems Associates.

O'Connell, M. (1988). *The gift of hospitality.* Evanston, IL: Center for Urban Affairs and Policy Research.

Pearpoint, J., Forest, M., & Snow, J. (1992). *The inclusion papers.* Toronto: Inclusion Press.

Prigatano, G. (1989). Work, love and play after brain injury. *Bulletin of Menninger Clinic, 53* (whole no. 5).

Rusch, F. (1979). Toward the validation of social/vocational survival skills. *Mental Retardation, 32*(2), 24–39.

Senge, P. (1990). *The fifth discipline.* New York: Doubleday.

Skrtic, T. (1986). The crisis in special educational knowledge: A perspective on perspective. *Focus on Exceptional Children, 18*(7), 68–79.

Wehman, P. (1975). Toward a social skills curriculum for developmentally disabled clients in vocational settings. *Rehabilitation Literature, 11,* 2–18.

Wehman, P., & Kregel, J. (1985). A supported work approach to competitive employment. *Journal of the Association for Persons with Severe Handicaps, 10,* 3–11.

Wirth, A. G. (1983). *Productive work in industry and schools: Becoming persons again.* Langham, MD: University Press of America.

Wolfensberger, W. (1972). *Normalization.* Toronto: National Institute on Mental Retardation.

Wolfensberger, W. (1983). *PASSING.* Toronto: National Institute on Mental Retardation.

Author Index

Subject Index

About the Editors

Ronald C. Savage, EdD

Ron Savage is a special educator who taught at both elementary and high school levels. He received his doctorate in education in 1979 from Boston University. Later, as a professor of education at Castleton State College (Vermont), he taught undergraduate and graduate courses in education, supervised student teachers, and coordinated graduate education programs. He co-founded the Vermont State Head Injury Association and served as its president. He then became clinical associate professor of neurology at the University of Medicine and Dentistry and associate professor of applied psychology at Rutgers University (New Jersey). Currently, he serves as program director of Hilltop Manor in Niskayuna, New York, one of the largest brain injury rehabilitation centers in the United States, serving children, adolescents, and young adults.

Savage co-founded the Special Education Task Force of the National Head Injury Foundation (NHIF). He presently serves as chairperson of the Pediatric Task Force for NHIF. Savage speaks and consults widely with state head injury associations, hospitals, state governments, educational agencies, and providers of brain injury rehabilitation. He is widely published in the area of traumatic brain injury rehabilitation and serves on several boards and committees of national and state organizations concerned with children and youth who have special needs.

Gary F. Wolcott, MEd

Gary Wolcott is a counseling psychologist who began his career working in the mental health field. He received his master's degree in counseling psychology from Northeastern University in 1976. Wolcott worked as Director of Education of the National Head Injury Foundation, facilitating its educational and professional services, from 1985 to 1989. Previously, he served as an administrator and program director of a number of human service agencies, including a 5-year period as Executive Director of a rehabilitation program that serves persons with multiple disabilities. Wolcott currently serves as an educational consultant and co-investigator with The Research and Training Center in Rehabilitation and Childhood Trauma, Department of Rehabilitation Medicine, Tufts University School of Medicine, Boston.

In 1989, he established Wolcott & Associates, a management and training consultation firm that provides services to organizations working with persons with acquired brain injuries. These services include staff training on acquired brain injury rehabilitation, quality assurance, strategic planning, accreditation, and advocacy for persons with neurologic disabilities. In addition, Wolcott develops programs and materials for parents, teachers, and administrators serving students with acquired brain injuries. He has created a series of training manuals for working with students following a traumatic injury, and is collaborating on a book for parents and students on vocational transition following high school.